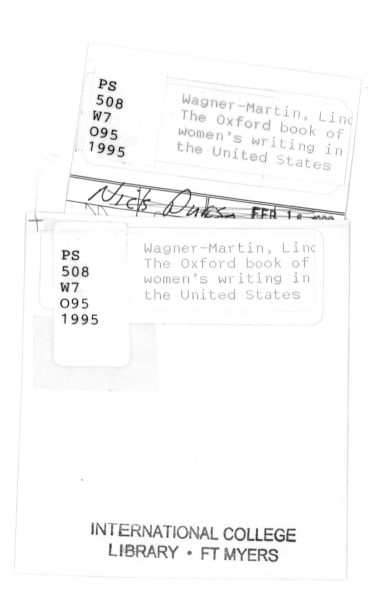

THE OXFORD BOOK OF
Women's Writing in the United States

THE OXFORD BOOK OF
Women's Writing
in the
United States

Edited by
Linda Wagner-Martin
Cathy N. Davidson

Oxford   New York
OXFORD UNIVERSITY PRESS
1995

Oxford University Press

Oxford   New York
Athens   Auckland   Bangkok   Bombay
Calcutta   Cape Town   Dar es Salaam   Delhi
Florence   Hong Kong   Istanbul   Karachi
Kuala Lumpur   Madras   Madrid   Melbourne
Mexico City   Nairobi   Paris   Singapore
Taipei   Tokyo   Toronto

and associated companies in
Berlin   Ibadan

Copyright © 1995 by Linda Wagner-Martin and Cathy N. Davidson

Published by Oxford University Press, Inc.,
200 Madison Avenue, New York, New York 10016

Oxford is a registered trademark of Oxford University Press

Library of Congress Cataloging-in-Publication Data
The Oxford book of women's writing in the United States
edited by Linda Wagner-Martin, Cathy N. Davidson.
p.   cm.   Includes index.
ISBN 0-19-508706-2
1. American literature—Women authors.   2. Women—United States
—Literary collections.   I. Wagner-Martin, Linda.
II. Davidson, Cathy N., 1949-   .
PS508.W7095   1995   810.8'09287—dc20   95-1499

9   8   7   6   5   4   3   2   1
Printed in the United States of America
on acid-free paper

CONTENTS

THE OXFORD BOOK OF
Women's Writing in the United States

INTRODUCTION

This collection of writing by women bears out the perception that women have been writing for hundreds of years—in diaries, letters, poetry, recipes, plays, and fiction. Whether it be Judith Sargent Murray's 1790 essay "On the Equality of the Sexes" or Abigail Adams's letter reminding her husband John to "remember the ladies" when he drafted governance documents for the rebellious colonies, women have recorded what is important to them. They have used language as a persuasive tool, as a way of remembering, and as a means of etching their deepest, fondest dreams. Writing on slips of paper or stationery; in personal journals or notebooks; and with pencil, pen, typewriter, and computer, women writers have created a verbal treasure older than the nation itself. This collection honors both the variety of women's writing and the variety of women's lives in America, from the beginnings to the present.

As most readers of writing by women have long recognized, the only real problem with acclaiming the work of women authors has been finding it. Many more women writers are "lost" than continue to appear in print—even when, during their own times, they were significant literary figures. Through its selections, and its grouping of works into "private" and "public" texts, this anthology makes available representative works by nearly a hundred women writers. Because there is so much good writing by women, we have chosen works that stand for a larger body of work: for instance, there is a poem by Sylvia Plath, but none by women poets often associated with her, such as Anne Sexton, Kathleen Spivack, or Anne Waldman. Similarly, a play by Alice Gerstenberg is included, but none by Lillian Hellman. A truly complete anthology of women's writing would comprise a volume as thick as its paired work, *The Oxford Companion to Women's Writing in the United States*. Our intention in selecting materials for this book was quite different: we hoped to build a book that, relieved of an obligation to be comprehensive, readers could simply enjoy.

We hope, too, that our collection speaks to the problems of categorizing women's writing within existing patterns in literary history. In the 1990s, the most significant writing is said to occur in the contemporary novel. Readers are most interested in the new long prose forms—novel, memoir, biography—

yet a hundred years ago, the poem was the most prestigious literary form. Women wrote a great deal of poetry. Just as readers' preferences have changed, so, too, has critical opinion about validating the forms in which authors have written. For most of recorded history, women wrote privately rather than publicly: they wrote letters (indeed, communicating with family members was one of their many responsibilities), they kept diaries, and they recorded important family events in Bibles and daybooks. But what they wrote was not, then, considered "literature." This anthology attempts to reveal the variety of private writing by including excerpts from women's letters, diaries, and autobiographical writings—even their recipes and the historical context for them—because today's readers understand how crucial such works were, and are. The voices of Anaïs Nin, Georgia O'Keeffe, Pat Mora, Natalie Barney, Harriet Jacobs, and others speak to today's readers, perhaps because of the intimacy of the forms in which they wrote.

More recently, women began creating public voices. Among the first women journalists were Margaret Fuller, Fanny Fern, and—before them— Judith Sargent Murray. Writing to effect social change—whether for women's rights or for alleviation of the suffering of the poor—was often the province of women writers. Anna Julia Cooper's pleas for equal education for women, particularly black women; Meridel Le Sueur's descriptions of unemployed women during the Great Depression; Mary Hunter Austin's and Marilou Awiakta's valorization of Native American life—these are only a few of the works included.

Because, beginning in the eighteenth and nineteenth centuries, most women writers in the United States worked to support themselves and their families, they wrote what would sell: they did not have the luxury of calling themselves writers and disappearing into attics for years while they learned the trade. Women who wrote, however, were dedicated professionals; and what they wrote and published shaped general literary taste. That taste, in turn, shaped the more frequently touted important literary texts, for the most part written by their male colleagues. Just as Nathaniel Hawthorne's *The Scarlet Letter* drew from a tradition of fiction, much of it by women writers, in which the sexual "sin" of the woman protagonist created the narrative, so many canonized texts of American letters have had their intellectual genesis in work written by women now long forgotten, work that was sometimes devalued because it was commercially successful.

Other writing by women has been lost because it did not fit into existing literary categories. As the editors spent several years traversing the vast terrain of women's writing, we were struck repeatedly by works that were anomalies. Among these were Susan Fenimore Cooper's lyric meditations on nature (the daughter of novelist James Fenimore Cooper, her works outsold those of

Henry David Thoreau during the mid-nineteenth century). A number of difficult-to-categorize works we finally grouped under the rubric "Acting Out." What literary category *is* Sojourner Truth's magnificent speech, "A'n't I a Woman?" Where do Paula Gunn Allen's "Kopis'taya," the chant for calling friendly spirits, or E. M. Broner's "ceremonies" of women's friendships belong? Our way of classifying these expressions of the writers' interactions with others is to emphasize the oral, the performance quality that links them. We move from the oral speech, to staged plays, to the more contemporary emphasis on the oral text as recorded and shaped by Anna Deavere Smith in *Fires in the Mirror,* her "play" about the Crown Heights, New York, racial conflict. In the second section of that division, we group texts relating to women's rituals and ceremonies, beginning with the oldest American forms, those from various Native American cultures, and ending with Broner's Jewish women's rituals and Luisah Teish's parallel ceremonies for the black extended family.

By allowing the categories for this book to grow from the writing itself, we hope the result is a lively, engaging, and inviting collection. This anthology luxuriates in some of the best writing U.S. women have produced, and its "politics" is its awareness that the best U.S. women's writing is, quite simply, some of the best writing in the world. More to the point, the collection avoids special pleadings of "diversity" because, once again, the women who wrote beautifully, poignantly, tenderly, passionately, humorously, or powerfully about America and American lives are a heterogenous group. Sui Sin Far's touching memoir about growing up "different" in the United States, like the powerful autobiography of Zitkala-Ša, whose mother was a Sioux, tells the reader more about "otherness" than any sociological treatise. Toni Morrison's purposefully enigmatic "Recitatif," a story in which the reader never knows for certain which character is black and which white, prompts us to question existing categories of difference. Janice Mirikitani's and Nellie Wong's poems about being young Asian-American women, like Alice Walker's meditation on the beauty of growing old, speak to all readers, as Jan Freeman's and Olga Broumas and Jane Miller's love poems speak to anyone who has ever known passion.

Throughout the book, we define women's writing as writing by women. Geographically, we have confined ourselves to literature written in the United States and in English; happily, the collection represents various geographical regions, since U.S. women writers have never been concentrated exclusively in the centers of publishing power. Chronologically, there is work from the colonial period to the immediate present: from Anne Bradstreet to Lucille Clifton and Michelle Cliff, Judith Ortiz Cofer and Carolyn Forché. Excellence has been our main criterion for selection. We have included both classics of U.S. women's writing (such as Susan Glaspell's *Trifles* and Charlotte Perkins Stetson Gilman's "The Yellow Wall-Paper") and works not yet known to many readers (the comic stories of Marietta Holley, Gish Jen, and Helena María Viramontes; Ursula K. Le Guin's postmodern parable; and the powerful essays of Mary Gordon, Martha Gellhorn, Anna Quindlen, and Gloria Steinem). We have included a section of erotica, because so much passionate writing by women has been lost. Just as women writers reflected on their love of nature and their role at the center of home and kitchen, so they wrote about their great capacity to love. We have placed the erotica at the end of the book grouped with excerpts from women's cookbooks, in a category we call "Bodily Pleasures." We hope that the tone of this concluding section, the enjoyment of life in all its component parts, flavors the book as a whole; and that its readers find pleasure—pleasure of all kinds—throughout its rich selections.

PART I

Short Fiction

❖

We think of American fiction as the most interesting and innovative writing being done in the world. Readers everywhere have marveled at the power of the short story as written by U.S. authors. During the late eighteenth and nineteenth centuries, much of our best short fiction came from the pens of women writers, whose skill in the form made them at least self-supporting, and often, famous. The host of new women's magazines meant that publishers needed a quantity of short fiction, and women who could write well about human situations were in great demand.

As the stories collected here show, women have produced an immense variety of excellent short fiction. So many short stories have been published in the past 150 years in the United States, many by women writers, that no complete history of the form has yet been written. The quantity is overwhelming, suggesting that there is something freeing, something liberating, in the brevity of the form. In investing herself in the short story, the writer (regardless of historical period or geographical location) has been willing to take on new challenges, often challenges of form—how to do something, how to express something that has never been said or written about before. Perhaps even more important, writers of the short story have been able to take on challenges of theme. There is a sense of privacy in the short story form, a realization that comparatively few people are going to see the work (even if it is eventually published in a collection): publishers care more about novels, reviewers care more about novels, and the general public cares more about novels. So there is a kind of anonymity in writing short stories, an anonymity that is a disguise. And being disguised is, itself, a way of freeing the psyche.

All writers are caught in the dilemma of what can be written about, what can be said—and women writers bear the heaviest burden of all, particularly when they write about sexual matters. What is "appropriate" for a woman writer to know, or, to know well enough to explore in writing? A hundred years ago, when unmarried, sheltered women were not supposed to know what passion was, women writers put their personal reputations on the line by describing sexual situations. Writing in the 1890s, Kate Chopin did not even try to publish her story "The Storm" (collected here under "Erotica").

The fiction that appears in this section of the book has been chosen to chart the excellence of the short story and novella forms as practiced, and often invented, by women writers. Some of the earliest of the fictions—Sarah Orne Jewett's and Alice Dunbar-Nelson's stories—probe questions of gender roles; and others interrogate received opinions of what are suitable behaviors for women. Mary Wilkins Freeman asks whether "Mother," who has for forty years been crying out for a new house, should move her family into her husband's new barn in protest? Should Chopin's young mother spend her money on purchases for herself instead of for her children? Should the unnamed protagonist who suffers post-partum depression in Gilman's story feel such immense guilt for wanting to write? Even though these are stories from the nineteenth century, they speak to today's readers about common situations and difficulties. Like the most contemporary of fictions, they feature protagonists who are faced with ambiguous decisions.

From the poignance of Hisaye Yamamoto's characterization of the Japanese-American mother in "Seventeen Syllables" to the brilliant triumph of Edith Wharton's twice-divorced heroine in "The Other Two," these stories chart the range of real life as women live it. The baffling endurance of Eudora Welty's aged protagonist in "A Worn Path," set against the maniacal egoism of Flannery O'Connor's even older character in "A Late Encounter with the Enemy," show the differences in the way people meet the process of aging— while Ursula K. Le Guin's parable ("May's Lion") plays with a similar theme and provides a narrative about the way fiction is created. Nella Larsen's focus on a male character in her story "Freedom" shifts the reader's attention, but not the impact of the fiction, much as Gish Jen's shaping "In the American Society" around a paternal definition of success forces the reader to question all aspects of the "American dream." Two evocative studies of the sheer horror of murder by Cynthia Ozick and Joyce Carol Oates show the way the author's control of form forces the reader to recognize such terror. Technically, in the way the words are arranged to affect the reader, these are classics of American fiction.

Zora Neale Hurston's assumed objectivity in "Sweat" makes the survival of her female protagonist its own kind of triumph. In her deft presentation of a common woman leading her own life, Helena María Viramontes redefines traditional notions of triumph or tragedy. And the stories by Tillie Olsen and Toni Morrison each probe the reader's usual definitions of race, friendship, and protagonist.

The last two selections in this section, Rebecca Harding Davis's *Life in the Iron-Mills* and Willa Cather's *Old Mrs. Harris*, are longer than most stories and are properly categorized as novellas. In the flurry of fiction writing that occurred during the latter half of the nineteenth century and the twentieth century entire, many writers found that their subject matter demanded more length than the incisive, single-effect form of most short stories. Not so long as a conventional novel, novellas (or *novelles* or short novels) ran from approximately 15,000 words to 50,000 words (or more). The term was never defined explicitly, but came to characterize a very long piece of short fiction.

Rather than using any simple consideration of length, however, most readers today categorize a work as a novella on the basis of its narrative complexity. In the novella form, the writer attempts to give readers much more than a glimpse of a character, a situation, or a culture. The construct is seldom as plot-driven as some short stories are—where the reader's attention may be focused almost entirely on "what happened next." In both *Life in the Iron-Mills* and *Old Mrs. Harris,* several characters grow and change, a seemingly simple situation melds into a set of linked incidents, and nearly complete cultures are re-created. The reader of each of these fictions is asked to comprehend the full picture of the character's life in its material context, so that the event that sparks both interaction and narrative is always contextualized and never the result of some *deus ex machina* randomness. In a comparatively short space, then, readers come to understand the hard labor and poverty of iron workers during a time when no labor laws protected them from the cavalier (and usually inhuman) treatment of mill owners; just as they understand the economic and human stress underlying an apparently bucolic pastoral existence.

Not all of the fictional works in this section are about women, but—suitably—many of them are. While many women have written successfully about male characters, the heart of their important fictional enterprise—to draw and order existence so that readers find not only reality but a kind of comfort in their recognition of that reality—lies in conveying the world of women's lives from the point of view of writers who themselves are leading such lives. The immense variety in the way they write about women's lives sparks the outpouring of fiction that today proves how talented, how ambitious, and how wise women writers in the United States have been, and are.

❖

Sarah Orne Jewett
(1849–1909)

Sarah Orne Jewett began writing and publishing short fiction in her teens. By the age of twenty, she had published a story in *Atlantic Monthly,* one of America's leading periodicals. Through this publication, she met the editor, James T. Fields, and his wife, Annie, an editor and author in her own right. The two women writers maintained a thirty-year relationship and, after James's death, lived part of each year together and traveled together extensively, both in Europe and the Caribbean.

Jewett is known for finely crafted, lyrical stories that often engage pressing social issues. Most of her stories are set in New England, often in southern Maine, where she was raised in middle-class comfort. Jewett was keenly aware of the changes wrought by industrialization, urbanization, and the various economic recessions that plagued the late nineteenth century, and she was sensitive to the plight of those rural inhabitants of the region who had less than she. She is probably best known for her collection, *A White Heron and Other Stories* (1886), and a semi-autobiographical novel, *A Country Doctor* (1884), both of which focus on such signature Jewett themes as women's relationship to nature, the obstacles faced by women, and the bonds they create among themselves.

"Tom's Husband" is one of Jewett's most overtly feminist stories. It humorously but also astutely examines gender issues through a classic example of marital role reversal.

❖

TOM'S HUSBAND

I shall not dwell long upon the circumstances that led to the marriage of my hero and heroine; though their courtship was to them, the only one that has ever noticeably approached the ideal, it had many aspects in which it was entirely commonplace in other people's eyes. While the world in general smiles at lovers with kindly approval and sympathy, it refuses to be aware of the unprecedented delight which is amazing to the lovers themselves.

But, as has been true in many other cases, when they were at last married, the most ideal of situations was found to have been changed to the most practical. Instead of having shared their original duties, and, as school-boys would say, going halves, they discovered that the cares of life had been doubled. This led to some distressing moments for both our friends; they understood suddenly that instead of dwelling in heaven they were still upon earth, and had made themselves slaves to new laws and limitations. Instead of being freer and happier than ever before, they had assumed new responsibilities; they had established a new household, and must fulfill in some way or another the obligations of it. They looked back with affection to their engagement; they had been longing to have each other to themselves, apart from the world, but it seemed that they never felt so keenly that they were still units in modern society. Since Adam and Eve were in Paradise, before the devil joined them, nobody has had a chance to imitate that unlucky couple. In some respects they told the truth when, twenty times a day, they said that life had never been so pleasant before; but there were mental reservations on either side which might have subjected them to the accusation of lying. Somehow, there was a little feeling of disappointment, and they caught themselves wondering—though they would have died sooner than confess it—whether they were quite so happy as they had expected. The truth was, they were much happier than people usually are, for they had an uncommon capacity for enjoyment. For a little while they were like a sail-boat that is beating and has to drift a few minutes before it can catch the wind and start off on the other tack. And they had the same feeling, too, that any one is likely to have who has been long pursuing some object of his ambition or desire. Whether it is a coin, or a picture, or a stray volume of some old edition of Shakespeare, or whether it is an office under government or a lover, when fairly in one's grasp there is a loss of the eagerness that was felt in pursuit. Satisfaction, even after one has dined well, is not so interesting and eager a feeling as hunger.

My hero and heroine were reasonably well established to begin with: they each had some money, though Mr. Wilson had most. His father had at one time been a rich man, but with the decline, a few years before, of manufacturing interests, he had become, mostly through the fault of others, somewhat involved; and at the time of his death his affairs were in such a condition that it was still a question whether a very large sum or a moderately large one would represent his estate. Mrs. Wilson, Tom's step-mother, was somewhat of an invalid; she suffered severely at times with asthma, but she was almost entirely relieved by living in another part of the country. While her husband lived, she had accepted her illness as inevitable, and rarely left home; but during the last few years she had lived in Philadelphia with her own people, making short and wheezing visits only from time to time, and had not undergone a voluntary period of suffering since the occasion of Tom's marriage, which she had entirely approved. She had a sufficient property of her own, and she and Tom were independent of each other in that way. Her only other step-child was a daughter, who had married a navy officer, and had at this time gone out to spend three years (or less) with her husband, who had been ordered to Japan.

It is not unfrequently noticed that in many marriages one of the persons who choose each other as partners for life is said to have thrown himself or herself away, and the relatives and friends look on with dismal forebodings and ill-concealed submission. In this case it was the wife who might have done so much better, according to public opinion. She did not think so herself, luckily, either before marriage or afterward, and I do not think it occurred to her to picture to herself the sort of career which would have been her alternative. She had been an only child, and had usually taken her own way. Some one once said that it was a great pity that she had not been obliged to work for her living, for she had inherited a most uncommon business talent, and, without being disreputably keen at a bargain, her insight into the practical working of affairs was very clear and far-reaching. Her father, who had also been a manufacturer, like Tom's, had often said it had been a mistake that she was a girl instead of a boy. Such executive ability as hers is often wasted in the more contracted sphere of women, and is apt to be more a disadvantage than a help. She was too independent and self-reliant for a wife; it would seem at first thought that she needed a wife herself more than she did a husband. Most men like best the women whose natures cling and appeal to theirs for protection. But Tom Wilson, while he did not wish to be protected himself, liked these very qualities in his wife which would have displeased some other men; to tell the truth, he was very much in love with his wife just as she was. He was a successful collector of almost everything but money, and during a great part of his life he had been an invalid, and he had grown, as he laughingly confessed, very old-womanish. He had been badly lamed, when a boy, by being caught in some machinery in his father's mill, near which he was idling one afternoon, and though he had almost entirely outgrown the effect of his injury, it had not been until after many years. He had been in college, but his eyes had given out there, and he had been obliged to leave in the middle of his junior year, though he had kept up a pleasant intercourse with the members of his class, with whom he had been a great favorite. He was a good deal of an idler in the world. I do not think his ambition, except in the case of securing Mary Dunn for his wife, had ever been distinct; he seemed to make the most he could of each day as it came, without making all his days' works tend toward some grand result, and go toward the upbuilding of some grand plan and purpose. He consequently gave no promise of being either distinguished or great. When his eyes would allow, he was an indefatigable reader; and although he would have said that he read only for amusement, yet he amused himself with books that were well worth the time he spent over them.

The house where he lived nominally belonged to his step-mother, but she had taken for granted that Tom would bring his wife home to it, and assured him that it should be to all intents and purposes his. Tom was deeply attached to the old place, which was altogether the pleasantest in town. He had kept bachelor's hall there most of the time since his father's death, and he had taken great pleasure, before his marriage, in refitting it to some extent, though it was already comfortable and furnished in remarkably good taste. People said of him that if it had not been for his illnesses, and if he had been a poor boy, he probably would have made something of himself. As it was, he was not very well known by the townspeople, being somewhat reserved, and not taking much interest in their every-day subjects of conversation. Nobody liked him so well as they liked his wife, yet there was no reason why he should be disliked enough to have much said about him.

After our friends had been married for some time, and had outlived the first strangeness of the new order of things, and had done their duty to their neighbors with so much apparent willingness and generosity that even Tom himself was liked a great deal better than he ever had been before, they were sitting together one stormy evening in the library, before the fire. Mrs. Wilson had been reading Tom the letters which had come to him by the night's mail. There was a long one from his sister in Nagasaki, which had been written with a good deal of ill-disguised reproach. She complained of the smallness of the income of her share in her father's estate, and said that she had been assured by American friends that the smaller mills were starting up everywhere, and beginning to do well again. Since so much of their money was invested in the factory, she had been surprised and sorry to find by Tom's last letters that he had seemed to have no idea of putting in a proper person as superintendent, and going to work again. Four per cent on her other property, which she had been told she must soon expect instead of eight, would make a great difference to her. A navy captain in a foreign port was obliged to entertain a great deal, and Tom must know that it cost them much more to live than it did him, and ought to think of their interests. She hoped he would talk over what was best to be done with their mother (who had been made executor, with Tom, of his father's will).

Tom laughed a little, but looked disturbed. His wife had said something to the same effect, and his mother had spoken once or twice in her letters of the prospect of starting the mill again. He was not a bit of a business man, and he did not feel certain, with the theories which he had arrived at of the state of the country, that it was safe yet to spend the money which would have to be spent in putting the mill in order. "They think that the minute it is going again we shall be making money hand over hand, just as father did when we were children," he said. "It is going to cost us no end of money before we can make anything. Before father died he meant to put in a good deal of new machinery, I remember. I don't know anything about the business myself, and I would have sold out long ago if I had had an offer that came anywhere near the value. The larger mills are the only ones that are good for anything now, and we should have to bring a crowd of French Canadians here; the day is past for the people who live in this part of the country to go into the factory again. Even the Irish all go West when they come into the country, and don't come to places like this any more."

"But there are a good many of the old work-people down in the village," said Mrs. Wilson. "Jack Towne asked me the other day if you weren't going to start up in the spring."

Tom moved uneasily in his chair, "I'll put you in for superintendent, if you like," he said, half angrily, whereupon Mary threw the newspaper at him; but by the time he had thrown it back he was in good humor again.

"Do you know, Tom," she said, with amazing seriousness, "that I believe I should like nothing in the world so much as to be the head of a large business? I hate keeping house,—I always did; and I never did so much of it in all my life put together as I have since I have been married. I suppose it isn't womanly to say so, but if I could escape from the whole thing I believe I should be perfectly happy. If you get rich when the mill is going again, I shall beg for a housekeeper, and shirk everything. I give you fair warning. I don't believe I keep this house half so well as you did before I came here."

Tom's eyes twinkled. "I am going to have that glory,—I don't think you do, Polly; but you can't say that I have not been forbearing. I certainly have not told you more than twice how we used to have things cooked. I'm not going to be your kitchen-colonel."

"Of course it seemed the proper thing to do," said his wife, meditatively; "but I think we should have been even happier than we have if I had been spared it. I have had some days of wretchedness that I shudder to think of. I never know what to have for breakfast; and I ought not to say it, but I don't mind the sight of dust. I look upon housekeeping as my life's great discipline"; and at this pathetic confession they both laughed heartily.

"I've a great mind to take it off your hands," said Tom. "I always rather liked it, to tell the truth, and I ought to be a better housekeeper,—I have been at it for five years; though housekeeping for one is different from what it is for two, and one of them a woman. You see you have brought a different element into my family. Luckily, the servants are pretty well drilled. I do think you upset them a good deal at first!"

Mary Wilson smiled as if she only half heard what he was saying. She drummed with her foot on the floor and looked intently at the fire, and presently gave it a vigorous poking. "Well?" said Tom, after he had waited patiently as long as he could.

"Tom! I'm going to propose something to you. I wish you would really do as you said, and take all the home affairs under your care, and let me start the mill. I am certain I could manage it. Of course I should get people who understood the thing to teach me. I believe I was made for it; I should like it above all things. And this is what I will do: I will bear the cost of starting it, myself,—I think I have money enough, or can get it; and if I have not put affairs in the right trim at the end of a year I will stop, and you may make some other arrangement. If I have, you and your mother and sister can pay me back."

"So I am going to be the wife, and you the husband," said Tom, a little indignantly; "at least, that is what people will say. It's a regular Darby and Joan affair, and you think you can do more work in a day than I can do in three. Do you know that you must go to town to buy cotton? And do you know there are a thousand things about it that you don't know?"

"And never will?" said Mary, with perfect good humor. "Why, Tom. I can learn as well as you, and a good deal better, for I like business, and you don't. You forget that I was always father's right-hand man after I was a dozen years old, and that you have let me invest my money and some of your own, and I haven't made a blunder yet."

Tom thought that his wife had never looked so handsome or so happy. "I don't care, I should rather like the fun of knowing what people will say. It is a new departure, at any rate. Women think they can do everything better than men in these days, but I'm the first man, apparently, who has wished he were a woman."

"Of course people will laugh," said Mary, "but they will say that it's just like me, and think I am fortunate to have married a man who will let me do as I choose. I don't see why it isn't sensible: you will be living exactly as you were before you married, as to home affairs; and since it was a good thing for you to know something about housekeeping then, I can't imagine why you shouldn't go on with it now, since it makes me miserable, and I am wasting a fine business talent while I do it. What do we care for people's talking about it?"

"It seems to me that it is something like women's smoking: it isn't wicked, but it isn't the custom of the country. And I don't like the idea of your going among business men. Of course I should be above going with you, and having people think I must be an idiot; they would say that you married a manufacturing interest, and I was thrown in. I can foresee that my pride is going to be humbled to the dust in every way," Tom declared in mournful tones, and began to shake with laughter. "It is one of your lovely castles in the air, dear Polly, but an old brick mill needs a better foundation than the clouds. No, I'll look around, and get an honest, experienced man for agent. I suppose it's the best thing we can do, for the machinery ought not to lie still any longer; but I mean to sell the factory as soon as I can. I devoutly wish it would take fire, for the insurance would be the best price we are likely to get. That is a famous letter from Alice! I am afraid the captain has been growling over his pay, or they have been giving too many little dinners on board ship. If we were rid of the mill, you and I might go out there this winter. It would be capital fun."

Mary smiled again in an absent-minded way. Tom had an uneasy feeling that he had not heard the end of it yet, but nothing more was said for a day or two. When Mrs. Tom Wilson announced, with no apparent thought of being contradicted, that she had entirely made up her mind, and she meant to see those men who had been overseers of the different departments, who still lived in the village, and have the mill put in order at once. Tom looked disturbed, but made no opposition; and soon after breakfast his wife formally presented him with a handful of keys, and told him there was some lamb in the house for dinner; and presently he heard the wheels of her little phaeton rattling off down the road. I should be untruthful if I tried to persuade any one that he was not provoked; he thought she would at least have waited for his formal permission, and at first he meant to take another horse, and chase her, and bring her back in disgrace, and put a stop to the whole thing. But something assured him that she knew what she was about, and he determined to let her have her own way. If she failed, it might do no harm, and this was the only ungallant thought he gave her. He was sure that she would do nothing unladylike, or be unmindful of his dignity; and he believed it would be looked upon as one of her odd, independent freaks, which always had won respect in the end, however much they had been laughed at in the beginning. "Susan," said he, as that estimable person went by the door with the dustpan, "you may tell Catherine to come to me for orders about the house, and you may do so yourself. I am going to take charge again, as I did before I was married. It is no trouble to me, and Mrs. Wilson dislikes it. Besides, she is going into business, and will have a great deal else to think of."

"Yes, sir; very well, sir," said Susan, who was suddenly moved to ask so many questions that she was utterly silent. But her master looked very happy; there was evidently no disapproval of his wife; and she went on up the stairs, and began to sweep them down, knocking the dust brush about excitedly, as if she were trying to kill a descending colony of insects.

Tom went out to the stable and mounted his horse, which had been waiting for him to take his customary after-breakfast ride to the post-office, and he galloped down the road in quest of the phaeton. He saw Mary talking with Jack Towne, who had been an overseer and a valued workman of his father's. He was looking much surprised and pleased.

"I wasn't caring so much about getting work, myself," he explained; "I've got what will carry me and my wife through; but it'll be better for the young folks about here to work near home. My nephews are wanting something to do; they were going to Lynn next week. I don't say but I should like to be to work in the old place again. I've sort of missed it, since we shut down."

"I'm sorry I was so long in overtaking you," said Tom, politely, to his wife.

"Well, Jack, did Mrs. Wilson tell you she's going to start the mill? You must give her all the help you can."

" 'Deed I will," said Mr. Towne, gallantly, without a bit of astonishment.

"I don't know much about the business yet," said Mrs. Wilson, who had been a little overcome at Jack Towne's lingo of the different rooms and machinery, and who felt an overpowering sense of having a great deal before her in the next few weeks. "By the time the mill is ready, I will be ready, too," she said, taking heart a little; and Tom, who was quick to understand her moods, could not help laughing, as he rode alongside. "We want a new barrel of flour, Tom, dear," she said, by way of punishment for his untimely mirth.

If she lost courage in the long delay, or was disheartened at the steady call for funds, she made no sign; and after a while the mill started up, and her cares were lightened, so that she told Tom that before next pay day she would like to go to Boston for a few days, and go to the theatre, and have a frolic and a rest. She really looked pale and thin, and she said she never worked so hard in all her life; but nobody knew how happy she was, and she was so glad she had married Tom, for some men would have laughed at it.

"I laughed at it," said Tom, meekly. "All is, if I don't cry by and by, because I am a beggar, I shall be lucky." But Mary looked fearlessly serene, and said that there was no danger at present.

It would have been ridiculous to expect a dividend the first year, though the Nagasaki people were pacified with difficulty. All the business letters came to Tom's address, and everybody who was not directly concerned thought that he was the motive power of the reawakened enterprise. Sometimes business people came to the mill, and were amazed at having to confer with Mrs. Wilson, but they soon had to respect her talents and her success. She was helped by the old clerk, who had been promptly recalled and reinstated, and she certainly did capitally well. She was laughed at, as she had expected to be, and people said they should think Tom would be ashamed of himself; but it soon appeared that he was not to blame, and what reproach was offered was on the score of his wife's oddity. There was nothing about the mill that she did not understand before very long, and at the end of the second year she declared a small dividend with great pride and triumph. And she was congratulated on her success, and every one thought of her project in a different way from the way they had thought of it in the beginning. She had singularly good fortune: at the end of the third year she was making money for herself and her friends faster than most people were, and approving letters began to come from Nagasaki. The Ashtons had been ordered to stay in that region, and it was evident that they were continually being obliged to entertain more instead of less. Their children were growing fast, too, and constantly becoming more expensive. The captain and his wife had already begun to congratulate themselves secretly that their two sons would in all probability come into possession, one day, of their uncle Tom's handsome property.

For a good while Tom enjoyed life, and went on his quiet way serenely. He was anxious at first, for he thought that Mary was going to make ducks and drakes of his money and her own. And then he did not exactly like the looks of the thing, either; he feared that his wife was growing successful as a business person at the risk of losing her womanliness. But as time went on, and he found there was no fear of that, he accepted the situation philosophically. He gave up his collection of engravings, having become more interested in one of coins and medals, which took up most of his leisure time. He often went to the city in pursuit of such treasures, and gained much renown in certain quarters as a numismatologist of great skill and experience. But at last his house (which had almost kept itself, and had given him little to do beside ordering the dinners, while faithful old Catherine and her niece Susan were his aids) suddenly became a great care to him. Catherine, who had been the main-stay of the family for many years, died after a short illness, and Susan must needs choose that time, of all others, for being married to one of the second hands in the mill. There followed a long and dismal season of experimenting, and for a time there was a procession of incapable creatures going in at one kitchen door and out of the other. His wife would not have liked to say so, but it seemed to her that Tom was growing fussy about the house affairs, and took more notice of those minor details than he used. She wished more than once, when she was tired, that he would not talk so much about the housekeeping; he seemed sometimes to have no other thought.

In the early days of Mrs. Wilson's business life, she had made it a rule to consult her husband on every subject of importance; but it had speedily proved to be a formality. Tom tried manfully to show a deep interest which he did not feel, and his wife gave up, little by little, telling him much about her affairs. She said that she liked to drop business when she came home in the evening; and at last she fell into the habit of taking a nap on the library sofa, while Tom, who could not use his eyes much by lamp-light, sat smoking or in utter idleness before the fire. When they were first married his wife had made it a rule that she should always read him the evening papers, and afterward they had always gone on with some book of history or philosophy, in which they were both interested. These evenings of their early married life had been charming to both of them, and from time to time one would say to the other that they ought to take up again the habit of reading together. Mary was so unaffectedly tired in the evening that Tom never liked to propose a walk; for, though he was not a man of peculiarly social nature, he had always been accustomed to pay an occasional evening visit to his neighbors in the village. And though he had little interest in the business world, and still less knowledge of it, after a while he wished that his wife would have more to say about what she was planning and doing, or how things were getting on. He thought that her chief aid, old Mr. Jackson, was far more in her thoughts than he. She was forever quoting Jackson's opinions. He did not like to find that she took it for granted that he was not interested in the welfare of his own property; it made him feel like a sort of pensioner and dependent, though, when they had guests at the house, which was by no means seldom, there was nothing in her manner that would imply that she thought herself in any way the head of the family. It was hard work to find fault with his wife in any way, though, to give him his due, he rarely tried.

But, this being a wholly unnatural state of things, the reader must expect to hear of its change at last, and the first blow from the enemy was dealt by an old woman, who lived nearby, and who called to Tom one morning, as he was driving down to the village in a great hurry (to post a letter, which ordered his agent to secure a long-wished-for ancient copper coin, at any price), to ask him if they had made yeast that week, and if she could borrow a cupful, as her own had met with some misfortune. Tom was instantly in a rage, and he mentally condemned her to some undeserved fate, but told her aloud to go and see the cook. This slight delay, besides being killing to his dignity, caused him to lose the mail, and in the end his much-desired copper coin. It was a hard day for him, altogether; it was Wednesday, and the first days of the week having been stormy the washing was very late. And Mary came home to dinner provokingly good-natured. She had met an old school-mate and her husband driving home from the mountains, and had first taken them over her factory, to their great amusement and delight, and then had brought them home to dinner. Tom greeted them cordially, and manifested his usual graceful hospitality; but the minute he saw his wife alone he said in a plaintive tone of rebuke, "I should think you might have remembered that the servants are unusually busy to-day. I do wish you would take a little interest in things at home. The women have been washing, and I'm sure I don't know what sort of a dinner we can give your friends. I wish you had thought to bring home some steak. I have been busy myself, and couldn't go down to the village. I thought we would only have a lunch."

Mary was hungry, but she said nothing, except that it would be all right,— she didn't mind; and perhaps they could have some canned soup.

She often went to town to buy or look at cotton, or to see some improvement in machinery, and she brought home beautiful bits of furniture and new pictures for the house, and showed a touching thoughtfulness in remembering Tom's fancies; but somehow he had an uneasy suspicion that she could get along pretty well without him when it came to the deeper wishes and hopes of her life, and that her most important concerns were all matters in which he had no share. He seemed to himself to have merged his life in his wife's; he lost his interest in things outside the house and grounds; he felt himself fast growing rusty and behind the times, and to have somehow missed a good deal in life; he had a suspicion that he was a failure. One day the thought rushed over him that his had been almost exactly the experience of most women, and he wondered if it really was any more disappointing and ignominious to him than it was to women themselves. "Some of them may be contented with it," he said to himself, soberly. "People think women are designed for such careers by nature, but I don't know why I ever made such a fool of myself."

Having once seen his situation in life from such a standpoint, he felt it day by day to be more degrading, and he wondered what he should do about it; and once, drawn by a new, strange sympathy, he went to the little family burying-ground. It was one of the mild, dim days that come sometimes in early November, when the pale sunlight is like the pathetic smile of a sad face, and he sat for a long time on the limp, frost-bitten grass beside his mother's grave.

But when he went home in the twilight his step-mother, who just then was making them a little visit, mentioned that she had been looking through some boxes of hers that had been packed long before and stowed away in the garret. "Everything looks very nice up there," she said, in her wheezing voice (which, worse than usual that day, always made him nervous), and added, without any intentional slight to his feelings, "I do think you have always been a most excellent housekeeper."

"I'm tired of such nonsense!" he exclaimed, with surprising indignation. "Mary, I wish you to arrange your affairs so that you can leave them for six months at least. I am going to spend this winter in Europe."

"Why, Tom, dear!" said his wife, appealingly. "I couldn't leave my business any way in the"—

But she caught sight of a look on his usually placid countenance that was something more than decision, and refrained from saying anything more.

And three weeks from that day they sailed.

1884

Alice Ruth Moore Dunbar-Nelson

(1875–1935)

Alice Ruth Moore Dunbar-Nelson was born in New Orleans, the child of a former slave mother—who may have had Indian blood—and a seaman who was probably of white Creole extraction. Growing up in a single-parent household, Alice attended public schools, graduated in 1892 from a two-year teacher's program at Straight College, and taught school in New Orleans; Medford, Massachusetts; Brooklyn, New York; and Wilmington, Delaware.

She began publishing poetry before she was twenty, and in 1895 her first book, *Violets and Other Tales*, appeared. Seeing one of her poems in print, the poet Paul Laurence Dunbar wrote to her. Their two-year correspondence led to their meeting, and to a two-year engagement; in 1898 they married. In 1899 Alice Dunbar published *The Goodness of St. Rocque and Other Stories,* her final collection of short stories.

The marriage ended in 1902, but Alice took on the role of Dunbar's widow after his death in 1906—even after she married the journalist Robert J. Nelson in 1916. Her middle and later years were spent as she worked as a journalist, and devoted herself to such public causes as help for adolescent girls in Harlem, women's suffrage, anti-lynching, and the National Federation of Colored Women's Clubs. She died in 1935.

"Tony's Wife," a study of racism among European immigrants, shows Dunbar-Nelson's awareness of the power of gender roles. Not marrying his common-law wife provided Tony with avenues to both control her and cast her off, leaving his small estate to his family. The author's sensitivity to ethnicity—given her own mixed lineage—prompted her to draw believable characters who often were subjected to prejudice because of their nationality or race.

❖

TONY'S WIFE

"Gimme fi' cents worth o'candy, please." It was the little Jew girl who spoke, and Tony's wife roused herself from her knitting to rise and count out the multi-hued candy which should go in exchange for the dingy nickel grasped in warm, damp fingers. Three long sticks, carefully wrapped in crispest brown paper, and a half dozen or more of pink candy fish for lagniappe, and the little Jew girl sped away in blissful contentment. Tony's wife resumed her knitting with a stifled sigh until the next customer should come.

A low growl caused her to look up apprehensively. Tony himself stood beetle-browned and huge in the small doorway.

"Get up from there," he muttered, "and open two dozen oysters right away; the Eliots want 'em." His English was unaccented. It was long since he had seen Italy.

She moved meekly behind the counter, and began work on the thick shells. Tony stretched his long neck up the street.

"Mr. Tony, mama wants some charcoal." The very small voice at his feet must have pleased him, for his black brows relaxed into a smile, and he poked the little one's chin with a hard, dirty finger, as he emptied the ridiculously small bucket of charcoal into the child's bucket, and gave a banana for lagniappe.

The crackling of shells went on behind, and a stifled sob arose as a bit of sharp edge cut into the thin, worn fingers that clasped the knife.

"Hurry up there, will you?" growled the black brows; "the Eliots are sending for the oysters."

She deftly strained and counted them, and, after wiping her fingers, resumed her seat, and took up the endless crochet work, with her usual stifled sigh.

Tony and his wife had always been in this same little queer old shop on Prytania Street, at least to the memory of the oldest inhabitant in the neighbourhood. When or how they came, or how they stayed, no one knew; it was enough that they were there, like a sort of ancestral fixture to the street. The neighbourhood was fine enough to look down upon these two tumble-down shops at the corner, kept by Tony and Mrs. Murphy, the grocer. It was a semi-fashionable locality, far up-town, away from the old-time French quarter. It was the sort of neighbourhood where millionaires live before their fortunes are made and fashionable, high-priced private schools flourish, where the small cottages are occupied by aspiring school-teachers and choir-singers. Such was this locality, and you must admit that it was indeed a condescension to tolerate Tony and Mrs. Murphy.

He was a great, black-bearded, hoarse-voiced, six-foot specimen of Italian humanity, who looked in his little shop and on the prosaic pavement of Prytania Street somewhat as Hercules might seem in a modern drawing-room. You instinctively thought of wild mountain-passes, and the gleaming dirks of bandit contadini in looking at him. What his last name was, no one knew. Someone had maintained once that he had been christened Antonio Malatesta, but that was unauthentic, and as little to be believed as that other wild theory that her name was Mary.

She was meek, pale, little, ugly, and German. Altogether part of his arms and legs would have very decently made another larger than she. Her hair was pale and drawn in sleek, thin tightness away from a pinched, pitiful face, whose dull cold eyes hurt you, because you knew they were trying to mirror sorrow, and could not because of their expressionless quality. No matter what the weather or what her other toilet, she always wore a thin little shawl of dingy brick-dust hue about her shoulders. No matter what the occasion or what the day, she always carried her knitting with her, and seldom ceased the incessant twist, twist of the shining steel among the white cotton meshes. She might put down the needles and lace into the spool-box long enough to open oysters, or wrap up fruit and candy, or count out wood and coal into infinitesimal portions, or do her housework; but the knitting was snatched with avidity at the first spare moment, and the worn, white, blue-marked fingers, half enclosed in kid-glove stalls for protection, would writhe and twist in and out again. Little girls just learning to crochet borrowed their patterns from Tony's wife, and it was considered quite a mark of advancement to have her inspect a bit of lace done by eager, chubby fingers. The ladies in larger houses, whose husbands would be millionaires some day, bought her lace, and gave it to their servants for Christmas presents.

As for Tony, when she was slow in opening his oysters or in cooking his red beans and spaghetti, he roared at her, and prefixed picturesque adjectives to her lace, which made her hide it under her apron with a fearsome look in her dull eyes.

He hated her in a lusty, roaring fashion, as a healthy beefy boy hates a sick cat and torments it to madness. When she displeased him, he beat her, and knocked her frail form on the floor. The children could tell when this had happened. Her eyes would be red, and there would be blue marks on her face and neck. "Poor Mrs. Tony," they would say, and nestle close to her. Tony did not roar at her for petting them, perhaps because they spent money on the multi-hued candy in glass jars on the shelves.

Her mother appeared upon the scene once, and stayed a short time; but Tony got drunk one day and beat her because she ate too much, and she disappeared soon after. Whence she came and where she departed, no one could tell, not even Mrs. Murphy, the Pauline Pry and Gazette of the block.

Tony had gout, and suffered for many days in roaring helplessness, the while his foot, bound and swathed in many folds of red flannel, lay on the chair before him. In proportion as his gout increased and he bawled from pure physical discomfort, she became light-hearted, and moved about the shop with real, brisk cheeriness. He could not hit her then without such pain that after one or two trials he gave up in disgust.

So the dull years had passed, and life had gone on pretty much the same for Tony and the German wife and the shop. The children came on Sunday evenings to buy the stick candy, and on week-days for coal and wood. The servants came to buy oysters for the larger houses, and to gossip over the counter about their employers. The little dry woman knitted, and the big man moved lazily in and out in his red flannel shirt, exchanged politics with the tailor next door through the window, or lounged into Mrs. Murphy's bar and drank fiercely. Some of the children grew up and moved away, and other little girls came to buy candy and eat pink lagniappe fishes, and the shop still thrived.

One day Tony was ill, more than the mummied foot of gout, or the wheeze of asthma; he must keep his bed and send for the doctor.

She clutched his arm when he came, and pulled him into the tiny room.

"Is it——is it anything much, doctor?" she gasped.

Æsculapius shook his head as wisely as the occasion would permit. She followed him out of the room into the shop.

"Do you——will he get well, doctor?"

Æsculapius buttoned up his frock coat, smoothed his shining hat, cleared his throat, then replied oracularly,

"Madam, he is completely burned out inside. Empty as a shell, madam, empty as a shell. He cannot live, for he has nothing to live on."

As the cobblestones rattled under the doctor's equipage rolling leisurely up Prytania Street, Tony's wife sat in her chair and laughed,—laughed with a hearty joyousness that lifted the film from the dull eyes and disclosed a sparkle beneath.

The drear days went by, and Tony lay like a veritable Samson shorn of his strength, for his voice was sunken to a hoarse, sibilant whisper, and his black eyes gazed fiercely from the shock of hair and beard about a white face. Life went on pretty much as before in the shop; the children paused to ask how Mr. Tony was, and even hushed the jingles on their bell hoops as they passed the door. Red-headed Jimmie, Mrs. Murphy's nephew, did the hard jobs, such as splitting wood and lifting coal from the bin; and in the intervals between tending the fallen giant and waiting on the customers, Tony's wife sat in her accustomed chair, knitting fiercely, with an inscrutable smile about her purple compressed mouth.

Then John came, introducing himself, serpent-wise, into the Eden of her bosom.

John was Tony's brother, huge and bluff too, but fair and blond, with the beauty of Northern Italy. With the same lack of race pride which Tony had displayed in selecting his German spouse, John had taken unto himself Betty, a daughter of Erin, aggressive, powerful, and cross-eyed. He turned up now, having heard of this illness, and assumed an air of remarkable authority at once.

A hunted look stole into the dull eyes, and after John had departed with blustering directions as to Tony's welfare, she crept to his bedside timidly.

"Tony," she said,—"Tony, you are very sick."

An inarticulate growl was the only response.

"Tony, you ought to see the priest; you mustn't go any longer without taking the sacrament."

The growl deepened into words.

"Don't want any priest; you're always after some snivelling old woman's fuss. You and Mrs. Murphy go on with your church; it won't make *you* any better."

She shivered under this parting shot, and crept back into the shop. Still the priest came next day.

She followed him in to the bedside and knelt timidly.

"Tony," she whispered, "here's Father Leblanc."

Tony was too languid to curse out loud; he only expressed his hate in a toss of the black beard and shaggy mane.

"Tony," she said nervously, "won't you do it now? It won't take long, and it will be better for you when you go——Oh, Tony, don't——don't laugh. Please, Tony, here's the priest."

But the Titan roared aloud: "No; get out. Think I'm a-going to give you a chance to grab my money now? Let me die and go to hell in peace."

Father Leblanc knelt meekly and prayed, and the woman's weak pleadings continued,——

"Tony, I've been true and good and faithful to you. Don't die and leave me no better than before. Tony, I do want to be a good woman once, a real-for-true married woman. Tony, here's the priest; say yes." And she wrung her ringless hands.

"You want my money," said Tony, slowly, "and you sha'n't have it, not a cent; John shall have it."

Father Leblanc shrank away like a fading spectre. He came next day and next day, only to see re-enacted the same piteous scene,—the woman pleading to be made a wife ere death hushed Tony's blasphemies, the man chuckling in pain-racked glee at the prospect of her bereaved misery. Not all the prayers of Father Leblanc nor the wailings of Mrs. Murphy could alter the determination of the will beneath the shock of hair; he gloated in his physical weakness at the tenacious grasp on his mentality.

"Tony," she wailed on the last day, her voice rising to a shriek in its eagerness, "tell them I'm your wife; it'll be the same. Only say it, Tony, before you die!"

He raised his head, and turned stiff eyes and gibbering mouth on her; then, with one chill finger pointing at John, fell back dully and heavily.

They buried him with many honours by the Society of Italia's Sons. John took possession of the shop when they returned home, and found the money hidden in the chimney corner.

As for Tony's wife, since she was not his wife after all, they sent her forth in the world penniless, her worn fingers clutching her bundle of clothes in nervous agitation, as though they regretted the time lost from knitting.

1899

Mary Wilkins Freeman
(1852–1930)

Mary Wilkins Freeman was one of the nineteenth-century middle-class women who needed the income from their short stories and novels to live. She supported herself and an aunt for many years, bringing her knowledge of New England women's lives into the fiction that would later be known as *realistic*. In her choice of characters, situations, and narrative strategies, Freeman aimed to write accessibly about human beings in the sometimes necessary conflicts of their daily lives. Her now classic story, "The Revolt of 'Mother,'" shows the long-suffering Sarah Penn pushed beyond her usual passive acceptance to a rebellion that surprises not only her children and husband, but their community. That Freeman maintains sympathy for all, even the complacent husband Adoniram, is the mark of her great ability to show individual behavior as part of a complex social system (here, the patriarchal and the agrarian).

Mary Wilkins led a successful writer's life until she was 49, when—after a ten-year courtship—she married Dr. Charles Freeman. They moved away from her home in Randolph, Massachusetts, the site of much of her fiction, to Metuchen, New Jersey. As her husband grew debilitated from alcoholism, he forced her to write for the income they needed to live. After twenty years of unhappiness, during which time he was often institutionalized, the couple separated. In 1926, Mary Wilkins Freeman was awarded the William Dean Howells Gold Medal for Fiction by the American Academy of Letters; that same year, with Edith Wharton, she was inducted into the National Institute of Arts and Letters (the first women members elected to that august body).

THE REVOLT OF "MOTHER"

"Father!"

"What is it?"

"What are them men diggin' over there in the field for?"

There was a sudden dropping and enlarging of the lower part of the old man's face, as if some heavy weight had settled therein; he shut his mouth tight, and went on harnessing the great bay mare. He hustled the collar on to her neck with a jerk.

"Father!"

The old man slapped the saddle upon the mare's back.

"Look here, father, I want to know what them men are diggin' over in the field for, an' I'm goin' to know."

"I wish you'd go into the house, mother, an' 'tend to your own affairs," the old man said then. He ran his words together, and his speech was almost as inarticulate as a growl.

But the woman understood; it was her most native tongue. "I ain't goin' into the house till you tell me what them men are doin' over there in the field," said she.

Then she stood waiting. She was a small woman, short and straight-waisted like a child in her brown cotton gown. Her forehead was mild and benevolent between the smooth curves of gray hair; there were meek downward lines about her nose and mouth; but her eyes, fixed upon the old man, looked as if the meekness had been the result of her own will, never of the will of another.

They were in the barn, standing before the wide open doors. The spring air, full of the smell of growing grass and unseen blossoms, came in their faces. The deep yard in front was littered with farm wagons and piles of wood; on the edges, close to the fence and the house, the grass was a vivid green, and there were some dandelions.

The old man glanced doggedly at his wife as he tightened the last buckles on the harness. She looked as immovable to him as one of the rocks in his pasture-land, bound to the earth with generations of blackberry vines. He slapped the reins over the horse, and started forth from the barn.

"*Father!*" said she.

The old man pulled up. "What is it?"

"I want to know what them men are diggin' over there in that field for."

"They're diggin' a cellar, I s'pose, if you've got to know."

"A cellar for what?"

"A barn."

"A barn? You ain't goin' to build a barn over there where we was goin' to have a house, father?"

The old man said not another word. He hurried the horse into the farm wagon, and clattered out of the yard, jouncing as sturdily on his seat as a boy.

The woman stood a moment looking after him, then she went out of the barn across a corner of the yard to the house. The house, standing at right angles with the great barn and a long reach of sheds and out-buildings, was infinitesimal compared with them. It was scarcely as commodious for people as the little boxes under the barn eaves were for doves.

A pretty girl's face, pink and delicate as a flower, was looking out of one of the house windows. She was watching three men who were digging over in the field which bounded the yard near the road line. She turned quietly when the woman entered.

"What are they digging for, mother?" said she. "Did he tell you?"

"They're diggin' for—a cellar for a new barn."

"Oh, mother, he ain't going to build another barn?"

"That's what he says."

A boy stood before the kitchen glass combing his hair. He combed slowly and painstakingly, arranging his brown hair in a smooth hillock over his forehead. He did not seem to pay any attention to the conversation.

"Sammy, did you know father was going to build a new barn?" asked the girl.

The boy combed assiduously.

"Sammy!"

He turned, and showed a face like his father's under his smooth crest of hair. "Yes, I s'pose I did," he said, reluctantly.

"How long have you known it?" asked his mother.

" 'Bout three months, I guess."

"Why didn't you tell of it?"

"Didn't think 'twould do no good."

"I don't see what father wants another barn for," said the girl, in her sweet, slow voice. She turned again to the window, and stared out at the digging men in the field. Her tender, sweet face was full of a gentle distress. Her forehead was as bald and innocent as a baby's, with the light hair strained back from it in a row of curl-papers. She was quite large, but her soft curves did not look as if they covered muscles.

Her mother looked sternly at the boy. "Is he goin' to buy more cows?" said she.

The boy did not reply; he was tying his shoes.

"Sammy, I want you to tell me if he's goin' to buy more cows."

"I s'pose he is."

"How many?"

"Four, I guess."

His mother said nothing more. She went into the pantry, and there was a clatter of dishes. The boy got his cap from a nail behind the door, took an old arithmetic from the shelf, and started for school. He was lightly built, but clumsy. He went out of the yard with a curious spring in the hips, that made his loose homemade jacket tilt up in the rear.

The girl went to the sink, and began to wash the dishes that were piled up there. Her mother came promptly out of the pantry, and shoved her aside. "You wipe 'em," said she; "I'll wash. There's a good many this mornin'."

The mother plunged her hands vigorously into the water, the girl wiped the plates slowly and dreamily. "Mother," said she, "don't you think it's too bad father's going to build that new barn, much as we need a decent house to live in?"

Her mother scrubbed a dish fiercely. "You ain't found out yet we're women-folks, Nanny Penn," said she. "You ain't seen enough of men-folks yet to. One of these days you'll find it out, an' then you'll know that we know only what men-folks think we do, so far as any use of it goes, an' how we'd ought to reckon men-folks in with Providence, an' not complain of what they do any more than we do of the weather."

"I don't care; I don't believe George is anything like that, anyhow," said Nanny. Her delicate face flushed pink, her lips pouted softly, as if she were going to cry.

"You wait an' see. I guess George Eastman ain't no better than other men. You hadn't ought to judge father, though. He can't help it, 'cause he don't look at things jest the way we do. An' we've been pretty comfortable here, after all. The roof don't leak—ain't never but once—that's one thing. Father's kept it shingled right up."

"I do wish we had a parlor."

"I guess it won't hurt George Eastman any to come to see you in a nice clean kitchen. I guess a good many girls don't have as good a place as this. Nobody's ever heard me complain."

"I ain't complained either, mother."

"Well, I don't think you'd better, a good father an' a good home as you've got. S'pose your father made you go out an' work for your livin'? Lots of girls have to that ain't no stronger an' better able to than you be."

Sarah Penn washed the frying-pan with a conclusive air. She scrubbed the outside of it as faithfully as the inside. She was a masterly keeper of her box of a house. Her one living-room never seemed to have in it any of the dust which the friction of life with inanimate matter produces. She swept, and there seemed to be no dirt to go before the broom; she cleaned, and one could see no difference. She was like an artist so perfect that he has apparently no art. To-day she got out a mixing bowl and a board, and rolled some pies, and there was no more flour upon her than upon her daughter who was doing finer work. Nanny was to be married in the fall, and she was sewing on some white cambric and embroidery. She sewed industriously while her mother cooked, her soft milk-white hands and wrists showed whiter than her delicate work.

"We must have the stove moved out in the shed before long," said Mrs. Penn. "Talk about not havin' things, it's been a real blessin' to be able to put a stove up in that shed in hot weather. Father did one good thing when he fixed that stove-pipe out there."

Sarah Penn's face as she rolled her pies had that expression of meek vigor which might have characterized one of the New Testament saints. She was making mince-pies. Her husband, Adoniram Penn, liked them better than any other kind. She baked twice a week. Adoniram often liked a piece of pie between meals. She hurried this morning. It had been later than usual when she began, and she wanted to have a pie baked for dinner. However deep a resentment she might be forced to hold against her husband, she would never fail in sedulous attention to his wants.

Nobility of character manifests itself at loop-holes when it is not provided with large doors. Sarah Penn's showed itself to-day in flaky dishes of pastry. So she made the pies faithfully, while across the table she could see, when she glanced up from her work, the sight that rankled in her patient and stead-fast soul—the digging of the cellar of the new barn in the place where Adon-iram forty years ago had promised her their new house should stand.

The pies were done for dinner. Adoniram and Sammy were home a few minutes after twelve o'clock. The dinner was eaten with serious haste. There was never much conversation at the table in the Penn family. Adoniram asked a blessing, and they ate promptly, then rose up and went about their work.

Sammy went back to school, taking soft sly lopes out of the yard like a rabbit. He wanted a game of marbles before school, and feared his father would give him some chores to do. Adoniram hastened to the door and called after him, but he was out of sight.

"I don't see what you let him go for, mother," said he. "I wanted him to help me unload that wood."

Adoniram went to work out in the yard unloading wood from the wagon. Sarah put away the dinner dishes, while Nanny took down her curl-papers and changed her dress. She was going down to the store to buy some more embroidery and thread.

When Nanny was gone, Mrs. Penn went to the door. "Father!" she called.

"Well, what is it!"

"I want to see you jest a minute, father."

"I can't leave this wood nohow. I've got to git it unloaded an' go for a load of gravel afore two o'clock. Sammy had ought to helped me. You hadn't ought to let him go to school so early."

"I want to see you jest a minute."

"I tell ye I can't, nohow, mother."

"Father, you come here." Sarah Penn stood in the door like a queen; she held her head as if it bore a crown; there was the patience which makes authority royal in her voice. Adoniram went.

Mrs. Penn led the way into the kitchen, and pointed to a chair. "Sit down, father," said she; "I've got somethin' I want to say to you."

He sat down heavily; his face was quite stolid, but he looked at her with restive eyes. "Well, what is it, mother?"

"I want to know what you're buildin' that new barn for, father?"

"I ain't got nothin' to say about it."

"It can't be you think you need another barn?"

"I tell ye I ain't got nothin' to say about it, mother; an' I ain't goin' to say nothin'."

"Be you goin' to buy more cows?"

Adoniram did not reply; he shut his mouth tight.

"I know you be, as well as I want to. Now, father, look here"—Sarah Penn had not sat down; she stood before her husband in the humble fashion of a Scripture woman—"I'm goin' to talk real plain to you; I never have sence I married you, but I'm goin' to now. I ain't never complained, an' I ain't goin' to complain now, but I'm goin' to talk plain. You see this room here, father; you look at it well. You see there ain't no carpet on the floor, an' you see the paper is all dirty, an' droppin' off the walls. We ain't had no new paper on it for ten year, an' then I put it on myself, an' it didn't cost but ninepence a roll. You see this room, father; it's all the one I've had to work in an' eat in an' sit in sence we was married. There ain't another woman in the whole town whose husband ain't got half the means you have but what's got better. It's all the room Nanny's got to have her company in; an' there ain't one of her mates but what's got better, an' their fathers not so able as hers is. It's all the room she'll have to be married in. What would you have thought, father, if we had had our weddin' in a room no better than this? I was married in my mother's parlor, with a carpet on the floor, an' stuffed furniture, an' a mahogany card-table. An' this is all the room my daughter will have to be married in. Look here, father!"

Sarah Penn went across the room as though it were a tragic stage. She flung open a door and disclosed a tiny bedroom, only large enough for a bed and bureau, with a path between. "There, father," said she—"there's all the room I've had to sleep in forty year. All my children were born there—the two that died, an' the two that's livin'. I was sick with a fever there."

She stepped to another door and opened it. It led into the small, ill-lighted pantry. "Here," said she, "is all the buttery I've got—every place I've got for my dishes, to set away my victuals in, an' to keep my milk-pans in. Father, I've been takin' care of the milk of six cows in this place, an' now you're goin' to build a new barn, an' keep more cows, an' give me more to do in it."

She threw open another door. A narrow crooked flight of stairs wound upward from it. "There, father," said she, "I want you to look at the stairs that go up to them two unfinished chambers that are all the places our son an' daughter have had to sleep in all their lives. There ain't a prettier girl in town nor a more ladylike one than Nanny, an' that's the place she has to sleep in. It ain't so good as your horse's stall; it ain't so warm an' tight."

Sarah Penn went back and stood before her husband. "Now, father," said she, "I want to know if you think you're doin' right an' accordin' to what you profess. Here, when we was married, forty year ago, you promised me faithful that we should have a new house built in that lot over in the field before the year was out. You said you had money enough, an' you wouldn't ask me to live in no such place as this. It is forty year now, an' you've been makin' more money, an' I've been savin' of it for you ever since, an' you ain't built no house yet. You've built sheds an' cow-houses an' one new barn, an' now you're goin' to build another. Father, I want to know if you think it's right. You're lodgin' your dumb beasts better than you are your own flesh an' blood. I want to know if you think it's right."

"I ain't got nothin' to say."

"You can't say nothin' without ownin' it ain't right, father. An' there's another thing—I ain't complained; I've got along forty year, an' I s'pose I should forty more, if it wa'n't for that—if we don't have another house. Nanny she can't live with us after she's married. She'll have to go somewheres else to live away from us, an' it don't seem as if I could have it so, noways, father. She wa'n't ever strong. She's got considerable color, but there wa'n't ever any backbone to her. I've always took the heft of everything off her, an' she ain't fit to keep house an' do everything herself. She'll be all worn out inside of a year. Think of her doin' all the washin' an' ironin' an' bakin' with them soft white hands an' arms, an' sweepin'! I can't have it so, noways, father."

Mrs. Penn's face was burning; her mild eyes gleamed. She had pleaded her little cause like a Webster; she had ranged from severity to pathos; but her opponent employed that obstinate silence which makes eloquence futile with mocking echoes. Adoniram arose clumsily.

"Father, ain't you got nothin' to say?" said Mrs. Penn.

"I've got to go off after that load of gravel. I can't stan' here talkin' all day."

"Father, won't you think it over, an' have a house built there instead of a barn?"

"I ain't got nothin' to say."

Adoniram shuffled out. Mrs. Penn went into her bedroom. When she came out, her eyes were red. She had a roll of unbleached cotton cloth. She spread it out on the kitchen table, and began cutting out some shirts for her husband. The men over in the field had a team to help them this afternoon; she could hear their halloos. She had a scanty pattern for the shirts; she had to plan and piece the sleeves.

Nanny came home with her embroidery, and sat down with her needle-work. She had taken down her curl-papers, and there was a soft roll of fair hair like an aureole over her forehead; her face was as delicately fine and clear as porcelain. Suddenly she looked up, and the tender red flamed all over her face and neck. "Mother," said she.

"What say?"

"I've been thinking—I don't see how we're goin' to have any—wedding in this room. I'd be ashamed to have his folks come if we didn't have anybody else."

"Mebbe we can have some new paper before then; I can put it on. I guess you won't have no call to be ashamed of your belongin's."

"We might have the wedding in the new barn," said Nanny, with gentle pettishness. "Why, mother, what makes you look so?"

Mrs. Penn had started, and was staring at her with a curious expression. She turned again to her work, and spread out a pattern carefully on the cloth. "Nothin'," said she.

Presently Adoniram clattered out of the yard in his two-wheeled dump cart, standing as proudly upright as a Roman charioteer. Mrs. Penn opened the door and stood there a minute looking out; the halloos of the men sounded louder.

It seemed to her all through the spring months that she heard nothing but the halloos and the noises of saws and hammers. The new barn grew fast. It was a fine edifice for this little village. Men came on pleasant Sundays, in their meeting suits and clean shirt bosoms, and stood around it admiringly. Mrs. Penn did not speak of it, and Adoniram did not mention it to her, although sometimes, upon a return from inspecting it, he bore himself with injured dignity.

"It's a strange thing how your mother feels about the new barn," he said, confidentially, to Sammy one day.

Sammy only grunted after an odd fashion for a boy; he had learned it from his father.

The barn was all completed ready for use by the third week in July. Adoniram had planned to move his stock in on Wednesday; on Tuesday he received a letter which changed his plans. He came in with it early in the morning. "Sammy's been to the post-office," said he, "an' I've got a letter from Hiram." Hiram was Mrs. Penn's brother, who lived in Vermont.

"Well," said Mrs. Penn, "what does he say about the folks?"

"I guess they're all right. He says he thinks if I come up country right off there's a chance to buy jest the kind of a horse I want." He stared reflectively out of the window at the new barn.

Mrs. Penn was making pies. She went on clapping the rolling-pin into the crust, although she was very pale, and her heart beat loudly.

"I dun' know but what I'd better go," said Adoniram. "I hate to go off jest now, right in the midst of hayin', but the ten-acre lot's cut, an' I guess Rufus an' the others can git along without me three or four days. I can't get a horse round here to suit me, nohow, an' I've got to have another for all that wood-haulin' in the fall. I told Hiram to watch out, an' if he got wind of a good horse to let me know. I guess I'd better go."

"I'll get out your clean shirt an' collar," said Mrs. Penn calmly.

She laid out Adoniram's Sunday suit and his clean clothes on the bed in the little bedroom. She got his shaving-water and razor ready. At last she buttoned on his collar and fastened his black cravat.

Adoniram never wore his collar and cravat except on extra occasions. He held his head high, with a rasped dignity. When he was all ready, with his coat and hat brushed, and a lunch of pie and cheese in a paper bag, he hesitated on the threshold of the door. He looked at his wife, and his manner was defiantly apologetic. "*If* them cows come to-day, Sammy can drive 'em into the new barn," said he; "an' when they bring the hay up, they can pitch it in there."

"Well," replied Mrs. Penn.

Adoniram set his shaven face ahead and started. When he had cleared the door-step, he turned and looked back with a kind of nervous solemnity. "I shall be back by Saturday if nothin' happens," said he.

"Do be careful, father," returned his wife.

She stood in the door with Nanny at her elbow and watched him out of sight. Her eyes had a strange, doubtful expression in them; her peaceful forehead was contracted. She went in, and about her baking again. Nanny sat sewing. Her wedding-day was drawing nearer, and she was getting pale and thin with her steady sewing. Her mother kept glancing at her.

"Have you got that pain in your side this mornin'?" she asked.

"A little."

Mrs. Penn's face, as she worked, changed, her perplexed forehead smoothed, her eyes were steady, her lips firmly set. She formed a maxim for herself, although incoherently with her unlettered thoughts. "Unsolicited opportunities are the guide-posts of the Lord to the new roads of life," she repeated in effect, and she made up her mind to her course of action.

"S'posin' I *had* wrote to Hiram," she muttered once, when she was in the pantry—"s'posin' I had wrote, an' asked him if he knew of any horse? But I didn't, an' father's goin' wa'n't none of my doin'. It looks like a providence." Her voice rang out quite loud at the last.

"What you talkin' about, mother?" called Nanny.

"Nothin'."

Mrs. Penn hurried her baking; at eleven o'clock it was all done. The load of hay from the west field came slowly down the cart track, and drew up at the new barn. Mrs. Penn ran out. "Stop!" she screamed—"stop!"

The men stopped and looked; Sammy upreared from the top of the load, and stared at his mother.

"Stop!" she cried out again. "Don't you put the hay in that barn; put it in the old one."

"Why, he said to put it in here," returned one of the hay-makers, wonderingly. He was a young man, a neighbor's son, whom Adoniram hired by the year to help on the farm.

"Don't you put the hay in the new barn; there's room enough in the old one, ain't there?" said Mrs. Penn.

"Room enough," returned the hired man, in his thick, rustic tones. "Didn't need the new barn, nohow, far as room's concerned. Well, I s'pose he changed his mind." He took hold of the horses' bridles.

Mrs. Penn went back to the house. Soon the kitchen windows were darkened, and a fragrance like warm honey came into the room.

Nanny laid down her work. "I thought father wanted them to put the hay into the new barn?" she said, wonderingly.

"It's all right," replied her mother.

Sammy slid down from the load of hay, and came in to see if dinner was ready.

"I ain't goin' to get a regular dinner to-day, as long as father's gone," said his mother. "I've let the fire go out. You can have some bread an' milk an' pie. I thought we could get along." She set out some bowls of milk, some bread and a pie on the kitchen table. "You'd better eat your dinner now," said she. "You might jest as well get through with it. I want you to help me afterward."

Nanny and Sammy stared at each other. There was something strange in their mother's manner. Mrs. Penn did not eat anything herself. She went into the pantry, and they heard her moving dishes while they ate. Presently she came out with a pile of plates. She got the clothes-basket out of the shed, and packed them in it. Nanny and Sammy watched. She brought out cups and saucers, and put them in with the plates.

"What you goin' to do, mother?" inquired Nanny, in a timid voice. A sense of something unusual made her tremble, as if it were a ghost. Sammy rolled his eyes over his pie.

"You'll see what I'm goin' to do," replied Mrs. Penn. "If you're through, Nanny, I want you to go up-stairs an' pack up your things; an' I want you, Sammy, to help me take down the bed in the bedroom."

"Oh, mother, what for?" gasped Nanny.

"You'll see."

During the next few hours a feat was performed by this simple, pious New England mother which was equal in its way to Wolfe's storming of the Heights of Abraham. It took no more genius and audacity of bravery for Wolfe to cheer his wondering soldiers up those steep precipices, under the sleeping eyes of the enemy, than for Sarah Penn, at the head of her children, to move all their little household goods into the new barn while her husband was away.

Nanny and Sammy followed their mother's instructions without a murmur; indeed, they were overawed. There is a certain uncanny and superhuman quality about all such purely original undertakings as their mother's was to them. Nanny went back and forth with her light loads, and Sammy tugged with sober energy.

At five o'clock in the afternoon the little house in which the Penns had lived for forty years had emptied itself into the new barn.

Every builder builds somewhat for unknown purposes, and is in a measure a prophet. The architect of Adoniram Penn's barn, while he designed it for the comfort of four-footed animals, had planned better than he knew for the comfort of humans. Sarah Penn saw at a glance its possibilities. These great box-stalls, with quilts hung before them, would make better bedrooms than the one she had occupied for forty years, and there was a tight carriage-room. The harness-room, with its chimney and shelves, would make a kitchen of her dreams. The great middle space would make a parlor, by-and-by, fit for a palace. Up-stairs there was as much room as down. With partitions and windows, what a house would there be! Sarah looked at the row of stanchions before the allotted space for cows, and reflected that she would have her front entry there.

At six o'clock the stove was up in the harness-room, the kettle was boiling, and the table set for tea. It looked almost as home-like as the abandoned house across the yard had ever done. The young hired man milked, and Sarah directed him calmly to bring the milk to the new barn. He came gaping, dropping little blots of foam from the brimming pails on the grass. Before the next morning he had spread the story of Adoniram Penn's wife moving into the new barn all over the little village. Men assembled in the store and talked it over, women with shawls over their heads scuttled into each other's houses before their work was done. Any deviation from the ordinary course of life in this quiet town was enough to stop all progress in it. Everybody paused to look at the staid, independent figure on the side track. There was a difference of opinion with regard to her. Some held her to be insane; some, of a lawless and rebellious spirit.

Friday the minister went to see her. It was in the forenoon, and she was at the barn door shelling peas for dinner. She looked up and returned his salutation with dignity, then she went on with her work. She did not invite him in. The saintly expression of her face remained fixed, but there was an angry flush over it.

The minister stood awkwardly before her, and talked. She handled the peas as if they were bullets. At last she looked up, and her eyes showed the spirit that her meek front had covered for a lifetime.

"There ain't no use talkin', Mr. Hersey," said she. "I've thought it all over an' over, an' I believe I'm doin' what's right. I've made it the subject of prayer, an' it's betwixt me an' the Lord an' Adoniram. There ain't no call for nobody else to worry about it."

"Well, of course, if you have brought it to the Lord in prayer, and feel satisfied that you are doing right, Mrs. Penn," said the minister, helplessly. His thin gray-bearded face was pathetic. He was a sickly man; his youthful confidence had cooled; he had to scourge himself up to some of his pastoral duties as relentlessly as a Catholic ascetic, and then he was prostrated by the smart.

"I think it's right jest as much as I think it was right for our forefathers to come over from the old country 'cause they didn't have what belonged to 'em," said Mrs. Penn. She arose. The barn threshold might have been Plymouth Rock from her bearing. "I don't doubt you mean well, Mr. Hersey," said she, "but there are things people hadn't ought to interfere with. I've been a member of the church for over forty year. I've got my own mind an' my own feet, an' I'm goin' to think my own thoughts an' go my own ways, an' nobody but the Lord is goin' to dictate to me unless I've a mind to have him. Won't you come in an' set down? How is Mis' Hersey?"

"She is well, I thank you," replied the minister. He added some more perplexed apologetic remarks; then he retreated.

He could expound the intricacies of every character study in the Scriptures, he was competent to grasp the Pilgrim Fathers and all historical innovators, but Sarah Penn was beyond him. He could deal with primal cases, but parallel ones worsted him. But, after all, although it was aside from his province, he wondered more how Adoniram Penn would deal with his wife than how the Lord would. Everybody shared the wonder. When Adoniram's four new cows arrived, Sarah ordered three to be put in the old barn, the other in the house shed where the cooking-stove had stood. That added to the excitement. It was whispered that all four cows were domiciled in the house.

Towards sunset on Saturday, when Adoniram was expected home, there was a knot of men in the road near the new barn. The hired man had milked, but he still hung around the premises. Sarah Penn had supper all ready. There were brown-bread and baked beans and a custard pie; it was the supper Adoniram loved on a Saturday night. She had a clean calico, and she bore herself imperturbably. Nanny and Sammy kept close at her heels. Their eyes were large, and Nanny was full of nervous tremors. Still there was to them more pleasant excitement than anything else. An inborn confidence in their mother over their father asserted itself.

Sammy looked out of the harness-room window. "There he is," he announced, in an awed whisper. He and Nanny peeped around the casing. Mrs. Penn kept on about her work. The children watched Adoniram leave the new horse standing in the drive while he went to the house door. It was fastened. Then he went around to the shed. That door was seldom locked, even when the family was away. The thought how her father would be confronted by the cow flashed upon Nanny. There was a hysterical sob in her throat. Adoniram emerged from the shed and stood looking about in a dazed fashion. His lips moved; he was saying something, but they could not hear what it was. The hired man was peeping around a corner of the old barn, but nobody saw him.

Adoniram took the new horse by the bridle and led him across the yard to the new barn. Nanny and Sammy slunk close to their mother. The barn doors rolled back, and there stood Adoniram, with the long mild face of the great Canadian farm horse looking over his shoulder.

Nanny kept behind her mother, but Sammy stepped suddenly forward, and stood in front of her.

Adoniram stared at the group. "What on airth you all down here for?" said he. "What's the matter over to the house?"

"We've come here to live, father," said Sammy. His shrill voice quavered out bravely.

"What"—Adoniram sniffed—"what is it smells like cookin'?" said he. He stepped forward and looked in the open door of the harness-room. Then he turned to his wife. His old bristling face was pale and frightened. "What on airth does this mean, mother?" he gasped.

"You come in here, father," said Sarah. She led the way into the harness-room and shut the door. "Now, father," said she, "you needn't be scared. I ain't crazy. There ain't nothin' to be upset over. But we've come here to live, an' we're goin' to live here. We've got jest as good a right here as new horses an' cows. The house wa'n't fit for us to live in any longer, an' I made up my mind I wa'n't goin' to stay there. I've done my duty by you forty year, an' I'm goin' to do it now; but I'm goin' to live here. You've got to put in some windows and partitions; an' you'll have to buy some furniture."

"Why, mother!" the old man gasped.

"You'd better take your coat off an' get washed—there's the wash-basin—an' then we'll have supper."

"Why, mother!"

Sammy went past the window, leading the new horse to the old barn. The old man saw him, and shook his head speechlessly. He tried to take off his coat, but his arms seemed to lack the power. His wife helped him. She poured some water into the tin basin, and put in a piece of soap. She got the comb and brush, and smoothed his thin gray hair after he had washed. Then she put the beans, hot bread, and tea on the table. Sammy came in, and the family drew up. Adoniram sat looking dazedly at his plate, and they waited.

"Ain't you goin' to ask a blessin', father?" said Sarah.

And the old man bent his head and mumbled.

All through the meal he stopped eating at intervals, and stared furtively at his wife; but he ate well. The home food tasted good to him, and his old frame was too sturdily healthy to be affected by his mind. But after supper he went out, and sat down on the step of the smaller door at the right of the barn, through which he had meant his Jerseys to pass in stately file, but which Sarah designed for her front house door, and he leaned his head on his hands.

After the supper dishes were cleared away and the milk-pans washed, Sarah went out to him. The twilight was deepening. There was a clear green glow in the sky. Before them stretched the smooth level of field; in the distance was a cluster of haystacks like the huts of a village; the air was very cool and calm and sweet. The landscape might have been an ideal one of peace.

Sarah bent over and touched her husband on one of his thin, sinewy shoulders. "Father!"

The old man's shoulders heaved: he was weeping.

"Why, don't do so, father," said Sarah.

"I'll—put up the—partitions, an'—everything you—want, mother."

Sarah put her apron up to her face; she was overcome by her own triumph.

Adoniram was like a fortress whose walls had no active resistance, and went down the instant the right besieging tools were used. "Why, mother," he said, hoarsely, "I hadn't no idee you was so set on't as all this comes to."

1891

40

Charlotte Perkins Stetson Gilman
(1860–1935)

Charlotte Perkins Stetson Gilman, one of the foremost feminist intellectuals of her day, wrote over fifteen books and nearly two hundred short stories and founded an influential women's rights magazine, *Forerunner*. Largely self-educated, Gilman's primary concern was the subservience of women within what she called "androcentric" society. In *Women and Economics* (1898) and her feminist utopia, *Herland* (1915), Gilman emphasizes that women must have "world work" beyond their traditional roles as wife and mother in order to maintain their emotional and intellectual independence.

After forming powerful relationships with a number of women, Gilman married Charles Walter Stetson in 1882. She fell into a deep depression after the birth of their daughter in 1885, which led her to consult Dr. S. Weir Mitchell, a famous physician who advocated the "rest cure" for ambitious women. Against Weir's advice, she resumed her writing career and was able to lift herself out of the mental condition that incapacitates the heroine of her haunting, autobiographical story, "The Yellow Wall-Paper" (1893).

After an amicable divorce in which she granted Stetson primary custody of their child, Charlotte supported herself by writing and lecturing, occupations that continued after her 1900 marriage to George Houghton Gilman. Following her husband's death in 1934, she moved to California where she lived with her daughter and Stetson's second wife. She was diagnosed with inoperable cancer soon after, made a formal farewell to her family and friends, and ended her life with chloroform.

❖

THE YELLOW WALL-PAPER

It is very seldom that mere ordinary people like John and myself secure ancestral halls for the summer.

A colonial mansion, a hereditary estate, I would say a haunted house, and reach the height of romantic felicity—but that would be asking too much of fate!

Still I will proudly declare that there is something queer about it.

Else, why should it be let so cheaply? And why have stood so long untenanted?

John laughs at me, of course, but one expects that in marriage.

John is practical in the extreme. He has no patience with faith, an intense horror of superstition, and he scoffs openly at any talk of things not to be felt and seen and put down in figures.

John is a physician, and *perhaps*—(I would not say it to a living soul, of course, but this is dead paper and a great relief to my mind—) *perhaps* that is one reason I do not get well faster.

You see he does not believe I am sick!

And what can one do?

If a physician of high standing, and one's own husband, assures friends and relatives that there is really nothing the matter with one but temporary nervous depression—a slight hysterical tendency[1]—what is one to do?

My brother is also a physician, and also of high standing, and he says the same thing.

So I take phosphates or phosphites—whichever it is, and tonics, and journeys, and air, and exercise, and am absolutely forbidden to "work" until I am well again.

Personally, I disagree with their ideas.

Personally, I believe that congenial work, with excitement and change, would do me good.

But what is one to do?

I did write for a while in spite of them; but it *does* exhaust me a good deal—having to be so sly about it, or else meet with heavy opposition.

I sometimes fancy that in my condition if I had less opposition and more society and stimulus—but John says the very worst thing I can do is to think about my condition, and I confess it always makes me feel bad.

So I will let it alone and talk about the house.

The most beautiful place! It is quite alone, standing well back from the road, quite three miles from the village. It makes me think of English places that you read about, for there are hedges and walls and gates that lock, and lots of separate little houses for the gardeners and people.

There is a *delicious* garden! I never saw such a garden—large and shady, full of box-bordered paths, and lined with long grape-covered arbors with seats under them.

There were greenhouses, too, but they are all broken now.

There was some legal trouble, I believe, something about the heirs and coheirs; anyhow, the place has been empty for years.

That spoils my ghostliness, I am afraid, but I don't care—there is something strange about the house—I can feel it.

---

[1]Many women's ailments were diagnosed as coming from the womb (*hyster*). This ineffectual diagnosis often led to mistreatment.

I even said so to John one moonlight evening, but he said what I felt was a *draught,* and shut the window.

I get unreasonably angry with John sometimes. I'm sure I never used to be so sensitive. I think it is due to this nervous condition.

But John says if I feel so, I shall neglect proper self-control; so I take pains to control myself—before him, at least, and that makes me very tired.

I don't like our room a bit. I wanted one downstairs that opened on the piazza and had roses all over the window, and such pretty old-fashioned chintz hangings! but John would not hear of it.

He said there was only one window and not room for two beds, and no near room for him if he took another.

He is very careful and loving, and hardly lets me stir without special direction.

I have a schedule prescription for each hour in the day; he takes all care from me, and so I feel basely ungrateful not to value it more.

He said we came here solely on my account, that I was to have perfect rest and all the air I could get. "Your exercise depends on your strength, my dear," said he, "and your food somewhat on your appetite; but air you can absorb all the time." So we took the nursery at the top of the house.

It is a big, airy room, the whole floor nearly, with windows that look all ways, and air and sunshine galore. It was nursery first and then playroom and gymnasium, I should judge; for the windows are barred for little children, and there are rings and things in the walls.

The paint and paper look as if a boys' school had used it. It is stripped off—the paper—in great patches all around the head of my bed, about as far as I can reach, and in a great place on the other side of the room low down. I never saw a worse paper in my life.

One of those sprawling flamboyant patterns committing every artistic sin.

It is dull enough to confuse the eye in following, pronounced enough to constantly irritate and provoke study, and when you follow the lame uncertain curves for a little distance they suddenly commit suicide—plunge off at outrageous angles, destroy themselves in unheard of contradictions.

The color is repellant, almost revolting; a smouldering unclean yellow, strangely faded by the slow-turning sunlight.

It is a dull yet lurid orange in some places, a sickly sulphur tint in others.

No wonder the children hated it! I should hate it myself if I had to live in this room long.

There comes John, and I must put this away,—he hates to have me write a word.

* * *

We have been here two weeks, and I haven't felt like writing before, since that first day.

I am sitting by the window now, up in this atrocious nursery, and there is nothing to hinder my writing as much as I please, save lack of strength.

John is away all day, and even some nights when his cases are serious.

I am glad my case is not serious!

But these nervous troubles are dreadfully depressing.

John does not know how much I really suffer. He knows there is no *reason* to suffer, and that satisfies him.

Of course it is only nervousness. It does weigh on me so not to do my duty in any way!

I meant to be such a help to John, such a real rest and comfort, and here I am a comparative burden already!

Nobody would believe what an effort it is to do what little I am able,—to dress and entertain, and order things.

It is fortunate Mary is so good with the baby. Such a dear baby!

And yet I *cannot* be with him, it makes me so nervous.

I suppose John never was nervous in his life. He laughs at me so about this wall-paper!

At first he meant to repaper the room, but afterwards he said that I was letting it get the better of me, and that nothing was worse for a nervous patient than to give way to such fancies.

He said that after the wall-paper was changed it would be the heavy bedstead, and then the barred windows, and then that gate at the head of the stairs, and so on.

"You know the place is doing you good," he said, "and really, dear, I don't care to renovate the house just for a three months' rental."

"Then do let us go downstairs," I said, "there are such pretty rooms there."

Then he took me in his arms and called me a blessed little goose, and said he would go down cellar, if I wished, and have it whitewashed into the bargain.

But he is right enough about the beds and windows and things.

It is an airy and comfortable room as any one need wish, and, of course, I would not be so silly as to make him uncomfortable just for a whim.

I'm really getting quite fond of the big room, all but that horrid paper.

Out of one window I can see the garden, those mysterious deep-shaded arbors, the riotous old-fashioned flowers, and bushes and gnarly trees.

Out of another I get a lovely view of the bay and a little private wharf belonging to the estate. There is a beautiful shaded lane that runs down there from the house. I always fancy I see people walking in these numerous paths and arbors, but John has cautioned me not to give way to fancy in the least.

44

He says that with my imaginative power and habit of story-making, a nervous weakness like mine is sure to lead to all manner of excited fancies, and that I ought to use my will and good sense to check the tendency. So I try.

I think sometimes that if I were only well enough to write a little it would relieve the press of ideas and rest me.

But I find I get pretty tired when I try.

It is so discouraging not to have any advice and companionship about my work. When I get really well, John says we will ask cousin Henry and Julia down for a long visit; but he says he would as soon put fireworks in my pillow-case as to let me have those stimulating people about now.

I wish I could get well faster.

But I must not think about that. This paper looks to me as if it *knew* what a vicious influence it had!

There is a recurrent spot where the pattern lolls like a broken neck and two bulbous eyes stare at you upside down.

I get positively angry with the impertinence of it and the everlastingness. Up and down and sideways they crawl, and those absurd, unblinking eyes are everywhere. There is one place where two breaths didn't match, and the eyes go all up and down the line, one a little higher than the other.

I never saw so much expression in an inanimate thing before, and we all know how much expression they have! I used to lie awake as a child and get more entertainment and terror out of blank walls and plain furniture than most children could find in a toy-store.

I remember what a kindly wink the knobs of our big, old bureau used to have, and there was one chair that always seemed like a strong friend.

I used to feel that if any of the other things looked too fierce I could always hop into that chair and be safe.

The furniture in this room is no worse than inharmonious, however, for we had to bring it all from downstairs. I suppose when this was used as a playroom they had to take the nursery things out, and no wonder! I never saw such ravages as the children have made here.

The wall-paper, as I said before, is torn off in spots, and it sticketh closer than a brother—they must have had perseverance as well as hatred.

Then the floor is scratched and gouged and splintered, the plaster itself is dug out here and there, and this great heavy bed which is all we found in the room, looks as if it had been through the wars.

But I don't mind it a bit—only the paper.

There comes John's sister. Such a dear girl as she is, and so careful of me! I must not let her find me writing.

She is a perfect and enthusiastic housekeeper, and hopes for no better profession. I verily believe she thinks it is the writing which made me sick!

But I can write when she is out, and see her a long way off from these windows.

There is one that commands the road, a lovely shaded winding road, and one that just looks off over the country. A lovely country, too, full of great elms and velvet meadows.

This wall-paper has a kind of subpattern in a different shade, a particularly irritating one, for you can only see it in certain lights, and not clearly then.

But in the places where it isn't faded and where the sun is just so—I can see a strange, provoking, formless sort of figure, that seems to skulk about behind that silly and conspicuous front design.

There's sister on the stairs!

Well, the Fourth of July is over! The people are all gone and I am tired out. John thought it might do me good to see a little company, so we just had mother and Nellie and the children down for a week.

Of course I didn't do a thing. Jennie sees to everything now.

But it tired me all the same.

John says if I don't pick up faster he shall send me to Weir Mitchell[2] in the fall.

But I don't want to go there at all. I had a friend who was in his hands once, and she says he is just like John and my brother, only more so!

Besides, it is such an undertaking to go so far.

I don't feel as if it was worth while to turn my hand over for anything, and I'm getting dreadfully fretful and querulous.

I cry at nothing, and cry most of the time.

Of course I don't when John is here, or anybody else, but when I am alone.

And I am alone a good deal just now. John is kept in town very often by serious cases, and Jennie is good and lets me alone when I want her to.

So I walk a little in the garden or down that lovely lane, sit on the porch under the roses, and lie down up here a good deal.

I'm getting really fond of the room in spite of the wall-paper. Perhaps *because* of the wall-paper.

It dwells in my mind so!

I lie here on this great immovable bed—it is nailed down, I believe—and follow that pattern about by the hour. It is as good as gymnastics, I assure you. I start, we'll say, at the bottom, down in the corner over there where it has not been touched, and I determine for the thousandth time that I *will* follow that pointless pattern to some sort of a conclusion.

I know a little of the principle of design, and I know this thing was not

[2]Dr. S. Weir Mitchell (1829–1914) invented a rest cure which consisted of bed rest, a diet of rich foods, and separation from stimuli. Gilman had herself undergone his treatment.

arranged on any laws of radiation, or alternation, or repetition, or symmetry, or anything else that I ever heard of.

It is repeated, of course, by the breadths, but not otherwise.

Looked at in one way each breadth stands alone, the bloated curves and flourishes—a kind of "debased Romanesque" with *delirium tremens*—go waddling up and down in isolated columns of fatuity.

But, on the other hand, they connect diagonally, and the sprawling outlines run off in great slanting waves of optic horror, like a lot of wallowing seaweeds in full chase.

The whole thing goes horizontally, too, at least it seems so, and I exhaust myself in trying to distinguish the order of its going in that direction.

They have used a horizontal breadth for a frieze, and that adds wonderfully to the confusion.

There is one end of the room where it is almost intact, and there, when the crosslights fade and the low sun shines directly upon it, I can almost fancy radiation after all,—the interminable grotesque seem to form around a common centre and rush off in headlong plunges of equal distraction.

It makes me tired to follow it. I will take a nap I guess.

I don't know why I should write this.

I don't want to.

I don't feel able.

And I know John would think it absurd. But I *must* say what I feel and think in some way—it is such a relief!

But the effort is getting to be greater than the relief.

Half the time now I am awfully lazy, and lie down ever so much.

John says I mustn't lose my strength, and has me take cod liver oil and lots of tonics and things, to say nothing of ale and wine and rare meat.

Dear John! He loves me very dearly, and hates to have me sick. I tried to have a real earnest reasonable talk with him the other day, and tell him how I wish he would let me go and make a visit to Cousin Henry and Julia.

But he said I wasn't able to go, nor able to stand it after I got there; and I did not make out a very good case for myself, for I was crying before I had finished.

It is getting to be a great effort for me to think straight. Just this nervous weakness I suppose.

And dear John gathered me up in his arms, and just carried me upstairs and laid me on the bed, and sat by me and read to me till it tired my head.

He said I was his darling and his comfort and all he had, and that I must take care of myself for his sake, and keep well.

He says no one but myself can help me out of it, that I must use my will and self-control and not let any silly fancies run away with me.

There's one comfort, the baby is well and happy, and does not have to occupy this nursery with the horrid wall-paper.

If we had not used it, that blessed child would have! What a fortunate escape! Why, I wouldn't have a child of mine, an impressionable little thing, live in such a room for worlds.

I never thought of it before, but it is lucky that John kept me here after all, I can stand it so much easier than a baby, you see.

Of course I never mention it to them any more—I am too wise,—but I keep watch of it all the same.

There are things in that paper that nobody knows but me, or ever will.

Behind that outside pattern the dim shapes get clearer every day.

It is always the same shape, only very numerous.

And it is like a woman stooping down and creeping about behind that pattern. I don't like it a bit. I wonder—I begin to think—I wish John would take me away from here!

It is so hard to talk with John about my case, because he is so wise, and because he loves me so.

But I tried it last night.

It was moonlight. The moon shines in all around just as the sun does.

I hate to see it sometimes, it creeps so slowly, and always comes in by one window or another.

John was asleep and I hated to waken him, so I kept still and watched the moonlight on that undulating wall-paper till I felt creepy.

The faint figure behind seemed to shake the pattern, just as if she wanted to get out.

I got up softly and went to feel and see if the paper *did* move, and when I came back John was awake.

"What is it, little girl?" he said. "Don't go walking about like that—you'll get cold."

I thought it was a good time to talk, so I told him that I really was not gaining here, and that I wished he would take me away.

"Why, darling!" said he, "our lease will be up in three weeks, and I can't see how to leave before.

"The repairs are not done at home, and I cannot possibly leave town just now. Of course if you were in any danger, I could and would, but you really are better, dear, whether you can see it or not. I am a doctor, dear, and I know. You are gaining flesh and color, your appetite is better, I feel really much easier about you."

"I don't weigh a bit more," said I, "nor as much; and my appetite may be better in the evening when you are here, but it is worse in the morning when you are away!"

"Bless her little heart!" said he with a big hug, "she shall be as sick as she pleases! But now let's improve the shining hours[3] by going to sleep, and talk about it in the morning!"

"And you won't go away?" I asked gloomily.

"Why, how can I, dear? It is only three weeks more and then we will take a nice little trip of a few days while Jennie is getting the house ready. Really dear you are better!"

"Better in body perhaps—" I began, and stopped short, for he sat up straight and looked at me with such a stern, reproachful look that I could not say another word.

"My darling," said he, "I beg of you, for my sake and for our child's sake, as well as for your own, that you will never for one instant let that idea enter your mind! There is nothing so dangerous, so fascinating, to a temperament like yours. It is a false and foolish fancy. Can you not trust me as a physician when I tell you so?"

So of course I said no more on that score, and we went to sleep before long. He thought I was asleep first, but I wasn't, and lay there for hours trying to decide whether that front pattern and the back pattern really did move together or separately.

On a pattern like this, by daylight, there is a lack of sequence, a defiance of law, that is a constant irritant to a normal mind.

The color is hideous enough, and unreliable enough, and infuriating enough, but the pattern is torturing.

You think you have mastered it, but just as you get well underway in following, it turns a back-somersault and there you are. It slaps you in the face, knocks you down, and tramples upon you. It is like a bad dream.

The outside pattern is a florid arabesque, reminding one of a fungus. If you can imagine a toadstool in joints, an interminable string of toadstools, budding and sprouting in endless convolutions—why, that is something like it.

That is, sometimes!

There is one marked peculiarity about this paper, a thing nobody seems to notice but myself, and that is that it changes as the light changes.

When the sun shoots in through the east window—I always watch for that first long, straight ray—it changes so quickly that I never can quite believe it.

---

[3]"How doth the little busy bee / Improve each shining hour" were platitudinous lines from a popular poem by Isaac Watts (1674–1748), "Against Idleness and Mischief."

That is why I watch it always.

By moonlight—the moon shines in all night when there is a moon—I wouldn't know it was the same paper.

At night in any kind of light, in twilight, candlelight, lamplight, and worst of all by moonlight, it becomes bars! The outside pattern I mean, and the woman behind it is as plain as can be.

I didn't realize for a long time what the thing was that showed behind, that dim sub-pattern, but now I am quite sure it is a woman.

By daylight she is subdued, quiet. I fancy it is the pattern that keeps her so still. It is so puzzling. It keeps me quiet by the hour.

I lie down ever so much now. John says it is good for me, and to sleep all I can.

Indeed he started the habit by making me lie down for an hour after each meal.

It is a very bad habit I am convinced, for you see I don't sleep.

And that cultivates deceit, for I don't tell them I'm awake—O no!

The fact is I am getting a little afraid of John.

He seems very queer sometimes, and even Jennie has an inexplicable look.

It strikes me occasionally, just as a scientific hypothesis,—that perhaps it is the paper!

I have watched John when he did not know I was looking, and come into the room suddenly on the most innocent excuses, and I've caught him several times *looking at the paper!* And Jennie too. I caught Jennie with her hand on it once.

She didn't know I was in the room, and when I asked her in a quiet, a very quiet voice, with the most restrained manner possible, what she was doing with the paper—she turned around as if she had been caught stealing, and looked quite angry—asked me why I should frighten her so!

Then she said that the paper stained everything it touched, that she had found yellow smooches on all my clothes and John's, and she wished we would be more careful!

Did not that sound innocent? But I know she was studying that pattern, and I am determined that nobody shall find it out but myself!

Life is very much more exciting now than it used to be. You see I have something more to expect, to look forward to, to watch. I really do eat better, and am more quiet than I was.

John is so pleased to see me improve! He laughed a little the other day, and said I seemed to be flourishing in spite of my wall-paper.

I turned it off with a laugh. I had no intention of telling him it was *because* of the wall-paper—he would make fun of me. He might even want to take me away.

I don't want to leave now until I have found it out. There is a week more, and I think that will be enough.

I'm feeling ever so much better! I don't sleep much at night, for it is so interesting to watch developments; but I sleep a good deal in the daytime.

In the daytime it is tiresome and perplexing.

There are always new shoots on the fungus, and new shades of yellow all over it. I cannot keep count of them, though I have tried conscientiously.

It is the strangest yellow, that wall-paper! It makes me think of all the yellow things I ever saw—not beautiful ones like buttercups, but old foul, bad yellow things.

But there is something else about that paper—the smell! I noticed it the moment we came into the room, but with so much air and sun it was not bad. Now we have had a week of fog and rain, and whether the windows are open or not, the smell is here.

It creeps all over the house.

I find it hovering in the dining-room, skulking in the parlor, hiding in the hall, lying in wait for me on the stairs.

It gets into my hair.

Even when I go to ride, if I turn my head suddenly and surprise it—there is that smell!

Such a peculiar odor, too! I have spent hours in trying to analyze it, to find what it smelled like.

It is not bad—at first, and very gentle, but quite the subtlest, most enduring odor I ever met.

In this damp weather it is awful, I wake up in the night and find it hanging over me.

It used to disturb me at first. I thought seriously of burning the house—to reach the smell.

But now I am used to it. The only thing I can think of that it is like is the *color* of the paper! A yellow smell.

There is a very funny mark on this wall, low down, near the mopboard. A streak that runs round the room. It goes behind every piece of furniture, except the bed, a long, straight, even *smooch*, as if it had been rubbed over and over.

I wonder how it was done and who did it, and what they did it for. Round and round and round—round and round and round—it makes me dizzy!

I really have discovered something at last.

Through watching so much at night, when it changes so, I have finally found out.

The front pattern *does* move—and no wonder! The woman behind shakes it!

Sometimes I think there are a great many women behind, and sometimes only one, and she crawls around fast, and her crawling shakes it all over.

Then in the very bright spots she keeps still, and in the very shady spots she just takes hold of the bars and shakes them hard.

And she is all the time trying to climb through. But nobody could climb through that pattern—it strangles so; I think that is why it has so many heads.

They get through, and then the pattern strangles them off and turns them upside down, and makes their eyes white!

If those heads were covered or taken off it would not be half so bad.

I think that woman gets out in the daytime!

And I'll tell you why—privately—I've seen her!

I can see her out of every one of my windows!

It is the same woman, I know, for she is always creeping, and most women do not creep by daylight.

I see her in that long shaded lane, creeping up and down. I see her in those dark grape arbors, creeping all around the garden.

I see her on that long road under the trees, creeping along, and when a carriage comes she hides under the blackberry vines.

I don't blame her a bit. It must be very humiliating to be caught creeping by daylight!

I always lock the door when I creep by daylight. I can't do it at night, for I know John would suspect something at once.

And John is so queer now, that I don't want to irritate him. I wish he would take another room! Besides, I don't want anybody to get that woman out at night but myself.

I often wonder if I could see her out of all the windows at once.

But, turn as fast as I can, I can only see out of one at one time.

And though I always see her, she *may* be able to creep faster than I can turn!

I have watched her sometimes away off in the open country, creeping as fast as a cloud shadow in a high wind.

If only that top pattern could be gotten off from the under one! I mean to try it, little by little.

I have found out another funny thing, but I shan't tell it this time! It does not do to trust people too much.

There are only two more days to get this paper off, and I believe John is beginning to notice. I don't like the look in his eyes.

And I heard him ask Jennie a lot of professional questions about me. She had a very good report to give.

She said I slept a good deal in the daytime.

John knows I don't sleep very well at night, for all I'm so quiet!

He asked me all sorts of questions, too, and pretended to be very loving and kind.

As if I couldn't see through him!

Still, I don't wonder he acts so, sleeping under this paper for three months.

It only interests me, but I feel sure John and Jennie are secretly affected by it.

Hurrah! This is the last day, but it is enough. John to stay in town over night, and won't be out until this evening.

Jennie wanted to sleep with me—the sly thing! but I told her I should undoubtedly rest better for a night all alone.

That was clever, for really I wasn't alone a bit! As soon as it was moonlight and that poor thing began to crawl and shake the pattern, I got up and ran to help her.

I pulled and she shook, I shook and she pulled, and before morning we had peeled off yards of that paper.

A strip about as high as my head and half around the room.

And then when the sun came and that awful pattern began to laugh at me, I declared I would finish it to-day!

We go away to-morrow, and they are moving all my furniture down again to leave things as they were before.

Jennie looked at the wall in amazement, but I told her merrily that I did it out of pure spite at the vicious thing.

She laughed and said she wouldn't mind doing it herself, but I must not get tired.

How she betrayed herself that time!

But I am here, and no person touches this paper but me,—not *alive!*

She tried to get me out of the room—it was too patent! But I said it was so quiet and empty and clean now that I believed I would lie down again and sleep all I could; and not to wake me even for dinner—I would call when I woke.

So now she is gone, and the servants are gone, and the things are gone, and there is nothing left but that great bedstead nailed down, with the canvas mattress we found on it.

We shall sleep downstairs to-night, and take the boat home to-morrow.

I quite enjoy the room, now it is bare again.

How those children did tear about here!

This bedstead is fairly gnawed!

But I must get to work.

I have locked the door and thrown the key down into the front path.

I don't want to go out, and I don't want to have anybody come in, till John comes.

I want to astonish him.

I've got a rope up here that even Jennie did not find. If that woman does get out, and tries to get away, I can tie her!

But I forgot I could not reach far without anything to stand on!

This bed will *not* move!

I tried to lift and push it until I was lame, and then I got so angry I bit off a little piece at one corner—but it hurt my teeth.

Then I peeled off all the paper I could reach standing on the floor. It sticks horribly and the pattern just enjoys it! All those strangled heads and bulbous eyes and waddling fungus growths just shriek with derision!

I am getting angry enough to do something desperate. To jump out of the window would be admirable exercise, but the bars are too strong even to try.

Besides I wouldn't do it. Of course not. I know well enough that a step like that is improper and might be misconstrued.

I don't like to *look* out of the windows even—there are so many of those creeping women, and they creep so fast.

I wonder if they all come out of that wall-paper as I did?

But I am securely fastened now by my well-hidden rope—you don't get *me* out in the road there!

I suppose I shall have to get back behind the pattern when it comes night, and that is hard!

It is so pleasant to be out in this great room and creep around as I please!

I don't want to go outside. I won't, even if Jennie asks me to.

For outside you have to creep on the ground, and everything is green instead of yellow.

But here I can creep smoothly on the floor, and my shoulder just fits in that long smooch around the wall, so I cannot lose my way.

Why there's John at the door!

It is no use, young man, you can't open it!

How he does call and pound!

Now he's crying for an axe.

It would be a shame to break down that beautiful door!

"John dear!" said I in the gentlest voice, "the key is down by the front steps, under a plantain leaf!"

That silenced him for a few moments.

Then he said—very quietly indeed, "Open the door, my darling!"

"I can't," said I. "The key is down by the front door under a plantain leaf!"

And then I said it again, several times, very gently and slowly, and said it so often that he had to go and see, and he got it of course, and came in. He stopped short by the door.

"What is the matter?" he cried. "For God's sake, what are you doing!"

I kept on creeping just the same, but I looked at him over my shoulder.

"I've got out at last," said I, "in spite of you and Jane. And I've pulled off most of the paper, so you can't put me back!"

Now why should that man have fainted? But he did, and right across my path by the wall, so that I had to creep over him every time!

1892

Marietta Holley

(1836–1926)

Marietta Holley was a political satirist who gained national attention with *My Opinions and Betsey Bobbet's* (1873), her first major prose work. In this and in several subsequent volumes, the conservative opinions of Josiah Allen and Betsey Bobbet are juxtaposed with the plain, folksy wisdom of Samantha (or, as she usually designates herself, "Josiah Allen's wife"), a believer in "wimmen's rights." Holley wrote over twenty volumes of prose, most of them in the vernacular humor tradition, and became as popular as her contemporary, Mark Twain. Using Samantha as her spokeswoman, she addressed all of the permutations of feminism as well as such issues as imperialism, racism, temperance, family violence, class pretensions, and the double sexual standard (the subject of "A Male Magdalene").

Holley was born and raised on a farm in Jefferson County, New York, the youngest of seven children. When her older brothers went West, Holley had to end her education and work to support the struggling family. She never lost touch with her humble origins. Even after her books brought fame, she eschewed celebrity, preferring to remain home in Jefferson County. Enjoying a lively correspondence with other writers and women's activists, Holley lived alone in a mansion built on her father's property until her death at eighty-nine years of age.

❖

A MALE MAGDALENE
from *Samantha vs. Josiah*

I attended a beautiful party yesterday; it wuz a anniversary, and carried on regardless of style and expense. Over seven wuz invited, besides the happy folks who gin the party. And the cookin' wuz, I do almost believe, as good as my own. That's dretful high praise, but Miss Chawgo deserves it. It wuz to celebrate their weddin' day, which occurred the year before at half past two, and dinner wuz on the table at exactly that hour.

There wuz Josiah and me, Miss Bizer Kipp and Lophemia, she that wuz Submit Tewksbury, and her husband, and Widder Bassett and her baby. That made a little over seven; the baby hadn't ort to count so high as a adult. The party wuz all in high sperits, and all dressed well and looked well, though Miss Bassett whispered to me that Miss Kipp had flammed out a little too much.

She wuz very dressy in a pink flowered shally with lots of ribbins kinder floatin', but she felt and said that she wuz celebratin' a very auspicious occasion with very dear friends, which made us lenitent to her. Weddin' anniversaries are now and agin happy and agreeable, and the male party here, Nelt Chawgo, how much! how much that young man had to be thankful for! yes indeed!

And Id'no but I might jest as well tell about it now as any time while in history's pages the gay party is settin' 'round the bountifully spread table.

I'll make the story short as possible. Most three years ago we had a new arrival in Jonesville, a young grocery man by the name of Nelson Chawgo; the young folks all called him Nelt. He bought out old uncle Simon Pettigrew, his good will and bizness, though so fur as the good will went I wouldn't paid a cent fur it, or not more than a cent, anyway. Uncle Sime abused his wife, wuz clost as the bark to a tree, and some mentioned the word "sand" in connection with his sugar, and "peas" with his coffee, and etcetery, etcetery. But his bizness wuz what might be called first rate; he had laid up money and retired triumphant at seventy-one.

But to resoom. Uncle Sime Pettigrew's place of bizness wuz a handsome one, a new brick block with stun granite trimmin's, some stained glass over the doors and winders, and everything else it needed for comfort and respectability. He had a big stock of goods and whoever bought 'em and set up bizness in that handsome new block would have been looked up to even if he had been an old man with a bald head, rumatiz and a wooden leg.

But when it wuz a young, handsome, unmarried man, you may imagin he made a sensation to once, and he wuz as handsome a chap as you would often see, light completed with sort o' melancholy blue eyes and curly brown hair and mustash.

The Jonesvillians and Loontowners went into ecstacies over him the first day he appeared in meetin', he wuz so beautiful. They acted fairly foolish; they praised him up so and wuz so enthusiastick. But it is my way to keep calmer and more demute. I will try to restrain my emotions if I have to tie a string to 'em and haul 'em back if I find 'em liable to go too fur. I never could bear anybody or anything that slopped over, from a oriter to a kettle of maple syrup, and I kep' holt of my faculties and common sense in this case, and several of the sisters in the meetin'-house got mad as hens at me, and importuned me sharp as to why I didn't go into spazzums of admiration over him.

And I sez, "He is sweet-lookin', I can't deny that, but there is a kinder weak and waverin' expression to his face that would cause me anxiety if I wuz his Ma."

But when I promulgated these idees to the other sistern, sister Bizer Kipp especially, she most took my head off. She said his face wuz "Bea-u-tiful, just perfection."

But I still repeated what I had said in a megum tone, and with my most megumest mean, but I agreed with her in a handsome way that Nelt wuz what would be called very, very sweet and winsome, and would be apt to attract female attention and be sought after. And so he wuz. As days rolled on he grew to be the rage in Jonesville, a he-belle, as you may say. Groceries lay in piles on wimmen's buttery shelves and sickness wuz rampant, caused by a too free use of raisins and cinnamon and all-spice. They are too dryin'.

And still the wimmen flocked to his counters as if they couldn't buy enough stuff, and they priced peanuts, and got samples of cast-steel soap, and acted. No place of amusement wuz considered agreeable or endurable without Nelt Chawgo; no party wuz gin without his name stood first on the list, and when he got there he wuz surrounded by a host of the fair sect showerin' attention on him, anxious to win a smile from him.

He wuz doin' dretful well in bizness, and doin' well in morals so fur as I knew. He wuz payin' attention in a sort of a languid, half-hearted way, to Lophemia Kipp. She wuz a pretty girl, sister Kipp's only child. It wuz very pleasin' to her Ma. Folks thought she wuz the one that had brought it about; she acted so triumphant and big feelin' about it, and told everybody how active Nelt wuz in the meetin'-house, and how well he wuz doin' in bizness, and how strong and stimulatin' his tea and coffee wuz.

Folks thought, as I say, that she had more to do about his payin' attention to Lophemia than she did, fur it wuz thought that she had gin her heart to young Jim Carter, old lawyer Carter's youngest boy. He had gone west on a ranch, and it wuz spozed he carried her heart with him. It wuz known he carried her picture, took standin', with a smile on the pretty lips and a happy glow in the eyes, rousted up it wuz spozed by young Jim himself. He went with her to the photographer's; that wuz known, too. Miss Kipp had boasted a sight about him, his good looks and his good bizness and his attentions to Lophemia till Nelt come.

Sister Kipp hain't megum, she is one of the too enthusiastick ones whose motto is not "Love me little love me long," but "Love me a immense quantity in a short time." It stands to reason that if the stream is over rapid the pond will run out sooner; if the stream meanders slow and stiddy, it will last longer.

Well, 'tennyrate she wuz all took up with Nelt Chawgo, and praisin' him up as she had to the very skies you may imagin my feelin's when one day she fairly bust into my settin'-room, out of breath and red in the face, and sez: "I've discovered the dretfulest thing! the awfulest, the most harrowin'! Nelt Chawgo, that young he-hussy, shall never enter my doors agin!"

"Whyee!" sez I, "what's the matter?"

Sez she, "He's a lost young man, a ruined feller!"

"Whyee!" sez I agin, and I sunk right down in my tracts in a rockin'-chair, she havin' sunken down in one opposite; and sez I, "I hain't mistrusted it. He has acted modest and moral; I can't believe it!"

"But it is so," sez he. "He has been ruined. Angerose Wilds, a dashin' young woman up in the town of Lyme, is responsible."

"I have hearn of her," sez I. "She had quite a lot of money left her, and is cuttin' a great swath."

"Well," sez sister Kipp, "she has deceived and ruined Nelt Chawgo, and then deserted him; it has all been proved out, and he shall never speak to Lophemia agin, the miserable outcaster!"

Well, I wuz dumbfoundered and horrowstruck like all the rest of Jonesville, but I, as my way is, made inquiries and investigations into the matter. And the next time I see Miss Kipp, and she begun to me awful about Nelt, runnin' him down all to nort, I sez to her, "I have found out some things that makes me feel more lenitent towards Nelson Chawgo."

Oh, how she glared at me. "Lenitent!" sez she, "I'd talk about lenity to that villian, that low ruined creeter!"

"Well," sez I, "I have inquired and found out that Angerose Wilds jest follered Nelt up with attentions and flatteries, and it is spozed up in Lyme that he wuz tempted and fell under a promise of marriage." And I spoke with considerable indignation about this woman who wuz beautiful and rich and holdin' her head high.

But Miss Kipp treated it light and sez: "Oh, young wimmen must sow their wild oats, and then they most always settle down and make the best of wives."

But agin I mentioned extenuatin' circumstances. Sez I, "Miss Wilds wuz noble and galliant in her bearin'; she wuz rich and handsome, and she turned his thoughtless head with her flatteries, and won his pure and unsophistocated heart, so it wuz like wax or putty in her designin' hands, and then at the last she turned her back on him and wouldn't have nothin' to say to him." But these mitigatin', extenuatin' circumstances didn't mitigate or extenuate a mite with Miss Kipp.

Sez she bitterly, "Couldn't he have repulsed her attentions? Couldn't he have kep' his manly modesty if he had been a mind to? Wuz there any need of his fallin' to the depths of infamy he sunk to? No, he is lost, he is ruined!" sez she.

Sez I, "Sister Kipp, don't talk so scornfully; don't say ruined," sez I. "Fall is a good word to use in such a case; folks can fall and git up agin—mebby he will. But ruined is a big word and a hard one; it don't carry any hope with it; it breathes of despair, agony and eternal loss."

"Well," sez she, "it ort to in his case. I shall draw my skirts away from him and go by on the other side. Before his ruin he wuz a sweet, lovely young man but now he is lost. I shall have nothin' to do with him, nor Lophemia shan't."

But I still tried to draw her attention to the facts I had promulgated that Miss Wilds, too, wuz not guiltless. But she wuz sot and wouldn't yield.

She said his sect wuz considered stronger-minded than our sect, with heftier brains and mightier wills, and so it stood to reason that if he wuz tempted by one of the weaker and more feather-brained, he could have saved himself and her, too, from ruin.

There wuz some sense in her talk, I had to admit that there wuz. But I kep' on wavin' my mantilly of charity as high as I could, hopin' that some of the folds, even if it wuzn't nothin' but the end of the tabs, might sort o' shadder Nelt a little, for he wuz indeed a object of pity.

And we couldn't none of us look ahead and see the thrillin' eppisode that wuz in front on him. No, a thick veil of despair seemed to hang down in front on him. And I didn't mistrust that it wuz my hands that wuz goin' to push that veil aside and let some rays lighten up the darkness. But more of that anon and bimeby.

When the news got out about Nelt Chawgo, Jonesville society wuz rent to its very twain. The two factions led on by Miss Kipp and Nelt's friends waged a fearful warfare, some jinin' one side and some the other.

Some on 'em, the old conservative ones, wuz for overlookin' the hull matter so fur as Nelt wuz concerned and throwin' the hull blame onto the female woman up to Lyme on the safe old ground, trod so long by the world at large, that he wuz a man and so such sin in him wuzn't a sin. It wuz sin in a woman, a deep and hopeless sin that forever barred the guilty one from the pail of respectable society.

But I held to the firm belief that if she carried the pail he ort to, and visey versey. My idee wuz that they ort to carry the pail between 'em. They said it wuz sin in the woman, a turrible and hopeless sin, but in him it wuzn't. It come under the head of wild oats, which when planted thick in youth and springin' up rank, prepared the ground for a rich after crop of moral graces.

This wuz old well-established doctrine that had been follered for years and years, so they felt it wuz safe.

But one night to a church sociable when Miss Kipp had brung the subject up and one of our foremost deacons, Deacon Henzy, wuz advancin' these ideas, she that wuz Nancy Butterick, who had come to Jonesville to deliver a lecture in the interests of the W. C. T. U., she sassed Deacon Henzy right back and sez she:

"The idee of thinkin' that the same sin when committed by a man and a woman ort to be laid entirely onto the party that is in the law classed with lunaticks and idiots." Sez she, "That hain't good logic. If a woman is a fool she hadn't ort to be expected to have her brain tapped and run wisdom and morality, and if she is a lunatick she might be expected to cut up and act."

She wuz educated high, Nancy wuz, and knew a sight in the first place, as folks have to, to amount to much, for all education can do anyway is to sharpen the tools that folks use to hew their way through the wilderness of life.

Sez she, "The male sect is in the eyes of the Law the gardeens of females, and ort to act like gardeens to 'em and try to curb their folly and wickedness and restrain it instead of takin' advantage of it, and fallin' victims to their weakness." Sez she, "When a oak tree falls it falls heavier than a creepin' vine, a creepin' up and hangin' to it, and it would be jest as sensible to lay the hull of the blame on the creeper for the fall of the oak, as to put the hull of the blame on the Lyme woman."

Why, she brung up lots of simelys that fairly bristled with eloquence, and Deacon Henzy sassed her back in his way of thinkin'; it wuz a sight to hear 'em talkin' pro and con. . . .

. . . I thought Jane Ann looked queer, but I went on and sez: "Oh, if that woman could look and see the wreck she has made of that once happy and good young man, it must be she would be struck with remorse. They say she is handsome and well off, and holds her head high, while her victim is dyin' under the contempt and scorn of the world. Nobody will associate with him. Why, my Josiah draws his pantaloons away from him for fear of the contamination of his touch. He's weighed down under the scorn of the world and his own remorse. He is ruined in his bizness, and he's goin' into the gallopin' consumption as fast as he can gallop."

Jane Ann gin me such a queer look here that I involuntary follered her gaze and looked at the handsome stranger. Her work had fell into her lap, her face wuz red as blood, and she busted into tears, sayin:

"I am Angerose Wilds! I am the guilty wretch that wuz the means of that sweet and innocent young creature's fall; I am the one to blame. But," sez she with her streamin' eyes lifted to mine, "I never realized until you brung it before me the extent of my crime, but I will atone for the evil as fur as I can. I will marry him and so do all I can to lift him up and make an honest man of him, and set him right in the eyes of the community. And," sez she, while the tears chased each other down her cheeks, "Poor Nelt! poor boy! how you have suffered; and I alone am the guilty cause!"

But here I interfered agin, held up by Justice and Duty. "Don't say, mom, that you alone are to blame; divide it into two bundles of guilt, take one on your own back and pack the other onto hisen. It hain't fair for one to bear it alone, male or female."

Josiah come that very minute and I had to bid them a hasty adoo. But the last words that galliant appearin' handsome woman whispered to me wuz: "I will make an honest man of him; I will marry him."

And if you'll believe it, she did. It all ended first rate, almost like a real novel story. It seems that woman wuz so smut with remorse when it wuz brought before her in a eloquent and forcible manner; and she realized the almost irreparable wrong she had committed aginst that lovely and innocent young man, she offered him the only reparation in her power; she offered him honorable marriage, which he accepted gladly, and they got married the next week, and he brought her to Jonesville the follerin' Monday, and they sot up housekeepin' in a handsome two-story-and-a-half house, and are doin' well and bid fair to make a respectable couple.

We buy the most of our groceries there; not all, for I am megum in groceries as well as in everything else. I buy some of the other grocer, not bein' willin' to hurt his fellin's, his wife bein' a member of the same meetin'-house. But Miss Kipp can't be megum any more than my own dear pardner can. She come 'round immegiate and unanimous, and said their marriage made 'em both all that could be desired. She buys all her groceries of him; she sez his tea is cheaper and takes a spunful less in a drawin'. But I don't believe it; I believe she steeps it longer. 'Tennyrate she bought of him all her fruit and candy and stuff for Lophemia Carter's weddin', which took place some time ago.

Well, this party I sot out to tell you about wuz to celebrate the first anniversary of the Chawgo and Wilds weddin', and wuz a joyful event.

After we got home Josiah wuz so nerved up (part on't wuz the strong coffee), that I had to read three truthful articles out of the scrap-book; he a settin' leanin back in his chair a listenin' and a makin' comments on each one on 'em as I finished readin' 'em.

His talk bein' some like the little pieces they play between songs, interludes, I believe they call 'em, only his talk wuzn't all the time melogious; no, indeed; fur from it. There wuz minor cords in it, and discords, and flats and sharps, yes indeed!

1906

Kate Chopin

(1851–1904)

Kate Chopin began writing after her husband's death; in part, she needed a means of supporting her six young children. Born to a wealthy St. Louis family, Kate O'Flaherty had been well-educated in Catholic schools, and had often thought of writing. After her debut in 1868, she married Oscar Chopin, a Creole cotton trader from New Orleans. There she lived a young socialite's life of husband- and child-centered enjoyment until his unexpected death in 1882.

Returning to St. Louis, Chopin began publishing fiction in magazines; in the brief years of her writing career, she published nearly a hundred stories. Her story collections—*Bayou Folk* (1894) and *A Night in Acadie* (1897)—were popular. Although readers thought of Chopin as a "local color" writer—because she used the Cajun and Creole patois for some of her characters' dialects—she was more obviously an important mainstream writer. Her accurate portraits of Victorian and turn-of-the-century women have never been equalled for their depiction of women's interior conflicts.

In a kindly way, "A Pair of Silk Stockings" charts those conflicts within the woman protagonist. Seemingly devoted to caring and providing for her young children, she here allows her hunger for beautiful things to dominate, and she spends her money on herself. Chopin's brief but startling story involves the reader in both questioning the actions of the character, and empathizing with her.

The same kind of surprise for the reader was evident in the second of Chopin's novels, her 1899 *The Awakening*. Even though world literature of the nineteenth century was filled with such passionate women as Flaubert's Emma Bovary, George Sand's Lelia, and Ibsen's Hedda Gabler, American readers objected to Chopin's Edna Pontellier leaving her role as wife and mother and searching for a self—both erotically and professionally. Chopin's admiration for Maupaussant, Flaubert, and other continental writers led her to write fiction that was far from provincial. If readers of her time found her scandalous, readers of today find her remarkable.

❖

A PAIR OF SILK STOCKINGS

Little Mrs. Sommers one day found herself the unexpected possessor of fifteen dollars. It seemed to her a very large amount of money, and the way in which it stuffed and bulged her worn old *porte-monnaie*[1] gave her a feeling of importance such as she had not enjoyed for years.

The question of investment was one that occupied her greatly. For a day or two she walked about apparently in a dreamy state, but really absorbed in speculation and calculation. She did not wish to act hastily, to do anything she might afterward regret. But it was during the still hours of the night when she lay awake revolving plans in her mind that she seemed to see her way clearly toward a proper and judicious use of the money.

A dollar or two should be added to the price usually paid for Janie's shoes, which would insure their lasting an appreciable time longer than they usually did. She would buy so and so many yards of percale for new shirt waists for the boys and Janie and Mag. She had intended to make the old ones do by skilful patching. Mag should have another gown. She had seen some beautiful patterns, veritable bargains in the shop windows. And still there would be left enough for new stockings—two pairs apiece—and what darning that would save for a while! She would get caps for the boys and sailor-hats for the girls. The vision of her little brood looking fresh and dainty and new for once in their lives excited her and made her restless and wakeful with anticipation.

The neighbors sometimes talked of certain "better days" that little Mrs. Sommers had known before she had ever thought of being Mrs. Sommers. She herself indulged in no such morbid retrospection. She had no time—no second of time to devote to the past. The needs of the present absorbed her every faculty. A vision of the future like some dim, gaunt monster sometimes appalled her, but luckily tomorrow never comes.

Mrs. Sommers was one who knew the value of bargains; who could stand for hours making her way inch by inch toward the desired object that was selling below cost. She could elbow her way if need be; she had learned to clutch a piece of goods and hold it and stick to it with persistence and determination till her turn came to be served, no matter when it came.

But that day she was a little faint and tired. She had swallowed a light luncheon—no! when she came to think of it, between getting the children fed and the place righted, and preparing herself for the shopping bout, she had actually forgotten to eat any luncheon at all!

She sat herself upon a revolving stool before a counter that was comparatively deserted, trying to gather strength and courage to charge through an eager multitude that was besieging breast-works of shirting and figured lawn. An all-gone limp feeling had come over her and she rested her hand aimlessly upon the counter. She wore no gloves. By degrees she grew aware that her

[1] Purse.

hand had encountered something very soothing, very pleasant to touch. She looked down to see that her hand lay upon a pile of silk stockings. A placard near by announced that they had been reduced in price from two dollars and fifty cents to one dollar and ninety-eight cents; and a young girl who stood behind the counter asked her if she wished to examine their line of silk hosiery. She smiled, just as if she had been asked to inspect a tiara of diamonds with the ultimate view of purchasing it. But she went on feeling the soft, sheeny luxurious things—with both hands now, holding them up to see them glisten, and to feel them glide serpent-like through her fingers.

Two hectic blotches came suddenly into her pale cheeks. She looked up at the girl.

"Do you think there are any eights-and-a-half among these?"

There were any number of eights-and-a-half. In fact, there were more of that size than any other. Here was a light-blue pair; there were some lavender, some all black and various shades of tan and gray. Mrs. Sommers selected a black pair and looked at them very long and closely. She pretended to be examining their texture, which the clerk assured her was excellent.

"A dollar and ninety-eight cents," she mused aloud. "Well, I'll take this pair." She handed the girl a five-dollar bill and waited for her change and for her parcel. What a very small parcel it was! It seemed lost in the depths of her shabby old shopping-bag.

Mrs. Sommers after that did not move in the direction of the bargain counter. She took the elevator, which carried her to an upper floor into the region of the ladies' waiting-rooms. Here, in a retired corner, she exchanged her cotton stockings for the new silk ones which she had just bought. She was not going through any acute mental process or reasoning with herself, nor was she striving to explain to her satisfaction the motive of her action. She was not thinking at all. She seemed for the time to be taking a rest from that laborious and fatiguing function and to have abandoned herself to some mechanical impulse that directed her actions and freed her of responsibility.

How good was the touch of the raw silk to her flesh! She felt like lying back in the cushioned chair and reveling for a while in the luxury of it. She did for a little while. Then she replaced her shoes, rolled the cotton stockings together and thrust them into her bag. After doing this she crossed straight over to the shoe department and took her seat to be fitted.

She was fastidious. The clerk could not make her out; he could not reconcile her shoes with her stockings, and she was not too easily pleased. She held back her skirts and turned her feet one way and her head another way as she glanced down at the polished, pointed-tipped boots. Her foot and ankle looked very pretty. She could not realize that they belonged to her and were a part of herself. She wanted an excellent and stylish fit, she told the young fellow who served her, and she did not mind the difference of a dollar or two more in the price so long as she got what she desired.

It was a long time since Mrs. Sommers had been fitted with gloves. On rare occasions when she had bought a pair they were always "bargains," so cheap that it would have been preposterous and unreasonable to have expected them to be fitted to the hand.

Now she rested her elbow on the cushion of the glove counter, and a pretty, pleasant young creature, delicate and deft of touch, drew a long-wristed "kid" over Mrs. Sommers's hand. She smoothed it down over the wrist and buttoned it neatly, and both lost themselves for a second or two in admiring contemplation of the little symmetrical gloved hand. But there were other places where money might be spent.

There were books and magazines piled up in the window of a stall a few paces down the street. Mrs. Sommers bought two high-priced magazines such as she had been accustomed to read in the days when she had been accustomed to other pleasant things. She carried them without wrapping. As well as she could she lifted her skirts at the crossings. Her stockings and boots and well fitting gloves had worked marvels in her bearing—had given her a feeling of assurance, a sense of belonging to the well-dressed multitude.

She was very hungry. Another time she would have stilled the cravings for food until reaching her own home, where she would have brewed herself a cup of tea and taken a snack of anything that was available. But the impulse that was guiding her would not suffer her to entertain any such thought.

There was a restaurant at the corner. She had never entered its doors; from the outside she had sometimes caught glimpses of spotless damask and shining crystal, and soft-stepping waiters serving people of fashion.

When she entered her appearance created no surprise, no consternation, as she had half feared it might. She seated herself at a small table alone, and an attentive waiter at once approached to take her order. She did not want a profusion; she craved a nice and tasty bite—a half dozen blue-points, a plump chop with cress, a something sweet—a crème-frappée, for instance; a glass of Rhine wine, and after all a small cup of black coffee.

While waiting to be served she removed her gloves very leisurely and laid them beside her. Then she picked up a magazine and glanced through it, cutting the pages with a blunt edge of her knife. It was all very agreeable. The damask was even more spotless than it had seemed through the window, and the crystal more sparkling. There were quiet ladies and gentlemen, who did not notice her, lunching at the small tables like her own. A soft, pleasing strain of music could be heard, and a gentle breeze was blowing through the window. She tasted a bite, and she read a word or two, and she sipped the amber wine and wiggled her toes in the silk stockings. The price of it made no difference. She counted the money out to the waiter and left an extra coin on his tray, whereupon he bowed before her as before a princess of royal blood.

There was still money in her purse, and her next temptation presented itself in the shape of a matinée poster.

It was a little later when she entered the theatre, the play had begun and the house seemed to her to be packed. But there were vacant seats here and there, and into one of them she was ushered, between brilliantly dressed women who had gone there to kill time and eat candy and display their gaudy attire. There were many others who were there solely for the play and acting. It is safe to say there was no one present who bore quite the attitude which Mrs. Sommers did to her surroundings. She gathered in the whole—stage and players and people in one wide impression, and absorbed it and enjoyed it. She laughed at the comedy and wept—she and the gaudy woman next to her wept over the tragedy. And they talked a little together over it. And the gaudy woman wiped her eyes and sniffled on a tiny square of filmy, perfumed lace and passed little Mrs. Sommers her box of candy.

The play was over, the music ceased, the crowd filed out. It was like a dream ended. People scattered in all directions. Mrs. Sommers went to the corner and waited for the cable car.

A man with keen eyes, who sat opposite to her, seemed to like the study of her small, pale face. It puzzled him to decipher what he saw there. In truth, he saw nothing unless he were wizard enough to detect a poignant wish, a powerful longing that the cable car would never stop anywhere, but go on and on with her forever.

1896

Edith Wharton

(1862–1937)

Edith Wharton, born to the wealthy New York Joneses, lived a conflicted life. Her family expected her to be a conventional debutante, summering at Newport and traveling in Europe; she, however, wanted to become a writer. In 1885, she married Teddy Wharton, a Bostonian thirteen years older than she, and attempted to combine both lives. After a breakdown in 1898, she finally found health in admitting her ambition, and began to lead a life conducive to writing.

From the outside, Edith Wharton's life looked glamorous. She and Teddy traveled abroad extensively; with income from *The House of Mirth*, she designed and built her dream home, The Mount, in Lenox, Massachusetts; and she became a highly successful writer. After *The House of Mirth* was a bestseller in 1905, she published an acclaimed novel every two or three years— from *Ethan Frome* in 1911 to *Custom of the Country, Summer, The Reef, The Age of Innocence* (for which she won the Pulitzer Prize for Fiction in 1921), and many others.

For all her professional success, however, her personal life was disappointing. A marriage devoid of any sexual comfort deteriorated into a painful alliance: Teddy's instability, infidelity, and mismanagement of her money— combined with her deep happiness during a brief affair with journalist Morton Fullerton—led her to divorce Wharton. Because a divorcée had no place in elite society, Wharton moved to France. There she established homes for children orphaned during World War I, and continued writing. "The Other Two" is a wry glimpse of an American woman with admirable panache; her several divorces have not ended her life, and even her third husband has enough sense of humor to enjoy her self-possession.

❖

THE OTHER TWO

Waythorn, on the drawing-room hearth, waited for his wife to come down to dinner.

It was their first night under his own roof, and he was surprised at his thrill of boyish agitation. He was not so old, to be sure—his glass gave him little more than the five-and-thirty years to which his wife confessed—but he had fancied himself already in the temperate zone; yet here he was listening for her step with a tender sense of all it symbolized, with some old trail of verse about the garlanded nuptial doorposts floating through his enjoyment of the pleasant room and the good dinner just beyond it.

They had been hastily recalled from their honeymoon by the illness of Lily Haskett, the child of Mrs. Waythorn's first marriage. The little girl, at Waythorn's desire, had been transferred to his house on the day of her mother's wedding, and the doctor, on their arrival, broke the news that she was ill with typhoid, but declared that all the symptoms were favorable. Lily could show twelve years of unblemished health, and the case promised to be a light one. The nurse spoke as reassuringly, and after a moment of alarm Mrs. Waythorn had adjusted herself to the situation. She was very fond of Lily—her affection for the child had perhaps been her decisive charm in Waythorn's eyes—but she had the perfectly balanced nerves which her little girl had inherited, and no woman ever wasted less tissue in unproductive worry. Waythorn was therefore quite prepared to see her come in presently, a little late because of a last look at Lily, but as serene and well-appointed as if her goodnight kiss had been laid on the brow of health. Her composure was restful to him; it acted as ballast to his somewhat unstable sensibilities. As he pictured her bending over the child's bed he thought how soothing her presence must be in illness: her very step would prognosticate recovery.

His own life had been a gray one, from temperament rather than circumstance, and he had been drawn to her by the unperturbed gaiety which kept her fresh and elastic at an age when most women's activities are growing either slack or febrile. He knew what was said about her; for, popular as she was, there had always been a faint undercurrent of detraction. When she had appeared in New York, nine or ten years earlier, as the pretty Mrs. Haskett whom Gus Varick had unearthed somewhere—was it in Pittsburgh or Utica?—society, while promptly accepting her, had reserved the right to cast a doubt on its own indiscrimination. Inquiry, however, established her undoubted connection with a socially reigning family, and explained her recent divorce as the natural result of a runaway match at seventeen; and as nothing was known of Mr. Haskett it was easy to believe the worst of him.

Alice Haskett's remarriage with Gus Varick was a passport to the set whose recognition she coveted, and for a few years the Varicks were the most popular couple in town. Unfortunately the alliance was brief and stormy, and this time the husband had his champions. Still, even Varick's stanchest supporters admitted that he was not meant for matrimony, and Mrs. Varick's grievances were of a nature to bear the inspection of the New York courts. A New York divorce is in itself a diploma of virtue, and in the semiwidowhood of this second separation Mrs. Varick took on an air of sanctity, and was allowed to confide her wrongs to some of the most scrupulous ears in town. But when it was known that she was to marry Waythorn there was a momentary reaction. Her best friends would have preferred to see her remain in the role of the injured wife, which was as becoming to her as crepe to a rosy complexion. True, a decent time had elapsed, and it was not even suggested that Waythorn had supplanted his predecessor. People shook their heads over him, however, and one grudging friend, to whom be affirmed that he took the step with his eyes open, replied oracularly: "Yes—and with your ears shut."

Waythorn could afford to smile at these innuendoes. In the Wall Street phrase, he had "discounted" them. He knew that society has not yet adapted itself to the consequences of divorce, and that till the adaptation takes place every woman who uses the freedom the law accords her must be her own social justification. Waythorn had an amused confidence in his wife's ability to justify herself. His expectations were fulfilled, and before the wedding took place Alice Varick's group had rallied openly to her support. She took it all imperturbably: she had a way of surmounting obstacles without seeming to be aware of them, and Waythorn looked back with wonder at the trivialities over which he had worn his nerves thin. He had the sense of having found refuge in a richer, warmer nature than his own, and his satisfaction, at the moment, was humorously summed up in the thought that his wife, when she had done all she could for Lily, would not be ashamed to come down and enjoy a good dinner.

The anticipation of such enjoyment was not, however, the sentiment expressed by Mrs. Waythorn's charming face when she presently joined him. Though she had put on her most engaging tea gown she had neglected to assume the smile that went with it, and Waythorn thought he had never seen her look so nearly worried.

"What is it?" he asked. "Is anything wrong with Lily?"

"No; I've just been in and she's still sleeping." Mrs. Waythorn hesitated. "But something tiresome has happened."

He had taken her two hands, and now perceived that he was crushing a paper between them.

"This letter?"

"Yes—Mr. Haskett has written—I mean his lawyer has written."

Waythorn felt himself flush uncomfortably. He dropped his wife's hands. "What about?"

"About seeing Lily. You know the courts—"

"Yes, yes," he interrupted nervously.

Nothing was known about Haskett in New York. He was vaguely supposed to have remained in the outer darkness from which his wife had been rescued, and Waythorn was one of the few who were aware that he had given up his business in Utica and followed her to New York in order to be near his little girl. In the days of his wooing, Waythorn had often met Lily on the doorstep, rosy and smiling, on her way "to see papa."

"I am so sorry," Mrs. Waythorn murmured.

He roused himself. "What does he want?"

"He wants to see her. You know she goes to him once a week."

"Well—he doesn't expect her to go to him now, does he?"

"No—he has heard of her illness; but he expects to come here."

"*Here?*"

Mrs. Waythorn reddened under his gaze. They looked away from each other.

"I'm afraid he has the right. . . . You'll see. . . ." She made a proffer of the letter.

Waythorn moved away with a gesture of refusal. He stood staring about the softly-lighted room, which a moment before had seemed so full of bridal intimacy.

"I'm so sorry," she repeated. "If Lily could have been moved—"

"That's out of the question," he returned impatiently.

"I suppose so."

Her lip was beginning to tremble, and he felt himself a brute.

"He must come, of course," he said. "When is—his day?"

"I'm afraid—tomorrow."

"Very well. Send a note in the morning."

The butler entered to announce dinner.

Waythorn turned to his wife. "Come—you must be tired. It's beastly, but try to forget about it," he said, drawing her hand through his arm.

"You're so good, dear. I'll try," she whispered back.

Her face cleared at once, and as she looked at him across the flowers, between the rosy candleshades, he saw her lips waver back into a smile.

"How pretty everything is!" she sighed luxuriously.

He turned to the butler. "The champagne at once, please. Mrs. Waythorn is tired."

In a moment or two their eyes met above the sparkling glasses. Her own were quite clear and untroubled: he saw that she had obeyed his injunction and forgotten.

II

Waythorn, the next morning, went downtown earlier than usual. Haskett was not likely to come till the afternoon, but the instinct of flight drove him forth. He meant to stay away all day—he had thoughts of dining at his club. As his door closed behind him he reflected that before he opened it again it would have admitted another man who had as much right to enter it as himself, and the thought filled him with a physical repugnance.

He caught the elevated at the employees' hour, and found himself crushed between two layers of pendulous humanity. At Eighth Street the man facing him wriggled out, and another took his place. Waythorn glanced up and saw that it was Gus Varick. The men were so close together that it was impossible to ignore the smile of recognition on Varick's handsome overblown face. And after all—why not? They had always been on good terms, and Varick had been divorced before Waythorn's attentions to his wife began. The two exchanged a word on the perennial grievance of the congested trains, and when a seat at their side was miraculously left empty the instinct of self-preservation made Waythorn slip into it after Varick.

The latter drew the stout man's breath of relief. "Lord—I was beginning to feel like a pressed flower." He leaned back, looking unconcernedly at Waythorn. "Sorry to hear that Sellers is knocked out again."

"Sellers?" echoed Waythorn, starting at his partner's name.

Varick looked surprised. "You didn't know he was laid up with the gout?"

"No. I've been away—I only got back last night." Waythorn felt himself reddening in anticipation of the other's smile.

"Ah—yes; to be sure. And Sellers' attack came on two days ago. I'm afraid he's pretty bad. Very awkward for me, as it happens, because he was just putting through a rather important thing for me."

"Ah?" Waythorn wondered vaguely since when Varick had been dealing in "important things." Hitherto he had dabbled only in the shallow pools of speculation, with which Waythorn's office did not usually concern itself.

It occurred to him that Varick might be talking at random, to relieve the strain of their propinquity. That strain was becoming momentarily more apparent to Waythorn, and when, at Cortlandt Street, he caught sight of an acquaintance and had a sudden vision of the picture he and Varick must present to an initiated eye, he jumped up with a muttered excuse.

"I hope you'll find Sellers better," said Varick civilly, and he stammered back: "If I can be of any use to you—" and let the departing crowd sweep him to the platform.

At his office he heard that Sellers was in fact ill with the gout, and would probably not be able to leave the house for some weeks.

"I'm sorry it should have happened so, Mr. Waythorn," the senior clerk said with affable significance. "Mr. Sellers was very much upset at the idea of giving you such a lot of extra work just now."

"Oh, that's no matter," said Waythorn hastily. He secretly welcomed the pressure of additional business, and was glad to think that, when the day's work was over, he would have to call at his partner's on the way home.

He was late for luncheon, and turned in at the nearest restaurant instead of going to his club. The place was full, and the waiter hurried him to the back of the room to capture the only vacant table. In the cloud of cigar smoke Waythorn did not at once distinguish his neighbors: but presently, looking about him, he saw Varick seated a few feet off. This time, luckily, they were too far apart for conversation, and Varick, who faced another way, had probably not even seen him; but there was an irony in their renewed nearness.

Varick was said to be fond of good living, and as Waythorn sat dispatching his hurried luncheon he looked across half enviously at the other's leisurely degustation of his meal. When Waythorn first saw him he had been helping himself with critical deliberation to a bit of Camembert at the ideal point of liquefaction, and now, the cheese removed, he was just pouring his *café double* from its little two storied earthen pot. He poured slowly, his ruddy profile bent over the task, and one beringed white hand steadying the lid of the coffeepot; then he stretched his other hand to the decanter of cognac at his elbow, filled a liqueur glass, took a tentative sip, and poured the brandy into his coffee cup.

Waythorn watched him in a kind of fascination. What was he thinking of—only of the flavor of the coffee and the liqueur? Had the morning's meeting left no more trace in his thoughts than on his face? Had his wife so completely passed out of his life that even this odd encounter with her present husband, within a week after her remarriage, was no more than an incident in his day? And as Waythorn mused, another idea struck him: had Haskett ever met Varick as Varick and he had just met? The recollection of Haskett perturbed him, and he rose and left the restaurant, taking a circuitous way out to escape the placid irony of Varick's nod.

It was after seven when Waythorn reached home. He thought the footman who opened the door looked at him oddly.

"How is Miss Lily?" he asked in haste.

"Doing very well, sir. A gentleman—"

"Tell Barlow to put off dinner for half an hour," Waythorn cut him off, hurrying upstairs.

He went straight to his room and dressed without seeing his wife. When he reached the drawing room she was there, fresh and radiant. Lily's day had been good; the doctor was not coming back that evening.

At dinner Waythorn told her of Seller's illness and of the resulting complications. She listened sympathetically, adjuring him not to let himself be overworked, and asking vague feminine questions about the routine of the office. Then she gave him the chronicle of Lily's day; quoted the nurse and doctor, and told him who had called to inquire. He had never seen her more serene and unruffled. It struck him, with a curious pang, that she was very happy in being with him, so happy that she found a childish pleasure in rehearsing the trivial incidents of her day.

After dinner they went to the library, and the servant put the coffee and liqueurs on a low table before her and left the room. She looked singularly soft and girlish in her rosy-pale dress, against the dark leather of one of his bachelor armchairs. A day earlier the contrast would have charmed him.

He turned away now, choosing a cigar with affected deliberation.

"Did Haskett come?" he asked, with his back to her.

"Oh, yes—he came."

"You didn't see him, of course?"

She hesitated a moment. "I let the nurse see him."

That was all. There was nothing more to ask. He swung round toward her, applying a match to his cigar. Well, the thing was over for a week, at any rate. He would try not to think of it. She looked up at him, a trifle rosier than usual, with a smile in her eyes.

"Ready for your coffee, dear?"

He leaned against the mantelpiece, watching her as she lifted the coffeepot. The lamplight struck a gleam from her bracelets and tipped her soft hair with brightness. How light and slender she was, and how each gesture flowed into the next! She seemed a creature all compact of harmonies. As the thought of Haskett receded, Waythorn felt himself yielding again to the joy of possessorship. They were his, those white hands with their flitting motions, his the light haze of hair, the lips and eyes. . . .

She set down the coffeepot, and reaching for the decanter of cognac, measured off a liqueur glass and poured it into his cup.

Waythorn uttered a sudden exclamation.

"What is the matter?" she said, startled.

"Nothing; only—I don't take cognac in my coffee."

"Oh, how stupid of me," she cried.

Their eyes met, and she blushed a sudden agonized red.

III

Ten days later, Mr. Sellers, still housebound, asked Waythorn to call on his way downtown.

The senior partner, with his swaddled foot propped up by the fire, greeted his associate with an air of embarrassment.

"I'm sorry, my dear fellow; I've got to ask you to do an awkward thing for me."

Waythorn waited, and the other went on, after a pause apparently given to the arrangement of his phrases: "The fact is, when I was knocked out I had just gone into a rather complicated piece of business for—Gus Varick."

"Well?" said Waythorn, with an attempt to put him at his ease.

"Well—it's this way: Varick came to me the day before my attack. He had evidently had an inside tip from somebody, and had made about a hundred thousand. He came to me for advice, and I suggested his going in with Vanderlyn."

"Oh, the deuce!" Waythorn exclaimed. He saw in a flash what had happened. The investment was an alluring one, but required negotiation. He listened quietly while Sellers put the case before him, and, the statement ended, he said: "You think I ought to see Varick?"

"I'm afraid I can't as yet. The doctor is obdurate. And this thing can't wait, I hate to ask you, but no one else in the office knows the ins and outs of it."

Waythorn stood silent. He did not care a farthing for the success of Varick's venture, but the honor of the office was to be considered, and he could hardly refuse to oblige his partner.

"Very well," he said, "I'll do it."

That afternoon, apprised by telephone, Varick called at the office. Waythorn, waiting in his private room, wondered what the others thought of it. The newspapers, at the time of Mrs. Waythorn's marriage, had acquainted their readers with every detail of her previous matrimonial ventures, and Waythorn could fancy the clerks smiling behind Varick's back as he was ushered in.

Varick bore himself admirably. He was easy without being undignified, and Waythorn was conscious of cutting a much less impressive figure. Varick had no experience of business, and the talk prolonged itself for nearly an hour while Waythorn set forth with scrupulous precision the details of the proposed transaction.

"I'm awfully obliged to you," Varick said as he rose. "The fact is I'm not used to having much money to look after, and I don't want to make an ass of myself—" He smiled, and Waythorn could not help noticing that there was something pleasant about his smile. "It feels uncommonly queer to have enough cash to pay one's bills. I'd have sold my soul for it a few years ago!"

Waythorn winced at the allusion. He had heard it rumored that a lack of funds had been one of the determining causes of the Varick separation, but it did not occur to him that Varick's words were intentional. It seemed more likely that the desire to keep clear of embarrassing topics had fatally drawn him into one. Waythorn did not wish to be outdone in civility.

"We'll do the best we can for you," he said. "I think this is a good thing you're in."

"Oh, I'm sure it's immense. It's awfully good of you—" Varick broke off, embarrassed. "I suppose the thing's settled now—but if—"

"If anything happens before Sellers is about, I'll see you again," said Waythorn quietly. He was glad, in the end, to appear the more selfpossessed of the two.

The course of Lily's illness ran smooth, and as the days passed Waythorn grew used to the idea of Haskett's weekly visit. The first time the day came round, he stayed out late, and questioned his wife as to the visit on his return. She replied at once that Haskett had merely seen the nurse downstairs, as the doctor did not wish anyone in the child's sickroom till after the crisis.

The following week Waythorn was again conscious of the recurrence of the day, but had forgotten it by the time he came home to dinner. The crisis of the disease came a few days later, with a rapid decline of fever, and the little girl was pronounced out of danger. In the rejoicing which ensued the thought of Haskett passed out of Waythorn's mind, and one afternoon, letting himself into the house with a latchkey, he went straight to his library without noticing a shabby hat and umbrella in the hall.

In the library he found a small effaced-looking man with a thinnish gray beard sitting on the edge of a chair. The stranger might have been a piano tuner, or one of those mysteriously efficient persons who are summoned in emergencies to adjust some detail of domestic machinery. He blinked at Waythorn through a pair of gold-rimmed spectacles and said mildly: "Mr. Waythorn, I presume? I am Lily's father."

Waythorn flushed. "Oh—" he stammered uncomfortably. He broke off, disliking to appear rude. Inwardly he was trying to adjust the actual Haskett to the image of him projected by his wife's reminiscences. Waythorn had been allowed to infer that Alice's first husband was a brute.

"I am sorry to intrude," said Haskett, with his over-the-counter politeness.

"Don't mention it," returned Waythorn, collecting himself. "I suppose the nurse has been told?"

"I presume so. I can wait," said Haskett. He had a resigned way of speaking, as though life had worn down his natural powers of resistance.

Waythorn stood on the threshold, nervously pulling off his gloves.

"I'm sorry you've been detained. I will send for the nurse," he said; and as he opened the door he added with an effort: "I'm glad we can give you a good report of Lily." He winced as the *we* slipped out, but Haskett seemed not to notice it.

"Thank you, Mr. Waythorn, it's been an anxious time for me."

"Ah, well, that's past. Soon she'll be able to go to you." Waythorn nodded and passed out.

In his own room he flung himself down with a groan. He hated the womanish sensibility which made him suffer so acutely from the grotesque chances of life. He had known when he married that his wife's former husbands were both living, and that amid the multiplied contacts of modern existence there were a thousand chances to one that he would run against one or the other, yet he found himself as much disturbed by his brief encounter with Haskett as though the law had not obligingly removed all difficulties in the way of their meeting.

Waythorn sprang up and began to pace the room nervously. He had not suffered half as much from his two meetings with Varick. It was Haskett's presence in his own house that made the situation so intolerable. He stood still, hearing steps in the passage.

"This way, please," he heard the nurse say. Haskett was being taken upstairs, then: not a corner of the house but was open to him. Waythorn dropped into another chair, staring vaguely ahead of him. On his dressing table stood a photograph of Alice, taken when he had first known her. She was Alice Varick then—how fine and exquisite he had thought her! Those were Varick's pearls about her neck. At Waythorn's insistence they had been returned before her marriage. Had Haskett ever given her any trinkets—and what had become of them, Waythorn wondered? He realized suddenly that he knew very little of Haskett's past or present situation; but from the man's appearance and manner of speech he could reconstruct with curious precision the surroundings of Alice's first marriage. And it startled him to think that she had, in the background of her life, a phase of existence so different from anything with which he had connected her. Varick, whatever his faults, was a gentleman, in the conventional, traditional sense of the term: the sense which at that moment seemed, oddly enough, to have most meaning to Waythorn. He and Varick had the same social habits, spoke the same language, understood the same allusions. But this other man . . . it was grotesquely uppermost in Waythorn's mind that Haskett had worn a made-up tie attached with an elastic. Why should that ridiculous detail symbolize the whole man? Waythorn was exasperated by his own paltriness, but the fact of the tie expanded, forced itself on him, became as it were the key to Alice's past. He could see her, as Mrs. Haskett, sitting in a "front parlor" furnished in plush, with a pianola, and copy of *Ben Hur* on the center table. He could see her going to the theater with Haskett—or perhaps even to a "Church Sociable"—she in a "picture hat" and Haskett in a black frock coat, a little creased, with the made-up tie on an elastic. On the way home they would stop and look at the illuminated shop windows, lingering over the photographs of New York actresses. On Sunday afternoons Haskett would take her for a walk, pushing Lily ahead of them in a white enameled perambulator, and Waythorn had a vision of the people they would stop and talk to. He could fancy how pretty Alice must have looked, in a dress adroitly constructed from the hints of a New York fashion paper, and how she must have looked down on the other women, chafing at her life, and secretly feeling that she belonged in a bigger place.

For the moment his foremost thought was one of wonder at the way in which she had shed the phase of existence which her marriage with Haskett implied. It was as if her whole aspect, every gesture, every inflection, every allusion, were a studied negation of that period of her life. If she had denied being married to Haskett she could hardly have stood more convicted of duplicity than in this obliteration of the self which had been his wife.

Waythorn started up, checking himself in the analysis of her motives. What right had he to create a fantastic effigy of her and then pass judgment on it? She had spoken vaguely of her first marriage as unhappy, had hinted, with becoming reticence, that Haskett had wrought havoc among her young illusions. . . . It was a pity for Waythorn's peace of mind that Haskett's very inoffensiveness shed a new light on the nature of those illusions. A man would rather think that his wife has been brutalized by her first husband than that the process has been reversed.

IV

"Mr. Waythorn, I don't like that French governess of Lily's."

Haskett, subdued and apologetic, stood before Waythorn in the library, revolving his shabby hat in his hand.

Waythorn, surprised in his armchair over the evening paper, stared back perplexedly at his visitor.

"You'll excuse my asking to see you," Haskett continued. "But this is my last visit, and I thought if I could have a word with you it would be a better way than writing to Mrs. Waythorn's lawyer."

Waythorn rose uneasily. He did not like the French governess either; but that was irrelevant.

"I am not so sure of that," he returned stiffly; "but since you wish it I will give your message to—my wife." He always hesitated over the possessive pronoun in addressing Haskett.

The latter sighed. "I don't know as that will help much. She didn't like it when I spoke to her."

Waythorn turned red. "When did you see her?" he asked.

"Not since the first day I came to see Lily—right after she was taken sick. I remarked to her then that I didn't like the governess."

Waythorn made no answer. He remembered distinctly that, after that first visit, he had asked his wife if she had seen Haskett. She had lied to him then, but she had respected his wishes since; and the incident cast a curious light on her character. He was sure she would not have seen Haskett that first day if she had divined that Waythorn would object, and the fact that she did not divine it was almost as disagreeable to the latter as the discovery that she had lied to him.

"I don't like the woman," Haskett was repeating with mild persistency. "She ain't straight, Mr. Waythorn—she'll teach the child to be underhand. I've noticed a change in Lily—she's too anxious to please—and she don't always tell the truth. She used to be the straightest child, Mr. Waythorn—" He broke off, his voice a little thick. "Not but what I want her to have a stylish education," he ended.

Waythorn was touched. "I'm sorry, Mr. Haskett; but frankly, I don't quite see what I can do."

Haskett hesitated. Then he laid his hat on the table, and advanced to the hearthrug, on which Waythorn was standing. There was nothing aggressive in his manner, but he had the solemnity of a timid man resolved on a decisive measure.

"There's just one thing you can do, Mr. Waythorn," he said. "You can remind Mrs. Waythorn that, by the decree of the courts, I am entitled to have a voice in Lily's bringing-up." He paused, and went on more deprecatingly: "I'm not the kind to talk about enforcing my rights, Mr. Waythorn. I don't know as I think a man is entitled to rights he hasn't known how to hold on to; but this business of the child is different. I've never let go there—and I never mean to."

The scene left Waythorn deeply shaken. Shamefacedly, in indirect ways, he had been finding out about Haskett; and all that he had learned was favorable. The little man, in order to be near his daughter, had sold out his share in a profitable business in Utica, and accepted a modest clerkship in a New York manufacturing house. He boarded in a shabby street and had few acquaintances. His passion for Lily filled his life. Waythorn felt that this exploration of Haskett was like groping about with a dark lantern in his wife's past; but he saw now that there were recesses his lantern had not explored. He had never inquired into the exact circumstances of his wife's first matrimonial rupture. On the surface all had been fair. It was she who had obtained the divorce, and the court had given her the child. But Waythorn knew how many ambiguities such a verdict might cover. The mere fact that Haskett retained a right over his daughter implied an unsuspected compromise. Waythorn was an idealist. He always refused to recognize unpleasant contingencies till he found himself confronted with them, and then he saw them followed by a spectral train of consequences. His next days were thus haunted, and he determined to try to lay the ghosts by conjuring them up in his wife's presence.

When he repeated Haskett's request a flame of anger passed over her face; but she subdued it instantly and spoke with a slight quiver of outraged motherhood.

"It is very ungentlemanly of him," she said.

The word grated on Waythorn. "That is neither here nor there. It's a bare question of rights."

She murmured: "It's not as if he could ever be a help to Lily—"

Waythorn flushed. This was even less to his taste. "The question is," he repeated, "what authority has he over her?"

She looked downward, twisting herself a little in her seat. "I am willing to see him—I thought you objected," she faltered.

In a flash he understood that she knew the extent of Haskett's claims. Perhaps it was not the first time she had resisted them.

"My objecting has nothing to do with it," he said coldly; "if Haskett has a right to be consulted you must consult him."

She burst into tears, and he saw that she expected him to regard her as a victim.

Haskett did not abuse his rights. Waythorn had felt miserably sure that he would not. But the governess was dismissed, and from time to time the little man demanded an interview with Alice. After the first outburst she accepted the situation with her usual adaptability. Haskett had once reminded Waythorn of the piano tuner, and Mrs. Waythorn, after a month or two, appeared to class him with that domestic familiar. Waythorn could not but respect the father's tenacity. At first he had tried to cultivate the suspicion that Haskett might be "up to" something, that he had an object in securing a foothold in the house. But in his heart Waythorn was sure of Haskett's single-mindedness; he even guessed in the latter a mild contempt for such advantages as his relation with the Waythorns might offer. Haskett's sincerity of purpose made him invulnerable, and his successor had to accept him as a lien on the property.

Mr. Sellers was sent to Europe to recover from his gout, and Varick's affairs hung on Waythorn's hands. The negotiations were prolonged and complicated; the first time that Varick had come to the house, and the surprise of seeing him, combined with the singular inopportuneness of his arrival, gave a new edge to Waythorn's blunted sensibilities. He stared at his visitor without speaking.

Varick seemed too preoccupied to notice his host's embarrassment.

"My dear fellow," he exclaimed in his most expansive tone, "I must apologize for tumbling in on you in this way, but I was too late to catch you downtown, and so I thought—"

He stopped short, catching sight of Haskett, and his sanguine color deepened to a flush which spread vividly under his scant blond hair. But in a moment he recovered himself and nodded slightly. Haskett returned the bow in silence, and Waythorn was still groping for speech when the footman came in carrying a tea table.

The intrusion offered a welcome vent to Waythorn's nerves. "What the deuce are you bringing this here for?" he said sharply.

"I beg your pardon, sir, but the plumbers are still in the drawing room, and Mrs. Waythorn said she would have tea in the library." The footman's perfectly respectful tone implied a reflection on Waythorn's reasonableness.

"Oh, very well," said the latter resignedly, and the footman proceeded to open the folding tea table and set out its complicated appointments. While this interminable process continued the three men stood motionless, watching it with a fascinated stare, till Waythorn, to break the silence, said to Varick, "Won't you have a cigar?"

He held out the case he had just tendered to Haskett, and Varick helped himself with a smile. Waythorn looked about for a match, and finding none, proffered a light from his own cigar. Haskett, in the background held his ground mildly, examining his cigar tip now and then, and stepping forward at the right moment to knock its ashes into the fire.

The footman at last withdrew, and Varick immediately began: "If I could just say half a word to you about this business—"

"Certainly," stammered Waythorn; "in the dining room—"

But as he placed his hand on the door it opened from without; and his wife appeared on the threshold.

She came in fresh and smiling, in her street dress and hat, shedding a fragrance from the boa which she loosened in advancing.

"Shall we have tea in here, dear?" she began; and then she caught sight of Varick. Her smile deepened, veiling a slight tremor of surprise.

"Why, how do you do?" she said with a distinct note of pleasure.

As she shook hands with Varick she saw Haskett standing behind him. Her smile faded for a moment, but she recalled it quickly, with a scarcely perceptible side glance at Waythorn.

"How do you do, Mr. Haskett?" she said, and shook hands with him a shade less cordially.

The three men stood awkwardly before her, till Varick, always the most self-possessed, dashed into an explanatory phrase.

"We—I had to see Waythorn a moment on business," he stammered, brick-red from chin to nape.

Haskett stepped forward with his air of mild obstinacy. "I am sorry to intrude; but you appointed five o'clock—" he directed his resigned glance to the timepiece on the mantel.

She swept aside their embarrassment with a charming gesture of hospitality.

"I'm so sorry—I'm always late; but the afternoon was so lovely." She stood drawing off her gloves, propitiatory and graceful, diffusing about her a sense of ease and familiarity in which the situation lost its grotesqueness. "But before talking business," she added brightly, "I'm sure everyone wants a cup of tea."

She dropped into her low chair by the tea table, and the two visitors, as if drawn by her smile, advanced to receive the cups she held out.

She glanced about for Waythorn, and he took the third cup with a laugh.

1904

Hisaye Yamamoto

(1921–   )

Hisaye Yamamoto was born in Redondo Beach, California, to Japanese immigrant parents. One of the *nisei* (second-generation Japanese Americans), she wrote often about the problems of divided national loyalties. Trying to maintain the traditions and beliefs of Japan while yet becoming "American" is here illustrated brilliantly in Tome Hayashi's accomplishment with writing *haiku* (a strictly measured Japanese poetic form of 17 syllables). Her daughter's indifference to her skill symbolizes the disdain of the *nisei* for the conflicts of the *issei* (first generation). In the riveting denouement of her mother's life story, Rosie begins to understand the pathos of that lost Japanese life, love, and honor. What has persevered—and given her life itself—is her mother's indomitable will.

Yamamoto wrote from childhood on, and contributed to Japanese-American newspapers until she and her family were incarcerated for three years in an internment camp in Arizona after the 1942 Japanese Relocation Act. Between 1948 and 1952, her short stories appeared in the annual *Best American Short Stories,* and during that period she received a John Hay Whitney Foundation Opportunity Award. But when literary critic Ivor Winters urged her to accept a Stanford University Writing Fellowship, she turned it down to work as a volunteer on a Catholic Worker rehabilitation farm on Staten Island, New York. She later married and returned to Los Angeles. Like many women writers with family responsibilities, Yamamoto did not publish a book until *Seventeen Syllables and Other Stories* appeared in 1988; in 1986 she received the American Book Award for Lifetime Achievement from the Before Columbus Foundation.

SEVENTEEN SYLLABLES

The first Rosie knew that her mother had taken to writing poems was one evening when she finished one and read it aloud for her daughter's approval. It was about cats, and Rosie pretended to understand it thoroughly and appreciate it no end, partly because she hesitated to disillusion her mother about the quantity and quality of Japanese she had learned in all the years now that she had been going to Japanese school every Saturday (and Wednesday, too, in the summer). Even so, her mother must have been skeptical about the depth of Rosie's understanding, because she explained afterwards about the kind of poem she was trying to write.

See, Rosie, she said, it was a *haiku*, a poem in which she must pack all her meaning into seventeen syllables only, which were divided into three lines of five, seven, and five syllables. In the one she had just read, she had tried to capture the charm of a kitten, as well as comment on the superstition that owning a cat of three colors meant good luck.

"Yes, yes, I understand. How utterly lovely," Rosie said, and her mother, either satisfied or seeing through the deception and resigned, went back to composing.

The truth was that Rosie was lazy; English lay ready on the tongue but Japanese had to be searched for and examined, and even then put forth tentatively (probably to meet with laughter). It was so much easier to say yes, yes, even when one meant no, no. Besides, this was what was in her mind to say: I was looking through one of your magazines from Japan last night, Mother, and towards the back I found some *haiku* in English that delighted me. There was one that made me giggle off and on until I fell asleep—

> *It is morning, and lo!*
> *I lie awake, comme il faut,*
> *sighing for some dough.*

Now, how to reach her mother, how to communicate the melancholy song? Rosie knew formal Japanese by fits and starts, her mother had even less English, no French. It was much more possible to say yes, yes.

It developed that her mother was writing the *haiku* for a daily newspaper, the *Mainichi Shimbun*, that was published in San Francisco. Los Angeles, to be sure, was closer to the farming community in which the Hayashi family lived and several Japanese vernaculars were printed there, but Rosie's parents said they preferred the tone of the northern paper. Once a week, the *Mainichi* would have a section devoted to *haiku*, and her mother became an extravagant contributor, taking for herself the blossoming pen name, Ume Hanazono.

So Rosie and her father lived for awhile with two women, her mother and Ume Hanazono. Her mother (Tome Hayashi by name) kept house, cooked, washed, and, along with her husband and the Carrascos, the Mexican family hired for the harvest, did her ample share of picking tomatoes out in the sweltering fields and boxing them in tidy strata in the cool packing shed. Ume Hanazono, who came to life after the dinner dishes were done, was an earnest, muttering stranger who often neglected speaking when spoken to and stayed busy at the parlor table as late as midnight scribbling with pencil on scratch paper or carefully copying characters on good paper with her fat, pale green Parker.

The new interest had some repercussions on the household routine. Before, Rosie had been accustomed to her parents and herself taking their hot baths early and going to bed almost immediately afterwards, unless her parents challenged each other to a game of flower cards or unless company dropped in. Now if her father wanted to play cards, he had to resort to solitaire (at which he always cheated fearlessly), and if a group of friends came over, it was bound to contain someone who was also writing *haiku*, and the small assemblage would be split in two, her father entertaining the non-literary members and her mother comparing ecstatic notes with the visiting poet.

If they went out, it was more of the same thing. But Ume Hanazono's life span, even for a poet's, was very brief—perhaps three months at most.

One night they went over to see the Hayano family in the neighboring town to the west, an adventure both painful and attractive to Rosie. It was attractive because there were four Hayano girls, all lovely and each one named after a season of the year (Haru, Natsu, Aki, Fuyu), painful because something had been wrong with Mrs. Hayano ever since the birth of her first child. Rosie would sometimes watch Mrs. Hayano, reputed to have been the belle of her native village, making her way about a room, stooped, slowly shuffling, violently trembling (*always* trembling), and she would be reminded that this woman, in this same condition, had carried and given issue to three babies. She would look wonderingly at Mr. Hayano, handsome, tall, and strong, and she would look at her four pretty friends. But it was not a matter she could come to any decision about.

On this visit, however, Mrs. Hayano sat all evening in the rocker, as motionless and unobtrusive as it was possible for her to be, and Rosie found the greater part of the evening practically anaesthetic. Too, Rosie spent most of it in the girls' room, because Haru, the garrulous one, said almost as soon as the bows and other greetings were over, "Oh, you must see my new coat!"

It was a pale plaid of grey, sand, and blue, with an enormous collar, and Rosie, seeing nothing special in it, said, "Gee, how nice."

"Nice?" said Haru, indignantly. "Is that all you can say about it? It's gorgeous! And so cheap, too. Only seventeen-ninety-eight, because it was a sale. The saleslady said it was twenty-five dollars regular."

"Gee," said Rosie. Natsu, who never said much and when she said anything said it shyly, fingered the coat covetously and Haru pulled it away.

"Mine," she said, putting it on. She minced in the aisle between the two large beds and smiled happily. "Let's see how your mother likes it."

She broke into the front room and the adult conversation and went to stand in front of Rosie's mother, while the rest watched from the door. Rosie's mother was properly envious. "May I inherit it when you're through with it?"

Haru, pleased, giggled and said yes, she could, but Natsu reminded gravely from the door, "You promised me, Haru."

Everyone laughed but Natsu, who shamefacedly retreated into the bedroom. Haru came in laughing, taking off the coat. "We were only kidding, Natsu," she said. "Here, you try it on now."

After Natsu buttoned herself into the coat, inspected herself solemnly in the bureau mirror, and reluctantly shed it, Rosie, Aki, and Fuyu got their turns, and Fuyu, who was eight, drowned in it while her sisters and Rosie doubled up in amusement. They all went into the front room later, because Haru's mother quaveringly called to her to fix the tea and rice cakes and open a can of sliced peaches for everybody. Rosie noticed that her mother and Mr. Hayano were talking together at the little table—they were discussing a *haiku* that Mr. Hayano was planning to send to the *Mainichi*, while her father was sitting at one end of the sofa looking through a copy of *Life*, the new picture magazine. Occasionally, her father would comment on a photograph, holding it toward Mrs. Hayano and speaking to her as he always did—loudly, as though he thought someone such as she must surely be at least a trifle deaf also.

The five girls had their refreshments at the kitchen table, and it was while Rosie was showing the sisters her trick of swallowing peach slices without chewing (she chased each slippery crescent down with a swig of tea) that her father brought his empty teacup and untouched saucer to the sink and said, "Come on, Rosie, we're going home now."

"Already?" asked Rosie.

"Work tomorrow," he said.

He sounded irritated, and Rosie, puzzled, gulped one last yellow slice and stood up to go, while the sisters began protesting, as was their wont.

"We have to get up at five-thirty," he told them, going into the front room quickly, so that they did not have their usual chance to hang onto his hands and plead for an extension of time.

Rosie, following, saw that her mother and Mr. Hayano were sipping tea and still talking together, while Mrs. Hayano concentrated, quivering, on raising the handleless Japanese cup to her lips with both her hands and lowering it back to her lap. Her father, saying nothing, went out the door, onto the bright porch, and down the steps. Her mother looked up and asked, "Where is he going?"

"Where is he going?" Rosie said. "He said we were going home now."

"Going home?" Her mother looked with embarrassment at Mr. Hayano and his absorbed wife and then forced a smile. "He must be tired," she said.

Haru was not giving up yet. "May Rosie stay overnight?" she asked, and

Natsu, Aki, and Fuyu came to reinforce their sister's plea by helping her make a circle around Rosie's mother. Rosie, for once having no desire to stay, was relieved when her mother, apologizing to the perturbed Mr. and Mrs. Hayano for her father's abruptness at the same time, managed to shake her head no at the quarter, kindly but adamant, so that they broke their circle and let her go.

Rosie's father looked ahead into the windshield as the two joined him. "I'm sorry," her mother said. "You must be tired." Her father, stepping on the starter, said nothing. "You know how I get when it's *haiku*," she continued, "I forget what time it is." He only grunted.

As they rode homeward silently, Rosie, sitting between, felt a rush of hate for both—for her mother for begging, for her father for denying her mother. I wish this old Ford would crash, right now, she thought, then immediately, no, no, I wish my father would laugh, but it was too late: already the vision had passed through her mind of the green pick-up crumpled in the dark against one of the mighty eucalyptus trees they were just riding past, of the three contorted, bleeding bodies, one of them hers.

Rosie ran between two patches of tomatoes, her heart working more rambunctiously than she had ever known it to. How lucky it was that Aunt Taka and Uncle Gimpachi had come tonight, though, how very lucky. Otherwise she might not have really kept her half-promise to meet Jesus Carrasco. Jesus was going to be a senior in September at the same school she went to, and his parents were the ones helping with the tomatoes this year. She and Jesus, who hardly remembered seeing each other at Cleveland High where there were so many other people and two whole grades between them, had become great friends this summer—he always had a joke for her when he periodically drove the loaded pick-up up from the fields to the shed where she was usually sorting while her mother and father did the packing, and they laughed a great deal together over infinitesimal repartee during the afternoon break for chilled watermelon or ice cream in the shade of the shed.

What she enjoyed most was racing him to see which could finish picking a double row first. He, who could work faster, would tease her by slowing down until she thought she would surely pass him this time, then speeding up furiously to leave her several sprawling vines behind. Once he had made her screech hideously by crossing over, while her back was turned, to place atop the tomatoes in her green-stained bucket a truly monstrous, pale green worm (it had looked more like an infant snake). And it was when they had finished a contest this morning, after she had pantingly pointed a green finger at the immature tomatoes evident in the lugs at the end of his row and he had returned the accusation (with justice), that he had startlingly brought up the matter of their possibly meeting outside the range of both their parents' dubious eyes.

"What for?" she had asked.

"I've got a secret I want to tell you," he said.

"Tell me now," she demanded.

"It won't be ready till tonight," he said.

She laughed. "Tell me tomorrow then."

"It'll be gone tomorrow," he threatened.

"Well, for seven hakes, what is it?" she had asked, more than twice, and when he had suggested that the packing shed would be an appropriate place to find out, she had cautiously answered maybe. She had not been certain she was going to keep the appointment until the arrival of mother's sister and her husband. Their coming seemed a sort of signal of permission, of grace, and she had definitely made up her mind to lie and leave as she was bowing them welcome.

So as soon as everyone appeared settled back for the evening, she announced loudly that she was going to the privy outside, "I'm going to the *benjo!*" and slipped out the door. And now that she was actually on her way, her heart pumped in such an undisciplined way that she could hear it with her ears. It's because I'm running, she told herself, slowing to a walk. The shed was up ahead, one more patch away, in the middle of the fields. Its bulk, looming in the dimness, took on a sinisterness that was funny when Rosie reminded herself that it was only a wooden frame with a canvas roof and three canvas walls that made a slapping noise on breezy days.

Jesus was sitting on the narrow plank that was the sorting platform and she went around to the other side and jumped backwards to seat herself on the rim of a packing stand. "Well, tell me," she said without greeting, thinking her voice sounded reassuringly familiar.

"I saw you coming out the door," Jesus said. "I heard you running part of the way, too."

"Uh-huh," Rosie said. "Now tell me the secret."

"I was afraid you wouldn't come," he said.

Rosie delved around on the chicken-wire bottom of the stall for number two tomatoes, ripe, which she was sitting beside, and came up with a leftover that felt edible. She bit into it and began sucking out the pulp and seeds. "I'm here," she pointed out.

"Rosie, are you sorry you came?"

"Sorry? What for?" she said. "You said you were going to tell me something."

"I will, I will," Jesus said, but his voice contained disappointment, and Rosie fleetingly felt the older of the two, realizing a brand-new power which vanished without category under her recognition.

"I have to go back in a minute," she said. "My aunt and uncle are here from Wintersburg. I told them I was going to the privy."

Jesus laughed. "You funny thing," he said. "You slay me!"

"Just because you have a bathroom *inside*," Rosie said. "Come on, tell me."

Chuckling, Jesus came around to lean on the stand facing her. They still could not see each other very clearly, but Rosie noticed that Jesus became very sober again as he took the hollow tomato from her hand and dropped it back into the stall. When he took hold of her empty hand, she could find no words to protest; her vocabulary had become distressingly constricted and she thought desperately that all that remained intact now was yes and no and oh, and even these few sounds would not easily out. Thus, kissed by Jesus, Rosie fell for the first time entirely victim to a helplessness delectable beyond speech. But the terrible, beautiful sensation lasted no more than a second, and the reality of Jesus' lips and tongue and teeth and hands made her pull away with such strength that she nearly tumbled.

Rosie stopped running as she approached the lights from the windows of home. How long since she had left? She could not guess, but gasping yet, she went to the privy in back and locked herself in. Her own breathing deafened her in the dark, close space, and she sat and waited until she could hear at last the nightly calling of the frogs and crickets. Even then, all she could think to say was oh, my, and the pressure of Jesus' face against her face would not leave.

No one had missed her in the parlor, however, and Rosie walked in and through quickly, announcing that she was next going to take a bath. "Your father's in the bathhouse," her mother said, and Rosie, in her room, recalled that she had not seen him when she entered. There had been only Aunt Taka and Uncle Gimpachi with her mother at the table, drinking tea. She got her robe and straw sandals and crossed the parlor again to go outside. Her mother was telling them about the *haiku* competition in the *Mainichi* and the poem she had entered.

Rosie met her father coming out of the bathhouse. "Are you through, Father?" she asked. "I was going to ask you to scrub my back."

"Scrub your own back," he said shortly, going toward the main house.

"What have I done now?" she yelled after him. She suddenly felt like doing a lot of yelling. But he did not answer, and she went into the bathhouse. Turning on the dangling light, she removed her denims and T-shirt and threw them in the big carton for dirty clothes standing next to the washing machine.

Her other things she took with her into the bath compartment to wash after her bath. After she had scooped a basin of hot water from the square wooden tub, she sat on the grey cement of the floor and soaped herself at exaggerated leisure, singing, "Red Sails in the Sunset" at the top of her voice and using da-da-da where she suspected her words. Then, standing up, still singing, for she was possessed by the notion that any attempt now to analyze would result in spoilage and she believed that the larger her volume the less she would be able to hear herself think, she obtained more hot water and poured it on until she was free of lather. Only then did she allow herself to step into the steaming vat, one leg first, then the remainder of her body inch by inch until the water no longer stung and she could move around at will.

She took a long time soaking, afterwards remembering to go around outside to stoke the embers of the tin-lined fireplace beneath the tub and to throw on a few more sticks so that the water might keep its heat for her mother, and when she finally returned to the parlor, she found her mother still talking *haiku* with her aunt and uncle, the three of them on another round of tea. Her father was nowhere in sight.

At Japanese school the next day (Wednesday, it was), Rosie was grave and giddy by turns. Preoccupied at her desk in the row for students on Book Eight, she made up for it at recess by performing wild mimicry for the benefit of her friend Chizuko. She held her nose and whined a witticism or two in what she considered was the manner of Fred Allen; she assumed intoxication and a British accent to go over the climax of the Rudy Vallee recording of the pub conversation about William Ewart Gladstone; she was the child Shirley Temple piping, "On the Good Ship Lollipop"; she was the gentleman soprano of the Four Inkspots trilling, "If I Didn't Care." And she felt reasonably satisfied when Chizuko wept and gasped, "Oh, Rosie, you ought to be in the movies!"

Her father came after her at noon, bringing her sandwiches of minced ham and two nectarines to eat while she rode, so that she could pitch right into the sorting when they got home. The lugs were piling up, he said, and the ripe tomatoes in them would probably have to be taken to the cannery tomorrow if they were not ready for the produce haulers tonight. "This heat's not doing them any good. And we've got no time for a break today."

It *was* hot, probably the hottest day of the year, and Rosie's blouse stuck damply to her back even under the protection of the canvas. But she worked as efficiently as a flawless machine and kept the stalls heaped, with one part of her mind listening in to the parental murmuring about the heat and the tomatoes and with another part planning the exact words she would say to Jesus when he drove up with the first load of the afternoon. But when at last she saw that the pick-up was coming, her hands went berserk and the tomatoes started falling in the wrong stalls, and her father said, "Hey, hey! Rosie, watch what you're doing!"

"Well, I have to go to the *benjo*," she said, hiding panic.

"Go in the weeds over there," he said, only half-joking.

"Oh, Father!" she protested.

"Oh, go on home," her mother said. "We'll make out for awhile."

In the privy Rosie peered through a knothole toward the fields, watching as much as she could of Jesus. Happily she thought she saw him look in the direction of the house from time to time before he finished unloading and went back toward the patch where his mother and father worked. As she was heading for the shed, a very presentable black car purred up the dirt driveway to the house and its driver motioned to her. Was this the Hayashi home, he wanted to know. She nodded. Was she a Hayashi? Yes, she said, thinking that he was a good-looking man. He got out of the car with a huge, flat package and she saw that he warmly wore a business suit. "I have something here for your mother then," he said, in a more elegant Japanese than she was used to.

She told him where her mother was and he came along with her, patting his face with an immaculate white handkerchief and saying something about the coolness of San Francisco. To her surprised mother and father, he bowed and introduced himself as, among other things, the *haiku* editor of the *Mainichi Shimbun,* saying that since he had been coming as far as Los Angeles anyway, he had decided to bring her the first prize she had won in the recent contest.

"First prize?" her mother echoed, believing and not believing, pleased and overwhelmed. Handed the package with a bow, she bobbed her head up and down numerous times to express her utter gratitude.

"It is nothing much," he added, "but I hope it will serve as a token of our great appreciation for your contributions and our great admiration of your considerable talent."

"I am not worthy," she said, falling easily into his style. "It is I who should make some sign of my humble thanks for being permitted to contribute."

"No, no, to the contrary," he said, bowing again.

But Rosie's mother insisted, and then saying that she knew she was being unorthodox, she asked if she might open the package because her curiosity was so great. Certainly she might. In fact, he would like her reaction to it, for personally, it was one of his favorite *Hiroshiges.*

Rosie thought it was a pleasant picture, which looked to have been sketched with delicate quickness. There were pink clouds, containing some graceful calligraphy, and a sea that was a pale blue except at the edges, containing four sampans with indications of people in them. Pines edged the water and on the far-off beach there was a cluster of thatched huts towered over by pine-dotted mountains of grey and blue. The frame was scalloped and gilt.

After Rosie's mother pronounced it without peer and somewhat prodded her father into nodding agreement, she said Mr. Kuroda must at least have a cup of tea after coming all this way, and although Mr. Kuroda did not want to impose, he soon agreed that a cup of tea would be refreshing and went along with her to the house, carrying the picture for her.

"Ha, your mother's crazy!" Rosie's father said, and Rosie laughed uneasily as she resumed judgment on the tomatoes. She had emptied six lugs when he broke into an imaginary conversation with Jesus to tell her to go and remind her mother of the tomatoes, and she went slowly.

Mr. Kuroda was in his shirtsleeves expounding some *haiku* theory as he munched a rice cake, and her mother was rapt. Abashed in the great man's presence, Rosie stood next to her mother's chair until her mother looked up inquiringly, and then she started to whisper the message, but her mother pushed her gently away and reproached, "You are not being very polite to our guest."

"Father says the tomatoes . . ." Rosie said aloud, smiling foolishly.

"Tell him I shall only be a minute," her mother said, speaking the language of Mr. Kuroda.

When Rosie carried the reply to her father, he did not seem to hear and she said again, "Mother says she'll be back in a minute."

"All right, all right," he nodded, and they worked again in silence. But suddenly, her father uttered an incredible noise, exactly like the cork of a bottle popping, and the next Rosie knew, he was stalking angrily toward the house, almost running in fact, and she chased after him crying, "Father! Father! What are you going to do?"

He stopped long enough to order her back to the shed. "Never mind!" he shouted, "Get on with the sorting!"

And from the place in the fields where she stood, frightened and vacillating, Rosie saw her father enter the house. Soon Mr. Kuroda came out alone, putting on his coat. Mr. Kuroda got into his car and backed out down the driveway onto the highway. Next her father emerged, also alone, something in his arms (it was the picture, she realized), and, going over to the bathhouse woodpile, he threw the picture on the ground and picked up the axe. Smashing the picture, glass and all (she heard the explosion faintly), he reached over for the kerosene that was used to encourage the bath fire and poured it over the wreckage. I am dreaming, Rosie said to herself, I am dreaming, but her father, having made sure that his act of cremation was irrevocable, was even then returning to the fields.

Rosie ran past him and toward the house. What had become of her mother? She burst into the parlor and found her mother at the back window watching the dying fire. They watched together until there remained only a feeble smoke under the blazing sun. Her mother was very calm.

"Do you know why I married your father?" she said without turning.

"No," said Rosie. It was the most frightening question she had ever been called upon to answer. Don't tell me now, she wanted to say, tell me tomorrow, tell me next week, don't tell me today. But she knew she would be told now, that the telling would combine with the other violence of the hot afternoon to level her life, her world to the very ground.

It was like a story out of the magazines illustrated in sepia, which she had consumed so greedily for a period until the information had somehow reached her that those wretchedly unhappy autobiographies, offered to her as the testimonials of living men and women, were largely inventions: Her mother, at nineteen, had come to America and married her father as an alternative to suicide.

At eighteen she had been in love with the first son of one of the well-to-do families in her village. The two had met whenever and wherever they could, secretly, because it would not have done for his family to see him favor her—her father had no money; he was a drunkard and a gambler besides. She had learned she was with child; an excellent match had already been arranged for her lover. Despised by her family, she had given premature birth to a stillborn son, who would be seventeen now. Her family did not turn her out, but she could no longer project herself in any direction without refreshing in them the memory of her indiscretion. She wrote to Aunt Taka, her favorite sister in America, threatening to kill herself if Aunt Taka would not send for her. Aunt Taka hastily arranged a marriage with a young man of whom she knew, but lately arrived from Japan, a young man of simple mind, it was said, but of kindly heart. The young man was never told why his unseen betrothed was so eager to hasten the day of meeting.

The story was told perfectly, with neither groping for words nor untoward passion. It was as though her mother had memorized it by heart, reciting it to herself so many times over that its nagging vileness had long since gone.

"I had a brother then?" Rosie asked, for this was what seemed to matter now; she would think about the other later, she assured herself, pushing back the illumination which threatened all that darkness that had hitherto been merely mysterious or even glamorous. "A half-brother?"

"Yes."

"I would have liked a brother," she said.

Suddenly, her mother knelt on the floor and took her by the wrists. "Rosie," she said urgently, "Promise me you will never marry!" Shocked more by the request than the revelation, Rosie stared at her mother's face. Jesus, Jesus, she called silently, not certain whether she was invoking the help of the son of the Carrascos or of God, until there returned sweetly the memory of Jesus' hand, how it had touched her and where. Still her mother waited for an answer, holding her wrists so tightly that her hands were going numb. She tried to pull free. Promise, her mother whispered fiercely, promise. Yes, yes, I promise, Rosie said. But for an instant she turned away, and her mother, hearing the familiar glib agreement, released her. Oh, you, you, you, her eyes and twisted mouth said, you fool. Rosie, covering her face, began at last to cry, and the embrace and consoling hand came much later than she expected.

1949

Nella Larsen
(1891–1964)

Nella Larsen was a major writer of the Harlem Renaissance. Her *Quicksand* (1928) and *Passing* (1929) were well received by the women writers associated with the powerful black arts movement, yet much about Larsen is mysterious. Trained as a nurse, in 1919 she married Elmer Imes, who had a doctorate in physics. From 1921 to 1926, she worked as a librarian in New York and began writing, finding in fiction a way to quell her doubts about both her abilities and her marriage.

Published in 1926 in *Young's Magazine*, "Freedom" presents in a somewhat conventional narrative Larsen's premise that marriage is a gamble: no one can force anyone else to be truthful about the past. As Thadious Davis tells Larsen's story in her 1994 *Nella Larsen, Novelist of the Harlem Renaissance,* she was the victim of both an untruthful, philandering husband and callously untruthful parents. When her family moved from place to place in Chicago, attempting to pass for white, they kept their (light-skinned) younger daughter with them but sent Nellie away to school. So rejected, Nellie had little stability, and throughout much of her life she assumed various identities and roles. (She published this story as "Allen Semi.")

"Freedom" is an important addition to Larsen's *oeuvre* because it describes the hold fantasy can take on a person's mind. When the unnamed protagonist goes to his bewildered death, the reader is—intentionally—left with questions about the power of love and will, questions much like those the conclusion of *Passing* evokes. Larsen's own later life was a pastiche of life abroad, painful love relationships, and inexplicable withdrawals from friends. She spent her last years as night supervisor of nurses in a New York hospital, her identity as writer forgotten.

FREEDOM

He wondered, as he walked deftly through the impassioned traffic on the Avenue, how she would adjust her life if he were to withdraw from it. . . . How peaceful it would be to have no woman in one's life! These months away took on the appearance of a liberation, a temporary recess from a hateful existence in which he lived in intimacy with someone he did not know and would not now have chosen. . . . He began, again, to speculate on the pattern her life would take without him. Abruptly, it flashed upon him that the vague irritation of many weeks was a feeling of smoldering resentment against her.

The displeasure that this realization caused him increased his ill humor and distaste. He began to dissect her with an acrimony that astonished himself. Her unanimated beauty seemed now only a thin disguise for an inert mind, and not for the serene beauty of soul which he had attributed to her. He suspected, too, a touch of depravity, perhaps only physical, but more likely mental as well. Reflection convinced him that her appeal for him was bounded by the senses, for witness his disgust and clarity of vision, now that they were separated. How could he have been so blinded? Why, for him she had been the universe; a universe personal and unheedful of outside persons or things. He had adored her in a slavish fashion. He groaned inwardly at his own mental caricature of himself, sitting dumb, staring at her in fatuous worship. What an ass he had been!

His work here was done, but what was there to prevent him from staying away for six months—a year—forever? . . . Never to see her again! . . . He stopped, irresolute. What would she do? He tried to construct a representation of her future without him. In his present new hatred, she became a creature irresistibly given to pleasure at no matter what cost. A sybarite! A parasite too!

He was prayerfully thankful that appreciation of his danger had come before she had sapped from him all physical and spiritual vitality. But her future troubled him even while he assured himself that he knew its road, and laughed ruefully at the picture of her flitting from mate to mate.

A feverish impatience gripped him. Somehow, he must contrive to get himself out of the slough into which his amorous folly had precipitated him. . . . Three years. Good God! At the moment, those three years seemed the most precious of his life. And he had foolishly thrown them away. He had drifted pleasantly, peacefully, without landmarks; would be drifting yet but for the death of a friend whose final affairs had brought him away. . . .

He started. Death! Perhaps she would die. How that would simplify matters for him. But no; she would not die. He laughed without amusement. She would not die; she would outlast him, damn her! . . . An angry resentment, sharp and painful as whiplash, struck him. Its passing left him calm and determined. . . .

He braced himself and continued to walk. He had decided; he would stay. With this decision, he seemed to be reborn, He felt cool, refreshed, as if he had stepped out from a warm, scented place into a cold, brisk breeze. He was happy. The world had turned to silver and gold, and life again became a magical adventure. Even the placards in the shops shone with the light of paradise upon them. One caught and held his eye. Travel . . . Yes, he would travel; lose himself in India, China, the South Seas . . . Radiance from the most battered vehicle and the meanest pedestrian. Gladness flooded him. He was free.

A year, thick with various adventures, had slid by since that spring day on which he had wrenched himself free. He had lived, been happy, and with no woman in his life. The break had been simple: a telegram hinting at prolonged business and indefinite return. There had been no reply. This had annoyed him, but he told himself it was what he had expected. He would not admit that, perhaps, he had missed her letter in his wanderings. He had persuaded himself to believe what he wanted to believe—that she had not cared. Actually, there had been confusion in his mind, a complex of thoughts which made it difficult to know what he really had thought. He had imagined that he shuddered at the idea that she had accepted the most generous offer. He pitied her. There was, too, a touch of sadness, a sense of something lost, which he irritably explained on the score of her beauty. Beauty of any kind always stirred him. . . . Too bad a woman like that couldn't be decent. He was well rid of her.

But what had she done? How had he taken it? His contemptuous mood visualized her at times, laughing merrily at some jest made by his successor, or again sitting silent, staring into the fire. He would be conscious of every detail of her appearance: her hair simply arranged, her soft dark eyes, her delicate chin propped on hands rivaling the perfection of La Gioconda's. Sometimes there would be a reversion to the emotions which had ensnared him, when he ached with yearning, when he longed for her again. Such moments were rare.

Another year passed, during which his life had widened, risen, and then crashed. . . .

Dead? How could she be dead? Dead in childbirth, they had told him, both his mistress and the child she had borne him. She had been dead on that spring day when, resentful and angry at her influence in his life, he had reached out toward freedom—to find only a mirage; for he saw quite plainly that now he would never be free. It was she who had escaped him. Each time he had cursed and wondered, it had been a dead woman whom he had cursed and about whom he had wondered. . . . He shivered; he seemed always to be cold now. . . .

Well rid of her! How well he had not known, nor how easily. She was dead. And he had cursed her. But one didn't curse the dead. . . . Didn't one? Damn her! Why couldn't she have lived, or why hadn't she died sooner? For long months he had wondered how she had arranged her life, and all the while she had done nothing but to complete it by dying.

The futility of all his speculations exasperated him. His old resentment returned. She *had* spoiled his life; first by living and then by dying. He hated the fact that she had finished with him, rather than he with her. He could not forgive her. . . . Forgive her? She was dead. He felt somehow that, after all, the dead did not care if you forgave them or not.

Gradually, his mind became puppet to a disturbing tension which drove it back and forth between two thoughts: he had left her; she was dead. These two facts became lodged in his mind like burrs pricking at his breaking faculties. As he recalled the manner of his leaving her, it seemed increasingly brutal. She had died loving him, bearing him a child, and he had left her. He tried to shake off the heavy mental dejection which weighed him down, but his former will and determination deserted him. The vitality of the past, forever dragging him down into black depression, frightened him. The mental fog, thick as soot, into which the news of her death had trapped him, appalled him. He must get himself out. A wild anger seized him. He began to think of his own death, self-inflicted, with feeling that defied analysis. His zest for life became swallowed up in the rising tide of sorrow and mental chaos which was engulfing him.

As autumn approached, with faint notice on his part, his anger and resentment retreated, leaving in their wake a gentle stir of regret and remorse. Imperceptibly, he grew physically weary; a strange sensation of loneliness and isolation enveloped him. A species of timidity came upon him; he felt an unhappy remoteness from people, and began to edge away from life.

His deepening sense of isolation drove him more and more back upon his memories. Sunk in his armchair before the fire, he passed the days and sometimes the nights, for he had lost count of these, merged as they were into one another.

His increasing mental haziness had rejected the fact of her death; often she was there with him, just beyond the firelight or the candlelight. She talked and laughed with him. Sometimes, at night, he woke to see her standing over him or sitting in his chair before the dying fire. By some mysterious process, the glory of the first love flamed again in him. He forgot that they had ever parted. His twisted memories visioned her with him in places where she had never been. He had forgotten all but the past and that was brightly distorted.

He sat waiting for her. He seemed to remember that she had promised to come. Outside, the street was quiet. She was late. Why didn't she come? Childish tears fell over his cold cheeks. He sat weeping in front of the sinking fire.

A nameless dread seized him; she would not come! In the agony of his disappointment, he did not see that the fire had died and the candles had sputtered out. He sat wrapped in immeasurable sadness. He knew that she would not come.

Something in this thought fired his disintegrating brain. She would not come; then he must go to her.

He rose, shaking with cold, and groped toward the door. Yes, he would go to her.

The gleam of a streetlight through a French window caught his attention. He stumbled toward it. His cold fingers fumbled a moment with the catch, but he tore it open with a spark of his old determination and power, and stepped out—and down to the pavement a hundred feet below.

1926

Zora Neale Hurston
(1891–1960)

During the past twenty years, Zora Neale Hurston has become the mother of black women writers. Another of America's lost women writers, Hurston's work was recovered by Alice Walker, who credited Hurston with being her literary foremother, and Robert Hemenway, her first biographer. Since the mid-1970s, Hurston's work (particularly her 1937 novel, *Their Eyes Were Watching God*) has become a mainstay in women's studies and American literature courses. The positive tone of much of her writing, her ability to draw women characters who are both believable and inspiring, and her clear-sighted presentation of black life in all its diversity has made her classic.

Born and reared in the all-black Florida town of Eatonville, Hurston grew up without racial self-consciousness. She attended Howard University and graduated from Barnard College, where she studied with anthropologists Franz Boas and Gladys Reichard. In that field, she received several Guggenheim fellowships to study folklore among blacks in the South and the Caribbean, and the results of her study are her books, *Mules and Men* (1935) and *Tell My Horse* (1938).

Living in New York during the Harlem Renaissance, Hurston believed she could also be a writer—an ambition she proved by winning prestigious prizes in both fiction and drama. "Sweat" is one of her 1926 stories, and while her positive tone is less apparent here, at least Delia has a kind of muted revenge, and stays secure in the house that her own sweat has earned. No longer taking abuse from her husband, Delia in effect forces him into the action that, ironically, leads to his death rather than to hers.

Hurston's publications in the 1930s—*Jonah's Gourd Vine, Their Eyes Were Watching God, Moses: Man of the Mountain*—made her a leading black novelist, but as the Chicago school (which included Richard Wright and Ralph Ellison, among others) grew in prominence, her pacific depictions of black characters came under attack. One has only to contrast Hurston's Janie in *Their Eyes Were Watching God* (1937) with Wright's Bigger Thomas in *Native Son* (1940) to see the immense contrast between the latter's writing as a directive for social action and Hurston's writing that drew black life as possible, existing almost separate from white power. Falling from literary fashion cost Hurston her livelihood, however, and she died a pauper's death after years of working as a maid in Florida.

❖

SWEAT

It was eleven o'clock of a Spring night in Florida. It was Sunday. Any other night, Delia Jones would have been in bed for two hours by this time. But she was a washwoman, and Monday morning meant a great deal to her. So she collected the soiled clothes on Saturday when she returned the clean things. Sunday night after church, she sorted and put the white things to soak. It saved her almost a half-day's start. A great hamper in the bedroom held the clothes that she brought home. It was so much neater than a number of bundles lying around.

She squatted on the kitchen floor beside the great pile of clothes, sorting them into small heaps according to color, and humming a song in a mournful key, but wondering through it all where Sykes, her husband, had gone with her horse and buckboard.

Just then something long, round, limp and black fell upon her shoulders and slithered to the floor beside her. A great terror took hold of her. It softened her knees and dried her mouth so that it was a full minute before she could cry out or move. Then she saw that it was the big bull whip her husband liked to carry when he drove.

She lifted her eyes to the door and saw him standing there bent over with laughter at her fright. She screamed at him.

"Sykes, what you throw dat whip on me like dat? You know it would skeer me—looks just like a snake, an' you knows how skeered Ah is of snakes."

"Course Ah knowed it! That's how come Ah done it." He slapped his leg with his hand and almost rolled on the ground in his mirth. "If you such a big fool dat you got to have a fit over a earth worm or a string, Ah don't keer how bad Ah skeer you."

"You ain't got no business doing it. Gawd knows it's a sin. Some day Ah'm gointuh drop dead from some of yo' foolishness. 'Nother thing, where you been wid mah rig? Ah feeds dat pony. He ain't fuh you to be drivin' wid no bull whip."

"You sho' is one aggravatin' nigger woman!" he declared and stepped into the room. She resumed her work and did not answer him at once. "Ah done tole you time and again to keep them white folks' clothes outa dis house."

He picked up the whip and glared at her. Delia went on with her work. She went out into the yard and returned with a galvanized tub and set it on the washbench. She saw that Sykes had kicked all of the clothes together again, and now stood in her way truculently, his whole manner hoping, *praying*, for an argument. But she walked calmly around him and commenced to re-sort the things.

"Next time, Ah'm gointer kick'em outdoors," he threatened as he struck a match along the leg of his corduroy breeches.

Delia never looked up from her work, and her thin, stooped shoulders sagged further.

"Ah ain't for no fuss t'night Sykes. Ah just come from taking sacrament at the church house."

He snorted scornfully. "Yeah, you just come from de church house on a Sunday night, but heah you is gone to work on them clothes. You ain't nothing but a hypocrite. One of them amen-corner Christians—sing, whoop, and shout, then come home and wash white folks' clothes on the Sabbath."

He stepped roughly upon the whitest pile of things, kicking them helter-skelter as he crossed the room. His wife gave a little scream of dismay, and quickly gathered them together again.

"Sykes, you quit grindin' dirt into these clothes! How can Ah git through by Sat'day if Ah don't start on Sunday?"

"Ah don't keer if you never git through. Anyhow, Ah done promised Gawd and a couple of other men, Ah ain't gointer have it in mah house. Don't gimme no lip neither, else Ah'll throw 'em out and put mah fist up side yo' head to boot."

Delia's habitual meekness seemed to slip from her shoulders like a blown scarf. She was on her feet; her poor little body, her bare knuckly hands bravely defying the strapping hulk before her.

"Looka heah, Sykes, you done gone too fur. Ah been married to you fur fifteen years, and Ah been takin' in washin' fur fifteen years. Sweat, sweat, sweat! Work and sweat, cry and sweat, pray and sweat!"

"What's that got to do with me?" he asked brutally.

"What's it got to do with you, Sykes? Mah tub of suds is filled yo' belly with vittles more times than yo' hands is filled it. Mah sweat is done paid for this house and Ah reckon Ah kin keep on sweatin' in it."

She seized the iron skillet from the stove and struck a defensive pose, which act surprised him greatly, coming from her. It cowed him and he did not strike her as he usually did.

"Naw you won't," she panted, "that ole snaggle-toothed black woman you runnin' with ain't comin' heah to pile up on *mah* sweat and blood. You ain't paid for nothin' on this place, and Ah'm gointer stay right heah till Ah'm toted out foot foremost."

"Well, you better quit gittin' me riled up, else they'll be totin' you out sooner than you expect. Ah'm so tired of you Ah don't know whut to do. Gawd! How Ah hates skinny wimmen!"

A little awed by this new Delia, he sidled out of the door and slammed the back gate after him. He did not say where he had gone, but she knew too

PART I   SHORT   FICTION

well. She knew very well that he would not return until nearly daybreak also. Her work over, she went on to bed but not to sleep at once. Things had come to a pretty pass!

She lay awake, gazing upon the debris that cluttered their matrimonial trail. Not an image left standing along the way. Anything like flowers had long ago been drowned in the salty stream that had been pressed from her heart. Her tears, her sweat, her blood. She had brought love to the union and he had brought a longing after the flesh. Two months after the wedding, he had given her the first brutal beating. She had the memory of his numerous trips to Orlando with all of his wages when he had returned to her penniless, even before the first year had passed. She was young and soft then, but now she thought of her knotty, muscled limbs, her harsh knuckly hands, and drew herself up into an unhappy little ball in the middle of the big feather bed. Too late now to hope for love, even if it were not Bertha it would be someone else. This case differed from the others only in that she was bolder than the others. Too late for everything except her little home. She had built it for her old days, and planted one by one the trees and flowers there. It was lovely to her, lovely.

Somehow, before sleep came, she found herself saying aloud: "Oh well, whatever goes over the Devil's back, is got to come under his belly. Sometime or ruther, Sykes, like everybody else, is gointer reap his sowing." After that she was able to build a spiritual earthworks against her husband. His shells could no longer reach her. AMEN. She went to sleep and slept until he announced his presence in bed by kicking her feet and rudely snatching the covers away.

"Gimme some kivah heah, an' git yo' damn foots over on yo' own side! Ah oughter mash you in yo' mouf fuh drawing dat skillet on me."

Delia went clear to the rail without answering him. A triumphant indifference to all that he was or did.

II

The week was as full of work for Delia as all other weeks, and Saturday found her behind her little pony, collecting and delivering clothes.

It was a hot, hot day near the end of July. The village men on Joe Clarke's porch even chewed cane listlessly. They did not hurl the cane-knots as usual. They let them dribble over the edge of the porch. Even conversation had collapsed under the heat.

"Heah come Delia Jones," Jim Merchant said, as the shaggy pony came 'round the bend of the road toward them. The rusty buckboard was heaped with baskets of crisp, clean laundry.

103

"Yep," Joe Lindsay agreed. "Hot or col', rain or shine, jes'ez reg'lar ez de weeks roll roun' Delia carries 'em an' fetches 'em on Sat'day."

"She better if she wanter eat," said Moss. "Syke Jones ain't wuth de shot an' powder hit would tek tuh kill 'em. Not to *huh* he ain't."

"He sho' ain't," Walter Thomas chimed in. "It's too bad, too, cause she wuz a right pretty li'l trick when he got huh. Ah'd uh mah'ied huh mahself if he hadnter beat me to it."

Delia nodded briefly at the men as she drove past.

"Too much knockin' will ruin *any* 'oman. He done beat huh 'nough tuh kill three women, let 'lone change they looks," said Elijah Moseley. "How Syke kin stommuck dat big black greasy Mogul he's layin' roun' wid, gits me. Ah swear dat eight-rock couldn't kiss a sardine can Ah done thowed out de back do' 'way las' yeah."

"Aw, she's fat, thass how come. He's allus been crazy 'bout fat women," put in Merchant. "He'd a' been tied up wid one long time ago if he could a' found one tuh have him. Did Ah tell yuh 'bout him come sidlin' roun' *mah* wife—bringin' her a basket uh peecans outa his yard fuh a present? Yessir, mah wife! She tol' him tuh take 'em right straight back home, 'cause Delia works so hard ovah dat washtub she reckon everything on de place taste lak sweat an' soapsuds. Ah jus' wisht Ah'd a' caught 'im 'roun' dere! Ah'd a' made his hips ketch on fiah down dat shell road."

"Ah know he done it, too. Ah sees 'im grinnin' at every 'oman dat passes," Walter Thomas said. "But even so, he useter eat some mighty big hunks uh humble pie tuh git dat li'l 'oman he got. She wuz ez pretty ez a speckled pup! Dat wuz fifteen years ago. He useter be so skeered uh losin' huh, she could make him do some parts of a husband's duty. Dey never wuz de same in de mind."

"There oughter be a law about him," said Lindsay. "He ain't fit tuh carry guts tuh a bear."

Clarke spoke for the first time. "'Tain't no law on earth dat kin make a man be decent if it ain't in 'im. There's plenty men dat takes a wife lak dey do a joint uh sugar-cane. It's round, juicy an' sweet when dey gits it. But dey squeeze an' grind, squeeze an' grind an' wring tell dey wring every drop uh pleasure dat's in 'em out. When dey's satisfied dat dey is wrung dry, dey treats 'em jes' lak dey do a cane-chew. Dey thows 'em away. Dey knows whut dey is doin' while dey is at it, an' hates theirselves fuh it but they keeps on hangin' after huh tell she's empty. Den dey hates huh fuh bein' a cane-chew an' in de way."

"We oughter take Syke an' dat stray 'oman uh his'n down in Lake Howell swamp an' lay on de rawhide till they cain't say Lawd a' mussy. He allus wuz uh ovahbearin niggah, but since dat white 'oman from up north done teached 'im how to run a automobile, he done got too beggety to live—an' we oughter kill 'im," Old Man Anderson advised.

A grunt of approval went around the porch. But the heat was melting their civic virtue and Elijah Moseley began to bait Joe Clarke.

"Come on, Joe, git a melon outa dere an' slice it up for yo' customers. We'se all sufferin' wid de heat. De bear's done got *me!*"

"Thass right, Joe, a watermelon is jes' whut Ah needs tuh cure de eppizudicks," Walter Thomas joined forces with Moseley. "Come on dere, Joe. We all is steady customers an' you ain't set us up in a long time. Ah chooses dat long, bowlegged Floridy favorite."

"A god, an' be dough. You all gimme twenty cents and slice away," Clarke retorted. "Ah needs a col' slice m'self. Heah, everybody chip in. Ah'll lend y'all mah meat knife."

The money was all quickly subscribed and the huge melon brought forth. At that moment, Sykes and Bertha arrived. A determined silence fell on the porch and the melon was put away again.

Merchant snapped down the blade of his jackknife and moved toward the store door.

"Come on in, Joe, an' gimme a slab uh sow belly an' uh pound uh coffee—almost fuhgot 'twas Sat'day. Got to git on home." Most of the men left also.

Just then Delia drove past on her way home, as Sykes was ordering magnificently for Bertha. It pleased him for Delia to see.

"Git whutsoever yo' heart desires, Honey. Wait a minute, Joe. Give huh two bottles uh strawberry soda-water, uh quart parched ground-peas, an' a block uh chewin' gum."

With all this they left the store, with Sykes reminding Bertha that this was his town and she could have it if she wanted it.

The men returned soon after they left, and held their watermelon feast.

"Where did Sykes Jones git da 'oman from nohow?" Lindsay asked.

"Ovah Apopka. Guess dey musta been cleanin' out de town when she lef'. She don't look lak a thing but a hunk uh liver wid hair on it."

"Well, she sho' kin squall," Dave Carter contributed. "When she gits ready tuh laff, she jes' opens huh mouf an' latches it back tuh de las' notch. No ole granpa alligator down in Lake Bell ain't got nothin' on huh."

III

Bertha had been in town three months now. Sykes was still paying her room-rent at Della Lewis'—the only house in town that would have taken her in. Sykes took her frequently to Winter Park to 'stomps'. He still assured her that he was the swellest man in the state.

"Sho' you kin have dat li'l ole house soon's Ah git dat 'oman outa dere. Everything b'longs tuh me an' you sho' kin have it. Ah sho' 'bominates uh skinny 'oman. Lawdy, you sho' is got one portly shape on you! You kin git *anything* you wants. Dis is *mah* town an' you sho' kin have it."

Delia's work-worn knees crawled over the earth in Gethsemane and up the rocks of Calvary many, many times during these months. She avoided the villagers and meeting places in her efforts to be blind and deaf. But Bertha nullified this to a degree, by coming to Delia's house to call Sykes out to her at the gate.

Delia and Sykes fought all the time now with no peaceful interludes. They slept and ate in silence. Two or three times Delia had attempted a timid friendliness, but she was repulsed each time. It was plain that the breaches must remain agape.

The sun had burned July to August. The heat streamed down like a million hot arrows, smiting all things living upon the earth. Grass withered, leaves browned, snakes went blind in shedding and men and dogs went mad. Dog days!

Delia came home one day and found Sykes there before her. She wondered, but started to go on into the house without speaking, even though he was standing in the kitchen door and she must either stoop under his arm or ask him to move. He made no room for her. She noticed a soap box beside the steps, but paid no particular attention to it, knowing that he must have brought it there. As she was stooping to pass under his outstretched arm, he suddenly pushed her backward, laughingly.

"Look in de box dere Delia, Ah done brung yuh somethin'!"

She nearly fell upon the box in her stumbling, and when she saw what it held, she all but fainted outright.

"Syke! Syke, mah Gawd! You take dat rattlesnake 'way from heah! You *gottuh.* Oh, Jesus, have mussy!"

"Ah ain't got tuh do nuthin' uh de kin'—fact is Ah ain't got tuh do nothin' but die. Tain't no use uh you puttin' on airs makin' out lak you skeered uh dat snake—he's gointer stay right heah tell he die. He wouldn't bite me cause Ah knows how tuh handle 'im. Nohow he wouldn't risk breakin' out his fangs 'gin *yo* skinny laigs."

"Naw, now Syke, don't keep dat thing 'round tryin' tuh skeer me tuh death. You knows Ah'm even feared uh earth worms. Thass de biggest snake Ah evah did see. Kill 'im Syke, please."

"Doan ast me tuh do nothin' fuh yuh. Goin' 'round tryin' tuh be so damn asterperious. Naw, Ah ain't gonna kill it. Ah think uh damn sight mo' uh him dan you! Dat's a nice snake an' anybody doan lak 'im kin jes' hit de grit."

The village soon heard that Sykes had the snake, and came to see and ask questions.

"How de hen-fire did you ketch dat six-foot rattler, Syke?" Thomas asked.

"He's full uh frogs so he cain't hardly move, thass how Ah eased up on 'm. But Ah'm a snake charmer an' knows how tuh handle 'em. Shux, dat ain't nothin'. Ah could ketch one eve'y day if Ah so wanted tuh."

"Whut he needs is a heavy hick'ry club leaned real heavy on his head. Dat's de bes' way tuh charm a rattlesnake."

"Naw, Walt, y'all jes' don't understand dese diamon' backs lak Ah do," said Sykes in a superior tone of voice.

The village agreed with Walter, but the snake stayed on. His box remained by the kitchen door with its screen wire covering. Two or three days later it had digested its meal of frogs and literally came to life. It rattled at every movement in the kitchen or the yard. One day as Delia came down the kitchen steps she saw his chalky-white fangs curved like scimitars hung in the wire meshes. This time she did not run away with averted eyes as usual. She stood for a long time in the doorway in a red fury that grew bloodier for every second that she regarded the creature that was her torment.

That night she broached the subject as soon as Sykes sat down to the table.

"Sykes, Ah wants you tuh take dat snake 'way fum heah. You done starved me an' Ah put up widcher, you done beat me an Ah took dat, but you done kilt all mah insides bringin' dat varmint heah."

Sykes poured out a saucer full of coffee and drank it deliberately before he answered her.

"A whole lot Ah keer 'bout how you feels inside uh out. Dat snake ain't goin' no damn wheah till Ah gits ready fuh 'im tuh go. So fur as beatin' is concerned, yuh ain't took near all dat you gointer take ef yuh stay 'round *me*."

Delia pushed back her plate and got up from the table. "Ah hates you, Sykes," she said calmly. "Ah hates you tuh de same degree dat Ah useter love yuh. Ah done took an' took till mah belly is full up tuh mah neck. Dat's de reason Ah got mah letter fum de church an' moved mah membership tuh Woodbridge—so Ah don't haftuh take no sacrament wid yuh. Ah don't wan- tuh see yuh 'round me atall. Lay 'round wid dat 'oman all yuh wants tuh, but gwan 'way fum me an' mah house. Ah hates yuh lak uh suck-egg dog."

Sykes almost let the huge wad of corn bread and collard greens he was chewing fall out of his mouth in amazement. He had a hard time whipping himself up to the proper fury to try to answer Delia.

"Well, Ah'm glad you does hate me. Ah'm sho' tiahed uh you hangin' ontuh me. Ah don't want yuh. Look at yuh stringey ole neck! Yo' rawbony laigs an' arms is enough tuh cut uh man tuh death. You looks jes' lak de devvul's doll-baby tuh *me*. You cain't hate me no worse dan Ah hates you. Ah been hatin' *you* fuh years."

"Yo' ole black hide don't look lak nothin' tuh me, but uh passle uh wrinkled up rubber, wid yo' big ole yeahs flappin' on each side lak uh paih uh buzzard wings. Don't think Ah'm gointuh be run 'way fum mah house neither. Ah'm goin' tuh de white folks 'bout *you*, mah young man, de very nex' time you lay yo' han's on me. Mah cup is done run ovah." Delia said this with no signs of fear and Sykes departed from the house, threatening her, but made not the slightest move to carry out any of them.

That night he did not return at all, and the next day being Sunday, Delia was glad she did not have to quarrel before she hitched up her pony and drove the four miles to Woodbridge.

She stayed to the night service—'love feast'—which was very warm and full of spirit. In the emotional winds her domestic trials were borne far and wide so that she sang as she drove homeward,

> *Jurden water, black an' col*
> *Chills de body, not de soul*
> *An' Ah wantah cross Jurden in uh calm time.*

She came from the barn to the kitchen door and stopped.

"Whut's de mattah, ol' Satan, you ain't kickin' up yo' racket?" She addressed the snake's box. Complete silence. She went on into the house with a new hope in its birth struggles. Perhaps her threat to go to the white folks had frightened Sykes! Perhaps he was sorry! Fifteen years of misery and suppression had brought Delia to the place where she would hope *anything* that looked towards a way over or through her wall of inhibitions.

She felt in the match-safe behind the stove at once for a match. There was only one there.

"Dat niggah wouldn't fetch nothin' heah tuh save his rotten neck, but he kin run thew whut Ah brings quick enough. Now he done toted off nigh on tuh haff uh box uh matches. He done had dat 'oman heah in mah house, too."

Nobody but a woman could tell how she knew this even before she struck the match. But she did and it put her into a new fury.

Presently she brought in the tubs to put the white things to soak. This time she decided she need not bring the hamper out of the bedroom; she would go in there and do the sorting. She picked up the pot-bellied lamp and went in. The room was small and the hamper stood hard by the foot of the white iron bed. She could sit and reach through the bedposts—resting as she worked.

"Ah wantah cross Jurden in uh calm time." She was singing again. The mood of the 'love feast' had returned. She threw back the lid of the basket almost gaily. Then, moved by both horror and terror, she sprang back toward the door. *There lay the snake in the basket!* He moved sluggishly at first, but even as she turned round and round, jumped up and down in an insanity of fear, he began to stir vigorously. She saw him pouring his awful beauty from the basket upon the bed, then she seized the lamp and ran as fast as she could to the kitchen. The wind from the open door blew out the light and the darkness added to her terror. She sped to the darkness of the yard, slamming the door after her before she thought to set down the lamp. She did not feel safe even on the ground, so she climbed up in the hay barn.

There for an hour or more she lay sprawled upon the hay a gibbering wreck.

Finally she grew quiet, and after that came coherent thought. With this stalked through her a cold, bloody rage. Hours of this. A period of introspection, a space of retrospection, then a mixture of both. Out of this an awful calm.

"Well, Ah done de bes' Ah could. If things ain't right, Gawd knows tain't mah fault."

She went to sleep—a twitch sleep—and woke up to a faint gray sky. There was a loud hollow sound below. She peered out. Sykes was at the wood-pile, demolishing a wire-covered box.

He hurried to the kitchen door, but hung outside there some minutes before he entered, and stood some minutes more inside before he closed it after him.

The gray in the sky was spreading. Delia descended without fear now, and crouched beneath the low bedroom window. The drawn shade shut out the dawn, shut in the night. But the thin walls held back no sound.

"Dat ol' scratch is woke up now!" She mused at the tremendous whirr inside, which every woodsman knows, is one of the sound illusions. The rattler is a ventriloquist. His whirr sounds to the right, to the left, straight ahead, behind, close under foot—everywhere but where it is. Woe to him who guesses wrong unless he is prepared to hold up his end of the argument! Sometimes he strikes without rattling at all.

Inside, Sykes heard nothing until he knocked a pot lid off the stove while trying to reach the match-safe in the dark. He had emptied his pockets at Bertha's.

The snake seemed to wake up under the stove and Sykes made a quick leap into the bedroom. In spite of the gin he had had, his head was clearing now.

"Mah Gawd!" he chattered, "ef Ah could on'y strack uh light!"

The rattling ceased for a moment as he stood paralyzed. He waited. It seemed that the snake waited also.

"Oh, fuh de light! Ah thought he'd be too sick"—Sykes was muttering to himself when the whirr began again, closer, right underfoot this time. Long before this, Sykes' ability to think had been flattened down to primitive instinct and he leaped—onto the bed.

Outside Delia heard a cry that might have come from a maddened chimpanzee, a stricken gorilla. All the terror, all the horror, all the rage that man possibly could express, without a recognizable human sound.

A tremendous stir inside there, another series of animal screams, the intermittent whirr of the reptile. The shade torn violently down from the window, letting in the red dawn, a huge brown hand seizing the window stick, great dull blows upon the wooden floor punctuating the gibberish of sound long after the rattle of the snake had abruptly subsided. All this Delia could see and hear from her place beneath the window, and it made her ill. She crept over to the four-o'clocks and stretched herself on the cool earth to recover.

She lay there. "Delia, Delia!" She could hear Sykes calling in a most despairing tone as one who expected no answer. The sun crept on up, and he called. Delia could not move—her legs had gone flabby. She never moved, he called, and the sun kept rising.

"Mah Gawd!" She heard him moan, "Mah Gawd fum Heben!" She heard him stumbling about and got up from her flower-bed. The sun was growing warm. As she approached the door she heard him call out hopefully, "Delia, is dat you Ah heah?"

She saw him on his hands and knees as soon as she reached the door. He crept an inch or two toward her—all that he was able, and she saw his horribly swollen neck and his one open eye shining with hope. A surge of pity too strong to support bore her away from that eye that must, could not, fail to see the tubs. He would see the lamp. Orlando with its doctors was too far. She could scarcely reach the chinaberry tree, where she waited in the growing heat while inside she knew the cold river was creeping up and up to extinguish that eye which must know by now that she knew.

1926

Tillie Olsen

(1913–   )

Tillie Lerner Olsen has written some of the most moving fiction of the twentieth century. In "O Yes" she portrays the dissolution of a childhood friendship between the black Parialee and the white (or at least passing) Carol, despite their mothers' closeness. Centered in the highly emotional black church service, the story (whose title replicates the call-and-response refrain of the service) moves impressionistically to describe the racist schools, the black characters' bonding through the creation of their own language, and the inevitable pain of girls growing up to face the restrictions of a middle-class culture. Years before the psychological work of Carol Gilligan and Jean Baker Miller, Olsen wrote convincingly about female adolescents' traumatic rites of passage.

The daughter of Russian activist immigrants, Olsen was educated (through the eleventh grade) in Nebraska. She worked as a domestic and in meat packing houses, and was jailed in Kansas City after attempting to organize packinghouse workers. A member of the Young Communist League, at nineteen she started her novel, *Yonnondio: From the Thirties* (1974); she also gave birth to a daughter. Later married to Jack Olsen, she bore three more children, always working outside her home to help support the family. By the 1950s, with time free to write again, Olsen became one of the key feminist voices. With her stories widely published, she helped recover the work of Rebecca Harding Davis, and spoke to the inevitable silencing of writers who lacked financial support in her ground-breaking book, *Silences* (1978). *Tell Me a Riddle* (1962) is her story collection.

O YES

1

They are the only white people there, sitting in the dimness of the Negro church that had once been a corner store, and all through the bubbling, swelling, seething of before the services, twelve-year-old Carol clenches tight her mother's hand, the other resting lightly on her friend, Parialee Phillips, for whose baptism she has come.

The white-gloved ushers hurry up and down the aisle, beckoning people to their seats. A jostle of people. To the chairs angled to the left for the youth choir, to the chairs angled to the right for the ladies' choir, even up to the

111

platform, where behind the place for the dignitaries and the mixed choir, the new baptismal tank gleams—and as if pouring into it from the ceiling, the blue-painted River of Jordan, God standing in the waters, embracing a brown man in a leopard skin and pointing to the letters of gold:

REJOICE

D   L

O

O   GOD IS LOVE   V

G   E

I AM THE WAY   THE TRUTH   THE LIFE

At the clear window, the crucified Christ embroidered on the starched white curtain leaps in the wind of the sudden singing. And the choirs march in. Robes of wine, of blue, of red.

"We stands and sings too," says Parialee's mother, Alva, to Helen; though already Parialee has pulled Carol up. Singing, little Lucinda Phillips fluffs out her many petticoats; singing, little Bubbie bounces up and down on his heels.

Any day now I'll reach that land of freedom,
Yes, o yes
Any day now, know that promised land

The youth choir claps and taps to accent the swing of it. Beginning to tap, Carol stiffens. "Parry, look. Somebody from school."

"Once more once," says Parialee, in the new way she likes to talk now.

"Eddie Garlin's up there. He's in my math."

"Couple cats from Franklin Jr. chirps in the choir. No harm or alarm."

Anxiously Carol scans the faces to see who else she might know, who else might know her, but looks quickly down to Lucinda's wide skirts, for it seems Eddie looks back at her, sullen or troubled, though it is hard to tell, faced as she is into the window of curtained sunblaze.

I know my robe will fit me well
I tried it on at the gates of hell

If it were a record she would play it over and over, Carol thought, to untwine the intertwined voices, to search how the many rhythms rock apart and yet are one glad rhythm.

When I get to heaven gonna sing and shout
Nobody be able to turn me out

"That's Mr. Chairback Evans going to invocate," Lucinda leans across Parry to explain. "He don't invoke good like Momma."

"Shhhh."

"Momma's the only lady in the church that invocates. She made the prayer last week. (Last month, Lucy.) I made the children's 'nouncement last time. (That was way back Thanksgiving.) And Bubbie's 'nounced too. Lots of times."

"Lucy-inda. SIT!"

Bible study announcements and mixed-choir practice announcements and Teen Age Hearts meeting announcements.

If Eddie said something to her about being there, worried Carol, if he talked to her right in front of somebody at school.

Messengers of Faith announcements and Mamboettes announcement and Committee for the Musical Tea.

Parry's arm so warm. Not realizing, starting up the old game from grade school, drumming a rhythm on the other's arm to see if the song could be guessed. "Parry, guess."

But Parry is pondering the platform.

The baptismal tank? "Parry, are you scared . . . the baptizing?"

"This cat? No." Shaking her head so slow and scornful, the barrette in her hair, sun fired, strikes a long rail of light. And still ponders the platform.

New Strangers Baptist Church invites you and Canaan Fair Singers announcements and Battle of Song and Cosmopolites meet. "O Lord, I couldn't find no ease," a solo. The ladies' choir:

O what you say seekers, o what you say seekers,
Will you never turn back no more?

The mixed choir sings:

Ezekiel saw that wheel of time
Every spoke was of humankind . . .

And the slim worn man in the pin-stripe suit starts his sermon On the Nature of God. How God is long-suffering. Oh, how long he has suffered. Calling the roll of the mighty nations, that rose and fell and now are dust for grinding the face of Man.

O voice of drowsiness and dream to which Carol does not need to listen.

As long ago. Parry warm beside her too, as it used to be, there in the classroom at Mann Elementary, and the feel of drenched in sun and dimness and dream. Smell and sound of the chalk wearing itself away to nothing, rustle of books, drumming tattoo of Parry's fingers on her arm: *Guess.*

And as the preacher's voice spins happy and free, it is the used-to-be play-yard. Tag. Thump of the volley ball. Ecstasy of the jump rope. Parry, do pepper. Carol, do pepper. Parry's bettern Carol, Carol's bettern Parry . . .

Did someone scream?

It seemed someone screamed—but all were sitting as before, though the sun no longer blared through the windows. She tried to see up where Eddie was, but the ushers were standing at the head of the aisle now, the ladies in white dresses like nurses or waitresses wear, the men holding their white-gloved hands up so one could see their palms.

"And God is Powerful," the preacher was chanting. "Nothing for him to scoop out the oceans and pat up the mountains. Nothing for him to scoop up the miry clay and create man. Man, I said, create Man."

The lady in front of her moaned "*O yes*" and others were moaning "*O yes.*"

"And when the earth mourned the Lord said, Weep not, for all will be returned to you, every dust, every atom. And the tired dust settles back, goes back. Until that Judgment Day. That great day."

"*O yes.*"

The ushers were giving out fans. Carol reached for one and Parry said: "What *you* need one for?" but she took it anyway.

"You think Satchmo can blow; you think Muggsy can blow; you think Dizzy can blow?" He was straining to an imaginary trumpet now, his head far back and his voice coming out like a trumpet.

"Oh Parry, he's so good."

"Well. Jelly jelly."

"Nothing to Gabriel on that great getting-up morning. And the horn wakes up Adam, and Adam runs to wake up Eve, and Eve moans; Just one more minute, let me sleep, and Adam yells, Great Day, woman, don't you know it's the Great Day?"

"*Great Day, Great Day,*" the mixed choir behind the preacher rejoices:

> *When our cares are past*
> *when we're home at last . . .*

"And Eve runs to wake up Cain." Running round the platform, stooping and shaking imaginary sleepers, "and Cain runs to wake up Abel." Looping, scalloping his voice—"Grea-aaa-aat Daaaay." All the choirs thundering:

Great Day
When the battle's fought
And the victory's won

Exultant spirals of sound. And Carol caught into it (Eddie forgotten, the game forgotten) chanting with Lucy and Bubbie: "*Great Day.*"

"Ohhhhhhhhhh," his voice like a trumpet again, "the re-unioning. Ohhhhhhhhh, the rejoicing. After the ages immemorial of longing."

Someone *was* screaming. And an awful thrumming sound with it, like feet and hands thrashing around, like a giant jumping of a rope.

"*Great Day.*" And no one stirred or stared as the ushers brought a little woman out into the aisle, screaming and shaking, just a little shrunk-up woman not much taller than Carol, the biggest thing about her her swollen hands and the cascades of tears wearing her face.

The shaking inside Carol too. Turning and trembling to ask: "What . . . that lady?" But Parry still ponders the platform; little Lucy loops the chain of her bracelet round and round; and Bubbie sits placidly, dreamily. Alva Phillips is up fanning a lady in front of her; two lady ushers are fanning other people Carol cannot see. And her mother, her mother looks in a sleep.

Yes. He raised up the dead from the grave. He made old death behave.

Yes. Yes. From all over, hushed.   *O Yes*

He was your mother's rock. Your father's mighty tower. And he gave us a little baby. A little baby to love.

I am so glad

Yes, your friend, when you're friendless. Your father when you're fatherless. Way maker. Door opener.

Yes

When it seems you can't go on any longer, he's there. You can, he says, you can.

Yes

And that burden you been carrying—ohhhhh that burden—not for always will it be. No, not for always.

Stay with me, Lord

I will put my Word in you and it is power. I will put my Truth in you and it is power.

O Yes

Out of your suffering I will make you to stand as a stone. A tried stone. Hewn out of the mountains of ages eternal.

Ohhhhhhhhhhhh. Out of the mire I will lift your feet. Your tired feet from so much wandering. From so much work and wear and hard times.

Yes

115

From so much journeying—and never the promised land. And I'll wash them in the well your tears made. And I'll shod them in the gospel of peace, and of feeling good. Ohhhhhhhhh.

O Yes.

Behind Carol, a trembling wavering scream. Then the thrashing. Up above, the singing:

> *They taken my blessed Jesus and flogged him to the woods*
> *And they made him hew out his cross and they dragged him to Calvary*
> *Shout brother, Shout shout shout. He never cried a word.*

Powerful throbbing voices. Calling and answering to each other.

> *They taken my blessed Jesus and whipped him up the hill*
> *With a knotty whip and a raggedy thorn he never cried a word*
> *Shout, sister. Shout shout shout. He never cried a word.*
>
> *Go tell the people the Saviour has risen*
> *Has risen from the dead and will live forevermore*
> *And won't have to die no more.*

Halleloo.

> *Shout, brother, shout*
> *We won't have to die no more!*

A single exultant lunge of shriek. Then the thrashing. All around a clapping. Shouts with it. The piano whipping, whipping air to a froth. Singing now.

> *I once was lost who now am found*
> *Was blind who now can see*

On Carol's fan, a little Jesus walked on wondrously blue waters to where bearded disciples spread nets out of a fishing boat. If she studied the fan—became it—it might make a wall around her. If she could make what was happening (*what* was happening?) into a record small and round to listen to far and far as if into a seashell—the stamp and rills and spirals all tiny (but never any screaming).

> *wade wade in the water*

Jordan's water is chilly and wild
I've got to get home to the other side
God's going to trouble the waters

The music leaps and prowls. Ladders of screamings. Drumming feet of ushers running. And still little Lucy fluffs her skirts, loops the chain on her bracelet; still Bubbie sits and rocks dreamily; and only eyes turn for an instant to the aisle as if nothing were happening. "Mother, let's go home," Carol begs, but her mother holds her so tight. Alva Phillips, strong Alva, rocking too and chanting, *O Yes*. No, do not look.

Wade,
Sea of trouble all mingled with fire
Come on my brethren it's time to go higher
Wade wade

The voices in great humming waves, slow, slow (when did it become the humming?), everyone swaying with it too, moving like in slow waves and singing, and up where Eddie is, a new cry, wild and open, "O help me, Jesus," and when Carol opens her eyes she closes them again, quick, but still can see the new known face from school (not Eddie), the thrashing, writhing body struggling against the ushers with the look of grave and loving support on their faces, and hear the torn, tearing cry: "Don't take me away, life everlasting don't take me away"

And now the rhinestones in Parry's hair glitter wicked; the white hands of the ushers, fanning, foam in the air; the blue-painted waters of Jordan swell and thunder; Christ spirals on his cross in the window—and she is drowned under the sluice of the slow singing and the sway.

So high up and forgotten the waves and the world, so stirless the deep cool green and the wrecks of what had been. Here now Hostess Foods, where Alva Phillips works her nights—but different from that time Alva had taken them through before work, for it is all sunken under water, the creaking loading platform where they had left the night behind; the closet room where Alva's swaddles of sweaters, boots, and cap hung, the long hall lined with pickle barrels, the sharp freezer door swinging open.

Bubbles of breath that swell. A gulp of numbing air. She swims into the chill room where the huge wheels of cheese stand, and Alva swims too, deftly oiling each machine: slicers and wedgers and the convey, that at her touch start to roll and grind. The light of day blazes up and Alva is holding a cup, saying: Drink this, baby.

"DRINK IT." Her mother's voice and the numbing air demanding her to pay attention. Up through the waters and into the car.

"That's right, lambie, now lie back." Her mother's lap.

"Mother."

"Shhhhh. You almost fainted, lambie."

Alva's voice. "You gonna be all right, Carol . . . Lucy, I'm telling you for the last time, you and Buford get back into that church. Carol is *fine*."

"Lucyinda, if I had all your petticoats I could float." Crying. "Why didn't you let me wear my full skirt with the petticoats, Mother."

"Shhhhh, lamb." Smoothing her cheek. "Just breathe, take long deep breaths."

". . . How you doing now, you little ol' consolation prize?" It is Parry, but she does not come in the car or reach to Carol through the open window: "No need to cuss and fuss. You going to be sharp as a tack, Jack."

Answering automatically: "And cool as a fool."

Quick, they look at each other.

"Parry, we have to go home now, don't we, Mother? I almost fainted, didn't I, Mother? . . . Parry, I'm sorry I got sick and have to miss your baptism."

"Don't feel sorry. I'll feel better you not there to watch. It was our mommas wanted you to be there, not me."

"Parry!" Three voices.

"Maybe I'll come over to play kickball after. If you feeling better. Maybe. Or bring the pogo." Old shared joys in her voice. "Or any little thing."

In just a whisper: "Or any little thing. Parry. Good-bye, Parry."

And why does Alva have to talk now?

"You all right? You breathin' deep like your momma said? Was it too close 'n hot in there? Did something scare you, Carrie?"

Shaking her head to lie, "No."

"I blames myself for not paying attention. You not used to people letting go that way. Lucy and Bubbie, Parialee, they used to it. They been coming since they lap babies."

"Alva, that's all right. Alva. Mrs. Phillips."

"You *was* scared. Carol, it's something to study about. You'll feel better if you understand."

Trying not to listen.

"You not used to hearing what people keeps inside, Carol. You know how music can make you feel things? Glad or sad or like you can't sit still? That was religion music, Carol."

"I have to breathe deep, Mother said."

"Not everybody feels religion the same way. Some it's in their mouth, but some it's like a hope in their blood, their bones. And they singing songs every word that's real to them, Carol, every word out of they own life. And the preaching finding lodgment in their hearts."

The screaming was tuning up in her ears again, high above Alva's patient voice and the waves lapping and fretting.

"Maybe somebody's had a hard week, Carol, and they locked up with it. Maybe a lot of hard weeks bearing down."

"Mother, my head hurts."

"And they're home, Carol, church is home. Maybe the only place they can feel how they feel and maybe let it come out. So they can go on. And it's all right."

"Please, Alva. Mother, tell Alva my head hurts."

"Get Happy, we call it, and most it's a good feeling, Carol. When you got all that locked up inside you."

"Tell her we have to go home. It's all right, Alva. Please, Mother. Say good-bye. Good-bye."

When I was carrying Parry and her father left me, and I fifteen years old, one thousand miles away from home, sin-sick and never really believing, as still I don't believe all, scorning, for what have it done to help, waiting there in the clinic and maybe sleeping, a voice called: Alva, Alva. So mournful and so sweet: Alva. Fear not, I have loved you from the foundation of the universe. And a little small child tugged on my dress. He was carrying a parade stick, on the end of it a star that outshined the sun. Follow me, he said. And the real sun went down and he hidden his stick. How dark it was, how dark. I could feel the darkness with my hands. And when I could see, I screamed. Dump trucks run, dumping bodies in hell, and a convey line run, never ceasing with souls, weary ones having to stamp and shove them along, and the air like fire. Oh I never want to hear such screaming. Then the little child jumped on a motorbike making a path no bigger than my little finger. But first he greased my feet with the hands of my momma when I was a knee baby. They shined like the sun was on them. Eyes he placed all around my head, and as I journeyed upward after him, it seemed I heard a mourning: "Mama Mama you must help carry the world." The rise and fall of nations I saw. And the voice called again Alva Alva, and I flew into a world of light, multitudes singing, Free, free, I am so glad.

2

Helen began to cry, telling her husband about it.

"You and Alva ought to have your heads examined, taking her there cold like that," Len said. "All right, wreck my best handkerchief. Anyway, now that she's had a bath, her Sunday dinner. . . ."

"And been fussed over," seventeen-year-old Jeannie put in.

"She seems good as new. Now *you* forget it, Helen."

"I can't. Something . . . deep happened. If only I or Alva had told her what it would be like. . . . But I didn't realize."

You don't realize a lot of things, Mother, Jeannie said, but not aloud.

"So Alva talked about it after instead of before. Maybe it meant more that way."

"Oh Len, she didn't listen."

"You don't know if she did or not. Or what there was in the experience for her. . . ."

Enough to pull that kid apart two ways even more, Jeannie said, but still not aloud.

"I was so glad she and Parry were going someplace together again. Now that'll be between them too. Len, they really need, miss each other. What happened in a few months? When I think of how close they were, the hours of makebelieve and dressup and playing ball and collecting. . . ."

"Grow up, Mother." Jeannie's voice was harsh. "Parialee's collecting something else now. Like her own crowd. Like jivetalk and rhythmandblues. Like teachers who treat her like a dummy and white kids who treat her like dirt; boys who think she's really something and chicks who. . . ."

"Jeannie, I know. It hurts."

"Well, maybe it hurts Parry too. Maybe. At least she's got a crowd. Just don't let it hurt Carol though, 'cause there's nothing she can do about it. That's all through, her and Parialee Phillips, put away with their paper dolls."

"No, Jeannie, no."

"It's like Ginger and me. Remember Ginger, my best friend in Horace Mann. But you hardly noticed when it happened to us, did you . . . because she was white? Yes, Ginger, who's got two kids now, who quit school year before last. Parry's never going to finish either. What's she got to do with Carrie any more? They're going different places. Different places, different crowds. And they're sorting. . . ."

"Now wait, Jeannie. Parry's just as bright, just as capable."

"They're in junior high, Mother. Don't you know about junior high? How they sort? And it's all where you're going. Yes and Parry's colored and Carrie's white. And you have to watch everything, what you wear and how you wear it and who you eat lunch with and how much homework you do and how you act to the teacher and what you laugh at. . . . And run with your crowd."

"It's that final?" asked Len. "Don't you think kids like Carol and Parry can show it doesn't *have* to be that way."

"They can't. They can't. They don't let you."

"No need to shout," he said mildly. "And who do you mean by 'they' and what do you mean by 'sorting'?"

How they sort. A foreboding of comprehension whirled within Helen. What was it Carol had told her of the Welcome Assembly the first day in junior high? The models showing How to Dress and How Not to Dress and half the girls in their loved new clothes watching their counterparts up on the stage—*their* straight skirt, their sweater, their earrings, lipstick, hairdo— "How Not to Dress," "a bad reputation for your school." It was nowhere in Carol's description, yet picturing it now, it seemed to Helen that a mute cry of violated dignity hung in the air. Later there had been a story of going to another Low 7 homeroom on an errand and seeing a teacher trying to wipe the forbidden lipstick off a girl who was fighting back and cursing. Helen could hear Carol's frightened, self-righteous tones: ". . . and I hope they expel her; she's the kind that gives Franklin Jr. a bad rep; she doesn't care about anything and always gets into fights." Yet there was nothing in these incidents to touch the heavy comprehension that waited. . . . Homework, the wonderings those times Jeannie and Carol needed help: "What if there's no one at home to give the help, and the teachers with their two hundred and forty kids a day can't or don't or the kids don't ask and they fall hopelessly behind, what then?"—but this too was unrelated. And what had it been that time about Parry? "Mother, Melanie and Sharon won't go if they know Parry's coming." Then of course you'll go with Parry, she's been your friend longer, she had answered, but where was it they were going and what had finally happened? Len, my head hurts, she felt like saying, in Carol's voice in the car, but Len's eyes were grave on Jeannie who was saying passionately:

"If you think it's so goddam important why do we have to live here where it's for real; why don't we move to Ivy like Betsy (yes, I know, money), where it's the deal to be buddies, in school anyway, three coloured kids and their father's a doctor or judge or something big wheel and one always gets elected President or head song girl or something to prove oh how we're democratic. . . . What do you want of that poor kid anyway? Make up your mind. Stay friends with Parry—but be one of the kids. Sure. Be a brain—but not a square. Rise on up, college prep, but don't get separated. Yes, stay one of the kids but. . . ."

"Jeannie. You're not talking about Carol at all, are you, Jeannie? Say it again. I wasn't listening. I was trying to think."

"She will not say it again," Len said firmly, "you look about ready to pull a Carol. One a day's our quota. And you, Jeannie, we'd better cool it. Too much to talk about for one session. . . . Here, come to the window and watch the Carol and Parry you're both all worked up about."

In the wind and the shimmering sunset light, half the children of the block are playing down the street. Leaping, bouncing, hallooing, tugging the kites of spring. In the old synchronized understanding, Carol and Parry kick, catch, kick, catch. And now Parry jumps on her pogo stick (the last time), Carol shadowing her, and Bubbie, arching his body in a semicircle of joy, bounding after them, high, higher, higher.

And the months go by and supposedly it is forgotten, except for the now and then when, self-important, Carol will say: I really truly did nearly faint, didn't I, Mother, that time I went to church with Parry?

And now seldom Parry and Carol walk the hill together. Melanie's mother drives by to pick up Carol, and the several times Helen has suggested Parry, too, Carol is quick to explain: "She's already left" or "She isn't ready; she'll make us late."

And after school? Carol is off to club or skating or library or someone's house, and Parry can stay for kickball only on the rare afternoons when she does not have to hurry home where Lucy, Bubbie, and the cousins wait to be cared for, now Alva works the four to twelve-thirty shift.

No more the bending together over the homework. All semester the teachers have been different, and rarely Parry brings her books home, for where is there space or time and what is the sense? And the phone never rings with: what you going to wear tomorrow, are you bringing your lunch, or come on over, let's design some clothes for the Katy Keane comic-book contest. And Parry never drops by with Alva for Saturday snack to or from grocery shopping.

And the months go by and the sorting goes on and seemingly it is over until that morning when Helen must stay home from work, so swollen and feverish is Carol with mumps.

The afternoon before, Parry had come by, skimming up the stairs, spilling books and binders on the bed: Hey frail, lookahere and wail, your momma askin for homework, what she got against YOU? . . . looking quickly once then not looking again and talking fast. . . . Hey, you bloomed. You gonna be your own pumpkin, hallowe'en? Your momma know yet it's mu-umps? And lumps. Momma says: no distress, she'll be by tomorrow morning see do you need anything while your momma's to work. . . . (Singing: *whole lotta shakin goin on*.) All your 'signments is inside; Miss Rockface says the teachers to write 'em cause I mightn't get it right all right.

But did not tell: Does your mother work for Carol's mother? Oh, you're neighbors! Very well, I'll send along a monitor to open Carol's locker but you're only to take these things I'm writing down, nothing else.

Now say after me: Miss Campbell is trusting me to be a good responsible girl. And go right to Carol's house. After school. Not stop anywhere on the way. Not lose anything. And only take. What's written on the list. You really gonna mess with that book stuff? Sign on *mine* says do-not-open-until-eX-mas. . . . That Mrs. Fernandez doll she didn't send nothin, she was the only, says feel better and read a book to report if you feel like and I'm the most for takin care for you; she's my most, wish I could get her but she only teaches 'celerated. . . . Flicking the old read books on the shelf but not opening to mock-declaim as once she used to . . . Vicky, Eddie's g.f. in Rockface office, she's on suspended for sure, yellin to Rockface: you bitchkitty don't you give me no more bad shit. That Vicky she can sure sling-ating-ring it. Staring out the window as if the tree not there in which they had hid out and rocked so often. . . . For sure. (*Keep mo-o-vin.*) Got me a new pink top and lilac skirt. Look sharp with this purple? Cinching in the wide belt as if delighted with what newly swelled above and swelled below. Wear it Saturday night to Sweet's, Modernaires Sounds of Joy, Leroy and Ginny and me goin if Momma'll stay home. IF. (*Shake my baby shake*). How come old folks still likes to party? Huh? Asking of Rembrandt's weary old face looking from the wall. How come (softly) you long-gone you. Touching her face to his quickly, lightly. NEXT mumps is your buddybud Melanie's turn to tote your stuff. *I'm* gettin the hoovus goovus. Hey you so unneat, don't care what you bed with. Removing the books and binders, ranging them on the dresser one by one, marking lipstick faces—bemused or mocking or amazed—on each paper jacket. Better. Fluffing out smoothing the quilt with exaggerated energy. Any little thing I can get, cause I gotta blow. Tossing up and catching their year-ago, arm-in-arm graduation picture, replacing it deftly, upside down, into its mirror crevice. Joe. Bring you joy juice or fizz water or kickapoo? Adding a frown line to one bookface. Twanging the paper fishkite, the Japanese windbell overhead, setting the mobile they had once made of painted eggshells and decorated straws to twirling and rocking. And is gone.

She talked to the lipstick faces after, in her fever, tried to stand on her head to match the picture, twirled and twanged with the violent overhead.

Sleeping at last after the disordered night. Having surrounded herself with the furnishings of that world of childhood she no sooner learned to live in comfortably, then had to leave.

The dollhouse stands there to arrange and rearrange; the shell and picture card collections to re-sort and remember; the population of dolls given away to little sister, borrowed back, propped all around to dress and undress and caress.

She has thrown off her nightgown because of the fever, and her just budding breast is exposed where she reaches to hold the floppy plush dog that had been her childhood pillow.

Not for anything would Helen have disturbed her. Except that in the unaccustomedness of a morning at home, in the bruised restlessness after the sleepless night, she clicks on the radio—and the storm of singing whirls into the room:

> *. . . sea of trouble all mingled with fire*
> *Come on my brethern we've got to go higher*
> *Wade, wade. . . .*

And Carol runs down the stairs, shrieking and shrieking. "Turn it off, Mother, turn it off." Hurling herself at the dial and wrenching it so it comes off in her hand.

"Ohhhhh," choked and convulsive, while Helen tries to hold her, to quiet.

"Mother, why did they sing and scream like that?"

"At Parry's church?"

"Yes." Rocking and strangling the cries. "I hear it all the time." Clinging and beseeching. ". . . What was it, Mother? Why?"

Emotion, Helen thought of explaining, *a characteristic of the religion of all oppressed peoples, yes your very own great-grandparents*—thought of saying. And discarded.

Aren't you now, haven't you had feelings in yourself so strong they had to come out some way? ("what howls restrained by decorum")—thought of saying. And discarded.

Repeat Alva: *hope . . . every word out of their own life. A place to let go. And church is home.* And discarded.

The special history of the Negro people—history?—just you try living what must be lived every day—thought of saying. And discarded.

And said nothing.

And said nothing.

And soothed and held.

"Mother, a lot of the teachers and kids don't like Parry when they don't even know what she's like. Just because . . ." Rocking again, convulsive and shamed. "And I'm not really her friend any more."

No news. Betrayal and shame. Who betrayed? Whose shame? Brought herself to say aloud: "But may be friends again. As Alva and I are."

The sobbing a whisper. "That girl Vicky who got that way when I fainted, she's in school. She's the one keeps wearing the lipstick and they wipe it off and she's always in trouble and now maybe she's expelled. Mother."

"Yes, lambie."

"She acts so awful outside but I remember how she was in church and whenever I see her now I have to wonder. And hear . . . like I'm her, Mother, like I'm her." Clinging and trembling. "Oh why do I have to feel it's happening to me too?

"Mother, I want to forget about it all, and not care—like Melanie. Why can't I forget? Oh why is it like it is and why do I have to care?"

Caressing, quieting.

Thinking: *caring asks doing. It is a long baptism into the seas of humankind, my daughter. Better immersion than to live untouched. . . . Yet how will you sustain?*

Why is it like it is?

Sheltering her daughter close, mourning the illusion of the embrace.

And why do I have to care?

While in her, her own need leapt and plunged for the place of strength that was not—where one could scream or sorrow while all knew and accepted, and gloved and loving hands waited to support and understand.

FOR MARGARET HEATON, WHO ALWAYS TAUGHT
1956

Flannery O'Connor
(1925–1964)

Flannery O'Connor created some of the most striking short fiction of the twentieth century. A native of Georgia, she had little in common with the Protestant fundamentalist (and often racist and sexist) culture of her area. A well-educated Catholic woman, O'Connor cultivated her difference from the residents of Milledgeville, Georgia, and in her work it is middle- and lower-class Southern whites who serve as targets for her devastating and often macabre humor. Her treatment of the aging General Sash in "A Late Encounter with the Enemy" is among her milder portraits. Here her critical eye falls instead on his enabling granddaughter, Sarah, whose graduation from college takes second place to her grandfather's perverse fantasies of fame and sexual prowess.

O'Connor's life, though short, was focused on her writing. When she was sixteen, her father died of lupus erythematosus, after being so debilitated from the ailment that he had not worked for several years. She received a B.A. from Georgia College and then took a master's degree at the University of Iowa Writers' Workshop. After moving to New York to work on her fiction, in 1950 she suffered her first attack of lupus. Returning home to live with her mother, she led a carefully monitored life. Though she could write only a few hours each day, she published two novels, *Wise Blood* (1952) and *The Violent Bear It Away* (1960), and two collections of stories, *A Good Man Is Hard to Find* (1955) and *Everything That Rises Must Converge* (1965). Since her death, collections of her reviews, letters, and essays (*Mystery and Manners*, 1969) have appeared.

❖

A LATE ENCOUNTER WITH THE ENEMY

General Sash was a hundred and four years old. He lived with his granddaughter, Sally Poker Sash, who was sixty-two years old and who prayed every night on her knees that he would live until her graduation from college. The General didn't give two slaps for her graduation but he never doubted he would live for it. Living had got to be such a habit with him that he couldn't conceive of any other condition. A graduation exercise was not exactly his idea of a good time, even if, as she said, he would be expected to sit on the stage in his uniform. She said there would be a long procession of teachers and students in their robes but that there wouldn't be anything to equal *him* in his uniform. He knew this well enough without her telling him, and as for the damm procession, it could march to hell and back and not cause him a quiver. He liked parades with floats full of Miss Americas and Miss Daytona Beaches and Miss Queen Cotton Products. He didn't have any use for processions and a procession full of schoolteachers was about as deadly as the River Styx to his way of thinking. However, he was willing to sit on the stage in his uniform so that they could see him.

Sally Poker was not as sure as he was that he would live until her graduation. There had not been any perceptible change in him for the last five years, but she had the sense that she might be cheated out of her triumph because she so often was. She had been going to summer school every year for the past twenty because when she started teaching, there were no such things as degrees. In those times, she said, everything was normal but nothing had been normal since she was sixteen, and for the past twenty summers, when she should have been resting, she had had to take a trunk in the burning heat to the state teacher's college; and though when she returned in the fall, she always taught in the exact way she had been taught not to teach, this was a mild revenge that didn't satisfy her sense of justice. She wanted the General at her graduation because she wanted to show what she stood for, or, as she said, "what all was behind her," and was not behind them. This *them* was not anybody in particular. It was just all the upstarts who had turned the world on its head and unsettled the ways of decent living.

She meant to stand on that platform in August with the General sitting in his wheel chair on the stage behind her and she meant to hold her head very high as if she were saying, "See him! See him! My kin, all you upstarts! Glorious upright old man standing for the old traditions! Dignity! Honor! Courage! See him!" One night in her sleep she screamed, "See him! See him!" and turned her head and found him sitting in his wheel chair behind her with a terrible expression on his face and with all his clothes off except the general's hat and she had waked up and had not dared to go back to sleep again that night.

For his part, the General would not have consented even to attend her graduation if she had not promised to see to it that he sit on the stage. He liked to sit on any stage. He considered that he was still a very handsome man. When he had been able to stand up, he had measured five feet four inches of pure game cock. He had white hair that reached to his shoulders behind and he would not wear teeth because he thought his profile was more striking without them. When he put on his full-dress general's uniform, he knew well enough that there was nothing to match him anywhere.

This was not the same uniform he had worn in the War between the States. He had not actually been a general in that war. He had probably been a foot soldier; he didn't remember what he had been; in fact, he didn't remember that war at all. It was like his feet, which hung down now shriveled at the very end of him, without feeling, covered with a blue-gray afghan that Sally Poker had crocheted when she was a little girl. He didn't remember the Spanish-American War in which he had lost a son; he didn't even remember the son. He didn't have any use for history because he never expected to meet it again. To his mind, history was connected with processions and life with parades and he liked parades. People were always asking him if he remembered this or that—a dreary black procession of questions about the past. There was only one event in the past that had any significance for him and that he cared to talk about; that was twelve years ago when he had received the general's uniform and had been in the premiere.

"I was in that preemy they had in Atlanta," he would tell visitors sitting on his front porch. "Surrounded by beautiful guls. It wasn't a thing local about it. It was nothing local about it. Listen here. It was a nashnul event and they had me in it—up onto the stage. There was no bob-tails at it. Every person at it had paid ten dollars to get in and had to wear his tuxseeder. I was in this uniform. A beautiful gul presented me with it that afternoon in a hotel room."

"It was in a suite in the hotel and I was in it too, Papa," Sally Poker would say, winking at the visitors. "You weren't alone with any young lady in a hotel room."

"Was, I'd a known what to do," the old General would say with a sharp look and the visitors would scream with laughter. "This was a Hollywood, California, gul," he'd continue. "She was from Hollywood, California, and didn't have any part in the pitcher. Out there they have so many beautiful guls that they don't need that they call them a extra and they don't use them for nothing but presenting people with things and having their pitchers taken. They took my pitcher with her. No, it was two of them. One on either side and me in the middle with my arms around each of them's waist and their waist ain't any bigger than a half a dollar."

Sally Poker would interrupt again. "It was Mr. Govisky that gave you the uniform, Papa, and he gave me the most exquisite corsage. Really, I wish you could have seen it. It was made with gladiola petals taken off and painted gold and put back together to look like a rose. It was exquisite. I wish you could have seen it, it was . . ."

"It was a big as her head," the General would snarl. "I was tellin it. They gimme this soward and they say, 'Now General, we don't want you to start a war on us. All we want you to do is march right up on that stage when you're innerduced tonight and answer a few questions. Think you can do that?' 'Think I can do it!' I say. 'Listen here. I was doing things before you were born,' and they hollered."

"He was the hit of the show," Sally Poker would say, but she didn't much like to remember the premiere on account of what had happened to her feet at it. She had bought a new dress for the occasion—a long black crepe dinner dress with a rhinestone buckle and a bolero—and a pair of silver slippers to wear with it, because she was supposed to go up on the stage with him to keep him from falling. Everything was arranged for them. A real limousine came at ten minutes to eight and took them to the theater. It drew up under the marquee at exactly the right time, after the big stars and the director and the author and the governor and the mayor and some less important stars. The police kept traffic from jamming and there were ropes to keep the people off who wouldn't go. All the people who couldn't go watched them step out of the limousine into the lights. Then they walked down the red and gold foyer and an usherette in a Confederate cap and little short skirt conducted them to their special seats. The audience was already there and a group of UDC members began to clap when they saw the General in his uniform and that started everybody to clap. A few more celebrities came after them and then the doors closed and the lights went down.

A young man with blond wavy hair who said he represented the motion-picture industry came out and began to introduce everybody and each one who was introduced walked up on the stage and said how really happy he was to be here for this great event. The General and his granddaughter were introduced sixteenth on the program. He was introduced as General Tennessee Flintrock Sash of the Confederacy, though Sally Poker had told Mr. Govisky that his name was George Poker Sash and that he had only been a major. She helped him up from his seat but her heart was beating so fast she didn't know whether she'd make it herself.

The old man walked up the aisle slowly with his fierce white head high and his hat held over his heart. The orchestra began to play the Confederate Battle Hymn very softly and the UDC members rose as a group and did not sit down again until the General was on the stage. When he reached the center of the stage with Sally Poker just behind him guiding his elbow, the orchestra burst out in a loud rendition of the Battle Hymn and the old man, with real stage presence, gave a vigorous trembling salute and stood at attention until the last blast had died away. Two of the usherettes in Confederate caps and short skirts held a Confederate and a Union flag crossed behind them.

The General stood in the exact center of the spotlight and it caught a weird moon-shaped slice of Sally Poker—the corsage, the rhinestone buckle and one hand clenched around a white glove and handkerchief. The young man with the blond wavy hair inserted himself into the circle of light and said he was *really* happy to have here tonight for this great event, one, he said, who had fought and bled in the battles they would soon see daringly reenacted on the screen, and "Tell me, General," he asked, "how old are you?"

"Niiiiiinnttty-two!" the General screamed.

The young man looked as if this were just about the most impressive thing that had been said all evening. "Ladies and gentlemen," he said, "let's give the General the biggest hand we've got!" and there was applause immediately and the young man indicated to Sally Poker with a motion of his thumb that she could take the old man back to his seat now so that the next person could be introduced; but the General had not finished. He stood immovable in the exact center of the spotlight, his neck thrust forward, his mouth slightly open, and his voracious gray eyes drinking in the glare and the applause. He elbowed his granddaughter roughly away. "How I keep so young," he screeched, "I kiss all the pretty guls!"

This was met with a great din of spontaneous applause and it was at just that instant that Sally Poker looked down at her feet and discovered that in the excitement of getting ready she had forgotten to change her shoes: two brown Girl Scout oxfords protruded from the bottom of her dress. She gave the General a yank and almost ran with him off the stage. He was very angry that he had not got to say how glad he was to be here for this event and on the way back to his seat, he kept saying as loud as he could, "I'm glad to be here at this preemy with all these beautiful guls!" but there was another celebrity going up the other aisle and nobody paid any attention to him. He slept through the picture, muttering fiercely every now and then in his sleep.

Since then, his life had not been very interesting. His feet were completely dead now, his knees worked like old hinges, his kidneys functioned when they would, but his heart persisted doggedly to beat. The past and the future were the same thing to him, one forgotten and the other not remembered; he had no more notion of dying than a cat. Every year on Confederate Memorial Day, he was bundled up and lent to the Capitol City Museum where he was displayed from one to four in a musty room full of old photographs, old uniforms, old artillery, and historic documents. All these were carefully preserved in glass cases so that children would not put their hands on them. He wore his general's uniform from the premiere and sat, with a fixed scowl, inside a small roped area. There was nothing about him to indicate that he was alive except an occasional movement in his milky gray eyes, but once when a bold child touched his sword, his arm shot forward and slapped the hand off in an instant. In the spring when the old homes were opened for pilgrimages, he was invited to wear his uniform and sit in some conspicuous spot and lend atmosphere to the scene. Some of these times he only snarled at the visitors but sometimes he told about the premiere and the beautiful girls.

If he had died before Sally Poker's graduation, she thought she would have died herself. At the beginning of the summer term, even before she knew if she would pass, she told the Dean that her grandfather, General Tennessee Flintrock Sash of the Confederacy, would attend her graduation and that he was a hundred and four years old and that his mind was still clear as a bell. Distinguished visitors were always welcome and could sit on the stage and be introduced. She made arrangements with her nephew, John Wesley Poker Sash, a Boy Scout, to come wheel the General's chair. She thought how sweet it would be to see the old man in his courageous gray and the young boy in his clean khaki—the old and the new, she thought appropriately—they would be behind her on the stage when she received her degree.

Everything went almost exactly as she had planned. In the summer while she was away at school, the General stayed with other relatives and they brought him and John Wesley, the Boy Scout, down to the graduation. A reporter came to the hotel where they stayed and took the General's picture with Sally Poker on one side of him and John Wesley on the other. The General, who had had his picture taken with beautiful girls, didn't think much of this. He had forgotten precisely what kind of event this was he was going to attend but he remembered that he was to wear his uniform and carry the sword.

On the morning of the graduation, Sally Poker had to line up in the academic procession with the B.S.'s in Elementary Education and she couldn't see to getting him on the stage herself—but John Wesley, a fat blond boy of ten with an executive expression, guaranteed to take care of everything. She came in her academic gown to the hotel and dressed the old man in his uniform. He was as frail as a dried spider. "Aren't you just thrilled, Papa?" she asked. "I'm just thrilled to death!"

"Put the sword across my lap, damm you," the old man said, "where it'll shine."

She put it there and then stood back looking at him. "You look just grand," she said.

"God damm it," the old man said in a slow monotonous certain tone as if he were saying it to the beating of his heart. "God damm every goddam thing to hell."

"Now, now," she said and left happily to join the procession.

The graduates were lined up behind the Science building and she found her place just as the line started to move. She had not slept much the night before and when she had, she had dreamed of the exercises, murmuring, "See him, see him?" in her sleep but waking up every time just before she turned her head to look at him behind her. The graduates had to walk three blocks in the hot sun in their black wool robes and as she plodded stolidly along she thought that if anyone considered this academic procession something impressive to behold, they need only wait until they saw that old General in his courageous gray and that clean young Boy Scout stoutly wheeling his chair across the stage with the sunlight catching the sword. She imagined that John Wesley had the old man ready now behind the stage.

The black procession wound its way up the two blocks and started on the main walk leading to the auditorium. The visitors stood on the grass, picking out their graduates. Men were pushing back their hats and wiping their foreheads and women were lifting their dresses slightly from the shoulders to keep them from sticking to their backs. The graduates in their heavy robes looked as if the last beads of ignorance were being sweated out of them. The sun blazed off the fenders of automobiles and beat from the columns of the buildings and pulled the eye from one spot of glare to another. It pulled Sally Poker's toward the big red Coca-Cola machine that had been set up by the side of the auditorium. Here she saw the General parked, scowling and hatless in his chair in the blazing sun while John Wesley, his blouse loose behind, his hip and cheek pressed to the red machine, was drinking a Coca-Cola. She broke from the line and galloped to them and snatched the bottle away. She shook the boy and thrust in his blouse and put the hat on the old man's head. "Now get him in there!" she said, pointing one rigid finger to the side door of the building.

For his part the General felt as if there were a little hole beginning to widen in the top of his head. The boy wheeled him rapidly down a walk and up a ramp and into a building and bumped him over the stage entrance and into position where he had been told and the General glared in front of him at heads that all seemed to flow together and eyes that moved from one face to another. Several figures in black robes came and picked up his hand and shook it. A black procession was flowing up each aisle and forming to stately music in a pool in front of him. The music seemed to be entering his head through the little hole and he thought for a second that the procession would try to enter it too.

He didn't know what procession this was but there was something familiar about it. It must be familiar to him since it had come to meet him, but he didn't like a black procession. Any procession that came to meet him, he thought irritably, ought to have floats with beautiful guls on them like the floats before the preemy. It must be something connected with history like they were always having. He had no use for any of it. What happened then wasn't anything to a man living now and he was living now.

When all the procession had flowed into the black pool, a black figure began orating in front of it. The figure was telling something about history and the General made up his mind he wouldn't listen, but the words kept seeping in through the little hole in his head. He heard his own name mentioned and his chair was shuttled forward roughly and the Boy Scout took a big bow. They called his name and the fat brat bowed. Goddam you, the old man tried to say, get out of my way, I can stand up!—but he was jerked back again before he could get up and take the bow. He supposed the noise they made was for him. If he was over, he didn't intend to listen to any more of it. If it hadn't been for the little hole in the top of his head, none of the words would have got to him. He thought of putting his finger up there into the hole to block them but the hole was a little wider than his finger and it felt as if it were getting deeper.

Another black robe had taken the place of the first one and was talking now and he heard his name mentioned again but they were not talking about him, they were still talking about history. "If we forget our past," the speaker was saying, "we won't remember our future and it will be as well for we won't have one." The General heard some of these words gradually. He had forgotten history and he didn't intend to remember it again. He had forgotten the name and face of his wife and the names and faces of his children or even if he had a wife and children, and he had forgotten the names of places and the places themselves and what had happened at them.

He was considerably irked by the hole in his head. He had not expected to have a hole in his head at this event. It was the slow black music that had put it there and though most of the music had stopped outside, there was still a little of it in the hole, going deeper and moving around in his thoughts, letting the words he heard into the dark places of his brain. He heard the words, Chickamauga, Shiloh, Johnston, Lee, and he knew he was inspiring all these words that meant nothing to him. He wondered if he had been a general at Chickamauga or at Lee. Then he tried to see himself and the horse mounted in the middle of a float full of beautiful girls, being driven slowly through downtown Atlanta. Instead, the old words began to stir in his head as if they were trying to wrench themselves out of place and come to life.

The speaker was through with that war and had gone on to the next one and now he was approaching another and all his words, like the black procession, were vaguely familiar and irritating. There was a long finger of music in the General's head, probing various spots that were words, letting in a little light on the words and helping them to live. The words began to come toward him and he said, Dammit! I ain't going to have it! and he started edging backwards to get out of the way. Then he saw the figure in the black robe sit down and there was a noise and the black pool in front of him began to rumble and to flow toward him from either side to the black slow music, and he said, Stop dammit! I can't do but one thing at a time! He couldn't protect himself from the words and attend to the procession too and the words were coming at him fast. He felt that he was running backwards and the words were coming at him like musket fire, just escaping him but getting nearer and nearer. He turned around and began to run as fast as he could but he found himself running toward the words. He was running into a regular volley of them and meeting them with quick curses. As the music swelled toward him, the entire past opened up on him out of nowhere and he felt his body riddled in a hundred places with sharp stabs of pain and he fell down, returning a curse for every hit. He saw his wife's narrow face looking at him critically through her round gold-rimmed glasses; he saw one of his squinting bald-headed sons; and his mother ran toward him with an anxious look; then a succession of places—Chickamauga, Shiloh, Marthasville—rushed at him as if the past were the only future now and he had to endure it. Then suddenly he saw that the black procession was almost on him. He recognized it, for it had been dogging all his days. He made such a desperate effort to see over it and find out what comes after the past that his hand clenched the sword until the blade touched the bone.

The graduates were crossing the stage in a long file to receive their scrolls and shake the president's hand. As Sally Poker, who was near the end, crossed, she glanced at the General and saw him sitting fixed and fierce, his eyes wide open, and she turned her head forward again and held it a perceptible degree higher and received her scroll. Once it was all over and she was out of the auditorium in the sun again, she located her kin and they waited together on a bench in the shade for John Wesley to wheel the old man out. That crafty scout had bumped him out the back way and rolled him at high speed down a flagstone path and was waiting now, with the corpse, in the long line at the Coca-Cola machine.

1953

Eudora Welty

(1909–   )

Eudora Welty has often been named as a serious contender for the Nobel Prize for Literature. The most prominent short fiction writer in the United States, she is known for a range of work that includes both the comic and the poignant, if not tragic. Famous worldwide for her short stories, the Mississippian captures elusive traits of characters so that they seem not only real, but freshly imagined. In the persona of Phoenix Jackson in "A Worn Path," Welty transfers her white middle-class understanding of family relationships in the South to the evocative portrait of the "very old and small" black woman. As with much of her work, this story is eminently successful.

An only child of Ohio parents who moved to Jackson before Eudora was born, Welty was educated at Mississippi State College for Women, the University of Wisconsin, and the Columbia University School of Business. During the Great Depression, she was a publicity assistant for the Works Progress Administration, where she became a good photographer and also learned to understand how crucial economic stability is for all people. *A Curtain of Green* (1941), her first story collection, was published in 1941, followed by *The Wide Net* (1943), *The Golden Apples* (1949), and her novels (*The Robber Bridegroom*, 1942; *The Ponder Heart*, 1954; *Losing Battles*, 1970; and *The Optimist's Daughter*, which won the Pulitzer Prize for Fiction in 1972). *One Writer's Beginnings*, her self-effacing memoir, appeared in 1984.

❖

A WORN PATH

It was December—a bright frozen day in the early morning. Far out in the country there was an old Negro woman with her head tied in a red rag, coming along a path through the pinewoods. Her name was Phoenix Jackson. She was very old and small and she walked slowly in the dark pine shadows, moving a little from side to side in her steps, with the balanced heaviness and lightness of a pendulum in a grandfather clock. She carried a thin, small cane made from an umbrella, and with this she kept tapping the frozen earth in front of her. This made a grave and persistent noise in the still air, that seemed meditative like the chirping of a solitary little bird.

She wore a dark stripped dress reaching down to her shoe tops, and an equally long apron of bleached sugar sacks, with a full pocket: all neat and tidy, but every time she took a step she might have fallen over her shoelaces, which dragged from her unlaced shoes. She looked straight ahead. Her eyes were blue with age. Her skin had a pattern all its own of numberless branching wrinkles and as though a whole little tree stood in the middle of her forehead, but a golden color ran underneath, and the two knobs of her cheeks were illumined by a yellow burning under the dark. Under the red rag her hair came down on her neck in the frailest of ringlets, still black, and with an odor like copper.

Now and then there was a quivering in the thicket. Old Phoenix said, "Out of my way, all you foxes, owls, beetles, jack rabbits, coons and wild animals! . . . Keep out from under these feet, little bob-whites . . . Keep the big wild hogs out of my path. Don't let none of those come running my direction. I got a long way." Under her small black-freckled hand her cane, limber as a buggy whip, would switch at the brush as if to rouse up any hiding things.

On she went. The woods were deep and still. The sun made the pine needles almost too bright to look at, up where the wind rocked. The cones dropped as light as feathers. Down in the hollow was the mourning dove—it was not too late for him.

The path ran up a hill. "Seem like there is chains about my feet, time I get this far," she said, in the voice of argument old people keep to use with themselves. "Something always take a hold of me on this hill—pleads I should stay."

After she got to the top she turned and gave a full, severe look behind her where she had come. "Up through pines," she said at length. "Now down through oaks."

Her eyes opened their widest, and she started down gently. But before she got to the bottom of the hill a bush caught her dress.

Her fingers were busy and intent, but her skirts were full and long, so that before she could pull them free in one place they were caught in another. It was not possible to allow the dress to tear. "I in the thorny bush," she said. "Thorns, you doing your appointed work. Never want to let folks pass, no sir. Old eyes thought you was a pretty little *green* bush."

Finally, trembling all over, she stood free, and after a moment dared to stoop for her cane.

"Sun so high!" she cried, leaning back and looking, while the thick tears went over her eyes. "The time getting all gone here."

At the foot of this hill was a place where a log was laid across the creek.

"Now comes the trial," said Phoenix.

Putting her right foot out, she mounted the log and shut her eyes. Lifting her skirt, leveling her cane fiercely before her, like a festival figure in some parade, she began to march across. Then she opened her eyes and she was safe on the other side.

"I wasn't as old as I thought," she said.

But she sat down to rest. She spread her skirts on the bank around her and folded her hands over her knees. Up above her was a tree in a pearly cloud of mistletoe. She did not dare to close her eyes, and when a little boy brought her a plate with a slice of marble-cake on it she spoke to him. "That would be acceptable," she said. But when she went to take it there was just her own hand in the air.

So she left that tree, and had to go through a barbed-wire fence. There she had to creep and crawl, spreading her knees and stretching her fingers like a baby trying to climb the steps. But she talked loudly to herself: she could not let her dress be torn now, so late in the day, and she could not pay for having her arm or her leg sawed off if she got caught fast where she was.

At last she was safe through the fence and risen up out in the clearing. Big dead trees, like black men with one arm, were standing in the purple stalks of the withered cotton field. There sat a buzzard.

"Who you watching?"

In the furrow she made her way along.

"Glad this not the season for bulls," she said, looking sideways, "and the good Lord made his snakes to curl up and sleep in the winter. A pleasure I don't see no two-headed snake coming around that tree, where it come once. It took a while to get by him, back in the summer."

She passed through the old cotton and went into a field of dead corn. It whispered and shook and was taller than her head. "Through the maze now," she said, for there was no path.

Then there was something tall, black, and skinny there, moving before her.

At first she took it for a man. It could have been a man dancing in the field. But she stood still and listened, and it did not make a sound. It was as silent as a ghost.

"Ghost," she said sharply, "who be you the ghost of? For I have heard of nary death close by."

But there was no answer—only the ragged dancing in the wind.

She shut her eyes, reached out her hand, and touched a sleeve. She found a coat and inside that an emptiness, cold as ice.

"You scarecrow," she said. Her face lighted. "I ought to be shut up for good," she said with laughter. "My senses is gone. I too old. I the oldest people I ever know. Dance, old scarecrow," she said, "while I dancing with you."

She kicked her foot over the furrow, and with mouth drawn down, shook her head once or twice in a little strutting way. Some husks blew down and whirled in streamers about her skirts.

Then she went on, parting her way from side to side with the cane, through the whispering field. At last she came to the end, to a wagon track where the silver grass blew between the red ruts. The quail were walking around like pullets, seeming all dainty and unseen.

"Walk pretty," she said. "This the easy place. This the easy going."

She followed the track, swaying through the quiet bare fields, through the little strings of trees silver in their dead leaves, past cabins silver from weather, with the doors and windows boarded shut, all like old women under a spell sitting there. "I walking in their sleep," she said, nodding her head vigorously.

In a ravine she went where a spring was silently flowing through a hollow log. Old Phoenix bent and drank. "Sweet-gum makes the water sweet," she said, and drank more. "Nobody know who made this well, for it was here when I was born."

The track crossed a swampy part where the moss hung as white as lace from every limb. "Sleep on, alligators, and blow your bubbles." Then the track went into the road.

Deep, deep the road went down between the high green-colored banks. Overhead the live-oaks met, and it was as dark as a cave.

A black dog with a lolling tongue came up out of the weeds by the ditch. She was meditating, and not ready, and when he came at her she only hit him a little with her cane. Over she went in the ditch, like a little puff of milkweed.

Down there, her senses drifted away. A dream visited her, and she reached her hand up, but nothing reached down and gave her a pull. So she lay there and presently went to talking. "Old woman," she said to herself, "that black dog come up out of the weeds to stall you off, and now there he sitting on his fine tail, smiling at you."

A white man finally came along and found her—a hunter, a young man, with his dog on a chain.

"Well, Granny!" he laughed. "What are you doing there?"

"Lying on my back like a June-bug waiting to be turned over, mister," she said, reaching up her hand.

He lifted her up, gave her a swing in the air, and set her down. "Anything broken, Granny?"

"No sir, them old dead weeds is springy enough," said Phoenix, when she had got her breath. "I thank you for your trouble."

"Where do you live, Granny?" he asked, while the two dogs were growling at each other.

"Away back yonder, sir, behind the ridge. You can't even see it from here."

"On your way home?"

"No sir, I going to town."

"Why, that's too far! That's as far as I walk when I come out myself, and I get something for my trouble." He patted the stuffed bag he carried, and there hung down a little closed claw. It was one of the bob-whites, with its beak hooked bitterly to show it was dead. "Now you go on home, Granny!"

"I bound to go to town, mister," said Phoenix. "The time come around."

He gave another laugh, filling the whole landscape. "I know you old colored people! Wouldn't miss going to town to see Santa Claus!"

But something held old Phoenix very still. The deep lines in her face went into a fierce and different radiation. Without warning, she had seen with her own eyes a flashing nickel fall out of the man's pocket onto the ground.

"How old are you, Granny?" he was saying.

"There is no telling, mister," she said, "no telling."

Then she gave a little cry and clapped her hands and said, "Git on away from here, dog! Look! Look at that dog!" She laughed as if in admiration. "He ain't scared of nobody. He a big black dog." She whispered, "Sic him!"

"Watch me get rid of that cur," said the man. "Sic him, Pete! Sic him!"

Phoenix heard the dogs fighting, and heard the man running and throwing sticks. She even heard a gunshot. But she was slowly bending forward by that time, further and further forward, the lids stretched down over her eyes, as if she were doing this in her sleep. Her chin was lowered almost to her knees. The yellow palm of her hand came out from the fold of her apron. Her fingers slid down and along the ground under the piece of money with the grace and care they would have in lifting an egg from under a setting hen. Then she slowly straightened up, she stood erect, and the nickel was in her apron pocket. A bird flew by. Her lips moved. "God watching me the whole time. I come to stealing."

The man came back, and his own dog panted about them. "Well, I scared him off that time," he said, and then he laughed and lifted his gun and pointed it at Phoenix.

She stood straight and faced him.

"Doesn't the gun scare you?" he said, still pointing it.

"No, sir, I seen plenty go off closer by, in my day, and for less than what I done," she said, holding utterly still.

He smiled, and shouldered the gun. "Well, Granny," he said, "you must be a hundred years old, and scared of nothing. I'd give you a dime if I had any money with me. But you take my advice and stay home, and nothing will happen to you."

"I bound to go on my way, mister," said Phoenix. She inclined her head in the red rag. Then they went in different directions, but she could hear the gun shooting again and again over the hill.

She walked on. The shadows hung from the oak trees to the road like curtains. Then she smelled wood-smoke, and smelled the river, and she saw a steeple and the cabins on their steep steps. Dozens of little black children whirled around her. There ahead was Natchez shining. Bells were ringing. She walked on.

In the paved city it was Christmas time. There were red and green electric lights strung and crisscrossed everywhere, and all turned on in the daytime. Old Phoenix would have been lost if she had not distrusted her eyesight and depended on her feet to know where to take her.

She paused quietly on the sidewalk where people were passing by. A lady came along in the crowd, carrying an armful of red-, green- and silver wrapped presents; she gave off perfume like the red roses in hot summer, and Phoenix stopped her.

"Please, missy, will you lace up my shoe?" She held up her foot.

"What do you want, Grandma?"

"See my shoe," said Phoenix. "Do all right for out in the country, but wouldn't look right to go in a big building."

"Stand still then, Grandma," said the lady. She put her packages down on the sidewalk beside her and laced and tied both shoes tightly.

"Can't lace 'em with a cane," said Phoenix. "Thank you, missy. I doesn't mind asking a nice lady to tie up my shoe, when I gets out on the street."

Moving slowly and from side to side, she went into the big building, and into a tower of steps, where she walked up and around and around until her feet knew to stop.

She entered a door, and there she saw nailed up on the wall the document that had been stamped with the gold seal and framed in the gold frame, which matched the dream that was hung up in her head.

"Here I be," she said. There was a fixed and ceremonial stiffness over her body.

"A charity case, I suppose," said an attendant who sat at the desk before her.

But Phoenix only looked above her head. There was sweat on her face, the wrinkles in her skin shone like a bright net.

"Speak up, Grandma," the woman said. "What's your name? We must have your history, you know. Have you been here before? What seems to be the trouble with you?"

Old Phoenix only gave a twitch to her face as if a fly were bothering her.

"Are you deaf?" cried the attendant.

But then the nurse came in.

"Oh, that's just old Aunt Phoenix," she said. "She doesn't come for herself—she has a little grandson. She makes these trips just as regular as clockwork. She lives away back off the Old Natchez Trace." She bent down. "Well, Aunt Phoenix, why don't you just take a seat? We won't keep you standing after your long trip." She pointed.

The old woman sat down, bolt upright in the chair.

"Now, how is the boy?" asked the nurse.

Old Phoenix did not speak.

"I said, how is the boy?"

But Phoenix only waited and stared straight ahead, her face very solemn and withdrawn into rigidity.

"Is his throat any better?" asked the nurse. "Aunt Phoenix, don't you hear me? Is your grandson's throat any better since the last time you came for the medicine?"

With her hands on her knees, the old woman waited, silent, erect and motionless, just as if she were in armor.

"You mustn't take up our time this way, Aunt Phoenix," the nurse said. "Tell us quickly about your grandson, and get it over. He isn't dead, is he?"

At last there came a flicker and then a flame of comprehension across her face, and she spoke.

"My grandson. It was my memory had left me. There I sat and forgot why I made my long trip."

"Forgot?" The nurse frowned. "After you came so far?"

Then Phoenix was like an old woman begging a dignified forgiveness for waking up frightened in the night. "I never did go to school, I was too old at the Surrender," she said in a soft voice. "I'm an old woman without an education. It was my memory fail me. My little grandson, he is just the same, and I forgot it in the coming."

"Throat never heals, does it?" said the nurse, speaking in a loud, sure voice to old Phoenix. By now she had a card with something written on it, a little list. "Yes. Swallowed lye. When was it?—January—two—three years ago—"

Phoenix spoke unasked now. "No, missy, he not dead, he just the same. Every little while his throat begin to close up again, and he not able to swallow. He not get his breath. He not able to help himself. So the time come around, and I go on another trip for the soothing medicine."

"All right. The doctor said as long as you came to get it, you could have it," said the nurse. "But it's an obstinate case."

"My little grandson, he sit up there in the house all wrapped up, waiting by himself." Phoenix went on. "We is the only two left in the world. He suffer and it don't seem to put him back at all. He got a sweet look. He going to last. He wear a little patch quilt and peep out holding his mouth open like a little bird. I remembers so plain now. I not going to forget him again, no, the whole enduring time. I could tell him from all the others in creation."

"All right." The nurse was trying to hush her now. She brought her a bottle of medicine. "Charity," she said, making a check mark in a book.

Old Phoenix held the bottle close to her eyes, and then carefully put it into her pocket.

"I thank you," she said.

"It's Christmas time, Grandma," said the attendant. "Could I give you a few pennies out of my purse?"

"Five pennies is a nickel," said Phoenix stiffly.

"Here's a nickel," said the attendant.

Phoenix rose carefully and held out her hand. She received the nickel and then fished the other nickel out of her pocket and laid it beside the new one. She stared at her palm closely, with her head on one side.

Then she gave a tap with her cane on the floor.

"This is what come to me to do," she said. "I going to the store and buy my child a little windmill they sells, made out of paper. He going to find it hard to believe there such a thing in the world. I'll march myself back where he waiting, holding it straight up in this hand."

She lifted her free hand, gave a little nod, turned around, and walked out of the doctor's office. Then her slow step began on the stairs, going down.

1941

Cynthia Ozick

(1928–   )

Cynthia Ozick has never avoided the controversial in her short fiction and her novel, *Trust* (1966). A regular contributor to the *New Yorker,* she has been, for many years, a writer's writer—in that other writers pay attention to what Ozick achieves. "The Shawl," which originally appeared in that magazine, is a most unusual story, approaching the horrors of the Holocaust through the intimate point of view of two women incarcerated in a death camp. In its unexpected brevity, and its careful focus on the dailiness of women's lives, the story combines the shock of the terror of imminent death with the deep agony of a mother's love bereft. The fiction also manages to draw two female protagonists, the mother Rosa and the younger Stella, who are quite different from each other—and unfortunately also different in their love for Rosa's child, Magda.

A native New Yorker, Ozick graduated from New York University and later earned an M.A. in English at Ohio State University. After her marriage, she taught for a time at New York University. Thoroughly educated in Jewish philosophy and lore, Ozick has increasingly focused on the Jewish world in her fiction. She also translates Yiddish poetry.

THE SHAWL

Stella, cold, cold, the coldness of hell. How they walked on the roads together, Rosa with Magda curled up between sore breasts, Magda wound up in the shawl. Sometimes Stella carried Magda. But she was jealous of Magda. A thin girl of fourteen, too small, with thin breasts of her own, Stella wanted to be wrapped in a shawl, hidden away, asleep, rocked by the march, a baby, a round infant in arms. Magda took Rosa's nipple, and Rosa never stopped walking, a walking cradle. There was not enough milk; sometimes Magda sucked air; then she screamed. Stella was ravenous. Her knees were tumors on sticks, her elbows chicken bones.

Rosa did not feel hunger; she felt light, not like someone walking but like someone in a faint, in trance, arrested in a fit, someone who is already a floating angel, alert and seeing everything, but in the air, not there, not touching the road. As if teetering on the tips of her fingernails. She looked into Magda's face through a gap in the shawl: a squirrel in a nest, safe, no one could reach her inside the little house of the shawl's windings. The face, very round, a pocket mirror of a face: but it was not Rosa's bleak complexion, dark like cholera, it was another kind of face altogether, eyes blue as air, smooth feathers of hair nearly as yellow as the Star sewn into Rosa's coat. You could think she was one of *their* babies.

Rosa, floating, dreamed of giving Magda away in one of the villages. She could leave the line for a minute and push Magda into the hands of any woman on the side of the road. But if she moved out of line they might shoot. And even if she fled the line for half a second and pushed the shawl-bundle at a stranger, would the woman take it? She might be surprised, or afraid; she might drop the shawl, and Magda would fall out and strike her head and die. The little round head. Such a good child, she gave up screaming, and sucked now only for the taste of the drying nipple itself. The neat grip of the tiny gums. One mite of a tooth tip sticking up in the bottom gum, how shining, an elfin tombstone of white marble gleaming there. Without complaining, Magda relinquished Rosa's teats, first the left, then the right; both were cracked, not a sniff of milk. The duct-crevice extinct, a dead volcano, blind eye, chill hole, so Magda took the corner of the shawl and milked it instead. She sucked and sucked, flooding the threads with wetness. The shawl's good flavor, milk of linen.

It was a magic shawl, it could nourish an infant for three days and three nights. Magda did not die, she stayed alive, although very quiet. A peculiar smell, of cinnamon and almonds, lifted out of her mouth. She held her eyes open every moment, forgetting how to blink or nap, and Rosa and sometimes Stella studied their blueness. On the road they raised one burden of a leg after another and studied Magda's face. "Aryan," Stella said, in a voice grown as thin as a string; and Rosa thought how Stella gazed at Magda like a young cannibal. And the time that Stella said "Aryan," it sounded to Rosa as if Stella had really said "Let us devour her."

But Magda lived to walk. She lived that long, but she did not walk very well, partly because she was only fifteen months old, and partly because the spindles of her legs could not hold up her fat belly. It was fat with air, full and round. Rosa gave almost all her food to Magda, Stella gave nothing; Stella was ravenous, a growing child herself, but not growing much. Stella did not menstruate. Rosa did not menstruate. Rosa was ravenous, but also not; she learned from Magda how to drink the taste of a finger in one's mouth. They were in a place without pity, all pity was annihilated in Rosa, she looked at Stella's bones without pity. She was sure that Stella was waiting for Magda to die so she could put her teeth into the little thighs.

Rosa knew Magda was going to die very soon; she should have been dead already, but she had been buried away deep inside the magic shawl, mistaken there for the shivering mound of Rosa's breasts; Rosa clung to the shawl as if it covered only herself. No one took it away from her. Magda was mute. She never cried. Rosa hid her in the barracks, under the shawl, but she knew that one day someone would inform; or one day someone, not even Stella, would steal Magda to eat her. When Magda began to walk Rosa knew that Magda was going to die very soon, something would happen. She was afraid to fall asleep; she slept with the weight of her thigh on Magda's body; she was afraid she would smother Magda under her thigh. The weight of Rosa was becoming less and less; Rosa and Stella were slowly turning into air.

Magda was quiet, but her eyes were horribly alive, like blue tigers. She watched. Sometimes she laughed—it seemed a laugh, but how could it be? Magda had never seen anyone laugh. Still, Magda laughed at her shawl when the wind blew its corners, the bad wind with pieces of black in it, that made Stella's and Rosa's eyes tear. Magda's eyes were always clear and tearless. She watched like a tiger. She guarded her shawl. No one could touch it; only Rosa could touch it. Stella was not allowed. The shawl was Magda's own baby, her pet, her little sister. She tangled herself up in it and sucked on one of the corners when she wanted to be very still.

Then Stella took the shawl away and made Magda die.

Afterward Stella said: "I was cold."

And afterward she was always cold, always. The cold went into her heart: Rosa saw that Stella's heart was cold. Magda flopped onward with her little pencil legs scribbling this way and that, in search of the shawl; the pencils faltered at the barracks opening, where the light began. Rosa saw and pursued. But already Magda was in the square outside the barracks, in the jolly light. It was the roll-call arena. Every morning Rosa had to conceal Magda under the shawl against a wall of the barracks and go out and stand in the arena with Stella and hundreds of others, sometimes for hours, and Magda, deserted, was quiet under the shawl, sucking on her corner. Every day Magda was silent, and so she did not die. Rosa saw that today Magda was going to die, and at the same time a fearful joy ran in Rosa's two palms, her fingers were on fire, she was astonished, febrile: Magda, in the sunlight, swaying on her pencil legs, was howling. Ever since the drying up of Rosa's nipples, ever since Magda's last scream on the road, Magda had been devoid of any syllable; Magda was a mute. Rosa believed that something had gone wrong with her vocal cords, with her windpipe, with the cave of her larynx; Magda was defective, without a voice; perhaps she was deaf; there might be something amiss with her intelligence; Magda was dumb. Even the laugh that came when the ash-stippled wind made a clown out of Magda's shawl was only the air-blown showing of her teeth. Even when the lice, head lice and body lice, crazed her so that she became as wild as one of the big rats that plundered the barracks at daybreak looking for carrion, she rubbed and scratched and kicked and bit and rolled without a whimper. But now Magda's mouth was spilling a long viscous rope of clamor.

"Maaaa—"

It was the first noise Magda had ever sent out from her throat since the drying up of Rosa's nipples.

"Maaaa . . . aaa!"

Again! Magda was wavering in the perilous sunlight of the arena, scribbling on such pitiful little bent shins. Rosa saw. She saw that Magda was grieving for the loss of her shawl, she saw that Magda was going to die. A tide of commands hammered in Rosa's nipples: Fetch, get, bring! But she did not know which to go after first, Magda or the shawl. If she jumped out into the arena to snatch Magda up, the howling would not stop, because Magda would still not have the shawl; but if she ran back into the barracks to find the shawl, and if she found it, and if she came after Magda holding it and shaking it, then she would get Magda back, Magda would put the shawl in her mouth and turn dumb again.

Rosa entered the dark. It was easy to discover the shawl. Stella was heaped under it, asleep in her thin bones. Rosa tore the shawl free and flew—she could fly, she was only air—into the arena. The sunheat murmured of another life, of butterflies in summer. The light was placid, mellow. On the other side of the steel fence, far away, there were green meadows speckled with dandelions and deep-colored violets; beyond them, even farther, innocent tiger lilies, tall, lifting their orange bonnets. In the barracks they spoke of "flowers," of "rain": excrement, thick turd-braids, and the slow stinking maroon waterfall that slunk down from the upper bunks, the stink mixed with a bitter fatty floating smoke that greased Rosa's skin. She stood for an instant at the margin of the arena. Sometimes the electricity inside the fence would seem to hum; even Stella said it was only an imagining, but Rosa heard real sounds in the wire; grainy sad voices. The farther she was from the fence, the more clearly the voices crowded at her. The lamenting voices strummed so convincingly, so passionately, it was impossible to suspect them of being phantoms. The voices told her to hold up the shawl, high; the voices told her to shake it, to whip with it, to unfurl it like a flag. Rosa lifted, shook, whipped, unfurled. Far off, very far, Magda leaned across her air-fed belly, reaching out with the rods of her arms. She was high up, elevated, riding someone's shoulder. But the shoulder that carried Magda was not coming toward Rosa and the shawl, it was drifting away, the speck of Magda was moving more and more into the smoky distance. Above the shoulder a helmet glinted. The light tapped the helmet and sparkled it into a goblet. Below the helmet a black body like a domino and a pair of black boots hurled themselves in the direction of the electrified fence. The electric voices began to chatter wildly. "Maamaa, maaa-maaa," they all hummed together. How far Magda was from Rosa now, across the whole square, past a dozen barracks, all the way on the other side! She was no bigger than a moth.

All at once Magda was swimming through the air. The whole of Magda traveled through loftiness. She looked like a butterfly touching a silver vine. And the moment Magda's feathered round head and her pencil legs and balloonish belly and zigzag arms splashed against the fence, the steel voices went mad in their growling, urging Rosa to run and run to the spot where Magda had fallen from her flight against the electrified fence; but of course Rosa did not obey them. She only stood, because if she ran they would shoot, and if she tried to pick up the sticks of Magda's body they would shoot, and if she let the wolf's screech ascending now through the ladder of her skeleton break out, they would shoot; so she took Magda's shawl and filled her own mouth with it, stuffed it in and stuffed it in, until she was swallowing up the wolf's screech and tasting the cinnamon and almond depth of Magda's saliva; and Rosa drank Magda's shawl until it dried.

1980

Joyce Carol Oates
(1938–   )

Joyce Carol Oates, one of America's most prolific authors, is a consummate artist. She has written well-crafted novels, stories, plays, poems, essays, and even a knowledgeable book about boxing. Born in rural upstate New York, she early began to write voluminously, producing a novel during each of the semesters in which she attended Syracuse University, majoring in English and philosophy. As a graduate student at the University of Wisconsin, she met Raymond Smith, whom she married in 1961. After several years teaching at the University of Detroit and the University of Windsor in southern Ontario, Canada, Oates now teaches at Princeton University, where she and Smith co-edit and publish the literary magazine *Ontario Review* and manage the Ontario Review Press.

"Gothic" is a word often used to describe Oates's fiction, and "Extenuating Circumstances" does not belie that description. Like the characters in such early works as *Expensive People* (1968) or *them* (1969) or more recent works such as *Black Water* (1992), the narrator of "Extenuating Circumstances" leads a life marked by extreme violence. The story is particularly interesting for its form. It is a tour de force written in a numbing stream-of-consciousness in which we are locked inside the psyche of the narrator whose self-justifications range from the banal to the self-deceived to the truly pitiable.

EXTENUATING CIRCUMSTANCES

Because it was a mercy. Because God even in His cruelty will sometimes grant mercy.

Because Venus was in the sign of Sagittarius.

Because you laughed at me, my faith in the stars. My hope.

Because he cried, you do not know how he cried.

Because at such times his little face was so twisted and hot, his nose running with mucus, his eyes so hurt.

Because in such he was his mother, and not you. Because I wanted to spare him such shame.

Because he remembered you, he knew the word *Daddy*.

Because watching TV he would point to a man and say *Daddy*—?

Because this summer has gone on so long, and no rain. The heat lightning flashing at night, without thunder.

Because in the silence, at night, the summer insects scream.

Because by day there are earth-moving machines and grinders operating hour upon hour razing the woods next to the playground. Because the red dust got into our eyes, our mouths.

Because he would whimper *Mommy?*—in that way that tore my heart.

Because last Monday the washing machine broke down, I heard a loud thumping that scared me, the dirty soapy water would not drain out. Because in the light of the bulb overhead he saw me holding the wet sheets in my hand crying *What can I do? What can I do?*

Because the sleeping pills they give me now are made of flour and chalk, I am certain.

Because I loved you more than you loved me even from the first when your eyes moved on me like candle flame.

Because I did not know this yet, yes I knew it but cast it from my mind.

Because there was shame in it. Loving you knowing you would not love me enough.

Because my job applications are laughed at for misspellings and torn to pieces as soon as I leave.

Because they will not believe me when listing my skills. Because since he was born my body is misshapen, the pain is always there.

Because I see that it was not his fault and even in that I could not spare him.

Because even at the time when he was conceived (in those early days we were so happy! so happy I am certain lying together on top of the bed the corduroy bedspread in that narrow jiggly bed hearing the rain on the roof that slanted down so you had to stoop being so tall and from outside on the street the roof with its dark shingles looking always wet was like a lowered brow over the windows on the third floor and the windows like squinting eyes and we would come home together from the University meeting at the Hardee's corner you from the geology lab or the library and me from Accounting where my eyes ached because of the lights with their dim flicker no one else could see and I was so happy your arm around my waist and mine around yours like any couple, like any college girl with her boyfriend, and walking *home*, yes it was *home*, I thought always it was *home*, we would look up at the windows of the apartment laughing saying who do you think lives there? what are their names? who are they? that cozy secret-looking room under the eaves where the roof came down, came down dripping black runny water I hear now drumming on this roof but only if I fall asleep during the day with my clothes on so tired so exhausted and when I wake up there is no rain, only the earth-moving machines and grinders in the woods so I must acknowledge *It is another time, it is time*) yes I knew.

Because you did not want him to be born.

Because he cried so I could hear him through the shut door, through all the doors.

Because I did not want him to be *Mommy*, I wanted him to be *Daddy* in his strength.

Because this washcloth in my hand was in my hand when I saw how it must be.

Because the checks come to me from the lawyer's office not from you. Because in tearing open the envelopes my fingers shaking and my eyes showing such hope I revealed myself naked to myself so many times.

Because to this shame he was a witness, he saw.

Because he was too young at two years to know. Because even so he knew.

Because his birthday was a sign, falling in the midst of Pisces.

Because in certain things he *was* his father, that knowledge in eyes that went beyond me in mockery of me.

Because one day he would laugh too as you have done.

Because there is no listing for your telephone and the operators will not tell me. Because in any of the places I know to find you, you cannot be found.

Because your sister has lied to my face, to mislead me. Because she who was once my friend, I believed, was never my friend.

Because I feared loving him too much, and in that weakness failing to protect him from hurt.

Because his crying tore my heart but angered me too so I feared laying hands upon him wild and unplanned.

Because he flinched seeing me. That nerve jumping in his eye.

Because he was always hurting himself, he was so clumsy falling off the swing hitting his head against the metal post so one of the other mothers saw and cried out *Oh! Oh look your son is bleeding!* and that time in the kitchen whining and pulling at me in a bad temper reaching up to grab the pot handle and almost overturning the boiling water in his face so I lost control slapping him shaking him by the arm *Bad! Bad! Bad! Bad!* my voice rising in fury not caring who heard.

Because that day in the courtroom you refused to look at me your face shut like a fist against me and your lawyer too, like I was dirt beneath your shoes. Like maybe he was not even your son but you would sign the papers as if he was, you are so superior.

Because the courtroom was not like any courtroom I had a right to expect, not a big dignified courtroom like on TV just a room with a judge's desk and three rows of six seats each and not a single window and even here that flickering light that yellowish-sickish fluorescent tubing making my eyes ache so I wore my dark glasses giving the judge a false impression of me, and I was sniffing, wiping my nose, every question they asked me I'd hear myself giggle so nervous and ashamed even stammering over my age and my name so you looked with scorn at me, all of you.

Because they were on your side, I could not prevent it.

Because in granting me child support payments, you had a right to move away. Because I could not follow.

Because he wet his pants, where he should not have, for his age.

Because it would be blamed on me. It *was* blamed on me.

Because my own mother screamed at me over the phone. She could not help me with my life she said, no one can help you with your life, we were screaming such things to each other as left us breathless and crying and I slammed down the receiver knowing that I had no mother and after the first grief I knew *It is better, so.*

Because he would learn that someday, and the knowledge of it would hurt him.

Because he had my hair coloring, and my eyes. That left eye, the weakness in it.

Because that time it almost happened, the boiling water overturned onto him, I saw how easy it would be. How, if he could be prevented from screaming, the neighbors would not know.

Because yes they would know, but only when I wanted them to know.

Because you would know then. Only when I wanted you to know.

Because then I could speak to you in this way, maybe in a letter which your lawyer would forward to you, or your sister, maybe over the telephone or even face to face. Because then you could not escape.

Because though you did not love him you could not escape him.

Because I have begun to bleed for six days quite heavily, and will then spot for another three or four. Because soaking the blood in wads of toilet paper sitting on the toilet my hands shaking I think of you who never bleed.

Because I am a proud woman, I scorn your charity.

Because I am not a worthy mother. Because I am so tired.

Because the machines digging in the earth and grinding trees are a torment by day, and the screaming insects by night.

Because there is no sleep.

Because he would only sleep, these past few months, if he could be with me in my bed.

Because he whimpered *Mommy!—Mommy don't!*

Because he flinched from me when there was no cause.

Because the pharmacist took the prescription and was gone such a long time, I knew he was telephoning someone.

Because at the drugstore where I have shopped for a year and a half they pretended not to know my name.

Because in the grocery store the cashiers stared smiling at me and at him pulling at my arm spilling tears down his face.

Because they whispered and laughed behind me, I have too much pride to respond.

Because he was with me at such times, he was a witness to such.

Because he had no one but his Mommy and his Mommy had no one but him. Which is so lonely.

Because I had gained seven pounds from last Sunday to this, the waist of my slacks is so tight. Because I hate the fat of my body.

Because looking at me naked now you would show disgust.

Because I *was* beautiful for you, why wasn't that enough?

Because that day the sky was dense with clouds the color of raw liver but yet there was no rain. Heat lightning flashing with no sound making me so nervous but no rain.

Because his left eye was weak, it would always be so unless he had an operation to strengthen the muscle.

Because I did not want to cause him pain and terror in his sleep.

Because you would pay for it, the check from the lawyer with no note.

Because you hated him, your son.

Because he was *our* son, you hated him.

Because you moved away. To the far side of the country I have reason to believe.

Because in my arms after crying he would lie so still, only one heart beating between us.

Because I knew I could not spare him from hurt.

Because the playground hurt our ears, raised red dust to get into our eyes and mouths.

Because I was so tired of scrubbing him clean, between his toes and beneath his nails, the insides of his ears, his neck, the many secret places of filth.

Because I felt the ache of cramps again in my belly, I was in a panic my period had begun so soon.

Because I could not spare him the older children laughing.

Because after the first terrible pain he would be beyond pain.

Because in this there is mercy.

Because God's mercy is for him, and not for me.

Because there was no one here to stop me.

Because my neighbors' TV was on so loud, I knew they could not hear even if he screamed through the washcloth.

Because you were not here to stop me, were you.

Because finally there is no one to stop us.

Because finally there is no one to save us.

152

Because my own mother betrayed me.

Because the rent would be due again on Tuesday which is the first of September. And by then I will be gone.

Because his body was not heavy to carry and to wrap in the down comforter, you remember that comforter, I know.

Because the washcloth soaked in his saliva will dry on the line and show no sign.

Because to heal there must be forgetfulness and oblivion.

Because he cried when he should not have cried but did not cry when he should.

Because the water came slowly to boil in the big pan, vibrating and humming on the front burner.

Because the kitchen was damp with steam from the windows shut so tight, the temperature must have been 100° F.

Because he did not struggle. And when he did, it was too late.

Because I wore rubber gloves to spare myself being scalded.

Because I knew I must not panic, and did not.

Because I loved him. Because love hurts so bad.

Because I wanted to tell you these things. Just like this.

1992

Helena María Viramontes

(1954–   )

Helena María Viramontes has impressed readers for the past decade with her tough yet poignant stories of urban barrios and of the borderland, the lives of Chicanas and their children in particular. Best known for such relentlessly powerful stories as "The Cariboo Cafe," "Neighbors," "The Broken Web," and "The Moths," she also writes a more palatable realistic fiction that shows the characters' abilities to cope with their often frustrating lives. In "Miss Clairol," Viramontes places her protagonist, Arlene, with her adolescent child, Champ, in the cosmetics aisle of a K-Mart, as Arlene gets ready for yet another of the dates (and the changes in hair color) that mark the stages in her life. As Champ watches the inevitable preparations, she senses that her own life will follow in some of the same patterns.

The daughter of working class parents in East Los Angeles, Viramontes was one of nine children in a household always open to new arrivals from Mexico. In her crowded yet supportive home, she saw the situations that comprised her earliest fiction—that written while she did her B.A. in English at Immaculate Heart College, and began taking courses in the creative writing program at University of California, Irvine. In 1985 her story collection, *The Moths and Other Stories*, appeared to good reviews. She also coedited *Chicana Creativity and Criticism: Charting New Frontiers in American Literature*, and is active in helping other women to find voice. One of the most interesting women writing today, Viramontes does not abandon her truly feminist focus in her eloquent speaking for the Hispanic culture that is so often her subject. She insists that women's lives, and women's development from girlhood to adulthood, are valuable topics for fiction.

❖

MISS CLAIROL

Arlene and Champ walk to K-Mart. The store is full of bins mounted with bargain buys from T-shirts to rubber sandals. They go to aisle 23, Cosmetics. Arlene, wearing bell bottom jeans two sizes too small, can't bend down to the Miss Clairol boxes, asks Champ.

–Which one mamá–says Champ, chewing her thumb nail.

–Shit, mija, I dunno.–Arlene smacks her gum, contemplating the decision.–Maybe I need a change, tú sabes. What do you think?–She holds up a few blond strands with black roots. Arlene has burned the softness of her hair with peroxide; her hair is stiff, breaks at the ends and she needs plenty of

Aqua Net hairspray to tease and tame her ratted hair, then folds it back into a high lump behind her head. For the last few months she has been a platinum "Light Ash" blond, before that a Miss Clairol "Flame" redhead, before that Champ couldn't even identify the color—somewhere between orange and brown, a "Sun Bronze." The only way Champ knows her mother's true hair color is by her roots which, like death, inevitably rise to the truth.

–I hate it, tú sabes, when I can't decide.–Arlene is wearing a pink, strapless tube top. Her stomach spills over the hip hugger jeans. Spits the gum onto the floor.–Fuck it.–And Champ follows her to the rows of nailpolish, next to the Maybelline rack of make-up, across the false eyelashes that look like insects on display in clear, plastic boxes. Arlene pulls out a particular color of nailpolish, looks at the bottom of the bottle for the price, puts it back, gets another. She has a tattoo of purple XXX's on her left finger like a ring. She finally settles for a purple-blackish color, Ripe Plum, that Champ thinks looks like the color of Frankenstein's nails. She looks at her own stubby nails, chewed and gnawed.

Walking over to the eyeshadows, Arlene slowly slinks out another stick of gum from her back pocket, unwraps and crumbles the wrapper into a little ball, lets it fall to her feet. Smacks the gum.

–Grandpa Ham used to make chains with these gum wrappers–she says, toeing the wrapper on the floor with her rubber sandals, her toes dotted with old nailpolish.–He started one, tú sabes, that went from room to room. That was before he went nuts–she says, looking at the price of magenta eyeshadow.– Sabes que? What do you think?–lifting the eyeshadow to Champ.

–I dunno–responds Champ, shrugging her shoulders the way she always does when she is listening to something else, her own heartbeat, what Gregorio said on the phone yesterday, shrugs her shoulders when Miss Smith says OFELIA, answer my question. She is too busy thinking of things people otherwise dismiss like parentheses, but sticks to her like gum, like a hole on a shirt, like a tattoo, and sometimes she wishes she weren't born with such adhesiveness. The chain went from room to room, round and round like a web, she remembers. That was before he went nuts.

–Champ. You listening? Or in lala land again?–Arlene has her arms akimbo on a fold of flesh, pissed.

–I said, I dunno.–Champ whines back, still looking at the wrapper on the floor.

–Well you better learn, tú sabes, and fast too. Now think, will this color go good with Pancha's blue dress?–Pancha is Arlene's comadre. Since Arlene has a special date tonight, she lent Arlene her royal blue dress that she keeps in a plastic bag at the end of her closet. The dress is made of chiffon, with satin-like material underlining, so that when Arlene first tried it on and strut-

155

ted about, it crinkled sounds of elegance. The dress fits too tight. Her plump arms squeeze through, her hips breathe in and hold their breath, the seams do all they can to keep the body contained. But Arlene doesn't care as long as it sounds right.

–I think it will–Champ says, and Arlene is very pleased.

–Think so? So do I mija.–

They walk out the double doors and Champ never remembers her mother paying.

It is four in the afternoon, but already Arlene is preparing for the date. She scrubs the tub, Art Labo on the radio, drops crystals of Jean Nate into the running water, lemon scent rises with the steam. The bathroom door ajar, she removes her top and her breasts flop and sag, pushes her jeans down with some difficulty, kicks them off, and steps in the tub.

–Mija. MIJA–she yells.–Mija, give me a few bobby pins.–She is worried about her hair frizzing and so wants to pin it up.

Her mother's voice is faint because Champ is in the closet. There are piles of clothes on the floor, hangers thrown askew and tangled, shoes all piled up or thrown on the top shelf. Champ is looking for her mother's special dress. Pancha says every girl has one at the end of her closet.

–Goddamn it Champ.–

Amidst the dirty laundry, the black hole of the closet, she finds nothing.

–NOW–

–Alright, ALRIGHT. Cheeze amá, stop yelling–says Champ, and goes in the steamy bathroom, checks the drawers. Hairbrushes jump out, rollers, strands of hair. Rummages through bars of soap, combs, eyeshadows, finds nothing; pulls open another drawer, powder, empty bottles of oil, manicure scissors, kotex, dye instructions crinkled and botched, finally, a few bobby pins.

After Arlene pins up her hair, she asks Champ,–Sabes que? Should I wear my hair up? Do I look good with it up?–Champ is sitting on the toilet.

–Yea, amá, you look real pretty.–

–Thanks mija–says Arlene.–Sabes que? When you get older I'll show you how you can look just as pretty–and she puts her head back, relaxes, like the Calgon commercials.

Champ lays on her stomach, T.V. on to some variety show with pogo stick dancers dressed in outfits of stretchy material and glitter. She is wearing one of Gregorio's white T-shirts, the ones he washes and bleaches himself so that the whiteness is impeccable. It drapes over her deflated ten year old body like a dress. She is busy cutting out Miss Breck models from the stacks of old magazines Pancha found in the back of her mother's garage. Champ collects the array of honey colored haired women, puts them in a shoe box with all her other special things.

Arlene is in the bathroom, wrapped in a towel. She has painted her eyebrows so that the two are arched and even, penciled thin and high. The magenta shades her eyelids. The towel slips, reveals one nipple blind from a cigarette burn, a date to forget. She rewraps the towel, likes her reflection, turns to her profile for additional inspection. She feels good, turns up the radio to . . . your love. For your loveeeee, I will do anything, I will do anything, forrr your love. For your kiss . . .

Champ looks on. From the open bathroom door, she can see Arlene, anticipation burning like a cigarette from her lips, sliding her shoulders to the ahhhh ahhhhh, and pouting her lips until the song ends. And Champ likes her mother that way.

Arlene carefully stretches black eyeliner, like a fallen question mark, outlines each eye. The work is delicate, her hand trembles cautiously, stops the process to review the face with each line. Arlene the mirror is not Arlene the face who has worn too many relationships, gotten too little sleep. The last touch is the chalky, beige lipstick.

By the time she is finished, her ashtray is full of cigarette butts, Champ's variety show is over, and Jackie Gleason's dancing girls come on to make kaleidoscope patterns with their long legs and arms. Gregorio is still not home, and Champ goes over to the window, checks the houses, the streets, corners, roams the sky with her eyes.

Arlene sits on the toilet, stretches up her nylons, clips them to her girdle. She feels good thinking about the way he will unsnap her nylons, and she will unroll them slowly, point her toes when she does.

Champ opens a can of Campbell soup, finds a perfect pot in the middle of a stack of dishes, pulls it out to the threatening rumble of the tower. She washes it out, pours the contents of the red can, turns the knob. After it boils, she puts the pot on the sink for it to cool down. She searches for a spoon.

Arlene is romantic. When Champ begins her period, she will tell her things that only women can know. She will tell her about the first time she made love with a boy, her awkwardness and shyness forcing them to go under the house, where the cool, refined soil made a soft mattress. How she closed her eyes and wondered what to expect, or how the penis was the softest skin she had ever felt against her, how it tickled her, searched for a place to connect. She was eleven and his name was Harry.

She will not not tell Champ that her first fuck was a guy named Puppet who ejaculated prematurely, at the sight of her apricot vagina, so plump and fuzzy.–Pendejo–she said–you got it all over me.–She rubbed the gooey substance off her legs, her belly in disgust. Ran home to tell Rat and Pancha, her mouth open with laughter.

Arlene powder puffs under her arms, between her breasts, tilts a bottle of *Love Cries* perfume and dabs behind her ears, neck and breasts for those tight caressing songs which permit them to grind their bodies together until she can feel a bulge in his pants and she knows she's in for the night.

Jackie Gleason is a bartender in a saloon. He wears a black bow tie, a white apron, and is polishing a glass. Champ is watching him, sitting in the radius of the gray light, eating her soup from the pot.

Arlene is a romantic. She will dance until Pancha's dress turns a different color, dance until her hair becomes undone, her hips jiggering and quaking beneath a new pair of hosiery, her mascara shadowing under her eyes from the perspiration of the ritual, dance spinning herself into Miss Clairol, and stopping only when it is time to return to the sewing factory, time to wait out the next date, time to change hair color. Time to remember or to forget.

Champ sees Arlene from the window. She can almost hear Arlene's nylons rubbing against one another, hear the crinkling sound of satin when she gets in the blue and white shark-finned Dodge. Champ yells goodbye. It all sounds so right to Arlene who is too busy cranking up the window to hear her daughter.

1988

Toni Morrison
(1931–   )

Toni Morrison, winner of the 1993 Nobel Prize for Literature, is widely regarded as one of America's greatest novelists. From her first novel, *The Bluest Eye* (1970), which tells the heart-wrenching story of a young Black girl who believes she would be lovable if only she had blue eyes, to *Beloved* (1987), a historically based story of a mother who would kill her children rather than return them to slavery, Morrison has dealt brilliantly and powerfully with the psychological, sociological, and spiritual deformations of racism in America. One of America's most lyrical prose stylists, Morrison is an intellectual who, in her nonfiction work *Playing in the Dark: Whiteness and the Literary Imagination* (1992) cogently analyzes the consequences of racism in American life and letters.

Born in a racially mixed, working-class neighborhood in Lorain, Ohio, she went on to earn a bachelor's and a master's degree from Howard University and Cornell University, respectively. She had two sons during her marriage to Jamaican architect Harold Morrison. As an editor at Random House, she worked to publish a number of African-American writers even as she continued to write her own fiction. She is currently a chaired professor at Princeton University.

"Recitatif," one of Morrison's few short stories, describes the changing dynamics in a long-term relationship between a white woman and an African-American woman without overtly telling the race of either character. Readers piece together racial identities from clues that force us to ask questions about the usual ways in which race is represented in literature.

RECITATIF

My mother danced all night and Roberta's was sick. That's why we were taken to St. Bonny's. People want to put their arms around you when you tell them you were in a shelter, but it really wasn't bad. No big long room with one hundred beds like Bellevue. There were four to a room, and when Roberta and me came, there was a shortage of state kids, so we were the only ones assigned to 406 and could go from bed to bed if we wanted to. And we wanted to, too. We changed beds every night and for the whole four months we were there we never picked one out as our own permanent bed.

It didn't start out that way. The minute I walked in and the Big Bozo introduced us, I got sick to my stomach. It was one thing to be taken out of your own bed early in the morning—it was something else to be stuck in a strange place with a girl from a whole other race. And Mary, that's my mother, she was right. Every now and then she would stop dancing long enough to tell me something important and one of the things she said was that they never washed their hair and they smelled funny. Roberta sure did. Smell funny, I mean. So when the Big Bozo (nobody ever called her Mrs. Itkin, just like nobody every said St. Bonaventure)—when she said, "Twyla, this is Roberta. Roberta, this is Twyla. Make each other welcome." I said, "My mother won't like you putting me in here."

"Good," said Bozo. "Maybe then she'll come and take you home."

How's that for mean? If Roberta had laughed I would have killed her, but she didn't. She just walked over to the window and stood with her back to us.

"Turn around," said the Bozo. "Don't be rude. Now Twyla. Roberta. When you hear a loud buzzer, that's the call for dinner. Come down to the first floor. Any fights and no movie." And then, just to make sure we knew what we would be missing, "*The Wizard of Oz.*"

Roberta must have thought I meant that my mother would be mad about my being put in the shelter. Not about rooming with her, because as soon as Bozo left she came over to me and said, "Is your mother sick too?"

"No," I said. "She just likes to dance all night."

"Oh," she nodded her head and I liked the way she understood things so fast. So for the moment it didn't matter that we looked like salt and pepper standing there and that's what the other kids called us sometimes. We were eight years old and got F's all the time. Me because I couldn't remember what I read or what the teacher said. And Roberta because she couldn't read at all and didn't even listen to the teacher. She wasn't good at anything except jacks, at which she was a killer: pow scoop pow scoop pow scoop.

We didn't like each other all that much at first, but nobody else wanted to play with us because we weren't real orphans with beautiful dead parents in the sky. We were dumped. Even the New York City Puerto Ricans and the upstate Indians ignored us. All kinds of kids were in there, black ones, white ones, even two Koreans. The food was good, though. At least I thought so. Roberta hated it and left whole pieces of things on her plate: Spam, Salisbury steak—even jello with fruit cocktail in it, and she didn't care if I ate what she wouldn't. Mary's idea of supper was popcorn and a can of Yoo-Hoo. Hot mashed potatoes and two weenies was like Thanksgiving for me.

It really wasn't bad, St. Bonny's. The big girls on the second floor pushed us around now and then. But that was all. They wore lipstick and eyebrow pencil and wobbled their knees while they watched TV. Fifteen, sixteen, even, some of them were. They were put-out girls, scared runaways most of them.

Poor little girls who fought their uncles off but looked tough to us, and mean. God did they look mean. The staff tired to keep them separate from the younger children, but sometimes they caught us watching them in the orchard where they played radios and danced with each other. They'd light out after us and pull our hair or twist our arms. We were scared of them, Roberta and me, but neither of us wanted the other one to know it. So we got a good list of dirty names we could shout back when we ran from them through the orchard. I used to dream a lot and almost always the orchard was there. Two acres, four maybe, of these little apple trees. Hundreds of them. Empty and crooked like beggar women when I first came to St. Bonny's but fat with flowers when I left. I don't know why I dreamt about that orchard so much. Nothing really happened there. Nothing all that important, I mean. Just the big girls dancing and playing the radio. Roberta and me watching. Maggie fell down there once. The kitchen woman with legs like parentheses. And the big girls laughed at her. We should have helped her up, I know, but we were scared of those girls with lipstick and eyebrow pencil. Maggie couldn't talk. The kids said she had her tongue cut out, but I think she was just born that way: mute. She was old and sandy-colored and she worked in the kitchen. I don't know if she was nice or not. I just remember her legs like parentheses and how she rocked when she walked. She worked from early in the morning till two o'clock, and if she was late, if she had too much cleaning and didn't get out till two-fifteen or so, she'd cut through the orchard so she wouldn't miss her bus and have to wait another hour. She wore this really stupid little hat—a kid's hat with ear flaps—and she wasn't much taller than we were. A really awful little hat. Even for a mute, it was dumb—dressing like a kid and never saying anything at all.

"But what about if somebody tries to kill her?" I used to wonder about that. "Or what if she wants to cry? Can she cry?"

"Sure," Roberta said. "But just tears. No sounds come out."

"She can't scream?"

"Nope. Nothing."

"Can she hear?"

"I guess."

"Let's call her," I said. And we did.

"Dummy! Dummy!" She never turned her head.

"Bow legs! Bow legs!" Nothing. She just rocked on, the chin straps of her baby-boy hat swaying from side to side. I think we were wrong. I think she could hear and didn't let on. And it shames me even now to think there was somebody in there after all who heard us call her those names and couldn't tell on us.

We got along all right, Roberta and me. Changed beds every night, got

F's in civics and communication skills and gym. The Bozo was disappointed in us, she said. Out of 130 of us state cases, 90 were under twelve. Almost all were real orphans with beautiful dead parents in the sky. We were the only ones dumped and the only ones with F's in three classes including gym. So we got along—what with her leaving whole pieces of things on her plate and being nice about not asking questions.

I think it was the day before Maggie fell down that we found out our mothers were coming to visit us on the same Sunday. We had been at the shelter twenty-eight days (Roberta twenty-eight and a half) and this was their first visit with us. Our mothers would come at ten o'clock in time for chapel, then lunch with us in the teacher's lounge. I thought if my dancing mother met her sick mother it might be good for her. And Roberta thought her sick mother would get a big bang out of a dancing one. We got excited about it and curled each other's hair. After breakfast we sat on the bed watching the road from the window. Roberta's socks were still wet. She washed them the night before and put them on the radiator to dry. They hadn't, but she put them on anyway because their tops were so pretty—scalloped in pink. Each of us had a purple construction-paper basket that we had made in craft class. Mine had a yellow crayon rabbit on it. Roberta's had eggs with wiggly lines of color. Inside were cellophane grass and just the jelly beans because I'd eaten the two marshmallow eggs they gave us. The Big Bozo came herself to get us. Smiling she told us we looked very nice and to come downstairs. We were so surprised by the smile we'd never seen before, neither of us moved.

"Don't you want to see your mommies?"

I stood up first and spilled the jelly beans all over the floor. Bozo's smile disappeared while we scrambled to get the candy up off the floor and put it back in the grass.

She escorted us downstairs to the first floor, where the other girls were lining up to file into the chapel. A bunch of grown-ups stood to one side. Viewers mostly. The old biddies who wanted servants and the fags who wanted company looking for children they might want to adopt. Once in a while a grandmother. Almost never anybody young or anybody whose face wouldn't scare you in the night. Because if any of the real orphans had young relatives they wouldn't be real orphans. I saw Mary right away. She had on those green slacks I hated and hated even more now because didn't she know we were going to chapel? And that fur jacket with the pocket linings so ripped she had to pull to get her hands out of them. But her face was pretty—like always, and she smiled and waved like she was the little girl looking for her mother—not me.

I walked slowly, trying not to drop the jelly beans and hoping the paper handle would hold. I had to use my last Chiclet because by the time I finished cutting everything out, all the Elmer's was gone. I am left-handed and the scissors never worked for me. It didn't matter, though; I might just as well have chewed the gum. Mary dropped to her knees and grabbed me, mashing the basket, the jelly beans, and the grass into her ratty fur jacket.

"Twyla, baby. Twyla, baby!"

I could have killed her. Already I heard the big girls in the orchard the next time saying, "Twyyyyyla, baby!" But I couldn't stay mad at Mary while she was smiling and hugging me and smelling of Lady Esther dusting powder. I wanted to stay buried in her fur all day.

To tell the truth I forgot about Roberta. Mary and I got in line for the traipse into chapel and I was feeling proud because she looked so beautiful even in those ugly green slacks that made her behind stick out. A pretty mother on earth is better than a beautiful dead one in the sky even if she did leave you all alone to go dancing.

I felt a tap on my shoulder, turned, and saw Roberta smiling. I smiled back, but not too much lest somebody think this visit was the biggest thing that ever happened in my life. Then Roberta said, "Mother, I want you to meet my roommate, Twyla. And that's Twyla's mother."

I looked up it seemed for miles. She was big. Bigger than any man and on her chest was the biggest cross I'd ever seen. I swear it was six inches long each way. And in the crook of her arm was the biggest Bible ever made.

Mary, simple-minded as ever, grinned and tried to yank her hand out of the pocket with the raggedy lining—to shake hands, I guess. Roberta's mother looked down at me and then looked down at Mary too. She didn't say anything, just grabbed Roberta with her Bible-free hand and stepped out of line, walking quickly to the rear of it. Mary was still grinning because she's not too swift when it comes to what's really going on. Then this light bulb goes off in her head and she says "That bitch!" really loud and us almost in the chapel now. Organ music whining; the Bonny Angels singing sweetly. Everybody in the world turned around to look. And Mary would have kept it up—kept calling names if I hadn't squeezed her hand as hard as I could. That helped a little, but she still twitched and crossed and uncrossed her legs all through service. Even groaned a couple of times. Why did I think she would come there and act right? Slacks. No hat like the grandmother and viewers, and groaning all the while. When we stood for hymns she kept her mouth shut. Wouldn't even look at the words on the page. She actually reached in her purse for a mirror to check her lipstick. All I could think of was that she really needed to be killed. The sermon lasted a year, and I knew the real orphans were looking smug again.

We were supposed to have lunch in the teachers' lounge, but Mary didn't bring anything, so we picked fur and cellophane grass off the mashed jelly beans and ate them. I could have killed her. I sneaked a look at Roberta. Her

WOMEN'S WRITING IN THE UNITED STATES

mother had brought chicken legs and ham sandwiches and oranges and a whole box of chocolate-covered grahams. Roberta drank milk from a thermos while her mother read the Bible to her.

Things are not right. The wrong food is always with the wrong people. Maybe that's why I got into waitress work later—to match up the right people with the right food. Roberta just let those chicken legs sit there, but she did bring a stack of grahams up to me later when the visit was over. I think she was sorry that her mother would not shake my mother's hand. And I liked that and I liked the fact that she didn't say a word about Mary groaning all the way through the service and not bringing any lunch.

Roberta left in May when the apple trees were heavy and white. On her last day we went to the orchard to watch the big girls smoke and dance by the radio. It didn't matter that they said, "Twyyyyyla, baby." We sat on the ground and breathed. Lady Esther. Apple blossoms. I still go soft when I smell one or the other. Roberta was going home. The big cross and the big Bible was coming to get her and she seemed sort of glad and sort of not. I thought I would die in that room of four beds without her and I knew Bozo had plans to move some other dumped kid in there with me. Roberta promised to write every day, which was really sweet of her because she couldn't read a lick so how could she write anybody. I would have drawn pictures and sent them to her but she never gave me her address. Little by little she faded. Her wet socks with the pink scalloped tops and her big serious-looking eyes— that's all I could catch when I tried to bring her to mind.

I was working behind the counter at the Howard Johnson's on the Thruway just before the Kingston exit. Not a bad job. Kind of a long ride from Newburgh, but okay once I got there. Mine was the second night shift—eleven to seven. Very light until a Greyhound checked in for breakfast around six-thirty. At that hour the sun was all the way clear of the hills behind the restaurant. The place looked better at night—more like shelter—but I loved it when the sun broke in, even if it did show all the cracks in the vinyl and the speckled floor looked dirty no matter what the mop boy did.

It was August and a bus crowd was just unloading. They would stand around a long while: going to the john, and looking at gifts and junk-for-sale machines, reluctant to sit down so soon. Even to eat. I was trying to fill the coffee pots and get them all situated on the electric burners when I saw her. She was sitting in a booth smoking a cigarette with two guys smothered in head and facial hair. Her own hair was so big and wild I could hardly see her face. But the eyes. I would know them anywhere. She had on a powder-blue halter and shorts outfit and earrings the size of bracelets. Talk about lipstick and eyebrow pencil. She made the big girls look like nuns. I couldn't get off

164

the counter until seven o'clock, but I kept watching the booth in case they got up to leave before that. My replacement was on time for a change, so I counted and stacked my receipts as fast as I could and signed off. I walked over to the booth, smiling and wondering if she would remember me. Or even if she wanted to remember me. Maybe she didn't want to be reminded of St. Bonny's or to have anybody know she was ever there. I know I never talked about it to anybody.

I put my hands in my apron pockets and leaned against the back of the booth facing them.

"Roberta? Roberta Fisk?"

She looked up. "Yeah?"

"Twyla."

She squinted for a second and then said, "Wow."

"Remember me?"

"Sure. Hey. Wow."

"It's been a while," I said, and gave a smile to the two hairy guys.

"Yeah. Wow. You work here?"

"Yeah," I said. "I live in Newburgh."

"Newburgh? No kidding?" She laughed then a private laugh that included the guys but only the guys, and they laughed with her. What could I do but laugh too and wonder why I was standing there with my knees showing out from under that uniform. Without looking I could see the blue and white triangle on my head, my hair shapeless in a net, my ankles thick in white oxfords. Nothing could have been less sheer than my stockings. There was this silence that came down right after I laughed. A silence it was her turn to fill up. With introductions, maybe, to her boyfriends or an invitation to sit down and have a Coke. Instead she lit a cigarette off the one she'd just finished and said, "We're on our way to the Coast. He's got an appointment with Hendrix." She gestured casually toward the boy next to her.

"Hendrix? Fantastic," I said. "Really fantastic. What's she doing now?"

Roberta coughed on her cigarette and the two guys rolled their eyes up at the ceiling.

"Hendrix. Jimi Hendrix, asshole. He's only the biggest—Oh, wow. Forget it."

I was dismissed without anyone saying goodbye, so I thought I would do it for her.

"How's your mother?" I asked. Her grin cracked her whole face. She swallowed. "Fine," she said. "How's yours?"

"Pretty as a picture," I said and turned away. The backs of my knees were damp. Howard Johnson's really was a dump in the sunlight.

* * *

James is as comfortable as a house slipper. He liked my cooking and I liked his big loud family. They have lived in Newburgh all of their lives and talk about it the way people do who have always known a home. His grandmother is a porch swing older than his father and when they talk about streets and avenues and buildings they call them names they no longer have. They still call the A & P Rico's because it stands on property once a mom and pop store owned by Mr. Rico. And they call the new community college Town Hall because it once was. My mother-in-law puts up jelly and cucumbers and buys butter wrapped in cloth from a dairy. James and his father talk about fishing and baseball and I can see them all together on the Hudson in a raggedy skiff. Half the population of Newburgh is on welfare now, but to my husband's family it was still some upstate paradise of a time long past. A time of ice houses and vegetable wagons, coal furnaces and children weeding gardens. When our son was born my mother-in-law gave me the crib blanket that had been hers.

But the town they remembered had changed. Something quick was in the air. Magnificent old houses, so ruined they had become shelter for squatters and rent risks, were bought and renovated. Smart IBM people moved out of their suburbs back into the city and put shutters up and herb gardens in their backyards. A brochure came in the mail announcing the opening of a Food Emporium. Gourmet food it said—and listed items the rich IBM crowd would want. It was located in a new mall at the edge of town and I drove out to shop there one day—just to see. It was late in June. After the tulips were gone and the Queen Elizabeth roses were open everywhere. I trailed my cart along the aisle tossing in smoked oysters and Robert's sauce and things I knew would sit in my cupboard for years. Only when I found some Klondike ice cream bars did I feel less guilty about spending James's fireman's salary so foolishly. My father-in-law ate them with the same gusto little Joseph did.

Waiting in the check-out line I heard a voice say, "Twyla!"

The classical music piped over the aisles had affected me and the woman leaning toward me was dressed to kill. Diamonds on her hand, a smart white summer dress. "I'm Mrs. Benson," I said.

"Ho. Ho. The Big Bozo," she sang.

For a split second I didn't know what she was talking about. She had a bunch of asparagus and two cartons of fancy water.

"Roberta!"

"Right."

"For heaven's sake. Roberta."

"You look great," she said.

"So do you. Where are you? Here? In Newburgh?"

"Yes. Over in Annandale."

I was opening my mouth to say more when the cashier called my attention to her empty counter.

"Meet you outside." Roberta pointed her finger and went into the express line.

I placed the groceries and kept myself from glancing around to check Roberta's progress. I remembered Howard Johnson's and looking for a chance to speak only to be greeted with a stingy "wow." But she was waiting for me and her huge hair was sleek now, smooth around a small, nicely shaped head. Shoes, dress, everything lovely and summery and rich. I was dying to know what happened to her, how she got from Jimi Hendrix to Annandale, a neighborhood full of doctors and IBM executives. Easy, I thought. Everything is so easy for them. They think they own the world.

"How long," I asked her. "How long have you been here?"

"A year. I got married to a man who lives here. And you, you're married too, right? Benson, you said."

"Yeah. James Benson."

"And is he nice?"

"Oh, is he nice?"

"Well, is he?" Roberta's eyes were steady as though she really meant the question and wanted an answer.

"He's wonderful, Roberta. Wonderful."

"So you're happy."

"Very."

"That's good," she said and nodded her head. "I always hoped you'd be happy. Any kids? I know you have kids."

"One. A boy. How about you?"

"Four."

"Four?"

She laughed. "Step kids. He's a widower."

"Oh."

"Got a minute? Let's have a coffee."

I thought about the Klondikes melting and the inconvenience of going all the way to my car and putting the bags in the trunk. Served me right for buying all that stuff I didn't need. Roberta was ahead of me.

"Put them in my car. It's right here."

And then I saw the dark blue limousine.

"You married a Chinaman?"

"No," she laughed. "He's the driver."

"Oh, my. If the Big Bozo could see you now."

We both giggled. Really giggled. Suddenly, in just a pulse beat, twenty years disappeared and all of it came rushing back. The big girls (whom we

167

called gar girls—Roberta's misheard word for the evil stone faces described in a civics class) there dancing in the orchard, the ploppy mashed potatoes, the double weenies, the Spam with pineapple. We went into the coffee shop holding on to one another and I tried to think why we were glad to see each other this time and not before. Once, twelve years ago, we passed like strangers. A black girl and a white girl meeting in a Howard Johnson's on the road and having nothing to say. One in a blue and white triangle waitress hat— the other on her way to see Hendrix. Now we were behaving like sisters separated for much too long. Those four short months were nothing in time. Maybe it was the thing itself. Just being there, together. Two little girls who knew what nobody else in the world knew—how not to ask questions. How to believe what had to be believed. There was politeness in that reluctance and generosity as well. Is your mother sick too? No, she dances all night. Oh—and an understanding nod.

We sat in a booth by the window and fell into recollection like veterans.

"Did you ever learn to read?"

"Watch." She picked up the menu. "Special of the day. Cream of corn soup. Entrées. Two dots and a wriggly line. Quiche. Chef salad, scallops . . ."

I was laughing and applauding when the waitress came up.

"Remember the Easter baskets?"

"And how we tried to *introduce* them?"

"Your mother with that cross like two telephone poles."

"And yours with those tight slacks."

We laughed so loudly heads turned and made the laughter harder to suppress.

"What happened to the Jimi Hendrix date?"

Roberta made a blow-out sound with her lips.

"When he died I thought about you."

"Oh, you heard about him finally?"

"Finally. Come on, I was a small-town country waitress."

"And I was a small-town country dropout. God, were we wild. I still don't know how I got out of there alive."

"But you did."

"I did. I really did. Now I'm Mrs. Kenneth Norton."

"Sounds like a mouthful."

"It is."

"Servants and all?"

Roberta held up two fingers.

"Ow! What does he do?"

"Computers and stuff. What do I know?"

"I don't remember a hell of a lot from those days, but Lord, St. Bonny's is as clear as daylight. Remember Maggie? The day she fell down and those gar girls laughed at her?"

Roberta looked up from her salad and stared at me. "Maggie didn't fall," she said.

"Yes, she did. You remember."

"No, Twyla. They knocked her down. Those girls pushed her down and tore her clothes. In the orchard."

"I don't—that's not what happened."

"Sure it is. In the orchard. Remember how scared we were?"

"Wait a minute. I don't remember any of that."

"And Bozo was fired."

"You're crazy. She was there when I left. You left before me."

"I went back. You weren't there when they fired Bozo."

"What?"

"Twice. Once for a year when I was about ten, another for two months when I was fourteen. That's when I ran away."

"You ran away from St. Bonny's?"

"I had to. What do you want? Me dancing in that orchard?"

"Are you sure about Maggie?"

"Of course I'm sure. You've blocked it, Twyla. It happened. Those girls had behavior problems, you know."

"Didn't they, though. But why can't I remember the Maggie thing?"

"Believe me. It happened. And we were there."

"Who did you room with when you went back?" I asked her as if I would know her. The Maggie thing was troubling me.

"Creeps. They tickled themselves in the night."

My ears were itching and I wanted to go home suddenly. This was all very well but she couldn't just comb her hair, wash her face and pretend everything was hunky-dory. After the Howard Johnson's snub. And no apology. Nothing.

"Were you on dope or what that time at Howard Johnson's?" I tried to make my voice sound friendlier than I felt.

"Maybe, a little. I never did drugs much. Why?"

"I don't know; you acted sort of like you didn't want to know me then."

"Oh, Twyla, you know how it was in those days: black—white. You know how everything was."

But I didn't know. I thought it was just the opposite. Busloads of blacks and whites came into Howard Johnson's together. They roamed together then: students, musicians, lovers, protesters. You got to see everything at Howard Johnson's and blacks were very friendly with whites in those days. But sitting there with nothing on my plate but two hard tomato wedges wondering about the melting Klondikes it seemed childish remembering the slight. We went to her car, and with the help of the driver, got my stuff into my station wagon.

"We'll keep in touch this time," she said.

"Sure," I said. "Sure. Give me a call."

"I will," she said, and then just as I was sliding behind the wheel, she leaned into the window. "By the way. Your mother. Did she ever stop dancing?"

I shook my head. "No. Never."

Roberta nodded.

"And yours? Did she ever get well?"

She smiled a tiny sad smile. "No. She never did. Look, call me, okay?"

"Okay," I said, but I knew I wouldn't. Roberta had messed up my past somehow with that business about Maggie. I wouldn't forget a thing like that. Would I?

Strife came to us that fall. At least that's what the paper called it. Strife. Racial strife. The word made me think of a bird—a big shrieking bird out of 1,000,000,000 B.C. Flapping its wings and cawing. Its eye with no lid always bearing down on you. All day it screeched and at night it slept on the rooftops. It woke you in the morning and from the *Today* show to the eleven o'clock news it kept you an awful company. I couldn't figure it out from one day to the next. I knew I was supposed to feel something strong, but I didn't know what, and James wasn't any help. Joseph was on the list of kids to be transferred from the junior high school to another one at some far-out-of-the-way place and I thought it was a good thing until I heard it was a bad thing. I mean I didn't know. All the schools seemed dumps to me, and the fact that one was nicer looking didn't hold much weight. But the papers were full of it and then the kids began to get jumpy. In August, mind you. Schools weren't even open yet. I thought Joseph might be frightened to go over there, but he didn't seem scared so I forgot about it, until I found myself driving along Hudson Street out there by the school they were trying to integrate and saw a line of women marching. And who do you suppose was in line, big as life, holding a sign in front of her bigger than her mother's cross? MOTHERS HAVE RIGHTS TOO! it said.

I drove on, and then changed my mind. I circled the block, slowed down, and honked my horn.

Roberta looked over and when she saw me she waved. I didn't wave back, but I didn't move either. She handed her sign to another woman and came over to where I was parked.

"Hi."

"What are you doing?"

"Picketing. What's it look like?"

"What for?"

"What do you mean, 'What for?' They want to take my kids and send them out of the neighborhood. They don't want to go."

"So what if they go to another school? My boy's being bussed too, and I don't mind. Why should you?"

"It's not about us, Twyla. Me and you. It's about our kids."

"What's more *us* than that?"

"Well, it is a free country."

"Not yet, but it will be."

"What the hell does that mean? I'm not doing anything to you."

"You really think that?"

"I know it."

"I wonder what made me think you were different."

"I wonder what made me think you were different."

"Look at them," I said. "Just look. Who do they think they are? Swarming all over the place like they own it. And now they think they can decide where my child goes to school. Look at them, Roberta. They're Bozos."

Roberta turned around and looked at the women. Almost all of them were standing still now, waiting. Some were even edging toward us. Roberta looked at me out of some refrigerator behind her eyes. "No, they're not. They're just mothers."

"And what am I? Swiss cheese?"

"I used to curl your hair."

"I hated your hands in my hair."

The women were moving. Our faces looked mean to them of course and they looked as though they could not wait to throw themselves in front of a police car, or better yet, into my car and drag me away by my ankles. Now they surrounded my car and gently, gently began to rock it. I swayed back and forth like a sideways yo-yo. Automatically I reached for Roberta, like the old days in the orchard when they saw us watching them and we had to get out of there, and if one of us fell the other pulled her up and if one of us was caught the other stayed to kick and scratch, and neither would leave the other behind. My arm shot out of the car window but no receiving hand was there. Roberta was looking at me sway from side to side in the car and her face was still. My purse slid from the car seat down under the dashboard. The four policemen who had been drinking Tab in their car finally got the message and strolled over, forcing their way through the women. Quietly, firmly they spoke. "Okay, ladies. Back in line or off the streets."

Some of them went away willingly; others had to be urged away from the car doors and the hood. Roberta didn't move. She was looking steadily at me.

I was fumbling to turn on the ignition, which wouldn't catch because the gearshift was still in drive. The seats of the car were a mess because the swaying had thrown my grocery coupons all over it and my purse was sprawled on the floor.

"Maybe I am different now, Twyla. But you're not. You're the same little state kid who kicked a poor old black lady when she was down on the ground. You kicked a black lady and you have the nerve to call me a bigot."

The coupons were everywhere and the guts of my purse were bunched under the dashboard. What was she saying? Black? Maggie wasn't black.

"She wasn't black," I said.

"Like hell she wasn't, and you kicked her. We both did. You kicked a black lady who couldn't even scream."

"Liar!"

"You're the liar! Why don't you just go on home and leave us alone, huh?"

She turned away and I skidded away from the curb.

The next morning I went into the garage and cut the side out of the carton our portable TV had come in. It wasn't nearly big enough, but after a while I had a decent sign: red spray-painted letters on a white background—AND SO DO CHILDREN****. I meant just to go down to the school and tack it up somewhere so those cows on the picket line across the street could see it, but when I got there, some ten or so others had already assembled—protesting the cows across the street. Police permits and everything. I got in line and we strutted in time on our side while Roberta's group strutted on theirs. That first day we were all dignified, pretending the other side didn't exist. The second day there was name calling and finger gestures. But that was about all. People changed signs from time to time, but Roberta never did and neither did I. Actually my sign didn't make sense without Roberta's. "And so do children what?" one of the women on my side asked me. Have rights, I said, as though it was obvious.

Roberta didn't acknowledge my presence in any way and I got to thinking maybe she didn't know I was there. I began to pace myself in the line, jostling people one minute and lagging behind the next, so Roberta and I could reach the end of our respective lines at the same time and there would be a moment in our turn when we would face each other. Still, I couldn't tell whether she saw me and knew my sign was for her. The next day I went early before we were scheduled to assemble. I waited until she got there before I exposed my new creation. As soon as she hoisted her MOTHERS HAVE RIGHTS TOO I began to wave my new one, which said, HOW WOULD YOU KNOW? I know she saw that one, but I had gotten addicted now. My signs got crazier each day, and the women on my side decided that I was a kook. They couldn't make heads or tails out of my brilliant screaming posters.

I brought a painted sign in queenly red with huge black letters that said, IS YOUR MOTHER WELL? Roberta took her lunch break and didn't come back for the rest of the day or any day after. Two days later I stopped going too and couldn't have been missed because nobody understood my signs anyway.

It was a nasty six weeks. Classes were suspended and Joseph didn't go to anybody's school until October. The children—everybody's children—soon got bored with that extended vacation they thought was going to be so great. They looked at TV until their eyes flattened. I spent a couple of mornings tutoring my son, as the other mothers said we should. Twice I opened a text from last year that he had never turned in. Twice he yawned in my face. Other mothers organized living room sessions so the kids would keep up. None of the kids could concentrate so they drifted back to *The Price Is Right* and *The Brady Bunch*. When the school finally opened there were fights once or twice and some sirens roared through the streets every once in a while. There were a lot of photographers from Albany. And just when ABC was about to send up a news crew, the kids settled down like nothing in the world had happened. Joseph hung my HOW WOULD YOU KNOW? sign in his bedroom. I don't know what became of AND SO DO CHILDREN****. I think my father-in-law cleaned some fish on it. He was always puttering around in our garage. Each of his five children lived in Newburgh and he acted as though he had five extra homes.

I couldn't help looking for Roberta when Joseph graduated from high school, but I didn't see her. It didn't trouble me much what she had said to me in the car. I mean the kicking part. I know I didn't do that, I couldn't do that. But I was puzzled by her telling me Maggie was black. When I thought about it I actually couldn't be certain. She wasn't pitch-black, I knew, or I would have remembered that. What I remembered was the kiddie hat, and the semicircle legs. I tried to reassure myself about the race thing for a long time until it dawned on me that the truth was already there, and Roberta knew it. I didn't kick her; I didn't join in with the gar girls and kick that lady, but I sure did want to. We watched and never tried to help her and never called for help. Maggie was my dancing mother. Deaf, I thought, and dumb. Nobody inside. Nobody who would hear you if you cried in the night. Nobody who could tell you anything important that you could use. Rocking, dancing, swaying as she walked. And when the gar girls pushed her down, and started roughhousing, I knew she wouldn't scream, couldn't—just like me—and I was glad about that.

We decided not to have a tree, because Christmas would be at my mother-in-law's house, so why have a tree at both places? Joseph was at SUNY New Paltz and we had to economize, we said. But at the last minute, I changed my mind. Nothing could be that bad. So I rushed around town looking for a tree, something small but wide. By the time I found a place, it was snowing and very late. I dawdled like it was the most important purchase in the world and the tree man was fed up with me. Finally I chose one and had it tied onto the trunk of the car. I drove away slowly because the sand trucks were not out yet and the streets could be murder at the beginning of a snowfall. Downtown the streets were wide and rather empty except for a cluster of people coming out of the Newburgh Hotel. The one hotel in town that wasn't built out of cardboard and Plexiglas. A party, probably. The men huddled in the snow were dressed in tails and the women had on furs. Shiny things glittered from underneath their coats. It made me tired to look at them. Tired, tired, tired. On the next corner was a small diner with loops and loops of paper bells in the window. I stopped the car and went in. Just for a cup of coffee and twenty minutes of peace before I went home and tried to finish everything before Christmas Eve.

"Twyla?"

There she was. In a silvery evening gown and dark fur coat. A man and another woman were with her, the man fumbling for change to put in the cigarette machine. The woman was humming and tapping on the counter with her fingernails. They all looked a little bit drunk.

"Well. It's you."

"How are you?"

I shrugged. "Pretty good. Frazzled. Christmas and all."

"Regular?" called the woman from the counter.

"Fine," Roberta called back and then, "Wait for me in the car."

She slipped into the booth beside me. "I have to tell you something, Twyla. I made up my mind if I ever saw you again, I'd tell you."

"I'd just as soon not hear anything, Roberta. It doesn't matter now, anyway."

"No," she said. "Not about that."

"Don't be long," said the woman. She carried two regulars to go and the man peeled his cigarette packs as they left.

"It's about St. Bonny's and Maggie."

"Oh, please."

"Listen to me. I really did think she was black. I didn't make that up. I really thought so. But now I can't be sure. I just remember her as old, so old. And because she couldn't talk—well, you know, I thought she was crazy. She'd been brought up in an institution like my mother was and like I thought I would be too. And you were right. We didn't kick her. It was the gar girls. Only them. But, well, I wanted to. I really wanted them to hurt her. I said we did it, too. You and me, but that's not true. And I don't want you to carry that around. It was just that I wanted to do it so bad that day—wanting to is doing it."

Her eyes were watery from the drinks she'd had, I guess. I know it's that way with me. One glass of wine and I start bawling over the littlest thing.

"We were kids, Roberta."

"Yeah. Yeah. I know, just kids."

"Eight."

"Eight."

"And lonely."

"Scared, too."

She wiped her cheeks with the heel of her hand and smiled. "Well, that's all I wanted to say."

I nodded and couldn't think of any way to fill the silence that went from the diner past the paper bells on out into the snow. It was heavy now. I thought I'd better wait for the sand trucks before starting home.

"Thanks, Roberta."

"Sure."

"Did I tell you? My mother, she never did stop dancing."

"Yes. You told me. And mine, she never got well." Roberta lifted her hands from the tabletop and covered her face with her palms. When she took them away she really was crying. "Oh shit, Twyla. Shit, shit, shit. What the hell happened to Maggie?"

1983

Gish Jen
(1955–   )

Gish Jen was born on Long Island, New York, one of five children of parents who were educated in Shanghai, China, and then emigrated to the United States during and after World War II. A graduate of Harvard University, Jen attended Stanford Business School. In 1980, she taught English to engineers in Shandung, China; from 1981 to 1983, she completed an MFA at the Iowa Writers' Workshop. She now lives in Cambridge, Massachusetts, with her husband and child.

Jen's stories appeared in *The Atlantic* and *The Best American Short Stories 1988*, but her first novel, *Typical American* in 1991, brought her to the attention of the reading public. ("In the American Society" tells part of the Ralph Chang story, which is "typical" in its emphasis on achieving the American dream in a 1950s mode.) Jen's wry humor makes what might seem tragedy into remarkably insightful episodes, bringing the narrative of suburban social climbing into a fresh context. In this story, the daughters of the Chang household, Mona and Callie—in their roles as narrators—almost usurp the position of protagonist. A continual, seemingly unstudied theme of racism and its effects on neighborliness and on the workplace dominates Jen's domestic story, making this fiction larger than it seems on first reading.

❖

IN THE AMERICAN SOCIETY

I. His Own Society

When my father took over the pancake house, it was to send my little sister Mona and me to college. We were only in junior high at the time, but my father believed in getting a jump on things. "Those Americans always saying it," he told us. "Smart guys thinking in advance." My mother elaborated, explaining that businesses took bringing up, like children. They could take years to get going, she said, years.

In this case, though, we got rich right away. At two months we were breaking even, and at four, those same hotcakes that could barely withstand the weight of butter and syrup were supporting our family with ease. My mother bought a station wagon with air conditioning, my father an oversized, red vinyl recliner for the back room; and as time went on and the business continued to thrive, my father started to talk about his grandfather and the village he had reigned over in China—things my father had never talked about when he worked for other people. He told us about the bags of rice his family would give out to the poor at New Year's, and about the people who came to beg, on their hands and knees, for his grandfather to intercede for the more wayward of their relatives. "Like that Godfather in the movie," he would tell us as, his feet up, he distributed paychecks. Sometimes an employee would get two green envelopes instead of one, which meant that Jimmy needed a tooth pulled, say, or that Tiffany's husband was in the clinker again.

"It's nothing, nothing," he would insist, sinking back into his chair. "Who else is going to take care of you people?"

My mother would mostly just sigh about it. "Your father thinks this is China," she would say, and then she would go back to her mending. Once in a while, though, when my father had given away a particularly large sum, she would exclaim, outraged, "But this here is the U—S—of—A!"—this apparently having been what she used to tell immigrant stock boys when they came in late.

She didn't work at the supermarket anymore; but she had made it to the rank of manager before she left, and this had given her not only new words and phrases, but new ideas about herself, and about America, and about what was what in general. She had opinions, now, on how downtown should be zoned; she could pump her own gas and check her own oil; and for all she used to chide Mona and me for being "copycats," she herself was now interested in espadrilles, and wallpaper, and most recently, the town country club.

"So join already," said Mona, flicking a fly off her knee.

My mother enumerated the problems as she sliced up a quarter round of watermelon: There was the cost. There was the waiting list. There was the fact that no one in our family played either tennis or golf.

"So what?" said Mona.

"It would be waste," said my mother.

"Me and Callie can swim in the pool."

"Plus you need that recommendation letter from a member."

"Come on," said Mona. "Annie's mom'd write you a letter in sec."

My mother's knife glinted in the early summer sun. I spread some more newspaper on the picnic table.

"Plus you have to eat there twice a month. You know what that means." My mother cut another, enormous slice of fruit.

"No, I don't know what that means," said Mona.

"It means Dad would have to wear a jacket, dummy," I said.

"Oh! Oh! Oh!" said Mona, clasping her hand to her breast. "Oh! Oh! Oh! Oh! Oh!"

We all laughed: my father had no use for nice clothes, and would wear only ten-year-old shirts, with grease-spotted pants, to show how little he cared what anyone thought.

"Your father doesn't believe in joining the American society," said my mother. "He wants to have his own society."

"So go to dinner without him." Mona shot her seeds out in long arcs over the lawn. "Who cares what he thinks?"

But of course we all did care, and knew my mother could not simply up and do as she pleased. For in my father's mind, a family owed its head a degree of loyalty that left no room for dissent. To embrace what he embraced was to love; and to embrace something else was to betray him.

He demanded a similar sort of loyalty of his workers, whom he treated more like servants than employees. Not in the beginning, of course. In the beginning all he wanted was for them to keep on doing what they used to do, and to that end he concentrated mostly on leaving them alone. As the months passed, though, he expected more and more of them, with the result that for all his largesse, he began to have trouble keeping help. The cooks and busboys complained that he asked them to fix radiators and trim hedges, not only at the restaurant, but at our house; the waitresses that he sent them on errands and made them chauffeur him around. Our head waitress, Gertrude, claimed that he once even asked her to scratch his back.

"It's not just the blacks don't believe in slavery," she said when she quit.

My father never quite registered her complaint, though, nor those of the others who left. Even after Eleanor quit, then Tiffany, then Gerald, and Jimmy, and even his best cook, Eureka Andy, for whom he had bought new glasses, he remained mostly convinced that the fault lay with them.

"All they understand is that assembly line," he lamented. "Robots, they are. They want to be robots."

There *were* occasions when the clear running truth seemed to eddy, when he would pinch the vinyl of his chair up into little peaks and wonder if he was doing things right. But with time he would always smooth the peaks back down; and when business started to slide in the spring, he kept on like a horse in his ways.

By the summer our dishboy was overwhelmed with scraping. It was no longer just the hashbrowns that people were leaving for trash, and the service was as bad as the food. The waitresses served up French pancakes instead of German, apple juice instead of orange, spilt things on laps, on coats. On the Fourth of July some greenhorn sent an entire side of fries slaloming down a lady's *massif centrale*. Meanwhile in the back room, my father labored through articles on the economy.

"What is housing starts?" he puzzled. "What is GNP?"

Mona and I did what we could, filling in as busgirls and bookkeepers and, one afternoon, stuffing the comments box that hung by the cashier's desk. That was Mona's idea. We rustled up a variety of pens and pencils, checked boxes for an hour, smeared the cards up with coffee and grease, and waited. It took a few days for my father to notice that the box was full, and he didn't say anything about it for a few days more. Finally, though, he started to complain of fatigue; and then he began to complain that the staff was not what it could be. We encouraged him in this—pointing out, for instance, how many dishes got chipped—but in the end all that happened was that, for the first time since we took over the restaurant, my father got it into his head to fire someone. Skip, a skinny busboy who was saving up for a sports-car, said nothing as my father mumbled on about the price of dishes. My father's hands shook as he wrote out the severance check; and he spent the rest of the day napping in his chair once it was over.

As it was going on midsummer, Skip wasn't easy to replace. We hung a sign in the window and advertised in the paper, but no one called the first week, and the person who called the second didn't show up for his interview. The third week, my father phoned Skip to see if he would come back, but a friend of his had already sold him a Corvette for cheap.

Finally a Chinese guy named Booker turned up. He couldn't have been more than thirty, and was wearing a lighthearted seersucker suit, but he looked as though life had him pinned: his eyes were bloodshot and his chest sunken, and the muscles of his neck seemed to strain with the effort of holding his head up. In a single dry breath he told us that he had never bussed tables but was willing to learn, and that he was on the lam from the deportation authorities.

"I do not want to lie to you," he kept saying. He had come to the United States on a student visa, had run out of money, and was now in a bind. He was loath to go back to Taiwan, as it happened—he looked up at this point, to be sure my father wasn't pro-KMT—but all he had was a phony social security card and a willingness to absorb all blame, should anything untoward come to pass.

"I do not think, anyway, that it is against law to hire me, only to be me," he said, smiling faintly.

Anyone else would have examined him on this, but my father conceived of laws as speed bumps rather than curbs. He wiped the counter with his sleeve, and told Booker to report the next morning.

"I will be good worker," said Booker.

"Good," said my father.

"Anything you want me to do, I will do."

My father nodded.

179

Booker seemed to sink into himself for a moment. "Thank you," he said finally. "I am appreciate your help. I am very, very appreciate for everything." He reached out to shake my father's hand.

My father looked at him. "Did you eat today?" he asked in Mandarin.

Booker pulled at the hem of his jacket.

"Sit down," said my father. "Please, have a seat."

My father didn't tell my mother about Booker, and my mother didn't tell my father about the country club. She would never have applied, except that Mona, while over at Annie's had let it drop that our mother wanted to join. Mrs. Lardner came by the very next day.

"Why, I'd be honored and delighted to write you people a letter," she said. Her skirt billowed around her.

"Thank you so much," said my mother. "But it's too much trouble for you, and also my husband is . . ."

"Oh, it's no trouble at all, no trouble at all. I tell you." She leaned forward so that her chest freckles showed. "I know just how it is. It's a secret of course, but you know, my natural father was Jewish. Can you see it? Just look at my skin."

"My husband," said my mother.

"I'd be honored and delighted," said Mrs. Lardner with a little wave of her hands. "Just honored and delighted."

Mona was triumphant. "See, Mom," she said, waltzing around the kitchen when Mrs. Lardner left. "What did I tell you? 'I'm just honored and delighted, just honored and delighted.' " She waved her hands in the air.

"You know, the Chinese have a saying," said my mother. "To do nothing is better than to overdo. You mean well, but you tell me now what will happen."

"I'll talk Dad into it," said Mona, still waltzing. "Or I bet Callie can. He'll do anything Callie says."

"I can try, anyway," I said.

"Did you hear what I said?" said my mother. Mona bumped into the broom closet door. "You're not going to talk anything; you've already made enough trouble." She started on the dishes with a clatter.

Mona poked diffidently at a mop.

I sponged off the counter. "Anyway," I ventured. "I bet our name'll never even come up."

"That's if we're lucky," said my mother.

"There's all these people waiting," I said.

"Good," she said. She started on a pot.

I looked over at Mona, who was still cowering in the broom closet. "In fact, there's some black family's been waiting so long, they're going to sue," I said.

My mother turned off the water. "Where'd you hear that?"

"Patty told me."

She turned the water back on, started to wash a dish, then put it back down and shut the faucet.

"I'm sorry," said Mona.

"Forget it," said my mother. "Just forget it."

Booker turned out to be a model worker, whose boundless gratitude translated into a willingness to do anything. As he also learned quickly, he soon knew not only how to bus, but how to cook, and how to wait table, and how to keep the books. He fixed the walk-in door so that it stayed shut, reupholstered the torn seats in the dining room, and devised a system for tracking inventory. The only stone in the rice was that he tended to be sickly; but, reliable even in illness, he would always send a friend to take his place. In this way we got to know Ronald, Lynn, Dirk, and Cedric, all of whom, like Booker, had problems with their legal status and were anxious to please. They weren't all as capable as Booker, though, with the exception of Cedric, whom my father often hired even when Booker was well. A round wag of a man who called Mona and me *shou hou*—skinny monkeys—he was a professed non-smoker who was nevertheless always begging drags off of other people's cigarettes. This last habit drove our head cook, Fernando, crazy, especially since, when refused a hit, Cedric would occasionally snitch one. Winking impishly at Mona and me, he would steal up to an ashtray, take a quick puff, and then break out laughing so that the smoke came rolling out of his mouth in a great incriminatory cloud. Fernando accused him of stealing fresh cigarettes too, even whole packs.

"Why else do you think he's weaseling around in the back of the store all the time," he said. His face was blotchy with anger. "The man is a frigging thief."

Other members of the staff supported him in this contention and joined in on an "Operation Identification," which involved numbering and initialing their cigarettes—even though what they seemed to fear for wasn't so much their cigarettes as their jobs. Then one of the cooks quit; and rather than promote someone, my father hired Cedric for the position. Rumors flew that he was taking only half the normal salary, that Alex had been pressured to resign, and that my father was looking for a position with which to placate Booker, who had been bypassed because of his health.

The result was that Fernando categorically refused to work with Cedric.

"The only way I'll cook with that piece of slime," he said, shaking his huge tattooed fist, "is if it's his ass frying on the grill."

My father cajoled and cajoled, to no avail, and in the end was simply forced to put them on different schedules.

The next week Fernando got caught stealing a carton of minute steaks. My father would not tell even Mona and me how he knew to be standing by the back door when Fernando was on his way out, but everyone suspected Booker. Everyone but Fernando, that is, who was sure Cedric had been the tip-off. My father held a staff meeting in which he tried to reassure everyone that Alex had left on his own, and that he had no intention of firing anyone. But though he was careful not to mention Fernando, everyone was so amazed that he was being allowed to stay that Fernando was incensed nonetheless.

"Don't you all be putting your bug eyes on me," he said. "*He's* the frigging crook." He grabbed Cedric by the collar.

Cedric raised an eyebrow. "Cook, you mean," he said.

At this Fernando punched Cedric in the mouth; and the words he had just uttered notwithstanding, my father fired him on the spot.

With everything that was happening, Mona and I were ready to be getting out of the restaurant. It was almost time: the days were still stuffy with summer, but our window shade had started flapping in the evening as if gearing up to go out. That year the breezes were full of salt, as they sometimes were when they came in from the East, and they blew anchors and docks through my mind like so many tumbleweeds, filling my dreams with wherries and lobsters and grainy-faced men who squinted, day in and day out, at the sky.

It was time for a change, you could feel it; and yet the pancake house was the same as ever. The day before school started my father came home with bad news.

"Fernando called police," he said, wiping his hand on his pant leg.

My mother naturally wanted to know what police; and so with much coughing and hawing, the long story began, the latest installment of which had the police calling immigration, and immigration sending an investigator. My mother sat stiff as whalebone as my father described how the man summarily refused lunch on the house and how my father had admitted, under pressure, that he knew there were "things" about his workers.

"So now what happens?"

My father didn't know. "Booker and Cedric went with him to the jail," he said. "But me, here I am." He laughed uncomfortably.

The next day my father posted bail for "his boys" and waited apprehensively for something to happen. The day after that he waited again, and the day after that he called our neighbor's law student son, who suggested my father call the immigration department under an alias. My father took his advice;

and it was thus that he discovered that Booker was right: it was illegal for aliens to work, but it wasn't to hire them.

In the happy interval that ensued, my father apologized to my mother, who in turn confessed about the country club, for which my father had no choice but to forgive her. Then he turned his attention back to "his boys."

My mother didn't see that there was anything to do.

"I like to talking to the judge," said my father.

"This is not China," said my mother.

"I'm only talking to him. I'm not give him money unless he wants it."

"You're going to land up in jail."

"So what else I should do?" My father threw up his hands. "Those are my boys."

"Your boys!" exploded my mother. "What about your family? What about your wife?"

My father took a long sip of tea. "You know," he said finally. "In the war my father sent our cook to the soldiers to use. He always said it—the province comes before the town, the town comes before the family."

"A restaurant is not a town," said my mother.

My father sipped at his tea again. "You know, when I first come to the United States, I also had to hide-and-seek with those deportation guys. If people did not helping me, I'm not here today."

My mother scrutinized her hem.

After a minute I volunteered that before seeing a judge, he might try a lawyer.

He turned. "Since when did you become so afraid like your mother?"

I started to say that it wasn't a matter of fear, but he cut me off.

"What I need today," he said, "is a son."

My father and I spent the better part of the next day standing in lines at the immigration office. He did not get to speak to a judge, but with much persistence he managed to speak to a judge's clerk, who tried to persuade him that it was not her place to extend him advice. My father, though, shamelessly plied her with compliments and offers of free pancakes until she finally conceded that she personally doubted anything would happen to either Cedric or Booker.

"Especially if they're 'needed workers,'" she said, rubbing at the red marks her glasses left on her nose. She yawned. "Have you thought about sponsoring them to become permanent residents?"

Could he do that? My father was overjoyed. And what if he saw to it right away? Would she perhaps put in a good word with the judge?

She yawned again, her nostrils flaring. "Don't worry," she said. "They'll get a fair hearing."

My father returned jubilant. Booker and Cedric hailed him as their savior, their Buddha incarnate. He was like a father to them, they said; and laughing and clapping, they made him tell the story over and over, sorting over the details like jewels. And how old was the assistant judge? And what did she say?

That evening my father tipped the paperboy a dollar and bought a pot of mums for my mother, who suffered them to be placed on the dining room table. The next night he took us all out to dinner. Then on Saturday, Mona found a letter on my father's chair at the restaurant.

DEAR MR. CHANG,
You are the grat boss. But, we do not like to trial, so will runing away now. Plese to excus us. People saying the law in America is fears like dragon. Here is only $140. We hope some day we can pay back the rest bale. You will getting intrest, as you diserving, so grat a boss you are. Thank you for every thing. In next life you will be burn in rich family, with no more pancaks.

> YOURS TRULEY,
> BOOKER + CEDRIC

In the weeks that followed my father went to the pancake house for crises, but otherwise hung around our house, fiddling idly with the sump pump and boiler in an effort, he said, to get ready for winter. It was as though he had gone into retirement, except that instead of moving south, he had moved to the basement. He even took to showering my mother with little attentions, and to calling her "old girl," and when we finally heard that the club had entertained all the applications it could for the year, he was so sympathetic that he seemed more disappointed than my mother.

II. In the American Society

Mrs. Lardner tempered the bad news with an invitation to a bon voyage "bash" she was throwing for a friend of hers who was going to Greece for six months.

"Do come," she urged. "You'll meet everyone, and then, you know, if things open up in the spring . . ." She waved her hands.

My mother wondered if it would be appropriate to show up at a party for someone they didn't know, but "the honest truth" was that this was an annual affair. "If it's not Greece, it's Antibes," sighed Mrs. Lardner. "We really just do it because his wife left him and his daughter doesn't speak to him, and poor Jeremy just feels so *unloved.*"

She also invited Mona and me to the goings on, as "*demi*-guests" to keep

Annie out of the champagne. I wasn't too keen on the idea, but before I could say anything, she had already thanked us for so generously agreeing to honor her with our presence.

"A pair of little princesses, you are!" she told us. "A pair of princesses!"

The party was that Sunday. On Saturday, my mother took my father out shopping for a suit. As it was the end of September, she insisted that he buy a worsted rather than a seersucker, even though it was only ten, rather than fifty percent off. My father protested that it was as hot as ever, which was true—a thick Indian summer had cozied murderously up to us—but to no avail. Summer clothes, said my mother, were not properly worn after Labor Day.

The suit was unfortunately as extravagant in length as it was in price, which posed an additional quandary, since the tailor wouldn't be in until Monday. The salesgirl, though, found a way of tacking it up temporarily.

"Maybe this suit not fit me," fretted my father.

"Just don't take your jacket off," said the salesgirl.

He gave her a tip before they left, but when he got home refused to remove the price tag.

"I like to asking the tailor about the size," he insisted.

"You mean you're going to *wear* it and then *return* it?" Mona rolled her eyes.

"I didn't say I'm return it," said my father stiffly. "I like to asking the tailor, that's all."

The party started off swimmingly, except that most people were wearing bermudas or wrap skirts. Still, my parents carried on, sharing with great feeling the complaints about the heat. Of course my father tried to eat a cracker full of shallots and burnt himself in an attempt to help Mr. Lardner turn the coals of the barbeque; but on the whole he seemed to be doing all right. Not nearly so well as my mother, though, who had accepted an entire cupful of Mrs. Lardner's magic punch, and seemed indeed to be under some spell. As Mona and Annie skirmished over whether some boy in their class inhaled when he smoked, I watched my mother take off her shoes, laughing and laughing as a man with a beard regaled her with navy stories by the pool. Apparently he had been stationed in the Orient and remembered a few words of Chinese, which made my mother laugh still more. My father excused himself to go to the men's room then drifted back and weighed anchor at the hors d'oeuvres table, while my mother sailed on to a group of women, who tinkled at length over the clarity of her complexion. I dug out a book I had brought.

Just when I'd cracked the spine, though, Mrs. Lardner came by to bewail her shortage of servers. Her caterers were criminals, I agreed; and the next thing I knew I was handing out bits of marine life, making the rounds as amiably as I could.

"Here you go, Dad," I said when I got to the hors d'oeuvres table.

"Everything is fine," he said.

I hesitated to leave him alone; but then the man with the beard zeroed in on him, and though he talked of nothing but my mother, I thought it would be okay to get back to work. Just that moment, though, Jeremy Brothers lurched our way, an empty, albeit corked, wine bottle in hand. He was a slim, well-proportioned man, with a Roman nose and small eyes and a nice manly jaw that he allowed to hang agape.

"Hello," he said drunkenly. "Pleased to meet you."

"Pleased to meeting you," said my father.

"Right," said Jeremy. "Right. Listen. I have this bottle here, this most recalcitrant bottle. You see that it refuses to do my bidding. I bid it open sesame, please, and it does nothing." He pulled the cork out with his teeth, then turned the bottle upside down.

My father nodded.

"Would you have a word with it please?" said Jeremy. The man with the beard excused himself. "Would you please have a goddamned word with it?"

My father laughed uncomfortably.

"Ah!" Jeremy bowed a little. "Excuse me, excuse me, excuse me. You are not my man, not my man at all." He bowed again and started to leave, but then circled back. "Viticulture is not your forte, yes I can see that, see that plainly. But may I trouble you on another matter? Forget the damned bottle." He threw it into the pool, and winked at the people he splashed. "I have another matter. Do you speak Chinese?"

My father said he did not, but Jeremy pulled out a handkerchief with some characters on it anyway, saying that his daughter had sent it from Hong Kong and that he thought the characters might be some secret message.

"Long life," said my father.

"But you haven't looked at it yet."

"I know what it says without looking." My father winked at me.

"You do?"

"Yes, I do."

"You're making fun of me, aren't you?"

"No, no, no," said my father, winking again.

"Who are you anyway?" said Jeremy.

His smile fading, my father shrugged.

"Who are you?"

My father shrugged again.

Jeremy began to roar. "This is my party, *my party,* and I've never seen you before in my life." My father backed up as Jeremy came toward him. *"Who are you? WHO ARE YOU?"*

Just as my father was going to step back into the pool, Mrs. Lardner came running up. Jeremy informed her that there was a man crashing his party.

"Nonsense," said Mrs. Lardner. "This is Ralph Chang, who I invited extra especially so he could meet you." She straightened the collar of Jeremy's peach-colored polo shirt for him.

"Yes, well, we've had a chance to chat," said Jeremy.

She whispered in his ear; he mumbled something; she whispered something more.

"I do apologize," he said finally.

My father didn't say anything.

"I do." Jeremy seemed genuinely contrite. "Doubtless you've seen drunks before, haven't you? You must have them in China."

"Okay," said my father.

As Mrs. Lardner glided off, Jeremy clapped his arm over my father's shoulders. "You know, I really am quite sorry, quite sorry."

My father nodded.

"What can I do, how can I make it up to you?"

"No thank you."

"No, tell me, tell me," wheedled Jeremy. "Tickets to casino night?" My father shook his head. "You don't gamble. Dinner at Bartholomew's?" My father shook his head again. "You don't eat." Jeremy scratched his chin. "You know, my wife was like you. Old Annabelle could never let me make things up—never, never, never, never, never."

My father wriggled out from under his arm.

"How about sport clothes? You are rather overdressed, you know, excuse me for saying so. But here." He took off his polo shirt and folded it up. "You can have this with my most profound apologies." He ruffled his chest hairs with his free hand.

"No thank you," said my father.

"No, take it, take it. Accept my apologies." He thrust the shirt into my father's arms. "I'm so very sorry, so very sorry. Please, try it on."

Helplessly holding the shirt, my father searched the crowd for my mother.

"Here, I'll help you off with your coat."

My father froze.

Jeremy reached over and took his jacket off. "Milton's, one hundred twenty-five dollars reduced to one hundred twelve-fifty," he read. "What a bargain, what a bargain!"

"Please give it back," pleaded my father. "Please."

"Now for your shirt," ordered Jeremy.

Heads began to turn.

"Take off your shirt."

"I do not take orders like a servant," announced my father.

"Take off your shirt, or I'm going to throw this jacket right into the pool, just right into this little pool here." Jeremy held it over the water.

"Go ahead."

"One hundred twelve-fifty," taunted Jeremy. "One hundred twelve . . ."

My father flung the polo shirt into the water with such force that part of it bounced back up into the air like a fluorescent fountain. Then it settled into a soft heap on top of the water. My mother hurried up.

"You're a sport!" said Jeremy, suddenly breaking into a smile and slapping my father on the back. "You're a sport! I like that. A man with spirit, that's what you are. A man with panache. Allow me to return to you your jacket." He handed it back to my father. "Good value you got on that, good value."

My father hurled the coat into the pool too. "We're leaving," he said grimly. "Leaving!"

"Now, Ralphie," said Mrs. Lardner, bustling up; but my father was already stomping off.

"Get your sister," he told me. To my mother: "Get your shoes."

"That was *great*, Dad," said Mona as we walked down to the car. "You were *stupendous*."

"Way to show 'em," I said.

"What?" said my father offhandedly.

Although it was only just dusk, we were in a gulch, which made it hard to see anything except the gleam of his white shirt moving up the hill ahead of us.

"It was all my fault," began my mother.

"Forget it," said my father grandly. Then he said, "The only trouble is I left those keys in my jacket pocket."

"Oh *no*," said Mona.

"Oh no is right," said my mother.

"So we'll walk home," I said.

"But how're we going to get into the *house*," said Mona.

The noise of the party churned through the silence.

"Someone has to going back," said my father.

"Let's go to the pancake house first," suggested my mother. "We can wait there until the party is finished, and then call Mrs. Lardner."

Having all agreed that that was a good plan, we started walking again.

"God, just think," said Mona. "We're going to have to *dive* for them."

My father stopped a moment. We waited.

"You girls are good swimmers," he said finally. "Not like me."

Then his shirt started moving again, and we trooped up the hill after it, into the dark.

1986

Ursula K. Le Guin
(1929–   )

Ursula K. Le Guin, whose mother was a writer and father an anthropologist, early learned the fascination of alternative worlds. In her fantasy and science fiction, as well as in poems and essays, Le Guin often creates and explores societies that operate by new rules and with different principles than those that condition middle-class Western life. In *The Left Hand of Darkness* (1969), which won both Hugo and Nebula awards for science fiction, the planet "Gethen" is a peaceful, sexually expressive world inhabited by "androgynes" who are free of usual gender roles. A more recent work, *Always Coming Home* (1985), employs fiction, poetry, graphics, and music to present a future (and futuristic) race.

The mother of three children, Le Guin left her doctoral studies in Renaissance literature to devote herself to her writing. She settled with her family in Portland, Oregon, where she has had a continuing interest in ecology and environmentalism, interests which are also prevalent in her fiction.

Her story "May's Lion" is neither science fiction nor fantasy, but it employs such familiar Le Guin techniques as repetition and lyrical language. Thematically, this is also classic Le Guin in that it stresses the urgent need to give voice to stories that have been repressed or discounted.

❖

MAY'S LION

Jim remembers it as a bobcat, and he was May's nephew, and ought to know. It probably was a bobcat. I don't think May would have changed her story, though you can't trust a good story-teller not to make the story suit herself, or get the facts to fit the story better. Anyhow she told it to us more than once, because my mother and I would ask for it; and the way I remember it, it was a mountain lion. And the way I remember May telling it is sitting on the edge of the irrigation tank we used to swim in, cement rough as a lava flow and hot in the sun, the long cracks tarred over. She was an old lady then with a long Irish upper lip, kind and wary and balky. She liked to come sit and talk with my mother while I swam; she didn't have all that many people to talk to. She always had chickens, in the chickenhouse very near the back door of the farmhouse, so the whole place smelled pretty strong of chickens, and as long as she could she kept a cow or two down in the old barn by the creek. The first of May's cows I remember was Pearl, a big handsome Holstein who gave fourteen or twenty-four or forty gallons or quarts of milk at a milking, whichever is right for a prize milker. Pearl was beautiful in my eyes when I was four or five years old; I loved and admired her. I remember how excited I was, how I reached upward to them, when Pearl or the workhorse Prince, for whom my love amounted to worship, would put an immense and sensitive muzzle through the three-strand fence to whisk a cornhusk from my fearful hand; and then the munching and the sweet breath and the big nose would be at the barbed wire again: the offering is acceptable. . . . After Pearl there was Rosie, a purebred Jersey. May got her either cheap or free because she was a runt calf, so tiny that May brought her home on her lap in the back of the car, like a fawn. And Rosie always looked like she had some deer in her. She was a lovely, clever little cow and even more willful than old May. She often chose not to come in to be milked. We would hear May calling and then see her trudging across our lower pasture with the bucket, going to find Rosie wherever Rosie had decided to be milked today on the wild hills she had to roam in, a hundred acres of our and Old Jim's land. Then May had a fox terrier named Pinky, who yipped and nipped and turned me against fox terriers for life, but he was long gone when the mountain lion came; and the black cats who lived in the barn kept discreetly out of the story. As a matter of fact now I think of it the chickens weren't in it either. It might have been quite different if they had been. May had quit keeping chickens after old Mrs. Walter died. It was just her all alone there, and Rosie and the cats down in the barn, and nobody else within sight or sound of the old farm. We were in our house up the hill only in the summer, and Jim lived in town, those years. What time of year it was I don't know, but I imagine the grass still green or just turning gold. And May was in the house, in the kitchen, where she lived entirely unless she was asleep or outdoors, when she heard this noise.

Now you need May herself, sitting skinny on the edge of the irrigation tank, seventy or eighty or ninety years old, nobody knew how old May was and she had made sure they couldn't find out, opening her pleated lips and letting out this noise—a huge, awful yowl, starting soft with a nasal hum and rising slowly into a snarling gargle that sank away into a sobbing purr. . . . It got better every time she told the story.

"It was some meow," she said.

So she went to the kitchen door, opened it, and looked out. Then she shut the kitchen door and went to the kitchen window to look out, because there was a mountain lion under the fig tree.

Puma, cougar, catamount; *Felis concolor*, the shy, secret, shadowy lion of the New World, four or five feet long plus a yard of black-tipped tail, weighs about what a woman weighs, lives where the deer live from Canada to Chile, but always shyer, always fewer, the color of dry leaves, dry grass.

There were plenty of deer in the Valley in the forties, but no mountain lion had been seen for decades anywhere near where people lived. Maybe way back up in the canyons; but Jim, who hunted, and knew every deer-trail in the hills, had never seen a lion. Nobody had, except May, now, alone in her kitchen.

"I thought maybe it was sick," she told us. "It wasn't acting right. I don't think a lion would walk right into the yard like that if it was feeling well. If I'd still had the chickens it'd be a different story maybe! But it just walked around some, and then it lay down there," and she points between the fig tree and the decrepit garage. "And then after a while it kind of meowed again, and got up and come into the shade right there." The fig tree, planted when the house was built, about the time May was born, makes a great, green, sweet-smelling shade. "It just laid there looking around. It wasn't well," says May.

She had lived with and looked after animals all her life; she had also earned her living for years as a nurse.

"Well, I didn't know exactly what to do for it. So I put out some water for it. It didn't even get up when I come out the door. I put the water down there, not so close to it that we'd scare each other, see, and it kept watching me, but it didn't move. After I went back in it did get up and tried to drink some water. Then it made that kind of meowowow. I do believe it come here because it was looking for help. Or just for company, maybe."

The afternoon went on, May in the kitchen, the lion under the fig tree.

But down in the barnyard by the creek was Rosie the cow. Fortunately the gate was shut, so she could not come wandering up to the house and meet the lion; but she would be needing to be milked, come six or seven o'clock, and that got to worrying May. She also worried how long a sick mountain lion might hang around, keeping her shut in the house. May didn't like being shut in.

"I went out a time or two, and went shoo!"

Eyes shining amidst fine wrinkles, she flaps her thin arms at the lion. "Shoo! Go on home now!"

But the silent wild creature watches her with yellow eyes and does not stir.

"So when I was talking to Miss Macy on the telephone, she said it might have rabies, and I ought to call the sheriff. I was uneasy then. So finally I did that, and they come out, those county police, you know. Two carloads."

Her voice is dry and quiet.

"I guess there was nothing else they knew how to do. So they shot it."

She looks off across the field Old Jim, her brother, used to plow with Prince the horse and irrigate with the water from this tank. Now wild oats and blackberry grow there. In another thirty years it will be a rich man's vineyard, a tax write-off.

"He was seven feet long, all stretched out, before they took him off. And so thin! They all said, 'Well, Aunt May, I guess you were scared there! I guess you were some scared!' But I wasn't. I didn't want him shot. But I didn't know what to do for him. And I did need to get to Rosie."

I have told this true story which May gave to us as truly as I could, and now I want to tell it as fiction, yet without taking it from her: rather to give it back to her, if I can do so. It is a tiny part of the history of the Valley, and I want to make it part of the Valley outside history. Now the field that the poor man plowed and the rich man harvested lies on the edge of a little town, houses and workshops of timber and fieldstone standing among almond, oak, and eucalyptus trees; and now May is an old woman with a name that means the month of May: Rains End. An old woman with a long, wrinkled-pleated upper lip, she is living alone for the summer in her summer place, a meadow a mile or so up in the hills above the little town. Sinshan. She took her cow Rose with her, and since Rose tends to wander she keeps her on a long tether down by the tiny creek, and moves her into fresh grass now and then. The summerhouse is what they call a nine-pole house, a mere frame of poles stuck in the ground—one of them is a live digger-pine sapling—with stick and matting walls, and mat roof and floors. It doesn't rain in the dry season, and the roof is just for shade. But the house and its little front yard where Rains End has her camp stove and clay oven and matting loom are well shaded by a fig tree that was planted there a hundred years or so ago by her grandmother.

Rains End herself has no grandchildren; she never bore a child, and her one or two marriages were brief and very long ago. She has a nephew and two grandnieces, and feels herself an aunt to all children, even when they are afraid of her and rude to her because she has got so ugly with old age, smelling as musty as a chickenhouse. She considers it natural for children to shrink away from somebody part way dead, and knows that when they're a little older and have got used to her they'll ask her for stories. She was for sixty years a member of the Doctors Lodge, and though she doesn't do curing any more people still ask her to help with nursing sick children, and the children come to long for the kind, authoritative touch of her hands when she bathes them to bring a fever down, or changes a dressing, or combs out bed-tangled hair with witch hazel and great patience.

So Rains End was just waking up from an early afternoon nap in the heat of the day, under the matting roof, when she heard a noise, a huge, awful yowl that started soft with a nasal hum and rose slowly into a snarling gargle that sank away into a sobbing purr. . . . And she got up and looked out from the open side of the house of sticks and matting, and saw a mountain lion under the fig tree. She looked at him from her house; he looked at her from his.

And this part of the story is much the same: the old woman; the lion; and, down by the creek, the cow.

It was hot. Crickets sang shrill in the yellow grass on all the hills and canyons, in all the chaparral. Rains End filled a bowl with water from an unglazed jug and came slowly out of the house. Halfway between the house and the lion she set the bowl down on the dirt. She turned and went back to the house.

The lion got up after a while and came and sniffed at the water. He lay down again with a soft, querulous groan, almost like a sick child, and looked at Rains End with the yellow eyes that saw her in a different way than she had ever been seen before.

She sat on the matting in the shade of the open part of her house and did some mending. When she looked up at the lion she sang under her breath, tunelessly; she wanted to remember the Puma Dance Song but could only remember bits of it, so she made a song for the occasion:

> You are there, lion.
> You are there, lion. . . .

As the afternoon wore on she began to worry about going down to milk Rose. Unmilked, the cow would start tugging at her tether and making a commotion. That was likely to upset the lion. He lay so close to the house now that if she came out that too might upset him, and she did not want to frighten him or to become frightened of him. He had evidently come for some reason, and it behoved her to find out what the reason was. Probably he was sick; his coming so close to a human person was strange, and people who behave strangely are usually sick or in some kind of pain. Sometimes, though, they are spiritually moved to act strangely. The lion might be a messenger, or might have some message of his own for her or her townspeople. She was more used to seeing birds as messengers; the four-footed people go about their own business. But the lion, dweller in the Seventh House, comes from the place dreams come from. Maybe she did not understand. Maybe someone else would understand. She could go over and tell Valiant and her family, whose summerhouse was in Gahheya meadow, farther up the creek; or she could go over to Buck's, on Baldy Knoll. But there were four or five adolescents there, and one of them might come and shoot the lion, to boast that he'd saved old Rains End from getting clawed to bits and eaten.

Mooooooo! said Rose, down by the creek, reproachfully.

The sun was still above the southwest ridge, but the branches of pines were across it and the heavy heat was out of it, and shadows were welling up in the low fields of wild oats and blackberry.

Moooooo! said Rose again, louder.

The lion lifted up his square, heavy head, the color of dry wild oats, and gazed down across the pastures. Rains End knew from that weary movement that he was very ill. He had come for company in dying, that was all.

"I'll come back, lion," Rains End sang tunelessly. "Lie still. Be quiet. I'll come back soon." Moving softly and easily, as she would move in a room with a sick child, she got her milking pail and stool, slung the stool on her back with a woven strap so as to leave a hand free, and came out of the house. The lion watched her at first very tense, the yellow eyes firing up for a moment, but then put his head down again with that little grudging, groaning sound. "I'll come back, lion," Rains End said. She went down to the creekside and milked a nervous and indignant cow. Rose could smell lion, and demanded in several ways, all eloquent, just what Rains End intended to *do?* Rains End ignored her questions and sang milking songs to her: "Su bonny, su bonny, be still my grand cow . . ." Once she had to slap her hard on the hip. "Quit that, you old fool! Get over! I am *not* going to untie you and have you walking into trouble! I won't let him come down this way."

She did not say how she planned to stop him.

She retethered Rose where she could stand down in the creek if she liked. When she came back up the rise with the pail of milk in hand, the lion had not moved. The sun was down, the air above the ridges turning clear gold. The yellow eyes watched her, no light in them. She came to pour the milk into the lion's bowl. As she did so, he all at once half rose up. Rains End started, and spilled some of the milk she was pouring. "Shoo! Stop that!" she whispered fiercely, waving her skinny arm at the lion. "Lie down now! I'm afraid of you when you get up, can't you see that, stupid? Lie down now, lion. There you are. Here I am. It's all right. You know what you're doing." Talking softly as she went, she returned to her house of stick and matting. There she sat down as before, in the open porch, on the grass mats.

The mountain lion made the grumbling sound, ending with a long sigh, and let his head sink back down on his paws.

Rains End got some cornbread and a tomato from the pantry box while there was still daylight left to see by, and ate slowly and neatly. She did not offer the lion food. He had not touched the milk, and she thought he would eat no more in the House of Earth.

From time to time as the quiet evening darkened and stars gathered thicker overhead she sang to the lion. She sang the five songs of *Going Westward to the Sunrise,* which are sung to human beings dying. She did not know if it was proper and appropriate to sing these songs to a dying mountain lion, but she did not know his songs.

Twice he also sang: once a quavering moan, like a house cat challenging another tom to battle, and once a long, sighing purr.

Before the Scorpion had swung clear of Sinshan Mountain, Rains End had pulled her heavy shawl around herself in case the fog came in, and had gone sound asleep in the porch of her house.

She woke with the grey light before sunrise. The lion was a motionless shadow, a little farther from the trunk of the fig tree than he had been the night before. As the light grew, she saw that he had stretched himself out full length. She knew he had finished his dying, and sang the fifth song, the last song, in a whisper, for him:

> The doors of the Four Houses
> are open.
> Surely they are open.

Near sunrise she went to milk Rose, and to wash in the creek. When she came back up to the house she went closer to the lion, though not so close as to crowd him, and stood for a long time looking at him stretched out in the long, tawny, delicate light. "As thin as I am!" she said to Valiant, when she went up to Gahheya later in the morning to tell the story and to ask help carrying the body of the lion off where the buzzards and coyotes could clean it.

It's still your story, Aunt May; it was your lion. He came to you. He brought his death to you, a gift; but the men with the guns won't take gifts, they think they own death already. And so they took from you the honor he did you, and you felt that loss. I wanted to restore it. But you don't need it. You followed the lion where he went, years ago now.

1983

Rebecca Harding Davis
(1831–1910)

Life in the Iron-Mills (1861) is not only a powerful novella of working-class life in a Virginia mill town, it is also, on several levels, an allegory of U.S. women's literature. Originally published to considerable acclaim in one of the nation's most prestigious magazines, *Atlantic Monthly,* it became merely a footnote to American literary history until 1972 when writer Tillie Olsen "rediscovered" it and wrote an Afterword for its republication by the Feminist Press, a press noted for many discoveries of forgotten women writers.

Published anonymously and narrated by someone whose gender is left unspecified, *Life in the Iron-Mills* was thought by many of its readers to have been written by a man. Many were surprised when a thirty-year-old woman, Rebecca Harding (1831–1910), was revealed to be the author of this gritty, powerful tale that is unflinching in its depiction of the destruction of body and spirit caused by industrialization. Her first published work, *Life in the Iron-Mills* was based on Rebecca Harding's experiences in Wheeling, Virginia, where she moved with her family when she was five years old. There she watched the workers on the streets, smelled the putrid air from the mills, and became sensitive to an aspect of life that few nineteenth-century white, middle-class women were aware of.

After she published this story, she received a fan letter from a journalist, Lemuel Clarke Davis. A correspondence ensued, and she married him in 1863 and moved to Philadelphia where she had three children and took care of the household tasks. Determined not to allow her family to fall into poverty as her husband repeatedly brought them to the brink of financial disaster, she wrote book after book for money. Prolific, she never again achieved the artistry of her first published work.

Life in the Iron-Mills has some of the formal characteristics of a mid-century America novel—an array of both major and minor characters who come into a complicated moral conflict that must be resolved by the end of the work. As a novella, however, the pacing is faster, the plot is more tightly constructed, and there is greater concision of both details and events. This novella is also unique in its perspective, its tone of moral outrage, its shifting point of view, its powerful prose style, and its relentless attention to class as a shaper of character. Perhaps most intriguing is the way in which Harding Davis dissects the unexamined class values and prejudices of the middle-class observers of the working poor, and dares the reader to overcome those prejudices in order to understand the artistic spirit and financial contingencies that move Hugh Wolfe, the novella's main character.

LIFE IN THE IRON-MILLS[1]

"Is this the end?
O Life, as futile, then, as frail!
What hope of answer or redress?"[2]

A cloudy day: do you know what that is in a town of iron-works?[3] The sky sank down before dawn, muddy, flat, immovable. The air is thick, clammy with the breath of crowded human beings. It stifles me. I open the window, and, looking out, can scarcely see through the rain the grocer's shop opposite, where a crowd of drunken Irishmen are puffing Lynchburg tobacco[4] in their pipes. I can detect the scent through all the foul smells ranging loose in the air.

The idiosyncrasy of this town is smoke. It rolls sullenly in slow folds from the great chimneys of the iron-foundries, and settles down in black, slimy pools on the muddy streets. Smoke on the wharves, smoke on the dingy boats, on the yellow river,—clinging in a coating of greasy soot to the house-front, the two faded poplars, the faces of the passers-by. The long train of mules, dragging masses of pig-iron through the narrow street, have a foul vapor hanging to their reeking sides. Here, inside, is a little broken figure of an angel pointing upward from the mantel-shelf; but even its wings are covered with smoke, clotted and black. Smoke everywhere! A dirty canary chirps desolately in a cage beside me. Its dream of green fields and sunshine is a very old dream—almost worn out, I think.

From the back-window I can see a narrow brick-yard sloping down to the riverside, strewed with rain-butts and tubs. The river, dull and tawny-colored, (*la belle rivière!*) drags itself sluggishly along, tired of the heavy weight of boats and coal-barges. What wonder? When I was a child, I used to fancy a look of weary, dumb appeal upon the face of the negro-like river slavishly bearing its burden day after day. Something of the same idle notion comes to me to-day, when from the street-window I look on the slow stream of human life creeping past, night and morning, to the great mills. Masses of men, with dull, besotted faces bent to the ground, sharpened here and there by pain or cunning; skin and muscle and flesh begrimed with smoke and ashes; stooping all night over boiling caldrons of metal, laired by day in dens of drunkenness

[1] Published originally in the *Atlantic Monthly* 7 (April 1861), pp. 430–451.
[2] A recasting of Tennyson's lines from sections XII and LVI of "In Memoriam A.H.H.," his lament for his dead friend.
[3] The town is usually thought to be Wheeling, Virginia (now West Virginia), which was the author's home.
[4] Cheap tobacco.

and infamy; breathing from infancy to death an air saturated with fog and grease and soot vileness for soul and body. What do you make of a case like that, amateur psychologist? You call it an altogether serious thing to be alive: to these men it is a drunken jest, a joke,—horrible to angels perhaps, to them commonplace enough. My fancy about the river was an idle one: it is no type of such a life. What if it be stagnant and slimy here? It knows that beyond there waits for it odorous sunlight,—quaint old gardens, dusky with soft, green foliage of apple-trees, and flushing crimson with roses,—air, and fields, and mountains. The future of the Welsh puddlers[5] passing just now is not so pleasant. To be stowed away, after his grimy work is done, in a hole in the muddy graveyard, and after that,——*not* air, nor green fields, nor curious roses.

Can you see how foggy the day is? As I stand here, idly tapping the window-pane, and looking out through the rain at the dirty back-yard and the coal-boats below, fragments of an old story float up before me,—a story of this old house into which I happened to come today. You may think it a tiresome story enough, as foggy as the day, sharpened by no sudden flashes of pain or pleasure.—I know: only the outline of a dull life, that long since, with thousands of dull lives like its own, was vainly lived and lost: thousands of them,—massed, vile, slimy lives, like those of the torpid lizards in yonder stagnant water-butt.—Lost? There is a curious point for you to settle, my friend, who study psychology in a lazy, *dilettante* way. Stop a moment. I am going to be honest. This is what I want you to do. I want you to hide your disgust, take no heed to your clean clothes, and come right down with me,—here, into the thickest of the fog and mud and foul effluvia. I want you to hear this story. There is a secret down here, in this nightmare fog, that has lain dumb for centuries: I want to make it a real thing to you. You, Egoist, or Pantheist, or Arminian,[6] busy in making straight paths for your feet on the hills, do not see it clearly,—this terrible question which men here have gone mad and died trying to answer. I dare not put this secret into words. I told you it was dumb. These men, going by with drunken faces and brains full of unawakened power, do not ask it of Society or of God. Their lives ask it; their deaths ask it. There is no reply. I will tell you plainly that I have a great hope; and I bring it to you to be tested. It is this: that this terrible dumb question is its own reply; that it is not the sentence of death we think it, but, from the very extremity of its darkness, the most solemn prophecy which the world has known of the Hope to come. I dare make my meaning no clearer, but will only tell my story. It will, perhaps, seem to you as foul and dark as this thick

---

[5] One who heats and stirs oxidizing substances into pig iron, changing it to wrought iron.
[6] One rejecting predestination. Davis's point is that the poverty of the workers prevents their developing any such intellectualized arguments.

vapor about us, and as pregnant with death; but if your eyes are free as mine are to look deeper, no perfume-tinted dawn will be so fair with promise of the day that shall surely come.

My story is very simple,—only what I remember of the life of one of these men,—a furnace-tender in one of Kirby & John's rolling-mills,—Hugh Wolfe. You know the mills? They took the great order for the Lower Virginia railroads there last winter; run usually with about a thousand men. I cannot tell why I choose the half-forgotten story of this Wolfe more than that of myriads of these furnace-hands. Perhaps because there is a secret underlying sympathy between that story and this day with its impure fog and thwarted sunshine,—or perhaps simply for the reason that this house is the one where the Wolfes lived. There were the father and son,—both hands, as I said, in one of Kirby & John's mills for making railroad-iron,—and Deborah, their cousin, a picker[7] in some of the cotton-mills. The house was rented then to half a dozen families. The Wolfes had two of the cellar-rooms. The old man, like many of the puddlers and feeders[8] of the mills, was Welsh,—had spent half of his life in the Cornish tin-mines. You may pick the Welsh emigrants, Cornish miners, out of the throng passing the windows, any day. They are a trifle more filthy; their muscles are not so brawny; they stoop more. When they are drunk, they neither yell, nor shout, nor stagger, but skulk along like beaten hounds. A pure, unmixed blood, I fancy: shows itself in the slight angular bodies and sharply-cut facial lines. It is nearly thirty years since the Wolfes lived here. Their lives were like those of their class: incessant labor, sleeping in kennel-like rooms, eating rank pork and molasses, drinking—God and the distillers only know what; with an occasional night in jail, to atone for some drunken excess. Is that all of their lives?—of the portion given to them and these their duplicates swarming the streets to-day?—nothing beneath?—all? So many a political reformer will tell you,—and many a private reformer, too, who has gone among them with a heart tender with Christ's charity, and come out outraged, hardened.

One rainy night, about eleven o'clock, a crowd of half-clothed women stopped outside of the cellar-door. They were going home from the cotton-mill.

"Good-night, Deb," said one, a mulatto, steadying herself against the gas-post. She needed the post to steady her. So did more than one of them.

"Dah's a ball to Miss Potts' to-night. Ye'd best come."

"Inteet, Deb, if hur 'll come, hur 'll hef fun," said a shrill Welsh voice in the crowd.

---

[7]A person who operates the machine that picks apart cotton fibers.
[8]One who pours melted iron into casting forms.

Two or three dirty hands were thrust out to catch the gown of the woman, who was groping for the latch of the door.

"No."

"No? Where's Kit Small, then?"

"Begorra![9] on the spools. Alleys behint, though we helped her, we dud. An wid ye! Let Deb alone! It's ondacent frettin' a quiet body. Be the powers, an' we'll have a night of it! there 'll be lashin's o' drink,—the Vargent[10] be blessed and praised for 't!"

They went on, the mulatto inclining for a moment to show fight, and drag the woman Wolfe off with them; but, being pacified, she staggered away.

Deborah groped her way into the cellar, and, after considerable stumbling, kindled a match, and lighted a tallow dip, that sent a yellow glimmer over the room. It was low, damp,—the earthen floor covered with a green, slimy moss,—a fetid air smothering the breath. Old Wolfe lay asleep on a heap of straw, wrapped in a torn horse-blanket. He was a pale, meek little man, with a white face and red rabbit-eyes. The woman Deborah was like him; only her face was even more ghastly, her lips bluer, her eyes more watery. She wore a faded cotton gown and a slouching bonnet. When she walked, one could see that she was deformed, almost a hunchback. She trod softly, so as not to waken him, and went through into the room beyond. There she found by the half-extinguished fire an iron saucepan filled with cold boiled potatoes, which she put upon a broken chair with a pint-cup of ale. Placing the old candlestick beside this dainty repast, she untied her bonnet, which hung limp and wet over her face, and prepared to eat her supper. It was the first food that had touched her lips since morning. There was enough of it, however: there is not always. She was hungry,—one could see that easily enough,—and not drunk, as most of her companions would have been found at this hour. She did not drink, this woman,—her face told that, too,—nothing stronger than ale. Perhaps the weak, flaccid wretch had some stimulant in her pale life to keep her up,—some love or hope, it might be, or urgent need. When that stimulant was gone, she would take to whiskey. Man cannot live by work alone. While she was skinning the potatoes, and munching them, a noise behind her made her stop.

"Janey!" she called, lifting the candle and peering into the darkness. "Janey, are you there?"

A heap of ragged coats was heaved up, and the face of a young girl emerged, staring sleepily at the woman.

"Deborah," she said, at last, "I'm here the night."

[9]Idiomatic form of "By God."
[10]The Virgin Mary.

"Yes, child. Hur's welcome," she said, quietly eating on.

The girl's face was haggard and sickly; her eyes were heavy with sleep and hunger; real Milesian eyes they were, dark, delicate blue, glooming out from black shadows with a pitiful fright.

"I was alone," she said, timidly.

"Where's the father?" asked Deborah, holding out a potato, which the girl greedily seized.

"He's beyant,—wid Haley,—in the stone house." (Did you ever hear the word *jail* from an Irish mouth?) "I came here. Hugh told me never to stay me-lone."

"Hugh?"

"Yes."

A vexed frown crossed her face. The girl saw it, and added quickly,—

"I have not seen Hugh the day, Deb. The old man says his watch lasts till the mornin'."

The woman sprang up, and hastily began to arrange some bread and flitch[11] in a tin pail, and to pour her own measure of ale into a bottle. Tying on her bonnet, she blew out the candle.

"Lay ye down, Janey dear," she said, gently, covering her with the old rags. "Hur can eat the potatoes, if hur's hungry."

"Where are ye goin', Deb? The rain's sharp."

"To the mill, with Hugh's supper."

"Let him bide till th' morn. Sit ye down."

"No, no,"—sharply pushing her off. "The boy'll starve."

She hurried from the cellar, while the child wearily coiled herself up for sleep. The rain was falling heavily, as the woman, pail in hand, emerged from the mouth of the alley, and turned down the narrow street, that stretched out, long and black, miles before her. Here and there a flicker of gas lighted an uncertain space of muddy footwalk and gutter; the long rows of houses, except an occasional lagerbier shop, were closed; now and then she met a band of mill-hands skulking to or from their work.

Not many even of the inhabitants of a manufacturing town know the vast machinery of system by which the bodies of workmen are governed, that goes on unceasingly from year to year. The hands of each mill are divided into watches that relieve each other as regularly as the sentinels of an army. By night and day the work goes on, the unsleeping engines groan and shriek, the fiery pools of metal boil and surge. Only for a day in the week, in half-courtesy to public censure, the fires are partially veiled; but as soon as the clock strikes midnight, the great furnaces break forth with renewed

---

[11]Very poor quality salt pork.

fury, the clamor begins with fresh, breathless vigor, the engines sob and shriek like "gods in pain."

As Deborah hurried down through the heavy rain, the noise of these thousand engines sounded through the sleep and shadow of the city like far-off thunder. The mill to which she was going lay on the river, a mile below the city-limits. It was far, and she was weak, aching from standing twelve hours at the spools. Yet it was her almost nightly walk to take this man his supper, though at every square she sat down to rest, and she knew she should receive small word of thanks.

Perhaps, if she had possessed an artist's eye, the picturesque oddity of the scene might have made her step stagger less, and the path seem shorter; but to her the mills were only "summat deilish[12] to look at by night."

The road leading to the mills had been quarried from the solid rock, which rose abrupt and bare on one side of the cinder-covered road, while the river, sluggish and black, crept past on the other. The mills for rolling iron are simply immense tent-like roofs, covering acres of ground, open on every side. Beneath these roofs Deborah looked in on a city of fires, that burned hot and fiercely in the night. Fire in every horrible form: pits of flame waving in the wind; liquid metal-flames writhing in tortuous streams through the sand; wide caldrons filled with boiling fire, over which bent ghastly wretches stirring the strange brewing; and through all, crowds of half-clad men, looking like revengeful ghosts in the red light, hurried, throwing masses of glittering fire. It was like a street in Hell. Even Deborah muttered, as she crept through, " 'T looks like t' Devil's place!" It did,—in more ways than one.

She found the man she was looking for, at last, heaping coal on a furnace. He had not time to eat his supper; so she went behind the furnace, and waited. Only a few men were with him, and they noticed her only by a "Hyur comes t' hunchback, Wolfe."

Deborah was stupid with sleep; her back pained her sharply; and her teeth chattered with cold, with the rain that soaked her clothes and dripped from her at every step. She stood, however, patiently holding the pail, and waiting.

"Hout, woman! ye look like a drowned cat. Come near to the fire,"—said one of the men, approaching to scrape away the ashes.

She shook her head. Wolfe had forgotten her. He turned, hearing the man, and came closer.

"I did no' think; gi' me my supper, woman."

She watched him eat with a painful eagerness. With a woman's quick instinct, she saw that he was not hungry,—was eating to please her. Her pale, watery eyes began to gather a strange light.

---

[12]Idiomatic for "somewhat devilish."

"Is't good, Hugh? T' ale was a bit sour, I feared."

"No, good enough." He hesitated a moment. "Ye're tired, poor lass! Bide here till I go. Lay down there on that heap of ash, and go to sleep."

He threw her an old coat for a pillow, and turned to his work. The heap was the refuse of the burnt iron, and was not a hard bed; the half-smothered warmth, too, penetrated her limbs, dulling their pain and cold shiver.

Miserable enough she looked, lying there on the ashes like a limp, dirty rag,—yet not an unfitting figure to crown the scene of hopeless discomfort and veiled crime: more fitting, if one looked deeper into the heart of things,— at her thwarted woman's form, her colorless life, her waking stupor that smothered pain and hunger,—even more fit to be a type of her class. Deeper yet if one could look, was there nothing worth reading in this wet, faded thing, half-covered with ashes? no story of a soul filled with groping passionate love, heroic unselfishness, fierce jealousy? of years of weary trying to please the one human being whom she loved, to gain one look of real heart-kindness from him? If anything like this were hidden beneath the pale, bleared eyes, and dull, washed-out-looking face, no one had ever taken the trouble to read its faint signs: not the half-clothed furnace-tender, Wolfe, certainly. Yet he was kind to her: it was his nature to be kind, even to the very rats that swarmed in the cellar: kind to her in just the same way. She knew that. And it might be that very knowledge had given to her face its apathy and vacancy more than her low, torpid life. One sees that dead, vacant look steal sometimes over the rarest, finest of women's faces,—in the very midst, it may be, of their warmest summer's day; and then one can guess at the secret of intolerable solitude that lies hid beneath the delicate laces and brilliant smile. There was no warmth, no brilliancy, no summer for this woman; so the stupor and vacancy had time to gnaw into her face perpetually. She was young, too, though no one guessed it; so the gnawing was the fiercer.

She lay quiet in the dark corner, listening, through the monotonous din and uncertain glare of the works, to the dull plash of the rain in the far distance,—shrinking back whenever the man Wolfe happened to look towards her. She knew, in spite of all his kindness, that there was that in her face and form which made him loathe the sight of her. She felt by instinct, although she could not comprehend it, the finer nature of the man, which made him among his fellow-workmen something unique, set apart. She knew, that, down under all the vileness and coarseness of his life, there was a groping passion for whatever was beautiful and pure,—that his soul sickened with disgust at her deformity even when his words were kindest. Through this dull consciousness, which never left her, came, like a sting, the recollection of the dark blue eyes and lithe figure of the little Irish girl she had left in the cellar. The recollection struck through even her stupid intellect with a vivid glow of beauty and of grace. Little Janey, timid, helpless, clinging to Hugh as her only friend: that was the sharp thought, the bitter thought, that drove into the glazed eyes a fierce light of pain. You laugh at it? Are pain and jealousy less savage realities down here in this place I am taking you to than in your own house or your own heart,—your heart, which they clutch at sometimes? The note is the same, I fancy, be the octave high or low.

If you could go into this mill where Deborah lay, and drag out from the hearts of these men the terrible tragedy of their lives, taking it as a symptom of the disease of their class, no ghost Horror would terrify you more. A reality of soul-starvation, of living death, that meets you every day under the besotted faces on the street,—I can paint nothing of this, only give you the outside outlines of a night, a crisis in the life of one man: whatever muddy depth of soul-history lies beneath you can read according to the eyes God has given you.

Wolfe, while Deborah watched him as a spaniel its master, bent over the furnace with his iron pole, unconscious of her scrutiny, only stopping to receive orders. Physically, Nature had promised the man but little. He had already lost the strength and instinct vigor of a man, his muscles were thin, his nerves weak, his face (a meek, woman's face) haggard, yellow with consumption. In the mill he was known as one of the girl-men: "Molly Wolfe" was his *sobriquet*.[13] He was never seen in the cockpit,[14] did not own a terrier, drank but seldom; when he did, desperately. He fought sometimes, but was always thrashed, pommelled to a jelly. The man was game enough, when his blood was up: but he was no favorite in the mill; he had the taint of school-learning on him,—not to a dangerous extent, only a quarter or so in the free-school in fact, but enough to ruin him as a good hand in a fight.

For other reasons, too, he was not popular. Not one of themselves, they felt that, though outwardly as filthy and ash-covered; silent, with foreign thoughts and longings breaking out through his quietness in innumerable curious ways: this one, for instance. In the neighboring furnace-buildings lay great heaps of the refuse from the ore after the pig-metal is run. *Korl* we call it here: a light, porous substance, of a delicate, waxen, flesh-colored tinge. Out of the blocks of this korl, Wolfe, in his off-hours from the furnace, had a habit of chipping and moulding figures,—hideous, fantastic enough but sometimes strangely beautiful: even the mill-men saw that, while they jeered at him. It was a curious fancy in the man, almost a passion. The few hours for rest he spent hewing and hacking with his blunt knife, never speaking, until his watch came again,—working at one figure for months, and, when it

---

[13]Nickname.
[14]The area where cockfights were held.

was finished, breaking it to pieces perhaps, in a fit of disappointment. A morbid, gloomy man, untaught, unled, left to feed his soul in grossness and crime, and hard, grinding labor.

I want you to come down and look at this Wolfe, standing there among the lowest of his kind, and see him just as he is, that you may judge him justly when you hear the story of this night. I want you to look back, as he does every day, at his birth in vice, his starved infancy; to remember the heavy years he has groped through as boy and man,—the slow, heavy years of constant, hot work. So long ago he began, that he thinks sometimes he has worked there for ages. There is no hope that it will ever end. Think that God put into this man's soul a fierce thirst for beauty,—to know it, to create it; to *be*— something, he knows not what,—other than he is. There are moments when a passing cloud, the sun glinting on the purple thistles, a kindly smile, a child's face, will rouse him to a passion of pain,—when his nature starts up with a mad cry of rage against God, man, whoever it is that has forced this vile, slimy life upon him. With all this groping, this mad desire, a great blind intellect stumbling through wrong, a loving poet's heart, the man was by habit only a coarse, vulgar laborer, familiar with sights and words you would blush to name. Be just: when I tell you about this night, see him as he is. Be just,— not like man's law, which seizes on one isolated fact, but like God's judging angel, whose clear, sad eye saw all the countless cankering days of this man's life, all the countless nights, when, sick with starving, his soul fainted in him, before it judged him for this night, the saddest of all.

I called this night the crisis of his life. If it was, it stole on him unawares. These great turning-days of life cast no shadow before, slip by unconsciously. Only a trifle, a little turn of the rudder, and the ship goes to heaven or hell.

Wolfe, while Deborah watched him, dug into the furnace of melting iron with his pole, dully thinking only how many rails the lump would yield. It was late,—nearly Sunday morning; another hour, and the heavy work would be done,—only the furnaces to replenish and cover for the next day. The workmen were growing more noisy, shouting, as they had to do, to be heard over the deep clamor of the mills. Suddenly they grew less boisterous,—at the far end, entirely silent. Something unusual had happened. After a moment, the silence came nearer; the men stopped their jeers and drunken choruses. Deborah, stupidly lifting up her head, saw the cause of the quiet. A group of five or six men were slowly approaching, stopping to examine each furnace as they came. Visitors often came to see the mills after night: except by growing less noisy, the men took no notice of them. The furnace where Wolfe worked was near the bounds of the works; they halted there hot and tired: a walk over one of these great foundries is no trifling task. The woman, drawing out of sight, turned over to sleep. Wolfe, seeing them stop, suddenly roused from his indifferent stupor, and watched them keenly. He knew some of them: the overseer, Clarke,—a son of Kirby, one of the mill-owners,—and a Doctor May, one of the town-physicians. The other two were strangers. Wolfe came closer. He seized eagerly every chance that brought him into contact with this mysterious class that shone down on him perpetually with the glamour of another order of being. What made the difference between them? That was the mystery of his life. He had a vague notion that perhaps to-night he could find it out. One of the strangers sat down on a pile of bricks, and beckoned young Kirby to his side.

"This *is* hot, with a vengeance. A match, please?"—lighting his cigar. "But the walk is worth the trouble. If it were not that you must have heard it so often, Kirby, I would tell you that your works look like Dante's Inferno."[15]

Kirby laughed.

"Yes. Yonder is Farinata himself in the burning tomb,"—pointing to some figure in the shimmering shadows.

"Judging from some of the faces of your men," said the other, "they bid fair to try the reality of Dante's vision, some day."

Young Kirby looked curiously around, as if seeing the faces of his hands for the first time.

"They're bad enough, that's true. A desperate set, I fancy. Eh, Clarke?"

The overseer did not hear him. He was talking of net profits just then,—giving, in fact, a schedule of the annual business of the firm to a sharp peering little Yankee, who jotted down notes on a paper laid on the crown of his hat: a reporter for one of the city-papers, getting up a series of reviews of the leading manufactories. The other gentlemen had accompanied them merely for amusement. They were silent until the notes were finished, drying their feet at the furnaces, and sheltering their faces from the intolerable heat. At last the overseer concluded with—

"I believe that is a pretty fair estimate, Captain."

"Here, some of you men!" said Kirby, "bring up those boards. We may as well sit down, gentlemen, until the rain is over. It cannot last much longer at this rate."

"Pig-metal,"—mumbled the reporter,—"um!—coal facilities,—um!—hands employed, twelve hundred,—bitumen,—um!—all right, I believe, Mr. Clarke;—sinking-fund,—what did you say was your sinking-fund?"

"Twelve hundred hands?" said the stranger, the young man who had first spoken. "Do you control their votes, Kirby?"

"Control? No." The young man smiled complacently. "But my father

---

[15]From Dante Alighieri's poem, describing the poet's imaginary journey to Hell. In the poem, Farinata degli Uberti is submerged in a burning tomb as punishment for heresy. While the visitors discuss Dante, the listening workers are completely excluded from the reference.

brought seven hundred votes to the polls for his candidate last November. No force-work, you understand,—only a speech or two, a hint to form themselves into a society, and a bit of red and blue bunting to make them a flag. The Invincible Roughs,—I believe that is their name. I forget the motto: 'Our country's hope,' I think."

There was a laugh. The young man talking to Kirby sat with an amused light in his cool gray eye, surveying critically the half-clothed figures of the puddlers, and the slow swing of their brawny muscles. He was a stranger in the city,—spending a couple of months in the borders of a Slave State, to study the institutions of the South,—a brother-in-law of Kirby's,—Mitchell. He was an amateur gymnast,—hence his anatomical eye; a patron, in a *blasé* way, of the prize-ring; a man who sucked the essence out of a science or philosophy in an indifferent, gentlemanly way; who took Kant, Novalis, Humboldt,[16] for what they were worth in his own scales; accepting all, despising nothing, in heaven, earth, or hell, but one-idead men; with a temper yielding and brilliant as summer water, until his Self was touched, when it was ice, though brilliant still. Such men are not rare in the States.

As he knocked the ashes from his cigar, Wolfe caught with a quick pleasure the contour of the white hand, the blood-glow of a red ring he wore. His voice, too, and that of Kirby's touched him like music,—low, even, with chording cadences. About this man Mitchell hung the impalpable atmosphere belonging to the thorough-bred gentlemen. Wolfe, scraping away the ashes beside him, was conscious of it, did obeisance to it with his artist sense, unconscious that he did so.

The rain did not cease. Clarke and the reporter left the mills; the others, comfortably seated near the furnace, lingered, smoking and talking in a desultory way. Greek would not have been more unintelligible to the furnace-tenders, whose presence they soon forgot entirely. Kirby drew out a newspaper from his pocket and read aloud some article, which they discussed eagerly. At every sentence, Wolfe listened more and more like a dumb, hopeless animal, with a duller, more stolid look creeping over his face, glancing now and then at Mitchell, marking acutely every smallest sign of refinement, then back to himself, seeing as in a mirror his filthy body, his more stained soul.

Never! He had no words for such a thought, but he knew now, in all the sharpness of the bitter certainty, that between them there was a great gulf never to be passed. Never!

The bell of the mills rang for midnight. Sunday morning had dawned. Whatever hidden message lay in the tolling bells floated past these men un-

[16]German philosopher, poet, and naturalist, respectively (German institutions of learning were considered superior to American). Davis suggests that Mitchell may be educated but doesn't know much about the human condition.

known. Yet it was there. Veiled in the solemn music ushering the risen Saviour was a key-note to solve the darkest secrets of a world gone wrong,—even this social riddle which the brain of the grimy puddler grappled with madly to-night.

The men began to withdraw the metal from the caldrons. The mills were deserted on Sundays, except by the hands who fed the fires, and those who had no lodgings and slept usually on the ash-heaps. The three strangers sat still during the next hour, watching the men cover the furnaces, laughing now and then at some jest of Kirby's.

"Do you know," said Mitchell, "I like this view of the works better than when the glare was fiercest? These heavy shadows and the amphitheatre of smothered fires are ghostly, unreal. One could fancy these red smouldering lights to be the half-shut eyes of wild beasts, and the spectral figures their victims in the den."

Kirby laughed. "You are fanciful. Come, let us get out of the den. The spectral figures, as you call them, are a little too real for me to fancy a close proximity in the darkness,—unarmed, too."

The others rose, buttoning their overcoats, and lighting cigars.

"Raining, still," said Doctor May, "and hard. Where did we leave the coach, Mitchell?"

"At the other side of the works.—Kirby, what's that?"

Mitchell started back, half-frightened, as, suddenly turning a corner, the white figure of a woman faced him in the darkness,—a woman, white, of giant proportions, crouching on the ground, her arms flung out in some wild gesture of warning.

"Stop! Make that fire burn there!" cried Kirby, stopping short.

The flame burst out, flashing the gaunt figure into bold relief.

Mitchell drew a long breath.

"I thought it was alive," he said, going up curiously.

The others followed.

"Not marble, eh?" asked Kirby, touching it.

One of the lower overseers stopped.

"Korl, Sir."

"Who did it?"

"Can't say. Some of the hands; chipped it out in off-hours."

"Chipped to some purpose, I should say. What a flesh-tint the stuff has! Do you see, Mitchell?"

"I see."

He had stepped aside where the light fell boldest on the figure, looking at it in silence. There was not one line of beauty or grace in it: a nude woman's form, muscular, grown coarse with labor, the powerful limbs instinct with some one poignant longing. One idea: there it was in the tense, rigid muscles, the clutching hands, the wild, eager face, like that of a starving wolf's. Kirby and Doctor May walked around it, critical, curious. Mitchell stood aloof, silent. The figure touched him strangely.

"Not badly done," said Doctor May. "Where did the fellow learn that sweep of the muscles in the arm and hand? Look at them! They are groping,—do you see?—clutching: the peculiar action of a man dying of thirst."

"They have ample facilities for studying anatomy," sneered Kirby, glancing at the half-naked figures.

"Look," continued the Doctor, "at this bony wrist, and the strained sinews of the instep! A working-woman,—the very type of her class."

"God forbid!" muttered Mitchell.

"Why?" demanded May. "What does the fellow intend by the figure? I cannot catch the meaning."

"Ask him," said the other, dryly. "There he stands,"—pointing to Wolfe, who stood with a group of men, leaning on his ash-rake.

The Doctor beckoned him with the affable smile which kind-hearted men put on, when talking to these people.

"Mr. Mitchell has picked you out as the man who did this,—I'm sure I don't know why. But what did you mean by it?"

"She be hungry."

Wolfe's eyes answered Mitchell, not the Doctor.

"Oh-h! But what a mistake you have made, my fine fellow! You have given no sign of starvation to the body. It is strong,—terribly strong. It has the mad, half-despairing gesture of drowning."

Wolfe stammered, glanced appealingly at Mitchell, who saw the soul of the thing, he knew. But the cool, probing eyes were turned on himself now,— mocking, cruel, relentless.

"Not hungry for meat," the furnace-tender said at last.

"What then? Whiskey?" jeered Kirby, with a coarse laugh.

Wolfe was silent a moment, thinking.

"I dunno," he said, with a bewildered look. "It mebbe. Summat to make her live, I think,—like you. Whiskey ull do it, in a way."

The young man laughed again. Mitchell flashed a look of disgust some-where,—not at Wolfe.

"May," he broke out impatiently, "are you blind? Look at that woman's face! It asks questions of God, and says, 'I have a right to know.' Good God, how hungry it is!"

They looked a moment; then May turned to the mill-owner:—

"Have you many such hands as this? What are you going to do with them? Keep them at puddling iron?"

Kirby shrugged his shoulders. Mitchell's look had irritated him.

"*Ce n'est pas mon affaire.*[17] I have no fancy for nursing infant geniuses. I suppose there are some stray gleams of mind and soul among these wretches. The Lord will take care of his own; or else they can work out their own salvation. I have heard you call our American system a ladder which any man can scale. Do you doubt it? Or perhaps you want to banish all social ladders, and put us all on a flat table-land,—eh, May?"

The Doctor looked vexed, puzzled. Some terrible problem lay hid in this woman's face, and troubled these men. Kirby waited for an answer, and, receiving none, went on, warming with his subject.

"I tell you, there's something wrong that no talk of '*Liberté*' or '*Egalité*'[18] will do away. If I had the making of men, these men who do the lowest part of the world's work should be machines,—nothing more,—hands. It would be kindness. God help them! What are taste, reason, to creatures who must live such lives as that?" He pointed to Deborah, sleeping on the ash-heap. "So many nerves to sting them to pain. What if God had put your brain, with all its agony of touch, into your fingers, and bid you work and strike with that?"

"You think you could govern the world better?" laughed the Doctor.

"I do not think at all."

"That is true philosophy. Drift with the stream, because you cannot dive deep enough to find bottom, eh?"

"Exactly," rejoined Kirby. "I do not think. I wash my hands of all social problems,—slavery, caste, white or black. My duty to my operatives has a narrow limit,—the pay-hour on Saturday night. Outside of that, if they cut korl, or cut each other's throats, (the more popular amusement of the two,) I am not responsible."

The Doctor sighed,—a good honest sigh, from the depths of his stomach.

"God help us! Who is responsible?"

"Not I, I tell you," said Kirby, testily. "What has the man who pays them money to do with their souls' concerns, more than the grocer or butcher who takes it?"

"And yet," said Mitchell's cynical voice, "look at her! How hungry she is!"

Kirby tapped his boot with his cane. No one spoke. Only the dumb face of the rough image looking into their faces with the awful question, "What shall we do to be saved?" Only Wolfe's face, with its heavy weight of brain, its weak, uncertain mouth, its desperate eyes, out of which looked the soul of

[17]Kirby echoes Pontius Pilate before the crucifixion of Jesus Christ: "It is not my affair."
[18]During the French Revolution, "Liberty" and "Equality" were rallying cries.

his class,—only Wolfe's face turned towards Kirby's. Mitchell laughed,—a cool, musical laugh.

"Money has spoken!" he said, seating himself lightly on a stone with the air of an amused spectator at a play. "Are you answered?"—turning to Wolfe his clear, magnetic face.

Bright and deep and cold as Arctic air, the soul of the man lay tranquil beneath. He looked at the furnace-tender as he had looked at a rare mosaic in the morning; only the man was the more amusing study of the two.

"Are you answered? Why, May, look at him! *De profundis clamavi.*[19] Or, to quote in English, 'Hungry and thirsty, his soul faints in him.' And so Money sends back its answer into the depths through you, Kirby! Very clear the answer, too!—I think I remember reading the same words somewhere:—washing your hands in Eau de Cologne, and saying, 'I am innocent of the blood of this man. See ye to it!' "

Kirby flushed angrily.

"You quote Scripture freely."

"Do I not quote correctly? I think I remember another line, which may amend my meaning: 'Inasmuch as ye did it unto one of the least of these, ye did it unto me.' Deist?[20] Bless you, man, I was raised on the milk of the Word. Now, Doctor, the pocket of the world having uttered its voice, what has the heart to say? You are a philanthropist, in a small way,—*n'est ce pas?*[21] Here, boy, this gentleman can show you how to cut korl better,—or your destiny. Go on, May!"

"I think a mocking devil possesses you to-night," rejoined the Doctor, seriously.

He went to Wolfe and put his hand kindly on his arm. Something of a vague idea possessed the Doctor's brain that much good was to be done here by a friendly word or two: a latent genius to be warmed into life by a waited-for sunbeam. Here it was: he had brought it. So he went on complacently:—

"Do you know, boy, you have it in you to be a great sculptor, a great man?—do you understand?" (talking down to the capacity of his hearer: it is a way people have with children, and men like Wolfe)—"to live a better, stronger life than I, or Mr. Kirby here? A man may make himself anything he chooses. God has given you stronger powers than many men,—me, for instance."

May stopped, heated, glowing with his own magnanimity. And it was magnanimous. The puddler had drunk in every word, looking through the

[19]From Psalm 130.1, the Latin can be translated, "Out of the depths I have cried unto thee."
[20]One who believes in God's creating the world, but then not meddling in human affairs.
[21]"Aren't you?"

Doctor's flurry, and generous heat, and self-approval, into his will, with those slow, absorbing eyes of his.

"Make yourself what you will. It is your right."

"I know," quietly. "Will you help me?"

Mitchell laughed again. The Doctor turned now, in a passion,—

"You know, Mitchell, I have not the means. You know, if I had, it is in my heart to take this boy and educate him for"—

"The glory of God, and the glory of John May."

May did not speak for a moment; then, controlled, he said,—

"Why should one be raised, when myriads are left?—I have not the money, boy," to Wolfe, shortly.

"Money?" He said it over slowly, as one repeats the guessed answer to a riddle, doubtfully. "That is it? Money?"

"Yes, money,—that is it," said Mitchell, rising, and drawing his furred coat about him. "You've found the cure for all the world's diseases.—Come, May, find your good-humor, and come home. This damp wind chills my very bones. Come and preach your Saint-Simonian[22] doctrines to-morrow to Kirby's hands. Let them have a clear idea of the rights of the soul, and I'll venture next week they'll strike for higher wages. That will be the end of it."

"Will you send the coach-driver to this side of the mills?" asked Kirby, turning to Wolfe.

He spoke kindly: it was his habit to do so. Deborah, seeing the puddler go, crept after him. The three men waited outside. Doctor May walked up and down, chafed. Suddenly he stopped.

"Go back, Mitchell! You say the pocket and the heart of the world speak without meaning to these people. What has its head to say? Taste, culture, refinement? Go!"

Mitchell was leaning against a brick wall. He turned his head indolently, and looked into the mills. There hung about the place a thick, unclean odor. The slightest motion of his hand marked that he perceived it, and his insufferable disgust. That was all. May said nothing, only quickened his angry tramp.

"Besides," added Mitchell, giving a corollary to his answer, "it would be of no use. I am not one of them."

"You do not mean"—said May, facing him.

"Yes, I mean just that. Reform is born of need, not pity. No vital movement of the people's has worked down, for good or evil; fermented, instead, carried up the heaving, cloggy mass. Think back through history, and you will know it. What will this lowest deep—thieves, Magdalens, negroes—do with the

[22] A kind of early socialism.

213

light filtered through ponderous Church creeds, Baconian theories, Goethe schemes? Some day, out of their bitter need will be thrown up their own light-bringer,—their Jean Paul, their Cromwell, their Messiah."[23]

"Bah!" was the Doctor's inward criticism. However, in practice, he adopted the theory; for, when, night and morning, afterwards, he prayed that power might be given these degraded souls to rise, he glowed at heart, recognizing an accomplished duty.

Wolfe and the woman had stood in the shadow of the works as the coach drove off. The Doctor had held out his hand in a frank, generous way, telling him to "take care of himself, and to remember it was his right to rise." Mitchell had simply touched his hat, as to an equal, with a quiet look of thorough recognition. Kirby had thrown Deborah some money, which she found, and clutched eagerly enough. They were gone now, all of them. The man sat down on the cinder-road, looking up into the murky sky.

"'T be late, Hugh. Wunnot hur come?"

He shook his head doggedly, and the woman crouched out of his sight against the wall. Do you remember rare moments when a sudden light flashed over yourself, your world, God? when you stood on a mountain-peak, seeing your life as it might have been, as it is? one quick instant, when custom lost its force and everyday usage? when your friend, wife, brother, stood in a new light? your soul was bared, and the grave,—a fore-taste of the nakedness of the Judgment Day? So it came before him, his life, that night. The slow tides of pain he had borne gathered themselves up and surged against his soul. His squalid daily life, the brutal coarseness eating into his brain, as the ashes into his skin: before, these things had been a dull aching into his consciousness; to-night, they were reality. He gripped the filthy red shirt that clung, stiff with soot, about him, and tore it savagely from his arm. The flesh beneath was muddy with grease and ashes,—and the heart beneath that! And the soul? God knows.

Then flashed before his vivid poetic sense the man who had left him,—the pure face, the delicate, sinewy limbs, in harmony with all he knew of beauty or truth. In his cloudy fancy he had pictured a Something like this. He had found it in this Mitchell, even when he idly scoffed at his pain: a Man all-knowing, all-seeing, crowned by Nature, reigning,—the keen glance of his eye falling like a sceptre on other men. And yet his instinct taught him that he too—He! He looked at himself with sudden loathing, sick, wrung his hands with a cry, and then was silent. With all the phantoms of his heated,

---

[23]As before, the first set of phrases, mentioning the British essayist Francis Bacon (1561–1624) and German writer Johann Wolfgang von Goethe (1749–1832), suggests the uselessness of their work to the laborers. The second set suggests that these people need leaders who will come from their own class.

ignorant fancy, Wolfe had not been vague in his ambitions. They were practical, slowly built up before him out of his knowledge of what he could do. Through years he had day by day made this hope a real thing to himself,—a clear, projected figure of himself, as he might become.

Able to speak, to know what was best, to raise these men and women working at his side up with him: sometimes he forgot this defined hope in the frantic anguish to escape,—only to escape,—out of the wet, the pain, the ashes, somewhere, anywhere,—only for one moment of free air on a hill-side, to lie down and let his sick soul throb itself out in the sunshine. But to-night he panted for life. The savage strength of his nature was roused; his cry was fierce to God for justice.

"Look at me!" he said to Deborah, with a low, bitter laugh, striking his puny chest savagely. "What am I worth, Deb? Is it my fault that I am no better? My fault? My fault?"

He stopped, stung with a sudden remorse, seeing her hunchback shape writhing with sobs. For Deborah was crying thankless tears, according to the fashion of women.

"God forgi' me, woman! Things go harder wi' you nor me. It's a worse share."

He got up and helped her to rise; and they went doggedly down the muddy street, side by side.

"It's all wrong," he muttered, slowly,—"all wrong! I dunnot understan'. But it'll end some day."

"Come home, Hugh!" she said, coaxingly; for he had stopped, looking around bewildered.

"Home,—and back to the mill!" He went on saying this over to himself, as if he would mutter down every pain in this dull despair.

She followed him through the fog, her blue lips chattering with cold. They reached the cellar at last. Old Wolfe had been drinking since she went out, and had crept nearer the door. The girl Janey slept heavily in the corner. He went up to her, touching softly the worn white arm with his fingers. Some bitterer thought stung him, as he stood there. He wiped the drops from his forehead, and went into the room beyond, livid, trembling. A hope, trifling, perhaps, but very dear, had died just then out of the poor puddler's life, as he looked at the sleeping, innocent girl,—some plan for the future, in which she had borne a part. He gave it up that moment, then and forever. Only a trifle, perhaps, to us: his face grew a shade paler,—that was all. But, somehow, the man's soul, as God and the angels looked down on it, never was the same afterwards.

Deborah followed him into the inner room. She carried a candle, which she placed on the floor, closing the door after her. She had seen the look on his face, as he turned away: her own grew deadly. Yet, as she came up to him, her eyes glowed. He was seated on an old chest, quiet, holding his face in his hands.

"Hugh!" she said, softly.

He did not speak.

"Hugh, did hur hear what the man said,—him with the clear voice? Did hur hear? Money, money,—that it wud do all?"

He pushed her away,—gently, but he was worn out; her rasping tone fretted him.

"Hugh!"

The candle flared a pale yellow light over the cobwebbed brick walls, and the woman standing there. He looked at her. She was young, in deadly earnest; her faded eyes, and wet, ragged figure caught from their frantic eagerness a power akin to beauty.

"Hugh, it is true! Money ull do it! Oh, Hugh, boy, listen till me! He said it true! It is money!"

"I know. Go back! I do not want you here."

"Hugh, it is t' last time. I'll never worrit hur again."

There were tears in her voice now, but she choked them back.

"Hear till me only to-night! If one of t' witch people wud come, them we heard of t' home, and gif hur all hur wants, what then? Say, Hugh!"

"What do you mean?"

"I mean money."

Her whisper shrilled through his brain.

"If one of t' witch dwarfs wud come from t' lane moors to-night, and gif hur money, to go out,—*out*, I say,—out, lad, where t' sun shines, and t' heath grows, and t' ladies walk in silken gownds, and God stays all t' time,—where t' man lives that talked to us to-night,—Hugh knows,—Hugh could walk there like a king!"

He thought the woman mad, tried to check her, but she went on, fierce in her eager haste.

"If *I* were t' witch dwarf, if I had t' money, wud hur thank me? Wud hur take me out o' this place wid hur and Janey? I wud not come into the gran' house hur wud build, to vex hur wid t' hunch,—only at night when t' shadows were dark, stand far off to see hur."

Mad? Yes! Are many of us mad in this way?

"Poor Deb! poor Deb!" he said, soothingly.

"It is here," she said, suddenly jerking into his hand a small roll. "I took it! I did it! Me, me!—not hur! I shall be hanged, I shall be burnt in hell, if anybody knows I took it! Out of his pocket, as he leaned against t' bricks. Hur knows?"

216

She thrust it into his hand, and then, her errand done, began to gather chips together to make a fire, choking down hysteric sobs.

"Has it come to this?"

That was all he said. The Welsh Wolfe blood was honest. The roll was a small green pocket-book containing one or two gold pieces, and a check for an incredible amount, as it seemed to the poor puddler. He laid it down, hiding his face again in his hands.

"Hugh, don't be angry wud me! It's only poor Deb,—hur knows?"

He took the long skinny fingers kindly in his.

"Angry? God help me, no! Let me sleep. I am tired."

He threw himself heavily down on the wooden bench, stunned with pain and weariness. She brought some old rags to cover him.

It was late on Sunday evening before he awoke. I tell God's truth, when I say he had then no thought of keeping this money. Deborah had hid it in his pocket. He found it there. She watched him eagerly, as he took it out.

"I must gif it to him," he said, reading her face.

"Hur knows," she said with a bitter sigh of disappointment. "But it is hur right to keep it."

His right! The word struck him. Doctor May had used the same. He washed himself, and went out to find this man Mitchell. His right! Why did this chance word cling to him so obstinately? Do you hear the fierce devils whisper in his ear, as he went slowly down the darkening street?

The evening came on, slow and calm. He seated himself at the end of an alley leading into one of the larger streets. His brain was clear to-night, keen, intent, mastering. It would not start back, cowardly, from any hellish temptation, but meet it face to face. Therefore the great temptation of his life came to him veiled by no sophistry, but bold, defiant, owning its own vile name, trusting to one bold blow for victory.

He did not deceive himself. Theft! That was it. At first the word sickened him; then he grappled with it. Sitting there on a broken cart-wheel, the fading day, the noisy groups, the church-bells' tolling passed before him like a panorama, while the sharp struggle went on within. This money! He took it out, and looked at it. If he gave it back, what then? He was going to be cool about it.

People going by to church saw only a sickly mill-boy watching them quietly at the alley's mouth. They did not know that he was mad, or they would not have gone by so quietly: mad with hunger; stretching out his hands to the world, that had given so much to them, for leave to live the life God meant him to live. His soul within him was smothering to death; he wanted so much, thought so much, and *knew*—nothing. There was nothing of which he was certain, except the mill and things there. Of God and heaven he had heard so little, that they were to him what fairy-land is to a child: something real, but not here; very far off. His brain, greedy, dwarfed, full of thwarted energy and unused powers, questioned these men and women going by, coldly, bitterly, that night. Was it not his right to live as they,—a pure life, a good, true-hearted life, full of beauty and kind words? He only wanted to know how to use the strength within him. His heart warmed, as he thought of it. He suffered himself to think of it longer. If he took the money?

Then he saw himself as he might be, strong, helpful, kindly. The night crept on, as this one image slowly evolved itself from the crowd of other thoughts and stood triumphant. He looked at it. As he might be! What wonder, if it blinded him to delirium,—the madness that underlies all revolution, all progress, and all fall?

You laugh at the shallow temptation? You see the error underlying its argument so clearly,—that to him a true life was one of full development rather than self-restraint? that he was deaf to the higher tone in a cry of voluntary suffering for truth's sake than in the fullest flow of spontaneous harmony? I do not plead his cause. I only want to show you the mote in my brother's eye: then you can see clearly to take it out.

The money,—there it lay on his knee, a little blotted slip of paper, nothing in itself; used to raise him out of the pit; something straight from God's hand. A thief! Well, what was it to be a thief? He met the question at last, face to face, wiping the clammy drops of sweat from his forehead. God made this money—the fresh air, too—for his children's use. He never made the difference between poor and rich. The Something who looked down on him that moment through the cool gray sky had a kindly face, he knew,—loved his children alike. Oh, he knew that!

There were times when the soft floods of color in the crimson and purple flames, or the clear depth of amber in the water below the bridge, had somehow given him a glimpse of another world than this,—of an infinite depth of beauty and of quiet somewhere,—somewhere,—a depth of quiet and rest and love. Looking up now, it became strangely real. The sun had sunk quite below the hills, but his last rays struck upward, touching the zenith. The fog had risen, and the town and river were steeped in its thick, gray damp; but overhead, the sun-touched smoke-clouds opened like a cleft ocean,—shifting, rolling seas of crimson mist, waves of billowy silver veined with blood-scarlet, inner depths unfathomable of glancing light. Wolfe's artist-eye grew drunk with color. The gates of that other world! Fading, flashing before him now! What, in that world of Beauty, Content, and Right, were the petty laws, the mine and thine, of mill-owners and mill-hands?

A consciousness of power stirred within him. He stood up. A man,—he thought, stretching out his hands,—free to work, to live, to love! Free! His right! He folded the scrap of paper in his hand. As his nervous fingers took it in, limp and blotted, so his soul took in the mean temptation, lapped it in fancied rights, in dreams of improved existences, drifting and endless as the cloud-seas of color. Clutching it, as if the tightness of his hold would strengthen his sense of possession, he went aimlessly down the street. It was his watch at the mill. He need not go, need never go again, thank God!—shaking off the thought with unspeakable loathing.

Shall I go over the history of the hours of that night? how the man wandered from one to another of his old haunts, with a half-consciousness of bidding them farewell,—lanes and alleys and backyards where the mill-hands lodged,—noting, with a new eagerness, the filth and drunkenness, the pigpens, the ash-heaps covered with potato-skins, the bloated, pimpled women at the doors,—with a new disgust, a new sense of sudden triumph, and, under all, a new, vague dread, unknown before, smothered down, kept under, but still there? It left him but once during the night, when, for the second time in his life, he entered a church. It was a sombre Gothic pile, where the stained light lost itself in far-retreating arches; built to meet the requirements and sympathies of a far other class than Wolfe's. Yet it touched, moved him uncontrollably. The distances, the shadows, the still, marble figures, the mass of silent kneeling worshippers, the mysterious music, thrilled, lifted his soul with a wonderful pain. Wolfe forgot himself, forgot the new life he was going to live, the mean terror gnawing underneath. The voice of the speaker strengthened the charm; it was clear, feeling, full, strong. An old man, who had lived much, suffered much; whose brain was keenly alive, dominant; whose heart was summer-warm with charity. He taught it to-night. He held up Humanity in its grand total; showed the great world-cancer to his people. Who could show it better? He was a Christian reformer; he had studied the age thoroughly; his outlook at man had been free, world-wide, over all time. His faith stood sublime upon the Rock of Ages; his fiery zeal guided vast schemes by which the gospel was to be preached to all nations. How did he preach it to-night? In burning, light-laden words he painted the incarnate Life, Love, the universal Man: words that became reality in the lives of these people,—that lived again in beautiful words and actions, trifling, but heroic. Sin, as he defined it, was a real foe to them; their trials, temptations, were his. His words passed far over the furnace-tender's grasp, toned to suit another class of culture; they sounded in his ears a very pleasant song in an unknown tongue. He meant to cure this world-cancer with a steady eye that had never glared with hunger, and a hand that neither poverty nor strychnine-whiskey[24] had taught to shake. In this morbid, distorted heart of the Welsh puddler he had failed.

[24]Impure and cheap whiskey that sometimes causes illness and death.

Wolfe rose at last, and turned from the church down the street. He looked up: the night had come on foggy, damp; the golden mists had vanished, and the sky lay dull and ash-colored. He wandered again aimlessly down the street, idly wondering what had become of the cloud-sea of crimson and scarlet. The trial-day of this man's life was over, and he had lost the victory. What followed was mere drifting circumstance,—a quicker walking over the path,—that was all. Do you want to hear the end of it? You wish me to make a tragic story out of it? Why, in the police-reports of the morning paper you can find a dozen such tragedies: hints of ship-wrecks unlike any that ever befell on the high seas; hints that here a power was lost to heaven,—that there a soul went down where no tide can ebb or flow. Commonplace enough the hints are,— jocose sometimes, done up in rhyme.

Doctor May, a month after the night I have told you of, was reading to his wife at breakfast from this fourth column of the morning-paper; an un- usual thing,—these police-reports not being, in general, choice reading for ladies; but it was only one item he read.

"Oh, my dear! You remember that man I told you of, that we saw at Kirby's mill?—that was arrested for robbing Mitchell? Here he is; just listen:—'Cir- cuit Court. Judge Day. Hugh Wolfe, operative in Kirby & John's Loudon Mills. Charge, grand larceny. Sentence, nineteen years hard labor in peniten- tiary.'—Scoundrel! Serves him right! After all our kindness that night! Picking Mitchell's pocket at the very time!"

His wife said something about the ingratitude of that kind of people, and then they began to talk of something else.

Nineteen years! How easy that was to read! What a simple word for Judge Day to utter! Nineteen years! Half a lifetime!

Hugh Wolfe sat on the window-ledge of his cell, looking out. His ankles were ironed. Not usual in such cases; but he had made two desperate efforts to escape. "Well," as Haley, the jailer, said, "small blame to him! Nineteen years' imprisonment was not a pleasant thing to look forward to." Haley was very good-natured about it, though Wolfe had fought him savagely.

"When he was first caught," the jailer said afterwards, in telling the story, "before the trial, the fellow was cut down at once,—laid there on that pallet like a dead man, with his hands over his eyes. Never saw a man so cut down in my life. Time of the trial, too, came the queerest dodge of any customer I ever had. Would choose no lawyer. Judge gave him one, of course. Gibson it was. He tried to prove the fellow crazy; but it wouldn't go. Thing was plain as day-light: money found on him. 'T was a hard sentence,—all the law allows; but it was for 'xample's sake. These mill-hands are gettin' onbearable. When the sentence was read, he just looked up, and said the money was his by rights, and that all the world had gone wrong. That night, after the trial, a gentleman came to see him here, name of Mitchell,—him as he stole from. Talked to him for an hour. Thought he came for curiosity, like. After he was gone, thought Wolfe was remarkable quiet, and went into his cell. Found him very low; bed all bloody. Doctor said he had been bleeding at the lungs. He was as weak as a cat; yet, if ye'll b'lieve me, he tried to get a-past me and get out. I just carried him like a baby, and threw him on the pallet. Three days after, he tried it again: that time reached the wall. Lord help you! he fought like a tiger,—giv' some terrible blows. Fightin' for life, you see; for he can't live long, shut up in the stone crib down yonder. Got a death-cough now. 'T took two of us to bring him down that day; so I just put the irons on his feet. There he sits, in there. Goin' to-morrow, with a batch more of 'em. That woman, hunchback, tried with him,—you remember?—she's only got three years. 'Complice. But *she's* a woman, you know. He's been quiet ever since I put on irons: giv' up, I suppose. Looks white, sick-lookin'. It acts different on 'em, bein' sentenced. Most of 'em gets reckless, devilish-like. Some prays awful, and sings them vile songs of the mills, all in a breath. That woman, now, she's desper't'. Been beggin' to see Hugh, as she calls him, for three days. I'm a-goin' to let her in. She don't go with him. Here she is in this next cell. I'm a-goin' now to let her in."

He let her in. Wolfe did not see her. She crept into a corner of the cell, and stood watching him. He was scratching the iron bars of the window with a piece of tin which he had picked up, with an idle, uncertain, vacant stare, just as a child or idiot would do.

"Tryin' to get out, old boy?" laughed Haley. "Them irons will need a crow-bar beside your tin, before you can open 'em."

Wolfe laughed, too, in a senseless way.

"I think I'll get out," he said.

"I believe his brain's touched," said Haley, when he came out.

The puddler scraped away with the tin for half an hour. Still Deborah did not speak. At last she ventured nearer, and touched his arm.

"Blood?" she said, looking at some spots on his coat with a shudder.

He looked up at her. "Why, Deb!" he said, smiling,—such a bright, boyish smile, that it went to poor Deborah's heart directly, and she sobbed and cried out loud.

"Oh, Hugh, lad! Hugh! dunnot look at me, when it wur my fault! To think I brought hur to it! And I loved hur so! Oh, lad, I dud!"

The confession, even in this wretch, came with the woman's blush through the sharp cry.

He did not seem to hear her,—scraping away diligently at the bars with the bit of tin.

Was he going mad? She peered closely into his face. Something she saw there made her draw suddenly back,—something which Haley had not seen, that lay beneath the pinched, vacant look it had caught since the trial, or the curious gray shadow that rested on it. That gray shadow,—yes, she knew what that meant. She had often seen it creeping over women's faces for months, who died at last of slow hunger or consumption. That meant death, distant, lingering: but this—Whatever it was the woman saw, or thought she saw, used as she was to crime and misery, seemed to make her sick with a new horror. Forgetting her fear of him, she caught his shoulders, and looked keenly, steadily, into his eyes.

"Hugh!" she cried, in a desperate whisper,—"oh, boy, not that! for God's sake, not *that!*"

The vacant laugh went off his face, and he answered her in a muttered word or two that drove her away. Yet the words were kindly enough. Sitting there on his pallet, she cried silently a hopeless sort of tears, but did not speak again. The man looked up furtively at her now and then. Whatever his own trouble was, her distress vexed him with a momentary sting.

It was market-day. The narrow window of the jail looked down directly on the carts and wagons drawn up in a long line, where they had unloaded. He could see, too, and hear distinctly the clink of money as it changed hands, the busy crowd of whites and blacks shoving, pushing one another, and the chaffering and swearing at the stalls. Somehow, the sound, more than anything else had done, wakened him up,—made the whole real to him. He was done with the world and the business of it. He let the tin fall, and looked out, pressing his face close to the rusty bars. How they crowded and pushed! And he,—he should never walk that pavement again! There came Neff Sanders, one of the feeders at the mill, with a basket on his arm. Sure enough, Neff was married the other week. He whistled, hoping he would look up; but he did not. He wondered if Neff remembered he was there,—if any of the boys thought of him up there, and thought that he never was to go down that old cinder-road again. Never again! He had not quite understood it before; but now he did. Not for days or years, but never!—that was it.

How clear the light fell on that stall in front of the market! and how like a picture it was, the dark-green heaps of corn, and the crimson beets, and golden melons! There was another with game: how the light flickered on that pheasant's breast, with the purplish blood dripping over the brown feathers! He could see the red shining of the drops, it was so near. In one minute he could be down there. It was just a step. So easy, as it seemed, so natural to go! Yet it could never be—not in all the thousands of years to come—that he should put his foot on that street again! He thought of himself with a sorrowful pity, as of some one else. There was a dog down in the market, walking after his master with such a stately, grave look!—only a dog, yet he could go backwards and forwards just as be pleased: he had good luck! Why, the very vilest cur, yelping there in the gutter, had not lived his life, had been free to act out whatever thought God had put into his brain; while he—No, he would not think of that! He tried to put the thought away, and to listen to a dispute between a countryman and a woman about some meat; but it would come back. He, what had he done to bear this?

Then came the sudden picture of what might have been, and now. He knew what it was to be in the penitentiary,—how it went with men there. He knew how in these long years he should slowly die, but not until soul and body had become corrupt and rotten,—how, when he came out, if he lived to come, even the lowest of the mill-hands would jeer him,—how his hands would be weak, and his brain senseless and stupid. He believed he was almost that now. He put his hand to his head with a puzzled, weary look. It ached, his head, with thinking. He tried to quiet himself. It was only right, perhaps; he had done wrong. But was there right or wrong for such as he? What was right? And who had ever taught him? He thrust the whole matter away. A dark, cold quiet crept through his brain. It was all wrong; but let it be! It was nothing to him more than the others. Let it be!

The door grated, as Haley opened it.

"Come, my woman! Must lock up for t'night. Come, stir yerself!"

She went up and took Hugh's hand.

"Good-night, Deb," he said, carelessly.

She had not hoped he would say more; but the tired pain on her mouth just then was bitterer than death. She took his passive hand and kissed it.

"Hur'll never see Deb again!" she ventured, her lips growing colder and more bloodless.

What did she say that for? Did he not know it? Yet he would not be impatient with poor old Deb. She had trouble of her own, as well as he.

"No, never again," he said, trying to be cheerful.

She stood just a moment, looking at him. Do you laugh at her, standing there, with her hunchback, her rags, her bleared, withered face, and the great despised love tugging at her heart?

"Come, you!" called Haley, impatiently.

She did not move.

"Hugh!" she whispered.

It was to be her last word. What was it?

"Hugh, boy, not THAT!"

He did not answer. She wrung her hands, trying to be silent, looking in his face in an agony of entreaty. He smiled again, kindly.

"It is best, Deb. I cannot bear to be hurted any more."

"Hur knows," she said, humbly.

.

"Tell my father good-bye; and—and kiss little Janey."

She nodded, saying nothing, looked in his face again, and went out of the door. As she went, she staggered.

"Drinkin' to-day?" broke out Haley, pushing her before him. "Where the Devil did you get it? Here, in with ye!" and he shoved her into her cell, next to Wolfe's, and shut the door.

Along the wall of her cell there was a crack low down by the floor, through which she could see the light from Wolfe's. She had discovered it days before. She hurried in now, and, kneeling down by it, listened, hoping to hear some sound. Nothing but the rasping of the tin on the bars. He was at his old amusement again. Something in the noise jarred on her ear, for she shivered as she heard it. Hugh rasped away at the bars. A dull old bit of tin, not fit to cut korl with.

He looked out of the window again. People were leaving the market now. A tall mulatto girl, following her mistress, her basket on her head, crossed the street just below, and looked up. She was laughing; but, when she caught sight of the haggard face peering out through the bars, suddenly grew grave, and hurried by. A free, firm step, a clear-cut olive face, with a scarlet turban tied on one side, dark, shining eyes, and on the head the basket poised, filled with fruit and flowers, under which the scarlet turban and bright eyes looked out half-shadowed. The picture caught his eye. It was good to see a face like that. He would try to-morrow, and cut one like it. *Tomorrow!* He threw down the tin, trembling, and covered his face with his hands. When he looked up again, the daylight was gone.

Deborah, crouching near by on the other side of the wall, heard no noise. He sat on the side of the low pallet, thinking. Whatever was the mystery which the woman had seen on his face, it came out now slowly, in the dark there, and became fixed,—a something never seen on his face before. The evening was darkening fast. The market had been over for an hour; the rumbling of the carts over the pavement grew more infrequent: he listened to each, as it passed, because he thought it was to be for the last time. For the same reason, it was, I suppose, that he strained his eyes to catch a glimpse of each passer-by, wondering who they were, what kind of homes they were going to, if they had children,—listening eagerly to every chance word in the street, as if—(God be merciful to the man! what strange fancy was this?)— as if he never should hear human voices again.

It was quite dark at last. The street was a lonely one. The last passenger, he thought, was gone. No,—there was a quick step: Joe Hill, lighting the lamps. Joe was a good old chap; never passed a fellow without some joke or other. He remembered once seeing the place where he lived with his wife. "Granny Hill" the boys called her. Bedridden she was; but so kind as Joe was to her! kept the room so clean!—and the old woman, when he was there, was laughing at "some of t' lad's foolishness." The step was far down the street; but he could see him place the ladder, run up, and light the gas. A longing seized him to be spoken to once more.

"Joe!" he called, out of the grating. "Good-bye, Joe!"

The old man stopped a moment, listening uncertainly; then hurried on. The prisoner thrust his hand out of the window, and called again, louder; but Joe was too far down the street. It was a little thing; but it hurt him,—this disappointment.

"Good-bye, Joe!" he called, sorrowfully enough.

"Be quiet!" said one of the jailers, passing the door, striking on it with his club.

Oh, that was the last, was it?

There was an inexpressible bitterness on his face, as he lay down on the bed, taking the bit of tin, which he had rasped to a tolerable degree of sharpness, in his hand,—to play with, it may be. He bared his arms, looking intently at their corded veins and sinews. Deborah, listening in the next cell, heard a slight clicking sound, often repeated. She shut her lips tightly, that she might not scream; the cold drops of sweat broke over her, in her dumb agony.

"Hur knows best," she muttered at last, fiercely clutching the boards where she lay.

If she could have seen Wolfe, there was nothing about him to frighten her. He lay quite still, his arms outstretched, looking at the pearly stream of moonlight coming into the window. I think in that one hour that came then he lived back over all the years that had gone before. I think that all the low, vile life, all his wrongs, all his starved hopes, came then, and stung him with a farewell poison that made him sick unto death. (He made neither moan nor cry, only turned his worn face now and then to the pure light, that seemed so far off, as one that said, "How long, O Lord? how long?")

The hour was over at last. The moon, passing over her nightly path, slowly came nearer, and threw the light across his bed on his feet. He watched it steadily, as it crept up, inch by inch, slowly. It seemed to him to carry with it a great silence. He had been so hot and tired there always in the mills! The years had been so fierce and cruel! There was coming now quiet and coolness and sleep. His tense limbs relaxed, and settled in a calm languor. The blood ran fainter and slow from his heart. (He did not think now with a savage anger of what might be and was not; he was conscious only of deep stillness creeping over him.) At first he saw a sea of faces: the mill-men,—women he had known, drunken and bloated,—Janeys timid and pitiful,—poor old Debs: then they floated together like a mist, and faded away, leaving only the clear, pearly moonlight.

Whether, as the pure light crept up the stretched-out figure, it brought with it calm and peace, who shall say? His dumb soul was alone with God in judgment. A Voice may have spoken for it from far-off Calvary, "Father, forgive them, for they know not what they do!" Who dare say? Fainter and fainter the heart rose and fell, slower and slower, the moon floated from behind a cloud, until, when at last its full tide of white splendor swept over the cell, it seemed to wrap and fold into a deeper stillness the dead figure that never should move again. Silence deeper than the Night! Nothing that moved, save the black, nauseous stream of blood dripping slowly from the pallet to the floor!

There was outcry and crowd enough in the cell the next day. The coroner and his jury, the local editors, Kirby himself, and boys with their hands thrust knowingly into their pockets and heads on one side, jammed into the corners. Coming and going all day. Only one woman. She came late, and outstayed them all. A Quaker, or Friend, as they call themselves. I think this woman was known by that name in heaven. A homely body, coarsely dressed in gray and white. Deborah (for Haley had let her in) took notice of her. She watched them all—sitting on the end of the pallet, holding his head in her arms—with the ferocity of a watch-dog, if any of them touched the body. There was no meekness, no sorrow, in her face; the stuff out of which murderers are made, instead. All the time Haley and the woman were laying straight the limbs and cleaning the cell, Deborah sat still, keenly watching the Quaker's face. Of all the crowd there that day, this woman alone had not spoken to her,—only once or twice had put some cordial to her lips. After they all were gone, the woman, in the same still, gentle way, brought a vase of wood-leaves and berries, and placed it by the pallet, then opened the narrow window. The fresh air blew in, and swept the woody fragrance over the dead face. Deborah looked up with a quick wonder.

"Did hur know my boy wud like it? Did hur know Hugh?"

"I know Hugh now."

The white fingers passed in a slow, pitiful way over the dead, worn face. There was a heavy shadow in the quiet eyes.

"Did hur know where they'll bury Hugh?" said Deborah in a shrill tone, catching her arm.

This had been the question hanging on her lips all day.

"In t' town-yard? Under t' mud and ash? T' lad 'll smother, woman! He wur born on t' lane[25] moor, where t' air is frick[26] and strong. Take hur out, for God's sake, take hur out where t' air blows!"

[25]Lonely.
[26]Fresh.

226

The Quaker hesitated, but only for a moment. She put her strong arm around Deborah and led her to the window.

"Thee sees the hills, friend, over the river? Thee sees how the light lies warm there, and the winds of God blow all the day? I live there,—where the blue smoke is, by the trees. Look at me." She turned Deborah's face to her own, clear and earnest. "Thee will believe me? I will take Hugh and bury him there to-morrow."

Deborah did not doubt her. As the evening wore on, she leaned against the iron bars, looking at the hills that rose far off, through the thick sodden clouds, like a bright, unattainable calm. As she looked, a shadow of their solemn repose fell on her face: its fierce discontent faded into a pitiful, humble quiet. Slow, solemn tears gathered in her eyes: the poor weak eyes turned so hopelessly to the place where Hugh was to rest, the grave heights looking higher and brighter and more solemn than ever before. The Quaker watched her keenly. She came to her at last, and touched her arm.

"When thee comes back," she said, in a low, sorrowful tone, like one who speaks from a strong heart deeply moved with remorse or pity, "thee shall begin thy life again,—there on the hills. I came too late; but not for thee,— by God's help, it may be."

Not too late. Three years after, the Quaker began her work. I end my story here. At evening-time it was light. There is no need to tire you with the long years of sunshine, and fresh air, and slow, patient Christ-love, needed to make healthy and hopeful this impure body and soul. There is a homely pine house, on one of these hills, whose windows overlook broad, wooded slopes and clover-crimsoned meadows,—niched into the very place where the light is warmest, the air freest. It is the Friends' meeting-house. Once a week they sit there, in their grave, earnest way, waiting for the Spirit of Love to speak, opening their simple hearts to receive His words. There is a woman, old, deformed, who takes a humble place among them: waiting like them: in her gray dress, her worn face, pure and meek, turned now and then to the sky. A woman much loved by these silent, restful people; more silent than they, more humble, more loving. Waiting: with her eyes turned to hills higher and purer than these on which she lives,—dim and far off now, but to be reached some day. There may be in her heart some latent hope to meet there the love denied her here,—that she shall find him whom she lost, and that then she will not be all-unworthy. Who blames her? Something is lost in the passage of every soul from one eternity to the other,—something pure and beautiful, which might have been and was not: a hope, a talent, a love, over which the soul mourns, like Esau deprived of his birthright. What blame to the meek Quaker, if she took her lost hope to make the hills of heaven more fair?

Nothing remains to tell that the poor Welsh puddler once lived, but this figure of the mill-woman cut in korl. I have it here in a corner of my library. I keep it hid behind a curtain,—it is such a rough, ungainly thing. Yet there are about it touches, grand sweeps of outline, that show a master's hand. Sometimes,—to-night, for instance,—the curtain is accidentally drawn back, and I see a bare arm stretched out imploringly in the darkness, and an eager, wolfish face watching mine: a wan, woful face, through which the spirit of the dead korl-cutter looks out, with its thwarted life, its mighty hunger, its unfinished work. Its pale, vague lips seem to tremble with a terrible question. "Is this the End?" they say,—"nothing beyond?—no more?" Why, you tell me you have seen that look in the eyes of dumb brutes,—horses dying under the lash. I know.

The deep of the night is passing while I write. The gas-light wakens from the shadows here and there the objects which lie scattered through the room: only faintly, though; for they belong to the open sunlight. As I glance at them, they each recall some task or pleasure of the coming day. A half-moulded child's head; Aphrodite; a bough of forest-leaves; music; work; homely fragments, in which lie the secrets of all eternal truth and beauty. Prophetic all! Only this dumb, woful face seems to belong to and end with the night. I turn to look at it. Has the power of its desperate need commanded the darkness away? While the room is yet steeped in heavy shadow, a cool, gray light suddenly touches its head like a blessing hand, and its groping arm points through the broken cloud to the far East, where, in the flickering, nebulous crimson, God has set the promise of the Dawn.

1861

Willa Cather

(1873–1945)

Willa Cather spent the first nine years of her life in a spacious farmhouse near Winchester, Virginia. The oldest of seven children, Willa felt great responsibility when the family's move to Webster County, Nebraska, placed them in a harsh, nearly primitive, environment. The severe winters tested the hardihood of not only the Cathers but also their neighbors, many of whom were Swedish, Russian, and Bohemian immigrants, who searched—sometimes desperately—for the "American dream."

After graduating from the University of Nebraska and working as a journalist, then moving, first to Pittsburgh and then to New York in order to write and work as an editor at *McClure's* magazine, Cather often re-created that stark Nebraska world. The endurance and spirit of such characters in her fiction as Alexandra (*O Pioneers!*, 1913), Antonia (*My Ántonia*, 1918), and the Foresters (*A Lost Lady*, 1923) have made her writing inseparable from American legend.

Not that Cather ever wrote predictable fiction. Her many readers worldwide continue to find new treasures among her consistently brilliant achievements. This 1932 novella, *Old Mrs. Harris*, is of particular interest because Cather focuses on both a young woman coming of age, and an older woman whose view of her culture privileges its continuity. Here, in what was her favorite story, Cather creates a healthy woman's community.

❖

OLD MRS. HARRIS

I

Mrs. David Rosen, cross-stitch in hand, sat looking out of the window across her own green lawn to the ragged, sunburned back yard of her neighbours on the right. Occasionally she glanced anxiously over her shoulder toward her shining kitchen, with a black and white linoleum floor in big squares, like a marble pavement.

"Will dat woman never go?" she muttered impatiently, just under her breath. She spoke with a slight accent—it affected only her *th's*, and, occasionally, the letter *v*. But people in Skyline thought this unfortunate, in a woman whose superiority they recognized.

Mrs. Rosen ran out to move the sprinkler to another spot on the lawn, and in doing so she saw what she had been waiting to see. From the house next

229

door a tall, handsome woman emerged, dressed in white broadcloth and a hat with white lilacs; she carried a sunshade and walked with a free, energetic step, as if she were going out on a pleasant errand.

Mrs. Rosen darted quickly back into the house, lest her neighbour should hail her and stop to talk. She herself was in her kitchen housework dress, a crisp blue chambray which fitted smoothly over her tightly corseted figure, and her lustrous black hair was done in two smooth braids, wound flat at the back of her head, like a braided rug. She did not stop for a hat—her dark, ruddy, salmon-tinted skin had little to fear from the sun. She opened the half-closed oven door and took out a symmetrically plaited coffee-cake, beautifully browned, delicately peppered over with poppy seeds, with sugary margins about the twists. On the kitchen table a tray stood ready with cups and saucers. She wrapped the cake in a napkin, snatched up a little French coffee-pot with a black wooden handle, and ran across her green lawn, through the alley-way and the sandy, unkept yard next door, and entered her neighbour's house by the kitchen.

The kitchen was hot and empty, full of the untempered afternoon sun. A door stood open into the next room; a cluttered, hideous room, yet somehow homely. There, beside a goodsbox covered with figured oilcloth, stood an old woman in a brown calico dress, washing her hot face and neck at a tin basin. She stood with her feet wide apart, in an attitude of profound weariness. She started guiltily as the visitor entered.

"Don't let me disturb you, Grandma," called Mrs. Rosen. "I always have my coffee at dis hour in the afternoon. I was just about to sit down to it when I thought: 'I will run over and see if Grandma Harris won't take a cup with me.' I hate to drink my coffee alone."

Grandma looked troubled,—at a loss. She folded her towel and concealed it behind a curtain hung across the corner of the room to make a poor sort of closet. The old lady was always composed in manner, but it was clear that she felt embarrassment.

"Thank you, Mrs. Rosen. What a pity Victoria just this minute went down town!"

"But dis time I came to see you yourself, Grandma. Don't let me disturb you. Sit down there in your own rocker, and I will put my tray on this little chair between us, so!"

Mrs. Harris sat down in her black wooden rocking-chair with curved arms and a faded cretonne pillow on the wooden seat. It stood in the corner beside a narrow spindle-frame lounge. She looked on silently while Mrs. Rosen uncovered the cake and delicately broke it with her plump, smooth, dusky-red hands. The old lady did not seem pleased,—seemed uncertain and apprehensive, indeed. But she was not fussy or fidgety. She had the kind of quiet, intensely quiet, dignity that comes from complete resignation to the chances of life. She watched Mrs. Rosen's deft hands out of grave, steady brown eyes.

"Dis is Mr. Rosen's favourite coffee-cake, Grandma, and I want you to try it. You are such a good cook yourself, I would like your opinion of my cake."

"It's very nice, ma'am," said Mrs. Harris politely, but without enthusiasm.

"And you aren't drinking your coffee; do you like more cream in it?"

"No, thank you. I'm letting it cool a little. I generally drink it that way."

"Of course she does," thought Mrs. Rosen, "since she never has her coffee until all the family are done breakfast!"

Mrs. Rosen had brought Grandma Harris coffee-cake time and again, but she knew that Grandma merely tasted it and saved it for her daughter Victoria, who was as fond of sweets as her own children, and jealous about them, moreover,—couldn't bear that special dainties should come into the house for anyone but herself. Mrs. Rosen, vexed at her failures, had determined that just once she would take a cake to "de old lady Harris," and with her own eyes see her eat it. The result was not all she had hoped. Receiving a visitor alone, unsupervised by her daughter, having cake and coffee that should properly be saved for Victoria, was all so irregular that Mrs. Harris could not enjoy it. Mrs. Rosen doubted if she tasted the cake as she swallowed it,—certainly she ate it without relish, as a hollow form. But Mrs. Rosen enjoyed her own cake, at any rate, and she was glad of an opportunity to sit quietly and look at Grandmother, who was more interesting to her than the handsome Victoria.

It was a queer place to be having coffee, when Mrs. Rosen liked order and comeliness so much: a hideous, cluttered room, furnished with a rocking-horse, a sewing-machine, an empty baby-buggy. A walnut table stood against a blind window, piled high with old magazines and tattered books, and children's caps and coats. There was a wash-stand (two wash-stands, if you counted the oilcloth-covered box as one). A corner of the room was curtained off with some black-and-red-striped cotton goods, for a clothes closet. In another corner was the wooden lounge with a thin mattress and a red calico spread which was Grandma's bed. Beside it was her wooden rocking-chair, and the little splint-bottom chair with the legs sawed short on which her darning-basket usually stood, but which Mrs. Rosen was now using for a tea-table.

The old lady was always impressive, Mrs. Rosen was thinking,—one could not say why. Perhaps it was the way she held her head,—so simply, unprotesting and unprotected; or the gravity of her large, deep-set brown eyes, a warm, reddish brown, though their look, always direct, seemed to ask nothing and hope for nothing. They were not cold, but inscrutable, with no kindling gleam of intercourse in them. There was the kind of nobility about her head that there is about an old lion's; an absence of self-consciousness, vanity, preoccupation—something absolute. Her grey hair was parted in the middle, wound in two little horns over her ears, and done in a little flat knot behind. Her mouth was large and composed,—resigned, the corners drooping. Mrs. Rosen had very seldom heard her laugh (and then it was a gentle, polite laugh which meant only politeness). But she had observed that whenever Mrs. Harris's grandchildren were about, tumbling all over her, asking for cookies, teasing her to read to them, the old lady looked happy.

As she drank her coffee, Mrs. Rosen tried one subject after another to engage Mrs. Harris's attention.

"Do you feel this hot weather, Grandma? I am afraid you are over the stove too much. Let those naughty children have a cold lunch occasionally."

"No'm, I don't mind the heat. It's apt to come on like this for a spell in May. I don't feel the stove. I'm accustomed to it."

"Oh, so am I! But I get very impatient with my cooking in hot weather. Do you miss your old home in Tennessee very much, Grandma?"

"No'm, I can't say I do. Mr. Templeton thought Colorado was a better place to bring up the children."

"But you had things much more comfortable down there, I'm sure. These little wooden houses are too hot in summer."

"Yes'm, we were more comfortable. We had more room."

"And a flower-garden, and beautiful old trees, Mrs. Templeton told me."

"Yes'm, we had a great deal of shade."

Mrs. Rosen felt that she was not getting anywhere. She almost believed that Grandma thought she had come on an equivocal errand, to spy out something in Victoria's absence. Well, perhaps she had! Just for once she would like to get past the others to the real grandmother,—and the real grandmother was on her guard, as always. At this moment she heard a faint miaow. Mrs. Harris rose, lifting herself by the wooden arms of her chair, said: "Excuse me," went into the kitchen, and opened the screen door.

In walked a large, handsome, thickly furred Maltese cat, with long whiskers and yellow eyes and a white star on his breast. He preceded Grandmother, waited until she sat down. Then he sprang up into her lap and settled himself comfortably in the folds of her full-gathered calico skirt. He rested his chin in his deep bluish fur and regarded Mrs. Rosen. It struck her that he held his head in just the way Grandmother held hers. And Grandmother now became more alive, as if some missing part of herself were restored.

"This is Blue Boy," she said, stroking him. "In winter, when the screen door ain't on, he lets himself in. He stands up on his hind legs and presses the thumb-latch with his paw, and just walks in like anybody."

"He's your cat, isn't he, Grandma?" Mrs. Rosen couldn't help prying just a little; if she could find but a single thing that was Grandma's own!

"He's our cat," replied Mrs. Harris. "We're all very fond of him. I expect he's Vickie's more'n anybody's."

"Of course!" groaned Mrs. Rosen to herself. "Dat Vickie is her mother over again."

Here Mrs. Harris made her first unsolicited remark. "If you was to be troubled with mice at any time, Mrs. Rosen, ask one of the boys to bring Blue Boy over to you, and he'll clear them out. He's a master mouser." She scratched the thick blue fur at the back of his neck, and he began a deep purring. Mrs. Harris smiled. "We call that spinning, back with us. Our children still say: 'Listen to Blue Boy spin,' though none of 'em is ever heard a spinning-wheel—except maybe Vickie remembers."

"Did you have a spinning-wheel in your own house, Grandma Harris?"

"Yes'm. Miss Sadie Crummer used to come and spin for us. She was left with no home of her own, and it was to give her something to do, as much as anything, that we had her. I spun a good deal myself, in my young days." Grandmother stopped and put her hands on the arms of her chair, as if to rise. "Did you hear a door open? It might be Victoria."

"No, it was the wind shaking the screen door. Mrs. Templeton won't be home yet. She is probably in my husband's store this minute, ordering him about. All the merchants down town will take anything from your daughter. She is very popular wid de gentlemen, Grandma."

Mrs. Harris smiled complacently. "Yes'm. Victoria was always much admired."

At this moment a chorus of laughter broke in upon the warm silence, and a host of children, as it seemed to Mrs. Rosen, ran through the yard. The hand-pump on the back porch, outside the kitchen door, began to scrape and gurgle.

"It's the children, back from school," said Grandma. "They are getting a cool drink."

"But where is the baby, Grandma?"

"Vickie took Hughie in his cart over to Mr. Holliday's yard, where she studies. She's right good about minding him."

Mrs. Rosen was glad to hear that Vickie was good for something.

Three little boys came running in through the kitchen; the twins, aged ten, and Ronald, aged six, who went to kindergarten. They snatched off their caps and threw their jackets and school bags on the table, the sewing-machine, the rocking-horse.

"Howdy do, Mrs. Rosen." They spoke to her nicely. They had nice voices, nice faces, and were always courteous, like their father. "We are going to play in our back yard with some of the boys, Gram'ma," said one of the twins respectfully, and they ran out to join a troop of schoolmates who were already shouting and racing over that poor trampled back yard, strewn with veloci-pedes and croquet mallets and toy wagons, which was such an eyesore to Mrs. Rosen.

Mrs. Rosen got up and took her tray.

"Can't you stay a little, ma'am? Victoria will be here any minute."

But her tone let Mrs. Rosen know that Grandma really wished her to leave before Victoria returned.

A few moments after Mrs. Rosen had put the tray down in her own kitchen, Victoria Templeton came up the wooden sidewalk, attended by Mr. Rosen, who had quitted his store half an hour earlier than usual for the plea-sure of walking home with her. Mrs. Templeton stopped by the picket fence to smile at the children playing in the back yard,—and it was a real smile, she was glad to see them. She called Ronald over to the fence to give him a kiss. He was hot and sticky.

"Was your teacher nice today? Now run in and ask Grandma to wash your face and put a clean waist on you."

II

That night Mrs. Harris got supper with an effort—had to drive herself harder than usual. Mandy, the bound girl[1] they had brought with them from the South, noticed that the old lady was uncertain and short of breath. The hours from two to four, when Mrs. Harris usually rested, had not been at all restful this afternoon. There was an understood rule that Grandmother was not to receive visitors alone. Mrs. Rosen's call, and her cake and coffee, were too much out of the accepted order. Nervousness had prevented the old lady from getting any repose during her visit.

After the rest of the family had left the supper table, she went into the dining-room and took her place, but she ate very little. She put away the food that was left, and then, while Mandy washed the dishes, Grandma sat down in her rocking-chair in the dark and dozed.

The three little boys came in from playing under the electric light (arc lights had been but lately installed in Skyline) and began begging Mrs. Harris to read *Tom Sawyer* to them. Grandmother loved to read, anything at all, the Bible or the continued story in the Chicago weekly paper. She roused herself, lit her brass "safety lamp," and pulled her black rocker out of its corner to the

[1]Household servant who is more a member of the family than an employee.

234

wash-stand (the table was too far away from her corner, and anyhow it was completely covered with coats and school satchels). She put on her old-fashioned silver-rimmed spectacles and began to read. Ronald lay down on Grandmother's lounge bed, and the twins, Albert and Adelbert, called Bert and Del, sat down against the wall, one on a low box covered with felt, and the other on the little sawed-off chair upon which Mrs. Rosen had served coffee. They looked intently at Mrs. Harris, and she looked intently at the book.

Presently Vickie, the oldest grandchild, came in. She was fifteen. Her mother was entertaining callers in the parlour, callers who didn't interest Vickie, so she was on her way up to her own room by the kitchen stairway.

Mrs. Harris looked up over her glasses. "Vickie, maybe you'd take the book awhile, and I can do my darning."

"All right," said Vickie. Reading aloud was one of the things she would always do toward the general comfort. She sat down by the wash-stand and went on with the story. Grandmother got her darning-basket and began to drive her needle across great knee-holes in the boys' stockings. Sometimes she nodded for a moment, and her hands fell into her lap. After a while the little boy on the lounge went to sleep. But the twins sat upright, their hands on their knees, their round brown eyes fastened upon Vickie, and when there was anything funny, they giggled. They were chubby, dark-skinned little boys, with round jolly faces, white teeth, and yellow-brown eyes that were always bubbling with fun unless they were sad,—even then their eyes never got red or weepy. Their tears sparkled and fell; left no trace but a streak on the cheeks, perhaps.

Presently old Mrs. Harris gave out a long snore of utter defeat. She had been overcome at last. Vickie put down the book. "That's enough for tonight. Grandmother's sleepy, and Ronald's fast asleep. What'll we do with him?"

"Bert and me'll get him undressed," said Adelbert. The twins roused the sleepy little boy and prodded him up the back stairway to the bare room without window blinds, where he was put into his cot beside their double bed. Vickie's room was across the narrow hallway; not much bigger than a closet, but, anyway, it was her own. She had a chair and an old dresser, and beside her bed was a high stool which she used as a lamp-table,—she always read in bed.

After Vickie went upstairs, the house was quiet. Hughie, the baby, was asleep in his mother's room, and Victoria herself, who still treated her husband as if he were her "beau," had persuaded him to take her down town to the ice-cream parlour. Grandmother's room, between the kitchen and the dining-room, was rather like a passage-way; but now that the children were upstairs and Victoria was off enjoying herself somewhere, Mrs. Harris could be sure of enough privacy to undress. She took off the calico cover from her lounge bed and folded it up, put on her nightgown and white nightcap.

Mandy, the bound girl, appeared at the kitchen door.

"Miz' Harris," she said in a guarded tone, ducking her head, "you want me to rub your feet for you?"

For the first time in the long day the old woman's low composure broke a little. "Oh, Mandy, I would take it kindly of you!" she breathed gratefully.

That had to be done in the kitchen; Victoria didn't like anybody slopping about. Mrs. Harris put an old checked shawl round her shoulders and followed Mandy. Beside the kitchen stove Mandy had a little wooden tub full of warm water. She knelt down and untied Mrs. Harris's garter strings and took off her flat cloth slippers and stockings.

"Oh, Miz' Harris, your feet an' legs is swelled turrible tonight!"

"I expect they air, Mandy. They feel like it."

"Pore soul!" murmured Mandy. She put Grandma's feet in the tub and, crouching beside it, slowly, slowly rubbed her swollen legs. Mandy was tired, too. Mrs. Harris sat in her nightcap and shawl, her hands crossed in her lap. She never asked for this greatest solace of the day; it was something that Mandy gave, who had nothing else to give. If there could be a comparison in absolutes, Mandy was the needier of the two,—but she was younger. The kitchen was quiet and full of shadow, with only the light from an old lantern. Neither spoke. Mrs. Harris dozed from comfort, and Mandy herself was half asleep as she performed one of the oldest rites of compassion.

Although Mrs. Harris's lounge had no springs, only a thin cotton mattress between her and the wooden slats, she usually went to sleep as soon as she was in bed. To be off her feet, to lie flat, to say over the psalm beginning: *"The Lord is my shepherd,"* was comfort enough. About four o'clock in the morning, however, she would begin to feel the hard slats under her, and the heaviness of the old homemade quilts, with weight but little warmth, on top of her. Then she would reach under her pillow for her little comforter (she called it that to herself) that Mrs. Rosen had given her. It was a tan sweater of very soft brushed wool, with one sleeve torn and ragged. A young nephew from Chicago had spent a fortnight with Mrs. Rosen last summer and had left this behind him. One morning, when Mrs. Harris went out to the stable at the back of the yard to pat Buttercup, the cow, Mrs. Rosen ran across the alley-way.

"Grandma Harris," she said, coming into the shelter of the stable, "I wonder if you could make any use of this sweater Sammy left? The yarn might be good for your darning."

Mrs. Harris felt of the article gravely. Mrs. Rosen thought her face brightened. "Yes'm, indeed I could use it. I thank you kindly."

She slipped it under her apron, carried it into the house with her, and concealed it under her mattress. There she had kept it ever since. She knew Mrs. Rosen understood how it was; that Victoria couldn't bear to have anything come into the house that was not for her to dispose of.

On winter nights, and even on summer nights after the cocks began to crow, Mrs. Harris often felt cold and lonely about the chest. Sometimes her cat, Blue Boy, would creep in beside her and warm that aching spot. But on spring and summer nights he was likely to be abroad skylarking, and this little sweater had become the dearest of Grandmother's few possessions. It was kinder to her, she used to think, as she wrapped it about her middle, than any of her own children had been. She had married at eighteen and had had eight children; but some died, and some were, as she said, scattered.

After she was warm in that tender spot under the ribs, the old woman could lie patiently on the slats, waiting for daybreak; thinking about the comfortable rambling old house in Tennessee, its feather beds and hand-woven rag carpets and splint-bottom chairs, the mahogany sideboard, and the marble-top parlour table; all that she had left behind to follow Victoria's fortunes.

She did not regret her decision; indeed, there had been no decision. Victoria had never once thought it possible that Ma should not go wherever she and the children went, and Mrs. Harris had never thought it possible. Of course she regretted Tennessee, though she would never admit it to Mrs. Rosen:—the old neighbours, the yard and garden she had worked in all her life, the apple trees she had planted, the lilac arbour, tall enough to walk in, which she had clipped and shaped so many years. Especially she missed her lemon tree, in a tub on the front porch, which bore little lemons almost every summer, and folks would come for miles to see it.

But the road had led westward, and Mrs. Harris didn't believe that women, especially old women, could say when or where they would stop. They were tied to the chariot of young life, and had to go where it went, because they were needed. Mrs. Harris had gathered from Mrs. Rosen's manner, and from comments she occasionally dropped, that the Jewish people had an altogether different attitude toward their old folks; therefore her friendship with this kind neighbour was almost as disturbing as it was pleasant. She didn't want Mrs. Rosen to think she was "put upon," that there was anything unusual or pitiful in her lot. To be pitied was the deepest hurt anybody could know. And if Victoria once suspected Mrs. Rosen's indignation, it would be all over. She would freeze her neighbour out, and that friendly voice, that quick pleasant chatter with the little foreign twist, would thenceforth be heard only at a distance, in the alley-way or across the fence. Victoria had a good heart, but she was terribly proud and could not bear the least criticism.

As soon as the grey light began to steal into the room, Mrs. Harris would get up softly and wash at the basin on the oilcloth-covered box. She would wet her hair above her forehead, comb it with a little bone comb set in a tin rim, do it up in two smooth little horns over her ears, wipe the comb dry, and put it away in the pocket of her full-gathered calico skirt. She left nothing lying about. As soon as she was dressed, she made her bed, folding her nightgown and nightcap under the pillow, the sweater under the mattress. She smoothed the heavy quilts, and drew the red calico spread neatly over all. Her towel was hung on its special nail behind the curtain. Her soap she kept in a tin tobacco-box; the children's soap was in a crockery saucer. If her soap or towel got mixed up with the children's, Victoria was always sharp about it. The little rented house was much too small for the family, and Mrs. Harris and her "things" were almost required to be invisible. Two clean calico dresses hung in the curtained corner; another was on her back, and a fourth was in the wash. Behind the curtain there was always a good supply of aprons; Victoria bought them at church fairs, and it was a great satisfaction to Mrs. Harris to put on a clean one whenever she liked. Upstairs, in Mandy's attic room over the kitchen, hung a black cashmere dress and a black bonnet with a long crêpe veil, for the rare occasions when Mr. Templeton hired a double buggy and horses and drove his family to a picnic or to Decoration Day exercises. Mrs. Harris rather dreaded these drives, for Victoria was usually cross afterwards.

When Mrs. Harris went out into the kitchen to get breakfast, Mandy always had the fire started and the water boiling. They enjoyed a quiet half-hour before the little boys came running down the stairs, always in a good humour. In winter the boys had their breakfast in the kitchen, with Vickie. Mrs. Harris made Mandy eat the cakes and fried ham the children left, so that she would not fast so long. Mr. and Mrs. Templeton breakfasted rather late, in the dining-room and they always had fruit and thick cream,—a small pitcher of the very thickest was for Mrs. Templeton. The children were never fussy about their food. As Grandmother often said feelingly to Mrs. Rosen, they were as little trouble as children could possibly be. They sometimes tore their clothes, of course, or got sick. But even when Albert had an abscess in his ear and was in such pain, he would lie for hours on Grandmother's lounge with his cheek on a bag of hot salt, if only she or Vickie would read aloud to him.

"It's true, too, what de old lady says," remarked Mrs. Rosen to her husband one night at supper, "dey are nice children. No one ever taught them anything, but they have good instincts, even dat Vickie. And think, if you please, of all the self-sacrificing mothers we know,—Fannie and Esther, to come near home; how they have planned for those children from infancy and given them every advantage. And now ingratitude and coldness is what dey meet with."

Mr. Rosen smiled his teasing smile. "Evidently your sister and mine have the wrong method. The way to make your children unselfish is to be comfortably selfish yourself."

"But dat woman takes no more responsibility for her children than a cat takes for her kittens. Nor does poor young Mr. Templeton, for dat matter. How can he expect to get so many children started in life, I ask you? It is not at all fair!"

Mr. Rosen sometimes had to hear altogether too much about the Templetons, but he was patient, because it was a bitter sorrow to Mrs. Rosen that she had no children. There was nothing else in the world she wanted so much.

III

Mrs. Rosen in one of her blue working dresses, the indigo blue that became a dark skin and dusky red cheeks with a tone of salmon colour, was in her shining kitchen, washing her beautiful dishes—her neighbours often wondered why she used her best china and linen every day—when Vickie Templeton came in with a book under her arm.

"Good day, Mrs. Rosen. Can I have the second volume?"

"Certainly. You know where the books are." She spoke coolly, for it always annoyed her that Vickie never suggested wiping the dishes or helping with such household work as happened to be going on when she dropped in. She hated the girl's bringing-up so much that sometimes she almost hated the girl.

Vickie strolled carelessly through the dining-room into the parlour and opened the doors of one of the big bookcases. Mr. Rosen had a large library, and a great many unusual books. There was a complete set of the Waverley Novels in German, for example; thick, dumpy little volumes bound in tooled leather, with very black type and dramatic engravings printed on wrinkled, yellowing pages. There were many French books, and some of the German classics done into English, such as Coleridge's translation of Schiller's *Wallenstein*.

Of course no other house in Skyline was in the least like Mrs. Rosen's; it was the nearest thing to an art gallery and a museum that the Templetons had ever seen. All the rooms were carpeted alike (that was very unusual), with a soft velvet carpet, little blue and rose flowers scattered on a rose-grey ground. The deep chairs were upholstered in dark blue velvet. The walls were hung with engravings in pale gold frames: some of Raphael's "Hours," a large soft engraving of a castle on the Rhine, and another of cypress trees about a Roman ruin, under a full moon. There were a number of water-colour sketches, made in Italy by Mr. Rosen himself when he was a boy. A rich uncle had taken him abroad as his secretary. Mr. Rosen was a reflective, unambitious man, who didn't mind keeping a clothing-store in a little Western town, so long as he had a great deal of time to read philosophy. He was the only unsuccessful member of a large, rich Jewish family.

Last August, when the heat was terrible in Skyline, and the crops were burned up on all the farms to the north, and the wind from the pink and yellow sand-hills to the south blew so hot that it singed the few green lawns in the town, Vickie had taken to dropping in upon Mrs. Rosen at the very hottest part of the afternoon. Mrs. Rosen knew, of course, that it was probably because the girl had no other cool and quiet place to go—her room at home under the roof would be hot enough! Now, Mrs. Rosen liked to undress and take a nap from three to five,—if only to get out of her tight corsets, for she would have an hour-glass figure at any cost. She told Vickie firmly that she was welcome to come if she would read in the parlour with the blind up only a little way, and would be as still as a mouse. Vickie came, meekly enough, but she seldom read. She would take a sofa pillow and lie down on the soft carpet and look up at the pictures in the dusky room, and feel a happy, pleasant excitement from the heat and glare outside and the deep shadow and quiet within. Curiously enough, Mrs. Rosen's house never made her dissatisfied with her own; she thought that very nice, too.

Mrs. Rosen, leaving her kitchen in a state of such perfection as the Templetons were unable to sense or to admire, came into the parlour and found her visitor sitting cross-legged on the floor before one of the bookcases.

"Well, Vickie, and how did you get along with *Wilhelm Meister?*"

"I liked it," said Vickie.

Mrs. Rosen shrugged. The Templetons always said that; quite as if a book or a cake were lucky to win their approbation.

"Well, *what* did you like?"

"I guess I liked all that about the theatre and Shakspere best."

"It's rather celebrated," remarked Mrs. Rosen dryly. "And are you studying every day? Do you think you will be able to win that scholarship?"

"I don't know. I'm going to try awful hard."

Mrs. Rosen wondered whether any Templeton knew how to try very hard. She reached for her work-basket and began to do cross-stitch. It made her nervous to sit with folded hands.

Vickie was looking at a German book in her lap, an illustrated edition of *Faust*. She had stopped at a very German picture of Gretchen entering the church, with Faustus gazing at her from behind a rose tree, Mephisto at his shoulder.

"I wish I could read this," she said, frowning at the black Gothic text. "It's splendid, isn't it?"

Mrs. Rosen rolled her eyes upward and sighed. "Oh, my dear, one of de world's masterpieces!"

That meant little to Vickie. She had not been taught to respect master-pieces, she had no scale of that sort in her mind. She cared about a book only because it took hold of her.

She kept turning over the pages. Between the first and second parts, in this edition, there was inserted the *Dies Iræ* hymn in full. She stopped and puzzled over it for a long while.

"Here is something I can read," she said, showing the page to Mrs. Rosen. Mrs. Rosen looked up from her cross-stitch.

"There you have the advantage of me. I do not read Latin. You might translate it for me."

Vickie began:

> *"Day of wrath, upon that day*
> *The world to ashes melts away,*
> *As David and the Sibyl say.*

"But that don't give you the rhyme; every line ought to end in two syllables."

"Never mind if it doesn't give the metre," corrected Mrs. Rosen kindly; "go on, if you can."

Vickie went on stumbling through the Latin verses, and Mrs. Rosen sat watching her. You couldn't tell about Vickie. She wasn't pretty, yet Mrs. Rosen found her attractive. She liked her sturdy build, and the steady vitality that glowed in her rosy skin and dark blue eyes,—even gave a springy quality to her curly reddish-brown hair, which she still wore in a single braid down her back. Mrs. Rosen liked to have Vickie about because she was never listless or dreamy or apathetic. A half-smile nearly always played about her lips and eyes, and it was there because she was pleased with something, not because she wanted to be agreeable. Even a half-smile made her cheeks dimple. She had what her mother called "a happy disposition."

When she finished the verses, Mrs. Rosen nodded approvingly. "Thank you, Vickie. The very next time I go to Chicago, I will try to get an English translation of *Faust* for you."

"But I want to read this one." Vickie's open smile darkened. "What I want is to pick up any of these books and just read them, like you and Mr. Rosen do."

The dusky red of Mrs. Rosen's cheeks grew a trifle deeper. Vickie never paid compliments, absolutely never; but if she really admired anyone, something in her voice betrayed it so convincingly that one felt flattered. When she dropped a remark of this kind, she added another link to the chain of responsibility which Mrs. Rosen unwillingly bore and tried to shake off—the irritating sense of being somehow responsible for Vickie, since, God knew, no one else felt responsible.

Once or twice, when she happened to meet pleasant young Mr. Templeton alone, she had tried to talk to him seriously about his daughter's future. "She has finished de school here, and she should be getting training of some sort; she is growing up," she told him severely.

He laughed and said in his way that was so honest, and so disarmingly sweet and frank: "Oh, don't remind me, Mrs. Rosen! I just pretend to myself she isn't. I want to keep my little daughter as long as I can." And there it ended.

Sometimes Vickie Templeton seemed so dense, so utterly unperceptive, that Mrs. Rosen was ready to wash her hands of her. Then some queer streak of sensibility in the child would make her change her mind. Last winter, when Mrs. Rosen came home from a visit to her sister in Chicago, she brought with her a new cloak of the sleeveless dolman type, black velvet, lined with grey and white squirrel skins, a grey skin next a white. Vickie, so indifferent to clothes, fell in love with that cloak. Her eyes followed it with delight whenever Mrs. Rosen wore it. She found it picturesque, romantic. Mrs. Rosen had been captivated by the same thing in the cloak, and had bought it with a shrug, knowing it would be quite out of place in Skyline; and Mr. Rosen, when she first produced it from her trunk, had laughed and said: "Where did you get that?—out of *Rigoletto?*" It looked like that—but how could Vickie know?

Vickie's whole family puzzled Mrs. Rosen; their feelings were so much finer than their way of living. She bought milk from the Templetons because they kept a cow—which Mandy milked,—and every night one of the twins brought the milk to her in a tin pail. Whichever boy brought it, she always called him Albert—she thought Adelbert a silly, Southern name.

One night when she was fitting the lid on an empty pail, she said severely:

"Now, Albert, I have put some cookies for Grandma in this pail, wrapped in a napkin. And they are for Grandma, remember, not for your mother or Vickie."

"Yes'm."

When she turned to him to give him the pail, she saw two full crystal globes in the little boy's eyes, just ready to break. She watched him go softly down the path and dash those tears away with the back of his hand. She was sorry. She hadn't thought the little boys realized that their household was somehow a queer one.

Queer or not, Mrs. Rosen liked to go there better than to most houses in the town. There was something easy, cordial, and carefree in the parlour that never smelled of being shut up, and the ugly furniture looked hospitable. One felt a pleasantness in the human relationships. These people didn't seem to know there were such things as struggle or exactness or competition in the world. They were always genuinely glad to see you, had time to see you, and were usually gay in mood—all but Grandmother, who had the kind of gravity that people who take thought of human destiny must have. But even she liked light-heartedness in others; she drudged, indeed, to keep it going.

There were houses that were better kept, certainly, but the housekeepers had no charm, no gentleness of manner, were like hard little machines, most of them; and some were grasping and narrow. The Templetons were not selfish or scheming. Anyone could take advantage of them, and many people did. Victoria might eat all the cookies her neighbour sent in, but she would give away anything she had. She was always ready to lend her dresses and hats and bits of jewellery for the school theatricals, and she never worked people for favours.

As for Mr. Templeton (people usually called him "young Mr. Templeton"), he was too delicate to collect his just debts. His boyish, eager-to-please manner, his fair complexion and blue eyes and young face, made him seem very soft to some of the hard old money-grubbers on Main Street, and the fact that he always said "Yes, sir," and "No, sir," to men older than himself furnished a good deal of amusement to bystanders.

Two years ago, when this Templeton family came to Skyline and moved into the house next door, Mrs. Rosen was inconsolable. The new neighbours had a lot of children, who would always be making a racket. They put a cow and a horse into the empty barn, which would mean dirt and flies. They strewed their back yard with packing-cases and did not pick them up.

She first met Mrs. Templeton at an afternoon card party, in a house at the extreme north end of the town, fully half a mile away, and she had to admit that her new neighbour was an attractive woman, and that there was something warm and genuine about her. She wasn't in the least willowy or languishing, as Mrs. Rosen had usually found Southern ladies to be. She was high-spirited and direct; a trifle imperious, but with a shade of diffidence, too, as if she were trying to adjust herself to a new group of people and to do the right thing.

While they were at the party, a blinding snowstorm came on, with a hard wind. Since they lived next door to each other, Mrs. Rosen and Mrs. Templeton struggled homeward together through the blizzard. Mrs. Templeton seemed delighted with the rough weather; she laughed like a big country girl whenever she made a mis-step off the obliterated sidewalk and sank up to her knees in a snow-drift.

"Take care, Mrs. Rosen," she kept calling, "keep to the right! Don't spoil your nice coat. My, ain't this real winter? We never had it like this back with us."

When they reached the Templeton's gate, Victoria wouldn't hear of Mrs. Rosen's going farther. "No, indeed, Mrs. Rosen, you come right in with me and get dry, and Ma'll make you a hot toddy while I take the baby."

By this time Mrs. Rosen had begun to like her neighbour, so she went in. To her surprise, the parlour was neat and comfortable—the children did not strew things about there, apparently. The hard-coal burner threw out a warm red glow. A faded, respectable Brussels carpet covered the floor, an old-fashioned wooden clock ticked on the walnut bookcase. There were a few easy chairs, and no hideous ornaments about. She rather liked the old oil-chromos[2] on the wall: "Hagar and Ishmael in the Wilderness," and "The Light of the World." While Mrs. Rosen dried her feet on the nickel base of the stove, Mrs. Templeton excused herself and withdrew to the next room,—her bedroom,—took off her silk dress and corsets, and put on a white challis négligée. She reappeared with the baby, who was not crying, exactly, but making eager, passionate, gasping entreaties,—faster and faster, tenser and tenser, as he felt his dinner nearer and nearer and yet not his.

Mrs. Templeton sat down in a low rocker by the stove and began to nurse him, holding him snugly but carelessly, still talking to Mrs. Rosen about the card party, and laughing about their wade home through the snow. Hughie, the baby, fell to work so fiercely that beads of sweat came out all over his flushed forehead. Mrs. Rosen could not help admiring him and his mother. They were so comfortable and complete. When he was changed to the other side, Hughie resented the interruption a little; but after a time he became soft and bland, as smooth as oil, indeed; began looking about him as he drew in his milk. He finally dropped the nipple from his lips altogether, turned on his mother's arm, and looked inquiringly at Mrs. Rosen.

"What a beautiful baby!" she exclaimed from her heart. And he was. A sort of golden baby. His hair was like sunshine, and his long lashes were gold

---

[2]Inexpensive imitation oil paintings also called oleographs which were color lithographs popular in the latter half of the nineteenth century.

over such gay blue eyes. There seemed to be a gold glow in his soft pink skin, and he had the smile of a cherub.

"We think he's a pretty boy," said Mrs. Templeton. "He's the prettiest of my babies. Though the twins were mighty cunning little fellows. I hated the idea of twins, but the minute I saw them, I couldn't resist them."

Just then old Mrs. Harris came in, walking widely in her full-gathered skirt and felt-soled shoes, bearing a tray with two smoking goblets upon it.

"This is my mother, Mrs. Harris, Mrs. Rosen," said Mrs. Templeton.

"I'm glad to know you, ma'am," said Mrs. Harris. "Victoria, let me take the baby, while you two ladies have your toddy."

"Oh, don't take him away, Mrs. Harris, please!" cried Mrs. Rosen.

The old lady smiled. "I won't. I'll set right here. He never frets with his grandma."

When Mrs. Rosen had finished her excellent drink, she asked if she might hold the baby, and Mrs. Harris placed him on her lap. He made a few rapid boxing motions with his two fists, then braced himself on his heels and the back of his head, and lifted himself up in an arc. When he dropped back, he looked up at Mrs. Rosen with his most intimate smile. "See what a smart boy I am!"

When Mrs. Rosen walked home, feeling her way through the snow by following the fence, she knew she could never stay away from a house where there was a baby like that one.

IV

Vickie did her studying in a hammock hung between two tall cottonwood trees over in the Roadmaster's green yard. The Roadmaster had the finest yard in Skyline, on the edge of the town, just where the sandy plain and the sage-brush began. His family went back to Ohio every summer, and Bert and Del Templeton were paid to take care of his lawn, to turn the sprinkler on at the right hours and to cut the grass. They were really too little to run the heavy lawn-mower very well, but they were able to manage because they were twins. Each took one end of the handle-bar, and they pushed together like a pair of fat Shetland ponies. They were very proud of being able to keep the lawn so nice, and worked hard on it. They cut Mrs. Rosen's grass once a week, too, and did it so well that she wondered why in the world they never did anything about their own yard. They didn't have city water, to be sure (it was expensive), but she thought they might pick up a few velocipedes and iron hoops, and dig up the messy "flower-bed," that was even uglier than the naked gravel spots. She was particularly offended by a deep ragged ditch, a miniature arroyo, which ran across the back yard, serving no purpose and looking very dreary.

One morning she said craftily to the twins, when she was paying them for cutting her grass:

"And, boys, why don't you just shovel the sand-pile by your fence into dat ditch, and make your back yard smooth?"

"Oh, no, ma'am," said Adelbert with feeling. "We like to have the ditch to build bridges over!"

Ever since vacation began, the twins had been busy getting the Roadmaster's yard ready for the Methodist lawn party. When Mrs. Holliday, the Roadmaster's wife, went away for the summer, she always left a key with the Ladies' Aid Society and invited them to give their ice-cream social at her place.

This year the date set for the party was June fifteenth. The day was a particularly fine one, and as Mr. Holliday himself had been called to Cheyenne on railroad business, the twins felt personally responsible for everything. They got out to the Holliday place early in the morning, and stayed on guard all day. Before noon the drayman brought a wagonload of card-tables and folding chairs, which the boys placed in chosen spots under the cottonwood trees. In the afternoon the Methodist ladies arrived and opened up the kitchen to receive the freezers of home-made ice-cream, and the cakes which the congregation donated. Indeed, all the good cake-bakers in town were expected to send a cake. Grandma Harris baked a white cake, thickly iced and covered with freshly grated coconut, and Vickie took it over in the afternoon.

Mr. and Mrs. Rosen, because they belonged to no church, contributed to the support of all, and usually went to the church suppers in winter and the socials in summer. On this warm June evening they set out early, in order to take a walk first. They strolled along the hard gravelled road that led out through the sage toward the sand-hills; tonight it led toward the moon, just rising over the sweep of dunes. The sky was almost as blue as at midday, and had that look of being very near and very soft which it has in desert countries. The moon, too, looked very near, soft and bland and innocent. Mrs. Rosen admitted that in the Adirondacks, for which she was always secretly homesick in summer, the moon had a much colder brilliance, seemed farther off and made of a harder metal. This moon gave the sage-brush plain and the drifted sand-hills the softness of velvet. All countries were beautiful to Mr. Rosen. He carried a country of his own in his mind, and was able to unfold it like a tent in any wilderness.

When they at last turned back toward the town, they saw groups of people, women in white dresses, walking toward the dark spot where the paper lanterns made a yellow light underneath the cottonwoods. High above, the rustling tree-tops stirred free in the flood of moonlight.

The lighted yard was surrounded by a low board fence, painted the dark red Burlington colour, and as the Rosens drew near, they noticed four children standing close together in the shadow of some tall elder bushes just outside the fence. They were the poor Maude children; their mother was the wash-woman, the Rosens' laundress and the Templetons'. People said that every one of those children had a different father. But good laundresses were few, and even the members of the Ladies' Aid were glad to get Mrs. Maude's services at a dollar a day, though they didn't like their children to play with hers. Just as the Rosens approached, Mrs. Templeton came out from the lighted square, leaned over the fence, and addressed the little Maudes.

"I expect you children forgot your dimes, now didn't you? Never mind, here's a dime for each of you, so come along and have your ice-cream."

The Maudes put out small hands and said: "Thank you," but not one of them moved.

"Come along, Francie" (the oldest girl was named Frances). "Climb right over the fence." Mrs. Templeton reached over and gave her a hand, and the little boys quickly scrambled after their sister. Mrs. Templeton took them to a table which Vickie and the twins had just selected as being especially private—they liked to do things together.

"Here, Vickie, let the Maudes sit at your table, and take care they get plenty of cake."

The Rosens had followed close behind Mrs. Templeton, and Mr. Rosen now overtook her and said in his most courteous and friendly manner: "Good evening, Mrs. Templeton. Will you have ice-cream with us?" He always used the local idioms, though his voice and enunciation made them sound alto-gether different from Skyline speech.

"Indeed I will, Mr. Rosen. Mr. Templeton will be late. He went out to his farm yesterday, and I don't know just when to expect him."

Vickie and the twins were disappointed at not having their table to them-selves, when they had come early and found a nice one; but they knew it was right to look out for the dreary little Maudes, so they moved close together and made room for them. The Maudes didn't cramp them long. When the three boys had eaten the last crumb of cake and licked their spoons, Francie got up and led them to a green slope by the fence, just outside the lighted circle. "Now set down, and watch and see how folks do," she told them. The boys looked to Francie for commands and support. She was really Amos Maude's child, born before he ran away to the Klondike, and it had been rubbed into them that this made a difference.

The Templeton children made their ice-cream linger out, and sat watching the crowd. They were glad to see their mother go to Mr. Rosen's table, and noticed how nicely he placed a chair for her and insisted upon putting a scarf about her shoulders. Their mother was wearing her new dotted Swiss, with many ruffles, all edged with black ribbon, and wide ruffly sleeves. As the twins watched her over their spoons, they thought how much prettier their mother was than any of the other women, and how becoming her new dress was. The children got as much satisfaction as Mrs. Harris out of Victoria's good looks.

Mr. Rosen was well pleased with Mrs. Templeton and her new dress, and with her kindness to the little Maudes. He thought her manner with them just right—warm, spontaneous, without anything patronizing. He always admired her way with her own children, though Mrs. Rosen thought it too casual. Being a good mother, he believed, was much more a matter of physical poise and richness than of sentimentalizing and reading doctor-books. To-night he was more talkative than usual, and in his quiet way made Mrs. Templeton feel his real friendliness and admiration. Unfortunately, he made other people feel it, too.

Mrs. Jackson, a neighbour who didn't like the Templetons, had been keeping an eye on Mr. Rosen's table. She was a stout square woman of imperturbable calm, effective in regulating the affairs of the community because she never lost her temper, and could say the most cutting things in calm, even kindly, tones. Her face was smooth and placid as a mask, rather good-humoured, and the fact that one eye had a cast and looked askance made it the more difficult to see through her intentions. When she had been lingering about the Rosens' table for some time, studying Mr. Rosen's pleasant attentions to Mrs. Templeton, she brought up a trayful of cake.

"You folks are about ready for another helping," she remarked affably.

Mrs. Rosen spoke. "I want some of Grandma Harris's cake. It's a white coconut, Mrs. Jackson."

"How about you, Mrs. Templeton, would you like some of your own cake?"

"Indeed I would," said Mrs. Templeton heartily. "Ma said she had good luck with it. I didn't see it. Vickie brought it over."

Mrs. Jackson deliberately separated the slices on her tray with two forks. "Well," she remarked with a chuckle that really sounded amiable, "I don't know but I'd like my cakes, if I kept somebody in the kitchen to bake them for me."

Mr. Rosen for once spoke quickly. "If I had a cook like Grandma Harris in my kitchen, I'd live in it!" he declared.

Mrs. Jackson smiled. "I don't know as we feel like that, Mrs. Templeton? I tell Mr. Jackson that my idea of coming up in the world would be to forget I had a cookstove, like Mrs. Templeton. But we can't all be lucky."

Mr. Rosen could not tell how much was malice and how much was stupidity. What he chiefly detected was self-satisfaction; the craftiness of the coarse-fibred country girl putting catch questions to the teacher. Yes, he

248

decided, the woman was merely showing off—she regarded it as an accomplishment to make people uncomfortable.

Mrs. Templeton didn't at once take it in. Her training was all to the end that you must give a guest everything you have, even if he happens to be your worst enemy, and that to cause anyone embarrassment is a frightful and humiliating blunder. She felt hurt without knowing just why, but all evening it kept growing clearer to her that this was another of those thrusts from the outside which she couldn't understand. The neighbours were sure to take sides against her, apparently, if they came often to see her mother.

Mr. Rosen tried to distract Mrs. Templeton, but he could feel the poison working. On the way home the children knew something had displeased or hurt their mother. When they went into the house, she told them to go upstairs at once, as she had a headache. She was severe and distant. When Mrs. Harris suggested making her some peppermint tea, Victoria threw up her chin.

"I don't want anybody waiting on me. I just want to be left alone." And she withdrew without saying good-night, or "Are you all right, Ma?" as she usually did.

Left alone, Mrs. Harris sighed and began to turn down her bed. She knew, as well as if she had been at the social, what kind of thing had happened. Some of those prying ladies of the Woman's Relief Corps, or the Woman's Christian Temperance Union, had been intimating to Victoria that her mother was "put upon." Nothing ever made Victoria cross but criticism. She was jealous of small attentions paid to Mrs. Harris, because she felt they were paid "behind her back" or "over her head," in a way that implied reproach to her. Victoria had been a belle in their own town in Tennessee, but here she was not very popular, no matter how many pretty dresses she wore, and she couldn't bear it. She felt as if her mother and Mr. Templeton must be somehow to blame; at least they ought to protect her from whatever was disagreeable—they always had!

V

Mrs. Harris wakened at about four o'clock, as usual, before the house was stirring, and lay thinking about their position in this new town. She didn't know why the neighbours acted so; she was as much in the dark as Victoria. At home, back in Tennessee, her place in the family was not exceptional, but perfectly regular. Mrs. Harris had replied to Mrs. Rosen, when that lady asked why in the world she didn't break Vickie in to help her in the kitchen: "We are only young once, and trouble comes soon enough." Young girls, in the South, were supposed to be carefree and foolish; the fault Grandmother found in Vickie was that she wasn't foolish enough. When the foolish girl married and began to have children, everything else must give way to that. She must be humoured and given the best of everything, because having children was hard on a woman, and it was the most important thing in the world. In Tennessee every young married woman in good circumstances had an older woman in the house, a mother or mother-in-law or an old aunt, who managed the household economies and directed the help.

That was the great difference; in Tennessee there had been plenty of helpers. There was old Miss Sadie Crummer, who came to the house to spin and sew and mend; old Mrs. Smith, who always arrived to help at butchering- and preserving-time; Lizzie, the coloured girl, who did the washing and who ran in every day to help Mandy. There were plenty more, who came whenever one of Lizzie's barefoot boys ran to fetch them. The hills were full of solitary old women, or women but slightly attached to some household, who were glad to come to Miz' Harris's for good food and a warm bed, and the little present that either Mrs. Harris or Victoria slipped into their carpet-sack when they went away.

To be sure, Mrs. Harris, and the other women of her age who managed their daughter's house, kept in the background; but it was their own background, and they ruled it jealously. They left the front porch and the parlour to the young married couple and their young friends; the old women spent most of their lives in the kitchen and pantries and back dining-room. But there they ordered life to their own taste, entertained their friends, dispensed charity, and heard the troubles of the poor. Moreover, back there it was Grandmother's own house they lived in. Mr. Templeton came of a superior family and had what Grandmother called "blood," but no property. He never so much as mended one of the steps to the front porch without consulting Mrs. Harris. Even "back home," in the aristocracy, there were old women who went on living like young ones—gave parties and drove out in their carriage and "went North" in the summer. But among the middle-class people and the country-folk, when a woman was a widow and had married daughters, she considered herself an old woman and wore full-gathered black dresses and a black bonnet and became a housekeeper. She accepted this estate unprotestingly, almost gratefully.

The Templetons' troubles began when Mr. Templeton's aunt died and left him a few thousand dollars, and he got the idea of bettering himself. The twins were little then, and he told Mrs. Harris his boys would have a better chance in Colorado—everybody was going West. He went alone first, and got a good position with a mining company in the mountains of southern Colorado. He had been bookkeeper in the bank in his home town, had "grown up in the bank," as they said. He was industrious and honourable, and the managers of the mining company liked him, even if they laughed at his polite, soft-spoken manners. He could have held his position indefinitely, and maybe got a promotion. But the altitude of that mountain town was too high for his family. All the children were sick there; Mrs. Templeton was ill most of the time and nearly died when Ronald was born. Hillary Templeton lost his courage and came north to the flat, sunny, semi-arid country between Wray and Cheyenne, to work for an irrigation project. So far, things had not gone well with him. The pinch told on everyone, but most on Grandmother. Here, in Skyline, she had all her accustomed responsibilities, and no helper but Mandy. Mrs. Harris was no longer living in a feudal society, where there were plenty of landless people glad to render service to the more fortunate, but in a snappy little Western democracy, where every man was as good as his neighbour and out to prove it.

Neither Mrs. Harris nor Mrs. Templeton understood just what was the matter; they were hurt and dazed, merely. Victoria knew that here she was censured and criticized, she who had always been so admired and envied! Grandmother knew that these meddlesome "Northerners" said things that made Victoria suspicious and unlike herself; made her unwilling that Mrs. Harris should receive visitors alone, or accept marks of attention that seemed offered in compassion for her state.

These women who belonged to clubs and Relief Corps lived differently, Mrs. Harris knew, but she herself didn't like the way they lived. She believed that somebody ought to be in the parlour, and somebody in the kitchen. She wouldn't for the world have had Victoria go about every morning in a short gingham dress, with bare arms, and a dust-cap on her head to hide the curling-kids, as these brisk housekeepers did. To Mrs. Harris that would have meant real poverty, coming down in the world so far that one could no longer keep up appearances. Her life was hard now, to be sure, since the family went on increasing and Mr. Templeton's means went on decreasing; but she certainly valued respectability above personal comfort, and she could go on a good way yet if they always had a cool pleasant parlour, with Victoria properly dressed to receive visitors. To keep Victoria different from these "ordinary" women meant everything to Mrs. Harris. She realized that Mrs. Rosen managed to be mistress of any situation, either in kitchen or parlour, but that was because she was "foreign." Grandmother perfectly understood that their neighbour had a superior cultivation which made everything she did an exercise of skill. She knew well enough that their own ways of cooking and cleaning were primitive beside Mrs. Rosen's.

If only Mr. Templeton's business affairs would look up, they could rent a larger house, and everything would be better. They might even get a German girl to come in and help—but now there was no place to put her. Grandmother's own lot could improve only with the family fortunes—any comfort for herself, aside from that of the family, was inconceivable to her; and on the other hand she could have no real unhappiness while the children were well, and good, and fond of her and their mother. That was why it was worth while to get up early in the morning and make her bed neat and draw the red spread smooth. The little boys loved to lie on her lounge and her pillows when they were tired. When they were sick, Ronald and Hughie wanted to be in her lap. They had no physical shrinking from her because she was old. And Victoria was never jealous of the children's wanting to be with her so much; that was a mercy!

Sometimes, in the morning, if her feet ached more than usual, Mrs. Harris felt a little low. (Nobody did anything about broken arches in those days, and the common endurance test of old age was to keep going after every step cost something.) She would hang up her towel with a sigh and go into the kitchen, feeling that it was hard to make a start. But the moment she heard the children running down the uncarpeted back stairs, she forgot to be low. Indeed, she ceased to be an individual, an old woman with aching feet; she became part of a group, became a relationship. She was drunk up into their freshness when they burst in upon her, telling her about their dreams, explaining their troubles with buttons and shoe-laces and underwear shrunk too small. The tired, solitary old woman Grandmother had been at daybreak vanished; suddenly the morning seemed as important to her as it did to the children, and the mornings ahead stretched out sunshiny, important.

VI

The day after the Methodist social, Blue Boy didn't come for his morning milk; he always had it in a clean saucer on the covered back porch, under the long bench where the tin wash-tubs stood ready for Mrs. Maude. After the children had finished breakfast, Mrs. Harris sent Mandy out to look for the cat.

The girl came back in a minute, her eyes big.

"Law me, Miz' Harris, he's awful sick. He's a-layin' in the straw in the barn. He's swallered a bone, or havin' a fit or somethin'."

Grandmother threw an apron over her head and went out to see for herself. The children went with her. Blue Boy was retching and choking, and his yellow eyes were filled up with rhume.

"Oh, Gram'ma, what's the matter?" the boys cried.

"It's the distemper. How could he have got it?" Her voice was so harsh that Ronald began to cry. "Take Ronald back to the house, Del. He might get bit. I wish I'd kept my word and never had a cat again!"

"Why, Gram'ma!" Albert looked at her. "Won't Blue Boy get well?"

"Not from the distemper, he won't."

"But Gram'ma, can't I run for the veter'nary?"

"You gether up an armful of hay. We'll take him into the coal-house, where I can watch him."

Mrs. Harris waited until the spasm was over, then picked up the limp cat and carried him to the coal-shed that opened off the back porch. Albert piled the hay in one corner—the coal was low, since it was summer—and they spread a piece of old carpet on the hay and made a bed for Blue Boy. "Now you run along with Adelbert. There'll be a lot of work to do on Mr. Holliday's yard, cleaning up after the sociable. Mandy an' me'll watch Blue Boy. I expect he'll sleep for a while."

Albert went away regretfully, but the drayman and some of the Methodist ladies were in Mr. Holliday's yard, packing chairs and tables and ice-cream freezers into the wagon, and the twins forgot the sick cat in their excitement. By noon they had picked up the last paper napkin, raked over the gravel walks where the salt from the freezers had left white patches, and hung the hammock in which Vickie did her studying back in its place. Mr. Holliday paid the boys a dollar a week for keeping up the yard, and they gave the money to their mother—it didn't come amiss in a family where actual cash was so short. She let them keep half the sum Mrs. Rosen paid for her milk every Saturday, and that was more spending money than most boys had. They often made a few extra quarters by cutting grass for other people, or by distributing handbills. Even the disagreeable Mrs. Jackson next door had remarked over the fence to Mrs. Harris: "I do believe Bert and Del are going to be industrious. They must have got it from you, Grandma."

The day came on very hot, and when the twins got back from the Roadmaster's yard, they both lay down on Grandmother's lounge and went to sleep. After dinner they had a rare opportunity; the Roadmaster himself appeared at the front door and invited them to go up to the next town with him on his railroad velocipede. That was great fun: the velocipede always whizzed along so fast on the bright rails, the gasoline engine puffing; and grasshoppers jumped up out of the sagebrush and hit you in the face like sling-shot bullets. Sometimes the wheels cut in two a lazy snake who was sunning himself on the track, and the twins always hoped it was a rattler and felt they had done a good work.

The boys got back from their trip with Mr. Holliday late in the afternoon. The house was cool and quiet. Their mother had taken Ronald and Hughie down town with her, and Vickie was off somewhere. Grandmother was not in her room, and the kitchen was empty. The boys went out to the back porch to pump a drink. The coal-shed door was open, and inside, on a low stool, sat Mrs. Harris beside her cat. Bert and Del didn't stop to get a drink; they felt ashamed that they had gone off for a gay ride and forgotten Blue Boy. They sat down on a big lump of coal beside Mrs. Harris. They would never have known that this miserable rumpled animal was their proud tom. Presently he went off into a spasm and began to froth at the mouth.

"Oh, Gram'ma, can't you do anything?" cried Albert, struggling with his tears. "Blue Boy was such a good cat—why has he got to suffer?"

"Everything that's alive has got to suffer," said Mrs. Harris. Albert put out his hand and caught her skirt, looking up at her beseechingly, as if to make her unsay that saying, which he only half understood. She patted his hand. She had forgot she was speaking to a little boy.

"Where's Vickie?" Adelbert asked aggrievedly. "Why don't she do something? He's part her cat."

Mrs. Harris sighed. "Vickie's got her head full of things lately; that makes people kind of heartless."

The boys resolved they would never put anything into their heads, then!

Blue Boy's fit passed, and the three sat watching their pet that no longer knew them. The twins had not seen much suffering; Grandmother had seen a great deal. Back in Tennessee, in her own neighbourhood, she was accounted a famous nurse. When any of the poor mountain people were in great distress, they always sent for Miz' Harris. Many a time she had gone into a house where five or six children were all down with scarlet fever or diphtheria, and done what she could. Many a child and many a woman she had laid out and got ready for the grave. In her primitive community the undertaker made the coffin—he did nothing more. She had seen so much misery that she wondered herself why it hurt so to see her tom-cat die. She had taken her leave of him, and she got up from her stool. She didn't want the boys to be too much distressed.

"Now you boys must wash and put on clean shirts. Your mother will be home pretty soon. We'll leave Blue Boy; he'll likely be easier in the morning." She knew the cat would die at sundown.

After supper, when Bert looked into the coal-shed and found the cat dead, all the family were sad. Ronald cried miserably, and Hughie cried because Ronald did. Mrs. Templeton herself went out and looked into the shed, and she was sorry, too. Though she didn't like cats, she had been fond of this one.

"Hillary," she told her husband, "when you go down town tonight, tell the Mexican to come and get that cat early in the morning, before the children are up."

The Mexican had a cart and two mules, and he hauled away tin cans and refuse to a gully out in the sage-brush.

Mrs. Harris gave Victoria an indignant glance when she heard this, and turned back to the kitchen. All evening she was gloomy and silent. She refused to read aloud, and the twins took Ronald and went mournfully out to play under the electric light. Later, when they had said good-night to their parents in the parlour and were on their way upstairs, Mrs. Harris followed them into the kitchen, shut the door behind her, and said indignantly:

"Air you two boys going to let that Mexican take Blue Boy and throw him onto some trash-pile?"

The sleepy boys were frightened at the anger and bitterness in her tone. They stood still and looked up at her, while she went on:

"You git up early in the morning, and I'll put him in a sack, and one of you take a spade and go to that crooked old willer tree that grows just where the sand creek turns off the road, and you dig a little grave for Blue Boy, an' bury him right."

They had seldom seen such resentment in their grandmother. Albert's throat choked up, he rubbed the tears away with his fist.

"Yes'm, Gram'ma, we will, we will," he gulped.

VII

Only Mrs. Harris saw the boys go out next morning. She slipped a bread-and-butter sandwich into the hand of each, but she said nothing, and they said nothing.

The boys did not get home until their parents were ready to leave the table. Mrs. Templeton made no fuss, but told them to sit down and eat their breakfast. When they had finished, she said commandingly:

"Now you march into my room." That was where she heard explanations and administered punishment. When she whipped them, she did it thoroughly.

She followed them and shut the door.

"Now, what were you boys doing this morning?"

"We went off to bury Blue Boy."

"Why didn't you tell me you were going?"

They looked down at their toes, but said nothing. Their mother studied their mournful faces, and her overbearing expression softened.

"The next time you get up and go off anywhere, you come and tell me beforehand, do you understand?"

"Yes'm."

She opened the door, motioned them out, and went with them into the parlour. "I'm sorry about your cat, boys," she said. "That's why I don't like to have cats around; they're always getting sick and dying. Now run along and play. Maybe you'd like to have a circus in the back yard this afternoon? And we'll all come."

The twins ran out in a joyful frame of mind. Their grandmother had been mistaken; their mother wasn't indifferent about Blue Boy, she was sorry. Now everything was all right, and they could make a circus ring.

They knew their grandmother got put out about strange things, anyhow. A few months ago it was because their mother hadn't asked one of the visiting preachers who came to the church conference to stay with them. There was no place for the preacher to sleep except on the folding lounge in the parlour, and no place for him to wash—he would have been very uncomfortable, and so would all the household. But Mrs. Harris was terribly upset that there should be a conference in the town, and they not keeping a preacher! She was quite bitter about it.

The twins called in the neighbour boys, and they made a ring in the back yard, around their turning-bar. Their mother came to the show and paid admission, bringing Mrs. Rosen and Grandma Harris. Mrs. Rosen thought if all the children in the neighbourhood were to be howling and running in a circle in the Templetons' back yard, she might as well be there, too, for she would have no peace at home.

After the dog races and the Indian fight were over, Mrs. Templeton took Mrs. Rosen into the house to revive her with cake and lemonade. The parlour was cool and dusky. Mrs. Rosen was glad to get into it after sitting on a wooden bench in the sun. Grandmother stayed in the parlour with them, which was unusual. Mrs. Rosen sat waving a palm-leaf fan—she felt the heat very much, because she wore her stays so tight—while Victoria went to make the lemonade.

"De circuses are not so good, widout Vickie to manage them, Grandma," she said.

"No'm. The boys complain right smart about losing Vickie from their plays. She's at her books all the time now. I don't know what's got into the child."

"If she wants to go to college, she must prepare herself, Grandma. I am agreeably surprised in her. I didn't think she'd stick to it."

Mrs. Templeton came in with a tray of tumblers and the glass pitcher all frosted over. Mrs. Rosen wistfully admired her neighbour's tall figure and good carriage; she was wearing no corsets at all today under her flowered organdie afternoon dress, Mrs. Rosen had noticed, and yet she could carry herself so smooth and straight—after having had so many children, too! Mrs. Rosen was envious, but she gave credit where credit was due.

When Mrs. Templeton brought in the cake, Mrs. Rosen was still talking to Grandmother about Vickie's studying. Mrs. Templeton shrugged carelessly.

"There's such a thing as overdoing it, Mrs. Rosen," she observed as she poured the lemonade. "Vickie's very apt to run to extremes."

"But, my dear lady, she can hardly be too extreme in dis matter. If she is to take a competitive examination with girls from much better schools than ours, she will have to do better than the others, or fail: no two ways about it. We must encourage her."

Mrs. Templeton bridled a little. "I'm sure I don't interfere with her studying, Mrs. Rosen. I don't see where she got this notion, but I let her alone."

Mrs. Rosen accepted a second piece of chocolate cake. "And what do you think about it, Grandma?"

Mrs. Harris smiled politely. "None of our people, or Mr. Templeton's either, ever went to college. I expect it is all on account of the young gentleman who was here last summer."

Mrs. Rosen laughed and lifted her eyebrows. "Something very personal in Vickie's admiration for Professor Chalmers we think, Grandma? A very sudden interest in de sciences, I should say!"

Mrs. Templeton shrugged. "You're mistaken, Mrs. Rosen. There ain't a particle of romance in Vickie."

"But there are several kinds of romance, Mrs. Templeton. She may not have your kind."

"Yes'm, that's so," said Mrs. Harris in a low, grateful voice. She thought that a hard word Victoria had said of Vickie.

"I didn't see a thing in that Professor Chalmers, myself," Victoria remarked. "He was a gawky kind of fellow, and never had a thing to say in company. Did you think he amounted to much?"

"Oh, widout doubt Doctor Chalmers is a very scholarly man. A great many brilliant scholars are widout de social graces, you know." When Mrs. Rosen, from a much wider experience, corrected her neighbour, she did so somewhat playfully, as if insisting upon something Victoria capriciously chose to ignore.

At this point old Mrs. Harris put her hands on the arms of the chair in preparation to rise. "If you ladies will excuse me, I think I will go and lie down a little before supper." She rose and went heavily out on her felt soles. She never really lay down in the afternoon, but she dozed in her own black rocker. Mrs. Rosen and Victoria sat chatting about Professor Chalmers and his boys.

Last summer the young professor had come to Skyline with four of his students from the University of Michigan, and had stayed three months, digging for fossils out in the sandhills. Vickie had spent a great many mornings at their camp. They lived at the town hotel, and drove out to their camp every day in a light spring-wagon. Vickie used to wait for them at the edge of the town, in front of the Roadmaster's house, and when the spring-wagon came rattling along, the boys would call: "There's our girl!", slow the horses, and give her a hand up. They said she was their mascot, and were very jolly with her. They had a splendid summer—found a great bed of fossil elephant bones, where a whole herd must once have perished. Later on they came upon the bones of a new kind of elephant, scarcely larger than a pig. They were greatly excited about their finds, and so was Vickie. That was why they liked her. It was they who told her about a memorial scholarship at Ann Arbor, which was open to any girl from Colorado.

VIII

In August Vickie went down to Denver to take her examinations. Mr. Holliday, the Roadmaster, got her a pass, and arranged that she should stay with the family of one of his passenger conductors.

For three days she wrote examination papers along with other contestants, in one of the Denver high schools, proctored by a teacher. Her father had given her five dollars for incidental expenses, and she came home with a box of mineral specimens for the twins, a singing top for Ronald, and a toy burro for Hughie.

Then began days of suspense that stretched into weeks. Vickie went to the post-office every morning, opened her father's combination box, and looked over the letters, long before he got down town—always hoping there might be a letter from Ann Arbor. The night mail came in at six, and after supper she hurried to the post-office and waited about until the shutter at the general-delivery window was drawn back, a signal that the mail had all been "distributed." While the tedious process of distribution was going on, she usually withdrew from the office, full of joking men and cigar smoke, and walked up and down under the big cottonwood trees that overhung the side street. When the crowd of men began to come out, then she knew the mail-bags were empty, and she went in to get whatever letters were in the Templeton box and take them home.

After two weeks went by, she grew down-hearted. Her young professor, she knew, was in England for his vacation. There would be no one at the University of Michigan who was interested in her fate. Perhaps the fortunate contestant had already been notified of her success. She never asked herself, as she walked up and down under the cottonwoods on those summer nights, what she would do if she didn't get the scholarship. There was no alternative. If she didn't get it, then everything was over.

During the weeks when she lived only to go to the post-office, she managed to cut her finger and get ink into the cut. As a result, she had a badly infected hand and had to carry it in a sling. When she walked her nightly beat under the cottonwoods, it was a kind of comfort to feel that finger throb; it was companionship, made her case more complete.

The strange thing was that one morning a letter came, addressed to Miss Victoria Templeton; in a long envelope such as her father called "legal size," with *"University of Michigan"* in the upper left-hand corner. When Vickie took it from the box, such a wave of fright and weakness went through her that she could scarcely get out of the post-office. She hid the letter under her striped blazer and went a weak, uncertain trail down the sidewalk under the big trees. Without seeing anything or knowing what road she took, she got to the Roadmaster's green yard and her hammock, where she always felt not on the earth, yet of it.

Three hours later, when Mrs. Rosen was just tasting one of those clear soups upon which the Templetons thought she wasted so much pains and good meat, Vickie walked in at the kitchen door and said in a low but somewhat unnatural voice:

"Mrs. Rosen, I got the scholarship."

Mrs. Rosen looked up at her sharply, then pushed the soup back to a cooler part of the stove.

"What is dis you say, Vickie? You have heard from de University?"

"Yes'm. I got the letter this morning." She produced it from under her blazer.

Mrs. Rosen had been cutting noodles. She took Vickie's face in two hot, plump hands that were still floury, and looked at her intently. "Is dat true, Vickie? No mistake? I am delighted—and surprised! Yes, surprised. Den you will *be* something, you won't just sit on de front porch." She squeezed the girl's round, good-natured cheeks, as if she could mould them into something definite then and there. "Now you must stay for lunch and tell us all about it. Go in and announce yourself to Mr. Rosen."

Mr. Rosen had come home for lunch and was sitting, a book in his hand, in a corner of the darkened front parlour where a flood of yellow sun streamed in under the dark green blind. He smiled his friendly smile at Vickie and waved her to a seat, making her understand that he wanted to finish his paragraph. The dark engraving of the pointed cypresses and the Roman tomb was on the wall just behind him.

Mrs. Rosen came into the back parlour, which was the dining-room, and began taking things out of the silver-drawer to lay a place for their visitor. She spoke to her husband rapidly in German.

He put down his book, came over, and took Vickie's hand.

"Is it true, Vickie? Did you really win the scholarship?"

"Yes, sir."

He stood looking down at her through his kind, remote smile—a smile in the eyes, that seemed to come up through layers and layers of something— gentle doubts, kindly reservations.

"Why do you want to go to college, Vickie?" he asked playfully.

"To learn," she said with surprise.

"But why do you want to learn? What do you want to do with it?"

"I don't know. Nothing, I guess."

"Then what do you want it for?"

"I don't know. I just want it."

For some reason Vickie's voice broke there. She had been terribly strung up all morning, lying in the hammock with her eyes tight shut. She had not been home at all, she had wanted to take her letter to the Rosens first. And now one of the gentlest men she knew made her choke by something strange and presageful in his voice.

"Then if you want it without any purpose at all, you will not be disappointed." Mr. Rosen wished to distract her and help her to keep back the tears. "Listen: a great man once said: *'Le but n'est rien; le chemin, c'est tout.'* That means: The end is nothing, the road is all. Let me write it down for you and give you your first French lesson."

He went to the desk with its big silver inkwell, where he and his wife wrote so many letters in several languages, and inscribed the sentence on a sheet of purple paper, in his delicately shaded foreign script, signing under it a name: *J. Michelet.*[3] He brought it back and shook it before Vickie's eyes. "There, keep it to remember me by. Slip it into the envelope with your college credentials—that is a good place for it." From his deliberate smile and the twitch of one eyebrow, Vickie knew he meant her to take it along as an antidote, a corrective for whatever colleges might do to her. But she had always known that Mr. Rosen was wiser than professors.

Mrs. Rosen was frowning, she thought that sentence a bad precept to give any Templeton. Moreover, she always promptly called her husband back to earth when he soared a little; though it was exactly for this transcendental quality of mind that she reverenced him in her heart, and thought him so much finer than any of his successful brothers.

"Luncheon is served," she said in the crisp tone that put people in their places. "And Miss Vickie, you are to eat your tomatoes with an oil dressing, as we do. If you are going off into the world, it is quite time you learn to like things that are everywhere accepted."

---

[3]French Romantic historian (1798–1874).

Vickie said: "Yes'm," and slipped into the chair Mr. Rosen had placed for her. Today she didn't care what she ate, though ordinarily she thought a French dressing tasted a good deal like castor oil.

IX

Vickie was to discover that nothing comes easily in this world. Next day she got a letter from one of the jolly students of Professor Chalmer's party, who was watching over her case in his chief's absence. He told her the scholarship meant admission to the freshman class without further examinations, and two hundred dollars toward her expenses; she would have to bring along about three hundred more to put her through the year.

She took this letter to her father's office. Seated in his revolving desk-chair, Mr. Templeton read it over several times and looked embarrassed.

"I'm sorry, daughter," he said at last, "but really, just now, I couldn't spare that much. Not this year. I expect next year will be better for us."

"But the scholarship is for this year, Father. It wouldn't count next year. I just have to go in September."

"I really ain't got it, daughter." He spoke, oh so kindly! He had lovely manners with his daughter and his wife. "It's just all I can do to keep the store bills paid up. I'm away behind with Mr. Rosen's bill. Couldn't you study here this winter and get along about as fast? It isn't that I wouldn't like to let you have the money if I had it. And with young children, I can't let my life insurance go."

Vickie didn't say anything more. She took her letter and wandered down Main Street with it, leaving young Mr. Templeton to a very bad half-hour.

At dinner Vickie was silent, but everyone could see she had been crying. Mr. Templeton told *Uncle Remus* stories to keep up the family morale and make the giggly twins laugh. Mrs. Templeton glanced covertly at her daughter from time to time. She was sometimes a little afraid of Vickie, who seemed to her to have a hard streak. If it were a love-affair that the girl was crying about, that would be so much more natural—and more hopeful!

At two o'clock Mrs. Templeton went to the Afternoon Euchre Club, the twins were to have another ride with the Roadmaster on his velocipede, the little boys took their nap on their mother's bed. The house was empty and quiet. Vickie felt an aversion for the hammock under the cottonwoods where she had been betrayed into such bright hopes. She lay down on her grandmother's lounge in the cluttered play-room and turned her face to the wall.

When Mrs. Harris came in for her rest and began to wash her face at the tin basin, Vickie got up. She wanted to be alone. Mrs. Harris came over to her while she was still sitting on the edge of the lounge.

"What's the matter, Vickie child?" She put her hand on her grand-daughter's shoulder, but Vickie shrank away. Young misery is like that, some-times.

"Nothing. Except that I can't go to college after all. Papa can't let me have the money."

Mrs. Harris settled herself on the faded cushions of her rocker. "How much is it? Tell me about it, Vickie. Nobody's around."

Vickie told her what the conditions were, briefly and dryly, as if she were talking to an enemy. Everyone was an enemy; all society was against her. She told her grandmother the facts and then went upstairs, refusing to be com-forted.

Mrs. Harris saw her disappear through the kitchen door, and then sat looking at the door, her face grave, her eyes stern and sad. A poor factory-made piece of joiner's work seldom has to bear a look of such intense, accusing sorrow; as if that flimsy pretence of "grained" yellow pine were the door shut against all young aspiration.

X

Mrs. Harris had decided to speak to Mr. Templeton, but opportunities for seeing him alone were not frequent. She watched out of the kitchen window, and when she next saw him go into the barn to fork down hay for his horse, she threw an apron over her head and followed him. She waylaid him as he came down from the hayloft.

"Hillary, I want to see you about Vickie. I was wondering if you could lay hand on any of the money you got for the sale of my house back home."

Mr. Templeton was nervous. He began brushing his trousers with a little whisk-broom he kept there, hanging on a nail.

"Why, no'm, Mrs. Harris. I couldn't just conveniently call in any of it right now. You know we had to use part of it to get moved up here from the mines."

"I know. But I thought if there was any left you could get at, we could let Vickie have it. A body'd like to help the child."

"I'd like to, powerful well, Mrs. Harris. I would, indeedy. But I'm afraid I can't manage it right now. The fellers I've loaned to can't pay up this year. Maybe next year—" He was like a little boy trying to escape a scolding, though he had never had a nagging word from Mrs. Harris.

She looked downcast, but said nothing.

"It's all right, Mrs. Harris," he took on his brisk business tone and hung up the brush. "The money's perfectly safe. It's well invested."

Invested; that was a word men always held over women, Mrs. Harris thought, and it always meant they could have none of their own money. She sighed deeply.

"Well, if that's the way it is—" She turned away and went back to the house on her flat heelless slippers, just in time; Victoria was at that moment coming out to the kitchen with Hughie.

"Ma," she said, "can the little boy play out here, while I go down town?"

XI

For the next few days Mrs. Harris was very sombre, and she was not well. Several times in the kitchen she was seized with what she called giddy spells, and Mandy had to help her to a chair and give her a little brandy.

"Don't you say nothin', Mandy," she warned the girl. But Mandy knew enough for that.

Mrs. Harris scarcely noticed how her strength was failing, because she had so much on her mind. She was very proud, and she wanted to do something that was hard for her to do. The difficulty was to catch Mrs. Rosen alone.

On the afternoon when Victoria went to her weekly euchre, the old lady beckoned Mandy and told her to run across the alley and fetch Mrs. Rosen for a minute.

Mrs. Rosen was packing her trunk, but she came at once. Grandmother awaited her in her chair in the play-room.

"I take it very kindly of you to come, Mrs. Rosen. I'm afraid it's warm in here. Won't you have a fan?" She extended the palm leaf she was holding.

"Keep it yourself, Grandma. You are not looking very well. Do you feel badly, Grandma Harris?" She took the old lady's hand and looked at her anxiously.

"Oh, no, ma'am! I'm as well as usual. The heat wears on me a little, maybe. Have you seen Vickie lately, Mrs. Rosen?"

"Vickie? No. She hasn't run in for several days. These young people are full of their own affairs, you know."

"I expect she's backward about seeing you, now that she's so discouraged."

"Discouraged? Why, didn't the child get her scholarship after all?"

"Yes'm, she did. But they write her she has to bring more money to help her out; three hundred dollars. Mr. Templeton can't raise it just now. We had so much sickness in that mountain town before we moved up here, he got behind. Pore Vickie's downhearted."

"Oh, that is too bad! I expect you've been fretting over it, and that is why you don't look like yourself. Now what can we do about it?"

Mrs. Harris sighed and shook her head. "Vickie's trying to muster courage to go around to her father's friends and borrow from one and another. But we ain't been here long—it ain't like we had old friends here. I hate to have the child do it."

Mrs. Rosen looked perplexed. "I'm sure Mr. Rosen would help her. He takes a great interest in Vickie."

"I thought maybe he could see his way to. That's why I sent Mandy to fetch you."

"That was right, Grandma. Now let me think." Mrs. Rosen put up her plump red-brown hand and leaned her chin upon it. "Day after tomorrow I am going to run on to Chicago for my niece's wedding." She saw her old friend's face fall. "Oh, I shan't be gone long; ten days, perhaps. I will speak to Mr. Rosen tonight, and if Vickie goes to him after I am off his hands, I'm sure he will help her."

Mrs. Harris looked up at her with solemn gratitude. "Vickie ain't the kind of girl would forget anything like that, Mrs. Rosen. Nor I wouldn't forget it."

Mrs. Rosen patted her arm. "Grandma Harris," she exclaimed, "I will just ask Mr. Rosen to do it for you! You know I care more about the old folks than the young. If I take this worry off your mind, I shall go away to the wedding with a light heart. Now dismiss it. I am sure Mr. Rosen can arrange this himself for you, and Vickie won't have to go about to these people here, and our gossipy neighbours will never be the wiser." Mrs. Rosen poured this out in her quick, authoritative tone, converting her *th's* into *d's,* as she did when she was excited.

Mrs. Harris's red-brown eyes slowly filled with tears—Mrs. Rosen had never seen that happen before. But she simply said, with quiet dignity: "Thank you, ma'am. I wouldn't have turned to nobody else."

"That means I am an old friend already, doesn't it, Grandma? And that's what I want to be. I am very jealous where Grandma Harris is concerned!" She lightly kissed the back of the purple-veined hand she had been holding, and ran home to her packing. Grandma sat looking down at her hand. How easy it was for these foreigners to say what they felt!

XII

Mrs. Harris knew she was failing. She was glad to be able to conceal it from Mrs. Rosen when that kind neighbour dashed in to kiss her good-bye on the morning of her departure for Chicago. Mrs. Templeton was, of course, present, and secrets could not be discussed. Mrs. Rosen, in her stiff little brown traveling-hat, her hands tightly gloved in brown kid, could only wink and nod to Grandmother to tell her all was well. Then she went out and climbed into the "hack" bound for the depot, which had stopped for a moment at the Templetons' gate.

Mrs. Harris was thankful that her excitable friend hadn't noticed anything unusual about her looks, and, above all, that she had made no comment. She got through the day, and that evening, thank goodness, Mr. Templeton took his wife to hear a company of strolling players sing *The Chimes of Normandy* at the Opera House. He loved music, and just now he was very eager to distract and amuse Victoria. Grandma sent the twins out to play and went to bed early.

Next morning, when she joined Mandy in the kitchen, Mandy noticed something wrong.

"You set right down, Miz' Harris, an' let me git you some whisky. Deed, ma'am, you look awful porely. You ought to tell Miss Victoria an' let her send for the doctor."

"No, Mandy, I don't want no doctor. I've seen more sickness than ever he has. Doctors can't do no more than linger you out, an' I've always prayed I wouldn't last to be a burden. You git me some whisky in hot water, and pour it on a piece of toast. I feel real empty."

That afternoon when Mrs. Harris was taking her rest, for once she lay down upon her lounge. Vickie came in, tense and excited, and stopped for a moment.

"It's all right, Grandma. Mr. Rosen is going to lend me the money. I won't have to go to anybody else. He won't ask Father to endorse my note, either. He'll just take my name." Vickie rather shouted this news at Mrs. Harris, as if the old lady were deaf, or slow of understanding. She didn't thank her; she didn't know her grandmother was in any way responsible for Mr. Rosen's offer, though at the close of their interview he had said: "We won't speak of our arrangement to anyone but your father. And I want you to mention it to the old lady Harris. I know she has been worrying about you."

Having brusquely announced her news, Vickie hurried away. There was so much to do about getting ready, she didn't know where to begin. She had no trunk and no clothes. Her winter coat, bought two years ago, was so outgrown that she couldn't get into it. All her shoes were run over at the heel and must go to the cobbler. And she had only two weeks in which to do everything! She dashed off.

Mrs. Harris sighed and closed her eyes happily. She thought with modest pride that with people like the Rosens she had always "got along nicely." It was only with the ill-bred and unclassified, like this Mrs. Jackson next door, that she had disagreeable experiences. Such folks, she told herself, had come out of nothing and knew no better. She was afraid this inquisitive woman might find her ailing and come prying round with unwelcome suggestions.

Mrs. Jackson did, indeed, call that very afternoon, with a miserable contribution of veal-loaf as an excuse (all the Templetons hated veal), but Mandy had been forewarned, and she was resourceful. She met Mrs. Jackson at the kitchen door and blocked the way.

"Sh-h-h, ma'am, Miz' Harris is asleep, havin' her nap. No'm, she ain't porely, she's as usual. But Hughie had the colic last night when Miss Victoria was at the show, an' kep' Miz' Harris awake."

Mrs. Jackson was loath to turn back. She had really come to find out why Mrs. Rosen drove away in the depot hack yesterday morning. Except at church socials, Mrs. Jackson did not meet people in Mrs. Rosen's set.

The next day, when Mrs. Harris got up and sat on the edge of her bed, her head began to swim, and she lay down again. Mandy peeped into the play-room as soon as she came downstairs, and found the old lady still in bed. She leaned over her and whispered:

"Ain't you feelin' well, Miz' Harris?"

"No, Mandy, I'm right porely," Mrs. Harris admitted.

"You stay where you air, ma'am. I'll git the breakfast fur the chillun, an' take the other breakfast in fur Miss Victoria an' Mr. Templeton." She hurried back to the kitchen, and Mrs. Harris went to sleep.

Immediately after breakfast Vickie dashed off about her own concerns, and the twins went to cut grass while the dew was still on it. When Mandy was taking the other breakfast into the dining-room, Mrs. Templeton came through the play-room.

"What's the matter, Ma? Are you sick?" she asked in an accusing tone.

"No, Victoria, I ain't sick. I had a little giddy spell, and I thought I'd lay still."

"You ought to be more careful what you eat, Ma. If you're going to have another bilious spell, when everything is so upset anyhow, I don't know what I'll do!" Victoria's voice broke. She hurried back into her bedroom, feeling bitterly that there was no place in that house to cry in, no spot where one could be alone, even with misery; that the house and the people in it were choking her to death.

Mrs. Harris sighed and closed her eyes. Things did seem to be upset, though she didn't know just why. Mandy, however, had her suspicions. While she waited on Mr. and Mrs. Templeton at breakfast, narrowly observing their manner toward each other and Victoria's swollen eyes and desperate expression, her suspicions grew stronger.

Instead of going to his office, Mr. Templeton went to the barn and ran out the buggy. Soon he brought out Cleveland, the black horse, with his harness on. Mandy watched from the back window. After he had hitched the horse to the buggy, he came into the kitchen to wash his hands.

While he dried them on the roller towel, he said in his most business-like tone:

"I likely won't be back tonight, Mandy. I have to go out to my farm, and I'll hardly get through my business there in time to come home."

Then Mandy was sure. She had been through these times before, and at such a crisis poor Mr. Templeton was always called away on important business. When he had driven out through the alley and up the street past Mrs. Rosen's, Mandy left her dishes and went in to Mrs. Harris. She bent over and whispered low:

"Miz' Harris, I 'spect Miss Victoria's done found out she's goin' to have another baby! It looks that way. She's gone back to bed."

Mrs. Harris lifted a warning finger. "Sh-h-h!"

"Oh yes'm, I won't say nothin'. I never do."

Mrs. Harris tried to face this possibility, but her mind didn't seem strong enough—she dropped off into another doze.

All that morning Mrs. Templeton lay on her bed alone, the room darkened and a handkerchief soaked in camphor tied round her forehead. The twins had taken Ronald off to watch them cut grass, and Hughie played in the kitchen under Mandy's eye.

Now and then Victoria sat upright on the edge of the bed, beat her hands together softly and looked desperately at the ceiling, then about at those frail, confining walls. If only she could meet the situation with violence, fight it, conquer it! But there was nothing for it but stupid animal patience. She would have to go through all that again, and nobody, not even Hillary, wanted another baby—poor as they were, and in this overcrowded house. Anyhow, she told herself, she was ashamed to have another baby, when she had a daughter old enough to go to college! She was sick of it all; sick of dragging this chain of life that never let her rest and periodically knotted and overpowered her; made her ill and hideous for months, and then dropped another baby into her arms. She had had babies enough; and there ought to be an end to such apprehensions some time before you were old and ugly.

She wanted to run away, back to Tennessee, and lead a free, gay life, as she had when she was first married. She could do a great deal more with freedom than ever Vickie could. She was still young, and she was still handsome; why must she be for ever shut up in a little cluttered house with children and fresh babies and an old woman and a stupid bound girl and a husband who wasn't very successful? Life hadn't brought her what she expected when she married Hillary Templeton; life hadn't used her right. She had tried to keep up appearances, to dress well with very little to do it on, to keep young for her husband and children. She had tried, she had tried! Mrs. Templeton buried her face in the pillow and smothered the sobs that shook the bed.

Hillary Templeton, on his drive out through the sage-brush, up into the farming country that was irrigated from the North Platte, did not feel altogether cheerful, though he whistled and sang to himself on the way. He was sorry Victoria would have to go through another time. It was awkward just now, too, when he was so short of money. But he was naturally a cheerful man, modest in his demands upon fortune, and easily diverted from unpleasant thoughts. Before Cleveland had travelled half the eighteen miles to the farm, his master was already looking forward to a visit with his tenants, an old German couple who were fond of him because he never pushed them in a hard year—so far, all the years had been hard—and he sometimes brought them bananas and such delicacies from town.

Mrs. Heyse would open her best preserves for him, he knew, and kill a chicken, and tonight he would have a clean bed in her spare room. She always put a vase of flowers in his room when he stayed overnight with them, and that pleased him very much. He felt like a youth out there, and forgot all the bills he had somehow to meet, and the loans he had made and couldn't collect. The Heyses kept bees and raised turkeys, and had honeysuckle vines running over the front porch. He loved all those things. Mr. Templeton touched Cleveland with the whip, and as they sped along into the grass country, sang softly:

> *"Old Jesse was a gem'man,*
> *Way down in Tennessee."*

XIII

Mandy had to manage the house herself that day, and she was not at all sorry. There wasn't a great deal of variety in her life, and she felt very important taking Mrs. Harris's place, giving the children their dinner, and carrying a plate of milk toast to Mrs. Templeton. She was worried about Mrs. Harris, however, and remarked to the children at noon that she thought somebody ought to "set" with their grandma. Vickie wasn't home for dinner. She had her father's office to herself for the day and was making the most of it, writing a long letter to Professor Chalmers. Mr. Rosen had invited her to have dinner with him at the hotel (he boarded there when his wife was away), and that was a great honour.

When Mandy said someone ought to be with the old lady, Bert and Del offered to take turns. Adelbert went off to rake up the grass they had been cutting all morning, and Albert sat down in the play-room. It seemed to him his grandmother looked pretty sick. He watched her while Mandy gave her toast-water with whisky in it, and thought he would like to make the room look a little nicer. While Mrs. Harris lay with her eyes closed, he hung up the caps and coats lying about, and moved away the big rocking-chair that stood by the head of Grandma's bed. There ought to be a table there, he believed, but the small tables in the house all had something on them. Upstairs, in the room where he and Adelbert and Ronald slept, there was a nice clean wooden cracker-box, on which they sat in the morning to put on their shoes and stockings. He brought this down and stood it on end at the head of Grandma's lounge, and put a clean napkin over the top of it.

She opened her eyes and smiled at him. "Could you git me a tin of fresh water, honey?"

He went to the back porch and pumped till the water ran cold. He gave it to her in a tin cup as she had asked, but he didn't think that was the right way. After she dropped back on the pillow, he fetched a glass tumbler from the cupboard, filled it, and set it on the table he had just manufactured. When Grandmother drew a red cotton handkerchief from under her pillow and wiped the moisture from her face, he ran upstairs again and got one of his Sunday-school handkerchiefs, linen ones, that Mrs. Rosen had given him and Del for Christmas. Having put this in Grandmother's hand and taken away the crumpled red one, he could think of nothing else to do—except to darken the room a little. The windows had no blinds, but flimsy cretonne curtains tied back—not really tied, but caught back over nails driven into the sill. He loosened them and let them hang down over the bright afternoon sunlight. Then he sat down on the low sawed-off chair and gazed about, thinking that now it looked quite like a sick-room.

It was hard for a little boy to keep still.

"Would you like me to read *Joe's Luck* to you, Gram'ma?" he said presently. "You might, Bertie."

He got the "boy's book" she had been reading aloud to them, and began where she had left off. Mrs. Harris liked to hear his voice, and she liked to look at him when she opened her eyes from time to time. She did not follow the story. In her mind she was repeating a passage from the second part of *Pilgrim's Progress*, which she had read aloud to the children so many times; the passage where Christiana and her band come to the arbour on the Hill of Difficulty: *"Then said Mercy, how sweet is rest to them that labour."*

At about four o'clock Adelbert came home, hot and sweaty from raking. He said he had got in the grass and taken it to their cow, and if Bert was reading, he guessed he'd like to listen. He dragged the wooden rocking-chair up close to Grandma's bed and curled up in it.

Grandmother was perfectly happy. She and the twins were about the same age; they had in common all the realest and truest things. The years between them and her, it seemed to Mrs. Harris, were full of trouble and unimportant. The twins and Ronald and Hughie were important. She opened her eyes.

"Where is Hughie?" she asked.

"I guess he's asleep. Mother took him into her bed."

"And Ronald?"

"He's upstairs with Mandy. There ain't nobody in the kitchen now."

"Then you might git me a fresh drink, Del."

"Yes'm, Gram'ma." He tiptoed out to the pump in his brown canvas sneakers.

When Vickie came home at five o'clock, she went to her mother's room, but the door was locked—a thing she couldn't remember ever happening before. She went into the play-room—old Mrs. Harris was asleep, with one of the twins on guard, and he held up a warning finger. She went into the kitchen. Mandy was making biscuits, and Ronald was helping her to cut them out.

"What's the matter, Mandy? Where is everybody?"

"You know your papa's away, Miss Vickie; an' your mama's got a headache, an' Miz' Harris has had a bad spell. Maybe I'll just fix supper for you an' the boys in the kitchen, so you won't all have to be runnin' through her room."

"Oh, very well," said Vickie bitterly, and she went upstairs. Wasn't it just like them all to go and get sick, when she had now only two weeks to get ready for school, and no trunk and no clothes or anything? Nobody but Mr. Rosen seemed to take the least interest, "when my whole life hangs by a thread," she told herself fiercely. What were families for, anyway?

After supper Vickie went to her father's office to read; she told Mandy to leave the kitchen door open, and when she got home she would go to bed without disturbing anybody. The twins ran out to play under the electric light with the neighbour boys for a little while, then slipped softly up the back stairs to their room. Mandy came to Mrs. Harris after the house was still.

"Kin I rub your legs fur you, Miz' Harris?"

"Thank you, Mandy. And you might get me a clean nightcap out of the press."

Mandy returned with it.

"Lawsie me! But your legs is cold, ma'am!"

"I expect it's about time, Mandy," murmured the old lady. Mandy knelt on the floor and set to work with a will. It brought the sweat out on her, and at last she sat up and wiped her face with the back of her hand.

"I can't seem to git no heat into 'em, Miz' Harris. I got a hot flat-iron on the stove; I'll wrap it in a piece of old blanket and put it to your feet. Why didn't you have the boys tell me you was cold, pore soul?"

Mrs. Harris did not answer. She thought it was probably a cold that neither Mandy nor the flat-iron could do much with. She hadn't nursed so many people back in Tennessee without coming to know certain signs.

After Mandy was gone, she fell to thinking of her blessings. Every night for years, when she said her prayers, she had prayed that she might never have a long sickness or be a burden. She dreaded the heart-ache and humiliation of being helpless on the hands of people who would be impatient under such a care. And now she felt certain that she was going to die tonight, without troubling anybody.

She was glad Mrs. Rosen was in Chicago. Had she been at home, she would certainly have come in, would have seen that her old neighbour was very sick, and bustled about. Her quick eye would have found out all Grandmother's little secrets: how hard her bed was, that she had no proper place to wash, and kept her comb in her pocket; that her night-gowns were patched and darned. Mrs. Rosen would have been indignant, and that would have made Victoria cross. She didn't have to see Mrs. Rosen again to know that Mrs. Rosen thought highly of her and admired her—yes, admired her. Those funny little pats and arch pleasantries had meant a great deal to Mrs. Harris.

It was a blessing that Mr. Templeton was away, too. Appearances had to be kept up when there was a man in the house; and he might have taken it into his head to send for the doctor, and stir everybody up. Now everything would be so peaceful. *"The Lord is my shepherd,"* she whispered gratefully. "Yes, Lord, I always spoiled Victoria. She was so much the prettiest. But nobody won't ever be the worse for it: Mr. Templeton will always humour her, and the children love her more than most. They'll always be good to her; she has that way with her."

Grandma fell to remembering the old place at home: what a dashing, high-spirited girl Victoria was, and how proud she had always been of her; how she used to hear her laughing and teasing out in the lilac arbour when Hillary Templeton was courting her. Toward morning all these pleasant reflections faded out. Mrs. Harris felt that she and her bed were softly sinking, through the darkness to a deeper darkness.

Old Mrs. Harris did not really die that night, but she believed she did. Mandy found her unconscious in the morning. Then there was a great stir and bustle; Victoria, and even Vickie, were startled out of their intense self-absorption. Mrs. Harris was hastily carried out of the play-room and laid in Victoria's bed, put into one of Victoria's best nightgowns. Mr. Templeton was sent for, and the doctor was sent for. The inquisitive Mrs. Jackson from next door got into the house at last—installed herself as nurse, and no one had the courage to say her nay. But Grandmother was out of it all, never knew that she was the object of so much attention and excitement. She died a little while after Mr. Templeton got home.

Thus Mrs. Harris slipped out of the Templeton's story; but Victoria and Vickie had still to go on, to follow the long road that leads through things unguessed at and unforeseeable. When they are old, they will come closer and closer to Grandma Harris. They will think a great deal about her, and remember things they never noticed; and their lot will be more or less like hers. They will regret that they heeded her so little; but they, too, will look into the eager, unseeing eyes of young people and feel themselves alone. They will say to themselves: "I was heartless, because I was young and strong and wanted things so much. But now I know."

1930

PART II

Poetry

❖

At the beginning of written language, there were two kinds of poems. The lyric, or song, expressed an emotion (we think of Sappho's beautiful lyrics, the earliest known fragments of evocative love songs). The narrative poem, or epic, told stories—and its role in people's lives was gradually usurped by the prose forms we now call fiction, both novel and short story. That many readers privilege poetry as the highest, most difficult, form of literary expression stems in part from the length of its history.

Poetry by women writers in the United States has a history as long as the inhabitation of the continent. The chants and songs of Native Americans (collected later in this volume under "Rituals and Ceremonies") typify the long tradition of oral poetry, just as the work of seventeenth-century poet Anne Bradstreet reflects the influence of Western European culture. Writing in approved literary forms, Bradstreet was hailed as the first American poet. Her sometimes wry tone showed that she knew how dangerous writing was for women, and her deft ability to write in the highest of poetic forms—the ode, the sonnet—and still express herself in a woman's voice showed her consummate ability.

From earliest times to the present, women poets insisted that their work express their lives, intellectual as well as domestic and personal. Serious women writers who worked in the conventions of poetry—so that they had fourteen lines in a sonnet, for instance, or four rhyming lines in a quatrain— were still able to speak eloquently about the significant ideas of their time. Phillis Wheatley's ode to the power of imagination equals anything produced by a learned British male poet; Bradstreet's genuine love poems stayed within proper poetic conventions but expressed her own voice. In more modern times, when Muriel Rukeyser (1913–1980) wrote about "The Poem as Mask," she challenged the notion that women's art needed to be bound by those conventions, and thereby broke women's poetry away from such prescriptions. Rukeyser insisted that poets speak "with their own music." It was not only all right for women's voices to sound different from men's; it was, in fact, necessary.

Whether or not the poet uses traditional form, the heart of any poem is its sense of completion. Howard Nemerov, poet laureate of the United States in 1988, once explained that a good poem should work the way a good joke does—with no one having to ask whether it is finished. Everything about the poem should mesh—its emotional tone, the words chosen to evoke that tone, the length of line and shape of stanza that echo the emotion expressed, and whatever narrative drive the idea of the poem takes. When that happens, the reader is convinced the poet is good, knows what she is doing, knows what is happening within the living form of the work itself.

The difficulty of women poets expressing their emotions is that a great deal of any person's emotional life is gendered. Women value life experiences—family, children, birth, death—differently than do men, or so today's psychoanalytic scholars suggest. Women also contextualize, and see themselves as participants in a larger culture, in a community, rather than viewing themselves as completely self-defined. When a woman writer takes up the theme of adolescence, then, because her view of herself depends on that net of relationships, she would most likely write about a persona who is involved with others—as illustrated by Carolyn Forché's moving "As Children Together" (1982), a poem written to a girlhood friend from Detroit, a friend she has lost track of in adult life. Similarly, Audre Lorde's (1934–1992) "Song for a Thin Sister" and Margaret Walker's "Lineage" (1942) connect the woman protagonist with other women in either a cultural or a familial context.

❖

O N E

Poetry from the Beginning

Poems written by women writers in the United States reflect the historical progression from British-dominated traditional style, exemplified here in the work of Anne Bradstreet (1612–1672) and Phillis Wheatley (1753–1784), through the idiosyncratic and song-like (or hymn-like) poems of Emily Dickinson (1830–1886), to the free-form, modernist writing of Amy Lowell (1874–1925) and others who followed the explosion of modern poetry early in the twentieth century. But poetry by women writers in the United States can never be charged with having only historical interest.

Women poets have often been responsible for wholesale changes in the form of the art as it is practiced in America. The ghosts of Bradstreet and Wheatley were difficult to escape for the first two hundred years of literature in the United States, and Emily Dickinson made the category of "poem" into something entirely different from the works of the so-called Fireside Poets who were her contemporaries. More influential than any other American poet except Walt Whitman, Dickinson changed the way readers expected poems to "mean." Her enigmatic phrasing, which made the entire structure of the poem into a metaphor, forced readers to be sensitive to what was only suggested, as well as what was written.

As Adrienne Rich pointed out twenty years ago, Emily Dickinson was one of the first women writers in the United States to make her life the profession of her art. By withdrawing from the community of Amherst, Massachusetts, Dickinson could give all her energy and imagination to her writing. Passionate and often acerbic, her poems enabled readers to understand the full range of a woman's emotional life.

Many modernist women poets drew from the free-verse conventions espoused by Ezra Pound, T. S. Eliot, and Robert Frost, but at the back of their terse yet lyric modern expression was the genius of Emily Dickinson. From Amy Lowell to Margaret Walker (1915–), Gwendolyn Brooks (1917–) to Ruth Stone (1915–), the themes of family, everyday life, and love—both heterosexual and lesbian—found new force in the brevity of modernist poetry. In the later poems of Maya Angelou (1928–) and Sylvia Plath (1932–1963), the currents of modernism come to an impasse. Angelou's soothing, hearty voice speaks with a clear resonance; Plath's macabre humor made of her personal tragedies a new kind of vehicle for women's anger. Her unmistakably personal voice turned readers' expectations on their ear, and served as a kind of closure for expression in the highly formal modernist mode.

❖

Anne Bradstreet

(1612–1672)

TO MY DEAR AND LOVING HUSBAND

If ever two were one, then surely we.
If ever man were loved by wife, then thee;
If ever wife was happy in a man,
Compare with me, ye women, if you can.
I prize thy love more than whole mines of gold
Or all the riches that the East doth hold.

My love is such that rivers cannot quench,
Nor ought but love from thee, give recompense.
Thy love is such I can no way repay,

275

The heavens reward thee manifold, I pray.
Then while we live, in love let's so persevere
That when we live no more, we may live ever.

1678

❖

THE FLESH AND THE SPIRIT

In secret place where once I stood
Close by the banks of Lacrim[1] flood,
I heard two sisters reason on
Things that are past and things to come;
One flesh was called, who had her eye
On worldly wealth and vanity;
The other Spirit, who did rear
Her thoughts unto a higher sphere:
Sister, quoth Flesh, what liv'st thou on,
Nothing but meditation?
Doth contemplation feed thee so
Regardlessly to let earth go?
Can speculation satisfy
Notion without reality?
Dost dream of things beyond the moon,
And dost thou hope to dwell there soon?
Hast treasures there laid up in store
That all in th' world thou count'st but poor?
Art fancy sick, or turned a sot
To catch at shadows which are not?
Come, come, I'll show unto thy sense,
Industry hath its recompense.
What canst desire, but thou may'st see
True substance in variety?
Dost honor like? Acquire the same,
As some to their immortal fame,
And trophies to thy name erect
Which wearing time shall ne'er deject.
For riches doth thou long full sore?

[1]Tear (from the Latin *lacrima*).

276

Behold enough of precious store.
Earth hath more silver, pearls, and gold,
Than eyes can see or hands can hold.
Affect's thou pleasure? Take thy fill,
Earth hath enough of what you will.
Then let not go, what thou may'st find
For things unknown, only in mind.

Spirit: Be still thou unregenerate part,
Disturb no more my settled heart,
For I have vowed (and so will do)
Thee as a foe still to pursue.
And combat with thee will and must,
Until I see thee laid in th' dust.
Sisters we are, yea, twins we be,
Yet deadly feud 'twixt thee and me;
For from one father are we not,
Thou by old Adam wast begot.
But my arise is from above,
Whence my dear Father I do love.
Thou speak'st me fair, but hat'st me sore,
Thy flatt'ring shows I'll trust no more,
How oft thy slave, hast thou me made,
When I believed what thou hast said,
And never had more cause of woe
Than when I did what thou bad'st do.
I'll stop mine ears at these thy charms,
And count them for my deadly harms.
Thy sinful pleasures I do hate,
Thy riches are to me no bait,
Thine honors do, nor will I love;
For my ambition lies above.
My greatest honor it shall be
When I am victor over thee,
And triumph shall with laurel head,
When thou my captive shalt be led,
How I do live, thou need'st not scoff,
For I have meat thou know'st not of;
The hidden manna I do eat,
The word of life it is my meat.
My thoughts do yield me more content

Than can thy hours in pleasure spent.
Nor are they shadows which I catch,
Nor fancies vain at which I snatch,
But reach at things that are so high,
Beyond thy dull capacity;
Eternal substance I do see,
With which enriched I would be.
Mine eye doth pierce the heavens and see
What is invisible to thee.
My garments are not silk nor gold,
Nor such like trash which earth doth hold,
But royal robes I shall have on,
More glorious than the glist'ring sun;
My crown not diamonds, pearls, and gold,
But such as angels' heads enfold.
The city where I hope to dwell,
There's none on earth can parallel;
The stately walls both high and strong,
Are made of precious jasper stone;
The gates of pearl, both rich and clear,
And angels are for porters there;
The streets thereof transparent gold,
Such as no eye did e'er behold;
A crystal river there doth run,
Which doth proceed from the Lamb's throne.
Of life, there are the waters sure,
Which shall remain forever pure,
Nor sun, nor moon, they have no need,
For glory doth from God proceed.
No candle there, nor yet torchlight,
For there shall be no darksome night.
From sickness and infirmity
For evermore they shall be free;
Nor withering age shall e'er come there,
But beauty shall be bright and clear;
This city pure is not for thee,
For things unclean there shall not be.
If I of heaven may have my fill,
Take thou the world and all that will.

1678

Phillis Wheatley
(1753–1784)

ON IMAGINATION

Thy various works, imperial queen, we see,
How bright their forms! how deck'd with pomp by thee!
Thy wond'rous acts in beauteous order stand,
And all attest how potent is thine hand.

From Helicon's[1] refulgent heights attend,
Ye sacred choir, and my attempts befriend:
To tell her glories with a faithful tongue,
Ye blooming graces, triumph in my song.

Now here, now there, the roving *Fancy* flies,
Till some lov'd object strikes her wand'ring eyes,
Whose silken fetters all the senses bind,
And soft captivity involves the mind.

Imagination! who can sing thy force?
Or who describe the swiftness of thy course?
Soaring through air to find the bright abode,
Th' empyreal palace of the thund'ring God,
We on thy pinions can surpass the wind,
And leave the rolling universe behind:
From star to star the mental optics rove,
Measure the skies, and range the realms above.
There in one view we grasp the mighty whole,
Or with new worlds amaze th' unbounded soul.

Though *Winter* frowns to *Fancy's* raptur'd eyes
The fields may flourish, and gay scenes arise;
The frozen deeps may break their iron bands,
And bid their waters murmur o'er the sands.
Fair *Flora* may resume her fragrant reign,
And with her flow'ry riches deck the plain;
Sylvanus may diffuse his honours round,

[1]Helicon was one of the Greek muses' earthly mountain homes.

And all the forest may with leaves be crown'd:
Show'rs may descend, and dews their gems disclose,
And nectar sparkle on the blooming rose.

  Such is thy pow'r, nor are thine orders vain,
O thou the leader of the mental train:
In full perfection all thy works are wrought,
And thine the sceptre o'er the realms of thought.
Before thy throne the subject-passions bow,
Of subject-passions sov'reign ruler Thou;
At thy command joy rushes on the heart,
And through the glowing veins the spirits dart.

  Fancy might now her silken pinions try
To rise from earth, and sweep th' expanse on high;
From *Tithon's*[2] bed now might *Aurora* rise,
Her cheeks all glowing with celestial dies,
While a pure stream of light o'erflows the skies.
The monarch of the day I might behold,
And all the mountains tipt with radiant gold,
But I reluctant leave the pleasing views,
Which *Fancy* dresses to delight the *Muse:*
Winter austere forbids me to aspire,
And northern tempests damp the rising fire;
They chill the tides of *Fancy's* flowing sea,
Cease then, my song, cease the unequal lay.

1773

❖

Emily Dickinson
(1830–1886)

THE SOUL SELECTS HER OWN SOCIETY

The Soul selects her own Society—
Then—shuts the Door—

'Tithon (i.e., Tithonus), husband to Aurora, goddess of the dawn, father of her black Ethiopian son, Memnon, whose death in battle is told in *The Iliad.*

To her divine Majority—
Present no more—

Unmoved—she notes the Chariots—pausing—
At her low Gate—
Unmoved—an Emperor be kneeling
Upon her Mat—

I've known her—from an ample nation—
Choose One—
Then—close the Valves of her attention—
Like Stone—

c.1862   *1890*

THIS IS MY LETTER TO THE WORLD

This is my letter to the World
That never wrote to Me—
The simple News that Nature told—
With tender Majesty

Her[1] Message is committed
To Hands I cannot see—
For love of Her—Sweet—countrymen—
Judge tenderly—of Me

1862

❖

MY LIFE HAD STOOD—A LOADED GUN

My Life had stood—a Loaded Gun—
In Corners—till a Day
The Owner passed—identified—
And carried Me away—

'Nature's

281

And now We roam in Sovereign Woods—
And now We hunt the Doe—
And every time I speak for Him—
The Mountains straight reply—

And do I smile, such cordial light
Upon the Valley glow—
It is as a Vesuvian face[2]
Had let its pleasure through—

And when at Night—Our good Day done—
I guard My Master's Head—
'Tis better than the Eider Duck's
Deep Pillow—to have shared—

To foe of His—I'm deadly foe—
None stir the second time—
On whom I lay a Yellow Eye—
Or an emphatic Thumb—

Though I than He—may longer live
He longer must—than I—
For I have but the power to kill,
Without—the power to die—

c.1863

❖

AFTER GREAT PAIN, A FORMAL
FEELING COMES

After great pain, a formal feeling comes—
The Nerves sit ceremonious, like Tombs—
The stiff Heart questions was it He, that bore,
And Yesterday, or Centuries before?

The Feet, mechanical, go round—
Of Ground, or Air, or Ought—

[2]Mount Vesuvius; i.e., volcanic

A Wooden way
Regardless grown,
A Quartz contentment, like a stone—

This is the Hour of Lead—
Remembered, if outlived,
As Freezing persons, recollect the Snow—
First—Chill—then Stupor—then the letting go—

c. 1862

❖

Amy Lowell
(1874–1925)

DECADE

When you came, you were like red wine and honey,
And the taste of you burnt my mouth with its sweetness.
Now you are like morning bread,
Smooth and pleasant.
I hardly taste you at all for I know your savour,
But I am completely nourished.

1919

❖

Muriel Rukeyser
(1913–1980)

THE POEM AS MASK

Orpheus

When I wrote of the women in their dances and wildness, it
    was a mask,
on their mountain, god-hunting, singing, in orgy,
it was a mask; when I wrote of the god,

283

fragmented, exiled from himself, his life, the love gone down
    with song,
it was myself, split open, unable to speak, in exile from myself.

There is no mountain, there is no god, there is memory
of my torn life, myself split open in sleep, the rescued child
beside me among the doctors, and a word
of rescue from the great eyes.

No more masks! No more mythologies!

Now, for the first time, the god lifts his hand,
the fragments join in me with their own music.

1968

❖

Margaret Walker
(1915–   )

LINEAGE

My grandmothers were strong.
They followed plows and bent to toil.
They moved through fields sowing seed.
They touched earth and grain grew.
They were full of sturdiness and singing.
My grandmothers were strong.

My grandmothers are full of memories
Smelling of soap and onions and wet clay
With veins rolling roughly over quick hands
They have many clean words to say.
My grandmothers were strong.
Why am I not as they?

1942

Gwendolyn Brooks

(1917–   )

RELIGION
from *Ulysses*

At home we pray every morning, we
get down on our knees in a circle,
holding hands, holding Love,
and we sing Hallelujah.

Then we go into the World.

Daddy *speeds*, to break bread with his Girl Friend.
Mommy's a Boss. And a lesbian.
(She too has a nice Girl Friend.)

My brothers and sisters and I come to school.
We bring knives pistols bottles, little boxes, and cans.

We talk to the man who's cool at the playground gate.
Nobody Sees us, nobody stops our sin.

Our teachers feed us geography.
We spit it out in a hurry.

Now we are coming home.

At home, we pray every evening, we
get down on our knees in a circle,
holding hands, holding Love.

And we sing Hallelujah.

1991

Ruth Stone
(1915–   )

IN AN IRIDESCENT TIME

My mother, when young, scrubbed laundry in a tub,
She and her sisters on an old brick walk
Under the apple trees, sweet rub-a-dub.
The bees came round their heads, the wrens made talk.
Four young ladies each with a rainbow board
Honed their knuckles, wrung their wrists to red,
Tossed back their braids and wiped their aprons wet.
The Jersey calf beyond the back fence roared;
And all the soft day, swarms about their pet
Buzzed at his big brown eyes and bullish head.
Four times they rinsed, they said. Some things they starched,
Then shook them from the baskets two by two,
And pinned the fluttering intimacies of life
Between the lilac bushes and the yew:
Brown gingham, pink, and skirts of Alice blue.

1959

❖

Maya Angelou
(1928–   )

WOMAN ME

Your smile, delicate
rumor of peace.
Deafening revolutions nestle in the
cleavage of
your breasts
Beggar-Kings and red-ringed Priests
seek glory at the meeting
of your thighs
A grasp of Lions, A lap of Lambs.

Your tears, jeweled
strewn a diadem
caused Pharaohs to ride
deep in the bosom of the
Nile. Southern spas lash fast
their doors upon the night when
winds of death blow down your name
A bride of hurricanes,
    A swarm of summer wind.

Your laughter, pealing tall
above the bells of ruined cathedrals.
Children reach between your teeth
for charts to live their lives.
A stomp of feet, A bevy of swift hands.

1975

❖

Sylvia Plath
(1932–1963)

LADY LAZARUS

I have done it again.
One year in every ten
I manage it——

A sort of walking miracle, my skin
Bright as a Nazi lampshade
My right foot

A paperweight,
My face a featureless, fine
Jew linen.

Peel off the napkin
O my enemy.
Do I terrify?——

The nose, the eye pits, the full set of teeth?
The sour breath
Will vanish in a day.

Soon, soon the flesh
The grave cave ate will be
At home on me

And I a smiling woman.
I am only thirty.
And like the cat I have nine times to die.

This is Number Three.
What a trash
To annihilate each decade.

What a million filaments.
The peanut-crunching crowd
Shoves in to see

Then unwrap me hand and foot——
The big strip tease.
Gentlemen, ladies

These are my hands
My knees.
I may be skin and bone,

Nevertheless, I am the same, identical woman.
The first time it happened I was ten.
It was an accident.

The second time I meant
To last it out and not come back at all.
I rocked shut

As a seashell.
They had to call and call
And pick the worms off me like sticky pearls.

Dying
Is an art, like everything else.
I do it exceptionally well.

I do it so it feels like hell.
I do it so it feels real.
I guess you could say I've a call.

It's easy enough to do it in a cell.
It's easy enough to do it and stay put.
It's the theatrical

Comeback in broad day
To the same place, the same face, the same brute
Amused shout:

'A miracle!'
That knocks me out.
There is a charge

For the eyeing of my scars, there is a charge
For the hearing of my heart——
It really goes.

And there is a charge, a very large charge
For a word or a touch
Or a bit of blood

Or a piece of my hair or my clothes.
So, so, Herr Doktor.
So, Herr Enemy.

I am your opus,
I am your valuable,
The pure gold baby

That melts to a shriek.
I turn and burn.
Do not think I underestimate your great concern.

Ash, ash—
You poke and stir.
Flesh, bone, there is nothing there——

A cake of soap,
A wedding ring,
A gold filling.

Herr God, Herr Lucifer
Beware
Beware.

Out of the ash
I rise with my red hair
And I eat men like air.

23–29 October 1962   *1965*

T W O

Contemporary Poetry

It seems fitting that we open the section of poetry by women that we call "contemporary" with work by a still-living poet who was a peer of Sylvia Plath's. When United States poetry split away from the formalism that most modernist writers used, Adrienne Rich (1929–) was one of the leaders of the defiant new direction. Her 1973 "Diving into the Wreck" became a talismanic poem, speaking as it did for the promise of more androgynous attitudes. Casting the woman persona in the Odyssean role of explorer muted gender expectations, and the sophisticated fusion of self and other, plural and singular, at the close of the poem spoke for the spirit of the 1970s and the 1980s.

Contemporary women's poetry has followed Muriel Rukeyser's urging to drop the polite, elite mask, and voice real concerns. Nellie Wong's parodic use of Elizabeth Barrett Browning's famous poem gave a new dimension to her lament for her Asian-American adolescence. Lucille Clifton (1936–), Audre Lorde (1934–1992), and Judith Ortiz Cofer (1952–) speak of both physical appearance and racial marginalization. Rita Dove's "Daystar" (1986) isolates the core of a female consciousness, the need for privacy and a time to think. Michelle Cliff's mixed form prose poem, "A History of Costume" (1985), reflects on the culturally inscribed mandates for a woman's appearance, set within an unspoken dialogue between mother and daughter.

In Cliff's rich experimentation, the sense of the immediate present strikes home. Janice Mirikitani (1942–) begins her dialogic tapestry in "Suicide Note" with a prose excerpt that explains the death of the Asian-American woman the poem describes. With the poem structured around alternating voices, the reader is brought actively into the narration. The chant-like "Remember" by Joy Harjo (1951–) reminds us of the two kinds of poetry—this, the oral lyric, a praisesong for community, life, and "the dance that language is"—juxtaposed with poems that have a more story-like narrative. In the last poem in the section, the work by Carolyn Forché (1950–), the lives of her persona and that of the friend of her youth take on the luminosity of a fully achieved narrative. Women writers of the past decade are fulfilling the promise that modernism suggested: at the height of their craft, women writers are among the most often recognized of United States poets.

❖

Adrienne Rich
(1929–)

DIVING INTO THE WRECK

First having read the book of myths,
and loaded the camera,
and checked the edge of the knife-blade,
I put on
the body-armor of black rubber
the absurd flippers
the grave and awkward mask.
I am having to do this
not like Cousteau with his
assiduous team
aboard the sun-flooded schooner
but here alone.

There is a ladder.
The ladder is always there
hanging innocently
close to the side of the schooner.
We know what it is for,
we who have used it.
Otherwise
it's a piece of maritime floss
some sundry equipment.

I go down.
Rung after rung and still
the oxygen immerses me
the blue light
the clear atoms
of our human air.
I go down.
My flippers cripple me,
I crawl like an insect down the ladder
and there is no one
to tell me when the ocean
will begin.

First the air is blue and then
it is bluer and then green and then
black I am blacking out and yet
my mask is powerful
it pumps my blood with power
the sea is another story
the sea is not a question of power
I have to learn alone
to turn my body without force
in the deep element.
And now: it is easy to forget
what I came for
among so many who have always
lived here
swaying their crenellated fans
between the reefs
and besides
you breathe differently down here.

I came to explore the wreck.
The words are purposes.
The words are maps.
I came to see the damage that was done
and the treasures that prevail.
I stroke the beam of my lamp
slowly along the flank
of something more permanent
than fish or weed

the thing I came for:
the wreck and not the story of the wreck
the thing itself and not the myth

the drowned face always staring
toward the sun
the evidence of damage
worn by salt and sway into this threadbare beauty
the ribs of the disaster
curving their assertion
among the tentative haunters.

This is the place.
And I am here, the mermaid whose dark hair
streams black, the merman in his armored body
We circle silently
about the wreck
we dive into the hold.
I am she: I am he

whose drowned face sleeps with open eyes
whose breasts still bear the stress
whose silver, copper, vermeil cargo lies
obscurely inside barrels
half-wedged and left to rot
we are the half-destroyed instruments
that once held to a course
the water-eaten log
the fouled compass

We are, I am, you are
by cowardice or courage
the one who find our way
back to this scene
carrying a knife, a camera
a book of myths
in which
our names do not appear.

1973

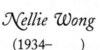

Nellie Wong

(1934–   )

WHEN I WAS GROWING UP

I know now that once I longed to be white.
How? you ask.
Let me tell you the ways.

when I was growing up, people told me
I was dark and I believed my own darkness
in the mirror, in my soul, my own narrow vision

> when I was growing up, my sisters
> with fair skin got praised
> for their beauty, and in the dark
> I fell further, crushed between high walls

when I was growing up, I read magazines
and saw movies, blonde movie stars, white skin,
sensuous lips and to be elevated, to become
a woman, a desirable woman, I began to wear
imaginary pale skin

> when I was growing up, I was proud
> of my English, my grammar, my spelling
> fitting into the group of smart children
> smart Chinese children, fitting in,
> belonging, getting in line

when I was growing up and went to high school,
I discovered the rich white girls, a few yellow girls,
their imported cotton dresses, their cashmere sweaters,
their curly hair and I thought that I too should have
what these lucky girls had

> when I was growing up, I hungered
> for American food, American styles,
> coded: white and even to me, a child
> born of Chinese parents, being Chinese
> was feeling foreign, was limiting,
> was unAmerican

when I was growing up and a white man wanted
to take me out, I thought I was special,
an exotic gardenia, anxious to fit
the stereotype of an oriental chick

> when I was growing up, I felt ashamed
> of some yellow men, their small bones,

295

their frail bodies, their spitting
on the streets, their coughing,
their lying in sunless rooms,
shooting themselves in the arms

when I was growing up, people would ask
if I were Filipino, Polynesian, Portuguese.
They named all colors except white, the shell
of my soul, but not my dark, rough skin

when I was growing up, I felt
dirty. I thought that god
made white people clean
and no matter how much I bathed,
I could not change, I could not shed
my skin in the gray water

when I was growing up, I swore
I would run away to purple mountains,
houses by the sea with nothing over
my head, with space to breathe,
uncongested with yellow people in an area
called Chinatown, in an area I later learned
was a ghetto, one of many hearts
of Asian America

I know now that once I longed to be white
How many more ways? you ask.
Haven't I told you enough?   *1981*

Lucille Clifton
(1936–   )

THE THIRTY EIGHTH YEAR

the thirty eighth year
of my life
plain as bread
round as a cake
an ordinary woman.

an ordinary woman.

i had expected to be
smaller than this,
more beautiful,
wiser in Afrikan ways,
more confident,
i had expected
more than this.

i will be forty soon.
my mother once was forty.

my mother died at forty four,
a woman of sad countenance
leaving behind a girl
awkward as a stork.
my mother was thick,
her hair was a jungle and
she was very wise
and beautiful
and sad.

i have dreamed dreams
for you mama
more than once.
i have wrapped me
in your skin
and made you live again
more than once.
i have taken the bones you hardened
and built daughters
and they blossom and promise fruit
like Afrikan trees.
i am a woman now.
an ordinary woman.

in the thirty eighth
year of my life,
surrounded by life,

a perfect picture of
blackness blessed,
i had not expected this
loneliness.

if it is western,
if it is the final
Europe in my mind,
if in the middle of my life
i am turning the final turn
into the shining dark
let me come to it whole
and holy
not afraid
not lonely

out of my mother's life
into my own.
into my own.

i had expected more than this.
i had not expected to be
an ordinary woman.

1974

❖

Audre Lorde
(1934–1992)

SONG FOR A THIN SISTER

Either heard or taught
as girls   we thought
that skinny was funny
or a little bit   silly

and   feeling a pull
toward the large and the colorful
I would joke you   when
you grew too thin.

But your new kind of hunger
makes me chilly   like danger
I see you forever retreating
shrinking   into a stranger
in flight
and growing up
Black   and fat
I was so sure that   skinny
was funny   or silly
but always
white.

1971

❖

Judith Ortiz Cofer
(1952–   )

WHAT THE GYPSY SAID
TO HER CHILDREN

We are like the dead
invisible to those who do not
want to see,
and color is our only protection against
the killing silence of their eyes,
the crimson of our tents pitched
like a scream
in the fields of our foes,
the amber warmth of our fires
where we gather to lift our voices
in the purple lament of our songs,
And beyond the scope of their senses
where all colors blend into one

we will build our cities of light,
we will carve them
out of the granite of their hatred,
with our own brown hands.

1983

❖

Rita Dove
(1952–   )

DAYSTAR

She wanted a little room for thinking:
but she saw diapers steaming on the line,
a doll slumped behind the door.

So she lugged a chair behind the garage
to sit out the children's naps.

Sometimes there were things to watch—
the pinched armor of a vanished cricket,
a floating maple leaf. Other days
she stared until she was assured
when she closed her eyes
she'd see only her own vivid blood.

She had an hour, at best, before Liza appeared
pouting from the top of the stairs.
And just *what* was mother doing
out back with the field mice? Why,

building a palace. Later
that night when Thomas rolled over and
lurched into her, she would open her eyes
and think of the place that was hers
for an hour—where

she was nothing,
pure nothing, in the middle of the day.

1986

Michelle Cliff
(1946–   )

A HISTORY OF COSTUME

*In the foreground a bird with a beautiful plume circles round
and round as if lost or giddy. There are red holes in its head
where there should be eyes. Another bird, tied to a stake, writhes
incessantly, for red ants devour it. Both are decoys. . . . It is in
the nesting season that the plumes are brightest, so, if we wish
to go on making pictures, we must imagine innumerable mouths
opening and shutting, until—as no parent bird comes to feed
them—the young birds rot where they sit. Then there are the
wounded birds, trailing leg or wing, as they flutter off to droop
or falter in the dust. But perhaps the most unpleasant sight that
we must make ourselves imagine is the sight of the bird tightly
held in one hand while another pierces the eyeballs with a feather.
But these hands—are they the hands of men or of women?*
VIRGINIA WOOLF, THE PLUMAGE BILL
The Woman's Leader, JULY 23, 1920

In the basement of the museum finery is on display; a history of costume,
open to the public. Plaster models—their heads swathed in varicolored nylon
stockings—are placed in rooms dedicated to periods of time.

I

My mother and I meet in public places—and move between
the swathed heads:
the faceless heads and covered bodies
the covered faces, the emblazoned bodies
the paisley-shawled bodies

cut off from
the undistinguished heads.

We came to this exhibit in part to connect, in part to recollect, but we hold
few memories in common; and our connections are limited by silences between us. Our common ground is the island where we were born—and we
speak in the language spoken there. And we bear a close resemblance, except
for eye-color.

II

We move into a room
filled with
    fans
    corsets
    parasols
    shoes
the covering of birds/the perimeters of whales/handles made from the tusks
of elephants/the work of the silkworm: to receive the lotusfoot.

The tiny shoes are lush: carefully designed,
    painstakingly executed.
Green silk bordered in red,
    embroidered with golden birds in flight.
Sewn perhaps by a mother for her daughter,
    according to custom.
And according to custom, also,
    fitted by that mother over time.

III

I start to talk about these feet, but our conversation slides into another room,
where a court dress of the eighteenth century is displayed: lapis blue silk sewn
with silver; cinched waist; hips spread outward supported by a cage; breasts
suggested by slight plaster mounds; small hands gesture toward the throat—
no legs are visible.

Behind this dress is a painting: Adélaïde Labille-Guiard—*Portrait of the Artist
with Two Pupils* (1785). The artist is at the center of the composition, before
a canvas; two students stand behind her, women. The artist, later absorbed
into silence, meant this work to show her dedication to teaching women;

devised a state plan for female education. And her work, because of her intent, was considered radical and dangerous.

I want to talk about this woman's work, but the painting hangs here because of what she wears; and this is what my mother notices.

IV

These rooms are crowded—with artificial light, canned music—women wander past the work of women become the trappings of women. Which women turned the birds-of-paradise into a knee-length frock?—the life-work of creatures worn during one evening. By whose direction? Who trapped the birds? What decoys were employed? Who killed them?

V

In a corner of one room are enormous ornamental combs. From a wall an etching mocks as women topple—fooled into imbalance. But look again: It is the women-alone who fall. At the left, serenely upright, a woman walks supported by a man; at the right a deliveryman hurries, a gigantic package carried on his head.

Together my mother and I remember women with filled market baskets; women who carry a week's wet laundry from the washing place; a woman we know who bears water on her head—each day for half a mile. And briefly— recalling the women of our common ground—we meet.

VI

And then the wigs: the hair of another woman. Jo's chestnut hair cut off. The plumage of an ostrich. To wear another woman's hair. To wear the feathers of a large flightless bird. To cover a head with hair that has been sold.

The women of Marie Antoinette's court: their elevated heads—and the rats they say lived in them. We talk about teased hair; knotted, split, sprayed hair; bleached, dyed, kinked, straightened, curled hair. My mother's hair streaked blonde.

VII

Inevitably we change places with the displays: How did they sit? How did they walk? How did they get their waists so small?

We see ourselves in riding habits: black velvet coat with thick red roses—the jacket of Queen Alexandra; heavily veiled top hat; high leather boots and slender crop—seated askew, the body placed to one side. Would we slide off? Would we use the whip? The first time—would we wash the blood off, or let it fade?

VIII

In a dimly lit room are camisoles, slips, all other underthings: these are soft cotton, pale flowers embroidered and connected with gentle pastel ribbons. I imagine women dressing and undressing—together in their white eyelet cotton camisoles, helping each other undo the ribbons. Perhaps napping during the afternoon of a nineteenth-century house party—lying side by side on large pillows, briefly released. Perhaps touching; stroking the ribcage bruised by stays; applying a hanky dipped in bay rum to the temples of another. Perhaps kissing her forehead after the application is done, perhaps taking her hand. Head on another's shoulder, drifting. To be waked too soon. I like to think of women making soft underclothes for their comfort—as they comfort each other.

IX

This dream is interrupted by the crimson silk pajamas of a harem woman: purple brocade coat trimmed in gold braid and galloon; coins suspended above her eyes.

X

This meeting-place is filled with stolen gold, silver, coral, pearls; with plundered skins, shells, bones, and teeth. Aspects of ornamental bondage, all used to maintain the costume.

XI

We reach the end of the exhibit: in a corner (American, nineteenth century) are a mourning couple; mother and daughter in identical black garb, the head of the mother swathed in black net; the tragedy of bombazine on a five-year-old likeness holding her mother's mourning hands.

1980

Janice Mirikitani
(1942–   )

SUICIDE NOTE

*. . . An Asian American college student was reported to have
jumped to her death from her dormitory window. Her body was
found two days later under a deep cover of snow. Her suicide
note contained an apology to her parents for having received less
than a perfect four point grade average . . .*

How many notes written . . .
ink smeared like birdprints in snow.

      not good enough   not pretty enough   not smart enough
dear mother and father.
I apologize
for disappointing you.
I've worked very hard,
              not good enough
harder, perhaps to please you.
If only I were a son, shoulders broad
as the sunset threading through pine,
I would see the light in my mother's
eyes, or the golden pride reflected
in my father's dream
of my wide, male hands worthy of work
and comfort.
I would swagger through life
muscled and bold and assured,
drawing praises to me
like currents in the bed of wind, virile
with confidence.
      not good enough   not strong enough   not good enough

I apologize.
Tasks do not come easily.
Each failure, a glacier.
Each disapproval, a bootprint.
Each disappointment,
ice above my river.
So I have worked hard.
                  not good enough
My sacrifice I will drop
bone by bone, perched
on the ledge of my womanhood,
fragile as wings.
                  not strong enough
It is snowing steadily
surely not good weather
for flying—this sparrow
sillied and dizzied by the wind
on the edge.
                  not smart enough
I make this ledge my altar
to offer penance.
This air will not hold me,
the snow burdens my crippled wings,
my tears drop like bitter cloth
softly into the gutter below.
    not good enough   not strong enough   not smart enough

              Choices thin as shaved
              ice. Notes shredded
              drift like snow

on my broken body,
covers me like whispers
of sorries
sorries.
Perhaps when they find me
they will bury
my bird bones beneath
a sturdy pine

and scatter my feathers like
unspoken song
over this white and cold and silent
breast of earth.

1987

❖

Joy Harjo
(1951–   )

REMEMBER

Remember the sky that you were born under,
know each of the star's stories.
Remember the moon, know who she is. I met her
in a bar once in Iowa City.
Remember the sun's birth at dawn, that is the
strongest point of time. Remember sundown
and the giving away to night.
Remember your birth, how your mother struggled
to give you form and breath. You are evidence of
her life, and her mother's, and hers.
Remember your father. He is your life, also.
Remember the earth whose skin you are:
red earth, black earth, yellow earth, white earth
brown earth, we are earth.
Remember the plants, trees, animal life who all have their
tribes, their families, their histories, too. Talk to them,
listen to them. They are alive poems.
Remember the wind. Remember her voice. She knows the
origin of this universe. I heard her singing Kiowa war
dance songs at the corner of Fourth and Central once.
Remember that you are all people and that all people
are you.
Remember that you are this universe and that this
universe is you.
Remember that all is in motion, is growing, is you.

Remember that language comes from this.
Remember the dance that language is, that life is.
Remember.

1983

❖

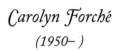

Carolyn Forché
(1950–)

AS CHILDREN TOGETHER

Under the sloped snow
pinned all winter with Christmas
lights, we waited for your father
to whittle his soap cakes
away, finish the whisky,
your mother to carry her coffee
from room to room closing lights
cubed in the snow at our feet.
Holding each other's
coat sleeves we slid down
the roads in our tight
black dresses, past
crystal swamps and the death
face of each dark house,
over the golden ice
of tobacco spit, the blue
quiet of ponds, with town
glowing behind the blind
white hills and a scant
snow ticking in the stars.
You hummed *blanche comme
la neige*[1] and spoke of Montreal
where a *quebeçoise* could sing,
take any man's face
to her unfastened blouse
and wake to wine

[1] French for "white as the snow," a traditional song of Quebec.

on the bedside table.
I always believed this,
Victoria, that there might
be a way to get out.

You were ashamed of that house,
its round tins of surplus flour,
chipped beef and white beans,
relief checks and winter trips
that always ended in deer
tied stiff to the car rack,
the accordion breath of your uncles
down from the north, and what
you called the stupidity
of the Michigan French.

Your mirror grew ringed
with photos of servicemen
who had taken your breasts
in their hands, the buttons
of your blouses in their teeth,
who had given you the silk
tassles of their graduation,
jackets embroidered with dragons
from the Far East. You kept
the corks that had fired
from bottles over their beds,
their letters with each city
blackened, envelopes of hair
from their shaved heads.
I am going to have it, you said.
Flowers wrapped in paper from carts
in Montreal, a plane lifting out
of Detroit, a satin bed, a table
cluttered with bottles of scent.

So standing in a platter of ice
outside a Catholic dance hall
you took their collars
in your fine chilled hands
and lied your age to adulthood.

I did not then have breasts of my own,
nor any letters from bootcamp
and when one of the men who had
gathered around you took my mouth
to his own there was nothing
other than the dance hall music
rising to the arms of iced trees.

I don't know where you are now, Victoria.
They say you have children, a trailer
in the snow near our town,
and the husband you found as a girl
returned from the Far East broken
cursing holy blood at the table
where nightly a pile of white shavings
is paid from the edge of his knife.

If you read this poem, write to me.
I have been to Paris since we parted.

1981

PART III

Public Lives

Women have participated fully in the development of the modern essay, a term coined by the French thinker Michel Eyquem de Montaigne (*Essais*, 1580) and popularized in England when philosopher Francis Bacon published his *Essays* (1597–1625) as "counsels for the successful conduct of life and the management of men." Since the sixteenth century, women such as Elizabeth Grymeston (known as the first woman essayist) have also focused on the successful conduct of life, but they have focused on the management of women as well as men. Writing essays that appeared in newspapers, magazines, and books, women have addressed a range of public issues (such as women's suffrage, racial violence, poverty, or war) and have also made formerly private concerns public (including aging, menstruation, or the unequal distribution of household tasks and childrearing duties).

There is no simple or clear-cut definition of this literary form. Usually (but not always) written in prose, the essay typically addresses public issues but may do so from either a personal or an impersonal perspective. Tone too may vary from polemical to satirical. The "formal essay" is usually a rigorously argued and logically constructed composition written explicitly to persuade or inform the reader. The "informal" or "familiar essay" is personal in voice and often light in tone. However, many essays blend these forms.

Through the essay as a genre women have moved outside the sphere of home and children to make their opinions known to the world at large. Writing for this larger public requires that a woman take herself seriously and be willing to speak out in her own voice (rather than masked behind a narrator or the characters in her novels). It also requires that a woman take herself seriously as an intellectual, as someone qualified to speak on matters of import to the public.

The essays included here exemplify the full range of styles, tones, and subjects of the genre. There are polemical, journalistic pieces like that by Judith Sargent Murray on sexual equality or Anna Quindlen on the vile ideologies of adolescent male sexual conquest, as well as pointedly satirical essays such as Gloria Steinem's "If Men Could Menstruate" and Judy Syfers' "I Want a Wife." Writing over a century apart, Margaret Fuller and Alice Walker each address issues of aging, while Mary Gordon and Marilou Awiakta interweave their personal stories with a larger story of origins and generations. Whether writing satirically or polemically, each of these essayists speaks her mind with passion and with power.

❖

O N E

Women and the Nation

Judith Sargent Murray (1751–1820) was one of the most famous patriots and feminists of the Revolutionary War era. Writing as "Constantia" and "The Gleaner," Murray filled the *Massachusetts Magazine* with essays on everything from religion to female equality. In the essay included here (written in 1779 and published in 1790), she especially champions female intellect, even slyly and wittily suggesting that, although she's making the case only for equality, she suspects that women are actually smarter than men.

In each of the essays in this section, a prominent thinker tackles an issue of import to the nation. The significance of Murray's writings is that she attempted to change public opinion precisely as the framers of the Constitution were deciding whether women should be included as full citizens in the new nation. She did not succeed in convincing them, but she did win over the hearts and minds of many women and men of her day. Similarly, writing in 1845, philosopher Margaret Fuller (1810–1850) criticizes the current forms of education for girls, and especially the argument that it is important to educate girls so that they will be better mothers for men. Instead, she advocates women's education for its own sake because she believes women should be honored for themselves. At a time when the "spinster" was a figure of ridicule, Fuller pays homage to the unmarried woman and adopts as a model a Native American woman who declared herself "betrothed to the Sun" and who lived apart, in her own wigwam, for the rest of her life.

"Fanny Fern"—Sara Payson (Willis) Parton (1811–1872)—was one of the most popular novelists and essayists of the mid-nineteenth century. Through her weekly column for the New York *Ledger,* she became the most influential woman journalist of her day. Although some of her work is within the nineteenth-century sentimental tradition, like many authors within that tradition she addressed critical social issues, including poverty, educational practices, labor reform, and woman's suffrage.

The daughter of former slaves, Ida B. Wells-Barnett (1862–1931) became the nation's most ardent voice against the heinous practice of lynching. In "The Case Stated" (1895) she notes that, in the thirty years since the end of the Civil War, some ten thousand African Americans have been killed by whites, without benefit of trial, while only three white men have been "tried, convicted, and executed" for murdering African Americans. Succinctly, forcefully, and eloquently, she exposes the extent of racial violence, especially in the South. In this and her other writings, Wells-Barnett pricked the conscience and raised the consciousness of the nation.

❖

Judith Sargent Murray
(1751–1820)

from *On the Equality of the Sexes*

Is it upon mature consideration we adopt the idea, that nature is thus partial in her distributions? Is it indeed a fact, that she hath yielded to one half of the human species so unquestionable a mental superiority? I know that to both sexes elevated understandings, and the reverse, are common. But, suffer me to ask, in what the minds of females are so notoriously deficient, or unequal. May not the intellectual powers be ranged under their four heads— imagination, reason, memory and judgement. The province of imagination has long since been surrendered up to us, and we have been crowned undoubted sovereigns of the regions of fancy. Invention is perhaps the most arduous effort of the mind; this branch of imagination hath been particularly ceded to us, and we have been time out of mind invested with that creative faculty. Observe the variety of fashions (here I bar the contemptuous smile) which distinguish and adorn the female world; how continually are they changing, insomuch that they almost render the whole man's assertion problematical, and we are ready to say, *there is something new under the sun*. Now, what a playfulness, what an exuberance of fancy, what strength of inventive imagination, doth this continual variation discover? Again, it hath been observed, that if the turpitude of the conduct of our sex, hath been ever so enormous, so extremely ready are we that the very first thought presents us with an apology so plausible, as to produce our actions even in an amiable light. Another instance of our creative powers, is our talent for slander; how ingenious are we at inventive scandal? what a formidable story can we in a moment fabricate merely from the force of a prolifick imagination? how many reputations, in the fertile brain of a female, have been utterly despoiled? how industrious are we at improving a hint? suspicion how easily do we convert into conviction, and conviction, embellished by the power of eloquence, stalks abroad to the surprise and confusion of unsuspecting innocence. Perhaps it

313

will be asked if I furnish these facts as instances of excellency in our sex. Certainly not; but as proofs of a creative faculty, of a lively imagination. Assuredly great activity of mind is thereby discovered, and was this activity properly directed, what beneficial effects would follow. Is the needle and kitchen sufficient to employ the operations of a soul thus organized? I should conceive not. Nay, it is a truth that those very departments leave the intelligent principle vacant, and at liberty for speculation. Are we deficient in reason? We can only reason from what we know, and if opportunity of acquiring knowledge hath been denied us, the inferiority of our sex cannot fairly be deduced from thence. Memory, I believe, will be allowed us in common, since every one's experience must testify, that a loquacious old woman is as frequently met with, as a communicative old man; their subjects are alike drawn from the fund of other times, and the transactions of their youth, or of maturer life, entertain, or perhaps fatigue you, in the evening of their lives. "But our judgment is not so strong—we do not distinguish so well." Yet it may be questioned, from what doth this superiority, in thus discriminating faculty of the soul, proceed. May we not trace its source in the difference of education, and continued advantages? Will it be said that the judgment of a male of two years old, is more sage than that of a female's of the same age? I believe the reverse is generally observed to be true. But from that period what partiality [how is the one exalted and the other depressed, by the contrary modes of education which are adopted] the one is taught to aspire, and the other is early confined and limited. As their years increase, the sister must be wholly domesticated, while the brother is led by the hand through all the flowery paths of science. Grant that their minds are by nature, equal; yet who shall wonder at the *apparent* superiority, if indeed custom becomes *second nature;* nay if it taketh place of nature, and that it doth the experience of each day will evince. At length arrived at womanhood; the uncultivated fair one feels a void, which the employments allotted her are by no means capable of filling. What can she do? to books, she may not apply; or if she doth, *to those only of the novel kind,* lest she merit the appellation of a *learned lady;* and what ideas have been affixed to this term, the observation of many can testify. Fashion, scandal and sometimes what is still more reprehensible, are then called in to her relief and who can say to what lengths the liberties she takes may proceed. Meantime she herself is most unhappy; she feels the want of a cultivated mind. Is she single, she in vain seeks to fill up time from sexual employments or amusements. Is she united to a person whose soul nature made equal to her own, education hath set him so far above her, that in those entertainments which are productive of such rational felicity, she is not qualified to accompany him. She experiences a mortifying consciousness of inferiority, which embitters every enjoyment. Doth the person to whom her adverse fate hath consigned her, possess a mind incapable of improvement she is equally wretched, in being so closely connected with an individual whom she cannot but despise. Now, was she permitted the same instructors as her brother, (with an eye however to their particular departments) for the employment of a rational mind an ample field would be opened. In astronomy she might catch a glimpse of the immensity of the Deity, and thence she would form amazing conceptions of the august and supreme Intelligence. In geography she would admire Jehova in the midst of his benevolence; thus adapting this globe to the various wants and amusements of its inhabitants. In natural philosophy she would adore the infinite majesty of heaven, clothed in condescension, and as she traversed the reptile world, she would hail the goodness of a creating God. A mind, thus filled, would have little room for the trifles with which our sex are, with too much justice, accused of amusing themselves, and they would thus be rendered fit companions for those, who should one day wear them as their crown. Fashions, in their variety, would then give place to conjectures, which might perhaps conduce to the improvement of the literary world; and there would be no leisure for slander or detraction. Reputation would not then be blasted, but serious speculations would occupy the lively imaginations of the sex. Unnecessary visits would be precluded, and that custom would only be indulged by way of relaxation, or to answer the demands of consanguinity and friendship. Females would become discreet, their judgments would be invigorated, and their partners for life being circumspectly chosen, an unhappy Hymen would then be as rare, as is now the reverse.

Will it be urged that those acquirements would supersede our domestick duties, I answer that every requisite in female economy is easily attained; and, with truth I can add, that when once attained, they require no further *mental attention*. Nay, while we are pursuing the needle, or the superintendency of the family, I repeat, that our minds are at full liberty for reflection; that imagination may exert itself in full vigor; and that if a just foundation early laid, our ideas will then be worthy of rational beings. If we were industrious we might easily find time to arrange them upon paper, or should avocations press too hard for such an indulgence, the hours allotted for conversation would at least become more refined and rational. Should it still be vociferated, "Your domestick employments are sufficient"—I would calmly ask, is it reasonable, that a candidate for immortality, for the joys of heaven, an intelligent being, who is to spend an eternity in contemplating the works of Deity, should at present be so degraded, as to be allowed no other ideas, than those which are suggested by the mechanism of a pudding, or the sewing of the seams of a garment? Pity that all such censures of female improvement do not go one step further, and deny their future existence; to be consistent they surely ought.

Yes, ye lordly, ye haughty sex, our souls are by nature *equal* to yours; the

315

same breath of God animates, enlivens, and invigorates us; and that we are not fallen lower than yourselves, let those witness who have greatly towered above the various discouragements by which they have been so heavily oppressed; and though I am unacquainted with the list of celebrated characters on either side, yet from the observations I have made in the contracted circle in which I have moved, I dare confidently believe, that from the commencement of time to the present day, there hath been as many females, as males, who, by the *mere force of natural powers,* have merited the crown of applause; who *thus unassisted,* have seized the wreath of fame. I know there are who assert, that as the animal powers of the one sex are superiour, of course their mental faculties also must be stronger; thus attributing strength of mind to the transient organization of this earth born tenement. But if this reasoning is just, man must be content to yield the palm to many of the brute creation, since by not a few of his brethren of the field, he is far surpassed in bodily strength. Moreover, was this argument admitted, it would prove too much, for occular demonstration evinceth, that there are many robust masculine ladies, and effeminate gentlemen. Yet I fancy that Mr. Pope, though clogged with an enervated body, and distinguished by a diminutive stature, could nevertheless lay claim to greatness of soul; and perhaps there are many other instances which might be adduced to combat so unphilosophical an opinion. Do we not often see, that when the clay built tabernacle is well nigh dissolved, when it is just ready to mingle with the parent soil, the immortal inhabitant aspires to, and even attaineth heights the most sublime, and which were before wholly unexplored. Besides, were we to grant that animal strength proved anything, taking into consideration the accustomed impartiality of nature, we should be induced to imagine, that she had invested the female mind with superiour strength as an equivalent for the bodily powers of man. But waving this however palpable advantage, for *equality* only, we wish to contend.

Constantia, 1790

❖

ℳargaret ℱuller
(1810–1850)

A WOMAN AT FORTY
from *Woman in the Nineteenth Century*

But to return to the thread of my subject.

Another sign of the times is furnished by the triumphs of Female Authorship. These have been great, and are constantly increasing. Women have taken possession of so many provinces for which men had pronounced them unfit, that, though these still declare there are some inaccessible to them, it is difficult to say just *where* they must stop.

The shining names of famous women have cast light upon the path of the sex, and many obstructions have been removed. When a Montague could learn better than her brother, and use her lore afterwards to such purpose as an observer, it seemed amiss to hinder women from preparing themselves to see, or from seeing all they could, when prepared. Since Somerville has achieved so much, will any young girl be prevented from seeking a knowledge of the physical sciences, if she wishes it? De Stael's name was not so clear of offense; she could not forget the Woman in the thought; while she was instructing you as a mind, she wished to be admired as a Woman; sentimental tears often dimmed the eagle glance. Her intellect, too, with all its splendor, trained in a drawing-room, fed on flattery, was tainted and flawed; yet its beams make the obscurest school-house in New England warmer and lighter to the little rugged girls who are gathered together on its wooden bench. They may never through life hear her name, but she is not the less their benefactress.

The influence has been such, that the aim certainly is, now, in arranging school instruction for girls, to give them as fair a field as boys. As yet, indeed, these arrangements are made with little judgment or reflection; just as the tutors of Lady Jane Grey, and other distinguished women of her time, taught them Latin and Greek, because they knew nothing else themselves, so now the improvement in the education of girls is to be made by giving them young men as teachers, who only teach what has been taught themselves at college, while methods and topics need revision for these new subjects, which could better be made by those who had experienced the same wants. Women are, often, at the head of these institutions; but they have, as yet, seldom been thinking women, capable of organizing a new whole for the wants of the time, and choosing persons to officiate in the departments. And when some portion of instruction of a good sort is got from the school, the far greater proportion which is infused from the general atmosphere of society contradicts its purport. Yet books and a little elementary instruction are not furnished in vain. Women are better aware how great and rich the universe is, not so easily blinded by narrowness or partial views of a home circle. "Her mother did so before her" is no longer a sufficient excuse. Indeed, it was never received as an excuse to mitigate the severity of censure, but was adduced as a reason, rather, why there should be no effort made for reformation.

Whether much or little has been done, or will be done,—whether women will add to the talent of narration the power of systematizing,—whether they will carve marble, as well as draw and paint,—is not important. But that it should be acknowledged that they have intellect which needs developing—that they should not be considered complete, if beings of affection and habit alone—is important.

Yet even this acknowledgment, rather conquered by Woman than proffered by Man, has been sullied by the usual selfishness. Too much is said of women being better educated, that they may become better companions and mothers *for men*. They should be fit for such companionship, and we have mentioned, with satisfaction, instances where it has been established. Earth knows no fairer, holier relation than that of a mother. It is one which, rightly understood, must both promote and require the highest attainments. But a being of infinite scope must not be treated with an exclusive view to any one relation. Give the soul free course, let the organization, both of body and mind, be freely developed, and the being will be fit for any and every relation to which it may be called. The intellect, no more than the sense of hearing, is to be cultivated merely that Woman may be a more valuable companion to Man, but because the Power who gave a power, by its mere existence signifies that it must be brought out toward perfection.

In this regard of self-dependence, and a greater simplicity and fulness of being, we must hail as a preliminary the increase of the class contemptuously designated as "old maids."

We cannot wonder at the aversion with which old bachelors and old maids have been regarded. Marriage is the natural means of forming a sphere, of taking root in the earth; it requires more strength to do this without such an opening; very many have failed, and their imperfections have been in every one's way. They have been more partial, more harsh, more officious and impertinent, than those compelled by severer friction to render themselves endurable. Those who have a more full experience of the instincts have a distrust as to whether the unmarried can be thoroughly human and humane, such as is hinted in the saying, "Old maids' and bachelors' children are well cared for," which derides at once their ignorance and their presumption.

Yet the business of society has become so complex, that it could now scarcely be carried on without the presence of these despised auxiliaries; and detachments from the army of aunts and uncles are wanted to stop gaps in every hedge. They rove about, mental and moral Ishmaelites, pitching their tents amid the fixed and ornamented homes of men.

In a striking variety of forms, genius of late, both at home and abroad, has paid its tribute to the character of the Aunt and the Uncle, recognizing in these personages the spiritual parents, who have supplied defects in the treatment of the busy or careless actual parents.

They also gain a wider, if not so deep experience. Those who are not intimately and permanently linked with others, are thrown upon themselves;

and, if they do not there find peace and incessant life, there is none to flatter them that they are not very poor, and very mean.

A position which so constantly admonishes, may be of inestimable benefit. The person may gain, undistracted by other relationships, a closer communion with the one. Such a use is made of it by saints and sibyls. Or she may be one of the lay sisters of charity, a canoness, bound by an inward vow,—or the useful drudge of all men, the Martha, much sought, little prized,—or the intellectual interpreter of the varied life she sees; the Urania of a half-formed world's twilight.

Or she may combine all these. Not "needing to care that she may please a husband," a frail and limited being, her thoughts may turn to the centre, and she may, by steadfast contemplation entering into the secret of truth and love, use it for the good of all men, instead of a chosen few, and interpret through it all the forms of life. It is possible, perhaps, to be at once a priestly servant and a loving muse.

Saints and geniuses have often chosen a lonely position, in the faith that if, undisturbed by the pressure of near ties, they would give themselves up to the inspiring spirit, it would enable them to understand and reproduce life better than actual experience could.

How many "old maids" take this high stand we cannot say: it is an unhappy fact that too many who have come before the eye are gossips rather, and not always good-natured gossips. But if these abuse, and none make the best of their vocation, yet it has not failed to produce some good results. It has been seen by others, if not by themselves, that beings, likely to be left alone, need to be fortified and furnished within themselves; and education and thought have tended more and more to regard these beings as related to absolute Being, as well as to others. It has been seen that, as the breaking of no bond ought to destroy a man, so ought the missing of none to hinder him from growing. And thus a circumstance of the time, which springs rather from its luxury than its purity, has helped to place women on the true platform.

Perhaps the next generation, looking deeper into this matter, will find that contempt is put upon old maids, or old women, at all, merely because they do not use the elixir which would keep them always young. Under its influence, a gem brightens yearly which is only seen to more advantage through the fissures Time makes in the casket. No one thinks of Michael Angelo's Persican Sibyl, or St. Theresa, or Tasso's Leonora, or the Greek Electra, as an old maid, more than of Michael Angelo or Canova as old bachelors, though all had reached the period in life's course appointed to take that degree.

See a common woman at forty; scarcely has she the remains of beauty, of any soft poetic grace which gave her attraction as Woman, which kindled the hearts of those who looked on her to sparkling thoughts, or diffused round her a roseate air of gentle love. See her, who was, indeed, a lovely girl, in the coarse, full-blown dahlia flower of what is commonly matron-beauty, "fat, fair, and forty," showily dressed, and with manners as broad and full as her frill or satin cloak. People observe, "How well she is preserved!" "She is a fine woman still," they say. This woman, whether as a duchess in diamonds, or one of our city dames in mosaics, charms the poet's heart no more, and would look much out of place kneeling before the Madonna. She "does well the honors of her house,"—"leads society,"—is, in short, always spoken and thought of upholstery-wise.

Or see that care-worn face, from which every soft line is blotted,—those faded eyes, from which lonely tears have driven the flashes of fancy, the mild white beam of a tender enthusiasm. This woman is not so ornamental to a tea-party; yet she would please better, in picture. Yet surely she, no more than the other, looks as a human being should at the end of forty years. Forty years! have they bound those brows with no garland? shed in the lamp no drop of ambrosial oil?

Not so looked the Iphigenia in Aulis. Her forty years had seen her in anguish, in sacrifice, in utter loneliness. But those pains were borne for her father and her country; the sacrifice she had made pure for herself and those around her. Wandering alone at night in the vestal solitude of her imprisoning grove, she has looked up through its "living summits" to the stars, which shed down into her aspect their own lofty melody. At forty she would not misbecome the marble.

Not so looks the Persica. She is withered; she is faded; the drapery that enfolds her has in its dignity an angularity, too, that tells of age, of sorrow, of a stern resignation to the *must*. But her eye, that torch of the soul, is untamed, and, in the intensity of her reading, we see a soul invincibly young in faith and hope. Her age is her charm, for it is the night of the past that gives this beacon-fire leave to shine. Wither more and more, black Chrysalid! thou dost but give the winged beauty time to mature its splendors!

Not so looked Victoria Colonna, after her life of a great hope, and of true conjugal fidelity. She had been, not merely a bride, but a wife, and each hour had helped to plume the noble bird. A coronet of pearls will not shame her brow; it is white and ample, a worthy altar for love and thought.

Even among the North American Indians, a race of men as completely engaged in mere instinctive life as almost any in the world, and where each chief, keeping many wives as useful servants, of course looks with no kind eye on celibacy in Woman, it was excused in the following instance mentioned by Mrs. Jameson. A woman dreamt in youth that she was betrothed to the Sun. She built her a wigwam apart, filled it with emblems of her alliance, and means of an independent life. There she passed her days, sustained by her own exertions, and true to her supposed engagement.

In any tribe, we believe, a woman, who lived as if she was betrothed to the Sun, would be tolerated, and the rays which made her youth blossom sweetly, would crown her with a halo in age.

There is, on this subject, a nobler view than heretofore, if not the noblest, and improvement here must coincide with that in the view taken of marriage. "We must have units before we can have union," says one of the ripe thinkers of the times.

1845

❖

Fanny Fern (Sara Payson [Willis] Parton)
(1811–1872)

THE WORKING-GIRLS OF NEW YORK
from *Folly As It Flies*

Nowhere more than in New York does the contest between squalor and splendor so sharply present itself. This is the first reflection of the observing stranger who walks its streets. Particularly is this noticeable with regard to its women. Jostling on the same pavement with the dainty fashionist is the care-worn working-girl. Looking at both these women, the question arises, which lives the more miserable life—she whom the world styles "fortunate," whose husband belongs to three clubs, and whose only meal with his family is an occasional breakfast, from year's end to year's end; who is as much a stranger to his own children as to the reader; whose young son of seventeen has already a detective on his track employed by his father to ascertain where and how he spends his nights and his father's money; swift retribution for that father who finds food, raiment, shelter, equipages for his household: but love, sympathy, companionship—never? Or she—this other woman—with a heart quite as hungry and unappeased, who also faces day by day the same appalling question: *Is this all life has for me?*

A great book is yet unwritten about women. Michelet has aired his wax-doll theories regarding them.[1] The defender of "woman's rights" has given us her views. Authors and authoresses of little, and big repute, have expressed themselves on this subject, and none of them as yet have begun to grasp it: men—because they lack spirituality, rightly and justly to interpret women; women—because they dare not, or will not tell us that which most interests

---

[1] Jules Michelet (1798–1894), a French historian, was something of a misogynist.

us to know. Who shall write this bold, frank, truthful book remains to be seen. Meanwhile woman's millennium is yet a great way off; and while it slowly progresses, conservatism and indifference gaze through their spectacles at the seething elements of to-day, and wonder "what ails all our women?"

Let me tell you what ails the working-girls. While yet your breakfast is progressing, and your toilet unmade, comes forth through Chatham Street and the Bowery, a long procession of them by twos and threes to their daily labor. Their breakfast, so called, has been hastily swallowed in a tenement house, where two of them share, in a small room, the same miserable bed. Of its quality you may better judge, when you know that each of these girls pays but three dollars a week for board, to the working man and his wife where they lodge.

The room they occupy is close and unventilated, with no accommodations for personal cleanliness, and so near to the little Flinegans that their Celtic night-cries are distinctly heard. They have risen unrefreshed, as a matter of course, and their ill-cooked breakfast does not mend the matter. They emerge from the doorway where their passage is obstructed by "nanny goats" and ragged children rooting together in the dirt, and pass out into the street. They shiver as the sharp wind of early morning strikes their temples. There is no look of youth on their faces; hard lines appear there. Their brows are knit; their eyes are sunken; their dress is flimsy, and foolish, and tawdry; always a hat, and feather or soiled artificial flower upon it; the hair dressed with an abortive attempt at style; a soiled petticoat; a greasy dress, a well-worn sacque or shawl, and a gilt breast-pin and earrings.

Now follow them to the large, black-looking building, where several hundred of them are manufacturing hoop-skirts. If you are a woman you have worn plenty; but you little thought what passed in the heads of these girls as their busy fingers glazed the wire, or prepared the spools for covering them, or secured the tapes which held them in their places. *You* could not stay five minutes in that room, where the noise of the machinery used is so deafening, that only by the motion of the lips could you comprehend a person speaking.

Five minutes! Why, these young creatures bear it, from seven in the morning till six in the evening; week after week, month after month, with only half an hour at midday to eat their dinner of a slice of bread and butter or an apple, which they usually eat in the building, some of them having come a long distance. As I said, the roar of machinery in that room is like the roar of Niagara. Observe them as you enter. Not one lifts her head. They might as well be machines, for any interest or curiosity they show, save always to know *what o'clock it is.* Pitiful! pitiful, you almost sob to yourself, as you look at these young girls. *Young?* Alas! it is only in years that they are young.

1868

Ida B. Wells-Barnett
(1862–1931)

THE CASE STATED

The student of American sociology will find the year 1894 marked by a pronounced awakening of the public conscience to a system of anarchy and outlawry which had grown during a series of ten years to be so common, that scenes of unusual brutality failed to have any visible effect upon the humane sentiments of the people of our land.

Beginning with the emancipation of the Negro, the inevitable result of unbridled power exercised for two and a half centuries, by the white man over the Negro, began to show itself in acts of conscienceless outlawry. During the slave *régime,* the Southern white man owned the Negro body and soul. It was to his interest to dwarf the soul and preserve the body. Vested with unlimited power over his slave, to subject him to any and all kinds of physical punishment, the white man was still restrained from such punishment as tended to injure the slave by abating his physical powers and thereby reducing his financial worth. While slaves were scourged mercilessly, and in countless cases inhumanly treated in other respects, still the white owner rarely permitted his anger to go so far as to take a life, which would entail upon him a loss of several hundred dollars. The slave was rarely killed, he was too valuable; it was easier and quite as effective, for discipline or revenge, to sell him "Down South."

But Emancipation came and the vested interests of the white man in the Negro's body were lost. The white man had no right to scourge the emancipated Negro, still less has he a right to kill him. But the Southern white people had been educated so long in that school of practice, in which might makes right, that they disdained to draw strict lines of action in dealing with the Negro. In slave times the Negro was kept subservient and submissive by the frequency and severity of the scourging, but, with freedom, a new system of intimidation came in vogue; the Negro was not only whipped and scourged; he was killed.

Not all nor nearly all of the murders done by white men, during the past thirty years in the South, have come to light, but the statistics as gathered and preserved by white men, and which have not been questioned, show that during these years more than ten thousand Negroes have been killed in cold blood, without the formality of judicial trial and legal execution. And yet, as evidence of the absolute impunity with which the white man dares to kill a Negro, the same record shows that during all these years, and for all these murders only three white men have been tried, convicted, and executed. As no white man has been lynched for the murder of colored people, these three executions are the only instances of the death penalty being visited upon white men for murdering Negroes.

Naturally enough the commission of these crimes began to tell upon the public conscience, and the Southern white man, as a tribute to the nineteenth century civilization, was in a manner compelled to give excuses for his barbarism. His excuses have adapted themselves to the emergency, and are aptly outlined by that greatest of all Negroes, Frederick Douglass, in an article of recent date, in which he shows that there have been three distinct eras of southern barbarism, to account for which three distinct excuses have been made.

The first excuse given to the civilized world for the murder of unoffending Negroes was the necessity of the white man to repress and stamp out alleged "race riots." For years immediately succeeding the war there was an appalling slaughter of colored people, and the wires usually conveyed to northern people and the world the intelligence, first, that an insurrection was being planned by Negroes, which, a few hours later, would prove to have been vigorously resisted by white men, and controlled with a resulting loss of several killed and wounded. It was always a remarkable feature in these insurrections and riots that only Negroes were killed during the rioting, and that all the white men escaped unharmed.

From 1865 to 1872, hundreds of colored men and women were mercilessly murdered and the almost invariable reason assigned was that they met their death by being alleged participants in an insurrection or riot. But this story at last wore itself out. No insurrection ever materialized; no Negro rioter was ever apprehended and proven guilty, and no dynamite ever recorded the black man's protest against oppression and wrong. It was too much to ask thoughtful people to believe this transparent story, and the southern white people at last made up their minds that some other excuse must be had.

Then came the second excuse, which had its birth during the turbulent times of reconstruction. By an amendment to the Constitution the Negro was given the right of franchise, and, theoretically at least, his ballot became his invaluable emblem of citizenship. In a government "of the people, for the people, and by the people," the Negro's vote became an important factor in all matters of state and national politics. But this did not last long. The southern white man would not consider that the Negro had any right which a white man was bound to respect, and the idea of a republican form of government in the southern states grew into general contempt. It was maintained that "This is a white man's government," and regardless of numbers, the white man should rule. "No Negro domination" became the new legend on the sanguinary banner of the sunny South, and under it rode the Ku Klux Klan, the Regulators, and the lawless mobs, which for any cause chose to murder one man or a dozen as suited their purpose best. It was a long, gory campaign; the blood chills and the heart almost loses faith in Christianity when one thinks of Yazoo, Hamburg, Edgefield, Copiah, and the countless massacres of defenceless Negroes, whose only crime was the attempt to exercise their right to vote.

But it was a bootless strife for colored people. The government which had made the Negro a citizen found itself unable to protect him. It gave him the right to vote, but denied him the protection which should have maintained that right. Scourged from his home; hunted through the swamps; hung by midnight raiders, and openly murdered in the light of day, the Negro clung to his right of franchise with a heroism which would have wrung admiration from the heart of savages. He believed that in that small white ballot there was a subtle something which stood for manhood as well as citizenship, and thousands of brave black men went to their graves, exemplifying the one by dying for the other.

The white man's victory soon became complete by fraud, violence, intimidation and murder. The franchise vouchsafed to the Negro grew to be a "barren ideality," and regardless of numbers, the colored people found themselves voiceless in the councils of those whose duty it was to rule. With no longer the fear of "Negro Domination" before their eyes, the white man's second excuse became valueless. With the Southern governments all subverted and the Negro actually eliminated from all participation in state and national elections, there could be no longer an excuse for killing Negroes to prevent "Negro Domination."

Brutality still continued; Negroes were whipped, scourged, exiled, shot and hung whenever and wherever it pleased the white man so to treat them, and as the civilized world with increasing persistency held the white people of the South to account for its outlawry, the murderers invented the third excuse—that Negroes had to be killed to avenge their assaults upon women. There could be framed no possible excuse more harmful to the Negro and more unanswerable if true in its sufficiency for the white man.

Humanity abhors the assailant of womanhood, and this charge upon the Negro at once placed him beyond the pale of human sympathy. With such unanimity, earnestness and apparent candor was this charge made and reiterated that the world has accepted the story that the Negro is the monster which the Southern white man has painted him. And today, the Christian world feels, that while lynching is a crime, and lawlessness and anarchy the certain precursors of a nation's fall, it can not by word or deed, extend sympathy or help to a race of outlaws, who might mistake their plea for justice and deem it an excuse for their continued wrongs.

The Negro has suffered much and is willing to suffer more. He recognizes that the wrongs of two centuries can not be righted in a day, and he tries to bear his burden with patience for to-day and be hopeful for to-morrow. But there comes a time when the veriest worm will turn, and the Negro feels to-day that after all the work he has done, all the sacrifices he has made, and all the suffering he has endured, if he did not, now, defend his name and man-hood from this vile accusation, he would be unworthy even of the contempt of mankind. It is to this charge he now feels he must make answer.

If the Southern people in defense of their lawlessness, would tell the truth and admit that colored men and women are lynched for almost any offense from murder to a misdemeanor, there would not now be the necessity for this defense. But when they intentionally, maliciously and constantly belie the record and bolster up these falsehoods by the words of legislators, preachers, governors and bishops, then the Negro must give to the world his side of the awful story.

A word as to the charge itself. In considering the third reason assigned by the Southern white people for the butchery of blacks, the question must be asked, what the white man means when he charges the black man with rape. Does he mean the crime which the statutes of the civilized states describe as such? Not by any means. With the Southern white man, any *mesalliance* ex-isting between a white woman and a colored man is a sufficient foundation for the charge of rape. The Southern white man says that it is impossible for a voluntary alliance to exist between a white woman and a colored man, and therefore, the fact of an alliance is a proof of force. In numerous instances where colored men have been lynched on the charge of rape, it was positively known at the time of lynching, and indisputably proven after the victim's death, that the relationship sustained between the man and woman was vol-untary and clandestine, and that in no court of law could even the charge of assault have been successfully maintained.

It was for the assertion of this fact, in the defense of her own race, that the writer hereof became an exile; her property destroyed and her return to her home forbidden under penalty of death, for writing the following editorial which was printed in her paper, *The Free Speech*, in Memphis, Tenn., May 21, 1892.

"Eight Negroes lynched since last issue of the 'Free Speech' one at Little Rock, Ark., last Saturday morning where the citizens broke (?) into the pen-itentiary and got their man; three near Anniston, Ala., one near New Orleans; and three at Clarksville, Ga., the last three for killing a white man, and five on the same old racket—the new alarm about raping white women. The same programme of hanging, then shooting bullets into the lifeless bodies was car-ried out to the letter. Nobody in this section of the country believes the old thread bare lie that Negro men rape white women. If Southern white men are not careful, they will over-reach themselves and public sentiment will have a reaction; a conclusion will then be reached which will be very damaging to the moral reputation of their women."

But threats cannot suppress the truth, and while the Negro suffers the soul deformity, resultant from two and a half centuries of slavery, he is no more guilty of this vilest of all vile charges than the white man who would blacken his name.

During all the years of slavery, no such charge was ever made, not even during the dark days of the rebellion, when the white man, following the fortunes of war went to do battle for the maintenance of slavery. While the master was away fighting to forge the fetters upon the slave, he left his wife and children with no protectors save the Negroes themselves. And yet during those years of trust and peril, no Negro proved recreant to his trust and no white man returned to a home that had been despoiled.

Likewise during the period of alleged "insurrection," and alarming "race riots," it never occurred to the white man, that his wife and children were in danger of assault. Nor in the Reconstruction era, when the hue and cry was against "Negro Domination," was there ever a thought that the domination would ever contaminate a fireside or strike to death the virtue of womanhood. It must appear strange indeed, to every thoughtful and candid man, that more than a quarter of a century elapsed before the Negro began to show signs of such infamous degeneration.

In his remarkable apology for lynching, Bishop Haygood, of Georgia, says: "No race, not the most savage, tolerates the rape of woman, but it may be said without reflection upon any other people that the Southern people are now and always have been most sensitive concerning the honor of their women—their mothers, wives, sisters and daughters." It is not the purpose of this defense to say one word against the white women of the South. Such need not be said, but it is their misfortune that the chivalrous white men of that section, in order to escape the deserved execration of the civilized world, should shield themselves by their cowardly and infamously false excuse, and call into question that very honor about which their distinguished priestly apologist claims they are most sensitive. To justify their own barbarism they assume a chivalry which they do not possess. True chivalry respects all womanhood, and no one who reads the record, as it is written in the faces of the million mulattoes in the South, will for a minute conceive that the southern white man had a very chivalrous regard for the honor due the women of his own race or respect for the womanhood which circumstances placed in his power. That chivalry which is "most sensitive concerning the honor of women" can hope for but little respect from the civilized world, when it con-

327

fines itself entirely to the women who happen to be white. Virtue knows no color line, and the chivalry which depends upon complexion of skin and texture of hair can command no honest respect.

When emancipation came to the Negroes, there arose in the northern part of the United States an almost divine sentiment among the noblest, purest and best white women of the North, who felt called to a mission to educate and Christianize the millions of southern ex-slaves. From every nook and corner of the North, brave young white women answered that call and left their cultured homes, their happy associations and their lives of ease, and with heroic determination went to the South to carry light and truth to the benighted blacks. It was a heroism no less than that which calls for volunteers for India, Africa and the Isles of the sea. To educate their unfortunate charges; to teach them the Christian virtues and to inspire in them the moral sentiments manifest in their own lives, these young women braved dangers whose record reads more like fiction than fact. They became social outlaws in the South. The peculiar sensitiveness of the southern white men for women, never shed its protecting influence about them. No friendly word from their own race cheered them in their work; no hospitable doors gave them the companionship like that from which they had come. No chivalrous white man doffed his hat in honor or respect. They were "Nigger teachers"—unpardonable offenders in the social ethics of the South, and were insulted, persecuted and ostracised, not by Negroes, but by the white manhood which boasts of its chivalry toward women.

And yet these northern women worked on, year after year, unselfishly, with a heroism which amounted almost to martyrdom. Threading their way through dense forests, working in school house, in the cabin and in the church, thrown at all times and in all places among the unfortunate and lowly Negroes, whom they had come to find and to serve, these northern women, thousands and thousands of them have spent more than a quarter of a century in giving to the colored people their splendid lessons for home and heart and soul. Without protection, save that which innocence gives to every good woman, they went about their work, fearing no assault and suffering none. Their chivalrous protectors were hundreds of miles away in their northern homes, and yet they never feared any "great dark faced mobs," they dared night or day to "go beyond their own roof trees." They never complained of assaults, and no mob was ever called into existence to avenge crimes against them. Before the world adjudges the Negro a moral monster, a vicious assailant of womanhood and a menace to the sacred precincts of home, the colored people ask the consideration of the silent record of gratitude, respect, protection and devotion of the millions of the race in the South, to the thousands of northern white women who have served as teachers and missionaries since the war.

The Negro may not have known what chivalry was, but he knew enough to preserve inviolate the womanhood of the South which was entrusted to his hands during the war. The finer sensibilities of his soul may have been crushed out by years of slavery, but his heart was full of gratitude to the white women of the North, who blessed his home and inspired his soul in all these years of freedom. Faithful to his trust in both of these instances, he should now have the impartial ear of the civilized world, when he dares to speak for himself as against the infamy wherewith he stands charged.

It is his regret, that, in his own defense, he must disclose to the world that degree of dehumanizing brutality which fixes upon America the blot of a national crime. Whatever faults and failings other nations may have in their dealings with their own subjects or with other people, no other civilized nation stands condemned before the world with a series of crimes so peculiarly national. It becomes a painful duty of the Negro to reproduce a record which shows that a large portion of the American people avow anarchy, condone murder and defy the contempt of civilization.

These pages are written in no spirit of vindictiveness, for all who give the subject consideration must concede that far too serious is the condition of that civilized government in which the spirit of unrestrained outlawry constantly increases in violence, and casts its blight over a continually growing area of territory. We plead not for the colored people alone, but for all victims of the terrible injustice which puts men and women to death without form of law. During the year 1894, there were 132 persons executed in the United States by due form of law, while in the same year, 197 persons were put to death by mobs who gave the victims no opportunity to make a lawful defense. No comment need be made upon a condition of public sentiment responsible for such alarming results.

The purpose of the pages which follow shall be to give the record which has been made, not by colored men, but that which is the result of compilations made by white men, of reports sent over the civilized world by white men in the South. Out of their own mouths shall the murderers be condemned. For a number of years the Chicago Tribune, admittedly one of the leading journals of America, has made a specialty of the compilation of statistics touching upon lynching. The data compiled by that journal and published to the world January 1st, 1894, up to the present time has not been disputed. In order to be safe from the charge of exaggeration, the incidents hereinafter reported have been confined to those vouched for by the Tribune.

Iola, 1895

T W O

The Struggle for Understanding

A high percentage of women's essays and journalism has to do with the uplift of women and their position in society. From earliest times, women writers have emphasized that women must have access to literacy and education, claiming justifiably that learning is a primary route to personal and economic self-sufficiency. Anna Julia Haywood Cooper's now-famous 1892 essay, "The Higher Education of Women," was controversial for its time— and not only because Cooper championed education for black women. Her acknowledging that educating women was "a rather dangerous experiment" was not just a rhetorical pose; at that time one of Harvard's leading faculty members was fighting hard against the creation of Radcliffe College (from its original designation as "the Harvard Annex," a non-degree granting unit of the men's college).

Other women writers attempted to describe lifestyles that were "other" to those of the mainstream, often male, culture. When Mary Hunter Austin wrote about a belief system that underlay Native American society, or Meridel Le Sueur described the lives of unemployed—and desperately poor—women during the Great Depression, they provided new information as a means of arguing their implicit points. What might be seen today as "political" writing was informed with the writers' urgent desire that readers understand actual situations.

Anna Julia Haywood Cooper (1858?–1964), born into slavery in North Carolina, was one of the leading black scholars and teachers of her time. Graduated from Oberlin College, Ohio, in 1884 (she began college after the death of her husband), she moved to Washington, D.C., where she taught science and mathematics at—and was principal of—Washington Colored High School (the M Street School). In 1892 she helped to organize the Colored Woman's League of Washington, D.C., and published the essay collection, *A Voice from the South*, from which the selection included here comes. Through her later years she remained active in black intellectual life, and in 1925 received a doctorate in French from the University of Paris.

Mary Hunter Austin (1868–1934) moved from Illinois to southern California in 1888, the same year she graduated from Blackburn College. After her marriage she began writing seriously; *The Land of Little Rain*, the first of her 27 books and several hundred essays, appeared in 1903. Her primary mission was to change social attitudes toward women, and toward the Native American and Hispanic cultures that remained enigmatic to many Americans. Austin was an early eco-feminist, as active in fights for water rights as for birth control and suffrage. Here she employs the metaphoric legends of a culture to explain the duality of good and evil.

Meridel Le Sueur (b. 1900) was a different kind of pioneer. In the midst of a literary establishment that was college-educated and at least middle class, Le Sueur wrote about the plight of the poor. Her focus on the lives of women, both white and of color, was also unusual; her long career of writing journalism, poetry, memoir, and fiction continues today—still innovative, still impassioned. The daughter of social activists from Iowa, Texas, Kansas, and Minnesota, Le Sueur negotiated difficult political times during the Great Depression. More recently, she has been active in Native American and civil rights, ecology, anti-war movements, and her own humane feminism.

❖

Anna Julia Haywood Cooper
(1858?–1964)

from *The Higher Education of Women*

In the very first year of our century, the year 1801, there appeared in Paris a book by Silvain Maréchal, entitled "Shall Woman Learn the Alphabet." The book proposes a law prohibiting the alphabet to women, and quotes authorities weighty and various, to prove that the woman who knows the alphabet has already lost part of her womanliness. The author declares that women can use the alphabet only as Moliére predicted they would, in spelling out the verb *amo;* that they have no occasion to peruse Ovid's *Ars Amoris,* since that is already the ground and limit of their intuitive furnishing; that Madame Guion would have been far more adorable had she remained a beautiful ignoramus as nature made her; that Ruth, Naomi, the Spartan woman, the Amazons, Penelope, Andromache, Lucretia, Joan of Arc, Petrarch's Laura, the daughters of Charlemagne, could not spell their names; while Sappho, Aspasia, Madame de Maintenon, and Madame de Stael could read altogether too well for their good; finally, that if women were once permitted to read Sophocles and work with logarithms, or to nibble at any side of the apple of knowledge, there would be an end forever to their sewing on buttons and embroidering slippers.

Please remember this book was published at the *beginning* of the Nineteenth Century. At the end of its first third, (in the year 1833) one solitary college in America decided to admit women within its sacred precincts, and organized what was called a "Ladies' Course" as well as the regular B.A. or Gentlemen's course.

It was felt to be an experiment—a rather dangerous experiment—and was adopted with fear and trembling by the good fathers, who looked as if they had been caught secretly mixing explosive compounds and were guiltily expecting every moment to see the foundations under them shaken and rent and their fair superstructure shattered into fragments.

But the girls came, and there was no upheaval. They performed their tasks modestly and intelligently. Once in a while one or two were found choosing the gentlemen's course. Still no collapse; and the dear, careful, scrupulous, frightened old professors were just getting their hearts out of their throats and preparing to draw one good free breath, when they found they would have to change the names of those courses; for there were as many ladies in the gentlemen's course as in the ladies', and a distinctively Ladies' Course, inferior in scope and aim to the regular classical course, did not and could not exist.

Other colleges gradually fell into line, and to-day there are one hundred and ninety-eight colleges for women, and two hundred and seven coeducational colleges and universities in the United States alone offering the degree of B.A. to women, and sending out yearly into the arteries of this nation a warm, rich flood of strong, brave, active, energetic, well-equipped, thoughtful women—women quick to see and eager to help the needs of this needy world—women who can think as well as feel, and who feel none the less because they think—women who are none the less tender and true for the parchment scroll they bear in their hands—women who have given a deeper, richer, nobler and grander meaning to the word "womanly" than any one-sided masculine definition could ever have suggested or inspired—women whom the world has long waited for in pain and anguish till there should be at last added to its forces and allowed to permeate its thought the complement of that masculine influence which has dominated it for fourteen centuries.

Since the idea of order and subordination succumbed to barbarian brawn and brutality in the fifth century, the civilized world has been like a child brought up by his father. It has needed the great mother heart to teach it to be pitiful, to love mercy, to succor the weak and care for the lowly.

Whence came this apotheosis of greed and cruelty? Whence this sneaking admiration we all have for bullies and prize-fighters? Whence the self-congratulation of "dominant" races, as if "dominant" meant "righteous" and carried with it a title to inherit the earth? Whence the scorn of so-called weak or unwarlike races and individuals, and the very comfortable assurance that it is their manifest destiny to be wiped out as vermin before this advancing civilization? As if the possession of the Christian graces of meekness, non-resistance and forgiveness, were incompatible with a civilization professedly based on Christianity, the religion of love! Just listen to this little bit of Barbarian brag:

> *As for Far Orientals, they are not of those who will survive.*
> *Artistic attractive people that they are, their civilization is like*
> *their own tree flowers, beautiful blossoms destined never to bear*
> *fruit. If these people continue in their old course, their earthly*
> *career is closed. Just as surely as morning passes into afternoon,*
> *so surely are these races of the Far East, if unchanged, destined*
> *to disappear before the advancing nations of the West. Vanish,*
> *they will, off the face of the earth, and leave our planet the*
> *eventual possession of the dwellers where the day declines. Unless*
> *their newly imported ideas really take root, it is from this whole*
> *world that Japanese and Koreans, as well as Chinese, will inevitably be excluded. Their Nirvana is already being realized;*
> *already, it has wrapped Far Eastern Asia in its winding sheet.—*
> Soul of the Far East—P. Lowell.

Delightful reflection for "the dwellers where day declines." A spectacle to make the gods laugh, truly, to see the scion of an upstart race by one sweep of his generalizing pen consigning to annihilation one-third the inhabitants of the globe—a people whose civilization was hoary headed before the parent elements that begot his race had advanced beyond nebulosity.

How like Longfellow's Iagoo, we Westerners are, to be sure! In the few hundred years we have had to strut across our allotted territory and bask in the afternoon sun, we imagine we have exhausted the possibilities of humanity. Verily, we are the people, and after us there is none other. Our God is power; strength, our standard of excellence, inherited from barbarian ancestors through a long line of male progenitors, the Law Salic permitting no feminine modifications.

Says one, "The Chinaman is not popular with us, and we do not like the Negro. It is not that the eyes of the one are set bias, and the other is darkskinned; but the Chinaman, the Negro is weak—*and Anglo Saxons don't like weakness.*"

The world of thought under the predominant man-influence, unmollified and unrestrained by its complementary force, would become like Daniel's fourth beast: "dreadful and terrible, and *strong* exceedingly;" "it had great iron teeth; it devoured and brake in pieces, and stamped the residue with the feet of it;" and the most independent of us find ourselves ready at times to fall down and worship this incarnation of power.

Mrs. Mary A. Livermore, a woman whom I can mention only to admire, came near shaking my faith a few weeks ago in my theory of the thinking woman's mission to put in the tender and sympathetic chord in nature's grand symphony, and counteract, or better, harmonize the diapason of mere strength and might.

She was dwelling on the Anglo-Saxon genius for power and his contempt for weakness, and described a scene in San Francisco which she had witnessed.

The incorrigible animal known as the American small-boy, had pounced upon a simple, unoffending Chinaman, who was taking home his work, and had emptied the beautifully laundried contents of his basket into the ditch. "And," said she, "when that great man stood there and blubbered before that crowd of lawless urchins, to any one of whom he might have taught a lesson with his two fists, *I didn't much care.*"

This is said like a man! It grates harshly. It smacks of the worship of the beast. It is contempt for weakness, and taken out of its setting it seems to contradict my theory. It either shows that one of the highest exponents of the Higher Education can be at times untrue to the instincts I have ascribed to the thinking woman and to the contribution she is to add to the civilized world, or else the influence she wields upon our civilization may be potent without being necessarily and always direct and conscious. The latter is the case. Her voice may strike a false note, but her whole being is musical with the vibrations of human suffering. Her tongue may parrot over the cold conceits that some man has taught her, but her heart is aglow with sympathy and loving kindness, and she cannot be true to her real self without giving out these elements into the forces of the world.

No one is in any danger of imagining Mark Antony "a plain blunt man," nor Cassius a sincere one—whatever the speeches they may make.

As individuals, we are constantly and inevitably, whether we are conscious of it or not, giving out our real selves into our several little worlds, inexorably adding our own true ray to the flood of starlight, quite independently of our professions and our masquerading; and so in the world of thought, the influence of thinking woman far transcends her feeble declamation and may seem at times even opposed to it.

A visitor in Oberlin once said to the lady principal, "Have you no rabble in Oberlin? How is it I see no police here, and yet the streets are as quiet and orderly as if there were an officer of the law standing on every corner."

Mrs. Johnston replied, "Oh, yes; there are vicious persons in Oberlin just as in other towns—*but our girls are our police.*"

With from five to ten hundred pure-minded young women threading the streets of the village every evening unattended, vice must slink away, like frost before the rising sun: and yet I venture to say there was not one in a hundred of those girls who would not have run from a street brawl as she would from a mouse, and who would not have declared she could never stand the sight of blood and pistols.

There is, then, a real and special influence of woman. An influence subtle and often involuntary, an influence so intimately interwoven in, so intricately interpenetrated by the masculine influence of the time that it is often difficult to extricate the delicate meshes and analyze and identify the closely clinging fibers. And yet, without this influence—so long as woman sat with bandaged eyes and manacled hands, fast bound in the clamps of ignorance and inaction, the world of thought moved in its orbit like the revolutions of the moon; with one face (the man's face) always out, so that the spectator could not distinguish whether it was disc or sphere.

Now I claim that it is the prevalence of the Higher Education among women, the making it a common everyday affair for women to reason and think and express their thought, the training and stimulus which enable and encourage women to administer to the world the bread it needs as well as the sugar it cries for; in short it is the transmitting the potential forces of her soul into dynamic factors that has given symmetry and completeness to the world's agencies. So only could it be consummated that Mercy, the lesson she teaches, and Truth, the task man has set himself, should meet together: that righteousness, or *rightness*, man's ideal,—and *peace*, its necessary 'other half,' should kiss each other.

We must thank the general enlightenment and independence of woman (which we may now regard as a *fait accompli*) that both these forces are now at work in the world, and it is fair to demand from them for the twentieth century a higher type of civilization than any attained in the nineteenth. Religion, science, art, economics, have all needed the feminine flavor; and literature, the expression of what is permanent and best in all of these, may be gauged at any time to measure the strength of the feminine ingredient. You will not find theology consigning infants to lakes of unquenchable fire long after women have had a chance to grasp, master, and wield its dogmas. You will not find science annihilating personality from the government of the Universe and making of God an ungovernable, unintelligible, blind, often destructive physical force; you will not find jurisprudence formulating as an axiom the absurdity that man and wife are one, and that one the man—that the married woman may not hold or bequeath her own property save as subject to her husband's direction; you will not find political economists declaring that the only possible adjustment between laborers and capitalists is that of selfishness and rapacity—that each must get all he can and keep all that he gets, while the world cries *laissez faire* and the lawyers explain, "it is the beautiful working of the law of supply and demand;" in fine, you will not find the law of love shut out from the affairs of men after the feminine half of the world's truth is completed.

Nay, put your ear now close to the pulse of the time. What is the keynote of the literature of these days? What is the banner cry of all the activities of the last half decade? What is the dominant seventh which is to add richness and tone to the final cadences of this century and lead by a grand modulation into the triumphant harmonies of the next? Is it not compassion for the poor and unfortunate, and, as Bellamy has expressed it, "indignant outcry against the failure of the social machinery as it is, to ameliorate the miseries of men!" Even Christianity is being brought to the bar of humanity and tried by the standard of its ability to alleviate the world's suffering and lighten and brighten its woe. What else can be the meaning of Matthew Arnold's saddening protest, "We cannot do without Christianity," cried he, "and we cannot endure it as it is."

When went there by an age, when so much time and thought, so much money and labor were given to God's poor and God's invalids, the lowly and unlovely, the sinning as well as the suffering—homes for inebriates and homes for lunatics, shelter for the aged and shelter for babes, hospitals for the sick, props and braces for the falling, reformatory prisons and prison reformatories, all show that a "mothering" influence from some source is leavening the nation.

Now please understand me. I do not ask you to admit that these benefactions and virtues are the exclusive possession of women, or even that women are their chief and only advocates. It may be a man who formulates and makes them vocal. It may be, and often is, a man who weeps over the wrongs and struggles for the amelioration: but that man has imbibed those impulses from a mother rather than from a father and is simply materializing and giving back to the world in tangible form the ideal love and tenderness, devotion and care that have cherished and nourished the helpless period of his own existence.

All I claim is that there is a feminine as well as a masculine side to truth; that these are related not as inferior and superior, not as better and worse, not as weaker and stronger, but as complements—complements in one necessary and symmetric whole. That as the man is more noble in reason, so the woman is more quick in sympathy. That as he is indefatigable in pursuit of abstract truth, so is she in caring for the interests by the way—striving tenderly and lovingly that not one of the least of these "little ones" should perish. That while we not unfrequently see women who reason, we say, with the coolness and precision of a man, and men as considerate of helplessness as a woman, still there is a general consensus of mankind that the one trait is essentially masculine and the other is peculiarly feminine. That both are needed to be worked into the training of children, in order that our boys may supplement their virility by tenderness and sensibility, and our girls may round out their gentleness by strength and self-reliance. That, as both are alike necessary in giving symmetry to the individual, so a nation or a race will degenerate into mere emotionalism on the one hand, or bullyism on the other, if dominated by either exclusively; lastly, and most emphatically, that the feminine factor can have its proper effect only through woman's development and education so that she may fitly and intelligently stamp her force on the forces of her day, and add her modicum to the riches of the world's thought. . . .

1892

❖

Mary Hunter Austin
(1868–1934)

THE COYOTE-SPIRIT AND THE WEAVING WOMAN

The Weaving Woman lived under the bank of the stony wash that cut through the country of the mesquite dunes. The Coyote-Spirit, which, you understand, is an Indian whose form has been changed to fit with his evil behavior, ranged from the Black Rock where the wash began to the white sands beyond Pahranagat; and the Goat-Girl kept her flock among the mesquites, or along the windy stretch of sage below the campoodie; but as the Coyote-Spirit never came near the wickiups by day, and the Goat-Girl went home the moment the sun dropped behind Pahranagat, they never met. These three are all that have to do with the story.

The Weaving Woman, whose work was the making of fine baskets of split willow and roots of yucca and brown grass, lived alone, because there was nobody found who wished to live with her, and because it was whispered among the wickiups that she was different from other people. It was reported that she had an infirmity of the eyes which caused her to see everything with rainbow fringes, bigger and brighter and better than it was. All her days were fruitful, a handful of pine nuts as much to make merry over as a feast; every lad who went by a-hunting with his bow at his back looked to be a painted brave, and every old woman digging roots as fine as a medicine man in all his feathers. All the faces at the campoodie, dark as the mingled sand and lava of the Black Rock country, deep lined with work and weather, shone for this singular old woman with the glory of the late evening light on Pahranagat. The door of her wickiup opened toward the campoodie with the smoke going up from cheerful hearths, and from the shadow of the bank where she sat to make baskets she looked down the stony wash where all the trails converged that led every way among the dunes, and saw an enchanted mesa covered with misty bloom and gentle creatures moving on trails that seemed to lead to the places where one had always wished to be.

Since all this was so, it was not surprising that her baskets turned out to be such wonderful affairs, and the tribesmen, though they winked and wagged their heads, were very glad to buy them for a haunch of venison or a bagful of mesquite meal. Sometimes, as they stroked the perfect curves of the bowls or traced out the patterns, they were heard to sigh, thinking how fine life would be if it were so rich and bright as she made it seem, instead of the dull occasion they had found it. There were some who even said it was a pity, since she was so clever at the craft, that the weaver was not more like other people, and no one thought to suggest that in that case her weaving would be no better than theirs. For all this the basket-maker did not care, sitting always happily at her weaving or wandering far into the desert in search of withes and barks and dyes, where the wild things showed her many a wonder hid from those who have not rainbow fringes to their eyes; and because she was not afraid of anything, she went farther and farther into the silent places until in the course of time she met the Coyote-Spirit.

Now a Coyote-Spirit, from having been a man, is continually thinking about men and wishing to be with them, and, being a coyote and of the wolf's breed, no sooner does he have his wish than he thinks of devouring. So as soon as this one had met the Weaving Woman he desired to eat her up, or to work her some evil according to the evil of his nature. He did not see any opportunity to begin at the first meeting, for on account of the infirmity of her eyes the woman did not see him as a coyote, but as a man, and let down her wicker water bottle for him to drink, so kindly that he was quite abashed. She did not seem in the least afraid of him, which is disconcerting even to a real coyote; though if he had been, she need not have been afraid of him in any case. Whatever pestiferous beast the Indian may think the dog of the wilderness, he has no reason to fear him except when by certain signs, as having a larger and leaner body, a sharper muzzle, and more evilly pointed ears, he knows him the soul of a bad-hearted man going about in that guise. There are enough of these Coyote-Spirits ranging in Mesquite Valley and over towards Funeral Mountains and about Pahranagat to give certain learned folk surmise as to whether there may not be a strange breed of wolves in that region; but the Indians know better.

When the Coyote-Spirit who had met the basket woman thought about it afterward, he said to himself that she deserved all the mischance that might come upon her for that meeting. "She knows," he said, "that this is my range, and whoever walks in a Coyote-Spirit's range must expect to take the consequences. She is not at all like the Goat-Girl."

The Coyote-Spirit had often watched the Goat-Girl from the top of Pahranagat, but because she was always in the open where no lurking-places were, and never far from the corn lands where the old men might be working, he had made himself believe he would not like that kind of a girl. Every morning he saw her come out of her leafy hut, loose the goats from the corral, which was all of cactus stems and broad leaves of prickly-pear, and lead them out among the wind-blown hillocks of sand under which the trunks of the mesquite flourished for a hundred years, and out of the tops of which the green twigs bore leaves and fruit; or along the mesa to browse on bitterbrush and the tops of scrubby sage. Sometimes she plaited willows for the coarser kinds of basketwork, or, in hot noonings while the flock dozed, worked herself collars and necklaces of white and red and turquoise-colored beads, and other times sat dreaming on the sand. But whatever she did, she kept far enough from the place of the Coyote-Spirit, who, now that he had met the Weaving Woman, could not keep his mind off her. Her hut was far enough from the campoodie so that every morning he went around by the Black Rock to see if she was still there, and there she sat weaving patterns in her baskets of all that she saw or thought. Now it would be the winding wash and the wattled huts beside it, now the mottled skin of the rattlesnake or the curled plumes of the quail.

At last the Coyote-Spirit grew so bold that when there was no one passing on the trail he would go and walk up and down in front of the wickiup. Then the Weaving Woman would look up from her work and give him the news of the season and the tribesmen in so friendly a fashion that he grew less and less troubled in his mind about working her mischief. He said in his evil heart that since the ways of such as he were known to the Indians,—as indeed they were, with many a charm and spell to keep them safe,—it could be no fault of his if they came to harm through too much familiarity. As for the Weaving Woman, he said, "She sees me as I am, and ought to know better," for he had not heard about the infirmity of her eyes.

Finally he made up his mind to ask her to go with him to dig for roots around the foot of Pahranagat, and if she consented,—and of course she did, for she was a friendly soul,—he knew in his heart what he would do. They went out by the mesa trail, and it was a soft and blossomy day of spring. Long wands of the creosote with shining fretted foliage were hung with creamy bells of bloom, and doves called softly from the Dripping Spring. They passed rows of owlets sitting by their burrows and saw young rabbits playing in their shallow forms. The Weaving Woman talked gayly as they went, as Indian women talk, with soft mellow voices and laughter breaking in between the words like smooth water flowing over stones. She talked of how the deer had shifted their feeding-grounds and of whether the quail had mated early that year as a sign of a good season, matters of which the Coyote-Spirit knew more than she, only he was not thinking of those things just then. Whenever her back was turned he licked his cruel jaws and whetted his appetite. They passed the level mesa, passed the tumbled fragments of the Black Rock and came to the sharp wall-sided cañons that showed the stars at noon from their deep wells of sombre shade, where no wild creature made its home and no birds ever sang. Then the Weaving Woman grew still at last because of the great stillness, and the Coyote-Spirit said in a hungry, whining voice,—

"Do you know why I brought you here?"

"To show me how still and beautiful the world is here," said the Weaving Woman, and even then she did not seem afraid.

"To eat you up," said the Coyote. With that he looked to see her fall quaking at his feet, and he had it in mind to tell her it was no fault but her own for coming so far astray with one of his kind, but the woman only looked at him and laughed. The sound of her laughter was like water in a bubbling spring.

"Why do you laugh?" said the Coyote, and he was so astonished that his jaws remained open when he had done speaking.

"How could you eat me?" said she. "Only wild beasts could do that."

"What am I, then?"

"Oh, you are only a man."

"I am a coyote," said he.

"Do you think I have no eyes?" said the woman. "Come!" For she did not understand that her eyes were different from other people's, what she really thought was that other people's were different from hers, which is quite another matter, so she pulled the Coyote-Spirit over to a rain-fed pool. In that country the rains collect in basins of the solid rock that grow polished with a thousand years of storm and give back from their shining side a reflection like a mirror. One such lay in the bottom of the black cañon, and the Weaving Woman stood beside it.

Now it is true of Coyote-Spirits that they are so only because of their behavior; not only have they power to turn themselves to men if they wish— but they do not wish, or they would not have become coyotes in the first place—but other people in their company, according as they think man-thoughts or beast-thoughts, can throw over them such a change that they have only to choose which they will be. So the basket-weaver contrived to throw the veil of her mind over the Coyote-Spirit, so that when he looked at himself in the pool he could not tell for the life of him whether he was most coyote or most man, which so frightened him that he ran away and left the Weaving Woman to hunt for roots alone. He ran for three days and nights, being afraid of himself, which is the worst possible fear, and then ran back to see if the basket-maker had not changed her mind. He put his head in at the door of her wickiup.

"Tell me, now, am I a coyote or a man?"

"Oh, a man," said she, and he went off to Pahranagat to think it over. In a day or two he came back.

"And what now?" he said.

"Oh, a man, and I think you grow handsomer every day."

That was really true, for what with her insisting upon it and his thinking about it, the beast began to go out of him and the man to come back. That night he went down to the campoodie to try and steal a kid from the corral, but it occurred to him just in time that a man would not do that, so he went back to Pahranagat and ate roots and berries instead, which was a true sign that he had grown into a man again. Then there came a day when the Weaving Woman asked him to stop at her hearth and eat. There was a savory smell going up from the cooking-pots, cakes of mesquite meal baking in the ashes, and sugary white buds of the yucca palm roasting on the coals. The man who had been a coyote lay on a blanket of rabbit skin and heard the cheerful snapping of the fire. It was all so comfortable and bright that somehow it made him think of the Goat-Girl.

"That is the right sort of a girl," he said to himself. "She has always stayed in the safe open places and gone home early. She should be able to tell me what I am," for he was not quite sure, and since he had begun to walk with men a little, he had heard about the Weaving Woman's eyes.

Next day he went out where the flock fed, not far from the corn lands, and Goat-Girl did not seem in the least afraid of him. So he went again, and the third day he said,—

"Tell me what I seem to you."

"A very handsome man," said she.

"Then will you marry me?" said he; and when the Goat-Girl had taken time to think about it she said yes, she thought she would.

Now, when the man who had been a coyote lay on the blanket of the Weaving Woman's wickiup, he had taken notice how it was made of willows driven into the ground around a pit dug in the earth, and the poles drawn together at the top, and thatched with brush, and he had tried at the foot of Pahranagat until he had built another like it; so when he had married the Goat-Girl, after the fashion of her tribe, he took her there to live. He was not now afraid of anything except that his wife might get to know that he

341

had once been a coyote. It was during the first month of their marriage that he said to her, "Do you know the basket-maker who lives under the bank of the stony wash? They call her the Weaving Woman."

"I have heard something of her and I have bought her baskets. Why do you ask?"

"It is nothing," said the man, "but I hear strange stories of her, that she associates with Coyote-Spirits and such creatures," for he wanted to see what his wife would say to that.

"If that is the case," said she, "the less we see of her the better. One cannot be too careful in such matters."

After that, when the man who had been a coyote and his wife visited the campoodie, they turned out of the stony wash before they reached the wickiup, and came in to the camp by another trail. But I have not heard whether the Weaving Woman noticed it.

1910

❖

Meridel Le Sueur
(1900–   )

WOMEN ARE HUNGRY

Let others sing of the hungry pain of Life,
Let others sing of the hungry pain of love,
I will sing of the hungry pain of hunger.

When you look at the unemployed women and girls you think instantly that there must be some kind of war. The men are gone away from the family; the family is disintegrating; the women try to hold it together, because women have most to do with the vivid life of procreation, food, and shelter. Deprived of their participation in that, they are beggars.

For this reason also they feel want and show it first: poverty is more personal to them than to men. The women looking for jobs or bumming on the road, or that you see waiting for a hand-out from the charities, are already mental cases as well as physical ones. A man can always get drunk, or talk to other men, no matter how broken he is in body and spirit; but a woman, ten to one, will starve alone in a hall bedroom until she is thrown out, and then she will sleep alone in some alley until she is picked up.

When the social fabric begins to give way it gives way from the bottom first. You can look at the bottom and see what is happening and what will continue to happen. The working-class family is going fast. The lower-middle-class family is also going, though not so fast. It is like a landslide. It is like a great chasm opening beneath the feet and swallowing the bottom classes first. The worker who lives from hand to mouth goes first, and then his family goes. The family rots, decays and goes to pieces with the woman standing last, trying to hold it together, and then going too. The man loses his job, cannot find another, then leaves. The older children try to get money, fail, and leave or are taken to the community farms. The mother stays with the little children helped by charity, until they too are sucked under by the diminishing dole and the growing terror.

Where are the women? There is the old woman who has raised her children, and they have all left her now, under the lash of hunger. There is the unattached woman, and the professional one, and the domestic servant. The latter went down two years ago. The professional woman began going down only recently. There are the young school girls—more than a million of them—who were graduated into unemployment two or three years ago. Many of them, particularly those coming from the industrial centers, who never went beyond grammar school, are now hoboes riding on the freights. Their ages run from eight to eighteen. They are the lost children.

You don't see women in bread lines. Statistics make unemployment abstract and not too uncomfortable. The human being is different. To be hungry is different than to count the hungry. There is a whole generation of young girls now who don't remember any boom days and don't believe in any Eldorado, or success, or prosperity. Their thin bones bear witness to a different thing. The women have learned something. Something is seeping into them that is going to make a difference for several generations. Something is happening to them.

II

Old and Young Mothers

We went up three flights of stairs and down a crooked corridor flanked by shut doors. There was not a sound. It was early afternoon. In that house there were about twenty families, and often four lived in one or two rooms, but now everything was pretty quiet. Everybody was taking a nap; the children had not yet come in from school. In the whole building only about five are employed regularly, and about two now and then in the Munsingwear just down the street; the rest are on charity. Six of these families are without men, just holding together like bees, in this huge desolate hive.

Anna, who lives on the top floor, is a cook and supports four people, her mother, sister, and two sons, on her $45 a month. Her man left three years ago to find a job in another city, and at first wrote now and then, and then didn't write at all, and now is lost. Anna comes home every Thursday to see her family, and the rest of the time she does not see them. This is Thursday, and she is home reading out of a Swedish Bible to her mother, who broke her leg last spring.

We listened at the door and then we knocked. The reading stopped. Anna opened the door. Leaning over a round table sat her old mother, her sister, her two blonde sons, and Mrs. Rose. Mrs. Rose is an elderly woman who has raised six tubercular children whose whereabouts she has not known for four years, since they were out of jobs. One was in a foundry in Pittsburgh, another on a wheat ranch in Montana. The other four were on the bum for a while and sometimes wrote her, but now they do not write. Mrs. Rose tries to support herself getting jobs as a housekeeper but has a hard time. Either she doesn't get paid at all or the man tries to sleep with her. She has hair that was hennaed a long time ago. She is lean and bitter and has a great deal of hate in her. She has nothing to do now, so she comes to talk to Anna and her mother in the afternoon and stays to eat there.

Many men have been killed making America. Many were killed laying the railroad, making docks, coal mines, felling the lumber, blasting the land. There were a lot of widows in the last century left to support their children with their physical labor. Everyone remembers many such women even in one small town. They were the women who took in washing, who scrubbed office buildings at night, or made the party dresses for the merchants' wives and daughters. Everyone remembers many such women and there are many who live in nobody's memory at all.

Anna's mother is such a woman. She had seven children, and her man was killed on the docks in Duluth while she was raising her children on the sand bar. After that she supported them herself, scrubbing office buildings every night until five-thirty. She sent them all through high-school, because in America education would lift them out of the physical labor of her class. Two of her sons were killed riding back and forth from coast to coast on the freight cars. Only one has a little property, a farm, but it is mortgaged and he is likely to lose it at any time now.

They all live in two attic rooms. You can see over the roofs of the town.

They begin to talk, as everyone does, of how to live. It is all nip and tuck. They are used to it, but you never get quite used to being trapped. At any time you may look up with amazement and see that you are trapped. "I've worked all my life," Anna's mother says, "with these arms and hands and sent seven children through high-school and now I can't get enough to eat."

The women all look at one another. The youngest boy, about four, is playing on the floor. The other boy is reading. They all look at the little boy, who looks like his father who was swallowed up, just as if some big crack had opened and swallowed him, or as if a war had devoured him whole. Mrs. Rose has lost all her children like that now. They all seem to be looking at something. Anna gets up to make supper of a sort.

"A person can't get paid nowadays for what a person does," Mrs. Rose says, and she begins telling about the last place she was working in, and the man was a widower with four children, and she worked like a dog for three months without any pay, and bacon rinds cooked with potato peelings most of the time because the garden had burnt up in the sun; and then she couldn't get a cent, not a red cent, and so now she is without work at all, and the cancer growing inside her, and nothing to show for her life and she might as well die.

Anna's mother sits with her broad arms over her stomach. She is full of words about it and pounding the Bible and saying she will write a letter to the President. "It's all in the Bible," she shouts, the tears going down her wrinkled face. "You cannot live by bread alone." She looks at the little boy again. "Anna, we left some milk for him. There will be a glass left. What are you going to feed him?" she cries. "He has got to have milk. You can't make bones with just bread. Everybody knows he has got to have milk."

The women all look at the child. Anna stops by the stove looking at the child. You can't feed a child cream tomorrow to make up for his not having milk today. They know that. Anna goes over and picks him up. It's really to feel his ribs and his legs.

It's hot in the room, all the heat goes up to the attic, and it's turned a bit warm out so they have left the door open, and women keep going by slowly in the hall to the lavatory. They have been going by heavily in the dark hall with swollen faces.

"There are four pregnant women in this attic," Anna's mother says bitterly. "If they knew . . . if they knew . . . they would cut their children out with a butcher knife. . . ."

"Mother!" Anna says. "Sh! they will hear. . . ."

"Better to hear it now than later, and only one has a man working now and then only for the city, and there hasn't been any snow yet this winter to speak of and besides the city is going broke and can't hire so many men."

"What do they do then?"

"Well, when you are going to have a baby you have got to have it. You go ahead and have it, whether a war is going on or not you go right ahead. They got so many women now having babies at the city hospital they only keep them eight days now. The better ones they turn out sooner. They got to have room. It's got so a woman can't have a baby. It's got so a woman is crazy to have a baby."

The other women look at her in fright. The child keeps on playing. Another pregnant woman goes slowly looming in the dark. Anna looks wildly at her two blonde boys. She gives her mother a cup of hot water with milk in it and sugar. The old lady cries pounding the Bible. "It says it all here. Under your own tree . . . it says. Every laborer is worthy of his hire. Every man should be under his own tree and should be paid at sundown. . . . "

Nobody knows what the poor suffer just for bread and burial. Nobody knows about it. Nobody has told about it. Nobody can know about how it feels unless you have been in it, the work there is, just for bread and burial.

The women look at one another. The child plays on the floor, never showing his bright face, his yellow hair shining. The snow keeps falling very softly outside the window.

We all seem to be sitting within some condition that we cannot get out of. Everyone is bright and ready for living and then cannot live.

Pretty soon it gets darker and people begin to come in, doors slam below and the smell of food comes up, and it smells terribly good when you know how hard it is to get, how it takes a whole life and all the energy of a man or a woman to get it for the born and the unborn and the dying, and how it takes some kind of splendid courage to still have children to keep alive when it is the way it is.

The winter evening settles slowly and the snow falls sadly.

The two bitter women tell about their lives in a loud voice and we listen, and something keeps going on and on, something that is killing us all and that nobody seems to stop.

You keep feeling how rich everything is except the thing of making a living. You feel how rich these women are in their necessity to have rich experience and then how they are crippled in their bright living, having too hard a world in which to get bread for the living and burial for the dead.

"I might have been a great singer," Anna's mother suddenly says softly. "Everyone said I might have been a great singer when I sang at Christmas in Sweden and everyone in Stockholm stopped on their way to listen. . . . "

"Is this all the milk?" Anna says pouring out half a glass.

"All the milk," the old woman screams. "My God, everybody knows you can't make bones out of water, doesn't everybody know that you can't make bones out of water? I took that woman next door a little milk. You can't make bones in her without something to eat, can you? Doesn't everybody in the world know that, you can't make bones, a woman can't make bones without the stuff to make it in her? . . . "

"Mama, mama, sit down," Anna cries. "Sit down, mama. Drink your pink tea, mama."

The woman next door, far gone in pregnancy, comes in. "Look, Anna, it is snowing. There will be some shoveling to do."

All the women turn to look at the feathery flakes drifting down. It will have to snow like this a long time before it makes any shoveling.

Milk went up two cents today. Milk is dearer.

III

Teacher

To get any relief work, if you are a teacher, and haven't had any work for a couple of years and have spent all your savings and let your insurance go and pawned everything you own, you have to go to the Board that is handling the relief work for teachers and *prove* to them that you are destitute. You not only have to be destitute but you have to prove it. They are both hard but the last is harder.

Nancy Sanderson's father had been a skilled glass blower. He had made pretty good money in his time before they invented a machine to take the place of the man. They lived pretty well and they always thought they were going to find some splendid new opportunity and go into business for themselves and be smart merchants and have the best house in town and servants. He educated all his six children because he knew that education was a thing that could get you on in America and anyone who had it could get what he wanted. So his four girls were school teachers and his two sons he educated to be engineers, and now they are all out of jobs. Old Sanderson fortunately is dead, but his daughters and his sons are not dead, except one daughter who is now dead because she chose it.

To prove you are destitute you have to go to the State House after having sent your application in before so it would be there ahead of you and everybody would know thoroughly about your being destitute, and then you have to put on your best things and go up there and see if they will give you one of those night classes for the unemployed, to teach. They are going to have classes for the unemployed, for adults, to keep up their ambition in this trying time; besides, it will employ a few teachers who, if they work steadily, will make as much as fifty dollars a month. Anyway, each State has appropriated so much money for this relief work. Some say it is a plan that comes from the educators who are afraid that they are not going to be supported so bountifully in the future, and are trying to make themselves important in the crisis. Some people wonder who is going to pay for it all anyway, whether the teachers will spend enough to put it back where it is taken out. Well, there is a lot of speculation, but probably there is a great deal too in the mind of a girl like Nancy Sanderson going up toward the State House on a frosty morning in a light spring suit to prove she is destitute.

She is alone, and it is hard for a lone woman to get much attention from the charities. She spent the last of her money last spring, all but about fifty dollars, and she does not know how she has been living. She has some friends who do not dream how destitute she has been. They ask her for dinner now and then but she eats so much, as you do when you are hungry, that it generally makes her sick afterwards. Well, there are ways of doing when you are destitute, and you get by some way and you don't know how you do it. A person can see you stand there and you look all right, but of course you have on quite a bit of rouge, but still you don't look starving or anything out of the usual and at the same time you may feel your knees dropping down and the greatest terror in the pit of your stomach. Lack of food is the best thing to give you terror. And, of course, Nancy's family always expected to get ahead, to better themselves. Never for a moment did they expect this.

So you feel very terrible going up to the capitol office building. You've gone up there a lot of times to get a position but that is different. Then you had your Ph.D. and your fur coat and the knowledge that you were going to get on in the world, and you didn't have to watch to see that your elbows did not come through and that your last pair of silk stockings did not spring into a run. The great building with the chariot of horses high above looks terrifying and you feel guilty, as if you had failed somehow and it must be your own fault.

You walk around a long time before you go in and then you go in and up the elevator without thinking and down the long hallway where women who have jobs are working, and you know who they are, like yourself nice girls who work very hard and save for a fur coat and to put some linen by in case of a wedding. And they are always looking to better themselves, too, in some mystical and obscure way that seldom comes about. A pang goes through you for what has happened to women.

There is a bench outside the door where people wait. The bench is full of rather thin but rouged women, waiting. You stand against the wall. Someone is in the office talking to the man who is in charge and there is a stenographer who goes to the huge file and hands him the application he wants.

You stand there. Perhaps there will be too many applications before yours. When you get in a big machine like this office building, then you don't think. You are in the machine. It can do what it likes. How many human lives are filed in a building like that! The woman in the office says desperately, "Twelve hundred new applications for work relief today . . ."

"Good Lord," the man says. He goes on talking in a loud desperate voice to the applicant who is a man and stands doggedly, twisting his cap and trying to answer. You can tell from the voices of both men that they are both caught in something, strained to the breaking point. The man who is asking the questions is part of a machine, too. He has to answer to someone higher up. "Well, you see," he shouts too loud, "you've got to answer these questions. You've got to answer them. You see, we'll give some of this work to someone who has a car, or a bank account, or owns a house, and then we'll be in dutch. . . ." The other man tries to answer in a low voice so no one will hear. He has had dreams, too. He has thought to have some power of his own, like any other man . . . Then another and another, all squirming, answering in low voices and going away and the man talking more shrilly.

Nancy Sanderson sat down, biting her teeth together, holding her wet hands tight in her lap. She looked all right. To look at her you would have thought she was all right. But hunger tears through you like a locomotive. You can hear your own heart like a trip hammer. You can hear your own blood in your ears like a cataract and you can't hear anything else. You are separated by your tremendous hunger from the ordinary world as if by a tragedy. You can't see what is happening. You can't hear what is being said.

The man was going over her application, trying to make it more definite. He was trying to be patient.

"You see, to get this, you have to prove absolute destitution."

"Yes," she said, wetting her tongue. When you don't eat the saliva begins to dry up in your mouth.

"Do you understand that?"

"Yes, I understand," she said again.

"Well, look here, you say you had fifty dollars left from your savings in the spring. Have you still got that?"

Where was that gone, fifty dollars? Why, fifty dollars doesn't last long.

"No, then what have you been living on? You must have been living on something. How have you been living?"

"I don't know," she cried in agony, and she felt all the starved blood rise and push against her throat like a million crying voices, but she did not cry out and she knew she must not cry because everyone would be embarrassed and they were all embarrassed already, as if they could not help something that was happening and they all felt ashamed and embarrassed.

"What have you been living on since?" the man suddenly shouted.

Everyone looked up, faces looking up from all around.

"I don't know," she barely said, and knowing all of them there squirming like worms when you uncover them.

"You've got to prove it, don't you understand that, you've got to prove it. . . ." The man seemed to be wild and shouting. "You've got to prove it."

She stood up amidst the eyes and saw the long corridor stretching out. She got up and started to walk as if she stepped among fetid and rotting bones and empty eye sockets. A silence followed her, and the people spoke to her in the common silence of hunger.

The manager got up and took a few steps after her, his pencil held out. "Wait," he said. "Perhaps something can be arranged. . . ." It sounded like a speech in a dream.

She went on down the white corridor so clean and white and warm, down into the rich lobby, out into the rich country with the fall light like gold upon the faces of the hungry people, and the horses of state gleaming and roaring into the sky, and she walked down past the nigger shanties and the Jewish tenements and people saw her walking and she looked all right so they paid no attention until she was dead.

When she came to the high bridge she let herself ease off into the air that was so sweet, as if you might skip winter.

They found her and took her to the morgue and of course they knew it was suicide.

1934

THREE

From the Personal to the Political

The essays in this section represent the full range of the essay genre—from the personal to the political—but also show, to quote the famous feminist dictum of the Seventies, that "the personal *is* the political." Environmentalism is the political issue addressed in "Longing to Die of Old Age" by Alice Walker (b. 1944), author of numerous novels, short stories, poems, and essays, including *The Color Purple* (1982, the first novel by a black woman to win the Pulitzer Prize). Walker talks about her long-lived ancestors like Mrs. Mary Poole, her "4-greats" grandmother, who lived from around 1800 to 1921, and then moves to her present community where cancer is as prevalent as the fertilizers and pesticides now used on gardens and on the tasteless vegetables available at the local supermarket. Similarly, novelist Mary Gordon (b. 1949) addresses the ambivalent nationalism of the immigrant upon visiting Ellis Island. Herself a daughter of a mother who is Irish and Italian and a father who is a Lithuanian Jew, she is haunted by the ghosts of the sixteen-million immigrants who came through that port as well as the 250,000 immigrants who were rejected. And in "Amazons in Appalachia," Marilou Awiakta searches for lost grandmothers who, according to a memoir written by Henry Timberlake in 1765, were "as famous in war, as powerful in the council." Combining genres—essay, poetry, a historical time line that she calls "a collage of possibilities"—Awiakta wonders what has happened to the daughters of the strong and powerful women described in the memoir and then answers, affirmatively, "We are here."

The last four pieces in this section are more journalistic in manner but use very different styles to address public issues. Gloria Steinem and Judy Syfers employ satire while Martha Gellhorn and Anna Quindlen write in a tone of passionate conviction and moral outrage. Steinem (b. 1934), the founder of *Ms.* magazine and one of the most influential feminists of the current wave of the U.S. women's movement, can be both devilishly witty (if men could menstruate, they "would brag about how long and how much") and crystal clear in her political point: "Logic has nothing to do with oppression." Writing in a similar tone and from similar premises, Judy Syfers (b. 1937) acknowledges that she wants a wife, and then details all that a wife contributes to a man's life. "My God," she asks, "who *wouldn't* want a wife?"

Novelist and reporter Martha Gellhorn (b. 1908) has been a fearless commentator on international issues, ranging from the Spanish Civil War to the poverty and starvation in drought- and war-ravaged Africa. Her powerful essay, "Last Words on Vietnam, 1987," exposes the "unvoiced agreement to

351

forget shame" that for too long has characterized the legacy of the Vietnam war. Finally, the section ends with a piece by Anna Quindlen (b. 1953), one of the country's most important newspaper columnists. She uses the recent case of a group of "high school jocks who measured their own self-worth in terms of how many meaningless sexual encounters they'd had" to deride the media's representation of women *and* men. So long as women are "sluts" and "boys will be boys," then our society will be subjected to gender violence of various kinds. Astutely and ingeniously, she ties the attitude toward these high school boys to the paranoia and homophobia arising from recent rulings about gays in the military. She issues a plea to the "good guys" to step forward from the shadows and protest the one-sided representation of themselves as a bunch of mindless, violent, sex-crazed maniacs. "Testosterone does not have to be toxic," she insists.

❖

Mary Gordon
(1949–   )

MORE THAN JUST A SHRINE: PAYING HOMAGE TO THE GHOSTS OF ELLIS ISLAND

I once sat in a hotel in Bloomsbury trying to have breakfast alone. A Russian with a habit of compulsively licking his lips asked if he could join me. I was afraid to say no; I thought it might be bad for détente. He explained to me that he was a linguist and that he always liked to talk to Americans to see if he could make any connection between their speech and their ethnic background. When I told him about my mixed ancestry—my mother is Irish and Italian, my father was a Lithuanian Jew—he began jumping up and down in his seat, rubbing his hands together and licking his lips even more frantically.

"Ah," he said, "so you are really somebody who comes from what is called the boiling pot of America." Yes, I told him; yes, I was; but I quickly rose to leave. I thought it would be too hard to explain to him the relation of the boiling potters to the main course, and I wanted to get to the British Museum. I told him that the only thing I could think of that united people whose backgrounds, histories, and points of view were utterly diverse was that their people had landed at a place called Ellis Island.

I didn't tell him that Ellis Island was the only American landmark I'd ever visited. How could I describe to him the estrangement I'd always felt from the kind of traveler who visits shrines to America's past greatness, those rebuilt forts with muskets behind glass and sabers mounted on the walls and gift shops selling maple sugar candy in the shape of Indian headdresses, those reconstructed villages with tables set for fifty and the Paul Revere silver gleaming? All that Americana—Plymouth Rock, Gettysburg, Mount Vernon, Valley Forge—it all inhabits for me a zone of blurred abstraction with far less hold on my imagination than the Bastille or Hampton Court. I suppose I've always known that my uninterest in it contains a large component of the willed: I am American, and those places purport to be my history. But they are not mine.

Ellis Island is, though; it's the one place I can be sure my people are connected to. And so I made a journey there to find my history, like any Rotarian traveling in his Winnebago to Antietam to find his. I had become part of that humbling democracy of people looking in some site for a past that has grown unreal. The monument I traveled to was not, however, a tribute to some old glory. The minute I set foot upon the island I could feel all that it stood for: insecurity, obedience, anxiety, dehumanization, the terrified and careful deference of the displaced. I hadn't traveled to the Battery and boarded a ferry across from the Statue of Liberty to raise flags or breathe a richer, more triumphant air. I wanted to do homage to the ghosts.

I felt them everywhere, from the moment I disembarked and saw the building with its high-minded brick, its hopeful little lawn, its ornamental cornices. The place was derelict when I arrived; it had not functioned for more than thirty years—almost as long as the time it had operated at full capacity as a major immigration center. I was surprised to learn what a small part of history Ellis Island had occupied. The main building was constructed in 1892, then rebuilt between 1898 and 1900 after a fire. Most of the immigrants who arrived during the latter half of the nineteenth century, mainly northern and western Europeans, landed not at Ellis Island but on the western tip of the Battery, at Castle Garden, which had opened as a receiving center for immigrants in 1855.

By the 1880s, the facilities at Castle Garden had grown scandalously inadequate. Officials looked for an island on which to build a new immigration center, because they thought that on an island immigrants could be more easily protected from swindlers and quickly transported to railroad terminals in New Jersey. Bedloe's Island was considered, but New Yorkers were aghast at the idea of a "Babel" ruining their beautiful new treasure, "Liberty Enlightening the World." The statue's sculptor, Frédéric-Auguste Bartholdi, reacted to the prospect of immigrants landing near his masterpiece in horror; he called it a "monstrous plan." So much for Emma Lazarus.

Ellis Island was finally chosen because the citizens of New Jersey petitioned the federal government to remove from the island an old naval powder magazine that they thought dangerously close to the Jersey shore. The explosives were removed; no one wanted the island for anything. It was the perfect place to build an immigration center.

I thought about the island's history as I walked into the building and made my way to the room that was the center in my imagination of the Ellis Island experience: the Great Hall. It had been made real for me in the stark, accusing photographs of Louis Hine and others, who took those pictures to make a point. It was in the Great Hall that everyone had waited—waiting, always, the great vocation of the dispossessed. The room was empty, except for me and a handful of other visitors and the park ranger who showed us around. I felt myself grow insignificant in that room, with its huge semicircular windows, its air, even in dereliction, of solid and official probity.

I walked in the deathlike expansiveness of the room's disuse and tried to think of what it might have been like, filled and swarming. More than sixteen million immigrants came through that room; approximately 250,000 were rejected. Not really a large proportion, but the implications for the rejected were dreadful. For some, there was nothing to go back to, or there was certain death; for others, who left as adventurers, to return would be to adopt in local memory the fool's role, and the failure's. No wonder that the island's history includes reports of three thousand suicides.

Sometimes immigrants could pass through Ellis Island in mere hours, though for some the process took days. The particulars of the experience in the Great Hall were often influenced by the political events and attitudes on the mainland. In the 1890s and the first years of the new century, when cheap labor was needed, the newly built receiving center took in its immigrants with comparatively little question. But as the century progressed, the economy worsened, eugenics became both scientifically respectable and popular, and World War I made American xenophobia seem rooted in fact.

Immigration acts were passed; newcomers had to prove, besides moral correctness and financial solvency, their ability to read. Quota laws came into effect, limiting the number of immigrants from southern and eastern Europe to less than 14 percent of the total quota. Intelligence tests were biased against all non-English-speaking persons, and medical examinations became increasingly strict, until the machinery of immigration nearly collapsed under its own weight. The Second Quota Law of 1924 provided that all immigrants be inspected and issued visas at American consular offices in Europe, rendering the center almost obsolete.

On the day of my visit, my mind fastened upon the medical inspections, which had always seemed to me most emblematic of the ignominy and terror the immigrants endured. The medical inspectors, sometimes dressed in uniforms like soldiers, were particularly obsessed with a disease of the eyes called trachoma, which they checked for by flipping back the immigrants' top eyelids with a hook used for buttoning gloves—a method that sometimes resulted in the transmission of the disease to healthy people. Mothers feared that if their children cried too much, their red eyes would be mistaken for a symptom of the disease and the whole family would be sent home. Those immigrants suspected of some physical disability had initials chalked on their coats. I remembered the photographs I'd seen of people standing, dumbstruck and innocent as cattle, with their manifest numbers hung around their necks and initials marked in chalk upon their coats: "E" for eye trouble, "K" for hernia, "L" for lameness, "X" for mental defects, "H" for heart disease.

I thought of my grandparents as I stood in the room: my seventeen-year-old grandmother, coming alone from Ireland in 1896, vouched for by a stranger who had found her a place as a domestic servant to some Irish who had done well. I tried to imagine the assault it all must have been for her; I've been to her hometown, a collection of farms with a main street—smaller than the athletic field of my local public school. She must have watched the New York skyline as the first- and second-class passengers were whisked off the gangplank with the most cursory of inspections while she was made to board a ferry to the new immigration center.

What could she have made of it—this buff-painted wooden structure with its towers and its blue slate roof, a place *Harper's Weekly* described as "a latter-day watering place hotel"? It would have been the first time she had heard people speaking something other than English. She would have mingled with people carrying baskets on their heads and eating foods unlike any she had ever seen—dark-eyed people, like the Sicilian she would marry ten years later, who came over with his family at thirteen, the man of the family, responsible even then for his mother and sister. I don't know what they thought, my grandparents, for they were not expansive people, nor romantic; they didn't like to think of what they called "the hard times," and their trip across the ocean was the single adventurous act of lives devoted after landing to security, respectability, and fitting in.

What is the potency of Ellis Island for someone like me—an American, obviously, but one who has always felt that the country really belonged to the early settlers, that, as J. F. Powers wrote in *Morte D'Urban*, it had been "handed down to them by the Pilgrims, George Washington and others, and that they were taking a risk in letting you live in it." I have never been the victim of overt discrimination; nothing I have wanted has been denied me because of the accidents of blood. But I suppose it is part of being an American to be engaged in a somewhat tiresome but always self-absorbing process of national definition. And in this process, I have found in traveling to Ellis

Island an important piece of evidence that could remind me I was right to feel my differentness. Something had happened to my people on that island, a result of the eternal wrongheadedness of American protectionism and the predictabilities of simple greed. I came to the island, too, so I could tell the ghosts that I was one of them, and that I honored them—their stoicism, and their innocence, the fear that turned them inward, and their pride. I wanted to tell them that I liked them better than I did the Americans who made them pass through the Great Hall and stole their names and chalked their weaknesses in public on their clothing. And to tell the ghosts what I have always thought: that American history was a very classy party that was not much fun until they arrived, brought the good food, turned up the music, and taught everyone to dance.

1985

❖

Alice Walker
(1944–   )

LONGING TO DIE OF OLD AGE

Mrs. Mary Poole, my "4-greats" grandmother, lived the entire nineteenth century, from around 1800 to 1921, and enjoyed exceptional health. The key to good health, she taught (this woman who as an enslaved person was forced to carry two young children, on foot, from Virginia to Georgia), was never to cover up the pulse at the throat. But, with the benefit of hindsight, one must believe that for her, as for generations of people after her, in our small farming community, diet played as large a role in her longevity and her health as loose clothing and fresh air.

For what did the old ones eat?

Well, first of all, almost nothing that came from a store. As late as my own childhood, in the fifties, at Christmas we had only raisins and perhaps bananas, oranges, and a peppermint stick, broken into many pieces, a sliver for each child; and during the year, perhaps, a half-dozen apples, nuts, and a bunch of grapes. All extravagantly expensive and considered rare. You ate *all* of the apple, sometimes, even, the seeds. Everyone had a vegetable garden; a garden as large as there was energy to work it. In these gardens people raised an abundance of food: corn, tomatoes, okra, peas and beans, squash, peppers, which they ate in summer and canned for winter. There was no chemical fertilizer. No one could have afforded it, had it existed, and there was no need for it. From the cows and pigs and goats, horses, mules, and fowl that people also raised, there was always ample organic manure.

Until I was grown I never heard of anyone having cancer.

In fact, at first cancer seemed to be coming from far off. For a long time if the subject of cancer came up, you could be sure cancer itself wasn't coming any nearer than to some congested place in the North, then to Atlanta, seventy-odd miles away, then to Macon, forty miles away, then to Monticello, twenty miles away. . . . The first inhabitants of our community to die of acknowledged cancer were almost celebrities, because of this "foreign" disease. But now, twenty-odd years later, cancer has ceased to be viewed as a visitor and is feared instead as a resident. Even the children die of cancer now, which, at least in the beginning, seemed a disease of the old.

Most of the people I knew as farmers left the farms (they did not own the land and were unable to make a living working for the white people who did) to rent small apartments in the towns and cities. They ceased to have gardens, and when they did manage to grow a few things they used fertilizer from boxes and bottles, sometimes in improbable colors and consistencies, which they rightly suspected, but had no choice but to use. Gone were their chickens, cows and pigs. Gone their organic manure.

To their credit, they questioned all that happened to them. Why must we leave the land? Why must we live in boxes with hardly enough space to breathe? (Of course, indoor plumbing seduced many a one.) Why must we buy all our food from the store? Why is the price of food so high—and it so tasteless? The collard greens bought in the supermarket, they said, "tasted like water."

The United States should have closed down and examined its every intention, institution, and law on the very first day a black woman observed that the collard greens tasted like water. Or when the first person of any color observed that store-bought tomatoes tasted more like unripened avocados than tomatoes.

The flavor of food is one of the clearest messages the Universe ever sends to human beings; and we have by now eaten poisoned warnings by the ton.

When I was a child growing up in middle Georgia in the forties and fifties, people still died of old age. Old age was actually a common cause of death. My parents inevitably visited dying persons over the long or short period of their decline; sometimes I went with them. Some years ago, as an adult, I accompanied my mother to visit a very old neighbor who was dying a few doors down the street, and though she was no longer living in the country, the country style lingered. People like my mother were visiting her constantly, bringing food, picking up and returning laundry, or simply stopping by to inquire how she was feeling and to chat. Her house, her linen, her skin all

357

glowed with cleanliness. She lay propped against pillows so that by merely turning her head she could watch the postman approaching, friends and relatives arriving, and, most of all, the small children playing beside the street, often in her yard, the sound of their play a lively music.

Sitting in the dimly lit, spotless room, listening to the lengthy but warm-with-shared-memories silences between my mother and Mrs. Davis was extraordinarily pleasant. Her white hair gleamed against her kissable black skin, and her bed was covered with one of the most intricately patterned quilts I'd ever seen—a companion to the dozen or more she'd stored in a closet, which, when I expressed interest, she invited me to see.

I thought her dying one of the most reassuring events I'd ever witnessed. She was calm, she seemed ready, her affairs were in order. She was respected and loved. In short, Mrs. Davis was having an excellent death. A week later, when she had actually died, I felt this all the more because she had left, in me, the indelible knowledge that such a death is possible. And that cancer and nuclear annihilation are truly obscene alternatives. And surely, teaching this very vividly is one of the things an excellent death is supposed to do.

To die miserably of self-induced sickness is an aberration we take as normal; but it is crucial that we remember and teach our children that there are other ways.

For myself, for all of us, I want a death like Mrs. Davis's. One in which we will ripen and ripen further, as richly as fruit, and then fall slowly into the caring arms of our friends and other people we know. People who will remember the good days and the bad, the names of lovers and grandchildren, the time sorrow almost broke, the time loving friendship healed.

It must become a right of every person to die of old age. And if we secure this right for ourselves, we can, coincidentally, assure it for the planet. And that, as they say, will be excellence, which is, perhaps, only another name for health.

1985

❖

Martha Gellhorn
(1908–   )

LAST WORDS ON VIETNAM, 1987

Forgetting is a normal human activity, although the usual result of forgetting mistakes and craven deeds is to repeat them. The collective forgetting of nations is something else: an unvoiced agreement to forget shame. Consensus amnesia was the American reaction, an almost instant reaction, to the Vietnam war. Perhaps the type of shame was divided as the country once divided: shame of defeat, the self-proclaimed patriots' view; shame of the war itself, the antiwar protesters' view. Amnesia worked well and unjustly for about twelve years. In American public consciousness twelve years is an aeon.

Amnesia erased the Vietnam veterans, all 2.8 million men; the small proportion of combat troops, who had a brutal record, together with the majority, non-combat support troops. Except for professional soldiers, marines, air force and sparse volunteers, amnesia deleted the fact that the huge majority of the veterans had been forcibly drafted and the huge majority were America's least privileged citizens, not exempt from Vietnam duty through attendance in college. Amnesia spared the men at the top, the men responsible for the war: the nation forgot to blame them. Amnesia even effaced the past. Whatever became of the rules governing nations that were established at the Nuremberg War Trials? The formal proscription, agreed by the U.S., against "the common plan or conspiracy," "crimes against peace," "war crimes," and "crimes against humanity." And amnesia simply blotted out the people of Vietnam, Cambodia and Laos.

Amnesia was convenient. Evidently it has served its purpose. Now America is standing tall, a remarkable feat that must astound backward foreigners. America can be proud. America is strong, as well it might be considering the Pentagon's budgets. America is not going to be pushed around by anyone again. (Did Vietnam invade America?) The outcome of the war is irrelevant to the unblemished high ideals that directed America into the war. The new look is righteousness. For a generation that had no experience of it, and for those Americans who cannot bear the thought that America was ever defeated, the Vietnam war is being rehabilitated.

To the extent that the President gives an emotional lead to the country, President Reagan stars in the revised Vietnam scenario. The key line in the change-over from amnesia to grandeur is President Reagan's "that noble cause." He has commended a comically grotesque movie hero, a Vietnam veteran called Rambo, as a model of American patriotism, the can-do man out there fighting single-handed to rescue imaginary American war prisoners from swarms of present-day murderous Vietnamese. The film itself would strain the credulity of a sensible five-year-old, but the country did not fall about laughing over Rambo. The scenario of Vietnam as a fine if failed crusade against communism suits a belligerent American attitude toward the rest of the world. The world is separated into enemies or followers. America is the biggest, the best, and knows best too. America is never wrong.

Again, Americans hear echoes of the Vietnam doctrine. Anti-communism is a religious faith, the President is its prophet and his supporters in government are its missionaries. True Americans believe without question in the faith and their President. Americans who oppose this doctrine as intrinsically wrong and dangerous to America and the world are unpatriotic, disloyal, heretics and (proof of sin) soft on communism. In a last effort to keep some of the record straight, I want to recall the real past, as I knew it.

Millions of Americans actively reviled the Vietnam war. (So did a multitude of non-Americans, objecting throughout the world.) In the early years of the war, when the voice of conscience was not loud in the land, the war-lovers named the war-haters "bleeding hearts," a sneering vulgarity that was new in the American language. Bleeding hearts increased in such numbers that two successive administrations saw them as enemies of the state and employed the FBI and the CIA to spy on American citizens exerting their legal right to protest against an illegal war. The police were freely and often violently used on anti-war demonstrators.

The homefolks were not alone in decrying the war. Veterans, returned from Vietnam and finished with their military service, declared their loathing of the war too. Passionate events marked the long passionate years of dissent. Two stand out as unique in American history. At Kent State University in conservative Ohio, a mass of students protesting peacefully if noisily were fired on by the National Guard. Four Americans, two girls and two boys, were killed for expressing their opinions. A thousand Vietnam veterans, wearing their old left-over uniforms, among them young men in wheelchairs, gathered at the Capitol in Washington and threw their war ribbons and medals on its steps: no fiercer gesture of contempt can be imagined. A civil war of conscience raged in America. The people who believed that America was about principles against the people who believed that America was about power.

I don't know when the phrase, "the most powerful man in the world" became automatically attached to the President of the United States. Did it begin with President Eisenhower or with President Kennedy? It has done no President good. On the contrary. A politician elevated to the highest office scarcely needs encouragement to egomania. The Imperial White House is not a good idea either.

The first and to date worst (though not last) result of the overweening use of Presidential power was the Vietnam war, a Presidential war. Not sanctioned as the constitution requires by Congress, it was waged on the strength of the famous Tonkin Bay Resolution, passed by Congress. Congress was stampeded into giving President Johnson an unprecedented authority by the report of a second attack on two American destroyers by North Vietnamese gunboats, 30 miles off the coast of Vietnam. It never happened, it was a non-incident.

A lie. The first attack had been harmless to American lives though insulting to American destroyers. The whole episode remains in doubt.

Washington waded into the Vietnam war with buoyant arrogance. Geopoliticians, those ominous fortune tellers, predicted that China would conquer all Southeast Asia if communism were not defeated in Vietnam. After which, the imagined threats were legion. Apparently no one stopped to think about the Vietnamese, who had already fought the Japanese and the French to get what they wanted: freedom from foreign domination. The Vietnam war would also prove to the world that the U.S. government had an iron will and "credibility," that mysterious word, and could be counted on to protect its allies, including an outstandingly corrupt puppet Asian dictatorship, masquerading as a democracy. In a horrifying way the Vietnam war was a show-off war, based on an ignorant fallacy.

Old-fashioned American ideals about the right of peoples to self-determination had been sloughed away in 1956 when the Vietnamese were denied the right to vote on their future. An international treaty, approved by the U.S. government, guaranteed this right. But we live in the tough real world now, don't we; we're not playing marbles, we're playing Superpowers.

Then the War in Vietnam ended. It seemed to leak away. After twelve years of covert two-faced involvement in Indo-China, and ten years of all-out American war, it was over. *And no one was responsible.* The grandees in Washington and Saigon—the politicians, the policy-makers, the planners, the administrators, the generals—just walked off. Nobody even said, "I'm sorry."

Fifty-eight thousand twenty-two Americans died in Vietnam, in combat and from non-combat hazards. 300,000 Americans were wounded; we are never told details of wounds and do not know how many of these were maimed for life. The war caused a special kind of casualty: trauma, men who came back physically intact, but could not live with their memories, with themselves, the mentally wounded. They had seen and done atrocities; it was an unclean war from the sleazy black market atmosphere of Saigon up to the burning hootches. American soldiers did not decide the methods for fighting the Vietnam war. Body counts and kill ratio dictated the methods. Those Americans who collected enemy ears and enjoyed the liberty to destroy—as in "search and destroy"—are chilling compatriots.

One pilot felt such revulsion from the murderous bombing of Vietnam that he refused to go on and was treated in military hospitals as insane, until his final discharge. Pilots and air crews in Vietnam distributed wholesale death and destruction. In scale, they committed far worse atrocities against helpless civilians than the infantrymen—napalm, white phosphorus, Agent Orange, antipersonnel bombs, the earth-shaking horror of carpet bombing—but were not condemned like the soldiers on the ground who committed atrocities by hand. Perhaps, after the war, some of them thought about it and condemned themselves; perhaps not.

These men were all obeying the orders of their superiors. The orders to bring to mind the Nazi theory of the successful practice of war: *schreklichkeit,* frightfulness. Frightfulness was defeated in Europe as in Southeast Asia. Aside from the irreparable damage it did to three Asian countries, I think it did irreparable damage to America in history.

The American army in Vietnam was an army of occupation, victims and victimizers both. Victims because they were wrongly sent 10,000 miles from home, to take part—even as mildly as storekeeper, clerk, cook—in a political war of aggression. Victimizers because they looked on the Vietnamese as a lesser breed, close to non-persons, gooks, sneaky, no doubt Vietcong at heart, acceptable as laundresses and bar girls. From this outlook, the hamlet barbarities were not unnatural.

The soldiers I saw in Vietnam and the American soldiers I knew in the Second World War in Europe might have come from different countries. Perhaps this is how you can tell a just war from an unjust war. Vietnam veterans felt bitterly that they were blamed for a rotten lost war. The blame was never theirs. The leaders should be judged; they led into evil. There have been no questions, no accounting to the American people. No one is responsible.

After long delay, a Vietnam War Memorial stands in Washington. Perhaps it was intended as part of the new gilding of the Vietnam war. I have not seen it except in photographs but I have heard much about it. I think it is inspired, I think it is perfect. That long handsome black stone wall condemns the war in Vietnam man by man, one at a time, name after name. The war is real because those names belonged to real men who lived with their names to identify them, and are now dead. I am told that people walk along the wall, reading names, and weep. So they should. Weep in sorrow, but also in anger. Why are these men dead? By what right and for what reason, were they sent off to be killed? The Vietnam memorial is a lesson in stone: mourn the dead, never excuse the war. Beware the glorifiers, for they will lead into evil again.

The American war in Vietnam destroyed three ancient civilizations. They had survived through millennia everything history can do, which is always plenty, but they could not survive us, who understood nothing about them, nor valued them, and do not grieve for them.

The whole of Vietnam, Cambodia and Laos is a war memorial. The Vietnamese have never been able to count their dead and wounded. Cambodians, subjected to 3,500 secret bombing raids, and Laotians who got whatever we were doling out, are a separate and unknown casualty toll. Outside opinion suggests two million Vietnamese dead and 4.5 million wounded. Given our weaponry and their lack of medical care, a tragic number of these must be amputees, the blind, the napalm deformed. Soldiers of the South Vietnamese Army, the Vietcong, the North Vietnamese Army account for a heavy share of the dead; no one can say how many hundreds of thousands. The bulk of the Vietnamese dead were peasants—more old men than young, women of all ages, children—who died of hunger and disease, died in massacres, died because they lived on that day's battleground, died because nightly "interdiction" artillery sprayed random shells over the countryside. Mainly they died under the fire and steel that rained from the skies. Vietnam is a small country, slightly larger than Norway. American planes dropped more tonnage of bombs on Vietnam, North and South, than was dropped in all theatres of war by all air forces in World War II.

We left behind in South Vietnam six and a half million destitute refugees, uprooted from their ancestral lands and traditions, with no homes to return to. Based on South Vietnam's official wartime Ministry of Health figures (surely not an overestimate) and projecting from their own forecasts, we left behind a pathetic army of some 300,000 orphans. There is no data that I know of to describe the conditions in North Vietnam but ten years of saturation bombing must have inflicted the same suffering.

Vietnam veterans deserve reparation, not re-packaging. Amends in care and money, according to need. A lot of generous rhetoric is floating about these days but not much else. It is infamous that the government left veterans, afflicted (like the Vietnamese) by the effects of Agent Orange, to struggle alone for compensation from the chemical manufacturers. Need exists; reparation is owed.

The Rambo re-packaging would be a bad joke (and surely is to Vietnam veterans) were it not that American teenagers, watching "Rambo II," have been heard to greet the film with screams of USA, USA, USA. As political indoctrination of kids, "Rambo" is unsound. More thoughtful re-packaging presents Vietnam combat troops as unfortunate young men fighting under horrendous conditions with great bravery, discredited by a few sadists and killers among them. This is a much happier image of themselves for Americans but it is full of peril: if the men were heroes, then the war tends to appear heroic. And it was not. It was a dirty big war like the dirty little war the French fought first.

In Vietnam war movies I have seen and the books I have read, Americans are the subject; the Vietnamese people and their country are background. This egocentricity implies that America and Americans were the major victims of the war. There has also been an odd note of self-pity in all these accounts of the war. Where is the pity for the Vietnamese? Where is there any sense of the war as a crime against the peasant people of Vietnam? Nobody deserves reparation more than the Vietnamese. We savaged them though they had never hurt us; and we have made no reparation to them, nothing.

We are the richest people in the world and they are among the poorest and we cannot find it in our hearts, our honor, to give them help—because the government of Vietnam is communist. And perhaps because they won. Vietnamese peasants are still punished for Superpower politics. They endured years of torment beyond our imagining, and kept their finest human qualities: kindness, dignity, courage. They are admirable people. What is the matter with us that we do not see our obligation to them? Have we forgotten our own humanity?

We could economize on our new MX ten-warhead nuclear missiles, for we certainly have enough already, turn over the saved billions to the Red Cross and ask it to manage a giant aid program for the impoverished people of Vietnam. Money is the least we can do. Instead, ever since the end of the Vietnam war, U.S. governments have harried the Vietnamese, economically and politically, with tireless spite. The U.S. has thus forced Vietnam into complete dependence on the Soviet Union; then castigates Vietnam. U.S. policy is nothing more than malign ill will toward a small distant country foundering in hardship because we ruined it and have done our best to keep it ruined. And China is our new ally in the persecution of Vietnam: the convoluted glory of geopolitics.

Vietnam is rarely in the news today, but a few years ago I saw a glimpse of it on TV: a children's hospital in Saigon, a shed. The little bodies were crowded three to a narrow wooden plank bed, just as they were in 1966. The doctor said sadly that he had few medicines, really nothing at all.

It is almost twenty-one years since I was in Vietnam and I can not forget any of it and never will, because I am American. The Presidents did not worry about the likes of me when they dumped a lifelong load of shame to fall where it might on the citizens. I remember with fury how we were lied to. Lyndon Johnson won a landslide election by promising not to send American boys to do the job Asian boys should do, though already the plans were made for sending American boys. Richard Nixon won a landslide election by promising that he had a plan to end the hated war, then proceeded to enlarge it for four years. American democracy needs an overhaul, re-tooling, there isn't much value in elections if the voters state their purpose at the polls and are promptly cheated afterwards.

It is not easy to be the citizen of a Superpower, nor is it getting easier. I would feel isolated with my shame if I were not sure that I belong, among millions of Americans, to a perennial minority of the nation. The obstinate bleeding hearts who will never agree that might makes right, and know that if the end justifies the means, the end is worthless. Power corrupts, an old truism, but why does it also make the powerful so stupid? Their power schemes become unstuck in time, at cruel cost to others; then the powerful put their stupid important heads together and invent the next similar schemes. A Saigon doctor, a poor man serving the poor, understood more about the real world than the power men in the White House. "All people are the same everywhere. They know what is justice and what is injustice."

Lest we forget.

1987

❖

Marilou Awiakta
(1936–   )

AMAZONS IN APPALACHIA

The reader will not be a little surprised to find the story of the Amazons not so great a fable as we imagined, many of the Cherokee women being as famous in war, as powerful in the council.
—HENRY TIMBERLAKE, MEMOIRS, *1765*

Are the spirits of these women accessible to us today? Yes! According to Albert Einstein, there is a dimension beyond time and space where time stands still—past, present and future are one. Native Americans have always known this dimension as "the time immemorial," a spiritual place we enter to commune intimately with all that is, a place abidingly real. Going there now, I return to my native mountains in East Tennessee and walk with the strong Cherokee grandmothers Timberlake met on his journey more than two centuries ago.

"Where are your women?"

The speaker is Attakullakulla, a Cherokee chief renowned for his shrewd and effective diplomacy. He has come to negotiate a treaty with the whites. Among his delegation are women "as famous in war, as powerful in the council." Their presence also has ceremonial significance: it is meant to show honor

365

to the other delegation. But that delegation is composed of males only; to them the absence of women is irrelevant, a trivial consideration.

To the Cherokee, however, reverence for women/Mother Earth/life/spirit is interconnected. Irreverence for one is likely to mean irreverence for all. Implicit in their chief's question, "Where are your women?" the Cherokee hear, "Where is your balance? What is your intent?" They see that balance is absent and are wary of the white men's motives. They intuit the mentality of destruction.

I turn to my own time. I look at the Congress, the Joint Chiefs of Staff, the Nuclear Regulatory Commission . . . at the hierarchies of my church, my university, my city, my children's school. "Where are your women?" I ask.

Wary and fearful, I call aside one of Attakullakulla's delegation. I choose her for the gray streak of experience in her hair, for her staunch hips and for the lively light in her eyes that indicates an alert, indomitable spirit. "Grandmother, I need your courage. Sing to me about your life."

Her voice has the clear, honing timbre of the mountains.

Song of the Grandmothers

I am Cherokee.
My people believe in the Spirit that unites all things.

I am woman. I am life force. My word has great value.
The man reveres me as he reveres Mother Earth and his own spirit.

The Beloved Woman is one of our principal chiefs.
Through her the Spirit often speaks to the people. In the Great
Council at the capital, she is a powerful voice.
Concerning the fate of hostages, her word is absolute.

Women share in all of life. We lead sacred dances. In
the Council we debate freely with men until an
agreement is reached. When the nation considers war,
we have a say, for we bear the warriors.

Sometimes I go into battle. I also plant and harvest.

I carry my own name and the name of my clan. If I
accept a mate, he and our children take the name of my
clan. If there is deep trouble between us, I am as free to

tell him to go as he is to leave. Our children and our
dwelling stay with me. As long as I am treated with
dignity, I am steadfast.

I love and work and sing.
I listen to the Spirit.
In all things I speak my mind.
I walk without fear.
I am Cherokee.

I feel the Grandmother's power. She sings of harmony, not dominance.
And her song rises from a culture that repeats the wise balance of nature: the
gender capable of bearing life is not separated from the power to sustain it.
A simple principle. Yet in spite—or perhaps because—of our vast progress in
science and technology, the American culture where I live has not grasped
this principle. In my county alone there are twenty-six hundred men who
refuse to pay child support, leaving their women and children with a hollow
name, bereft of economic means and sometimes even of a safe dwelling. On
the national level, the U.S. Constitution still does not include equal rights for
women.

The Grandmother can see this dimension of time and space as well as I—
its imbalance, its irreverence, its sparse presence of women in positions of
influence. And she can hear the brave women who sing for harmony and for
transforming power. "My own voice is small, Grandmother, and I'm afraid.
You live in a culture that believes in your song. How can you understand what
women of my time have to cope with?"

Grasping my chin gently, the Grandmother turns my face back toward the
treaty council. "Listen to Attakullakulla's question again. When he says,
'Where are your women?' look into the eyes of the white delegation and you
will see what I saw."

On the surface, hardness—the hardness of mind split from spirit, the eyes
of conquerors. Beyond the surface, stretching future decades deep, are crumpled treaties. Rich farms laid waste. And, finally, the Cherokee, goaded by
soldiers along a snowbound trail toward Oklahoma—a seemingly endless line
of women, men and children, wrapped in coats and blankets, their backs
bowed against the cold. In the only gesture of disdain left to them, they refuse
to look their captors in the face.

Putting my arms around the Grandmother, I lay my head on her shoulder.
Through touch we exchange sorrow, despair that anything really changes. I'm
ashamed that I've shown so little courage. She is sympathetic. But from the
pressure of her arms I also feel the stern, beautiful power that flows from all

the Grandmothers, as it flows from our mountains themselves. It says, "Dry your tears. Get up. Do for yourself or do without. Work for the day to come. Be joyful."

"Joyful, Grandmother?" I draw away. "Sorrow, yes. Work, yes. We must work . . . up to the end. But such a hardness is bearing down on my people. Already soldiers are gathering. Snow has begun to fall. This time we will walk the Trail of Fire. With the power of the atom, they can make the world's people walk it. How can you speak of joy?"

"Because, for those who die, death is death. A Trail of Tears for the Cherokee, a Trail of Fire for all—it is the same. But without joy, there is no hope. Without hope, the People have no chance to survive. Women know how to keep hope alive . . . at least *some* women do."

The reproach stings and angers me . . . because she is right. My joy, my hope *are* lost. I don't know how to find them again. Silently, my thoughts flow toward her. Hers flow back to me, strong, without anger.

"Come," she says.

"Where?"

"To Chota—the capital—to see the Beloved Woman."

I've heard of her—Nanyehi—"Whom many call a spirit person/immortal or 'the Path.' " Nanyehi, whom the whites call Nancy Ward and hold in great respect . . . the Beloved Woman whose advice and counsel are revered through the Cherokee nation. She is said to have a "queenly and commanding presence," as well as remarkable beauty, with skin the color and texture of the wild rose.

Not ready . . . I'm not ready for this. Following the Grandmother along the forest trail, I sometimes walk close, sometimes lag behind. Puny—that's what I am. Puny, puny, puny—the worst charge that can be leveled at any mountain woman, red, white or black. It carries pity, contempt, reproach. When we meet, the Beloved Woman will see straight into my spirit. I dread to feel the word in her look.

I know about her courage. She works ceaselessly for harmony with white settlers, interpreting the ways of each people to the other. From her uncle and mentor, Attakullakulla, she has learned diplomacy and the realities of power. She understands that the Cherokee ultimately will be outnumbered and that war will bring sure extinction. She counsels them to channel their energies from fighting into more effective government and better food production. To avoid bloodshed, she often risks censure and misunderstanding to warn either side of an impending attack, then urges resolution by arbitration. In the councils she speaks powerfully on two major themes: "Work for peace. Do not sell your land."

All the while, she knows the odds . . .

As the Grandmother and I pass through my hometown of Oak Ridge, I look at the nest of nuclear reactors there and weigh the odds of survival—for all people. The odds are small. But not impossible. My own song for harmony and reverence with the atom is a small breath. But it may combine with others to make a warm and mighty wind, powerful enough to transform the hardness and cold into life. It is not impossible.

I walk closer to the Grandmother. In this timeless dimension, we could move more rapidly, but she paces my spirit, holding it to a thoughtful rhythm as we cross several ridges and go down into the Tellico Valley. We walk beside the quiet, swift waters of the Little Tennessee River. Chota is not far off.

What time and space will the Grandmother choose for me to meet the Beloved Woman? I imagine a collage of possibilities:

1755 . . . Nanyehi fights beside her husband in a battle against the Creeks. When he is killed, she takes his rifle and leads the Cherokee to victory. Afterward, warriors sing of her deeds at Chota and the women and men of the Great Council award her the high office she will hold for more than half a century. She is seventeen, the mother of a son and a daughter.

1776 . . . Having captured the white woman, Mrs. Lydia Bean, Cherokee warriors tie her to the stake. Just as they light the fire, Nanyehi arrives on the scene, crying, "No woman will be burned at the stake while I am Beloved Woman!" Her word is absolute. Mrs. Bean goes free. She teaches dairying to Nanyehi, who in turn teaches it to the Cherokee.

1781 . . . At the Long Island Treaty Council, Nanyehi is the featured speaker. "Our cry is for peace; let it continue. . . . This peace must last forever. Let your women's sons be ours; our sons be yours. Let your women hear our words." (Note: No white women are present.)

Colonel William Christian responds to her, "Mother, we have listened well to your talk. . . . No man can hear it without being moved by it. . . . Our women shall hear your words . . . We will not meddle with your people if they will be still and quiet at home and let us live in peace."

Although the majority of Cherokee and whites hold the peace, violence and bloodshed continue among dissenting factions.

1785 . . . The Hopewell Treaty Council convenes in South Carolina. Attending the council are four commissioners appointed by Congress, thirty-six chiefs and about a thousand Cherokee delegates. Again the Beloved Woman speaks eloquently. Knowing full well the pattern of strife that precedes this council, she bases her talk on positive developments. "I take you by the hand in real friendship. . . . I look on you and the red people as my children. Your having determined on peace is most pleasant to me, for I have seen much trouble during the late war. . . . We are now under the protection of Congress and shall have no more disturbance. The talk I have given you is from the young warriors I have raised in my town, as well as myself. They rejoice that we have peace, and hope the chain of friendship will nevermore be broken."

Hope—that quality so necessary for survival. The Beloved Woman never loses hope. Perhaps I will learn the source of her strength by sharing her private moments: I may see her bend in joy over her newborn second daughter (fathered by the white trader Bryant Ward, to whom she is briefly married in the late 1750s) or hear her laugh among her grandchildren and the many orphans to whom she gives a home. Or I may stand beside her in 1817 as she composes her last message to her people. Too ill at age seventy-nine to attend the council, she sends the last message by her son. Twenty years before it begins, she sees the Trail of Tears loom ahead and her words have one theme: "My children, do not part with any more of our lands . . . it would be like destroying your mothers."

The Grandmother's hand on my arm halts my imagings. We stand at the edge of a secluded clearing, rimmed with tall pines. In the center is a large log house, and around it women—many women—move through sun and shadow. Some walk in the clearing. Others cluster on the porch, talking quietly, or sit at the edge of the forest in meditation. Not far from us, a woman who is combing another's hair leans forward to whisper, and their laughter rises into the soughing pines.

A great weaving is going on here, a deep bonding . . .

"This is the menstrual lodge," says the Grandmother. "When our power sign is with us we come here. It is a sacred time—a time for rest and meditation. No one is allowed to disturb our harmony. No warrior may even cross our path. In the menstrual lodge many things are known, many plans are made . . ."

"And the Beloved Woman?"

"She is here."

"What year is this, Grandmother?"

"It is not a year; it is a *season*—you and the Beloved Woman are meeting when each of you is in her forty-seventh season." From the expression on my face the Grandmother knows I appreciate the wisdom of her choice: Four and seven are the sacred numbers of the Cherokee, four symbolizing the balance of the four directions. It is the season when no women should be or can afford to be puny. The Grandmother nods. Motioning me to wait, she goes toward the lodge, threading her way through the women with a smile of recognition here, the touch of outstretched fingers there.

With my hands behind my hips, I lean against the stout, wiry-haired trunk of a pine. Its resinous scent clears my mind. These women are not the Amazons of the Greek fable. While they are independent and self-defined, they do not hate men or use them only at random for procreation. They do not elevate their daughters, then kill, cripple or make servants of their sons. But did the Greek patriarchs tell the truth? If Attakullakulla had asked them, "Where are your women?" they would have answered with a shrug. I'm wary of the Greeks bearing fables. Although there is little proof that they described the Amazons accurately, ample evidence suggests that they encountered—and resented—strong women like my Grandmothers and characterized them as heinous in order to justify destroying them (a strategy modern patriarchs also use).

In any case, why should I bother with distant Greeks and their nebulous fables when I have the spirits of the Grandmothers, whose roots are struck deep in my native soil and whose strength is as tangible and tenacious as the amber-pitched pine at my back?

Like the husk of a seed, my Western education/conditioning splits, and my spirit sends up a green shoot. With it comes a long-buried memory: I am twelve years old. Mother has told me that soon I will be capable of bearing life. "Think of it, Marilou. It's a sacred power, a great responsibility." I think . . . and wait for the power sign. It comes. Mother announces to my father, "Our little girl is a woman now. . . ." He smiles, "Well . . . mighty fine." In the evening we have a dinner in my honor. Steam from corn on the cob, fried chicken, green beans and cornbread mingles in my mind with the private odor, warm and pungent, that Mother describes as "fresh" (the rural term for mammals in season). I feel wholesome, proud, in harmony with the natural order.

I am ready now to meet the Beloved Woman . . .

"What was it like," you ask, "to be in her presence?"

"Come. I will show you." It is midnight, June, the full moon. Behind a farmhouse near the Kentucky border, you and I walk barefoot through the coarse grass. Crickets and treefrogs are drowsy. Birds are quiet. And we are enveloped in a powerful, sweet odor that transforms the night. Too pungent to be honeysuckle. Too fecund for roses. It recalls a baby's breath just after nursing, along with the memory of something warm and private that lingers at the edge of the mind. . . .

371

Sniffing the air, we seek the source—and find it. The cornfield in bloom. Row on row of sturdy stalks, with their tassels held up to the moon. Silently, in slow rhythm, we make our way into the field. The faint rustle of growing plants flows around and through us until, when we stop by a tall stalk, there seems no division between flesh and green. We rub the smooth, sinewy leaves on our cheeks and touch a nubile ear, where each grain of pollen that falls from the tassle will make a kernel, strong and turgid with milk. Linking arms around the stalk, we lift our faces to the drifting pollen and breathe the spirit of Selu Corn-Mother—the powerful, joyous, nurturing odor of one complete-in-herself.

"Where are your women?"

We are here.

1992

❖

Gloria Steinem
(1934–)

IF MEN COULD MENSTRUATE

Living in India made me understand that a white minority of the world has spent centuries conning us into thinking a white skin makes people superior, even though the only thing it really does is make them more subject to ultra-violet rays and wrinkles.

Reading Freud made me just as skeptical about penis envy. The power of giving birth makes "womb envy" more logical, and an organ as external and unprotected as the penis makes men very vulnerable indeed.

But listening recently to a woman describe the unexpected arrival of her menstrual period (a red stain had spread on her dress as she argued heatedly on the public stage) still made me cringe with embarrassment. That is, until she explained that, when finally informed in whispers of the obvious event, she had said to the all-male audience, "and you should be *proud* to have a menstruating woman on your stage. It's probably the first real thing that's happened to this group in years!"

Laughter. Relief. She had turned a negative into a positive. Somehow her story merged with India and Freud to make me finally understand the power of positive thinking. Whatever a "superior" group has will be used to justify its superiority, and whatever an "inferior" group has will be used to justify its plight. Black men were given poorly paid jobs because they were said to be "stronger" than white men, while all women were relegated to poorly paid jobs because they were said to be "weaker." As the little boy said when asked if he wanted to be a lawyer like his mother, "Oh no, that's women's work." Logic has nothing to do with oppression.

So what would happen if suddenly, magically, men could menstruate and women could not?

Clearly, menstruation would become an enviable, boast-worthy, masculine event:

Men would brag about how long and how much.

Young boys would talk about it as the envied beginning of manhood. Gifts, religious ceremonies, family dinners, and stag parties would mark the day.

To prevent monthly work loss among the powerful, Congress would fund a National Institute of Dysmenorrhea. Doctors would research little about heart attacks, from which men were hormonally protected, but everything about cramps.

Sanitary supplies would be federally funded and free. Of course, some men would still pay for the prestige of such commercial brands as Paul Newman Tampons, Muhammad Ali's Rope-a-Dope Pads, John Wayne Maxi Pads, and Joe Namath Jock Shields—"For Those Light Bachelor Days."

Statistical surveys would show that men did better in sports and won more Olympic medals during their periods.

Generals, right-wing politicians, and religious fundamentalists would cite menstruation ("*men*-struation") as proof that only men could serve God and country in combat ("You have to give blood to take blood"), occupy high political office ("Can women be properly fierce without a monthly cycle governed by the planet Mars?"), be priests, ministers, God Himself ("He gave this blood for our sins"), or rabbis ("Without a monthly purge of impurities, women are unclean").

Male liberals or radicals, however, would insist that women are equal, just different; and that any woman could join their ranks if only she were willing to recognize the primacy of menstrual rights ("Everything else is a single issue") or self-inflict a major wound every month ("You *must* give blood for the revolution").

Street guys would invent slang ("He's a three-pad man") and "give fives" on the corner with some exchange like, "Man, you lookin' *good!*"

"Yeah, man, I'm on the rag!"

TV shows would treat the subject openly. (*Happy Days:* Richie and Potsie try to convince Fonzie that he is still "The Fonz," though he has missed two periods in a row. *Hill Street Blues:* The whole precinct hits the same cycle.)

So would newspapers. (SUMMER SHARK SCARE THREATENS MENSTRUAT-ING MEN. JUDGE CITES MONTHLIES IN PARDONING RAPIST.) And so would movies. (Newman and Redford in *Blood Brothers!*)

Men would convince women that sex was *more* pleasurable at "that time of the month." Lesbians would be said to fear blood and therefore life itself, though all they needed was a good menstruating man.

Medical schools would limit women's entry ("they might faint at the sight of blood").

Of course, intellectuals would offer the most moral and logical arguments. Without that biological gift for measuring the cycles of the moon and planets, how could a woman master any discipline that demanded a sense of time, space, mathematics—or the ability to measure anything at all? In philosophy and religion, how could women compensate for being disconnected from the rhythm of the universe? Or for their lack of symbolic death and resurrection every month?

Menopause would be celebrated as a positive event, the symbol that men had accumulated enough years of cyclical wisdom to need no more.

Liberal males in every field would try to be kind. The fact that "these people" have no gift for measuring life, the liberals would explain, should be punishment enough.

And how would women be trained to react? One can imagine right-wing women agreeing to all these arguments with a staunch and smiling maso-chism. ("The ERA would force housewives to wound themselves every month": Phyllis Schlafly. "Your husband's blood is as sacred as that of Jesus—and so sexy, too!": Marabel Morgan.) Reformers and Queen Bees would adjust their lives to the cycles of the men around them. Feminists would explain endlessly that men, too, needed to be liberated from the false idea of Martian aggressiveness, just as women needed to escape the bonds of "menses-envy." Radical feminists would add that the oppression of the nonmenstrual was the pattern for all other oppressions. ("Vampires were our first freedom fighters!") Cultural feminists would exalt a female bloodless imagery in art and literature. Socialist feminists would insist that, once capitalism and imperialism were overthrown, women would menstruate, too. ("If women aren't yet menstru-ating in Russia," they would explain, "it's only because true socialism can't exist within capitalist encirclement.")

In short, we would discover, as we should already guess, that logic is in the eye of the logician. (For instance, here's an idea for theorists and logi-cians: If women are supposed to be less rational and more emotional at the beginning of our menstrual cycle when the female hormone is at its lowest level, then why isn't it logical to say that, in those few days, women behave the most like the way men behave all month long? I leave further improvisations up to you.)*

The truth is that, if men could menstruate, the power justifications would go on and on.

If we let them.

1983

Judy Syfers
(1937–   )

WHY I WANT A WIFE

I belong to that classification of people known as wives. I am A Wife. And, not altogether incidentally, I am a mother.

Not too long ago a male friend of mine appeared on the scene fresh from a recent divorce. He had one child, who is, of course, with his ex-wife. He is obviously looking for another wife. As I thought about him while I was ironing one evening, it suddenly occurred to me that I, too, would like to have a wife. Why do I want a wife?

I would like to go back to school so that I can become economically independent, support myself, and, if need be, support those dependent upon me. I want a wife who will work and send me to school. And while I am going to school I want a wife to take care of my children. I want a wife to keep track of the children's doctor and dentist appointments. And to keep track of mine, too. I want a wife to make sure my children eat properly and are kept clean. I want a wife who will wash the children's clothes and keep them mended. I want a wife who is a good nurturant attendant to my children, who arranges for their schooling, makes sure that they have an adequate social life with their peers, takes them to the park, the zoo, etc. I want a wife who takes care of the children when they are sick, a wife who arranges to be around when the children need special care, because, of course, I cannot miss classes at school. My wife must arrange to lose time at work and not lose the job. It may mean a small cut in my wife's income from time to time, but I guess I can tolerate that. Needless to say, my wife will arrange and pay for the care of the children while my wife is working.

I want a wife who will take care of *my* physical needs. I want a wife who will keep my house clean. A wife who will pick up after me. I want a wife

*With thanks to Stan Pottinger for many of the improvisations already here.

who will keep my clothes clean, ironed, mended, replaced when need be, and who will see to it that my personal things are kept in their proper place so that I can find what I need the minute I need it. I want a wife who cooks the meals, a wife who is a *good* cook. I want a wife who will plan the menus, do the necessary grocery shopping, prepare the meals, serve them pleasantly, and then do the cleaning up while I do my studying. I want a wife who will care for me when I am sick and sympathize with my pain and loss of time from school. I want a wife to go along when our family takes a vacation so that someone can continue to care for me and my children when I need a rest and change of scene.

I want a wife who will not bother me with rambling complaints about a wife's duties. But I want a wife who will listen to me when I feel the need to explain a rather difficult point I have come across in my course of studies. And I want a wife who will type my papers for me when I have written them.

I want a wife who will take care of the details of my social life. When my wife and I are invited out by my friends, I want a wife who will take care of the babysitting arrangements. When I meet people at school that I like and want to entertain, I want a wife who will have the house clean, will prepare a special meal, serve it to me and my friends, and not interrupt when I talk about the things that interest me and my friends. I want a wife who will have arranged that the children are fed and ready for bed before my guests arrive so that the children do not bother us.

And I want a wife who knows that sometimes I need a night out by myself.

I want a wife who is sensitive to my sexual needs, a wife who makes love passionately and eagerly when I feel like it, a wife who makes sure that I am satisfied. And, of course, I want a wife who will not demand sexual attention when I am not in the mood for it. I want a wife who assumes the complete responsibility for birth control, because I do not want more children. I want a wife who will remain sexually faithful to me so that I do not have to clutter up my intellectual life with jealousies. And I want a wife who understands that *my* sexual needs may entail more than strict adherence to monogamy. I must, after all, be able to relate to people as fully as possible.

If, by chance, I find another person more suitable as a wife than the wife I already have, I want the liberty to replace my present wife with another one. Naturally, I will expect a fresh, new life; my wife will take the children and be solely responsible for them so that I am left free.

When I am through with school and have a job, I want my wife to quit working and remain at home so that my wife can more fully and completely take care of a wife's duties.

My God, who *wouldn't* want a wife?

1971

Anna Quindlen
(1953–   )

THE GOOD GUYS

Before another television talk show hands out money to chat with the members of the Spur Posse, the low-life band of high school jocks who measured their own self-worth in terms of how many meaningless sexual encounters they'd had, the people who produce and host the shows should acknowledge something about their guests.

And that is that as surely as if they were paying white supremacists to come on and spew garbage about black people, they are enriching those who happily represent the worst and most distorted view of an entire class of human beings. And I don't mean women, although the teen-aged members of this sexual street gang treated girls like garbage while they were passing them around and trashing them afterwards.

The Posse members reflect a demeaning and insulting view of men, and the good guys, wherever they are, should rise up and say that that view stinks.

The ethos of this bunch of boys from a California suburb is part of a continuum that has played itself out over the last few months. Their cousins, metaphorically speaking, were the jocks in Glen Ridge, N.J., who were accused of using, among other things, a baseball bat on a retarded neighbor in a group sexual assault in the basement of a tidy family home.

Three of these guys were convicted, but not before a theme emerged clearly in their defense: "boys will be boys," according to one attorney. It is the same theme that suffuses the Lakewood story, and it is this: that young men are incapable of bringing either responsibility or humanity to their sexual activity.

Part of the defense in the Glen Ridge case, and part of the discussion of the Spur Posse, is that the sexual revolution made a lot of this happen, aided and abetted by MTV and Hollywood violence. And probably the culture has made it more open, more egregious.

But at base it all feels like something at least as old as I am. The girls get called sluts. And the boys get flown first class to some big city to brag on national television, the electronic-age version of standing around in the locker room talking about what a pig she was. People always blame the girl; she should have said no. A monosyllable, but conventional wisdom has always been that boys can't manage it.

Interestingly enough, the "boys will be boys" ethos has also been a big part of the debate over gay people in the military. Although women are several times more likely than men to be discharged from the service because of sexual orientation, there has been nary a word about barracks full of women soldiers terrified of lesbian sneak attacks.

Virtually all the fear fantasies have focused on gay men who will not be able to keep their hands off straight ones, despite the fact that gay men have usually done just that. That's because straight men have been projecting onto gay ones a stereotype that is demeaning to both: that male sexuality is by nature predatory.

But don't ever forget that in the Glen Ridge case, there were boys who walked away from that basement because they thought what was happening was wrong. Don't forget that what happened in Lakewood, the conspicuous consumption of other people, was less a matter of sex than a cross between a track meet and a slave auction.

Some of the mothers of Spur Posse members, who used their evanescent high school jock popularity to entice and then discard girls, were crushed to hear that their sons had been so cold in their attitude toward women. And no wonder. Sex aside, this was basically a question of whether your kids had grown up to be cruel or kind.

But one blowhard father bragged, "Nothing my boy did was anything that any red-blooded American boy wouldn't do at his age." That, thankfully, is not true. Boys may have sex earlier now, with more impunity, with a more casual commitment, in a cultural environment saturated with soft porn and cinematic violence.

But that doesn't mean that all of them, or even most of them, use their sexual encounters, as the boys in Lakewood and Glen Ridge did, for casual cruelty and intentional degradation. The good guys should stand up and say that. The talk shows should put them on and stop handing out payoffs to a bunch of losers who give all men a bad name. Testosterone does not have to be toxic.

1993

PART IV

Acting Out

❖

Women writers, as a matter of course, have changed, manipulated, and defied accepted literary categories precisely because new forms are necessary to address new issues, specifically, women's issues rarely raised in writing by men. An especially striking example of the breaking of literary conventions occurs in writing that partakes of the oral tradition. Although literary critics customarily maintain a hierarchical (and typically arbitrary) division between oral and written modes of expression, this section of our book is designed to acknowledge the variety and brilliance of the oral tradition in its many manifestations in women's literary creation.

We have subdivided the section into three parts—"Plays," "Speeches and Performance Pieces," and "Rituals and Ceremonies"—to show continuities between the various ways in which women have chosen to act out and speak out. Not only are the oral forms interconnected, but they also are often inspired by one another in profound ways that defy usual genre definitions.

The plays of Alice Gerstenberg (1893–1972) and Susan Glaspell (1882–1948) may look like conventional drama to the contemporary reader but, in fact, they revolutionized modern drama in America. Both playwrights employed a number of devices (such as Gerstenberg's reliance on masks) for which Eugene O'Neill is typically given credit, and both of their one-act plays not only feature women characters but also are *about* women's voices. Each play in its own way treats the visible versus the hidden language of women and the ways in which women speak among themselves versus the ways they speak in the presence of men. They make way for Genny Lim's 1989 drama, which gives voice to the silenced, whether a prostitute or a ghost.

The borders between drama, speech, performance piece, ritual, and ceremony are permeable, and we would like readers to see the selections in the second and third sections of "Acting Out" as variations on the more formally defined plays in the first part. Sojourner Truth (1797–1883), who escaped from slavery to freedom in 1827, became one of the most famous abolitionists in her day by singing gospel songs and reciting her powerful "Ain't I a Woman" speech in churches and auditoriums all over America. Understanding the link between speech and performance, Anna Deavere Smith (b. 1950), in her epic "In Search of America" series, has interviewed thousands of people about historical events, and then employed their words in her one-woman shows. Her plays are pastiches of reenacted voices that both honor their subjects and create theater from the ritual cadences—the poetry—of the spoken word.

Finally, we include a selection of beautiful prayers and vision quests that are part of the so-called traditional culture of Native Americans while also including two pieces by contemporary Native American writers, Paula Gunn Allen (b. 1939) and Wendy Rose (b. 1948), that draw from those traditions while creating new ones. The final selections show the ways in which rituals and ceremonies are important to a range of other genres (fictional and nonfictional) and are part of *all* women's lives, not just those of Native Americans. What links Sojourner Truth with Laurie Anderson (b. 1947) or the Arapaho Pipe Keeper with E. M. Broner (b. 1930) is the urgency and the significance of their acting and speaking out.

O N E

Plays

Women have long written for the theater. Colonial playwright Mercy Warren is only one of many early U.S. women writers whose reputation was made on the boards. The affinity between women's writing and drama may exist in part because of the play's reliance on both spoken word and visualized interaction (the "real" life that most women are, of necessity, immersed in) and in part because, historically, movements for social change have used theatrical productions to persuade audiences (as was the case during the suffrage movement). For whatever reasons, women writers' contributions to the development of American theater are influential and numerous.

The writing of both Alice Gerstenberg (1885–1972) and Susan Glaspell (1882–1948), in fact, may be said to have created twentieth century American drama as we know it. In 1911, Gerstenberg's *Overtones*, an innovative play about the split consciousnesses of two women characters—represented as four speakers on stage—foreshadowed what was to be a key element in modernist theater, the psychological study of character. *Overtones* was produced in the United States by the Washington Square Players, and starred Lily Langtry in its London production.

Eugene O'Neill, protégé of Susan Glaspell at the Provincetown Players theater, later became famous for his interrogation of characters' motives, whether in *Emperor Jones, Desire under the Elms*, or *Mourning Becomes Electra*. Glaspell's 1916 *Trifles*, like the Gerstenberg play, preceded any of O'Neill's work. When Glaspell wrote the one-act play, trying to script a new kind of drama for the incipient Provincetown group, she created a form that became famous for its complex and layered character interaction, as well as its implicit criticism of patriarchal power (shown here in the apparent dominance of the men's cultural roles).

Just as Gerstenberg stayed active in theater, particularly in the Chicago little theater and children's theater movements, so did Glaspell. Among her later plays were *Inheritors, The Verge*, and *Alison's House*, a recreation of Emily Dickinson's life, which won the Pulitzer Prize for Drama in 1931. Both women also wrote fiction; in fact, Glaspell wrote a short story version of *Trifles* in 1917, titled "A Jury of Her Peers."

Jenny Lim's (b. 1946) contemporary play, *Bitter Cane*, is in some ways the flowering of the early modernist experiments. Hard-hitting in its succinct dialogue, Lim's study of male–female relationships in inimical cultural settings (here, Chinese men brought to work on Hawaian sugarcane plantations) interrogates the flawed colonial oligarchy. Deft and incisive, *Bitter Cane* both creates sympathy for the poverty (both financial and emotional) of the men forced to work in virtual slavery, and warns the reader that the narrative is not simply history. Like many other impressive women playwrights today, Lim writes about truly significant themes with both precision and poetry.

❖

Alice Gerstenberg

(1893–1972)

OVERTONES

TIME: *The present.*

SCENE: HARRIET'S *fashionable living room. The door at the back leads to the hall. In the center a tea table with a high-backed chair at each side.*

   HARRIET'S *gown is a light, "jealous" green. Her counterpart,* HETTY, *wears a gown of the same design but in a darker shade.* MARGARET *wears a gown of lavender chiffon while her counterpart,* MAGGIE, *wears a gown of the same design in purple, a purple scarf veiling her face. Chiffon is used to give a sheer effect, suggesting a possibility of primitive and cultured selves merging into one woman. The primitive and cultured selves never come into actual physical contact but try to sustain the impression of mental conflict.* HARRIET *never sees*

HETTY, *never talks to her but rather thinks aloud looking into space.* HETTY, *however, looks at* HARRIET, *talks intently and shadows her continually. The same is true of* MARGARET *and* MAGGIE. *The voices of the cultured women are affected and lingering, the voices of the primitive impulsive and more or less staccato.*

When the curtain rises HARRIET *is seated right of tea table, busying herself with the tea things.*

HETTY: Harriet. (*There is no answer*) Harriet, my other self. (*There is no answer*) My trained self.

HARRIET: (*Listens intently*) Yes?

(*From behind* HARRIET'S *chair* HETTY *rises slowly*)

HETTY: I want to talk to you.

HARRIET: Well?

HETTY: (*Looking at* HARRIET *admiringly*) Oh, Harriet, you are beautiful today.

HARRIET: Am I presentable, Hetty?

HETTY: Suits me.

HARRIET: I've tried to make the best of the good points.

HETTY: My passions are deeper than yours. I can't keep on the mask as you do. I'm crude and real, you are my appearance in the world.

HARRIET: I am what you wish the world to believe you are.

HETTY: You are the part of me that has been trained.

HARRIET: I am your educated self.

HETTY: I am the rushing river; you are the ice over the current.

HARRIET: I am your subtle overtones.

HETTY: But together we are one woman, the wife of Charles Goodrich.

HARRIET: There I disagree with you, Hetty, I alone am his wife.

HETTY: (*Indignantly*) Harriet, how can you say such a thing!

HARRIET: Certainly. I am the one who flatters him. I have to be the one who talks to him. If I gave you a chance you would tell him at once that you dislike him.

HETTY: (*Moving away*) I don't love him, that's certain.

HARRIET: You leave all the fibbing to me. He doesn't suspect that my calm, suave manner hides your hatred. Considering the amount of scheming it causes me it can safely be said that he is my husband.

HETTY: Oh, if you love him—

HARRIET: I? I haven't any feelings. It isn't my business to love anybody.

HETTY: Then why need you object to calling him my husband?

HARRIET: I resent your appropriation of a man who is managed only through the cleverness of my artifice.

HETTY: You may be clever enough to deceive him, Harriet, but I am still the one who suffers. I can't forget he is my husband. I can't forget that I might have married John Caldwell.

HARRIET: How foolish of you to remember John, just because we met his wife by chance.

HETTY: That's what I want to talk to you about. She may be here at any moment. I want to advise you about what to say to her this afternoon.

HARRIET: By all means tell me now and don't interrupt while she is here. You have a most annoying habit of talking to me when people are present. Sometimes it is all I can do to keep my poise and appear *not* to be listening to you.

HETTY: Impress her.

HARRIET: Hetty, dear, is it not my custom to impress people?

HETTY: I hate her.

HARRIET: I can't let her see that.

HETTY: I hate her because she married John.

HARRIET: Only after you had refused him.

HETTY: (*Turning to* HARRIET) Was it my fault that I refused him?

HARRIET: That's right, blame me.

HETTY: It was your fault. You told me he was too poor and never would be able to do anything in painting. Look at him now, known in Europe, just returned from eight years in Paris, famous.

HARRIET: It was too poor a gamble at the time. It was much safer to accept Charles's money and position.

HETTY: And then John married Margaret within the year.

HARRIET: Out of spite.

HETTY: Freckled, gauky-looking thing she was, too.

HARRIET: (*A little sadly*) Europe improved her. She was stunning the other morning.

HETTY: Make her jealous today.

HARRIET: Shall I be haughty or cordial or caustic or—

HETTY: Above all else you must let her know that we are rich.

HARRIET: Oh, yes, I do that quite easily now.

HETTY: You must put it on a bit.

HARRIET: Never fear.

HETTY: Tell her I love my husband.

HARRIET: My husband—

HETTY: Are you going to quarrel with me?

HARRIET: (*Moves away*) No, I have no desire to quarrel with you. It is quite too uncomfortable. I couldn't get away from you if I tried.

HETTY: (*Stamping her foot and following* HARRIET) You were a stupid fool to make me refuse John, I'll never forgive you—never—

HARRIET: (*Stopping and holding up her hand*) Don't get me all excited. I'll be in no condition to meet her properly this afternoon.

HETTY: (*Passionately*) I could choke you for robbing me of John.

HARRIET: (*Retreating*) Don't muss me!

HETTY: You don't know how you have made me suffer.

HARRIET: (*Beginning to feel the strength of* HETTY'S *emotion surge through her and trying to conquer it*) It is not my business to have heartaches.

HETTY: You're bloodless. Nothing but sham—sham—while I—

HARRIET: (*Emotionally*) Be quiet! I can't let her see that I have been fighting with my inner self.

HETTY: And now after all my suffering you say it has cost you more than it has cost me to be married to Charles. But it's the pain here in my heart—I've paid the price—I've paid—Charles is not your husband!

HARRIET: (*Trying to conquer emotion*) He is.

HETTY: (*Follows* HARRIET) He isn't.

HARRIET: (*Weakly*) He is.

HETTY: (*Towering over* HARRIET) He isn't! I'll kill you!

HARRIET: (*Overpowered, sinks into a chair*) Don't—don't you're stronger than I—you're—

HETTY: Say he's mine.

HARRIET: He's ours.

HETTY: (*The telephone rings*) There she is now.

(HETTY *hurries to 'phone but* HARRIET *regains her supremacy*)

HARRIET: (*Authoritatively*) Wait! I can't let the telephone girl down there hear my real self. It isn't proper. (*At phone*) Show Mrs. Caldwell up.

HETTY: I'm so excited, my heart's in my mouth.

HARRIET: (*At the mirror*) A nice state you've put my nerves into.

HETTY: Don't let her see you're nervous.

HARRIET: Quick, put the veil on, or she'll see you shining through me.

(HARRIET *takes a scarf of chiffon that has been lying over the back of a chair and drapes it on* HETTY, *covering her face. The chiffon is the same color of their gowns but paler in shade so that it pales* HETTY'S *darker gown to match* HARRIET'S *lighter one. As* HETTY *moves in the following scene the chiffon falls away revealing now and then the gown of deeper dye underneath.*)

HETTY: Tell her Charles is rich and fascinating—boast of our friends, make her feel she needs us.

HARRIET: I'll make her ask John to paint us.

HETTY: That's just my thought—if John paints our portrait—

HARRIET: We can wear an exquisite gown—

HETTY: And make him fall in love again and—

HARRIET: (*Schemingly*) Yes. (MARGARET *parts the portières back center and extends her hand.* MARGARET *is followed by her counterpart* MAGGIE) Oh, Margaret, I'm so glad to see you!

HETTY: (*To* MAGGIE) That's a lie.

MARGARET: (*In superficial voice throughout*) It's enchanting to see you, Harriet.

MAGGIE: (*In emotional voice throughout*) I'd bite you, if I dared.

HARRIET: (*To* MARGARET) Wasn't our meeting a stroke of luck?

MARGARET: (*Coming down left of table*) I've thought of you so often, Harriet; and to come back and find you living in New York.

HARRIET: (*Coming down right of table*) Mr. Goodrich has many interests here.

MAGGIE: (*To* MARGARET) Flatter her.

MARGARET: I know, Mr. Goodrich is so successful.

HETTY: (*To* HARRIET) Tell her we're rich.

HARRIET: (*To* MARGARET) Won't you sit down?

MARGARET: (*Takes a chair*) What a beautiful cabinet!

HARRIET: Do you like it? I'm afraid Charles paid an extravagant price.

MAGGIE: (*To* HETTY) I don't believe it.

MARGARET: (*Sitting down. To* HARRIET) I am sure he must have.

HARRIET: (*Sitting down*) How well you are looking, Margaret.

HETTY: Yes, you are not. There are circles under your eyes.

MAGGIE: (*To* HETTY) I haven't eaten since breakfast and I'm hungry.

MARGARET: (*To* HARRIET) How well you are looking, too.

MAGGIE: (*To* HETTY) You have hard lines about your lips, are you happy?

HETTY: (*To* HARRIET) Don't let her know that I'm unhappy.

HARRIET: (*To* MARGARET) Why shouldn't I look well? My life is full, happy, complete—

MAGGIE: I wonder.

HETTY: (*In* HARRIET'S *ear*) Tell her we have an automobile.

MARGARET: (*To* HARRIET) My life is complete, too.

MAGGIE: My heart is torn with sorrow; my husband cannot make a living. He will kill himself if he does not get an order for a painting.

MARGARET: (*Laughs*) You must come and see us in our studio. John has been doing some excellent portraits. He cannot begin to fill his orders.

HETTY: (*To* HARRIET) Tell her we have an automobile.

HARRIET: (*To* MARGARET) Do you take lemon in your tea?

MAGGIE: Take cream. It's more filling.

MARGARET: (*Looking nonchalantly at tea things*) No, cream, if you please. How cozy!

MAGGIE: (*Glaring at tea things*) Only cakes! I could eat them all!

HARRIET: (*To* MARGARET) How many lumps?

MAGGIE: (*To* MARGARET) Sugar is nourishing.

MARGARET: (*To* HARRIET) Three, please. I used to drink very sweet coffee in Turkey and ever since I've—

HETTY: I don't believe you were ever in Turkey.

MAGGIE: I wasn't, but it is none of your business.

HARRIET: (*Pouring tea*) Have you been in Turkey? Do tell me about it.

MAGGIE: (*To* MARGARET) Change the subject.

MARGARET: (*To* HARRIET) You must go there. You have so much taste in dress you would enjoy seeing their costumes.

MAGGIE: Isn't she going to pass the cake?

MARGARET: (*To* HARRIET) John painted several portraits there.

HETTY: (*To* HARRIET) Why don't you stop her bragging and tell her we have an automobile?

HARRIET: (*Offers cake across the table to* MARGARET) Cake?

MAGGIE: (*Stands back of* MARGARET, *shadowing her as* HETTY *shadows* HARRIET, MAGGIE *reaches claws out for the cake and groans with joy*) At last!

(*But her claws do not touch the cake.*)

MARGARET: (*With a graceful, nonchalant hand places cake upon her plate and bites at it slowly and delicately*) Thank you.

HETTY: (*To* HARRIET) Automobile!

MAGGIE: (*To* MARGARET) Follow up the costumes with the suggestion that she would make a good model for John. It isn't too early to begin getting what you came for.

MARGARET: (*Ignoring* MAGGIE) What delicious cake.

HETTY: (*Excitedly to* HARRIET) There's your chance for the auto.

HARRIET: (*Nonchalantly to* MARGARET) Yes, it is good cake, isn't it? There are always a great many people buying it at Harper's. I sat in

my automobile fifteen minutes this morning waiting for
my chauffeur to get it.

MAGGIE: (*To* MARGARET) Make her order a portrait.

MARGARET: (*To* HARRIET) If you stopped at Harper's you must have noticed
the new gowns at Henderson's. Aren't the shop windows
alluring these days?

HARRIET: Even my chauffeur notices them.

MAGGIE: I know you have an automobile, I heard you the first time.

MARGARET: I notice gowns now with an artist's eye as John does. The one
you have on, my dear, is very paintable.

HETTY: Don't let her see you're anxious to be painted.

HARRIET: (*Nonchalantly*) Oh, it's just a little model.

MAGGIE: (*To* MARGARET) Don't seem anxious to get the order.

MARGARET: (*Nonchalantly*) Perhaps it isn't the gown itself but the way you
wear it that pleases the eye. Some people can wear any-
thing with grace.

HETTY: Yes, I'm very graceful.

HARRIET: (*To* MARGARET) You flatter me, my dear.

MARGARET: On the contrary, Harriet, I have an intense admiration for you.
I remember how beautiful you were—as a girl. In fact, I
was quite jealous when John was paying you so much attention.

HETTY: She is gloating because I lost him.

HARRIET: Those were childhood days in a country town.

MAGGIE: (*To* MARGARET) She's trying to make you feel that John was only a
country boy.

MARGARET: Most great men have come from the country. There is a fair
chance that John will be added to the list.

HETTY: I know it and I am bitterly jealous of you.

HARRIET: Undoubtedly he owes much of his success to you. Margaret, your
experience in economy and your ability to endure hardship.
Those first few years in Paris must have been a struggle.

MAGGIE: She is sneering at your poverty.

MARGARET: Yes, we did find life difficult at first, not the luxurious start a
girl has who marries wealth.

HETTY: (*To* HARRIET) Deny that you married Charles for his money.

(HARRIET *deems it wise to ignore* HETTY'S *advice*)

MARGARET: But John and I are so congenial in our tastes, that we were im-
pervious to hardship or unhappiness.

HETTY: (*In anguish*) Do you love each other? Is it really true?

HARRIET: (*Sweetly*) Did you have all the romance of starving for his art?

387

MAGGIE: (*To* MARGARET) She's taunting you. Get even with her.

MARGARET: Not for long. Prince Rier soon discovered John's genius, and introduced him royally to wealthy Parisians who gave him many orders.

HETTY: (*To* MAGGIE) Are you telling the truth or are you lying?

HARRIET: If he had so many opportunities there, you must have had great inducements to come back to the States.

MAGGIE: (*To* HETTY) We did, but not the kind you think.

MARGARET: John became the rage among Americans traveling in France, too, and they simply insisted upon his coming here.

HARRIET: Whom is he going to paint here?

MAGGIE: (*Frightened*) What names dare I make up?

MARGARET: (*Calmly*) Just at present Miss Dorothy Ainsworth of Oregon is posing. You may not know the name, but she is the daughter of a wealthy miner who found gold in Alaska.

HARRIET: I dare say there are many Western people we have never heard of.

MARGARET: You must have found social life in New York very interesting, Harriet, after the simplicity of our home town.

HETTY: (*To* MAGGIE) There's no need to remind us that our beginnings were the same.

HARRIET: Of course Charles's family made everything delightful for me. They are so well connected.

MAGGIE: (*To* MARGARET) Flatter her.

MARGARET: I heard it mentioned yesterday that you had made yourself very popular. Some one said you were very clever!

HARRIET: (*Pleased*) Who told you that?

MAGGIE: Nobody!

MARGARET: (*Pleasantly*) Oh, confidences should be suspected—respected, I mean. They said, too, that you are gaining some reputation as a critic of art.

HARRIET: I make no pretences.

MARGARET: Are you and Mr. Goodrich interested in the same things, too?

HETTY: No!

HARRIET: Yes, indeed, Charles and I are inseparable.

MAGGIE: I wonder.

HARRIET: Do have another cake.

MAGGIE: (*In relief*) Oh, yes.

> (*Again her claws extend but do not touch the cake*)

MARGARET: (*Takes cake delicately*) I really shouldn't—after my big luncheon. John took me to the Ritz and we are invited to the Bed-

fords' for dinner—they have such a magnificent house near
the drive—I really shouldn't, but the cakes are so good.

MAGGIE: Starving!

HARRIET: (*To* MARGARET) More tea?

MAGGIE: Yes!

MARGARET: No, thank you. How wonderfully life has arranged itself for you.
Wealth, position, a happy marriage, every opportunity to
enjoy all pleasures; beauty, art—how happy you must be.

HETTY: (*In anguish*) Don't call me happy. I've never been happy since I gave
up John. All these years without him—a future without
him—no—no—I shall win him back—away from you—
away from you—

HARRIET: (*Does not see* MAGGIE *pointing to cream and* MARGARET *stealing some*)
I sometimes think it is unfair for anyone to be as happy as
I am. Charles and I are just as much in love now as when
we married. To me he is just the dearest man in the world.

MAGGIE: (*Passionately*) My John is. I love him so much I could die for him.
I'm going through hunger and want to make him great
and he loves me. He worships me!

MARGARET: (*Leisurely to* HARRIET) I should like to meet Mr. Goodrich. Bring
him to our studio. John has some sketches to show. Not
many, because all the portraits have been purchased by the
subjects. He gets as much as four thousand dollars now.

HETTY: (*To* HARRIET) Don't pay that much.

HARRIET: (*To* MARGARET) As much as that?

MARGARET: It is not really too much when one considers that John is in the
foremost ranks of artists today. A picture painted by him
now will double and treble in value.

MAGGIE: It's a lie. He is growing weak with despair.

HARRIET: Does he paint all day long?

MAGGIE: No, he draws advertisements for our bread.

MARGARET: (*To* HARRIET) When you and your husband come to see us, telephone first—

MAGGIE: Yes, so he can get the advertisements out of the way.

MARGARET: Otherwise you might arrive while he has a sitter, and John refuses to let me disturb him then.

HETTY: Make her ask for an order.

HARRIET: (*To* MARGARET) Le Grange offered to paint me for a thousand.

MARGARET: Louis Le Grange's reputation isn't worth more than that.

HARRIET: Well, I've heard his work well mentioned.

MAGGIE: Yes, he is doing splendid work.

MARGARET: Oh, dear me, no. He is only praised by the masses. He is accepted not at all by artists themselves.

HETTY: (*Anxiously*) Must I really pay the full price?

HARRIET: Le Grange thought I would make a good subject.

MAGGIE: (*To* MARGARET) Let her fish for it.

MARGARET: Of course you would. Why don't you let Le Grange paint you, if you *trust* him?

HETTY: She doesn't seem anxious to have John do it.

HARRIET: But if Le Grange isn't accepted by artists, it would be a waste of time to pose for him, wouldn't it?

MARGARET: Yes, I think it would.

MAGGIE: (*Passionately to* HETTY *across back of table*) Give us the order. John is so despondent he can't endure much longer. Help us! Help me! Save us!

HETTY: (*To* HARRIET) Don't seem too eager.

HARRIET: And yet if he charges only a thousand one might consider it.

MARGARET: If you really wish to be painted, why don't you give a little more and have a portrait really worth while? John might be induced to do you for a little below his usual price considering that you used to be such good friends.

HETTY: (*In glee*) Hurrah!

HARRIET: (*Quietly to* MARGARET) That's very nice of you to suggest—of course I don't know—

MAGGIE: (*In fear*) For God's sake, say yes.

MARGARET: (*Quietly to* HARRIET) Of course, I don't know whether John would. He is very peculiar in these matters. He sets his value on his work and thinks it beneath him to discuss price.

HETTY: (*To* MAGGIE) You needn't try to make us feel small.

MARGARET: Still, I might quite delicately mention to him that inasmuch as you have many influential friends you would be very glad to—to—

MAGGIE: (*To* HETTY) Finish what I don't want to say.

HETTY: (*To* HARRIET) Help her out.

HARRIET: Oh, yes, introductions will follow the exhibition of my portrait. No doubt I—

HETTY: (*To* HARRIET) Be patronizing.

HARRIET: No doubt I shall be able to introduce your husband to his advantage.

MAGGIE: (*Relieved*) Saved.

MARGARET: If I find John in a propitious mood I shall take pleasure, for your sake, in telling him about your beauty. Just as you are sitting now would be a lovely pose.

MAGGIE: (*To* MARGARET) We can go now.

HETTY: (*To* HARRIET) Don't let her think she is doing us a favor.

HARRIET: It will give me pleasure to add my name to your husband's list of patronesses.

MAGGIE: (*Excitedly to* MARGARET) Run home and tell John the good news.

MARGARET: (*Leisurely to* HARRIET) I little guessed when I came for a pleasant chat about old times that it would develop into business arrangements. I had no idea, Harriet, that you had any intention of being painted. By Le Grange, too. Well, I came just in time to rescue you.

MAGGIE: (*To* MARGARET) Run home and tell John. Hurry, hurry!

HETTY: (*To* HARRIET) You managed the order very neatly. She doesn't suspect that you wanted it.

HARRIET: Now if I am not satisfied with my portrait I shall blame you. Margaret, dear. I am relying upon your opinion of John's talent.

MAGGIE: (*To* MARGARET) She doesn't suspect what you came for. Run home and tell John!

HARRIET: You always had a brilliant mind, Margaret.

MARGARET: Ah, it is you who flatter, now.

MAGGIE: (*To* MARGARET) You don't have to stay so long. Hurry home!

HARRIET: Ah, one does not flatter when one tells the truth.

MARGARET: (*Smiles*) I must be going or you will have me completely under your spell.

HETTY: (*Looks at clock*) Yes, do go. I have to dress for dinner.

HARRIET: (*To* MARGARET) Oh, don't hurry.

MAGGIE: (*To* HETTY) I hate you!

MARGARET: (*To* HARRIET) No, really I must, but I hope we shall see each other often at the studio. I find you so stimulating.

HETTY: (*To* MAGGIE) I hate you!

HARRIET: (*To* MARGARET) It is indeed gratifying to find a kindred spirit.

MAGGIE: (*To* HETTY) I came for your gold.

MARGARET: (*To* HARRIET) How delightful it is to know you again.

HETTY: (*To* MAGGIE) I am going to make you and your husband suffer.

HARRIET: My kind regards to John.

MAGGIE: (*To* HETTY) He has forgotten all about you.

MARGARET: (*Rises*) He will be so happy to receive them.

HETTY: (*To* MAGGIE) I can hardly wait to talk to him again.

391

HARRIET: I shall wait, then, until you send me word?

MARGARET: (*Offering her hand*) I'll speak to John about it as soon as I can and tell you when to come.

(HARRIET *takes* MARGARET'S *hand affectionately.* HETTY *and* MAGGIE *rush at each other, throw back their veils, and fling their speeches fiercely at each other.*)

HETTY: I love him—I love him—

MAGGIE: He's starving—I'm starving—

HETTY: I'm going to take him away from you—

MAGGIE: I want your money—and your influence.

HETTY and MAGGIE: I'm going to rob you—rob you.

(*There is a cymbal crash, the lights go out and come up again slowly, leaving only* MARGARET *and* HARRIET *visible.*)

MARGARET: (*Quietly to* HARRIET) I've had such a delightful afternoon.

HARRIET: (*Offering her hand*) It has been a joy to see you.

MARGARET: (*Sweetly to* HARRIET) Good-bye.

HARRIET: (*Sweetly to* MARGARET *as she kisses her*) Good-bye, my dear.

CURTAIN

1913

Susan Glaspell

(1882–1948)

TRIFLES: A PLAY IN ONE ACT

Characters

GEORGE HENDERSON. *County Attorney*
HENRY PETERS. *Sheriff*
LEWIS HALE. *Neighboring Farmer*
MRS. PETERS
MRS. HALE

Scene

The kitchen in the now abandoned farmhouse of JOHN WRIGHT, *a gloomy kitchen, and left without having been put in order—unwashed pans under the sink, a loaf of bread outside the breadbox, a dish towel on the table—other signs of incompleted work. At the rear the outer door opens and the* SHERIFF *comes in followed by the* COUNTY ATTORNEY *and* HALE. *The* SHERIFF *and* HALE *are men in middle life, the* COUNTY ATTORNEY *is a young man; all are much bundled up and go at once to the stove. They are followed by two women—the* SHERIFF'S *wife first; she is a slight wiry woman, a thin nervous face.* MRS. HALE *is larger and would ordinarily be called more comfortable looking, but she is disturbed now and looks fearfully about as she enters. The women have come in slowly, and stand close together near the door.*

COUNTY ATTORNEY: [*Rubbing his hands.*] This feels good. Come up to the fire, ladies.

MRS. PETERS: [*After taking a step forward.*] I'm not—cold.

SHERIFF: [*Unbuttoning his overcoat and stepping away from the stove as if to mark the beginning of official business.*] Now, Mr. Hale, before we move things about, you explain to Mr. Henderson just what you saw when you came here yesterday morning.

COUNTY ATTORNEY: By the way, has anything been moved? Are things just as you left them yesterday?

SHERIFF: [*Looking about.*] It's just the same. When it dropped below zero last night I thought I'd better send Frank out this morning to make a fire for us—no use getting pneumonia with a big case on, but I told him not to touch anything except the stove—and you know Frank.

COUNTY ATTORNEY: Somebody should have been left here yesterday.

SHERIFF: Oh—yesterday. When I had to send Frank to Morris Center for that man who went crazy—I want you to know I had my hands full yesterday, I knew you could get back from Omaha by today and as long as I went over everything here myself—

COUNTY ATTORNEY: Well, Mr. Hale, tell just what happened when you came here yesterday morning.

HALE: Harry and I had started to town with a load of potatoes. We came along the road from my place and as I got here I said, "I'm going to see if I can't get John Wright to go in with me on a party telephone." I spoke to Wright about it once before and he put me off, saying folks talked too much anyway, and all he asked was peace and quiet—I guess you know about how much he talked himself; but I thought maybe if I went to the house and talked about it before his wife, though I said to Harry that I didn't know as what his wife wanted made much difference to John—

COUNTY ATTORNEY: Let's talk about that later, Mr. Hale. I do want to talk about that, but tell now just what happened when you got to the house.

HALE: I didn't hear or see anything: I knocked at the door, and still it was all quiet inside. I knew they must be up, it was past eight o'clock. So I knocked again, and I thought I heard some-body say, "Come in." I wasn't sure, I'm not sure yet, but I opened the door—this door [*Indicating the door by which the two women are still standing*] and there in that rocker— [*Pointing to it.*] sat Mrs. Wright.
[*They all look at the rocker.*]

COUNTY ATTORNEY: What—was she doing?

HALE: She was rockin' back and forth. She had her apron in her hand and was kind of—pleating it.

COUNTY ATTORNEY: And how did she—look?

HALE: Well, she looked queer.

COUNTY ATTORNEY: How do you mean—queer?

HALE: Well, as if she didn't know what she was going to do next. And kind of done up.

COUNTY ATTORNEY: How did she seem to feel about your coming?

HALE: Why, I don't think she minded—one way or other. She didn't pay much attention. I said, "How do, Mrs. Wright, it's cold, ain't it?" And she said, "Is it?"—and went on kind of pleating at her apron. Well, I was surprised; she didn't ask me to come up to the stove, or to set down, but just sat there, not even looking at me, so I said, "I want to see John." And then she—laughed. I guess you would call it a laugh. I thought of Harry and the team outside, so I said a little sharp: "Can't I see John?" "No," she says, kind o' dull like. "Ain't he home?" says I. "Yes," says she, "he's home." "Then why can't I see him?" I asked her, out of patience. " 'Cause he's dead," says she. *"Dead?"* says I. She just nodded her head, not getting a bit excited, but rockin' back and forth. "Why—where is he?" says I, not knowing what to say. She just pointed upstairs—like that [*Himself pointing to the room above*]. I got up, with the idea of going up there. I walked from there to here—then I says, "Why, what did he die of?" "He died of a rope round his neck," says she, and just went on pleatin' at her apron. Well, I went out and called Harry. I thought I might—need help. We went upstairs and there he was lyin'—

COUNTY ATTORNEY: I think I'd rather have you go into that upstairs, where you can point it all out. Just go on now with the rest of the story.

HALE: Well, my first thought was to get that rope off. It looked . . . [*Stops, his face twitches.*] . . . but Harry, he went up to him, and he said, "No, he's dead all right, and we'd better not touch anything." So we went back down stairs. She was still sitting that same way. "Has anybody been notified?" I asked. "No," says she, unconcerned. "Who did this, Mrs. Wright?" said Harry. He said it businesslike—and she stopped pleatin' of her apron. "I don't know," she says. "You don't *know?*" says Harry. "No," says she. "Weren't you sleepin' in the bed with him?" says Harry. "Yes," says she, "but I was on the inside." "Somebody slipped a rope round his neck and strangled him and you didn't wake up?" says Harry. "I didn't wake up," she said after him. We must 'a looked as if we didn't see how that could be, for after a minute she said, "I sleep sound." Harry was going to ask her more questions but I said maybe we ought to let her tell her story first to the coroner, or the sheriff, so Harry went fast as he could to Rivers' place, where there's a telephone.

COUNTY ATTORNEY: And what did Mrs. Wright do when she knew that you had gone for the coroner?

HALE: She moved from that chair to this one over here [*Pointing to a small chair in the corner.*] and just sat there with her hands held together and looking down, I got a feeling that I ought to make some conversation, so I said I had come in to see if John wanted to put in a telephone, and at that she started to laugh, and then she stopped and looked at me—scared. [*The* COUNTY ATTORNEY, *who has had his notebook out, makes a note.*] I dunno, maybe it wasn't scared. I wouldn't like to say it was. Soon Harry got back, and then Dr. Lloyd came, and you, Mr. Peters, and so I guess that's all I know that you don't.

COUNTY ATTORNEY: [*Looking around.*] I guess we'll go upstairs first—and then out to the barn and around there. [*To the* SHERIFF] You're convinced that there was nothing important here— nothing that would point to any motive.

SHERIFF: Nothing here but kitchen things.

[*The* COUNTY ATTORNEY, *after again looking around the kitchen, opens the door of a cupboard closet. He gets up on a chair and looks on a shelf. Pulls his hand away, sticky.*]

COUNTY ATTORNEY: Here's a nice mess.

[*The women draw nearer.*]

MRS. PETERS: [*To the other woman.*] Oh, her fruit; it did freeze. [*To the* COUNTY ATTORNEY] She worried about that when it turned so cold. She said the fire'd go out and her jars would break.

SHERIFF: Well, can you beat the women! Held for murder and worryin' about her preserves.

COUNTY ATTORNEY: I guess before we're through she may have something more serious than preserves to worry about.

HALE: Well, women are used to worrying over trifles.

[*The two women move a little closer together.*]

COUNTY ATTORNEY: [*With the gallantry of a young politician.*] And yet, for all their worries, what would we do without the ladies? [*The women do not unbend. He goes to the sink, takes a dipperful of water from the pail and pouring it into a basin, washes his hands. Starts to wipe them on the roller towel, turns it for a cleaner place.*] Dirty towels! [*Kicks his foot against the pans under the sink.*] Not much of a housekeeper, would you say, ladies?

MRS. HALE: [*Stiffly.*] There's a great deal of work to be done on a farm.

COUNTY ATTORNEY: To be sure. And yet [*With a little bow to her*] I know
there are some Dickson county farmhouses which do not
have such roller towels.

[*He gives it a pull to expose its full length again.*]

MRS. HALE: Those towels get dirty awful quick. Men's hands aren't always as
clean as they might be.

COUNTY ATTORNEY: Ah, loyal to your sex, I see. But you and Mrs. Wright
were neighbors. I suppose you were friends, too.

MRS. HALE: [*Shaking her head.*] I've not seen much of her of late years. I've
not been in this house—it's more than a year.

COUNTY ATTORNEY: And why was that? You didn't like her?

MRS. HALE: I liked her all well enough. Farmers' wives have their hands full,
Mr. Henderson. And then—

COUNTY ATTORNEY: Yes—?

MRS. HALE: [*Looking about.*] It never seemed a very cheerful place.

COUNTY ATTORNEY: No—it's not cheerful. I shouldn't say she had the home-
making instinct.

MRS. HALE: Well, I don't know as Wright had, either.

COUNTY ATTORNEY: You mean that they didn't get on very well?

MRS. HALE: No, I don't mean anything. But I don't think a place'd be any
cheerfuller for John Wright's being in it.

COUNTY ATTORNEY: I'd like to talk more of that a little later. I want to get
the lay of things upstairs now.

[*He goes to the left, where three steps lead to a stair door.*]

SHERIFF: I suppose anything Mrs. Peters does'll be all right. She was to take
in some clothes for her, you know, and a few little things.
We left in such a hurry yesterday.

COUNTY ATTORNEY: Yes, but I would like to see what you take, Mrs. Peters,
and keep an eye out for anything that might be of use
to us.

MRS. PETERS: Yes, Mr. Henderson.

[*The women listen to the men's steps on the stairs, then look
about the kitchen.*]

MRS. HALE: I'd hate to have men coming into my kitchen, snooping around
and criticising.

[*She arranges the pans under sink which the* COUNTY ATTOR-
NEY *had shoved out of place.*]

MRS. PETERS: Of course it's no more than their duty.

MRS. HALE: Duty's all right, but I guess that deputy sheriff that came out to
make the fire might have got a little of this on. [*Gives the*

397

roller towel a pull.] Wish I'd thought of that sooner. Seems
mean to talk about her for not having things slicked up
when she had to come away in such a hurry.

MRS. PETERS: [*Who has gone to a small table in the left rear corner of the room,
and lifted one end of a towel that covers a pan.*] She had
bread set.
[*Stands still.*]

MRS. HALE: [*Eyes fixed on a loaf of bread beside the breadbox, which is on a low
shelf at the other side of the room. Moves slowly toward it.*]
She was going to put this in there. [*Picks up loaf, then
abruptly drops it. In a manner of returning to familiar
things.*] It's a shame about her fruit. I wonder if it's all
gone. [*Gets up on the chair and looks.*] I think there's some
here that's all right, Mrs. Peters. Yes—here; [*Holding it toward the window.*] this is cherries, too. [*Looking again.*] I
declare I believe that's the only one. [*Gets down, bottle in
her hand. Goes to the sink and wipes it off on the outside.*]
She'll feel awful bad after all her hard work in the hot
weather. I remember the afternoon I put up my cherries
last summer.
[*She puts the bottle on the big kitchen table, center of the room.
With a sigh, is about to sit down in the rocking-chair. Before
she is seated realizes what chair it is; with a slow look at it,
steps back. The chair which she has touched rocks back and
forth.*]

MRS. PETERS: Well, I must get those things from the front room closet. [*She
goes to the door at the right, but after looking into the other
room, steps back.*] You coming with me, Mrs. Hale? You
could help me carry them.
[*They go in the other room; reappear,* MRS. PETERS *carrying a
dress and skirt,* MRS. HALE *following with a pair of shoes.*]

MRS. PETERS: My, it's cold in there.
[*She puts the clothes on the big table, and hurries to the stove.*]

MRS. HALE: [*Examining her skirt.*] Wright was close. I think maybe that's
why she kept so much to herself. She didn't even belong to
the Ladies Aid. I suppose she felt she couldn't do her part,
and then you don't enjoy things when you feel shabby. She
used to wear pretty clothes and be lively, when she was
Minnie Foster, one of the town girls singing in the choir.
But that—oh, that was thirty years ago. This all you was
to take in?

MRS. PETERS: She said she wanted an apron. Funny thing to want, for there isn't much to get you dirty in jail, goodness knows. But I suppose just to make her feel more natural. She said they was in the top drawer in this cupboard. Yes, here. And then her little shawl that always hung behind the door. [*Opens stair door and looks.*] Yes, here it is. [*Quickly shuts door leading upstairs.*]

MRS. HALE: [*Abruptly moving toward her.*] Mrs. Peters?

MRS. PETERS: Yes, Mrs. Hale?

MRS. HALE: Do you think she did it?

MRS. PETERS: [*In a frightened voice.*] Oh, I don't know.

MRS. HALE: Well, I don't think she did. Asking for an apron and her little shawl. Worrying about her fruit.

MRS. PETERS: [*Starts to speak, glances up, where footsteps are heard in the room above. In a low voice.*] Mr. Peters says it looks bad for her. Mr. Henderson is awful sarcastic in a speech and he'll make fun of her sayin' she didn't wake up.

MRS. HALE: Well, I guess John Wright didn't wake when they was slipping that rope under his neck.

MRS. PETERS: No, it's strange. It must have been done awful crafty and still. They say it was such a—funny way to kill a man, rigging it all up like that.

MRS. HALE: That's just what Mr. Hale said. There was a gun in the house. He says that's what he can't understand.

MRS. PETERS: Mr. Henderson said coming out that what was needed for the case was a motive; something to show anger, or—sudden feeling.

MRS. HALE: [*Who is standing by the table.*] Well, I don't see any signs of anger around here. [*She puts her hand on the dish towel which lies on the table, stands looking down at table, one half of which is clean, the other half messy.*] It's wiped to here. [*Makes a move as if to finish work, then turns and looks at loaf of bread outside the breadbox. Drops towel. In that voice of coming back to familiar things.*] Wonder how they are finding things upstairs. I hope she had it a little more red-up up there. You know, it seems kind of *sneaking*. Locking her up in town and then coming out here and trying to get her own house to turn against her!

MRS. PETERS: But Mrs. Hale, the law is the law.

MRS. HALE: I s'pose 'tis. [*Unbuttoning her coat.*] Better loosen up your things, Mrs. Peters. You won't feel them when you go out.

[MRS. PETERS *takes off her fur tippet, goes to hang it on hook at back of room, stands looking at the under part of the small corner table.*]

MRS. PETERS: She was piecing a quilt.

[*She brings the large sewing basket and they look at the bright pieces.*]

MRS. HALE: It's log cabin pattern. Pretty, isn't it? I wonder if she was goin' to quilt it or just knot it?

[*Footsteps have been heard coming down the stairs. The SHERIFF enters followed by HALE and the COUNTY ATTORNEY.*]

SHERIFF: They wonder if she was going to quilt it or just knot it!

[*The men laugh; the women look abashed.*]

COUNTY ATTORNEY: [*Rubbing his hands over the stove.*] Frank's fire didn't do much up there, did it? Well, let's go out to the barn and get that cleared up.

[*The men go outside.*]

MRS. HALE: [*Resentfully.*] I don't know as there's anything so strange, our takin' up our time with little things while we're waiting for them to get the evidence. [*She sits down at the big table smoothing out a block with decision.*] I don't see as it's anything to laugh about.

MRS. PETERS: [*Apologetically.*] Of course they've got awful important things on their minds.

[*Pulls up a chair and joins MRS. HALE at the table.*]

MRS. HALE: [*Examining another block.*] Mrs. Peters, look at this one. Here, this is the one she was working on, and look at the sewing! All the rest of it has been so nice and even. And look at this! It's all over the place! Why, it looks as if she didn't know what she was about!

[*After she has said this they look at each other, then start to glance back at the door. After an instant MRS. HALE has pulled at a knot and ripped the sewing.*]

MRS. PETERS: Oh, what are you doing, Mrs. Hale?

MRS. HALE: [*Mildly.*] Just pulling out a stitch or two that's not sewed very good. [*Threading a needle.*] Bad sewing always made me fidgety.

MRS. PETERS: [*Nervously.*] I don't think we ought to touch things.

MRS. HALE: I'll just finish up this end. [*Suddenly stopping and leaning forward.*] Mrs. Peters?

MRS. PETERS: Yes. Mrs. Hale?

MRS. HALE: What do you suppose she was so nervous about?

MRS. PETERS: Oh—I don't know. I don't know as she was nervous. I sometimes sew awful queer when I'm just tired. [MRS. HALE *starts to say something, looks at* MRS. PETERS, *then goes on sewing.*] Well, I must get these things wrapped up. They may be through sooner than we think. [*Putting apron and other things together.*] I wonder where I can find a piece of paper, and string.

MRS. HALE: In that cupboard, maybe.

MRS. PETERS: [*Looking in cupboard.*] Why, here's a birdcage. [*Holds it up.*] Did she have a bird, Mrs. Hale?

MRS. HALE: Why, I don't know whether she did or not—I've not been here for so long. There was a man around last year selling canaries cheap, but I don't know as she took one; maybe she did. She used to sing real pretty herself.

MRS. PETERS: [*Glancing around.*] Seems funny to think of a bird here. But she must have had one, or why would she have a cage? I wonder what happened to it.

MRS. HALE: I s'pose maybe the cat got it.

MRS. PETERS: No, she didn't have a cat. She's got that feeling some people have about cats—being afraid of them. My cat got in her room and she was real upset and asked me to take it out.

MRS. HALE: My sister Bessie was like that. Queer, ain't it?

MRS. PETERS: [*Examining the cage.*] Why, look at this door. It's broke. One hinge is pulled apart.

MRS. HALE: [*Looking to.*] Looks as if someone must have been rough with it.

MRS. PETERS: Why, yes.

[*She brings the cage forward and puts it on the table.*]

MRS. HALE: I wish if they're going to find any evidence they'd be about it. I don't like this place.

MRS. PETERS: But I'm awful glad you came with me, Mrs. Hale. It would be lonesome for me sitting here alone.

MRS. HALE: It would, wouldn't it? [*Dropping her sewing.*] But I tell you what I do wish, Mrs. Peters. I wish I had come over sometimes when *she* was here. I—[*Looking around the room.*]—wish I had.

MRS. PETERS: But of course you were awful busy, Mrs. Hale—your house and your children.

MRS. HALE: I could've come. I stayed away because it weren't cheerful—and that's why I ought to have come. I—I've never liked this place. Maybe because it's down in a hollow and you don't see the road. I dunno what it is but it's a lonesome place

401

and always was. I wish I had come over to see Minnie
Foster sometimes. I can see now—
[*Shakes her head.*]

MRS. PETERS: Well, you mustn't reproach yourself, Mrs. Hale. Somehow we
just don't see how it is with other folks until—something
comes up.

MRS. HALE: Not having children makes less work—but it makes a quiet
house, and Wright out to work all day, and no company
when he did come in. Did you know John Wright, Mrs.
Peters?

MRS. PETERS: Not to know him; I've seen him in town. They say he was a
good man.

MRS. HALE: Yes—good; he didn't drink, and kept his word as well as most, I
guess, and paid his debts. But he was a hard man, Mrs.
Peters. Just to pass the time of day with him—[*Shivers.*]
Like a raw wind that gets to the bone. [*Pauses, her eye fall-
ing on the cage.*] I should think she would'a wanted a bird.
But what do you suppose went with it?

MRS. PETERS: I don't know, unless it got sick and died.
[*She reaches over and swings the broken door, swings it again.
Both women watch it.*]

MRS. HALE: You weren't raised round here, were you? [MRS. PETERS *shakes
her head.*] You didn't know—her?

MRS. PETERS: Not till they brought her yesterday.

MRS. HALE: She—come to think of it, she was kind of like a bird herself—
real sweet and pretty, but kind of timid and—fluttery.
How—she—did—change. [*Silence; then as if struck by a
happy thought and relieved to get back to every day things.*]
Tell you what, Mrs. Peters, why don't you take the quilt in
with you? It might take up her mind.

MRS. PETERS: Why, I think that's a real nice idea, Mrs. Hale. There couldn't
possibly be any objection to it, could there? Now, just what
would I take? I wonder if her patches are in here—and her
things.
[*They look in the sewing basket.*]

MRS. HALE: Here's some red. I expect this has got sewing things in it.
[*Brings out a fancy box.*] What a pretty box. Looks like
something somebody would give you. Maybe her scissors
are in here. [*Opens box. Suddenly puts her hand to her nose.*]
Why—[MRS. PETERS *bends nearer, then turns her face away.*]
There's something wrapped up in this piece of silk.

MRS. PETERS: Why, this isn't her scissors.

MRS. HALE: [*Lifting the silk.*] Oh, Mrs. Peters—it's—
[MRS. PETERS *bends closer.*]

MRS. PETERS: It's the bird.

MRS. HALE: [*Jumping up.*] But, Mrs. Peters—look at it! Its neck! Look at its neck! It's all—other side *to.*

MRS. PETERS: Somebody—wrung—its—neck.
[*Their eyes meet. A look of growing comprehension, of horror. Steps are heard outside.* MRS. HALE *slips box under quilt pieces, and sinks into her chair. Enter* SHERIFF *and* COUNTY ATTORNEY, MRS. PETERS *rises.*]

COUNTY ATTORNEY: [*As one turning from serious things to little pleasantries.*] Well, ladies have you decided whether she was going to quilt it or knot it?

MRS. PETERS: We think she was going to—knot it.

COUNTY ATTORNEY: Well, that's interesting, I'm sure. [*Seeing the birdcage.*] Has the bird flown?

MRS. HALE: [*Putting more quilt pieces over the box.*] We think the—cat got it.

COUNTY ATTORNEY: [Preoccupied.] Is there a cat?
[MRS. HALE *glances in a quick covert way at* MRS. PETERS.]

MRS. PETERS.: Well, not *now.* They're superstitious, you know. They leave.

COUNTY ATTORNEY: [*To* SHERIFF PETERS, *continuing an interrupted conversation.*] No sign at all of anyone having come from the outside. Their own rope. Now let's go up again and go over it piece by piece. [*They start upstairs.*] It would have to have been someone who knew just the—[MRS. PETERS *sits down.* *The two women sit there not looking at one another, but as if peering into something and at the same time holding back. When they talk now it is in the manner of feeling their way over strange ground, as if afraid of what they are saying, but as if they can not help saying it.*]

MRS. HALE: She liked the bird. She was going to bury it in that pretty box.

MRS. PETERS: [*In a whisper.*] When I was a girl—my kitten—there was a boy took a hatchet, and before my eyes—and before I could get there—[*Covers her face an instant.*] If they hadn't held me back I would have—[*Catches herself, looks upstairs where steps are heard, falters weakly.*]—hurt him.

MRS. HALE: [*With a slow look around her.*] I wonder how it would seem never to have had any children around. [*Pause.*] No, Wright wouldn't like the bird—a thing that sang. She used to sing. He killed that, too.

MRS. PETERS: [*Moving uneasily.*] We don't know who killed the bird.

MRS. HALE: I knew John Wright.

MRS. PETERS: It was an awful thing was done in this house that night, Mrs. Hale. Killing a man while he slept, slipping a rope around his neck that choked the life out of him.

MRS. HALE: His neck. Choked the life out of him.

[*Her hand goes out and rests on the birdcage.*]

MRS. PETERS: [*With rising voice.*] We don't know who killed him. We don't know.

MRS. HALE: [*Her own feeling not interrupted.*] If there'd been years and years of nothing, then a bird to sing to you, it would be awful— still, after the bird was still.

MRS. PETERS: [*Something within her speaking.*] I know what stillness is. When we homesteaded in Dakota, and my first baby died—after he was two years old, and me with no other then—

MRS. HALE: [*Moving.*] How soon do you suppose they'll be through, looking for the evidence?

MRS. PETERS: I know what stillness is. [*Pulling herself back.*] The law has got to punish crime, Mrs. Hale.

MRS. HALE: [*Not as if answering that.*] I wish you'd seen Minnie Foster when she wore a white dress with blue ribbons and stood up there in the choir and sang. [*A look around the room.*] Oh, I *wish* I'd come over here once in a while! That was a crime! That was a crime! Who's going to punish that?

MRS. PETERS: [*Looking upstairs.*] We mustn't—take on.

MRS. HALE: I might have known she needed help! I know how things can be—for women. I tell you, it's queer, Mrs. Peters. We live close together and we live far apart. We all go through the same things—it's all just a different kind of the same thing. [*Brushes her eyes; noticing the bottle of fruit, reaches out for it.*] If I was you I wouldn't tell her her fruit was gone. Tell her it ain't. Tell her it's all right. Take this in to prove it to her. She—she may never know whether it was broke or not.

MRS. PETERS: [*Takes the bottle, looks about for something to wrap it in; takes petticoat from the clothes brought from the other room, very nervously begins winding this around the bottle. In a false voice.*] My, it's a good thing the men couldn't hear us. Wouldn't they just laugh! Getting all stirred up over a little thing like a—dead canary. As if that could have anything to do with—with—wouldn't they *laugh!*

[*The men are heard coming down stairs.*]

MRS. HALE: [*Under her breath.*] Maybe they would—maybe they wouldn't.

COUNTY ATTORNEY: No, Peters, it's all perfectly clear except a reason for doing it. But you know juries when it comes to women. If there was some definite thing. Something to show—something to make a story about—a thing that would connect up with this strange way of doing it—

[*The women's eyes meet for an instant. Enter HALE from outer door.*]

HALE: Well, I've got the team around. Pretty cold out there.

COUNTY ATTORNEY: I'm going to stay here a while by myself. [*To the SHERIFF.*] You can send Frank out for me, can't you? I want to go over everything. I'm not satisfied that we can't do better.

SHERIFF: Do you want to see what Mrs. Peters is going to take in?

[*The COUNTY ATTORNEY goes to the table, picks up the apron, laughs.*]

COUNTY ATTORNEY: Oh, I guess they're not very dangerous things the ladies have picked out. [*Moves a few things about, disturbing the quilt pieces which cover the box. Steps back.*] No, Mrs. Peters doesn't need supervising. For that matter, a sheriff's wife is married to the law. Ever think of it that way, Mrs. Peters?

MRS. PETERS: Not—just that way.

SHERIFF: [*Chuckling.*] Married to the law. [*Moves toward the other room.*] I just want you to come in here a minute, George. We ought to take a look at these windows.

COUNTY ATTORNEY: [*Scoffingly.*] Oh, windows!

SHERIFF: We'll be right out, Mr. Hale.

[*HALE goes outside. The SHERIFF follows the COUNTY ATTORNEY into the other room. Then MRS. HALE rises, hands tight together, looking intensely at MRS. PETERS, whose eyes make a slow turn, finally meeting MRS. HALE'S. A moment MRS. HALE holds her, then her own eyes point the way to where the box is concealed. Suddenly MRS. PETERS throws back quilt pieces and tries to put the box in the bag she is wearing. It is too big. She opens box, starts to take bird out, cannot touch it, goes to pieces, stands there helpless. Sound of a knob turning in the other room. MRS. HALE snatches the box and puts it in the pocket of her big coat. Enter COUNTY ATTORNEY and SHERIFF.*]

COUNTY ATTORNEY: [*Facetiously.*] Well, Henry, at least we found out that she was not going to quilt it. She was going to—what is it you call it, ladies?

MRS. HALE: [*Her hand against her pocket.*] We call it—knot it, Mr. Henderson.

CURTAIN

1916

Genny Lim
(1946–   )

BITTER CANE

Characters

LAU HING JUO, the ghost of a middle-aged cane cutter
LI-TAI, a prostitute in her mid-thirties
KAM SU, a cane cutter in his early thirties
WING CHUNG KUO, the sixteen-year-old son of LAU HING
FOOK MING, a middle-aged Chinese luna (foreman)

Scene One

(*China. A bare stage.* WING *is packing to leave for America. There are several tightly wrapped cloth bundles on the floor, ready to go.*)

Voiceover of HIS OLD MOTHER: Listen well, young man, and understand.
You are my blood, my color, the offshoot and stem of my bones. There is no place on this earth where you can walk without shadow. The rain will pelt your shoulders like stones. The burning sun shall torment your flesh. Life is difficult and short. But the gods have given us laughter and song to forget our troubles.

You must remember, my only son, never to dishonor yourself. Do not be idle, do not wander aimlessly, without destination. Do not throw dust upon the gods' faces. Do not spill black ink on the ancestral graves. You have been formed, shaped like a thorn from my womb. You grow like the wound in my soul. Now it is up to you, my son. Do not kill me with shame as did your father. Will you break the cycle of pain or will you pursue another grievous lifetime? Beware of tigers everywhere. Snakes lie among the leaves like snares. The sun and wind carry the seeds of memory. Do not forget my words. They are all I have to leave you. (*Enter a funeral procession in a Chinese village during the mid-1800s. The drone of tantric Buddhist chants mingled with the weeping and wailing of women fill the air. White-robed mourners march across the stage bearing a litter with the shrouded body, paper effigies, and palace, symbolizing wealth and status in the afterlife. The objects are lowered to the*

407

ground in a funeral pyre. WING *approaches and halts apart from the rest. He presses his hands in prayer and bows three times. The mourners turn together and watch him in silence.* WING *takes up his bundles and exits. Blackout.*)

Scene Two

(*Storm over Oahu. Kahuku sugarcane plantation. A weary, middle-aged Chinese traveler, wearing white and a coolie hat, enters carrying a wrapped bundle. His movements should be stylized and suggestive of another world. He stops, listens, and puts down his bundle.*)

LAU HING (*attentively*): Listen to that. Sounds like it's never goin' to stop. Hear it hammering down the tin roofs? Drilling through cracks, dripping down walls, fillin' empty tins on the floor? Yu-chiang, the master of floods, remembers our sins. (*miming*) Sometimes he cups the ocean in his hands and hurls a tidal wave! (*howling of wind*) Hear him growling? (*pauses*) There's nothing more lonely than the sound of wind and rain. But, once it stops, you're back in the fields, knuckling under the sun. Just when you think you'll collapse, you look up and there she'll be, the cane witch. Smiling at you from behind high stalks; long, black hair shining, naked brown arms beckoning you. You blink your eyes twice to see if you're dreaming and she laughs. You don't know where she came from or who she is, but you want her. You want her so bad you can feel your heart trembling. You chase her through row after row of cane till you're breathless. When you finally catch up to her, she spins around and looks at you. Her two dark eyes are caverns. You reach to enter, but a stabbing pain pierces your heart and she disappears. There's no trace of her. All you see is a lizard darting through the leaves. And the faint smell of pikake.
(*Woman's laughter and sound of rain.* LAU *crosses downstage left, where he remains for the rest of the play. Light goes up on a wooden shack room with a vanity, a bed and a few feminine, Victorian articles. The set should be evocative, not literal. On the bed,* LI-TAI *is giggling as* KAM SU *tickles her.*)

KAM: Teach me!

LI-TAI: I'm not Hawaiian.

KAM (*lifting her camisole*): Then you need exposure. (*kisses her navel*)

408

LI-TAI (*laughing*): Piko.

KAM (*tickling*): Piko, piko, piko!

LI-TAI: Diu-mao-gwai!

KAM: Who you calling a drunk?

LI-TAI (*puts out her palm in a no-nonsense manner*): My money?
> (*Realizing the rules have changed,* KAM *irritably picks up a fifth of whiskey from her dresser and takes several snorts. She grabs it from him and puts it back.*)

KAM: Payday is Saturday. I'll pay you then.

LI-TAI (*irate*): What do you think I am? You pay me now!

KAM: I got one year left on my contract. (*digs into his pocket and hands her several coins*) One more lousy year. (*meaningfully*) Then I'm free.

LI-TAI (*looks at the coins with disgust*): Fifty cents! Is that all you got?

KAM: Have a heart, Li-Tai. I came all this way in the storm!

LI-TAI: And you can go back in it!

KAM: Please . . .

LI-TAI (*indignant*): You wouldn't do this to a haole woman!

KAM (*cajoling*): Just this once. I'm begging you!

LI-TAI (*contemptuously*): Jawk-gee! Do you think you're catching a pig?

KAM (*desperately*): As a countryman!

LI-TAI (*throws the coins on the floor in anger*): Get out.

KAM (*explodes*): You think you so high and mighty? You think you too good for me, huh? Well I'll tell you something. You and that Pake luna are nothing but a pair of blood-sucking leeches!

LI-TAI: You are dirt!
> (*She slaps him. He grabs her violently, forces her onto the bed, grabbing her bound feet. She struggles helplessly underneath him.*)

KAM (*aroused*): Crippled woman, where can you go? You have no feet—only petals for toes.
> (*She spits at him. He twists her ankles. She clenches her teeth in pain.*)

KAM: You can only submit! (*He bites the tip of her foot as if it was a delicacy.*) Like fish out of water.
> (*She struggles free and in a frenzy, gathers his coins and flings them at him.*)

LI-TAI: Take your crumbs and get out!

KAM: Why spit on your own kind? Do you think you're better than me?

LI-TAI (*contemptuously*): Shit is better than you. (*hysterically*) Get out! Get out!

KAM (*pointing his finger*): One day, you'll be sorry.

> (*He exits, slamming the door violently. She takes his shirt, opens the door, and hurls it out. We hear him yell from outside.*)

KAM (*offstage*): Pake snake! Mercenary whore!

LI-TAI (*screaming*): Fook will kill you if you ever come back here!

> (*She slams the door shut, leaning against it with eyes shut. She takes big gulps from the whiskey bottle. She goes slowly to the bed, sits, then lights the opium lamp on the bedside table and prepares the pipe. She takes deep tokes. The drug has an almost immediate calming effect on her. She picks up a cricket cage from her bed table and studies it with intense fascination. The room fills with smoke and the crescendo of rain, then the sound of a cane worker singing:*)

Hawaii, Hawaii
so far, far from home,
Hawaii, Hawaii
My bones ache and my heart breaks
thinking about the ones I left behind.

> (*The light fades on LI-TAI and comes up on KAM in the field, holding a machete and singing:*)

Hawaii, Hawaii
so far, far from home,
For every cane I cut, there are a thousand more
With so many days to pay.
Hawaii, Hawaii
Don't let me die of misery.
Don't bury me under the cane fields.

> (*LAU HING watches him silently from a distance. KAM wipes his brow with his sleeve, then hacks the stalks with vengeance.*)

KAM: Goddam sonovabitches! (*throws his whole body into cutting motion*) Take that! (*again striking*) And that, son-a-va-bitch!

> (*A CHINESE LUNA enters with a new worker.*)

LUNA (*to* KAM): Less mouth, more action! (*indicating newcomer*) I want you to teach this boy to cut cane. Make sure he doesn't cut the tops high. I want the stubs nice and low. Show him the

right way. Stack 'em straight. No sloppy piles. No cheat-
ing. I got eyes. We'll have to lop this field by Saturday—
otherwise, overtime.

KAM: No overtime! Our contract says no overtime Sunday!

LUNA: I'm boss here! If I say you work, you work. If I say you work overtime, you work overtime. Understand?

KAM (*stubbornly*): I understand the contract.

LUNA: Well now, I wouldn't want to violate your contract. If you don't like
working Sundays, you can work nights.

KAM: No dinner, no work!

LUNA: No work, no pay! You got that, Chinaboy? (*waiting for response*) Now
get back to work. That's what we pay you for.

(LUNA *exits.* KAM *takes the machete and lands it with force.*)

KAM: You haole lap-dog! (*strikes*) Profit from the blood of your countrymen!
(*strikes*) Traitor to the white devils! (*strikes*) Bastard! (*to*
WING) Back up! Look out for flying splinters. You're liable
to lose an eye or nose! You want to learn how to cut cane,
boy? This is how we cut. Nice and deep. Down to the
bone. They want the juice in that stalk. Don't let it run to
the ground. The bottom's where the vein's at. Easy. Nice
and sweet for the mill to grind. If you can cut one, you can
cut eight! Just think of each cane stalk as Fook Ming's
skinny neck . . . Aiii-ee-eee!!!
(*A final angry blow. Fade out.*)

Scene Three

(*Dinnertime outside the plantation shack.* KAM *is too wound up to eat.* WING, *by
comparison, wolfs down his bowl as if starved. There are two small packets beside
each of their bowls.*)

WING (*with disappointment*): Is this all we get for dinner?

KAM (*with a bitter laugh*): What did you expect? A king's nine-course ban-
quet? Cod fillet and shark fin soup? Deep-fried quail and
tender, boneless barley duck? Ha ha. You'd better get used
to limp salt cabbage and cold rice, cause you're gonna be
eating a lot of it. (*pushes his bowl toward* WING) Go ahead,
eat, friend.

WING (*eagerly seizes* KAM's *bowl*): Thank you.

KAM: Welcome to Kahuku, the land of bitter cane. I am Kam Su. Better
known as Kam-a Su-tra. And who are you?

WING: Wing. Wing Chun.

KAM: You look like someone I know. (*slapping mosquitoes*) I must have sweet blood. I'm being crucified! (*laughs*) Like Jesus.

WING: I got stung by a wasp in the field. (*rubbing his ear*) Who is Jesus?

KAM: Christ. Wrap your head. The nests are hidden in the leaves. (*points to his unopened packet;* WING *hands it to him*) Jesus Christ. Nailed on a cross by his own gentle kind. Friendship is a rare thing. Greater love hath no man than this, that a man lay down his life for his friends. (*preparing his pipe*) And there are those who profit from the misery of their own. Judas saith unto him, not Iscariot.

WING (*perplexed*): What the hell are you talking about?

KAM: Christian delirium. Don't mind me. When the sun hits, I start babbling that holy drivel. (*takes a puff*) The only book we could get was the Bible. We recited passages from Matthew, Mark, Luke, and John, like little schoolboys, trying to keep our minds off sex. It only made it worse. (KAM *points to* WING's *unused packet*) Aren't you going to open yours?

(WING *shakes his head disinterestedly.*)

KAM: Then why don't I trade my rice for your powder?

(WING *shrugs and shoves his packet toward* KAM. KAM *eagerly takes it.*)

KAM: I give you a month before you're as depraved as the rest of us. Disciples of the golden poppy.

WING (*offended*): Don't be so sure.

KAM (surly): Oh? You don't shit?

WING (*stubbornly*): Every man's different.

KAM (*cynically*): I don't agree. I say all men are the same. Deaf and dumb. You come out of a hole, you go into a hole. Eventually you disappear. Like the cane. (*takes out his pipe and opens the packet of powder*) You're no different. (*puts the powder in the bowl of the pipe*) You came to make money and return to the village rich. When your contract's up, you'll go home and pick a wife. That's what we all thought. You'll see. The seasons pass without fail. Each day follows the next. You plant, you cut, you harvest, you haul, and you don't ask questions. Like a dumb plow ox. The only thing you got to break the monotony is gambling, opium, or women. Euphoria or Christianity. Take your pick. Can you think of anything more depressing than praying to

some limp haole hanging from a cross? (*laughs*) He probably never understood a word of Chinese anyway! (*taps his
pipe, then lights it*)

WING: Why did you stop believing?

KAM: When I realized this White God wanted no graven images before
him. Father DeCarlo snatched up Kwan Kung and hurled
him on the ground. There was no way on earth, I'd let
him burn Kwan Kung! I carried him all the way with me
from China. Why that'd be like spittin' on my father's
grave! Father DeCarlo couldn't believe the endless string
of curses I shouted at him. If their God was going to be so
greedy, I said, I'd just as soon stay pagan. It was stupid to
think of myself as Christian anyway. You can't spin silk
out of cotton, no more than you can teach a pigeon to
swim. Soon as I pay my debt, I'm going back. I have no
illusions about this place. (*cheerfully*) I'll just spend whatever time I have left, playing, not praying. (*shrugs*) If
opium is evil, the white man's the devil. He gave it to us
and it's him who's keeping us here. (*puffing*) Most of the
fellas take any woman they can get their hands on. You
can't drain away your manhood. Why wait five or seven
years for a village girl? Some of the fellas marry Hawaiian
girls. Some even marry prostitutes!

WING: Not me. I'm going to make my village proud.

(WING *takes out a knife and a hunk of wood from his pocket
and starts whittling.* LAU *simultaneously takes out an invisible
knife and his cutting movements repeat* WING's.)

KAM: Look at the bastard talking! (*mocking him*) I'm going to make my
mother proud! What are you anyhow? Mexican? (*amused*)
You still a virgin? (*patronizing*) Listen, you don't have to
be ashamed. No one's perfect. I was once one too. But
once you've tasted wine (*a quick tug at his crotch*), you never
lose your thirst. (*smirks*) Know what I mean? You want a
woman?

WING: I'll wait till I marry.

KAM (*disgustedly*): Did you leave your dick in China? Is that what you're
carving? Wake up! I got just the woman for you, China-
boy. She can wrap her gaze around you till you think
you're seeing double. She's a snake beauty. With a deadly
bite.

WING: She must be a bad woman.

413

KAM: There are two kinds of women. The kind that reminds you of your mother and the kind every mother fears for her son. The first kind you marry and the other kind you lust. As long as you don't confuse the two, you'll be fine—know what I mean?

WING (*laughs*): Oh you're a real expert, aren't you, Kam?

KAM (*a casual wave of the hand*): Ah, I don't trust any woman. I don't let 'em get the better of me. If you're smart, you won't either. You gotta keep your knuckle on 'em. Don't take any chances. When you see a woman cry that's a sign of surrender. She'll be like that piece of wood in your hand. You can carve her into any shape you desire. (WING *laughs with disdain.*) She'll worship you like Jesus.

WING (*laughing*): You're full of dung!

KAM: Hey take it from me! I know what I'm talking about. Every woman wants you to suck her dainty earlobes. She wants you to caress her creamy thighs and pinch her nipples till she cries with pain. And when you bite those tiny dewdrop feet with your teeth, she'll ache with such pleasure, she'll think she was just born! She'll arch her back up in a half-moon and that's when you'll know, the gate of heaven is open. She's ready for you to plunge into the heart of the flower. (*with a big self-satisfied sigh*) The secret of seduction, according to the analects of Master Kama Sutra, is mystification. (*both are laughing conspiratorially*) Now how about it, country poke? (*lascivious grin*) Ready to dip your brush?

WING (*shaking his head nervously*): No.

KAM: You turnip, I give you one month before you come sweating!

WING (*stubbornly*): Not me, I'm no red lotus-chaser!

KAM (*with knowing certainty*): We'll see about that, Chinaboy. Anyone who whittles the way you do has got to have an itch! (*laughs*) (*Fade out.*)

Scene Four

(*Night time. Cicadas. Outside* LI-TAI'S *cabin. There is the sound of a couple's laughter from inside. The two men, outside, are hiding behind bushes, spying.* LAU *joins them unnoticed.*)

WING (*anxiously*): What if he doesn't leave?

KAM: Then you go and knock.

WING (*nervously*): What do I say?

KAM (*impatiently*): Why does a man go to a woman in the middle of the
night? You don't have to say nothin,' stupid!

WING (*misgivings*): Maybe we should go.

KAM (*irate*): You think we walked three miles for nothin'? You crazy!

WING (*nervous*): Maybe this isn't such a good idea.

KAM: Shoot! I do it all the time. The lunas, they know we sneak away. They
turn the other way. It just makes their job easier, that's all.
(*craning to see*) I wonder who's in there with her?

WING: It sounds like a man's voice!

KAM: Oh, you don't say?

(*Lights off on two men and up on* FOOK *and* LI-TAI *in bed,
drinking. He is slightly intoxicated. The room is lit by a single
kerosene lamp.*)

FOOK (*stroking her in pleased tones*): You have the body of a virgin. Tight and
firm as a stalk of cane. No one would suspect you were
over thirty-five.

LI-TAI: I'm not.

FOOK (*grinning possessively*): You can't keep secrets from me, Li-Tai.

LI-TAI: Did you bring me a treat today?

FOOK: I'm going to wind up in the poorhouse over you, Li-Tai!

LI-TAI: Come on, give Li-Li some candy!

FOOK (*reaches into the pocket of his garment at bedside and takes out an envelope, which he reluctantly hands her*): That's all you get.
(*She grabs the envelope.*)

LI-TAI: My delicious poppy!

FOOK (*shaking his head*): My poor little slave! (*he slowly gets dressed and out of
bed*) What will become of you?

LI-TAI (*annoyed*): Why do you always talk to yourself?

FOOK (*defensively*): I take good care of you Li-Tai. If it wasn't for me, you'd
be stuck in a brothel. You should be grateful.

LI-TAI: Shall I get on my hands and knees?

FOOK: Is that the position you like? (*matter-of-factly*) Do you have my
money?
(*She crosses to the drawer and takes out some money, which she
hands to a suspicious* FOOK.)

FOOK: Is that all?

LI-TAI (*nervously*): Business is slow.

FOOK: You're smoking up my profits.

LI-TAI (*turns her back*): Don't start!

FOOK: Then be straight with me!

LI-TAI: I want a cicada.

FOOK: What? Another damn cicada? What happened to the last one?

LI-TAI: It died.

FOOK: I despise those ugly insects!

LI-TAI (*sadly holds the empty cage up*): That's all I have.

FOOK (*amused*): You're such a child, Li-Tai. (*he tries to kiss her, but she turns her cheek*) You enjoy wearing me down, don't you? Don't you?

LI-TAI (*wearily*): Shouldn't you be going?

FOOK (*aroused*): I ought to turn you over my knees and spank you. Do you realize that in another year, I'll have enough to buy some land of my own? The rest of these coolies don't have the smarts to do anything but smoke and gamble. They have no ambition. They'll never make a cent because they're not willing to invest time to make money. Not me. Sugar is a good cash crop and prices are climbing. Soon I'll be a planter, not a luna. I'll have my own plantation and I'll hire my own men. We'll have money enough so you won't have to sleep with anyone but me. (*possessively*) I hate the thought of other men touching you. Especially Kam. You're not seeing that scoundrel anymore, are you? (*she shakes her head; he speaks desiringly*) You're spoiled. French perfume, cigarettes, silk stockings . . . in the middle of nowhere. You fancy yourself a lady, don't you, Li-Tai?

LI-TAI: I have my ways. (*to herself*) Sometimes I wonder which is more oppressive—the heat of the sun or the lust of a man.

FOOK: You know you couldn't survive here without me, Li-Tai. Don't forget where you were when I rescued you. You didn't have one decent outfit to your name and you were frail as a bean thread. It was easy as picking fruit off the ground. If I hadn't taken you, you would have rotted. (*pauses*) We'll be loading the mules tomorrow . . . I'll be back Sunday. (*pinches her cheek*) Be nice.

LI-TAI: Bring my cicada!

FOOK (*annoyed*): I'm jealous. (*with amusement*) Imagine that! Jealous of a cicada! A damned cicada. (*He exits.*)

(*The porch door opens slightly.*)

KAM: Look, someone's coming!

WING: Can you see who?

KAM: Shh.

(*The* CHINESE LUNA *stumbles out drunk and leaves in the darkness.*)

KAM: It's that sonuvabitch Fook Ming! (*under his breath*) That no-good

416

bitch! She goes for that stuffed cock. (*pushes* WING *toward
the door*) Go on, now's your chance!

WING (*resisting*): Don't push me!

KAM: You got cold feet?

WING: I just don't like to be pushed.

KAM: Alright, all right. (*starts to leave*)

WING: Hey, where you going?

KAM: To see somebody.

WING: Yeah? Who?

KAM (*giving him the nod*): What are you waiting for? Someone to take you
by the hand? (*reassuringly*) Okay, I'll wait till you go in.

WING (*pats* KAM *on shoulder*): Thanks Kam.

KAM: Remember, take your time, kid. Take a deep breath. Remember what
I told you! (*he watches* WING *approach her door*) And don't
forget to tell her who sent you!
(*Light fades on* KAM. WING *takes a deep breath and knocks.*)

LI-TAI (*calling from inside*): Who is it?

WING (*clearing his throat*): My name is Wing Chun . . . Kuo.
(*The light inside the cabin comes up as* LI-TAI *slowly opens the
door. She motions him to enter. He stands there awkwardly.*)

LI-TAI (*stares at him with immediate recognition*): You?

WING (*captivated*): I hope it's not too late.

LI-TAI (*glancing around nervously*): I thought I heard voices. (*returning curiously to* WING) You new?

WING: Yes. Three weeks.

LI-TAI: Hoi-ping?

WING (*surprised*): Yes. How did you know?

LI-TAI (*matter-of-factly*): By the way you talk.

WING (*impressed*): You're clever.

LI-TAI (*examining him*): You're good-looking. You look mixed.

WING: I'm Chinese, same as you. I was the best farmer back home.

LI-TAI: I believe it. (*looks at his hands*) Are you good with your hands?

WING (*surprised*): Yes. I can carve things.

LI-TAI (*impressed*): Ah, an artist! (*sounding his name*) Wing Chun. My name
is Li-Tai.

WING: Li-Tai. That's pretty. (*pauses*) Where you from?

LI-TAI (*abruptly*): Look. I know you're not here to gossip. You have two dollars?
(*He fumbles in his pocket and without looking hands her several bills. She smirks at his naivete and quickly tucks it in her
kimono pocket.*)

417

LI-TAI: Sit down.
> (*He sits.*)

LI-TAI: Want something to drink?

WING: Some tea would be nice, thank you.

LI-TAI (*amused laugh*): Tea? How old are you?

WING: Twenty.

LI-TAI (*frowning*): You're lying.

WING (*embarrassed*): Sixteen.

LI-TAI: This your first time?
> (*He nods with embarrassment. She takes a whiskey bottle, uncorks it, pours a glass, and hands it to him.*)

LI-TAI: Drink it. It'll give you confidence.
> (*He takes a big swallow and chokes. She laughs at him.*)

LI-TAI: Slow down. What's your hurry? (*smiling*) Talk to me.

WING (*still embarrassed*): About what?

LI-TAI: About you.

WING (*blushing*): There's not much to tell.

LI-TAI: Why not?

WING (*takes a gulp, then blurts*): My name is Wing and I like to eat duck gizzards.
> (*She bursts out laughing, then he laughs, too.*)

WING: On the first day of school, I remember the teacher asked us to introduce ourselves.

LI-TAI: And that was what you said.

WING: I couldn't think of anything else!

LI-TAI (*mockingly*): You still can't.

WING (*frustrated*): I don't know why I'm so tongue-tied. (*finishes his glass*)

LI-TAI: Talking is not important. (*refills his glass*) There are other ways to communicate. (*pours herself one, clicks his glass, then slumps on the bed with her glass in a provocative manner*) Your parents have a bride picked out for you yet?

WING: No. (*pauses*) My parents are dead.

LI-TAI: I'm sorry.

WING: My father died here. At Kahuku.

LI-TAI: Oh? (*surprised*) What was his name?

WING: Lau Hing. Kuo Lau Hing.
> (*She freezes at the recognition of his name.*)

WING: He was one of those Sandalwood boys who never made it back.

LI-TAI (*trembling*): How old were you when he left?

WING: I was just a baby.
> (*Struck by the resemblance, she cups his face with her hands.*)

LI-TAI: Let me look at you!

WING (*embarrassed*): What's the matter? Why are you looking at me like that?

LI-TAI (*marveling*): You remind me of someone.

WING: I'm as good as any man on Kahuku.

LI-TAI (*disdainfully*): The average man here is a pig. You don't want to be like them, do you?

WING: One flop in the family is enough. It's no secret. Lau Hing was a bum.

LI-TAI: How can a son talk about his own father in that way?

WING: And how can a father treat his family that way? Why should I pretend he was somebody he wasn't? (*somberly*) He was nobody to me. Nothing.

LI-TAI (*stung with guilt*): Your mother? She loved him?

WING (*disgustedly*): She died. He lied to her. He lied to her every month for two years! When he got tired of lying, he stopped writing altogether. She didn't hear from him again. Then one day, she gets this letter saying he's dead. (*bitterly*) You want to know what killed him? (*pauses*) Opium. The money he should have sent home, he squandered on himself! (*pauses*) They shipped his trunk back. She thought it was his bones. When she opened it, she fainted. The box was empty except for his hat and a few personal belongings. His body was never recovered they said, because he had drowned in the ocean. (*with cruel irony*) That's why I'm here. To redeem a dead man.

LI-TAI: You think you'll succeed?

WING: I'm not sending my ghost in an empty box home. Life is too short! (*listening to the sound of rain*) It's raining again.

LI-TAI: It's always raining. There's no escape. (*with a sense of foreboding*) You do what you can to forget. And survive. (*picks up a fan and begins moodily fanning herself*) I can't decide what's more boring. Living out here in the middle of nowhere or raising chickens in a puny plot back home.

WING: Why did you come here?

LI-TAI: A lady in the village told me that Hawai'i was paradise. She said there was hardly anything to do there but suck on big, fat, juicy sugarcane—sweeter than honey. I was crazy for cane and waited for the day to come here. When my mother died, my father remarried. My new mother didn't like a girl with bound feet who talked back. So I told her to send

419

me to Hawai'i. She sold me to a rich old merchant on the Big Island. I cried and begged to go back home. But I was his number four concubine. His favorite. Four is a bad luck number. So when the old man suffered a stroke in my bedroom, they, of course, blamed it on me. Number one wife, who was always jealous of me, picked up my red slippers and threw them at my face. Then she beat me with a bamboo rod and called me a good-for-nothing slave girl! (*laughs bitterly*) They lit firecrackers when Fook Ming took me. To rid my evil spirit. Some paradise. (*moved by* WING'S *look of compassion*) Tell me, what do they say about me?

WING (*blushing*): Who?

LI-TAI: The men. What do the men say about Li-Tai?

      (LAU HING *crosses from the wing toward* LI-TAI.)

WING: Nothing, (*admiringly*) Just that you're beautiful.

LAU (*passionately*): You're beautiful!

      (LI-TAI *turns and sees* LAU.)

LI-TAI: Who sent you here?

WING: No one, I swear!

LI-TAI (*frightened by* LAU'S *apparition*): Why do you come? (*cautiously*) What do you want from me?

WING (*apologetic and earnest*): I came to you because I need a woman.

LAU (*echoing simultaneously*): I came to you because I need a woman.

LI-TAI (*scornfully*): How much is your pleasure worth? Two dollars? All the money you have?

WING (*ardently*): Everything!

LAU: Everything!

LI-TAI (*with a nervous laugh*): So you need a woman. But not just any woman? (*crosses to a table and lights a candle in a glass holder*) You want one with experience? One who can guide you into manhood? (*puts out the kerosene lamp, picks up the candle, and turns to him*) Someone who can open your eyes and wipe the clouds from them. (*crosses to him*) Because you're not a little boy anymore. (*continues her cross to the bed*) And Mama can't help you. (*places candle on bedside table, then lies down*) But I can. (*coyly*) Come here.

      (*He takes a nervous breath and crosses to her. He halts in front of her.* LAU *turns and watches them.*)

LI-TAI: Are you afraid of me?

      (*She reaches for him and pulls him down to his knees. She puts his hand to her face and he slowly strokes her cheek as if dis-*

covering a woman's skin for the first time. He continues touching and stroking her face, neck, arms, and shoulders, gently and innocently.)

LI-TAI: You're pure as the lily's hidden leaf. (*gazing intently at him*) I see little torches flickering in your eyes!

WING (*with nervous passion*): They burn for you.

LI-TAI: You should stay away from fire.

WING: Why? We sacrifice to the gods with fire.

LI-TAI: Forget the gods. There's only you and I here. And the huge ocean, which surrounds us.

(She pulls him to her. She takes his hands and examines them as if remembering something from the past. She gently presses them to her cheeks. Then she pulls him alongside her on the bed. He removes her embroidered slippers, gently, then caresses her feet. LAU approaches the pair, mesmerized.)

WING: Does that feel good? (*she moans softly*) They're so tiny.

LI-TAI (*sighs*): Oh your hands . . . they feel like water!

LAU (*echoing*): . . . they feel like water!

LI-TAI (*matter-of-factly*): I'm made for pleasure. Not marriage. Family, cooking, raising babies. I wouldn't be good for that. (*a sad laugh*) I'm only good for one thing. (*provocatively*) And you, what are you good for?

(He kisses her feet. By now, LAU is standing a short distance from the couple, watching and experiencing every nuance of gesture as if reliving it. She leans over and unfastens his shirt. She takes in his young torso and gently runs her fingers over him. He takes her fingertips and gently bites them. She withdraws her hands, unloosens the kimono around her shoulders till it reveals her nakedness. LAU HING moves in closer to watch. WING reaches to touch her, but she coyly pulls away and re-covers herself with the kimono. He pulls her to him and pulls open her kimono as if unveiling a miracle. Struck by this first experience of womanly beauty, he stares in awe of her.)

LAU (*passionately*): You're beautiful!

(WING takes her into his arms. We hear the pounding rain amid her soft moans as they kiss. Fade out.)

Scene Five

(Downstage left.)

LAU: "When a dog comes, then riches . . . When a pig comes, then woes . . . When a cat comes, run quickly . . . And buy mourning

421

clothes." *(whittles with a carving knife the final touches to a puppet as he speaks)* Chance. Everything, chance! Every gambler knows it. Every farmer knows it. If nature's not with you, you're just out of luck. One flood can wipe your field clean; one disease can finish you off. You see the cane? They grow straight and tall against the wind. Just give them plenty of sunshine and water. But if blight comes *(indicating, with stylized gestures, the puppet's futile struggle with supernatural forces),* there's nothing can save it. *(to the puppet)* It's the hand of Yuk Wong Dai Dei. Heaven and earth. No man on earth can stop him. If a man does you wrong you can kill him. But once cane rot sets in, who do you blame?
(Fade out.)

Scene Six

(The next morning. LI-TAI *awakens beside* WING. *She contemplates his slumbering face. She raises her hand lovingly to stroke his features but refrains to keep from disturbing him. She throws on a light robe and climbs out of bed.* WING *stirs.)*

WING *(looks around, disoriented, then horrified):* Oh my god, it's morning! How could I fall asleep! *(gets up and starts frantically putting on his clothes)* I gotta get back.

LI-TAI *(calmly):* Wait. I'll fix breakfast. You can't work on an empty stomach.

WING: Next time.

LI-TAI *(resolutely):* Maybe there won't be a next time.

WING *(confused):* I don't understand.

LI-TAI *(a bit forcefully):* Stay here.

WING: I can't. *(reassuringly)* Look, I'll be back.

LI-TAI *(skeptically):* When?

WING: Next Saturday?

LI-TAI *(demanding):* Tomorrow!

WING *(embarrassed):* I-I . . . can't afford . . .

LI-TAI *(offended):* I won't take your money. I don't want it. Just don't treat me like some whore.

WING *(taking her by the shoulder):* What's gotten into you?

LI-TAI *(pulling away):* You tell me. *(sarcastically)* You're a man. Oh what's the use! The sun flattens down on you like an iron and all you can do is lie there and whimper. *(a sigh of disgust)* Some paradise.

WING: You give in to bitterness.

LI-TAI: They said, "You will never want to leave!" *(with bitter irony)* I never asked to come. *(reminiscing)* I was only twenty when I came to Kahuku . . . *(turning away from him)* . . . and the easy life. I've been here too long! *(gesturing at the landscape)* Like those mountains that never move. *(thinking aloud)* What do you think happens to us when we die?

WING *(decisively):* We go on living in the afterlife.

LI-TAI: No we don't. We wither and die.

WING: Don't you believe in immortality?

LI-TAI *(firmly):* No.

WING: Everything lives in the soul.

LI-TAI: Everything dies in the heart.

WING: That's not Chinese!

LI-TAI: Maybe I'm not Chinese.

WING: Don't you believe in fate?

LI-TAI: No.

WING: Why not?

LI-TAI: Because fate is destiny. I don't believe in destiny. It's our own hand that pulls us down, not some god's. We answer to ourselves.

WING: I don't know about that . . . *(romantically)* I was lying in the dark, unable to sleep, so I listened to sounds. The soft feet of rain, the rustling of boughs and leaves, ten thousand voices of crickets . . . I heard the grass talk to the wind. I heard the cicada's song.

LI-TAI *(amused):* What did it sing?

WING: It sang good evening to the stars.

LI-TAI: And what did the stars answer?

WING: The stars answered that they were lonely.

LI-TAI: Why were they lonely?

WING: Because they shined alone in the sky.

LI-TAI *(laughing):* Did they sing in Chinese?

WING: In a language beyond words. Did you ever try, when you were a kid, to pick out one star in the sky, then try to find that same star the next night? You can't. But you keep looking anyhow. When I first looked at you, I had this feeling fate brought us together. *(looks at her meaningfully)* Things happen for a reason.

LI-TAI: I don't believe that. Things just happen. We make them happen. We stumble into traps. We live, we die.

WING *(intrigued):* You're not like the women back home.

LI-TAI: They all think like one person. The young girls talk like old women and the old women are ignorant and superstitious. In China you're born old before you can walk. As a woman you're allowed to do only one thing. Please men. I've spent my whole life doing that! *(matter-of-factly)* You see this body? It's not mine. It belongs to Kahuku Plantation. My skin even smells like burnt cane!

WING: And what about your heart?

LI-TAI: I cut it out. Long ago.

WING: Then what was it I felt last night? *(with certainty)* I've known you before.

LI-TAI: Last night I was drunk! So were you. *(begins primping before the mirror)* What happened to all the years? I look in the mirror and count each new gray hair. *(sadly)* Time has no respect for a woman.

WING *(looking at her reflection from behind):* You have a beautiful face, a true face. With features that sing. *(tenderly)* Your brows describe the mists of Kweilin.

LI-TAI *(laughs):* What do my wrinkles reveal?

WING: The soft rays of the moon.

LI-TAI: A waning moon?

WING: No. A full one. *(dramatically)* I was reborn last night.

LI-TAI *(laughing):* Don't make me laugh.

WING: I mean it. *(puts his arms shyly around her)*

LI-TAI: Don't be foolish. *(scoffing)* I'm old enough to be your mother!

WING: The soul has no age.

LI-TAI *(sighs):* You remind me of a man I loved fifteen years ago.

WING: Who was that?

LI-TAI *(elusively):* A man who was a cicada. *(thoughtfully)* Did you know the cicada dies after he mates?

WING *(optimistically):* Yes, but he is resurrected from the grave he leaves behind.

> (WING *kisses her, then exits. A spot on* LAU, *kneeling in the cabin. He is folding a red Chinese robe in a ceremonial manner. She gives a start. Fade out).*

Scene Seven

(Break time. Several weeks have passed. KAM *enters mopping the sweat off his face as he puts down his machete.* WING *follows exhausted and lays his machete down.* KAM *ladles some water from a barrel for himself, then for* WING.)

WING: Thanks for covering me.

KAM: Sonuvabitch! Is it her again? How can you afford to go so much?

WING *(worried):* What did you tell the boss?

KAM *(facetiously):* I said you were in the outhouse with diarrhea.

WING *(gloomily):* Very funny.

KAM: I'm not covering for you anymore. I'm warning you!

WING: Okay, okay! *(nervously)* What do you know about Li-Tai?

KAM *(suspiciously):* Why?

WING *(with a deep breath):* I want to marry her.

KAM *(shocked):* You're joking! *(contemptuously)* She's a prostitute.

WING: Different flowers have a way with different eyes. *(defensively)* Besides, you said yourself some of the men marry prostitutes.

KAM *(angrily):* Listen, kid, you don't know what you're talking about. You don't go marry the first prostitute you jump in bed with. That's crazy! Soak your head in cold water and get back to the fields. *(nastily)* Did she tell you who she is?

WING: I don't care about the past.

KAM: Oh you don't, do you? Did she tell you she's Fook Ming's concubine? Huh? Did she tell you how he keeps her in that cabin all to himself? How he visits her on Sundays and Mondays? How the rest of the week he sets her up with the men?

WING *(stubbornly):* I don't care about him.

KAM *(shaking his head):* You're not the first you know. Don't think you're the only one who's tried. *(nastily)* More men have crawled into Li-Tai's bed than lice. They don't call her "The Cocoon" for nothing. She's used up. You stay away. I'm telling you, she's no good. She's poison. *(shaming him)* What would your parents think? You chasing after a slut?

WING *(grabs KAM angrily by the collar):* Don't call her names, you hear me? You're jealous because you want her too!

KAM *(confessing guiltily):* That's right. I want her too. I'd be lying if I said I didn't.

WING: Are you in love with her?

KAM *(angrily):* What man around here isn't in love with Li-Tai? What man here doesn't want her? The question is what man is crazy enough to give everything up for her?

WING: I am.

KAM *(sighs):* I know. That's what worries me. *(pauses)* You don't know the danger you're in. I seen one fella waste himself over her. He was a top cutter too. The best on Kahuku. Worked like the devil to buy her off Fook Ming, but when she re-

425

fused him, he went mad. He deserted one night, went to her cabin, but she just laughed at him. He couldn't take it. Went completely insane. Poor Lau Hing.

WING *(paling)*: Lau Hing Kuo?

KAM *(surprised)*: Yeah, that was his name. Did you know him?

WING *(softly)*: He was my father.

KAM *(hits himself in the head)*: I talk too much.

WING: Then my father never went back to China because of her?

KAM *(shaking his head)*: Li-Tai bewitched him. He was so heart-broken, he killed himself.

WING *(with shame)*: If it's true, then I should hate her.

KAM *(gravely)*: It's true. Everybody knows about Li-Tai and your father.

> (LAU *crosses behind* WING. WING *stands there frozen in utter disbelief and shock.* KAM *shakes his head desparingly.*)

KAM: You ask me, you've jumped from the net into the frying pan! When you think of what you left to come here, it makes no damn difference. Back home you'd plow the field and pray for rain. Even though you might not eat, at least it's your land. Here, you don't starve, but you work like an ox for some other sonuvabitch's land. Not only that, you don't live like a normal man. *(with indignation)* Look at me, I should be married by now. I should have a wife to screw. I should have a roomful of kids to take care of me in my old age. Instead I waste my time gambling, smoking opium, and falling in love with prostitutes. Like Li Tai.

(Fade out.)

Scene Eight

(The magical song of a flute fills the air. On stage right, LAU is on his hands and knees stalking a cicada. At his side are LI-TAI's cricket cage and his wrapped bundle. He mimes catching the insect and carefully putting it in the cage, eyeing it with fascination. As the light comes up on the men stage left, LAU sits back in reverie, listening to the cicada's song. It is three months later on the plantation. The men are bedraggled from a long day of cane loading. WING ladles water into tin cups for each of them.)

KAM *(massaging his aching shouder as he grumbles)*: God sits on his holy ass, while we labor like ants! If we die, who cares? *(with disgust)* Look at this hand! Can't even grip the machete. Can't even hold a pair of chopsticks, it's so swollen. *(trying to make a fist to curse the sky)* I may be an insignificant speck, but I got some feelings! (*mopping his forehead with his sleeve*) There must be all of ten suns out there! Each one burns hotter then the rest. We're ants pushing crumbs. No matter how many rows we level, we're always behind. The cane's as endless as sky. (*observing the sullen, hard-working* WING) Except you, you're inhuman. You blast through that jungle like you got a bee up your ass. You got endurance, Wing, but you also got no consideration. (*a warning tone*) Making it hard on the rest of us, you know? No one can pair up with you! They say you cut ahead and cause their cane to fall. (*with begrudging admiration*) You hit the stalk, it falls. Other fellas hit five, six times, it just shakes. You got one swift machete—like you been born to it. You gonna make me lose face, little brother! (*scolding*) All work and no play's unnatural, Wing. Go to town. Relax. (*raising an eyebrow*) Meet some new friends, yeah? (*pauses*) Come with me tonight! There's some tall, yellow-haired wahine with mango breasts and asses like bread-fruit. Lots of huluhulu. Hairy legs are beastly.

WING (*disinterested*): You go ahead, Kam.

KAM (*exasperated*): Goddam, Wing, Li-Tai's not the only woman in the world! You'd think she was Kwan Yin on earth! There's lots more where she comes from. She's common as opihi!

WING (*spins around with fists clenched*): Shut your mouth or I'll kill you!

KAM (*holding his arms up to protect himself*): Hold it, boy! I'm only trying to help. I was the one who introduced you to her! (*guiltily*) That's why I feel responsible. That's why when the fellas talk, I'm the one who defends you.

WING (*annoyed*): Why should you defend me?

KAM: They say things about you and her.

WING: What do I care what those bastards say?

KAM: They say, "Like father, like son."

WING (*with angry suspicion*): How do they know Lau's my father? I never told anyone. (*grabbing him angrily by the collar*) Except you.

KAM (*uneasily*): Maybe she told them!

WING (*threatening*): You're lying!

KAM (*a matter-of-fact confession*): Anyhow they were bound to find out, even if I didn't tell. (*struggling free*) Since you came along, she's stopped seeing anybody else. (*pauses*) They say you cursed her.

427

WING (*confused*): What the hell are you talking about?

KAM: Li-Tai is fading. She's an opium eater. You haven't been over there, have you? (*no reply*) She's consumed. She's wasted to nothing. The same way your father did. They say you caused it, to avenge him. I told them they were crazy. Fook's the one who's no good. He's the haoles' bootlicker. He's turned her into a ghost.

(FOOK MING *enters, crossing to* WING.)

FOOK: You fellas did decent work. I'm gonna let you off early this afternoon to make up for last night.

BOTH MEN (*mechanically*): Thank you. (*Both men turn to go.*)

FOOK: Oh, Wing. (WING *remains*) I been watching you. You're strong worker. In fact, one of the best cutters Kahuku's ever had. I like the way you go about your business. No funny stuff. Not like the others. I have to ride whip on 'em to keep 'em awake. You don't give me problems. You're solid, steady. No tricks. The big boss likes you. I like you too. (*studying* WING) I want you to be my back-up boy. You get a raise from three to four dollars a month. You keep the men in line, you see to it the harvest is in on time. Can you handle it?

WING (*with mechanical politeness*): Yes sir.

FOOK: Good. I think I can trust you. (*confidentially*) Let me warn you. Once you leave China, it's every Chinaman for himself. The minute you turn your back, there's always someone in the shadow, waiting to stick a knife in you. I would be careful of my friends if I were you. That Kam is a troublemaker. Friendship runs thin with him. Take it from me, the only real thing here . . . (*drops a silver dollar at* WING's *foot*) . . . is this.

(*Fade out.*)

Scene Nine

(*Nighttime. The song of a cicada fills the silence.* LI-TAI *is lying on the bed in an opium stupor. There is a loud knocking on the door. It is* WING *returning after an absence.* LI-TAI *appears oblivious to the noise, but the banging continues.*)

LI-TAI (*shouting*): Go away! Go away!

(*The door opens.* WING *stands in the doorway staring, shocked at the spectacle of* LI-TAI *in her degenerated, euphoric state. She does not appear aware of his presence.*)

WING: Li-Tai!
> (*She recognizes his voice but doesn't stir.*)

WING: It's me, Wing. (*approaching tentatively*) I hear you're sick.

LI-TAI (*to herself*): Three months.

WING (*confessing*): I tried to put you out of my mind.

LI-TAI: Who are you?

WING (*bewildered at her unkempt state*): What's happened to you? Why are you doing this?

LI-TAI: What are you doing here?

WING (*with resolve*): I want to know something. (*demanding*) I need to know.
> (*She absently picks up the pipe.*)

WING: You knew he was my father.

LI-TAI (*distractedly*): What are you talking about?

WING (*impatient*): Quit pretending. Lau Hing Quo. I told you he was my father! (*seizes the pipe violently*)

LI-TAI (*grabbing for the pipe*): Give me that!
> (*He jerks it away from her.*)

LI-TAI: Damn you, give it to me!

WING (*accusatory*): You were my father's lover, weren't you?

LI-TAI (*evasively*): I had many lovers!

WING (*resentfully*): Then he never meant anything to you, did he? You used him. (*hurt*) The same way you used me. (*rage mounting*) You knew he was my father, but you didn't care. I told you who my father was and yet you made love to me. How could you? What kind of a woman are you?

LI-TAI (*coldly*): You're not man enough to know.

WING: You bitch! (*slaps her on the cheek and then is stunned by his own violence*) I-I never hit a woman before!

LI-TAI (*evenly*): Lau Hing never hit me.

WING (*jealously*): How else was my father better than me?

LI-TAI (*acidly*): He knew how to treat a woman.

WING (*grabs the pipe and plays a sadistic keep-away with her*): How badly do you want this? Enough to inch over here on your belly? Show your true self, Li-Tai! Show me your white belly! Show me how you can crawl. (*sadistically*) CRAWL! I want you to crawl to me! (*tormenting*) Tell me, lizard woman, I want to know! (*with increasing cruelty*) Tell me how he treated you! (*grabbing her by the hair*) Was he better than me, huh?
> (*She fights her tears.*)

429

WING: Or have you already forgotten? (*lets go of her in disgust, snaps the pipe in two*) Here, bitch! (*throws it on the floor*)
(*She crawls to the broken pipe.*)

WING: Why don't you kill yourself. Get it over with!

LI-TAI (*demanding*): No, you kill me! Kill me! That's what you want, isn't it? (*picks up the broken pipe and stares absently at it*) I waited. I left the porch light on. I listened for your footsteps, your knock. I didn't sleep or eat. All I heard was the cicada. And the wind. Then it struck me that all my life I have done nothing but wait for a man. I waited for your father. And I waited for you.

WING (*accusatory*): You killed him!

LI-TAI (*with a sad laugh*): He wanted to marry me. (*cynically*) What kind of a future would we have had? A plantation runaway and a pei-pa girl?

WING: He was obsessed with you.

LI-TAI: He was obsessed with escaping.

WING: You were his dream. He betrayed everything for you.

LI-TAI: Go ahead and believe what you want. What does it matter now? (*listening*) Did you know if there was no sound, there would be nothing to measure time? Sometimes everything becomes so still, even the heart stops beating. Your mind just crawls inside itself like a hole.

WING (*bitterly*): For you he destroyed mother.

LI-TAI: He never loved her.

WING: You're spiteful. Hateful.

LI-TAI: I thought you were different. But you're not. If I'm spiteful and hateful, it's because you men made me this way. Lau was kind. I thought you were too. But you're cruel. Lau understood me, because he was different too. He had mixed blood. It runs in you too. They called him Heungsan Jai, "Sandalwood Boy," from Sandalwood Mountains. (*pauses*) I knew you were your father's son before you even told me. His face was etched on yours. You came in from his shadow.

WING: My father would have gone back, if it wasn't for you.

LI-TAI (*sadly*): You hate me, don't you? Don't you think I've suffered? How can you be so righteous? So sure of me. It wasn't because of me. It was your family. Lau swore he'd never go back. They treated him like dirt!

WING: Stop lying!

LI-TAI: Your grandfather brought a Hawaiian mistress back with him to China and she died shortly after giving birth to your father. When your grandfather died, the property was divided, and your father was cheated out of his share of land. Because he was a half-breed. Lau's marriage was arranged by a relative he barely knew. He never loved your mother. Lau loved me!

WING (*yelling*): Shut up!

LI-TAI: Look at yourself in the mirror, "Sandalwood Boy"! Find what's missing!

WING (*snatches the broken pipe and violently hurls the pieces against the wall*): SHUT UP! SHUT UP! (*jealously*) He still haunts you.

LI-TAI: He's dead.

WING: Tell me one thing. I've got to know. Do you love me, Li-Tai? Or is it my father you love?

LI-TAI: When you didn't come, I wanted to die. Is that love?

WING: Answer me!

LI-TAI: I love you.

WING: When I came here, I wanted to kill you. I wanted to hurt you. Then I took one look at you and I knew I couldn't pretend. I can't hate you, Li-Tai. (*pauses*) Give this up!

LI-TAI: I can't.

WING: Give up Fook Ming!

LI-TAI (*with a bitter laugh*): Fook Ming is impotent. I give him the illusion of virility. For that he pays me.

WING (*indicating her state*): This is how he pays you!

LI-TAI: It's my choice.

WING: Leave him.

LI-TAI: Don't be foolish.

WING: I'll leave Kahuku and take you with me. We'll go to Honolulu.

LI-TAI: Look at me! I'm not a young woman.

WING: You're scared. Everyone on this plantation is scared!

LI-TAI: Yes I am. I look in the mirror, but the lines and shadows don't go away. I think I'm looking at a stranger, then I realize the stranger is me. The young woman I thought I was is gone. Just a memory.

WING (*fervently*): If we can't change our past lives, then let us, at least, have our future! (*pauses*) Remember what I said about fate bringing us together? I believe it now more than ever.

LI-TAI (*trembling*): No.

WING: There's nothing to be afraid of. Trust me.

431

LI-TAI: It's too late.

WING: Don't you want to be happy?

LI-TAI: Happy? I thought only babies and idiots were happy!

WING: I'm good with my hands. I have skills. I can find a job in Honolulu. Back home, I carved the temple statues. I made Kwan Yin so beautiful, she brought tears to the villagers' eyes. My Kwan Kung was so fierce he frightened away temple thieves. If I can't do wood carving I can always farm. I heard about some rice farmers who are doing real well in marsh-land near Waikiki. And some taro planters in a valley called Manoa too. (*bitterly*) I can do more than cut cane!

LI-TAI (*worried*): What about Fook Ming?

WING: He won't be able to find us. We'll change our names and our family histories. We'll start all over.

LI-TAI (*thoughtfully*): I like that. I like the idea of starting over.

WING: I'll build you a house with twenty rooms and a courtyard with fruit trees and night-blooming jasmine. We'll plant seeds wher-ever we go and I'll carve the eight immortals over our front door so fate will smile upon us.

LI-TAI (*wistful*): You dream!

WING: I'll come for you on the ninth day of the ninth moon.

(*Lights fade on couple and light comes up on* LAU *with his bundle at his feet.*)

LAU: Everything can be understood in a moment, even if nothing is seen. (*holds up the red robe*) This robe belongs to someone on this side. I will take it to her. (*fondles the garment as if it were alive and makes the sleeves dance sensuously before his eyes*) Every night her empty robe dances in the wind and her sleeves get tangled in the boughs. The moon has just come to light her small house. (*he listens*) Listen to the wind. It's the only voice among the leaves. See how quiet the air has become! Darkness awaits her. (*he turns towards cabin*)

(*Fade out.*)

Scene Ten

(*Three weeks later in the heavy rain of the afternoon. Distant thunder.* LI-TAI *is packing. There is a knock on the door.*)

LI-TAI (*with nervous anticipation and indecision about what to do with the suit-case*): Wing?

(*The knocking continues. She quickly hides the suitcase under the bed, then opens the door. She is surprised to see a rain-soaked* KAM.)

LI-TAI: What are you doing here?

KAM (*awkwardly*): May I come in, Li-Tai?

LI-TAI: I thought I told you never to come back.

KAM (*with urgency*): It's important Li-Tai. It concerns you and Wing Chun.

LI-TAI (*suspiciously*): Come in.

(KAM *enters.*)

KAM (*brushing wet hair from his forehead*): Something has been bothering me. (*pauses*) I know the last time we left on bad terms. I have no hard feelings. I hope you don't either. (*groping*) After all, we're all Chinese, aren't we? We all came here for the same reason—why shouldn't we all get along and help each other?

LI-TAI: Get to the point, Kam.

KAM (*nervously*): Do you have some water?

LI-TAI (*pours him a glass*): Sit down.

KAM (*gulping gratefully*): Thank you. (*sits*) I want to apologize.

LI-TAI (*skeptical*): That's decent of you.

KAM: For those things I said to you. I've come to talk about you and Wing.

LI-TAI (*icily*): What concern is that of yours?

KAM: I only want to help, Li-Tai. (*rubbing his knees*) You don't know how hard it is for a man. Thousands of miles from home. Nothing to look at but field after rotten field of cane and empty sky. (*painfully*) You're a beautiful woman. Men fall in love with you. (*pauses*) It's no wonder Wing follows his father's footsteps . . .

LI-TAI (*upset*): I won't listen to this.

KAM: First Lau Hing, now Wing. Who next, Li-Tai?

LI-TAI: Get out!

KAM: Do you know that Wing is Lau Hing's son?

LI-TAI (*shaken*): Is this what you've come to tell me?

KAM: You must stop seeing Wing.

LI-TAI: You can't stop me!

KAM (*scrutinizing her*): It doesn't make a difference to you then? Why did you do it?

LI-TAI (*angrily*): You were the one who sent him here! Have you forgotten?

KAM (*defensively*): Do you think I'd be so vile as to do something like that if I'd known? I sent him as a gesture. A kind of peace of-

433

fering. I know I'm pretty low-down, but I'm not the devil. I don't play with the gods' rules, no more than I can change what's happened. (*pauses*) It's not for me to judge. That is up to heaven. (*pauses*) But think of what you're doing. Think! Wing wants to make good. Not like his father. In ten years he had gone from top cutter at Kahuku to a skeleton. (*pauses*) They blamed you for his suicide, Li-Tai.

(*Light on* LAU HING *standing in the plantation.*)

LI-TAI (*bitterly*): Of course. If a man is weak, it's the fault of the woman. Do you think I have the power to change men's lives? Am I the one who profits from the cane? Am I the one who put you here? Why don't you blame yourself? I'll tell you why. Because you're all scared! (*pauses*) At least Lau Hing had the guts to escape. (*painfully*) He deserted and came to me. He wanted me to run away with him. I refused. I was scared. Not him. He was ready to give up everything for his freedom. But I couldn't. (*ashamed*) I was a coward. What kind of a life would we have? Taking in laundry, shoveling horse dung, scrubbing white folks' dirt? I told him I wanted more than he could give. I told him I didn't want to see him anymore. (*pauses*) He stared at me as if I was mad. Then he left. I didn't see him again. (*pauses*) Then one day I was walking by the water ditch. I heard a moan. When I got close, I saw Lau Hing lying there on the ground . . .

(*A spot on* LAU *twisting the puppet's limbs as if trying to tear them apart. Then he drops the puppet in a fit of despair and gives a wrenching, soundless cry of pain.*)

LI-TAI (*distraught*): He was rolling in mud, kicking his feet up in the air and drooling like a baby. It was revolting! I turned and ran. I ran all the way home without stopping. I still can see him, lying there, vivid as ever. He disappeared soon after. They said he'd drowned himself. His body was never found.

(*Fade on* LAU *staring absently at the inert puppet.*)

KAM (*sadly*): One cannot trifle with the world. Lau failed his family. He failed you.

LI-TAI (*solemnly*): No. That's a lie. Lau didn't fail me. (*pauses*) I was the one who failed him. I promised to go with him, but in the end I didn't have the courage.

KAM: You were right not to go with him. What a fool!

LI-TAI: Even though I loved him, even though I wanted to, I couldn't face what was on the other side.

KAM: You've survived. That's enough.

LI-TAI: No, it isn't enough.

KAM: For godsakes, if I can stumble through the day half-awake, I'm ahead! The moment I'm awake, I'm pulled by the smell of cane and the lash of the whip. What choice do I have? I cut that cane and I don't ask questions. I get my four dollars and I spend it. That's life.

LI-TAI: No. Life is going after what you want, no matter what. (*pauses*) I was only six when my mother died. They led me to a small fire. I had to jump over for purification. But I was terrified. I screamed hysterically. I can still see their angry faces. (*pauses*) That day Lau insisted I run away with him to the mainland, I became terrified. The idea of freedom was as frightening as death.

KAM: The problem with you, Li-Tai, is you think too much. You should have been born a man.

LI-TAI: Men want to believe there's a difference between the way men and women think when there isn't.

KAM (*admonishing*): For a girl, to be without talent is itself a virtue.

LI-TAI (*curtly*): Virtue without talent is worthless. One may as well be an insect.

KAM (*amused*): I admire a headstrong woman. (*swallowing*) You've been through a lot. You don't need no more troubles. Neither do I. In nine months my contract will be up. Then I'll be a free man. (*building up courage*) I'm not a rich man. I'm not a young man, but I can take care of you. I can satisfy you . . . (*puts a nervous hand on her leg; she pulls away*) You won't even let me touch you! Do I repulse you? (*cruelly*) I bet you open up for the young ones . . . like Wing!

LI-TAI (*pulling away*): Get out!

KAM (*guiltily*): I'm sorry. I didn't mean it.

LI-TAI (*contemptuously*): You're wasting my time. Get out.

KAM (*rising*): I can give you a decent life. I can take you away from this. (*angrily*) What can that kid give you, huh? A grave in Kahuku? Is that what you want? Don't be stupid. You're no rosebud. Look at yourself.

(LAU *enters carrying the cricket cage in one hand and the red robe folded over his arm. He watches* LI-TAI *from across the room.*)

KAM: You're a stubborn woman, Li-Tai. (*pauses*) Good afternoon. (*bows stiffly*) Thanks for the water. This rain never lets up, does it? (*wipes his sweaty palms on his pants, then exits*)
(LI-TAI *crosses to the bed and pulls a suitcase out from underneath.* LAU *crosses with the bundle and folded kimono on top. She looks up, startled, at* LAU.)

LI-TAI: Lau Hing! Why are you here?

LAU: I've left Kahuku.

LI-TAI: You deserted.

LAU: You're coming with me, Li-Tai.

LI-TAI: I'm not going with you, Lau.

LAU: You promised.

LI-TAI: I've changed my mind.

LAU: Why?

LI-TAI: I'm a woman, Lau. There's nothing out there but desolation.

LAU: This life is good enough for you?

LI-TAI: What can you give me?

LAU (*presenting her with the bundle*): My soul.

LI-TAI (*terrified*): No!

LAU: You must return my bones. These bones are weary. They have waited so long for the earth. I have carried them all these years. An empty grave awaits me across the ocean. I cannot rest until these bones return to China. I must journey home. Come with me, Li-Tai. It is time. I have come to free you. I was a prisoner of Kahuku, just as you are. Now together we can walk through water and fire. (*extends his arms*) Come!

LI-TAI: I can't go with you Lau. (*with resolve*) I'm going with Wing!

LAU: Wing is my flesh. (*whispering*) He was sent here. You are the only one who can help him. Don't be afraid, Li-Tai! Trust me. Trust yourself. (*approaches her*) Remember the little girl? Go back to her. She needs you. Can't you hear her calling? You must save her. Jump! The flames won't hurt you. From water to fire. Jump! Over ocean into air. Reach! Into your heart. Into the heart of heaven. Redemption lies there. Li-Tai, come!
(LAU *hands her the bundle, which she accepts. He then removes the red robe on top and holds it up for her to wear. She crosses to him in trancelike submission. He helps her slowly and ceremoniously into the open fire robe. Fade out.*)

Scene Eleven

(*Outside* LI-TAI'S *cabin. Dusk.* WING *approaches with a hastily wrapped bundle thrown over his shoulder. He is suddenly cut off by* FOOK MING, *approaching from the opposite direction.*)

FOOK (*suspiciously*): You going someplace?

WING: I'm going to see Li-Tai.

FOOK: What are you doing with that goddam bundle? (*no reply*) Are you planning on going somewhere, Wing?

WING: Fook Ming, I don't want any trouble.

FOOK: Don't tell me you're running away? You've only been here a year!

WING: I can't finish my contract.

FOOK: Why, that's too bad. You have only four years to go. You owe Ka-huku thirteen hundred dollars for passage, room, and board.

WING: I will pay it back.

FOOK: You will pay it back. Right here on Kahuku! (*anger increasing*) Why did you stop here? (*yells*) Answer me, you sonuvabitch!

WING: I'm taking Li-Tai with me.

FOOK: Over my dead body. (*seething*) You think you can come here, still wet behind the ears and scheme for my woman behind my back?

WING: She doesn't love you.

FOOK (*exploding*): Li-Tai is mine! I own her. Every hair on her body, every inch of her flesh and bones is paid for in gold.

WING: You don't own her soul.

FOOK (*laughing uproariously*): So you, Wing Chun, have come to claim her soul, huh? What a hero. Too stupid to know you should never meddle with another man's property. It's a shame you have to learn the hard way. Because now, Wing boy . . . (*pulls out a knife*) . . . I will have to kill you! (*They struggle with the knife.* FOOK *is about to stab* WING, *when* KAM SU *suddenly appears and grabs* FOOK *from behind. The knife falls to the ground,* WING *seizes it.*)

FOOK (*desperately*): Don't do it, Wing. Don't kill me! Please! You won't get away with it. You'll hang! (*Just as* WING *is about to plunge the knife into* FOOK, WING *comes to his senses and drops the knife on the ground.* KAM *suddenly retrieves the knife and plunges it into* FOOK'S *belly.* FOOK

437

stares at him for one moment before he crumples and falls dead.)

KAM *(staring at the lifeless body)*: That's for every man who's died on Kahuku. For every goddam wasted life! *(to a shocked WING)* I know where you're going! You're making a mistake.

WING: I got nothing against you. Leave me alone.

KAM *(angrily)*: She was mine until you came along! *She was mine!!*

WING *(steadily)*: I don't want to fight you, Kam.

KAM *(with an ironical laugh)*: When my contract was up, I was going back to China. I was going to take her with me.

WING: She doesn't love you, Kam.

KAM: She would have come, if you hadn't spoiled everything! *(with growing desperation)* I know Li-Tai. She would have come with me. I know she would have!

WING *(trying to reason)*: You could come with us.

KAM *(deeply offended)*: I ought to kill you!

WING: You got one murder on your hands, Kam. You want another? Is it worth it?

KAM *(laughing bitterly)*: I'm a free man today. Do you know what that means? That means I can walk off this plantation and never look back. That means I can change my name and become a new man. Who knows? I might even get rich! *(reaches inside his pocket)* I got nothing holding me back! *(hysterically, he pulls out a fistful of coins, which spills onto the ground)* You see this money? I got more! I been saving for this day, kid! Look at me, look at me! Do I look like a Gold Mountain Boy? Do I look prosperous to you? *(pauses)* Or do I look like some dried-up sinner? *(throws the money on the ground as if it was dirt)* Take it! Take it! Take this dirty money! Take it!

WING: I can't take your money, Kam.

KAM *(commanding)*: Give it to her!

WING: She doesn't want it, either!

KAM *(suspiciously)*: You're speaking for her now, huh? *(a surly nod)* So that's the way it is. I might have known. *(confessing frankly)* I wanted to kill you and her. That's why I came. To put a stop to everything. But when I saw Fook, everything came to a head. I had to put a stop to everything. I had to. *(sincerely)* You understand? It had to be done. *(WING nods)* I don't want to know where you're going or what you're going to do. *(KAM turns to leave)*

WING: Where you going?

KAM *(stops to think):* Honolulu. I like the sound of that name. Ho-no-lu-lu. Sounds like a woman's name. Maybe I can start a gambling house there. *(grins)* Who knows?

WING *(shaking his head):* I don't understand you, Kam.

KAM *(with an ironic laugh):* I don't understand myself! *(an afterthought)* Oh, a word of advice. Watch out for the haoles if you go to Honolulu. They are a two-faced, cunning lot. I heard tell about a fella who bought a plot of land for a taro patch from some haoles. As it turned out, they didn't even own the land. It was owned by the Church. But by the time he found out, he had already planted and seeded the whole damn plot! So watch out. They'll crucify you.

WING: I will.

(They bow farewell to each other. KAM *runs off. Fade out.)*

Scene Twelve

*(*LI-TAI'S *cabin. Night. Cicadas.* LI-TAI *is dying. She is lying in bed in the red robe and* LAU'S *bundle is at her feet.)*

WING *(rushing over to her in alarm, taking her hands):* Li-Tai! Li-Tai!

LI-TAI *(very weakly):* Wing, I'm sorry. I can't go with you. There's little time.

WING *(determinedly):* I won't leave without you!

LI-TAI: You must. Or everything will have been a loss. I have a message for you. *(points to the bundle at her feet)* You must take this to Kwantung and bury it. They are the bones of your father. He gave them to me for safe burial. Lau died before he could fulfill his duty as a husband and father. Now you must complete his task. Now you are the keeper of his bones. Return home with them. Your father has waited a long time. *(squeezes his hand)* So have I. *(pauses)* Go home, Wing. Go home before it's too late.

WING *(desperately):* Don't leave me, Li-Tai, don't leave me!

LI-TAI: You were right from the first. We are old souls, you and I. Our destinies were locked. But now you have a chance to be free. Don't wander as your father and I did. Return these bones where they belong. They are part of you, Wing. Part of me. Home. I am ready to go home. Now. Home . . .

(She loses consciousness. Her fingers fall limp from his hands and she dies. WING *struggles against breaking down. Calmly,*

439

*he places one final kiss on her lips and covers her slowly with
the blanket. He turns his attention then to the bundle, lifts it
ceremoniously with the growing revelation of its intrinsic
meaning. He carries the bundle in his arms, as if it was alive,
outside. He stares sadly into the horizon. We hear the mournful melody of* KAM'S *voice from afar:)*

Hawaii, Hawaii
so far, far from home,
Hawaii, Hawaii
My bones ache and my heart breaks,
thinking about the one I left behind.

Hawaii, Hawaii
so far, far from home,
Hawaii, Hawaii
Don't let me die of misery.
Don't bury me under the cane fields
of Hawaii, Hawaii . . .

(Fade out.)

END OF PLAY

1989

TWO

Speeches and Performance Pieces

"Ain't I a woman?" Sojourner Truth (1797–1883) asked her primarily white, middle-class audiences as she toured the nation, gaining support for the abolitionist cause. If women are frail, then what gender is Sojourner Truth who, displaying a muscled bicep, demands: "Look at my arm! I have ploughed and planted, and gathered into barns, and no man could head me!" Mother of thirteen children, this woman exhorts with her voice and her body, forcing her listeners to reconsider definitions of "woman" and to reexamine the racial and gender assumptions that define "femininity" in U.S. culture.

In Truth's speech, the dialogue is with the audience. Alice Childress (1920–1994)—playwright, novelist, actor, and director—uses all the devices of theater to enact, in a prose work, a conversation between Marge and Tessie. Everything from ellipses to designate the pauses that would occur in an actual conversation, colloquial expressions, and a sentence structure that mimics conversational English signals that this is writing-as-speech or speech-as-writing, a blurred genre that exists on the page but that encourages the reader to *articulate* its message. Is Childress partaking of an oral or a written tradition here? Is it fiction or theater?

The work of Laurie Anderson (b. 1947) and Anna Deavere Smith (b. 1950)—two of America's most important contemporary performance artists—raises a host of other genre questions. When a piece originally performed on stage is then written down, are we reading or listening the page? Is it a different piece on the page than it was on the stage? Is it prose or poetry?

We invite readers to read/hear these intriguing works and to try to answer these questions for themselves. But we suggest that the only full answer to these questions is, quite simply and complexly, "yes."

Sojourner Truth

(1797–1883)

AIN'T I A WOMAN?

Well, children, where there is so much racket there must be something out of kilter. I think that 'twixt the negroes of the South and the women at the

North, all talking about rights, the white men will be in a fix pretty soon. But what's all this here talking about?

That man over there says that women need to be helped into carriages, and lifted over ditches, and to have the best place everywhere. Nobody ever helps me into carriages, or over mud-puddles, or gives me any best place! And ain't I a woman? Look at me! Look at my arm! I have ploughed and planted, and gathered into barns, and no man could head me! And ain't I a woman? I could work as much and eat as much as a man—when I could get it—and bear the lash as well! And ain't I a woman? I have borne thirteen children, and seen them most all sold off to slavery, and when I cried out with my mother's grief, none but Jesus heard me! And ain't I a woman?

Then they talk about this thing in the head: what's this they call it? [Intellect, someone whispers.] That's it, honey. What's that got to do with women's rights or negro's rights? If my cup won't hold but a pint, and yours holds a quart, wouldn't you be mean not to let me have my little half-measure full?

Then that little man in black there, he says women can't have as much rights as men, 'cause Christ wasn't a woman! Where did your Christ come from? Where did your Christ come from? From God and a woman! Man had nothing to do with Him.

If the first woman God ever made was strong enough to turn the world upside down all alone, these women together ought to be able to turn it back, and get it right side up again! And now they is asking to do it, the men better let them.

Obliged to you for hearing me, and now old Sojourner ain't got nothing more to say.

1881–1886

Alice Childress

(1920–1994)

MEN IN YOUR LIFE

No, Marge, I don't think you have any more hard luck with men than anybody else. Neither do I go in for this downin' of men all the time like they are so many strange bein's or enemies. I think men are people the same as women and you will run into some bad characters in this life be they men or women!
. . . Well, I'm in perfect agreement with that! A lot of men *do* think that they are just the cock o' the walk and oughta have the last word about everything! There are also a lot of them that look down on women and make fun of everything we say and do. I'm tellin' you they really can rile me when they end up sayin' something like, "Women! can't live with 'em or without, bless their souls!" Of course, rilin' is what they usually got in mind when they say those things.

But, Marge, we women are also the first ones that get a crack at these men. . . . Well, I mean, ain't we the ones that get to raise them from the time they are babies? While it's true that a heap of women have drawn some sad pick of husbands, it is also true that they raise their sons to make somebody else a mighty poor kinda spouse!

It is not a easy thing to raise a boy so's that he'll be as close to right as you can make him! It takes more than a bit of commonsense and a whole lot of tryin'. If I had a son, I would want him to be fair and square and good and worthwhile and at the same time not let anybody walk over him. Well, you know how Marie can hang-dog her husband around! . . . No, that is not at all necessary, and he shouldn't allow it! I would raise a son of mine to think for himself and get a good feelin' for the right and wrong of things! And I think a little application of the golden rule toward everybody oughta get him off to a good start! . . . Sure, everybody *says* they live by the golden rule, but how many people really and truly treat other folks like they'd like to be treated themselves? Not too many, you can be sure, 'cause everybody wants the tip-top best for themselves and then a *little bit more!*

I stopped off to see Tessie the other day in order to go over her club minutes. You know, I would never have gone if I thought Clarence was gonna be home from work that day! He can make me so mad 'til it ain't funny!

That man can say and do some of the worst kinda things! In the first place, he is *grumpy*. Yes, always frownin' up and mumblin' under his breath about nothin' in particular! . . . That alone would get me in a fistfight or a strait-jacket or both! I couldn't stand somebody goin', "mumble-mumble-make me

443

sick-mumble-mumble-my dinner-mumble mumble-tired of this. . . ." Yes, that's the way he goes on all the time! And don't let her have a visitor 'cause that's when he'll do it most!

It gets real embarrassin' to sit around pretendin' that you don't notice it. Lots of times when I've been there he would come walkin' in and say, "Where's my dinner?" before he would say good evenin' to anybody! And no matter how I try to recollect I can never remember a time when I could say I saw him laughin'!

The other day she went in the kitchen when he called her, and I could hear him sayin' "Where's that ten dollars I gave you last week?" And Tessie was whisperin' soft-like so's I couldn't hear what she was sayin', but it was plain to see that he was mad 'cause she wanted to pay out two dollars for club dues. When I left, I said, "Good night folks!" and he says, "mumble-mumble-night." Like it was killin' him to even do that much. He acts that way with everybody but mostly with Tessie!

I'll never forget the time when I went out with his brother Wallace! He was supposed to be takin' me out on this bang-up dinner date! Honey, as soon as we got in the restaurant he says, "The hash is real good in this place, they make it better than any other restaurant."

. . . No, dear, I wasn't payin' him no mind! I hadn't asked him to take me out to dinner! Neither had I told him to pick out a expensive restaurant, so I went ahead and ordered me some spring lamb chops with a salad on the side! I can stand a *broke* man but I dearly detest a *cheap* man! And he was just pure *cheap!*

Next thing he started lookin' in his newspaper for a good movie and the way he told it everything that was playin' at the high-priced picture houses was *no good,* but there was a couple of fine things showin' in the neighborhood places! So, since he'd asked me what *I* wanted to see, I picked out the exact one I had in mind. However, I didn't pick it out 'til I had ordered me a cocktail!

Then you should have heard him twistin' and turnin'! Started talkin' 'bout how long he'd been alone since his wife died and how he really *needed* somebody and things like that. I just sat there sippin' and noddin' in a understandin' way, but every once in a while I'd take a peek at my watch 'cause it was gettin' mighty close to bein' too late to catch a movie.

Next thing you know, he starts talkin' about *wastin'* our time. He says, "We're both grown and there ain't no need of us wastin' each other's time if we're not gonna get anywhere!" . . . Honey, I caught on real fast! He was lettin' me know that he didn't *want* to go to the movies unless I would come on out and declare how obligin' I was gonna be in the love-makin' department! . . .

So I says, "It's gettin' late Wallace, I have a splittin' headache and I think I'd better get on back home before we waste any more time *or* money!" And that was that! . . . Yes, he took me home and when we got to my door he says, "Do you want to give me a little kiss?" I just looked at him real calm-like and says, "Get off of that act, Wallace. You can tell whether somebody wants to kiss you or not, you don't have to ask! Now look at me and tell me whether I want to kiss you or not!" He didn't say another word, all he did was turn around and go on home!

I hate any man to be creepin' and pinchin' along tryin' all kinds of tricks and foolishness with me. . . . Of course, he had money, Marge! He has been workin' on a good steady job for the last fifteen years and ain't never missed a day's work in all that time. . . . Tessie was the one who really talked me into goin' out with him 'cause she told me I ought to go out with a "good steady fellow who has a reliable job."

I guess she was takin' a dig at Eddie 'cause he is a salesman and don't seem to be doin' so hot at sellin' them race-records and books. But I'll take Eddie any day and you can *have* Wallace! Eddie is the kind of man I like. He doesn't play any games or try no four-flushin'!

Whenever Eddie's in town I have a grand time and even a letter from him is worth more than a whole evenin' with somebody else. Sometimes he will say, "Well, honey, there ain't but five dollars in the cash register so let's try and stretch it into a good time!" And he can figure out a lot of swell things to do. We will go dancin' and then have a few beers and take the subway home or sometimes walk even! But the whole time we're laughin' and talkin' and enjoyin' ourselves so much 'til you couldn't believe how happy I feel!

Some Sunday afternoons Eddie is *broke* and then we go walkin' and he will take me up to a pawnshop window and turn it into a regular movin' picture show. . . . Well, I mean he will make up stories about the things that he sees in the window and try to figure out who they belonged to in the first place and how they happen to be in the pawnshop window now. . . . Oh, foolishness stories like, "I see where some cat had to pawn his saxophone, now why do you think he did that?" And I'll say, "To pay his room-rent!" And he'll say, "No, he got a letter tellin' him that if he came to East Jalappi, there would be a fine old steady job waitin' for him, so he hocked his horn in order to buy a ticket, only when he got off the boat he didn't have no horn to play so the poor old guy is hangin' 'round Jalappi tryin' to save up enough money to buy him a second-hand horn, and this horn is hangin' here in the window tryin' to tempt some youngster into takin' up music so that he can get to Jalappi some day himself!"

I like him to tell me them pawnshop stories. He can tell electric-iron stories, radio stories, ring stories, suitcase stories, silverware stories, and all manner of tales about cocktail shakers, toasters, suits and overcoats, cameras and all such things as that!

Eddie will do me favors, too. Like goin' downtown to buy things that I don't have time to pick up, washin' dishes for me, mindin' my cousin's kids so's she can go to church and a whole lot of other things like that. But what I really like about him is that sometimes when I ask him to do a lot of things, one comin' right after the other, he will say, "You runnin' a good thing in the ground, and furthermore I don't feel like it, what do you take me for?" I'm glad when he does that, too, 'cause just like I don't want nobody walkin' all over me, I sure wouldn't have any use for a man that's gonna let people trample him!

Marge, you know Eddie has loaned me money, too. But the first time he tried to borrow some from me, I got real scared 'cause you do hear so many stories 'bout how men try to take advantage of women sometimes by gettin' their money away from them. . . . Yes, I loaned it to him, but I worried him to death until I got it back. When he returned it, he said, "Whew! I don't *never* want to borrow *nothin'* from you no more 'cause it's too much of a strain!"

I felt a little bit shamed about that, but now we don't never have that kind of trouble no more 'cause all the time we know we can depend on each other no matter what happens! . . . Yes, we have been talkin' 'bout gettin' married, but neither one of us got enough change to start up family life in the way we'd want it to be, and you know how you can start puttin' things off 'til everything is shaped up just right.

But I get to thinkin' awful deep sometimes. And when Eddie is away, I start picturin' his easy-goin', happy ways, how he likes children, how he looks at me so that I don't have to wonder how he feels, how he never had to ask for a "little kiss" but knew when was the right time to kiss me, how he loves people, how he hates meanness and ugliness—how he wants me to get out of other folks' kitchens, when I think on all of that and stand him up side of those steady, reliable guys like Clarence and Wallace, it seems like Wallace and Clarence don't look so hot!

Yes, I think I will marry Eddie 'cause the only, single thing we will have to worry about is bein' poor. . . . Yes, that is a pretty big thing to have to worry about all the time, but if a man gives you all of the very best that he has to offer, all the time, what more could a woman want? . . .

1956

Laurie Anderson
(1947–   )

from *United States*

Themes for the Pictures

I had this dream . . . and in it my mother is sitting there cutting out pictures of hamsters from magazines. In some of the pictures, the hamsters are pets, and in some of them, hamsters are just somewhere in the background. And she's got a whole pile of these cedar chips—you know the kind: the kind from the bottoms of hamster cages—and she's gluing them together into frames for the pictures. She glues them together, and frames the pictures, and hangs them up over the fireplace—that's more or less her method. And suddenly I realize that this is just her way of telling me that I should become a structuralist filmmaker—which I had, you know, planned to do anyway . . .

Dog Show

I dreamed I was a dog in a dog show.
And my father came to the dog show.
And he said: That's a really good dog.
I like that dog.

And then all my friends came and I
was thinking:
No one has ever looked at me like this
for so long.
No one has ever stared at me like this
for so long
for such a long time
for so long.

Democratic Way

I dreamed that I was Jimmy Carter's lover, and I was somewhere, I guess in the White House . . . and there were lots of other women there, too . . . and they were supposed to be his lovers too . . . but I never even saw Jimmy Carter . . . and none of the other women ever saw him either . . .

And there was this big discussion going on because Jimmy had decided to open up the presidential elections to the dead. That is, that anyone who had ever lived would have the opportunity to become President. He said he thought it would be more democratic that way.

The more choice you had

The more democratic it would be.

from New Jersey Turnpike

I was living out in West Hollywood when the Hollywood Strangler was strangling women. He was strangling women all over town, but he was particularly strangling them in West Hollywood. Every night there was a panel discussion on TV about the strangler—speculations about his habits, his motives, his methods. One thing was clear about him: He only strangled women when they were alone, or with other women. The panel members would always end the show by saying, "Now, for all you women, listen, don't go outside without a man. Don't walk out to your car, don't even take out the garbage by yourself. Always go with a man." Then one of the eyewitnesses identified a policeman as one of the suspects. The next night, the chief of police was on the panel. He said, "Now, girls, whatever happens, do not stop for a police officer. Stay in your car. If a police officer tries to stop you, do not stop. Keep driving and under no circumstances should you get out of your car." For a few weeks, half the traffic in L.A. was doing twice the speed limit.

New York Social Life

Well I was lying in bed one morning, trying to think of a good reason to get up, and the phone rang and it was Geri and she said: Hey, hi! How are you? What's going on? How's your work?

Oh fine. You know, just waking up but it's fine, it's going okay, how's yours?

Oh a lot of work, you know, I mean, I'm trying to make some money too. Listen, I gotta get back to it, I just thought I'd call to see how you are . . .

And I said: Yeah, we should really get together next week. You know, have lunch, and talk. And she says: Yeah, uh, I'll be in touch. Okay?

Okay.

Uh, listen, take care.

Okay. Take it easy.

Bye bye.

Bye now. And I get up, and the phone rings and it's a man from Cleveland

and he says: Hey, hi! How are you? Listen, I'm doing a performance series and I'd like you to do something in it. Uh, you know, you could make a little money. I mean, I don't know how I *feel* about your work, you know, it's not really my style, it's kind of trite, but listen, it's *just* my opinion, don't take it personally. So listen, I'll be in town next week. I gotta go now, but I'll give you a call, and we'll have lunch, and we can discuss a few things.

And I hang up and it rings again and I don't answer it and I go out for a walk and I drop in at the gallery and they say: Hey, hi. How are you?

Oh fine. You know.

How's your work going?

Okay. I mean . . .

You know, it's not like it was in the sixties. I mean, those were the days, there's just no money around now, you know, survive, produce, stick it out, it's a jungle out there, just gotta keep working.

And the phone rings and she says: Oh excuse me, will you? Hey, hi! How are you? Uh-huh. How's your work? *Good.* Well, listen, stick it out, I mean, it's not the sixties, you know, listen, I gotta go now, but, uh, lunch would be great. Fine, next week? Yeah. Very busy now, but next week would be fine, okay? Bye bye.

Bye now.

And I go over to Magoo's, for a bite, and I see Frank and I go over to his table and I say:

Hey Frank. Hi, how are you? How's your work? Yeah, mine's okay too. Listen, I'm broke you know, but, uh, working. . . . Listen, I gotta go now, uh, we should *really* get together, you know. Why don't you drop by sometime? Yeah, that would be great. Okay. Take care.

Take it easy.

I'll see you.

I'll call you.

Bye now.

Bye bye.

And I go to a party and everyone's sitting around wearing these party hats and it's really awkward and no one can think of anything to say. So we all move around—fast—and it's: Hi! How are you? Where've you been? Nice to see you. Listen, I'm sorry I missed your thing last week, but we should really get together, you know, maybe next week. I'll call you. I'll see you.

Bye bye.

And I go home and the phone rings and it's Alan and he says: You know, I'm gonna have a show on, uh, cable TV and it's gonna be about loneliness, you know, people in the city who for whatever sociological, psychological, philosophical reasons just can't seem to communicate, you know, The Gap,

The Gap, uh, it'll be a talk show and people'll phone in but we will say at the beginning of each program: Uh, listen, don't call in with your *personal* problems because we don't want to hear them.

And I'm going to sleep and it rings again and it's Mary and she says: Hey, Laurie, how are you? Listen, uh, I just called to say hi. . . . Uh, yeah, well don't worry. Uh, listen, just keep working. I gotta go now. I know it's late but we should really get together next week maybe and have lunch and talk and. . . . Listen, Laurie, uh, if you want to talk before then, uh, I'll leave my answering machine on . . . and just give me a ring . . . anytime.

False Documents

I went to a palm reader and the odd thing about the reading was that everything she told me was totally wrong. She said I loved airplanes, that I had been born in Seattle, that my mother's name was Hilary. But she seemed so sure of the information that I began to feel like I'd been walking around with these false documents permanently tattooed to my hands. It was very noisy in the parlor and members of her family kept running in and out. They were speaking a high, clicking kind of language that sounded a lot like Arabic. Books and magazines in Arabic were strewn all over the floor. It suddenly occurred to me that maybe there was a translation problem—that maybe she was reading my hand from right to left instead of left to right.

Thinking of mirrors, I gave her my other hand. Then she put her other hand out and we sat there for several minutes in what I assumed was some kind of participatory ritual. Finally I realized that her hand was out because she was waiting for money.

Red Hot

My sister and I used to play this game called Red Hot.
And in Red Hot, the ceiling is suddenly about a
thousand degrees.
And there's no gravity.
Gravity doesn't exist anymore.
And you're trying not to float up to the ceiling
so you have to hold on to things.
You have to hold on to sheets, pillows, chairs,
anything so that you won't go floating up to that ceiling.

I guess it's not what anyone would call a very
competitive game.
You know what I mean?
Mainly, we just sweated a lot
and we were really glad when it was all over
and the ceiling cooled back down again.

1984

Anna Deavere Smith

(1950–   )

ROSLYN MALAMUD
THE COUP
from *Fires in the Mirror*

(Spring. Midafternoon. The sunny kitchen of a huge, beautiful house on Eastern Parkway in Crown Heights. It's a large, very well-equipped kitchen. We
are sitting at a table in a breakfast nook area, which is separated by shelves
from the cooking area. There is a window to the side. There are newspapers
on the chair at the far side of the table. Mrs. Malamud offers me food at the
beginning of the interview. We are drinking coffee. She is wearing a sweatshirt
with a large sequined cat. Her tennis shoes have matching sequined cats. She
has on a black skirt and is wearing a wig. Her nails are manicured. She has
beautiful eyes that sparkle are very warm, and a very resonant voice. There is
a lot of humor in her face.)

Do you know what happened in August here?
You see when you read the newspapers.
I mean my son filmed what was going on,
but when you read the newspapers . . .
Of course I was here
I couldn't leave my house.
I only would go out early during the day.
The police were barricading here.
You see,
I wish
I could just like
go on television.
I wanna scream to the whole world.
They said
that the Blacks were rioting against the Jews in Crown
    Heights
and that the Jews were fighting back.

Do you know that the Blacks who came here to riot were
  not my
neighbors?
I don't love my neighbors.
I don't know my Black neighbors.
There's one lady on President Street—
Claire—
I adore her.
She's my girl friend's next-door neighbor.
I've had a manicure
done in her house and we sit and kibbitz
and stuff
but I don't know them.
I told you we don't mingle socially
because of the difference
of food
and religion
and what have you here.
But
the people in this community
want exactly
what I want out of life.
They want to live
in nice homes.
They all go to work.
They couldn't possibly
have houses here
if they didn't
generally—They have
two,
um,
incomes
that come in.
They want to send their kids to college.

They wanna live a nice quiet life.
They wanna shop for their groceries and cook their meals
    and go to
their Sunday picnics!
They just want to have decent homes and decent lives!
The people who came to riot here
were brought here
by this famous
Reverend Al Sharpton,
which I'd like to know who ordained him?
He brought in a bunch of kids
who didn't have jobs in
the summertime.
I wish you could see the *New York Times,*
unfortunately it was on page twenty,
I mean, they interviewed
one of the Black girls on Utica Avenue.
She said,
"The guys will make you pregnant
at night
and in the morning not know who you are."
(*Almost whispering*)
And if you're sitting on a front stoop and it's very, very hot
and you have no money
and you have nothing to do with your time
and someone says, "Come on, you wanna riot?"
You know how kids are.
The fault lies with the police department.
The police department did nothing to stop them.
I was sitting here in the front of the house
when bottles were being thrown
and the sergeant tells five hundred policemen
with clubs and helmets and guns
to duck.
And I said to him,

"You're telling them to duck?
What should I do?
I don't have a club and a gun."
Had they put it—
stopped it on the first night
this kid who came from Australia . . .
(*She sucks her teeth*)
You know,
his parents were Holocaust survivors, he didn't have to die.
He worked,
did a lot of research in Holocaust studies.
He didn't have to die.
What happened on Utica Avenue
was an accident.
JEWISH PEOPLE
DO NOT DRIVE VANS INTO SEVEN-YEAR-OLD BOYS.
YOU WANT TO KNOW SOMETHING? BLACK PEOPLE
   DO NOT DRIVE
VANS INTO SEVEN-YEAR-OLD BOYS.
HISPANIC PEOPLE DON'T DRIVE VANS INTO
   SEVEN-YEAR-OLD BOYS.
IT'S JUST NOT DONE.
PEOPLE LIKE JEFFREY DAHMER MAYBE THEY DO IT.
BUT AVERAGE CITIZENS DO NOT GO OUT AND TRY
   TO KILL
(*Sounds like a laugh but it's just a sound*)
SEVEN-YEAR-OLD BOYS.
It was an accident!
But it was allowed to fester and to steam and all that.
When you come here do you see anything that's going on,
   riots?
No.
But Al Sharpton and the likes of him like *Dowerty*,
who by the way has been in prison
and all of a sudden he became Reverend *Dowerty*—

they once did an exposé on him—
but
these guys live off of this,
you understand?
People are not gonna give them money,
contribute to their causes
unless they're out there rabble-rousing.
My Black neighbors?
I mean I spoke to them.
They were hiding in their houses just like I was.
We were scared.
I was scared!
I was really frightened.
I had five hundred policemen standing in front of my house
every day
I had mounted police,
but I couldn't leave my block,
because when it got dark I couldn't come back in.
I couldn't meet anyone for dinner.
Thank God, I told you my children were all out of town.
My son was in Russia.
The coup
was exactly the same day as the riot
and I was very upset about it.
He was in Russia running a summer camp
and I was very concerned when I had heard about that.
I hadn't heard from him
that night the riot started.
When I did hear from him I told him to stay in Russia,
  he'd be safer
there than here.
And he was.

1993

THREE
Rituals and Ceremonies

The end of an era almost always prompts people to reflect on their values, to consider the meaning of life. It is not, then, surprising that, as we near the end of the century, there is more and more interest in spirituality, in the rituals and ceremonies that shape our lives. We see this profoundly in the pieces included here by poet and novelist Paula Gunn Allen (b. 1939), as well as by poet, painter, and anthropologist Wendy Rose (b. 1948), both of whom plumb the rituals and ceremonies of their heritage (Laguna Sioux for Allen, and Hopi for Rose) for inspiration for their poetry.

This section begins with a selection of traditional Native American rituals, prayers, and ceremonies, but the "gathering of spirits," to borrow the title (and the ancestral allusion) in Allen's poem, must not be considered solely the province of Native Americans. To see ritual as exclusive to Native American cultures is to create an Other, marginalized and separate, and to deny that which is deeply spiritual within all cultures. Thus George Ella Lyon (in a 1982 poem that reminds us that wit and ritual are not opposites) plumbs the Bible and Baptist tradition to create poetry from the ritual of foot-washing, each person humble before the other in preparation for communion.

Similarly, the ritual act of washing is powerfully invoked by Gloria Naylor (b. 1950) in *The Women of Brewster Place* (1982), a "novel in seven stories" that often reads like poetry. Ciel, a mother whose only child has just died of accidental electrocution, is brought back to life by her friend Mattie, who bathes her, washing away as much sorrow as she can. Here a friend's ablutions take over when religion fails to penetrate the abyss of grief that envelops Ciel: "There was no prayer, no bended knee or sackcloth supplication in those words, but a blasphemous fireball that shot forth and went smashing against the gates of heaven, raging and kicking, demanding to be heard."

We end this section with selections from two recent books, *Jambalaya* (1985) by Luisah Teish (b. 1948) and *The Telling* (1993) by E. M. Broner (b. 1930), that consciously reformulate rituals for women, one from an African-American and one from a Jewish heritage. *Jambalaya* is made up of instructions, recipes, prayers, and invocations that contemporary women may use to be in touch with the "extended family" that includes one's community and even one's ancestors. *The Telling* recounts the Passover seders that Broner prepares each year for a group of feminists in New York, as well as other rituals she and her community of women have created to commemorate the joys and the sorrows of their lives.

As important as the specific traditions that evoke the rituals in this section

457

are the "ceremonies of community" that remind all of us that we are not just brain and body. As Broner says, "It takes a lot of communal blessings to make a journey successful, to make one wish come true."

NATIVE AMERICAN RITUAL

Document 1: Kiowa Prayers

Prayers were an integral part of all Indians' lives long before they came in contact with Europeans. In this account, Reverend Hazel Botone, a retired Kiowa Indian Methodist minister, describes the aboriginal Kiowas' conceptualization of prayer.

Our people, the stories say, we came from somewhere up north. Our people were named after White Bear, a lot of animals up north. Our people prayed and gave sacrifices, not knowing who the true God was. No one told them. They don't read. They don't speak English.

Our people have always been praying people. That's one thing we had all the time, praying. You see a tree begin to leaf, you pray. You see somethin' comin' up—flowers—whatever it is. They always say, "Whoever makes it, whoever someone is that is making these things to come up—the grass— someone that is makin' the grain to come." They knew there was somebody powerful behind it. So they always prayed, always, but they didn't say, "Our Father in heaven," or "Dear God in heaven, listen to my prayer."

Document 2: The Medicine Bundle

Every tribe had at least one "medicine bundle," which served as the physical locus for the supernatural treatment of disease. The bundle was made up of what appeared to be odds and ends of the medicine reserve. It was to be available to those who needed it.

The following account of Myrtle Lincoln, an eighty-two-year-old Arapaho woman, was given in an interview December 22, 1969. Her story centers on the special care and taboos of the medicine bundle.

I don't know how many they had, but I know my mother-in-law had one. And we couldn't take the ashes out while that thing was in there. And it had a certain person that was blessed . . . to take it out. Nobody else couldn't touch that thing. My mother-in-law used to take it out before we take the ashes out. And we wasn't supposed to make a noise in there. And every morning when she gets up she'd take a hatchet and hit that tipi pole over there, so when those kids make a noise, well, it wouldn't bother that thing . . . She used to hit it . . . about four times and then . . . when these kids make a noise it wouldn't bother that medicine bag. Used to have to hit that pole every morning.

I don't know how she got it . . . at times she would get maybe tongue and then, you know, them shank bones, and put it on top of that medicine bag . . . She used to say she was feeding the spirit and then the next day she'd take it and cook it and we used to eat it.

It was just wrapped up . . . I never did touch it. I had a respect for that. I used to even keep my kids from running in and out from there.

They not supposed to open them unless they were all together and somebody make a pledge. It took lot of things for them to open them. Never did see it opened. When she handled that thing we had to keep the kids quiet. It wasn't just so you could go over there and pick it up and all that. She used to pray before she touch it. Now when she's going to bring it in she prays . . . to the Lord.

When asked what happened to the mother-in-laws's medicine bag, she answered:

I don't know . . . When the old man died and then she died, . . . none of us couldn't handle it. We left it at the house and I don't know who got it. I don't know who it could have went to. But my understanding was that Henry Lincoln and Chase Harrington—and there was a black man that used to stay around here. I guess they went after it and they sold it here in the drugstore. Here in Canton. And just think—all three of them were gone. One had a stroke and one didn't know where he was at. He was just out of his head. And he just talk until he died. And this black man, they had to take him to rest home. I guess he used to just scream and jump. See, that's what got them—because they bothered that medicine bag. And this Chase Harrington, he went to bed one night and he didn't *ever* get up again. He died in his sleep.

When asked if there were any reason why the medicine bundle would be opened, she explained:

If they made a pledge for some sick people—if their folks would get well, and they want this one to be painted with whatever paint was in them—in that bag. And they used to give horses and things and cook big dinner. And maybe inside of this sweat lodge, that's where they open it. Nobody ever had anything to do with it. They had a respect for it. They didn't make fun of it or anything. In a way they had a respect for that and . . . nobody used to talk about that. And now I'm crazy to be talking about it.

There [are] only two I knew something about. You know, I used to see them when they take care of them. And when they take them out—when they walk with them—they didn't walk fast. If you walk fast, well, the storm used to come up. They used to be easy with them.

Document 3: Vision Quest

Mary Poafybitty Neido, or Sanapia, the Comanche Eagle Doctor, tells about her vision quest at age seventeen. The four-day ordeal required fasting and solitary meditation while ghosts attempted to frighten and harass her to the point that she would renounce her medicine. She relates in this account what was expected of her. In spite of her failure to stay in the mountains for the required time, she passed the test and was declared a full-fledged medicine woman.

Just sit around, don't eat. You have to go out there by yourself and pray. And then when you pray and then you come back . . . you have to go down to the creek and wash all your sins away, something bad in you. You have to go down to the creek and take a bath. And then they paint you . . . all your face with red paint, you know, that rock paint that they grind, they put it all over your face and your arms and your feet, from your knees down, they paint you up like that.

They gave all that medicine to me. They showed me and they told me how to run it and everything like that. They told me all about that before I fasted. You supposed to go way up there in the hills and sleep up there by yourself. But me I was afraid to go up there by myself. I was afraid to go up there, but you supposed to go up there in the hills, and pray and cry and talk and . . . somebody come to you. They say,

"Somebody will come to you way in the middle of the night. They going to push you and kick you and they do things like that, but don't get scared. Just lay there and let them do what they want to you—just kick you around and slap you and all that. They fighting you for your medicine. They don't want you to have that. It's ghosts."

That's what they said.

I said, "I don't want to go up there. Them ghosts might catch me."

That's what I told them. I didn't want to go out. I didn't go out there. I was afraid to sleep up there in the mountains by myself. I just go up there and come back.

Document 4: Ghost Sickness

Ghost Sickness was not generally prevalent in the Plains area, but ghosts sometimes struck particularly vulnerable Comanche and Kiowa-Apache

persons by deforming them. The following account, which was recorded on June 15, 1967, is that of Sanapia, in which she describes the victims of ghost sickness.

[They had a] . . . twisted mouth and twisted eyes. Sometimes their eyes would go up on the left side this way and your mouth would be twisted the other way, and just look like your face get all twisted . . . They would be paralyzed on their arms, or the whole bottom half of their body and be twisted. And do you know what the Indians call that? They call it Ghost-Done-It. Ghost twisted person's face like that. In the night time they come right up on you. If you look at them like that they do that to you. The ghost. The Indians believe that. They believe they're ghosts.

When Sanapia agreed to treat a stricken individual, the person was required to bring a ritual payment consisting of dark green cloth, a commercially obtained bag of Bull Durham tobacco, and four corn-shuck cigarette "papers." She here describes how the contract with the patient was sealed and then gives a detailed account of the treatment. If this treatment failed, she then offered prayers from the Bible. And if this did not get the desired results, she held a special peyote meeting for the patient.

They would get this leaf or corn shuck and they roll their cigarette with that Bull Durham smoke. They wrap it up and light it and they give it to me and say,

"Here take this smoke. Pity me and get me well. I'm tired of this face all twisted up, tired of my legs paralyzed. I can't walk, can't do nothing. I want you to pity me and get me well."

And so I take it. I get a puff on it four times, just four times, and I say,

"Alright, I'll pity you. I'll see what I could do for you . . . Go in there and wash your face and your hands and you come and I'll doctor you."

Chew that medicine and put it on your hands and rub it like that (between the palms) and rub their face with it and their hands—out of my mouth what I chew this medicine . . . Then I would blow this medicine on their face and I would doctor them. Today I doctor three times, and tomorrow I doctor them three times, that's six. And if it's real bad I go ahead and doctor them till I doctor them eight times.

So, I start—tomorrow morning and noon and supper, and the next morning I'm through with them. Take them out there before daylight, and I do all the Indian ways what my mother and my uncle told me to do . . . And in the morning when they get up they ain't a thing wrong with them. They alright. Their face get alright. Their mouth get alright. They don't slobber no more. And then you bring the coals to the front of the house wherever they are, or go to the fireplace and put that cedar on there, and there's another kind of medicine that we mix together and then we just tell whoever it is that's sick—bend over like that. They inhale all that smoke. Take that feather and put it over the fire like that and smoke that feather—that's eagle feather. And take that and smoke that and we fan them all over from head to feet— all over their body. Four this way and four that way and turn around and eight in the back and on top of their head like that. Just fan that bad stuff away from them. That's what that smoke for. And after they do that, they alright. They get well.

Document 5: Special Doctoring

A grandmother's special powers are described in this account by Richard Manus, a Cherokee, in an interview February 8, 1969.

My grandmother was . . . what they call a witch doctor. And anytime they got an Indian in court, if he was an Indian, . . . they'd call my grandmother and she'd make tobacco and she'd have them smoking it in that courthouse. And she claimed that she mixing up that lawyer, the judge in that way. I know they said, (ninety)-five percent of them came clear anyhow. And they'd drop the cases or something. They'd never stick 'em. And I know that she'd go to every trial they had. They used her. And every trial they had, that's the way she went along. And I can look back now and see what she was doing and I presume I guess it was working. I don't know. It looks that a way to me now.

My grandmother was a mid-wife doctor. And she was a doctor of all trades. And right up there, right up above this spring, it's solid rock bottom and there's a place in there that's got a kind of wash stand like and a dish pan, but it's big. And I've seen her take people with running sores and all kinds. . . . And right yonder what I'm talking about now, she'd take them over there and she'd bathe them in there. And of course she'd take some kind of herb and when she got through bathing them, she'd wash them down with those herbs and she'd cure those people.

Document 6: Praying

Annie Hawk, a seventy-seven-year-old Cheyenne woman, relates the importance of prayer before beading or quilling. It is important to note here that Annie was a Baptist. From my long acquaintance with her, my perception is that her idea of "the man up there" was a fusion of the Christian God and the Great Spirit—which one was not important to her. The following account was given to the author in January 1977.

My grandmother, my mother's grandmother [*sic*], was a very important woman. She was selected by the Cheyennes. The others selected her to tan hides and make a tipi. That's because she was the oldest woman in camp, and the most respected. She tan a big bull hide and heifer hide, a yearling hide and calf hide—five hides she used to make that tipi. There was a few buffalo left then. That was before I was born—a long time ago—before my mother was born. I think in '77, that is 1877 or 1878. And before she started quilling, that is feather work with porcupine quills, she prayed for four days. And she didn't eat, fasted you know. And then she knew that everything was goin' to be alright. She knew the spirits wouldn't get mad or nothin' bad would happen. Then she spent a whole year quilling it.

That's what I do when I make special moccasins. Pray, that is, to the man up there. Say, some designs only women can wear and if somebody else gets 'em, I don't want nothin' bad happenin' to me. And [chuckle] sometimes I just pray for good luck.

Document 7: Arapaho Pipe Keeper

Rose Birdshead, daughter of Suzy Tallbear and sister of Amanda Tallbear Bates, Keepers of the Sacred Pipe, tells about growing up in a family which held an honored position in the Arapaho tribe. Here she describes the purpose of the pipe and its use.

Amanda Bates was my sister. She was older than I was, about nine years. My mother passed the pipe on to her. She knew she was getting up in years and she knew that she would have to pass it to her daughter because it has to stay in the family. It went to her and then it was coming to me. They always have public acknowledgment of that, you know, like at some Indian gathering. They have dance and they recognize it, and I've never done that. But it is mine now.

They don't have the ceremonies anymore. You just know who the chiefs are. But they do not go through that ceremony about the pipe. They have a pipe, but they don't smoke it. When they made treaties, you know, or made peace with a tribe, that was their way of introducing themselves to the other tribe.

And everybody had one language, and that was the sign language. Everybody knew the sign language. That is how they conversed. That's how they knew about the next person even though they don't talk the same language. So that pipe was used for that. And then it was like anybody going into a real estate office or something or signing a binding contract. Well, this pipe represented the same thing in that order. Why you smoke with them, and that's an agreement and you cannot break it.

You have to handle that pipe like it's something sacred. We're not supposed to drop that pipe. They say it's an ill omen to drop it. It's the last thing down here the Arapaho tribe has. All the rest of the lodges and that is gone. But they held on to the pipe.

They used the pipe at the Sun Dance. There are priests, they call them, who are in charge of all that. They know their duties and the pipe is used more in there than you see it any place else. They use it all through the ceremony.

My mother had it. It was given to her when she was quite a young maiden. They choose them according to their backgrounds, and who they are. See her grandfather, her mother's father was—I don't say he's the greatest priest, but he was the oldest. And his name was No One Knows, because no one knows who he is or where he came from like that. So his name was No One Knows. He was a great priest. I hate to say great, because there is no great priest.

She grew up in, well to me, it must have been something wonderful, because when I was growing up my sister and, well, there were a lot of things we couldn't do. You know how young kids will go do something and think nothing of it. And we couldn't do those things and I used to wonder why.

And on Sunday, I was just a little girl then, I'd want to go swimming. Oh, the kids were just havin' a ball. And here come my mother just ready to give me a lickin'. I'd have to go back and clean up and put on a buckskin dress. I didn't know it was such a great honor to wear a buckskin dress. I hated those things. They were hot, them leggins and the fringes. You parade around them in the Sun Dance. And today I just think what a great honor it is to see these Indians, especially when they're so beautiful in them.

That's the kind of life I had. I rebelled. I was the one that rebelled. I wanted to do what everyone else was doing.

And of course we were brought up in the Christian way. We belonged to the northern Baptist church. My father was a deacon and he more or less helped take care of the services with us.

Amanda got into goin' to this church, active and in the women's club meetings. At that time they were really good. They taught you somethin', you know. Of course we learned all that in school, but you come out and you try to practice it when you get home, and that's what she done. She was teaching how to bead and how to do craft work that young people didn't know but wanted to learn.

I believe it was about '63 or '64 when my mother gave her the pipe, because you know my mother was able to be up and around then. The last two years before her death she wasn't able to go places. So she gave that over to her daughter. That is still a Sacred Pipe that the Arapahos hold.

She sat with the chiefs. When they go have their meetings and discuss something important that they had meetings about, she was with them. She always sat with the chiefs.

And the pipe, it was passed to me. I will pass it on to one of my daughters, not sons because, well, it first was passed to a lady. It couldn't pass to a boy. I've got three daughters, but the one I had in mind is—she just lives a few miles from me. That's who I had in mind. And I've got a younger daughter. You know she would be a fine person, such a nice outgoing person. But she clings more to the, you know, white way. My other daughter understands the Indian culture.

My sister was a beautiful person. And you know after she got that pipe, she never would get mad at anybody. No matter what happened, she would always be so calm. And that's kinda the Indian way, kinda sacred. She always took care of me, you know, took the responsibility. And because she was that way, that's why she was chosen. I was the one who rebelled. I just never could understand why my mother was so strict with us. I wish I had understood.

Traditional

Paula Gunn Allen

(1939–   )

KOPIS'TAYA
(A GATHERING OF SPIRITS)

Because we live in the browning season
the heavy air blocking our breath,
and in this time when living
is only survival, we doubt the voices
that come shadowed on the air,
that weave within our brains
certain thoughts, a motion that is soft,
imperceptible, a twilight rain
soft feather's fall, a small body
dropping into its nest, rustling, murmuring,
settling in for the night.

Because we live in the hardedged season,
where plastic brittle and gleaming shines
and in this space that is cornered and angled,
we do not notice wet, moist, the significant
drops falling in perfect spheres
that are the certain measures of our minds;
almost invisible, those tears,
soft as dew, fragile, that cling to leaves,
petals, roots, gentle and sure,
every morning.

We are the women of daylight; of clocks and steel
foundrys, of drugstores and streetlights,
of superhighways that slice our days in two.
Wrapped around in glass and steel we ride
our lives; behind dark glasses we hide our eyes,
our thoughts, shaded, seem obscure, smoke
fills our minds, whisky husks our songs,
polyester cuts our bodies from our breath,
our feet from the welcoming stones of earth.

Our dreams are pale memories of themselves,
and nagging doubt is the false measure of our days.

Even so, the spirit voices are singing,
their thoughts are dancing in the dirty air.
Their feet touch the cement, the asphalt
delighting, still they weave dreams upon our
shadowed skulls, if we could listen.
If we could hear.
Let's go then. Let's find them. Let's
listen for the water, the careful gleaming drops
that glisten on the leaves, the flowers. Let's
ride the midnight, the early dawn. Feel the wind
striding through our hair. Let's dance
the dance of feathers, the dance of birds.

1986

Wendy Rose
(1948–)

NAMING POWER

They think
I am stronger than I am.
>I would tell this like a story
>but where a story should begin
>I am left standing in the beat
>of my silences.
There has to be someone to name you.

There must be hands
to raise you sun-high, old voices
to sing you in,
>warm fingers to touch you and give
>the ancient words that bind you to
>yourself, ogres with yucca stalks
>your uncles in disguise waiting
>as you learn to walk.
There has to be someone to name you.

These words have thundered in my body
for thirty years; like amnesia this way
of being a fragment,
>unfired pottery with poster paint
>splashed on dayglo pink, banana yellow,
>to hide the crumbling cracking commonness
>of porous insides, left in the storeroom
>for a quick tourist sale (they will make
>their buck or two from me but I will never
>be among them)
There has to be someone to name you.

I will choose the tongue
for my songs. I am
a young woman still
>joining hands with the moon, a creature
>of blood and it's the singing of the blood
>that matters, the singing of songs

to keep thunder around us, to hollow out
the sage-spotted hills, to starve
not for rabbit stew but
for being remembered.
There has to be someone to name you.

Aging with the rock
of this ancient land
I give myself to the earth,
merge
              my red feet on the mesa like rust, root
              in this place with my mothers before me,
              balance end by end like a rainbow
              between the two points of my birth, dance
              into shapes that search the sky for clouds
              filled with fertile water.

              Across asphalt canyons, bridging river
              after river, a thirty year old woman
is waiting for her name.

1994

George Ella Lyon
(1949–   )

THE FOOT-WASHING

"I wouldn't take the bread and wine if I didn't wash feet."
OLD REGULAR BAPTIST

They kneel on the slanting floor
before feet white as roots.
humble as tree stumps.
Men before men
women before women
to soothe the sourness
bound in each other's journeys.
Corns, calluses, bone knobs
all received and rinsed
given back clean
to Sunday shoes and hightops.

This is how they prepare
for the Lord's Supper,
singing and carrying a towel
and a basin of water,
praying while kids put soot
in their socks—almost as good
as nailing someone in the outhouse.

Jesus started it: He washed feet
after Magdalen dried His ankles
with her hair. "If I wash thee not,
thou hast no part with me."
All servants, they bathe
flesh warped to its balance.
God of the rootwad,
Lord of the bucket in the well.

1982

Gloria Naylor

(1950–)

from *The Women of Brewster Place*

After the funeral the well-meaning came to console and offer their dog-eared faith in the form of coconut cakes, potato pies, fried chicken, and tears. Ciel sat in the bed with her back resting against the headboard; her long thin fingers, still as midnight frost on a frozen pond, lay on the covers. She acknowledged their kindnesses with nods of her head and slight lip movements, but no sound. It was as if her voice was too tired to make the journey from the diaphragm through the larynx to the mouth.

Her visitors' impotent words flew against the steel edge of her pain, bled slowly, and returned to die in the senders' throats. No one came too near. They stood around the door and the dressing table, or sat on the edges of the two worn chairs that needed upholstering, but they unconsciously pushed themselves back against the wall as if her hurt was contagious.

A neighbor woman entered in studied certainty and stood in the middle of the room. "Child, I know how you feel, but don't do this to yourself. I lost one, too. The Lord will . . ." And she choked, because the words were jammed down into her throat by the naked force of Ciel's eyes. Ciel had opened them fully now to look at the woman, but raw fires had eaten them worse than lifeless—worse than death. The woman saw in that mute appeal for silence the ragings of a personal hell flowing through Ciel's eyes. And just as she went to reach for the girl's hand, she stopped as if a muscle spasm had overtaken her body and, cowardly, shrank back. Reminiscences of old, dried-over pains were no consolation in the face of this. They had the effect of cold beads of water on a hot iron—they danced and fizzled up while the room stank from their steam.

Mattie stood in the doorway, and an involuntary shudder went through her when she saw Ciel's eyes. Dear God, she thought, she's dying, and right in front of our faces.

"Merciful Father, no!" she bellowed. There was no prayer, no bended knee or sackcloth supplication in those words, but a blasphemous fireball that shot forth and went smashing against the gates of heaven, raging and kicking, demanding to be heard.

"No! No! No!" Like a black Brahman cow, desperate to protect her young, she surged into the room, pushing the neighbor woman and the others out of her way. She approached the bed with her lips clamped shut in such force that the muscles in her jaw and the back of her neck began to ache.

She sat on the edge of the bed and enfolded the tissue-thin body in her huge ebony arms. And she rocked. Ciel's body was so hot it burned Mattie when she first touched her, but she held on and rocked. Back and forth, back and forth—she had Ciel so tightly she could feel her young breasts flatten against the buttons of her dress. The black mammoth gripped so firmly that the slightest increase of pressure would have cracked the girl's spine. But she rocked.

And somewhere from the bowels of her being came a moan from Ciel, so high at first it couldn't be heard by anyone there, but the yard dogs began an unholy howling. And Mattie rocked. And then, agonizingly slow, it broke its way through the parched lips in a spaghetti-thin column of air that could be faintly heard in the frozen room.

Ciel moaned. Mattie rocked. Propelled by the sound, Mattie rocked her out of that bed, out of that room, into a blue vastness just underneath the sun and above time. She rocked her over Aegean seas so clean they shone like crystal, so clear the fresh blood of sacrificed babies torn from their mother's arms and given to Neptune could be seen like pink froth on the water. She rocked her on and on, past Dachau, where soul-gutted Jewish mothers swept their children's entrails off laboratory floors. They flew past the spilled brains of Senegalese infants whose mothers had dashed them on the wooden sides of slave ships. And she rocked on.

She rocked her into her childhood and let her see murdered dreams. And she rocked her back, back into the womb, to the nadir of her hurt, and they found it—a slight silver splinter, embedded just below the surface of the skin. And Mattie rocked and pulled—and the splinter gave way, but its roots were deep, gigantic, ragged, and they tore up flesh with bits of fat and muscle tissue clinging to them. They left a huge hole, which was already starting to pus over, but Mattie was satisfied. It would heal.

The bile that had formed a tight knot in Ciel's stomach began to rise and gagged her just as it passed her throat. Mattie put her hand over the girl's mouth and rushed her out the now-empty room to the toilet. Ciel retched yellowish-green phlegm, and she brought up white lumps of slime that hit the seat of the toilet and rolled off, splattering onto the tiles. After a while she heaved only air, but the body did not seem to want to stop. It was exorcising the evilness of pain.

Mattie cupped her hands under the faucet and motioned for Ciel to drink and clean her mouth. When the water left Ciel's mouth, it tasted as if she had been rinsing with a mild acid. Mattie drew a tub of hot water and undressed Ciel. She let the nightgown fall off the narrow shoulders, over the pitifully thin breasts and jutting hipbones. She slowly helped her into the water, and it was like a dried brown autumn leaf hitting the surface of a puddle.

And slowly she bathed her. She took the soap, and, using only her hands, she washed Ciel's hair and the back of her neck. She raised her arms and cleaned the armpits, soaping well the downy brown hair there. She let the soap slip between the girl's breasts, and she washed each one separately, cupping it in her hands. She took each leg and even cleaned under the toenails. Making Ciel rise and kneel in the tub, she cleaned the crack in her behind, soaped her pubic hair, and gently washed the creases in her vagina—slowly, reverently, as if handling a newborn.

She took her from the tub and toweled her in the same manner she had been bathed—as if too much friction would break the skin tissue. All of this had been done without either woman saying a word. Ciel stood there, naked, and felt the cool air play against the clean surface of her skin. She had the sensation of fresh mint coursing through her pores. She closed her eyes and the fire was gone. Her tears no longer fried within her, killing her internal organs with their steam. So Ciel began to cry—there, naked, in the center of the bathroom floor.

Mattie emptied the tub and rinsed it. She led the still-naked Ciel to a chair in the bedroom. The tears were flowing so freely now Ciel couldn't see, and she allowed herself to be led as if blind. She sat on the chair and cried—head erect. Since she made no effort to wipe them away, the tears dripped down her chin and landed on her chest and rolled down to her stomach and onto her dark pubic hair. Ignoring Ciel, Mattie took away the crumpled linen and made the bed, stretching the sheets tight and fresh. She beat the pillows into a virgin plumpness and dressed them in white cases.

And Ciel sat. And cried. The unmolested tears had rolled down her parted thighs and were beginning to wet the chair. But they were cold and good. She put out her tongue and began to drink in their saltiness, feeding on them. The first tears were gone. Her thin shoulders began to quiver, and spasms circled her body as new tears came—this time, hot and stinging. And she sobbed, the first sound she'd made since the moaning.

Mattie took the edges of the dirty sheet she'd pulled off the bed and wiped the mucus that had been running out of Ciel's nose. She then led her freshly wet, glistening body, baptized now, to the bed. She covered her with one sheet and laid a towel across the pillow—it would help for a while.

And Ciel lay down and cried. But Mattie knew the tears would end. And she would sleep. And morning would come.

1980

Luisah Teish

(1948–   )

THE SIXTH WORK: RITUALS FOR THE EXTENDED FAMILY
from *Jambalaya*

Following are rituals and exercises for attunement with your ancestors. By *attunement*, I mean sacred acts that will help you to realize your kinship with them. *None* of the exercises that follow are an invitation to possession. While direct possession is ultimately desirable, I feel it would be irresponsible to put such instructions in a book.

Pouring Libations

Libations should always be poured for the ancestors. Remember that the continuous creation of the *Da* is fluid. Water, juices, or alcohol can all be used. Simply pour the liquid on the ground or floor of the altar three times and say, "May my hands be fresh. May the road be clear. May the house be clean."

After your ancestors have drank, each person should take a sip of the liquid.

First Feast

Your first feast for the ancestors should be as elaborate as your means allow. There's only one rule on cooking for the *eguns*—no salt. Salt repels spirits, and you are asking them to focus some attention on you. Coffee, bread, sweets, fruit, soup, stews, meats, and so on—they eat it all. It is good to cook a special something characteristic of their and your motherland, such as cornbread, challah bread, scones, tortillas.

At this first feast, lay all the food on your altar and bless the food. Then take a small portion from each dish and place it on a saucer. Breathe on the food and touch it to the top of your head, your heart, and your pubis. Put a white candle in the center of the food, light it, and place it in a corner of the room. Then say,

"O blood of my blood. This is your child _____ (*name yourself, all others name themselves*). I bring you _____ (*name the foods*) for your nourishment. Know that you are loved and respected. Accept this offering for our good. Watch over your descendant: Let there be no death, let there be no illness, let there be no accident, let there be no upheaval, let there be no poverty, let there be no ill fate (*name all attributes you want to dispel*). Stand fast for me, for my good fortune, for my wealth, for my happiness, for my home, for my health (*name all the attributes you want to attract*).

"Thank you, blood of my blood. Thank you, O mighty dead."

The traditional Yoruba invocation is much longer than this one. But we are talking to kind spirits who are appreciative of our attention, so you can begin with this humble invocation. Later you will write your own.

Attendance

You should have as many of your family members in attendance as possible. If they are far away or are hostile to your spiritual practice, have friends represent them. After the ritual, call your mother. You need not tell her what you are doing, just call to say Hi.

After this first feast, develop the habit of taking a small saucer of food out of the pot *before* dinner is served. If you make this a weekly habit, the *eguns* will be happy.

Do you find yourself habitually dropping food while cooking? Do yams seem to fly from your fingers and slide across the kitchen floor? Maybe it's time to feed your ancestors.

I have said that cooking for your ancestors is simple. It is, with one exception. Do not think that you can *impose* your diet on them. It won't work for long.

I knew a woman who tried to force her ancestors to keep a vegetarian diet. The oracle kept saying that they were not satisfied. I suggested she make some meatballs for them. She did and got "great good fortune" from the oracle. I could advise her this way because I'd tried to impose a pork-free diet on my ancestors, but much to my disgust they insisted on pork chops to accompany their greens, yams, and cornbread.

By now a few of you are saying, "This is absurd! Why should I give food to somebody who can't eat it?" Remember, everything including food is made of energy. You are simply returning energy to those who gave you the energy of existence. Feed them, and they'll feed you.

The day after your first feast, take the food on the saucer and place it at the foot of a tree, or throw it in the compost heap. Give it back to Eartha, and She'll give it back to you in the forms of fruit, flowers, and vegetables.

Weekly Feast

The prayer for the weekly feast can be very simple. Again, touch the food to head, heart, and pubis before speaking. Use the lists you made in the Fifth Work. *For known ancestors:* "Blessed be the name of _____ who goes before me."

For unknown ancestors: "Honor to all those who died by _____ (*name the manner of death*). Love and Respect."

The Extended Family

I love the practice of extending the family to include people not related "by blood." Extended family is how the runaway slaves made their way to freedom. It is the way humble people have always functioned. Today the pressures of urban living—economic deprivation and loneliness—make this practice more than a courtesy. If we are to survive as whole human beings, the extended family must become the norm.

Any mentality that sets people apart from each other is the same mentality that gave rise to the slave trade, Nazi Germany, Hiroshima-Nagasaki, the massacre of the Native American, the Salem witch hunts, and many other atrocities too numerous and heartbreaking to mention. Now this demon mentality is being extended to the entire planet through the nuclear weapons game.

But through proper use of the *nommo* we can turn this ill fate around. We can affect the spirits of those who are possessed by the demon. We can activate the *Da* and debilitate the monster. We must make the whole of humanity our extended family. Here are two prayers to use; or write your own prayers.

Prayer for the Living

"To my kindred _____ (name the persons and places where they live).
May the blessing of the spirit be upon you.
May you be your best self.
May you walk in beauty.
May your guides be with you
at every crossroads.
May you be honorably greeted when you arrive.

Prayer for the Yet Unborn

"Come reside with us, those who are born to _____ (*name the attribute you wish to see birthed*, such as to stop the holocaust, to end world hunger, to create beauty). We eagerly await you."

Self-Blessing

1. *The ancestral bath.* Choose an herb native to your motherland (mine is magnolia). Steep it into a tea. Take a bath in the tea. While bathing read the stories you wrote about your family.
2. *Self-esteem chant.* Choose a nicely scented oil (I like vanilla). Place a container of the oil on a plate. Melt the bottom of two white candles

and stick them on the plate on both sides of the oil. Recite the self-esteem chant over the oil.

Now sit or stand before your *egun* altar and make a small cross on your body with the oil. Say, "I thank you for my _____ (*name and anoint body parts*), which are mine by your grace."

This exercise is important because women have been taught to be supercritical of their bodies. If you are alienated from your body, this will help you to overcome that alienation. If you already like your body, you'll feel even better. Personally, I am grateful for my eyes, a gift from my father's family. Having Moma's hips has its advantages. But my struggle is learning to love my hair, which has been the bane of my existence since childhood.

Sweet Silences

Your ancestors altar can be used as a meditation space. Following are two exercises for sweet silences.

1. *Water-gazing.* Sit in front of your altar and water-gaze.
2. *The sacred kiss.* Kneel in front of your altar. Open your hands so that the four fingers are close to each other and the thumbs are extended. Press the pointer fingers and the thumbs of both hands against each other until they form a diamond, or vulva-womb. Hold the vulva-womb directly over the top of your head. Inhale. Place the vulva-womb on the floor (earth). Exhale. Kiss the sacred portal that brought you into this world.

Joyful Noises

1. Make or buy a percussion instrument (drum, rattle, tambourine, cowbell, claves, bottle and spoon). Sit or stand before your altar. Tap out a rhythm that feels ancient and natural to you.
2. Create a rhythm by clapping your hands and stamping your feet. Play with the sound of the letter *O*.
3. Chant your grandmother's name repeatedly. Change the sound at times. Let the chant crescendo and then softer.
4. Walk *Damballah* in front of your altar. Make hissing and rattling sounds.

(Please be aware that all these exercises *can* be done in a wheelchair. Kiss the vulva-womb from an upright position by simply placing it in front of your lips. Do *Damballah* by pushing the chest forward, down, back, and up.)

It may seem to you that some of these exercises are theater games. It is true that "She Who Whispers" has advised me to make them simple and attractive.

But they are more than psychological devices to make you feel good. They are expenditures of energy consciously directed toward your ancestors. As you perform them, be aware that your subconscious is working in the assembly line to the racial consciousness and the collective unconscious. Be mindful of the inspiration that comes during and after these exercises.

1985

E. M. Broner

(1930–   )

THE CEREMONIES OF COMMUNITY
from *The Telling*

For more than fifteen years we have been present for one another for birthing ceremonies, re-empowerment ceremonies, to comfort after heartbreak, to re-assure after a hysterectomy, to be there when hearing of the loss of a parent.

As with Bella's Hug-In, the seder women knew how to honor and nurture one another, and we did it dramatically.

1978. FOR PHYLLIS. AFTER THE CIRCUMCISION.

On January 13, 1978, I flew from Detroit to New York for a ceremony: "Returning the Boy Child to the Women of the Family."

Phyllis had asked me to perform the ceremony after the circumcision of her new son, Ariel. She knew that, during the circumcision, the name of the father and all the illustrious male ancestors back to the tenth generation would be spoken. But none of the women who had borne the illustrious sons of the family would be mentioned by name. They were mere conduits.

Phyllis had phoned me at Wayne State University to request that I retrieve the child from the men and return him to the women of the family.

Chesler's apartment on West End Avenue was celebratory, with a table laid with delicatessen fare, with bagels, cheeses, honey cakes, and schnapps whiskey, for a *l'haim,* a toast to life.

Besides the father, the *mohel,* the one to circumcise, and the father's friends, stood the contingent of women: Phyllis, her mother, her aunt, her friends, including Erica Jong, who drove in from Connecticut, in the early stages of her pregnancy, and Gloria Steinem, who flew in from Washington, D.C., where she was on a writing grant. New York women, like publicist Selma Shapiro, lent their presence to this ritual.

After the baby was circumcised and the tiny yarmulke was placed on his head and he was told, "Now you're a Jew," I said, "It is time for us."

We took the baby away from the men.

We crowded into the study, sitting in a tight circle.

I introduced Ariel's grandmother and aunt to the group.

"The rest of us are his godmothers," I said.

Around the room the women blessed him.

"May you be tender," I said, "and, although you bruise, may you not bruise others."

Others said, "May you never feel more pain than you do on this day of circumcision."

"May you be strong enough to be the son of a feminist."

"May your mother be your friend all your shared life." It was Gloria, I believe, who blessed him that way.

"I bless you with laughter. You will need it."

"May you honor the women of your life as we honor you."

I asked that we present Ariel with something both useful and magical, a growing part of ourselves, whether it be a strand, curl, tendril, a nail clipping. For we were gathered here to weave together, to thatch, to patch.

I pulled out my tape, scissors, and card of red oaktag paper.

"This will be for Ariel in case he ever needs a spell, god-spell, magic," I said.

I cut the first strand of hair from my head and taped it upon this page of life and passed down the card. Each woman present cut her hair for Ariel— the gray of his grandmothers and aunt, black of his mother, blond of Gloria, brown of Erica.

We lit candles for Ariel and presented him with this hairy card of great power.

1979. FOR BELLA. AFTER THE FIRING.

It was the next year, 1979.

I would meet Bella Abzug as a result of Firing Friday, when, in Washington, on January 12th, President Jimmy Carter fired Bella. She had been co-chair of his National Advisory Committee on Women.

She had raised the funding for a meeting in Houston, Texas, the National Women's Conference, which would spawn a generation of new women politicians.

Hamilton Jordan, before Bella's meeting with Carter, phoned the press, "Boys, wanna have some fun? We're gonna fire Bella!"

The press was already gathered when Bella, unknowing, spoke to President Carter about the effect on women when there were cuts in social programs while the defense budget was being increased.

Her tone was strident, her finger employed like that of a *melamed*, a teacher. Neither the New York voice nor the pointing index finger pleased the southern president. It was not how ladies comported themselves.

Her firing in 1979 by the president had some of the effect of the treatment of Anita Hill by the Senate Judiciary Committee in 1991, shock at the arrogance of office holders.

In Detroit there was a luncheon to honor her work on women's behalf and to hear her story. I was to be poet laureate and sat at her table.

She said to us at her table, "Know what that ____ Jordan told me? He said, 'You know why (your husband) Martin is ill? You never stayed home. He had one heart attack already. You should stay home and take care of him.' "

That was January 30th, 1978, when I rose and read Bella a New Ten Commandments.

"These are the Male Commandments," I said:

1) Thou shalt not replace a man in Congress.
2) Thou shalt not run for Senate.
3) Thou shalt not have opinions before the president.
4) Thou shalt not be of energy and ambition.
5) Thou shalt not have a history of successful endeavor.
6) Thou shalt not spread compassion from outside thine own house, especially not unto the poor, the tired, the weary, the Black, the women, the gays.
7) Thou shalt have no vision, and if thou hast, let it be tunnel vision.
8) Thou shalt not raise thy voice above men, for in doing so, we would distract them from prayer and power.
9) Thou shalt not enter a room surrounded by friends, but singly, modestly, inconspicuously.
10) Thou shalt not let defeat strengthen thee.

I said to the women of Detroit, "We must be Tablet Breakers and New Rule Makers. Thou Shalt Not was written by men. This is how women speak:

1) Thou shalt enter the ancient Forbidden City of Washington, D.C.
2) Thou shalt replace the marble statues and oil portraits of men with the living presence of women.
3) Thou shalt honor thy women leaders that their days be long in the land.
4) Thou shalt educate thy daughters and honor them as we do our sons.
5) Thou shalt write and recite thine own history and place our founding mothers within its covers.
6) Thou shalt work mightily at replacing those who dishonor thee, whether they be from the city, the state, or head of the party.
7) Thou shalt remove those from office who would remove thee from the right to thine own body.
8) Thou shalt become as an army in the land.
9) Thou shalt invoke the names of thy foremothers: the judge Deborah, the warriors Yael, Judith, and the mighty Bella.

481

10) Thou shalt go forth with timbrel and song to right the ancient wrong.

Yet, it would be Bella who was to work at connecting the Carter-Kennedy forces at the next Democratic convention, so all could unite behind President Carter.

But some of us could not forget the need to humiliate the bravest and best of us.

1982. FOR A SEDER SISTER. AFTER HEARTBREAK.
SITTING SHIVAH FOR A LOST LOVE.
One Seder Sister has a broken heart.

Her lover, sixty-three, has gone to find a woman, twenty-three. Our friend, forty-three, thinks life is over, unfair; it's a man's world.

She cannot cease from weeping.

Her features are dissolving in the saltwater.

Her coloring has changed to boiled red.

She, a great beauty, has dulled her eyes, her hair, her soul.

So we gather to sit *shivah,* to hold a wake, on the day the lover weds his young woman.

We bring two items with us: a tape recorder and a cooked chicken.

We sit in a circle and speak into the machine.

We remind the bereaved of truth.

We remind the bereaved of her lost self.

We correct memory.

We reclaim the past.

The friend has been swept away. We must regather her, sweep her up, bring her back to us.

We remind our friend of who she is, how she is still whole.

We each remember the lost love. We correct our friend's memory.

We embrace in holy circle. We drink wine to the reunited wholeness of our friend.

We acknowledge amputation, separation as part of life.

We eat the cooked chicken. Ordinary routines go on.

We speak of work, of dreams, of visions.

The friend weeps and is embraced, and the tears wash away loss.

Our friend may wear a sign of mourning, besides her reddened eyes and heaving chest.

We cut a black armband and give it to our friend with a finite time in which to mourn.

And to end it.

1984. FOR ESTHER. AFTER THE OPERATION.

In Spring of 1984 I had a hysterectomy. My children came to bid farewell to their former abode, the twin sons complaining that it had been crowded in there.

I was dressed in white like a bride.

A *minyan*, a group of ten, women in this case, led by Phyllis and Lilly, gathered at our loft, carrying fruit—figs and dates, apricots and nuts, the firstfruits of the season for it was *Shavuoth*, the Holiday of Weeks, the time of first harvest.

The women placed me in the center of their circle and fed me as they said I had fed others, inside me and around my table.

Then the *minyan* of women spoke on:

Having a Womb and Using It
Having a Womb and Losing It
Having a Womb and Not Using It

And we spoke of what happens to one's womb—the fruit of the womb, firstfruit aborted, uterine cancer.

And we also spoke of what we suffered to be feminine—the boned, wired bras; the large curlers that strained our necks as we tried to straighten our hair.

And we declared an end to bone, wire, and plastic as a way of enhancing our beauty.

Then the women declared me Crone and said that the words I would utter would henceforth be considered wise.

A womb is like an accordian, expanding for as many as are contained within it. We declared an external womb, with which to care for, to aid those in need.

1987. FOR ESTHER. IN MOURNING.

My father died in 1987. He was a journalist, a gentle man. My father expected the *Kaddish*, the Mourner's Prayer, to be said for him by his sons, for daughters are not customarily the *Kaddish* of their parents.

I, the eldest, did not wish to abdicate my responsibility. The only place one could mourn daily was in an Orthodox synagogue.

I phoned one in the neighborhood.

"Oh," said the voice on the telephone, "we don't allow our women to mourn."

I thought of women with brimming eyes and fixed smiles.

I found a place nearby to say my Kaddish prayer.

But the men did not welcome my daily presence and hid themselves from me by turning their backs on me or hid me from them by pulling a curtain across the women's bench in our tiny prayer room.

I had been there for some weeks, either embattled or slowly making a few allies, when I decided to have an action.

I wrote my Seder Sisters and others at the beginning of March.

DEAR MINYAN MATES:

As most of you know, I have been saying *Kaddish* for my father for six weeks at an Orthodox *shul*. It's been an education for all of us. I, who am counted or discounted as half-a-man, the others who thought they were safe on an island of males.

I now need you, my sisters. I wish to have a *minyan* of women to attend the mourning service, Sunday, March 29th (1987).

Michele said, "I vowed I would never go to a synagogue that separated the men from the women, but, for Esther, I went. I know what it is to lose a parent and to need to mourn."

My sisters came: Letty with her hair primly back; Michele rushing down from the Upper East Side; Bea, from Westbeth, annoyed that I, a feminist, had placed myself in such a position. Edith walked over from her studio on 14th. Phyllis hired a car and drove in from Brooklyn early in the morning. Lilly Rivlin took time out from her busy schedule and new job at New Israel Fund to come to *shul*. Nahama came to add her voice to my *Kaddish*.

Bella was not going to be in town. "I said *Kaddish* for my father when I was thirteen all those years ago," she said, "when I was a girl and nobody did it. And I found out I would do what I needed to do and nobody could stop me. Next time you need me, call upon me and I'll come."

We filled the room with our presence and our voices.

When the prayers were finished, I sponsored a *kiddish*, with lox and herring and bagels and the men rushed into the room to eat. Some took little packets of food home with them to their lonely apartments.

"Remember how it was," one fellow said to the others, "when the women would come afterwards and make a spread and it was so comfortable?"

I was to stay the course, another nine months, strengthened by that memory of the women claiming their ancient right to mourn.

1988. FOR PHYLLIS. IN SUPPORT.

Lilly called the Seder Sisters, "Phyllis needs support."

Lilly arranges the support session at the Canadian Mission. We are there to join her in a meal. Then we rise, go into the living room, and surround

Phyllis. She falls into us, against us. And we protect her. We catch her. Lilly reads instructions about Trust, about Falling, about Getting Up, about Pulling Oneself Up.

Phyllis smiles her radiant smile.

If only we could have permanent effect.

1990. 1991. FOR NAHAMA. THE JOURNEY.

In late July of 1990, Bob and I open the door of our loft to greet wise women and some gentle men. We form a circle around a very pregnant young woman, Nahama, who sits enthroned on a sculptured chair, hand-carved by her brother Adam. She sits there to receive the blessings of the gathered for the ceremony "Blessing the Journey from Water to Air."

Rabbi Pamela Hoffman, a recent graduate of Jewish Theological Seminary, has come to help us expedite. Rabbi Pam reads the angel's blessings, those that surround us: on the right, Michael, God's gift; on the left, Gabriel, the strength of God; behind us, Uriel, the light of God; before us, Raphael, the health of God.

We sing a song by Cantor Debbie Friedman replete with blessings from the *Shekhinah*.

May you be blessed
beneath the wings of the *Shekhinah*.
Be blessed with love,
be blessed with peace.

And we sing another song from Debbie Friedman (from the tape *You Shall Be a Blessing*, Sounds Write Productions, 1989, available from Jewish Family Productions). The song, with words by Savina Teubal, is based on the words God spoke to Abraham: "Go forth," *Lech Lecha*. It gives women permission to cross borders into the feminine, *Lechi Lach*.

L'chi Lach (f)
to a land that I will show you
Lech L'cha (m)
to a place you do not know
L'chi Lach
on your journey I will bless you
and you shall be a blessing
L'chi Lach.

Phyllis Chesler blesses Nahama, stroking her hand and arm, reading from her own memoir, *With Child* (New York: Crowell, 1979), I see a carapace forming around Nahama. I begin to see her taking her place as the person she will be.

All of our friends who are able come to bless her.

Michele writes from Toronto, "I do not believe in God, so I can't be a godmother. But I believe in books, so I'll be her book fairy."

Lilly Rivlin gives her a silver *Chamsa,* a hand amulet, that Lilly has worn as protection. From now on, it will protect Nahama on her journey.

Mary Gordon gives her a Mexican wooden angel to bless her.

And, properly blessed, holding the silver *Chamsa* in her hand, Nahama goes into her hard travail and bears a golden-haired girl.

And there is trouble. Congenital problems.

We phone Letty, who calls a pediatric neurosurgeon in Los Angeles for advice.

Bea and Edith make the soothing sounds of comfort every day on the phone.

Lilly comes one hard night with Chinese take-out for everyone.

About nine months after the initial Journey ceremony, I speak to Cantor Debbie Friedman on the phone to California.

Debbie and I share the keynote speech at the Timbrels of Miriam Conference at the University of Judaism in Los Angeles. By phone and fax, we plan our interweaving of story and song. "The Journey from Water to Air" will be part of the presentation.

"Write another blessing song, using all the angels, to bless my daughter and her daughter," I request.

Debbie writes:

> *May our right hand draw us closer to our*
> *   Godliness.*
> *May our left hand give us strength to face each day.*
> *And before us, may our vision light our paths*
> *   ahead.*
> *And behind us, may well-being heal our way.*
>
> *All around us is Shekhinah.*
> *All around is Shekhinah.*
>
> *On my right, Michael.*
> *On my left, Gabriel.*

And before me, Uriel.
And behind me, Raphael.

All around us is Shekhinah.
All around us is Shekhinah.

There is reprieve. The child grows extraordinarily and, more importantly, normally.

When we have our seder The Plagues We Live Under, Nahama said to the group, "You may think I would list the problems of Alexandra as a plague. But it turned out to be a blessing of friendship. I quote what Letty told me when I asked her for help, 'That's what we're all here for.' "

It takes a lot of communal blessings to make a journey successful, to make one wish come true.

Those are our dramatic appearances for one another.

1993

PART V

Private Lives

Historians insist that we learn most about the everyday lives of women through private papers—letters, diaries, journals. Even in eras when it was considered unseemly and certainly "unfeminine" for women to publish their work, women recorded, interpreted, and commented upon their lives and the life of their times in their journals and letters. At least since the latter part of the eighteenth century, when paper and ink became affordable to middle-class Americans, young girls have been encouraged to keep a private record of their lives while adult women have typically assumed the role of correspondent, keeping in touch with family members and friends no longer living near by. The role of family communicator is one many women continue to play today, although the telephone and e-mail have diminished opportunities for future historians of women's lives.

The memoir is a more formal and public extension of the journal (in which private observations are recorded) and the letter (which has a clear audience). From the Latin word for "memory" or "remembering," a memoir records the world through the subjective lens of an all-seeing "I"/eye. While a diary or a journal is typically arranged by day or week (time providing the chief structuring device), a memoir or autobiography can have any number of organizing principles. It might evolve to show the ways in which the young child matures into the writing adult (similar to the *bildungsroman*, the novel of the "building" or education of the protagonist). Or it might begin with the adult authorial presence and then use flashbacks to recapture and present salient moments and events from the past. Yet even with its more formal narrative structure, the memoir often strives for a tone of intimacy and immediacy—a "You Are There" quality—that we associate with the most vivid diaries and letters. In all of these forms, the writer projects a personality. Indeed, sometimes the vividness of that keenly remembering and communicating self is more important than any events actually described.

In the selections included here, we have a range of voices and personalities. Some of the selections are written by famous women (such as Abigail Adams, who would become the nation's second First Lady); others, by women who are not remembered in standard histories or, indeed, who remain anonymous today. No matter. All speak with a presence, an immediate and urgent voice that is vivid, intense, and direct.

❖

O N E

The Republic of Women's Letters

Letters, such as the three included here, are typical of the formal, political epistles written by women in the late eighteenth and nineteenth centuries. Two are written by famous women, one under the pseudonym Matilda, but all indicate (contrary to stereotype) that women were engaged powerfully in the social and political life of their day. Although the ideology of "separate spheres" encouraged women to see the home as their sole province, Abigail Adams, Matilda, and Sarah Moore Grimké all knew that it was their right— even their duty—to speak about, and sometimes against, the world of events beyond domesticity.

Although Abigail (Smith) Adams (1744–1818) wrote letters throughout her life, including a number of passionate love letters to her husband John Adams, the second President of the United States, the one reprinted here is one of the most famous in American history. In this letter, she implores her husband to "Remember the Ladies" in the new "code of laws" that he will help to make in the wake of American independence from England. She even threatens to foment a rebellion of her own—a rebellion of women—if women continue to be excluded from the nation by being denied political "represen-tation." Sadly, the letter was treated almost as a joke by her husband. The ladies were not remembered in the new U.S. constitution.

The epistle by Matilda, written to the editors of *Freedom's Journal*, advances the cause of improved education for women. The author insists that it is long past the time when it is sufficient for a woman to know how to "darn a stocking, and cook a pudding well." She uses the public forum of the "letter to the editor" to make a case that women be encouraged to read, to study subjects including mathematics and history, and to teach their daughters these subjects as well.

The final letter in this section is from the pen of Sarah Moore Grimké (1792–1873) and written to her sister Angelina Emily. The Grimké sisters, both essayists, were influential reformers, concentrating especially on abolition and women's rights. Born in Charleston, South Carolina, daughters of a prominent slaveholder, they were educated according to their station—that is, in elite girls' schools were they learned piano playing, needlework, and other arts befitting upper-class women. However, secretly and on their own, they versed themselves in Latin, law, history, and other subjects. The two sisters rebelled against their background to such an extent that Sarah went to Philadelphia where she became a Quaker minister, followed by Angelina, who was expelled from her Episcopal congregation for her beliefs and behavior. When she moved to Philadelphia, like Sarah, she devoted her life to anti-slavery and women's rights issues. In letters to one another, the sisters worked out many of the ideas and political positions that would help to change the course of American history.

Abigail Adams
(1744–1818)

TO JOHN ADAMS

March 31, 1776

I long to hear that you have declared an independancy—and by the way in the new Code of Laws which I suppose it will be necessary for you to make I desire you would Remember the Ladies, and be more generous and favourable to them than your ancestors. Do not put such unlimited power into the hands of the Husbands. Remember all Men would be tyrants if they could. If perticuliar care and attention is not paid to the Laidies we are determined to foment a Rebelion, and will not hold ourselves bound by any Laws in which we have no voice, or Representation.

That your Sex are Naturally Tyrannical is a Truth so thoroughly established as to admit of no dispute, but such of you as wish to be happy willingly give up the harsh title of Master for the more tender and endearing one of Friend. Why then, not put it out of the power of the vicious and the Lawless to use us with cruelty and indignity with impunity. Men of Sense in all Ages abhor those customs which treat us only as the vassals of your Sex. Regard us then as Beings placed by providence under your protection and in immitation of the Supreem Being make use of that power only for our happiness.

Matilda

(nineteenth century)

LETTER TO THE EDITORS
of *Freedom's Journal*

MESSRS. EDITORS   August, 1827

Will you allow a female to offer a few remarks upon a subject that
you must allow to be all-important? I don't know that in any of your
papers, you have said sufficient upon the education of females. I hope
you are not to be classed with those, who think that our mathematical
knowledge should be limited to "fathoming the dish-kettle," and that
we have acquired enough of history, if we know that our grandfather's
father lived and died. 'Tis true the time has been, when to darn a
stocking, and cook a pudding well, was considered the end and aim
of a woman's being. But those were days when ignorance blinded
men's eyes. The diffusion of knowledge has destroyed those degrading opinions, and men of the present age, allow, that we have minds
that are capable and deserving of culture. There are difficulties, and
great difficulties in the way of our advancement; but that should only
stir us to greater efforts. We possess not the advantages with those
of our sex, whose skins are not colored like our own; but we can
improve what little we have, and make our one talent produce two-
fold. The influence that we have over the male sex demands, that our
minds should be instructed and improved with the principles of education and religion, in order that this influence should be properly
directed. Ignorant ourselves, how can we be expected to form the
minds of our youth, and conduct them in the paths of knowledge?
How can we "teach the young idea to shoot" if we have [no knowl-
edge] ourselves? I would address myself to all mothers, and say to
them, that while it is necessary to possess a knowledge of cookery,
and the various mysteries of pudding-making, something more is
requisite. It is their bounden duty to store their daughters' minds
with useful learning. They should be made to devote their leisure
time to reading books, whence they would derive valuable information, which could never be taken from them. I will no longer trespass
on your time and patience. I merely throw out these hints, in order
that some more able pen will take up the subject.

                                                        MATILDA

Sarah Moore Grimké
(1792–1873)

LETTER XV: MAN EQUALLY GUILTY WITH WOMAN IN THE FALL

Uxbridge, 10th Mo. 20th, 1837

MY DEAR SISTER,

It is said that "modern Jewish women light a lamp every Friday evening, half an hour before sunset, which is the beginning of their Sabbath, in remembrance of their original mother, who first extinguished the lamp of righteousness,—to remind them of their obligation to rekindle it." I am one of those who always admit, to its fullest extent, the popular charge, that woman brought sin into the world. I accept it as a powerful reason, why woman is bound to labor with double diligence, for the regeneration of that world she has been intrumental in ruining.

But, although I do not repel the imputation, I shall notice some passages in the sacred Scriptures, where this transaction is mentioned, which prove, I think, the identity and equality of man and woman, and that there is no difference in their guilt in the view of that God who searcheth the heart and trieth the reins of the children of men. In Is. 43:27, we find the following passage—"Thy first father hath sinned, and thy teachers have transgressed against me"—which is synonymous with Rom. 5:12. "Wherefore, as by ONE MAN sin entered into the world, and death by sin, &c." Here man and woman are included under one term, and no distinction is made in their criminality. The circumstances of the fall are again referred to in 2 Cor. 11:3—"But I fear lest, by any means, as the serpent *beguiled* Eve through his subtility, so your mind should be beguiled from the simplicity that is in Christ." Again, 1st Tim. 2:14–"Adam *was not deceived;* but the woman being *deceived,* was in the transgression." Now, whether the fact, that Eve was beguiled and deceived, is a proof that her crime was of deeper dye than Adam's, who was not deceived, but was fully aware of the consequences of sharing in her transgression, I shall leave the candid reader to determine.

My present object is to show, that, as woman is charged with all the sin that exists in the world, it is her solemn duty to labor for its

493

extinction; and that this she can never do effectually and extensively, until her mind is disenthralled of those shackles which have been riveted upon her by a *"corrupt public opinion, and a perverted interpretation of the holy Scriptures."* Woman must feel that she is the equal, and is designed to be the fellow laborer of her brother, or she will be studying to find out the *imaginary* line which separates the sexes, and divides the duties of men and women into two distinct classes, a separation not even hinted at in the Bible, where we are expressly told, "there is neither male nor female, for ye are all one in Christ Jesus" [Gal. 3:28].

My views on this subject are so much better embodied in the language of a living author than I can express them, that I quote the passage entire: "Woman's rights and man's rights are *both* contained in the *same* charter, and held by the *same* tenure. *All rights* spring out of the *moral* nature: they are both the root and the offspring of *responsibilities.* The physical constitution is the mere *instrument* of the *moral* nature; sex is a mere *incident* of this constitution, a provision necessary to this *form* of existence; its *only* design, not to give, nor to take away, nor in any respect to modify or even *touch* rights or responsibilities in any sense, except so far as the peculiar offices of each sex may afford less or more *opportunity* and ability for the exercise of rights, and the discharge of responsibilities; but merely to continue and enlarge the human department of God's government. Consequently, I know nothing of *man's* rights, or *woman's* rights; *human* rights are all that I recognise. The doctrine, that the *sex of the body* presides over and administers upon the rights and responsibilities of the moral, immortal nature, is to my mind a doctrine kindred to blasphemy, *when seen in its intrinsic nature.* It breaks up utterly the *relations* of the two natures, and reverses their functions; exalting the animal nature into a monarch, and humbling the moral into a slave; making the former a proprietor, and the latter its property."

To perform our duties, we must comprehend our rights and responsibilities; and it is because we do not understand, that we now fall so far short in the discharge of our obligations. Unaccustomed to think for ourselves, and to search the sacred volume, to see how far we are living up to the design of Jehovah in our creation, we have rested satisfied with the sphere marked out for us by man, never detecting the fallacy of that reasoning which forbids woman to exercise some of her noblest faculties, and stamps with the reproach of indelicacy those actions by which women were formerly dignified and exalted in the church.

I should not mention this subject again, if it were not to point out to my sisters what seems to me an irresistible conclusion from the literal interpretation of St. Paul, without reference to the context, and the peculiar circumstances and abuses which drew forth the expressions, "I suffer not a woman to teach"—"Let your women keep silence in the church," [1 Cor. 14:34], i.e. congregation. It is manifest, that if the apostle meant what his words imply, when taken in the strictest sense, then women have no right to *teach* Sabbath or day schools, or to open their lips to sing in the assemblies of the people; yet young and delicate women are engaged in all these offices; they are expressly trained to exhibit themselves, and raise their voices to a high pitch in the choirs of our places of worship. I do not intend to sit in judgment on my sisters for doing these things; I only want them to see, that they are as really infringing a *supposed* divine command, by instructing their pupils in the Sabbath or day schools, and by singing in the congregation, as if they were engaged in preaching the unsearchable riches of Christ to a lost and perishing world. Why, then, are we permitted to break this injunction in some points, and so sedulously warned not to overstep the bounds set for us by our *brethren* in another? Simply, as I believe, because in the one case we subserve *their* views and *their* interests, and act *in subordination to them;* whilst in the other, we come in contact with their interests, and claim to be on an equality with them in the highest and most important trust ever committed to man, namely, the ministry of the world. It is manifest, that if women were permitted to be ministers of the gospel, as they unquestionably were in the primitive ages of the Christian church, it would interfere materially with the present organized system of spiritual power and ecclesiastical authority, which is now vested solely in the hands of men. It would either show that all the paraphernalia of theological seminaries, &c. &c. to prepare men to become evangelists, is wholly unnecessary, or it would create a necessity for similar institutions in order to prepare women for the same office; and this would be an encroachment on that learning, which our kind brethren have so ungenerously monopolized. I do not ask any one to believe my statements, or adopt my conclusions, because they are mine; but I do earnestly entreat my sisters to lay aside their prejudices, and examine these subjects *for themselves,* regardless of the "traditions of men," because they are intimately connected with their duty and their usefulness in the present important crisis.

All who know any thing of the present system of benevolent and religious operations, know that women are performing an important

part in them, in *subserviency to men,* who guide our labors, and are
often the recipients of those benefits of education we toil to confer,
and which we rejoice they can enjoy, although it is their mandate
which deprives us of the same advantages. Now, whether our brethren have defrauded us intentionally, or unintentionally, the wrong we
suffer is equally the same. For years, they have been spurring us up
to the performance of our duties. The immense usefulness and the
vast influence of woman have been eulogized and called into exercise,
and many a blessing has been lavished upon us, and many a prayer
put up for us, because we have labored by day and by night to clothe
and feed and educate young men, whilst our own bodies sometimes
suffer for want of comfortable garments, and our minds are left in
almost utter destitution of that improvement which we are toiling to
bestow upon the brethren. . . .

I have now, my dear sister, completed my series of letters. I am
aware, they contain some new views; but I believe they are based on
the immutable truths of the Bible. All I ask for them is, the candid
and prayerful consideration of Christians. If they strike at some of
our bosom sins, our deep-rooted prejudices, our long cherished opinions, let us not condemn them on that account, but investigate them
fearlessly and prayerfully, and not shrink from the examination; because, if they are true, they place heavy responsibilities upon women.
In throwing them before the public, I have been actuated solely by
the belief, that if they are acted upon, they will exalt the character
and enlarge the usefulness of my own sex, and contribute greatly to
the happiness and virtue of the other. [That there is] a root of bitterness continually springing up in families and troubling the repose
of both men and women, must be manifest to even a superficial observer; and I believe it is the mistaken notion of the inequality of the
sexes. As there is an assumption of superiority on the one part, which
is not sanctioned by Jehovah, there is an incessant struggle on the
other to rise to that degree of dignity, which God designed women
to possess in common with men, and to maintain those rights and
exercise those privileges which every woman's common sense, apart
from the prejudices of education, tells her are inalienable; they are a
part of her moral nature, and can only cease when her immortal mind
is extinguished.

One word more. I feel that I am calling upon my sex to sacrifice
what has been, what is still dear to their hearts, the adulation, the
flattery, the attentions of trifling men. I am asking them to repel these
insidious enemies whenever they approach them; to manifest by their

conduct, that, although they value highly the society of pious and intelligent men, they have no taste for idle conversation, and for that silly preference which is manifested for their personal accommodation, often at the expense of great inconvenience to their male companions. As an illustration of what I mean, I will state a fact.

I was traveling lately in a stage coach. A gentleman, who was also a passenger, was made sick by riding with his back to the horses. I offered to exchange seats, assuring him it did not affect me at all unpleasantly; but he was too polite to permit a lady to run the risk of being discommoded. I am sure he meant to be very civil, but I really thought it was a foolish piece of civility. This kind of attention encourages selfishness in woman, and is only accorded as a sort of quietus, in exchange for those *rights* of which we are deprived. Men and women are equally bound to cultivate a spirit of accommodation; but I exceedingly deprecate her being treated like a spoiled child, and sacrifices made to her selfishness and vanity. In lieu of these flattering but injurious attentions, yielded to her as an inferior, as a mark of benevolence and courtesy, I want my sex to claim nothing from their brethren but what their brethren may justly claim from them, in their intercourse as Christians. I am persuaded woman can do much in this way to elevate her own character. And that we may become duly sensible of the dignity of our nature, only a little lower than the angels, and bring forth fruit to the glory and honor of Emanuel's name, is the fervent prayer of

THINE IN THE BONDS OF WOMANHOOD,

T W O

Women in the Nineteenth Century

In the nineteenth century, when middle- or upper-class women were un-
avoidably restricted to activities suitable to their "sheltered" lives, the diary
became the mark of the woman's gentility. Louisa May Alcott (1832–1888)
was provided early with books for recording her inner life (notice the emphasis
on morality and goodness in these pages from her pre-teen writings). In the
separate spheres women and men chose to inhabit, women were to be upright,
beneficent, and—at all times—a force for good.

Alcott's mature writing (such as *Work*) remains overshadowed by the books
for adolescent readers she wrote, literally, to feed her family: *Little Women,
Rose in Bloom, Little Men,* and *Jo's Boys* illustrate the mandate that women's
writing be instructive and supportive. The very popular nature writer, Susan
Fenimore Cooper (1813–1894), chose to follow those same injunctions; and
her often reprinted *Rural Hours,* first published in 1850, easily outsold Henry
David Thoreau's *Walden.* Both were meditations on the natural world.

Cooper, the daughter of novelist James Fenimore Cooper, like Alcott, the
daughter of educator-philosopher Bronson Alcott, was a highly educated
woman. Cooper in Cooperstown, New York, served as amanuensis for her
father. Never married, she spent her long life in humanitarian service, and
occasionally worked at her own writing.

Running parallel with this suitably genteel strain of well-born, white wom-
en's writing was the slave narrative—sometimes written by the slaves themselves, and sometimes by white (abolitionist) writers who were eager for
horrific tales to aid the anti-slave cause. One of the most important of the
autobiographical slave narratives is that written by Harriet Jacobs (1813?–
1897), who wrote under the pseudonym Linda Brent. *Incidents in the Life of
a Slave Girl,* published in 1861, was a shocking account because it explained
Jacobs's choice to be sexually active, though unmarried, as a means of resisting
the advances of her owner's father, a prominent physician in Edenton, North
Carolina. In the slave narrative, writing for private and personal satisfaction
(motivation for keeping a diary) had to give way to the urgent need to explain
the conditions of slavery—including its often hidden narratives of rape and
unnecessary separation of family members.

As letters from Frances E. W. Harper (1825–1911) and Elizabeth Ramsey
(ca. 1800), and the excerpt from the Civil War diary kept by Mary Boykin
Chesnut (1823–1886) show, the latter part of the nineteenth century in the
United States was dominated by the struggle over slavery, states' rights, and

both the Civil War and its aftermath. Women's writing, like men's, reflects that crucible.

❖

Louisa May Alcott
DIARY
(1832–1888)

1843

September 1st.—I rose at five and had my bath. I love cold water! Then we had our singing-lesson with Mr. Lane. After breakfast I washed dishes, and ran on the hill till nine, and had some thoughts,—it was so beautiful up there. Did my lessons,—wrote and spelt and did sums; and Mr. Lane read a story, "The Judicious Father": How a rich girl told a poor girl not to look over the fence at the flowers, and was cross to her because she was unhappy. The father heard her do it, and made the girls change clothes. The poor one was glad to do it, and he told her to keep them. But the rich one was very sad; for she had to wear the old ones a week, and after that she was good to shabby girls. I liked it very much, and I shall be kind to poor people.

Father asked us what was God's noblest work. Anna said *men*, but I said *babies*. Men are often bad; babies never are. We had a long talk, and I felt better after it, and *cleared up.*

We had bread and fruit for dinner. I read and walked and played till supper-time. We sung in the evening. As I went to bed the moon came up very brightly and looked at me. I felt sad because I have been cross today, and did not mind Mother. I cried, and then I felt better, and said that piece from Mrs. Sigourney, "I must not tease my mother." I get to sleep saying poetry,— I know a great deal.

Thursday, 14th.—Mr. Parker Pillsbury came, and we talked about the poor slaves. I had a music lesson with Miss P. I hate her, she is so fussy. I ran in the wind and played be a horse, and had a lovely time in the woods with Anna and Lizzie. We were fairies, and made gowns and paper wings. I "flied" the highest of all. In the evening they talked about travelling. I thought about Father going to England, and said this piece of poetry I found in Byron's poems:—

> "When I left thy shores, O Naxos,
>   Not a tear in sorrow fell;
> Not a sigh or faltered accent
>   Told my bosom's struggling swell."

499

It rained when I went to bed, and made a pretty noise on the roof.

A Sample of our Lessons.

"What virtues do you wish more of?" asks Mr. L. [Louisa's father]. I answer:—

Patience,	Love,	Silence,
Obedience,	Generosity,	Perseverance,
Industry,	Respect,	Self-denial.

"What vices less of?"

Idleness,	Wilfulness,	Vanity,
Impatience,	Impudence,	Pride,
Selfishness,	Activity,	Love of cats.

Mr. L.   L. (Louisa)

SOCRATES.   ALCIBIADES.

How can you get what you need? By trying.
How do you try? By resolution and perseverance.
How gain love? By gentleness.
What is gentleness? Kindness, patience, and care for other people's feelings.
Who has it? Father and Anna.
Who means to have it? Louisa, if she can.
(She never got it.—L.M.A.)
Write a sentence about anything. "I hope it will rain; the garden needs it."
What are the elements of hope? Expectation, desire, faith.
What are the elements in wish? Desire.
What is the difference between faith and hope? "Faith can believe without seeing; hope is not sure, but tries to have faith when it desires."

What are the most valuable kinds of self-denial? Appetite, temper.

How is self-denial of temper known? If I control my temper, I am respectful and gentle, and every one sees it.
What is the result of this self-denial? Every one loves me, and I am happy.
Why use self-denial? For the good of myself and others.
How shall we learn this self-denial? By resolving, and then trying *hard*.
What then do you mean to do? To resolve and try.
(Here the record of these lessons end, and poor little Alcibiades went to work and tried till fifty, but without any very great success, in spite of all the help Socrates and Plato gave her.—L.M.A.)

CONCORD, *Thursday.*—I had an early run in the woods before the dew was off the grass. The moss was like velvet, and as I ran under the arches of yellow and red leaves I sang for joy, my heart was so bright and the world so beautiful. I stopped at the end of the walk and saw the sunshine out over the wide "Virginia meadows."

It seemed like going through a dark life or grave into heaven beyond. A very strange and solemn feeling came over me as I stood there, with no sound but the rustle of the pines, no one near me, and the sun so glorious, as for me alone. It seemed as if I *felt* God as I never did before, and I prayed in my heart that I might keep that happy sense of nearness in my life.

[I have, for I most sincerely think that the little girl "got religion" that day in the wood when dear mother Nature led her to God.—L. M. A., 1885.]

Thirteen Years Old.

Fruitlands, 1846

March,—I have at last got the little room I have wanted so long, and am very happy with it. It does me good to be alone, and mother has made it very pretty and neat for me. My work-basket and desk are by the window, and my closet is full of dried herbs that smell very nice. The door that opens into the garden will be very pretty in summer, and I can run off to the woods when I like.

I have made a plan for my life, as I am in my teens, and no more a child. I am old for my age, and don't care much for girl's things. People think I'm wild and queer; but mother understands and helps me. I have not told any one about my plan; but I'm going to *be* good. I've made so many resolutions, and written sad notes, and cried over my sins, and it doesn't seem to do any good! Now I'm going to *work really*, for I feel a true desire to improve, and be a help and comfort, not a care and sorrow, to my dear mother.

Susan Fenimore Cooper
(1813–1894)

AFTERNOON IN THE WOODS
from *Rural Hours*

Saturday, [July] 28th.—Passed the afternoon in the woods.

What a noble gift to man are the forests! What a debt of gratitude and admiration we owe for their utility and their beauty!

How pleasantly the shadows of the wood fall upon our heads, when we turn from the glitter and turmoil of the world of man! The winds of heaven seem to linger amid these balmy branches, and the sunshine falls like a blessing upon the green leaves; the wild breath of the forest, fragrant with bark and berry, fans the brow with grateful freshness; and the beautiful wood-light, neither garish nor gloomy, full of calm and peaceful influences, sheds repose over the spirit. The view is limited, and the objects about us are uniform in character; yet within the bosom of the woods the mind readily lays aside its daily littleness, and opens to higher thoughts, in silent consciousness that it stands alone with the works of God. The humble moss beneath our feet, the sweet flowers, the varied shrubs, the great trees, and the sky gleaming above in sacred blue, are each the handiwork of God. They were all called into being by the will of the Creator, as we now behold them, full of wisdom and goodness. Every object here has a deeper merit than our wonder can fathom; each has a beauty beyond our full perception; the dullest insect crawling about these roots lives by the power of the Almighty; and the discolored shreds of last year's leaves wither away upon the lowly herbs in a blessing of fertility. But it is the great trees, stretching their arms above us in a thousand forms of grace and strength, it is more especially the trees which fill the mind with wonder and praise.

Of the infinite variety of fruits which spring from the bosom of the earth, the trees of the wood are the greatest in dignity. Of all the works of the creation which know the changes of life and death, the trees of the forest have the longest existence. Of all the objects which crown the gray earth, the woods preserve unchanged, throughout the greatest reach of time, their native character: the works of man are ever varying their aspect; his towns and his fields alike reflect the unstable opinions, the fickle wills and fancies of each passing generation; but the forests on his borders remain to-day the same [as] they were ages of years since. Old as the everlasting hills, during thousands of seasons they have put forth and laid down their verdure in calm obedience to the decree which first bade them cover the ruins of the Deluge.

But, although the forests are great and old, yet the ancient trees within their bounds must each bend individually beneath the doom of every earthly existence; they have their allotted period when the mosses of Time gather upon their branches; when, touched by decay, they break and crumble to dust. Like man, they are decked in living beauty; like man, they fall a prey to death; and while we admire their duration, so far beyond our own brief years, we also acknowledge that especial interest which can only belong to the graces of life and to the desolation of death. We raise our eyes, and we see collected in one company vigorous trunks, the oak, the ash, the pine, firm in the strength of maturity; by their side stand a young group, elm, and birch, and maple, their supple branches playing in the breezes, gay and fresh as youth itself; and yonder, rising in unheeded gloom, we behold a skeleton trunk, an old fir, every branch broken, every leaf fallen,—dull, still, sad, like the finger of Death.

It is the peculiar nature of the forest, that life and death may ever be found within its bounds, in immediate presence of each other; both with ceaseless, noiseless, advances, aiming at the mastery; and if the influences of the first be most general, those of the last are the most striking. Spring, with all her wealth of life and joy, finds within the forest many a tree unconscious of her approach; a thousand young plants springing up about the fallen trunk, the shaggy roots, seek to soften the gloomy wreck with a semblance of the verdure it bore of old; but ere they have thrown their fresh and graceful wreaths over the mouldering wood, half their own tribe wither and die with the year. We owe to this perpetual presence of death an impression, calm, solemn, almost religious in character, a chastening influence, beyond what we find in the open fields. But this subdued spirit is far from gloomy or oppressive, since it never fails to be relieved by the cheerful animation of living beauty. Sweet flowers grow beside the fallen trees, among the shattered branches, the season through; and the freedom of the woods, the unchecked growth, the careless position of every tree, are favorable to a thousand wild beauties, and fantastic forms, opening to the mind a play of fancy which is in itself cheering and enlivening, like the bright sunbeams which checker with golden light the shadowy groves. That character of rich variety also, stamped on all the works of the creation, is developed in the forest in clear and noble forms; we are told that in the field we shall not find two blades of grass exactly alike, that in the garden we shall not gather two flowers precisely similar, but in those cases the lines are minute, and we do not seize the truth at once; in the woods, however, the same fact stands recorded in bolder lines; we cannot fail to mark this great variety of detail among the trees; we see it in their trunks, their branches, their foliage; in the rude knots, the gnarled roots; in the mosses and lichens which feed upon their bark; in their forms, their coloring, their shadows. And within all this luxuriance of varied beauty, there dwells a sweet quiet, a noble harmony, a calm repose, which we seek in vain elsewhere, in so full a measure.

1850

❖

Harriet Ann Jacobs
(1813?–1897)

THE TRIALS OF GIRLHOOD
from *Incidents in the Life of a Slave Girl*

5

During the first years of my service in Dr. Flint's family, I was accustomed to share some indulgences with the children of my mistress. Though this seemed to me no more than right, I was grateful for it, and tried to merit the kindness by the faithful discharge of my duties. But I now entered on my fifteenth year—a sad epoch in the life of a slave girl. My master began to whisper foul words in my ear. Young as I was, I could not remain ignorant of their import. I tried to treat them with indifference or contempt. The master's age, my extreme youth, and the fear that his conduct would be reported to my grandmother, made him bear this treatment for many months. He was a crafty man, and resorted to many means to accomplish his purposes. Sometimes he had stormy, terrific ways, that made his victims tremble; sometimes he assumed a gentleness that he thought must surely subdue. Of the two, I preferred his stormy moods, although they left me trembling. He tried his utmost to corrupt the pure principles my grandmother had instilled. He peopled my young mind with unclean images, such as only a vile monster could think of. I turned from him with disgust and hatred. But he was my master. I was compelled to live under the same roof with him—where I saw a man forty years my senior daily violating the most sacred commandments of nature. He told me I was his property; that I must be subject to his will in all things. My soul revolted against the mean tyranny. But where could I turn for protection? No matter whether the slave girl be as black as ebony or as fair as her mistress. In either case, there is no shadow of law to protect her from insult, from violence, or even from death; all these are inflicted by fiends who bear the shape of men. The mistress, who ought to protect the helpless victim, has no other feelings towards her but those of jealousy and rage. The degradation, the wrongs, the vices, that grow out of slavery, are more than I can describe. They are greater than you would willingly believe. Surely, if you credited one half the truths that are told you concerning the helpless millions suffering in this cruel bondage, you at the north would not help to tighten the yoke. You surely would refuse to do for the master, on your own soil, the mean and cruel work which trained bloodhounds and the lowest class of white do for him at the south.

Every where the years bring to all enough of sin and sorrow; but in slavery the very dawn of life is darkened by these shadows. Even the little child, who is accustomed to wait on her mistress and her children, will learn, before she is twelve years old, why it is that her mistress hates such and such a one among the slaves. Perhaps the child's own mother is among those hated ones. She listens to violent outbreaks of jealous passion, and cannot help understanding what is the cause. She will become prematurely knowing in evil things. Soon she will learn to tremble when she hears her master's footfall. She will be compelled to realize that she is no longer a child. If God has bestowed beauty upon her, it will prove her greatest curse. That which commands admiration in the white woman only hastens the degradation of the female slave. I know that some are too much brutalized by slavery to feel the humiliation of their position; but many slaves feel it most acutely, and shrink from the memory of it. I cannot tell how much I suffered in the presence of these wrongs, nor how I am still pained by the retrospect. My master met me at every turn, reminding me that I belonged to him, and swearing by heaven and earth that he would compel me to submit to him. If I went out for a breath of fresh air, after a day of unwearied toil, his footsteps dogged me. If I knelt by my mother's grave, his dark shadow fell on me even there. The light heart which nature had given me became heavy with sad forebodings. The other slaves in my master's house noticed the change. May of them pitied me; but none dared to ask the cause. They had no need to inquire. They knew too well the guilty practices under that roof; and they were aware that to speak of them was an offence that never went unpunished.

I longed for some one to confide in. I would have given the world to have laid my head on my grandmother's faithful bosom, and told her all my troubles. But Dr. Flint swore he would kill me, if I was not as silent as the grave. Then, although my grandmother was all in all to me, I feared her as well as loved her. I had been accustomed to look up to her with a respect bordering upon awe. I was very young, and felt shamefaced about telling her such impure things, especially as I knew her to be very strict on such subjects. Moreover, she was a woman of a high spirit. She was usually very quiet in her demeanor;

but if her indignation was once roused, it was not very easily quelled. I had been told that she once chased a white gentleman with a loaded pistol, because he insulted one of her daughters. I dreaded the consequences of a violent outbreak; and both pride and fear kept me silent. But though I did not confide in my grandmother, and even evaded her vigilant watchfulness and inquiry, her presence in the neighborhood was some protection to me. Though she had been a slave, Dr. Flint was afraid of her. He dreaded her scorching rebukes. Moreover, she was known and patronized by many people; and he did not wish to have his villainy made public. It was lucky for me that I did not live on a distant plantation, but in a town not so large that the inhabitants were ignorant of each other's affairs. Bad as are the laws and customs in a slaveholding community, the doctor, as a professional man, deemed it prudent to keep up some outward show of decency.

O, what days and nights of fear and sorrow that man caused me! Reader, it is not to awaken sympathy for myself that I am telling you truthfully what I suffered in slavery. I do it to kindle a flame of compassion in your hearts for my sisters who are still in bondage, suffering as I once suffered.

I once saw two beautiful children playing together. One was a fair white child; the other was her slave, and also her sister. When I saw them embracing each other, and heard their joyous laughter, I turned sadly away from the lovely sight. I foresaw the inevitable blight that would fall on the little slave's heart. I knew how soon her laughter would be changed to sighs. The fair child grew up to be a still fairer woman. From childhood to womanhood her pathway was blooming with flowers, and overarched by a sunny sky. Scarcely one day of her life had been clouded when the sun rose on her happy bridal morning.

How had those years dealt with her slave sister, the little playmate of her childhood? She, also, was very beautiful; but the flowers and sunshine of love were not for her. She drank the cup of sin, and shame, and misery, whereof her persecuted race are compelled to drink.

In view of these things, why are ye silent, ye free men and women of the north? Why do your tongues falter in maintenance of the right? Would that I had more ability! But my heart is so full, and my pen is so weak! There are noble men and women who plead for us, striving to help those who cannot help themselves. God bless them! God give them strength and courage to go on! God bless those, every where, who are laboring to advance the cause of humanity!

1861

❖

Frances Ellen Watkins Harper
(1825–1911)

TO JOHN BROWN

Kendalville, Indiana
November 25, [1859]

DEAR FRIEND

Although the hands of Slavery throw a barrier between you and me, and it may not be my privilege to see you in your prison-house, Virginia has no bolts or bars through which I dread to send you my sympathy. In the name of the young girl sold from the warm clasp of a mother's arms to the clutches of a libertine or a profligate,—in the name of the slave mother, her heart rocked to and fro by the agony of her mournful separations,—I thank you, that you have been brave enough to reach out your hands to the crushed and blighted of my race. You have rocked the bloody Bastile; and I hope that from your sad fate great good may arise to the cause of freedom. Already from your prison has come a shout of triumph against the giant sin of our country. The hemlock is distilled with victory when it is pressed to the lips of Socrates. The Cross becomes a glorious ensign when Calvary's page-browed sufferer yields up his life upon it. And, if Universal Freedom is ever to be the dominant power of the land, your bodies may be only her first stepping stones to dominion. I would prefer to see Slavery go down peaceably by men breaking off their sins by righteousness and their iniquities by showing justice and mercy to the poor; but we cannot tell what the future may bring forth. God writes national judgments upon national sins; and what may be slumbering in the storehouse of divine justice we do not know. We may earnestly hope that your fate will not be a vain lesson, that it will intensify our hatred of Slavery and love of freedom, and that your martyr grave will be a sacred altar upon which men will record their vows of undying hatred to that system which tramples on man and bids defiance to God. I have written to your dear wife, and sent her a few dollars, and I pledge myself to you that I will continue to assist her. May the ever-blessed God shield you and your fellow-prisoners in the darkest hour. Send my sympathy to your fellow-prisoners; tell them to be of good courage; to seek a refuge in the Eternal God, and lean upon His everlasting arms for a sure support. If any of them, like you, have a wife or children that I can help, let them send me word.

❖

Elizabeth Ramsey

(ca. 1800)

TO LOUISA PICQUET

Wharton County, Texas, March 8, 1859

MY DEAR DAUGHTER,

I a gane take my pen in hand to drop a few lines.

I have written to you twice, but I hav not yet received an answer from you I can not imagin why you do not writ. I feel very much troubel. I fear you hav not recived my letters or you would hav written; I sent to my little grand children a ring also a button in my first letter. I want you to writ to me on recept of this letter, whether you hav ever received the letters and presents or not. I said in my letter to you that Col. Horton would let you have me for 1000 dollars or a woman that could fill my place; I think you could get one cheaper [in St. Louis] that would fill my place than to pay him the money; I am anxios to hav you to make this trade.

You have no Idea, what my feelings are. I hav not spent one happy moment since I received your kind letter. It is true I was more than rejoyest to hear from you my Dear child; but my feelings on this subject are in Expressible. No one but a mother can tell my feelings. In regard to your Brother John Col. Hurton is willing for you to hav him for a boy a fifteen years old or fifteen hundred dollars. I think that 1000 dollars is too much for me. You must writ very kind to Col. Horton and try to Get me for less money. I think you can change his Price by writing Kindly to him aske him in a kind manner to let you hav me for less. I think you can soften his heart and he will let you hav me for less than he has offered me to you for.

You Brother John sends his love to you and 100 kisses to your little son; Kiss my Dear little children 100 times for me particuler

Elizabeth. Say to her that she must writ to her grand mar ofton; I want you to hav your ambrotipe [photograph] taken also your children and send them to me. I would giv this world to see you and my sweet little children; may God bless you my Dear child and protect you is my prayer.

YOUR AFFECTIONATE MOTHER,
ELIZABETH RAMSEY

❖

Mary Boykin Chesnut
(1823–1886)

DIARY

August 26, 1861

... Now, this assemblage of army women or Confederate matrons talked pretty freely today. Let us record. . . .

"You people who have been everywhere, stationed all over the U.S.—states, frontiers—been to Europe and all that, tell us homebiding ones: are our men worse than the others? Does Mrs. Stowe know? You know?"

"No, Lady Mary Montagu[1] did. After all, only men and women—everywhere! But Mrs. Stowe's exceptional cases may be true. You can pick out horrors from any criminal court record or newspaper in any country."

"You see, irresponsible men, county magnates, city millionaires, princes, &c do pretty much as they please. They are above law and morals."

Russell once more, to whom London and Paris and India have been an everyday sight—and every night, too, streets and all—for him to go on in indignation because there are women on negro plantations who were not vestal virgins! Negro women are married and after marriage behave as well as other people. Marrying is the amusement of their life. They take life easily. So do their class everywhere. Bad men are hated here as elsewhere.

"I hate slavery. I hate a man who—You say there are no more fallen women on a plantation than in London, in proportion to numbers. What do you say to this? A magnate who runs a hideous black harem and its consequences under the same roof with his lovely white wife and his beautiful and accomplished daughters? He holds his head as high and poses as the model of all human virtues to these poor women whom God and the laws have given him.

---

[1]Lady Mary (Wortley) Montagu, wife of an adviser to George I, recorded her society in her *Letters.* In the first volume (1763) appears the sentence, "This world consists of men, women, and Herveys."

From the height of his awful majesty he scolds and thunders at them, as if he never did wrong in his life.

"Fancy such a man finding his daughter reading *Don Juan.* 'You with that unmoral book!' And he orders her out of his sight.

"You see, Mrs. Stowe did not hit the sorest spot. She makes Legree[2] a bachelor. Remember George II and his like."

"Oh, I knew half a Legree, a man said to be as cruel as Legree—but the other half of him did not correspond. He was a man of polished manners. And the best husband and father and member of the church in the world."

"Can that be so?"

"Yes, I know it. Exceptional case, that sort of thing, always."

"And I knew the dissolute half of Legree well. He was high and mighty. But the kindest creature to his slaves—and the unfortunate results of his bad ways were not sold, had not to jump over ice blocks. They were kept in full view and provided for handsomely in his will.

"His wife and daughters in the might of their purity and innocence are supposed never to dream of what is as plain before their eyes as the sunlight, and they play their parts of unsuspecting angels to the letter. They prefer to adore their father as model of all earthly goodness."

"Well, yes. If he is rich, he is the fountain from whence all blessings flow."

"The one I have in my eye—my half of Legree, the dissolute half—was so furious in his temper and thundered his wrath so at the poor women they were glad to let him do as he pleased in peace, if they could only escape his everlasting faultfinding and noisy bluster. Making everybody so uncomfortable."

"*Now.* Now, do you know any woman of this generation who would stand that sort of thing?"

"No, never—not for one moment. The make-believe angels were of the last century. We know—and we won't have it."

"Condition of women is improving, it seems. These are old-world stories."

"Women were brought up not to judge their fathers or their husbands. They took them as the Lord provided—and were thankful."

"If they should not go to heaven, after all—think of what lives most women lead."

"No heaven, no purgatory, no——, the other thing—never. I believe in future rewards and punishments."

"How about the wives of drunkards? I heard a woman say once to a friend of her husband, tell it as a cruel matter of fact, without bitterness, without comment: 'Oh, you have not seen him. He is changed. He has not gone to

---

[2]Simon Legree, the villain in Stowe's *Uncle Tom's Cabin.*

bed sober in thirty years.' She has had her purgatory—if not what Mrs.——
calls 'the other thing'—here in this world. We all know what a drunken man
is. To think, *for no crime* a person may be condemned to live with one thirty
years."

"You wander from the question I asked. Are Southern men worse because
of the slave system and the—facile black women?"

"Not a bit. They see too much of them. The barroom people don't drink.
The confectionary people loathe candy. They are sick of the black sight of
them."

"You think a nice man from the South is the nicest thing in the world."

"I know it. Put him by any other man and see!"

"And you say no saints and martyrs now—those good women who stand
by bad husbands? Eh?"

"No use to mince matters—no use to pick words—everybody knows the
life of a woman whose husband drinks."

"Some men have a hard time, too. I know women who are—well, the very
devil and all his imps."

"And have you not seen girls cower and shrink away from a fierce brute of
a father? Men are dreadful animals."

"Seems to me those of you who are hardest on men here are soft enough
with them when they are present. Now, everybody knows I am 'the friend of
man,' and I defend them behind their backs, as I take pleasure in their society—well—before their faces." . . .

THREE

Turning the Century

Memoirs and letters testify to the range of women's experiences and emotions, as exemplified by the private documents included in this section, which range from love letters to poignant accounts of cultural assimilation. The love letters are by two of America's more intriguing women, Natalie Barney (1876–1972) and Emma Goldman (1869–1940). Barney, a beautiful American hieress, was a Golden Girl who escaped to Europe in 1899 where she lived among the Parisian demimonde until her death. Poet, playwright, and essayist, she also hosted a brilliant salon for American and European women writers and intellectuals, a number of whom she took as her lovers. This unabashed love letter is to Liane de Pougy, one of the most brilliant and literary Parisian courtesans. By contrast, Goldman was a powerful activist, anarchist, lecturer, editor, writer, and publisher. She would have despised much about Barney's life as frivolous. Yet, as we see in her letter, Goldman, too, had a passionate side. Here she writes to Dr. Ben Reitman, a married man whom she met in 1908 and with whom she continued to have an affair until 1917.

The three memoirs included here also document a range of American lives. Zitkala-Ša (Gertrude Bonnin, 1876–1938) published installments of her memoir in *Atlantic* magazine in 1900 (and then collected the pieces in 1921 in *American Indian Stories*). These exquisitely crafted memoirs recount in vivid detail the child's devastating removal from home, her first encounters with the white world, and her tragic realization that she can never again go home to her Sioux life and ways. Similarly, in the memoir by Sui Sin Far (Edith Maud Eaton, 1865–1914), we are shown the painful process of assimilation and understand racism through the eyes of a young Eurasian girl. Finally, the anonymous "My Life, An Illinois Farmer's Wife" reveals the drudgery of her existence and the hard lot experienced by women in rural America.

❖

Natalie Barney

(1876–1972)

TO LIANE DE POUGY

1899

MY LIANE,

Since you are spiritually happy and physically chaste, I must be that way too . . . To tire myself out (I know more agreeable, but less innocent, ways), I take long rides.

Yesterday I went twenty-eight kilometers looking for some beauty on which to feast my eyes, tired of the monotony of my surroundings. I saw pipes, piles of stones, old women and cows. I also saw some sheep: one of them refused to walk like or with the others . . . and they were beating him. A moral lesson which I certainly don't appreciate. Was I like that sheep? The voice of my reason sharply answers yes. Then there were villages where I felt I had to dismount to taste their cider and the patois of the region.

Two years ago I would have found these inns picturesque, but now they simply seem dirty. A sure sign of age, when uncleanliness no longer has any artistic appeal. Must I confess that I have never known the youthful madness of he who sang: "In a loft, how happy one is at twenty." I'm still only twenty-three, but I already think that one is better off "elsewhere." In your bed, for example.

In coming here, I was hoping that the Bretons would look something like you. Still another disillusionment. . . . But I do see you, my beloved, in the flowers of your country. These things that I respect are independent of time and are all over. They grow as easily in the immense garden of the Infinite as in the secret of your soul. While I kiss, nibble and inhale the ones around me, do you know what I'm thinking about?

It's time for me to take another ride on my horse. Good-bye. Your . . . and for always.

NATTY

❖

Emma Goldman
(1869–1940)

TO BEN REITMAN

September 27, 1908

You have opened up the prison gates of my womanhood. And all the passion that was unsatisfied in me for so many years, leaped into a wild reckless storm boundless as the sea. . . . Can you then imagine that I could stay away from you? What is love, family ties, the power of association to the wanderer in the desert. His mind is bent on the spring that will quench his thirst. . . . Yet, if I were asked to choose between a world of understanding and the spring that fills my body with fire, I should have to choose the spring. It is life, sunshine, music, untold ecstasy. The Spring, oh ye Gods, that have tortured my body all these years, I will give you my soul only let me drink, drink from the Spring of my master lover. . . . There. You have the confession of a starved tortured being, my Ben.

❖

Zitkala-Ša (Gertrude Bonnin)
(1876–1938)

from *The School Days of an Indian Girl*

I.

The Land of Red Apples.

There were eight in our party of bronzed children who were going East with the missionaries. Among us were three young braves, two tall girls, and we three little ones, Judéwin, Thowin, and I.

We had been very impatient to start on our journey to the Red Apple Country, which, we were told, lay a little beyond the great circular horizon of the Western prairie. Under a sky of rosy apples we dreamt of roaming as freely and happily as we had chased the cloud shadows on the Dakota plains.

We had anticipated much pleasure from a ride on the iron horse, but the throngs of staring palefaces disturbed and troubled us.

On the train, fair women, with tottering babies on each arm, stopped their haste and scrutinized the children of absent mothers. Large men, with heavy bundles in their hands, halted near by, and riveted their glassy blue eyes upon us.

I sank deep into the corner of my seat, for I resented being watched. Directly in front of me, children who were no larger than I hung themselves upon the backs of their seats, with their bold white faces toward me. Sometimes they took their forefingers out of their mouths and pointed at my moccasined feet. Their mothers, instead of reproving such rude curiosity, looked closely at me, and attracted their children's further notice to my blanket. This embarrassed me, and kept me constantly on the verge of tears.

I sat perfectly still, with my eyes downcast, daring only now and then to shoot long glances around me. Chancing to turn to the window at my side, I was quite breathless upon seeing one familiar object. It was the telegraph pole which strode by at short paces. Very near my mother's dwelling, along the edge of a road thickly bordered with wild sunflowers, some poles like these had been planted by white men. Often I had stopped, on my way down the road, to hold my ear against the pole, and, hearing its low moaning, I used to wonder what the paleface had done to hurt it. Now I sat watching for each pole that glided by to be the last one.

In this way I had forgotten my uncomfortable surroundings, when I heard one of my comrades call out my name. I saw the missionary standing very near, tossing candies and gums into our midst. This amused us all, and we tried to see who could catch the most of the sweetmeats.

Though we rode several days inside of the iron horse, I do not recall a single thing about our luncheons.

It was night when we reached the school grounds. The lights from the windows of the large buildings fell upon some of the icicled trees that stood beneath them. We were led toward an open door, where the brightness of the lights within flooded out over the heads of the excited palefaces who blocked our way. My body trembled more from fear than from the snow I trod upon.

Entering the house, I stood close against the wall. The strong glaring light in the large whitewashed room dazzled my eyes. The noisy hurrying of hard shoes upon a bare wooden floor increased the whirring in my ears. My only safety seemed to be in keeping next to the wall. As I was wondering in which direction to escape from all this confusion, two warm hands grasped me firmly, and in the same moment I was tossed high in midair. A rosy-cheeked paleface woman caught me in her arms. I was both frightened and insulted by such trifling. I stared into her eyes, wishing her to let me stand on my own feet, but she jumped me up and down with increasing enthusiasm. My mother had never made a plaything of her wee daughter. Remembering this I began to cry aloud.

They misunderstood the cause of my tears, and placed me at a white table loaded with food. There our party were united again. As I did not hush my crying, one of the older ones whispered to me, "Wait until you are alone in the night."

It was very little I could swallow besides my sobs, that evening.

"Oh, I want my mother and my brother Dawée! I want to go to my aunt!" I pleaded; but the ears of the palefaces could not hear me.

From the table we were taken along an upward incline of wooden boxes, which I learned afterward to call a stairway. At the top was a quiet hall, dimly lighted. Many narrow beds were in one straight line down the entire length of the wall. In them lay sleeping brown faces, which peeped just out of the coverings. I was tucked into bed with one of the tall girls, because she talked to me in my mother tongue and seemed to soothe me.

I had arrived in the wonderful land of rosy skies, but I was not happy, as I had thought I should be. My long travel and the bewildering sights had exhausted me. I fell asleep, heaving deep, tired sobs. My tears were left to dry themselves in streaks, because neither my aunt nor my mother was near to wipe them away.

II.

The Cutting of My Long Hair.

The first day in the land of apples was a bitter-cold one; for the snow still covered the ground, and the trees were bare. A large bell rang for breakfast, its loud metallic voice crashing through the belfry overhead and into our sensitive ears. The annoying clatter of shoes on bare floors gave us no peace. The constant clash of harsh noises, with an undercurrent of many voices murmuring an unknown tongue, made a bedlam within which I was securely tied. And though my spirit tore itself in struggling for its lost freedom, all was useless.

A paleface woman, with white hair, came up after us. We were placed in a line of girls who were marching into the dining room. These were Indian girls, in stiff shoes and closely clinging dresses. The small girls wore sleeved aprons and shingled hair. As I walked noiselessly in my soft moccasins, I felt like sinking to the floor, for my blanket had been stripped from my shoulders. I looked hard at the Indian girls, who seemed not to care that they were even more immodestly dressed than I, in their tightly fitting clothes. While we marched in, the boys entered at an opposite door. I watched for the three young braves who came in our party. I spied them in the rear ranks, looking as uncomfortable as I felt.

A small bell was tapped, and each of the pupils drew a chair from under the table. Supposing this act meant they were to be seated, I pulled out mine and at once slipped into it from one side. But when I turned my head, I saw that I was the only one seated, and all the rest at our table remained standing. Just as I began to rise, looking shyly around to see how chairs were to be used, a second bell was sounded. All were seated at last, and I had to crawl back into my chair again. I heard a man's voice at one end of the hall, and I looked around to see him. But all the others hung their heads over their plates. As I glanced at the long chain of tables, I caught the eyes of a paleface woman upon me. Immediately I dropped my eyes, wondering why I was so keenly watched by the strange woman. The man ceased his mutterings, and then a third bell was tapped. Every one picked up his knife and fork and began eating. I began crying instead, for by this time I was afraid to venture anything more.

But this eating by formula was not the hardest trial in that first day. Late in the morning, my friend Judéwin gave me a terrible warning. Judéwin knew a few words of English; and she had overheard the paleface woman talk about cutting our long, heavy hair. Our mothers had taught us that only unskilled warriors who were captured had their hair shingled by the enemy. Among our people, short hair was worn by mourners, and shingled hair by cowards!

We discussed our fate some moments, and when Judéwin said, "We have to submit, because they are strong," I rebelled.

"No, I will not submit! I will struggle first!" I answered.

I watched my chance, and when no one noticed I disappeared. I crept up the stairs as quietly as I could in my squeaking shoes,—my moccasins had been exchanged for shoes. Along the hall I passed, without knowing whither I was going. Turning aside to an open door, I found a large room with three white beds in it. The windows were covered with dark green curtains, which made the room very dim. Thankful that no one was there, I directed my steps toward the corner farthest from the door. On my hands and knees I crawled under the bed, and cuddled myself in the dark corner.

From my hiding place I peered out, shuddering with fear whenever I heard footsteps near by. Though in the hall loud voices were calling my name, and I knew that even Judéwin was searching for me, I did not open my mouth to answer. Then the steps were quickened and the voices became excited. The sounds came nearer and nearer. Women and girls entered the room. I held my breath and watched them open closet doors and peep behind large trunks. Some one threw up the curtains, and the room was filled with sudden light. What caused them to stoop and look under the bed I do not know. I remember

517

being dragged out, though I resisted by kicking and scratching wildly. In spite of myself, I was carried downstairs and tied fast in a chair.

I cried aloud, shaking my head all the while until I felt the cold blades of the scissors against my neck, and heard them gnaw off one of my thick braids. Then I lost my spirit. Since the day I was taken from my mother I had suffered extreme indignites. People had stared at me. I had been tossed about in the air like a wooden puppet. And now my long hair was shingled like a coward's! In my anguish I moaned for my mother, but no one came to comfort me. Not a soul reasoned quietly with me, as my own mother used to do; for now I was only one of many little animals driven by a herder.

IV.

The Devil.

Among the legends the old warriors used to tell me were many stories of evil spirits. But I was taught to fear them no more than those who stalked about in material guise. I never knew there was an insolent chieftain among the bad spirits, who dared to array his forces against the Great Spirit, until I heard this white man's legend from a paleface woman.

Out of a large book she showed me a picture of the white man's devil. I looked in horror upon the strong claws that grew out of his fur-covered fingers. His feet were like his hands. Trailing at his heels was a scaly tail tipped with a serpent's open jaws. His face was a patchwork: he had bearded cheeks, like some I had seen palefaces wear; his nose was an eagle's bill, and his sharp-pointed ears were pricked up like those of a sly fox. Above them a pair of cow's horns curved upward. I trembled with awe, and my heart throbbed in my throat, as I looked at the king of evil spirits. Then I heard the paleface woman say that this terrible creature roamed loose in the world, and that little girls who disobeyed school regulations were to be tortured by him.

That night I dreamt about this evil divinity. Once again I seemed to be in my mother's cottage. An Indian woman had come to visit my mother. On opposite sides of the kitchen stove, which stood in the center of the small house, my mother and her guest were seated in straight-backed chairs. I played with a train of empty spools hitched together on a string. It was night, and the wick burned feebly. Suddenly I heard some one turn our door-knob from without.

My mother and the woman hushed their talk, and both looked toward the door. It opened gradually. I waited behind the stove. The hinges squeaked as the door was slowly, very slowly pushed inward.

Then in rushed the devil! He was tall! He looked exactly like the picture I had seen of him in the white man's papers. He did not speak to my mother, because he did not know the Indian language, but his glittering yellow eyes were fastened upon me. He took long strides around the stove, passing behind the woman's chair. I threw down my spools, and ran to my mother. He did not fear her, but followed closely after me. Then I ran round and round the stove, crying aloud for help. But my mother and the woman seemed not to know my danger. They sat still, looking quietly upon the devil's chase after me. At last I grew dizzy. My head revolved as on a hidden pivot. My knees became numb, and doubled under my weight like a pair of knife blades without a spring. Beside my mother's chair I fell in a heap. Just as the devil stooped over me with outstretched claws my mother awoke from her quiet indifference, and lifted me on her lap. Whereupon the devil vanished, and I was awake.

On the following morning I took my revenge upon the devil. Stealing into the room where a wall of shelves was filled with books, I drew forth The Stories of the Bible. With a broken slate pencil I carried in my apron pocket, I began by scratching out his wicked eyes. A few moments later, when I was ready to leave the room, there was a ragged hole in the page where the picture of the devil had once been.

V.

Iron Routine.

A loud-clamoring bell awakened us at half-past six in the cold winter mornings. From happy dreams of Western rolling lands and unlassoed freedom we tumbled out upon chilly bare floors back again into a paleface day. We had short time to jump into our shoes and clothes, and wet our eyes with icy water, before a small hand bell was vigorously rung for roll call.

There were too many drowsy children and too numerous orders for the day to waste a moment in any apology to nature for giving her children such a shock in the early morning. We rushed downstairs, bounding over two high steps at a time, to land in the assembly room.

A paleface woman, with a yellow-covered roll book open on her arm and a gnawed pencil in her hand, appeared at the door. Her small, tired face was coldly lighted with a pair of large gray eyes.

She stood still in a halo of authority, while over the rim of her spectacles her eyes pried nervously about the room. Having glanced at her long list of names and called out the first one, she tossed up her chin and peered through the crystals of her spectacles to make sure of the answer "Here."

Relentlessly her pencil black-marked our daily records if we were not present to respond to our names, and no chum of ours had done it successfully for us. No matter if a dull headache or the painful cough of slow consumption had delayed the absentee, there was only time enough to mark the tardiness. It was next to impossible to leave the iron routine after the civilizing machine had once begun its day's buzzing; and as it was inbred in me to suffer in silence rather than to appeal to the ears of one whose open eyes could not see my pain, I have many times trudged in the day's harness heavy-footed, like a dumb sick brute.

Once I lost a dear classmate. I remember well how she used to mope along at my side, until one morning she could not raise her head from her pillow. At her deathbed I stood weeping, as the paleface woman sat near her moistening the dry lips. Among the folds of the bedclothes I saw the open pages of the white man's Bible. The dying Indian girl talked disconnectedly of Jesus the Christ and the paleface who was cooling her swollen hands and feet.

I grew bitter, and censured the woman for cruel neglect of our physical ills. I despised the pencils that moved automatically, and the one teaspoon which dealt out, from a large bottle, healing to a row of variously ailing Indian children. I blamed the hard-working, well-meaning, ignorant woman who was inculcating in our hearts her superstitious ideas. Though I was sullen in all my little troubles, as soon as I felt better I was ready again to smile upon the cruel woman. Within a week I was again actively testing the chains which tightly bound my individuality like a mummy for burial.

The melancholy of those black days has left so long a shadow that it darkens the path of years that have since gone by. These sad memories rise above those of smoothly grinding school days. Perhaps my Indian nature is the moaning wind which stirs them now for their present record. But, however tempestuous this is within me, it comes out as the low voice of a curiously colored seashell, which is only for those ears that are bent with compassion to hear it.

VII.

Incurring My Mother's Displeasure.

In the second journey to the East I had not come without some precautions. I had a secret interview with one of our best medicine men, and when I left his wigwam I carried securely in my sleeve a tiny bunch of magic roots. This possession assured me of friends wherever I should go. So absolutely did I believe in its charms that I wore it through all the school routine for more than a year. Then, before I lost my faith in the dead roots, I lost the little buckskin bag containing all my good luck.

At the close of this second term of three years I was the proud owner of my first diploma. The following autumn I ventured upon a college career against my mother's will.

I had written for her approval, but in her reply I found no encouragement.

She called my notice to her neighbors' children, who had completed their education in three years. They had returned to their homes, and were then talking English with the frontier settlers. Her few words hinted that I had better give up my slow attempt to learn the white man's ways, and be content to roam over the prairies and find my living upon wild roots. I silenced her by deliberate disobedience.

Thus, homeless and heavy-hearted, I began anew my life among strangers.

As I hid myself in my little room in the college dormitory, away from the scornful and yet curious eyes of the students, I pined for sympathy. Often I wept in secret, wishing I had gone West, to be nourished by my mother's love, instead of remaining among a cold race whose hearts were frozen hard with prejudice.

During the fall and winter seasons I scarcely had a real friend, though by that time several of my classmates were courteous to me at a safe distance.

My mother had not yet forgiven my rudeness to her, and I had no moment for letter-writing. By daylight and lamplight, I spun with reeds and thistles, until my hands were tired from their weaving, the magic design which promised me the white man's respect.

At length, in the spring term, I entered an oratorical contest among the various classes. As the day of competition approached, it did not seem possible that the event was so near at hand, but it came. In the chapel the classes assembled together, with their invited guests. The high platform was carpeted, and gayly festooned with college colors. A bright white light illumined the room, and outlined clearly the great polished beams that arched the domed ceiling. The assembled crowds filled the air with pulsating murmurs. When the hour for speaking arrived all were hushed. But on the wall the old clock which pointed out the trying moment ticked calmly on.

One after another I saw and heard the orators. Still, I could not realize that they longed for the favorable decision of the judges as much as I did. Each contestant received a loud burst of applause, and some were cheered heartily. Too soon my turn came, and I paused a moment behind the curtains for a deep breath. After my concluding words, I heard the same applause that the others had called out.

Upon my retreating steps, I was astounded to receive from my fellow-students a large bouquet of roses tied with flowing ribbons. With the lovely flowers I fled from the stage. This friendly token was a rebuke to me for the hard feelings I had borne them.

Later, the decision of the judges awarded me the first place. Then there was a mad uproar in the hall, where my classmates sang and shouted my name at the top of their lungs; and the disappointed students howled and brayed in fearfully dissonant tin trumpets. In this excitement, happy students rushed

521

forward to offer their congratulations. And I could not conceal a smile when they wished to escort me in a procession to the students' parlor, where all were going to calm themselves. Thanking them for the kind spirit which prompted them to make such a proposition, I walked alone with the night to my own little room.

A few weeks afterward, I appeared as the college representative in another contest. This time the competition was among orators from different colleges in our State. It was held at the State capital, in one of the largest opera houses.

Here again was a strong prejudice against my people. In the evening, as the great audience filled the house, the student bodies began warring among themselves. Fortunately, I was spared witnessing any of the noisy wrangling before the contest began. The slurs against the Indian that stained the lips of our opponents were already burning like a dry fever within my breast.

But after the orations were delivered a deeper burn awaited me. There, before that vast ocean of eyes, some college rowdies threw out a large white flag, with a drawing of a most forlorn Indian girl on it. Under this they had printed in bold black letters words that ridiculed the college which was represented by a "squaw." Such worse than barbarian rudeness embittered me. While we waited for the verdict of the judges, I gleamed fiercely upon the throngs of palefaces. My teeth were hard set, as I saw the white flag still floating insolently in the air.

Then anxiously we watched the man carry toward the stage the envelope containing the final decision.

There were two prizes given, that night, and one of them was mine!

The evil spirit laughed within me when the white flag dropped out of sight, and the hands which hurled it hung limp in defeat.

Leaving the crowd as quickly as possible, I was soon in my room. The rest of the night I sat in an armchair and gazed into the crackling fire. I laughed no more in triumph when thus alone. The little taste of victory did not satisfy a hunger in my heart. In my mind I saw my mother far away on the Western plains, and she was holding a charge against me.

1900–1901

Sui Sin Far (Edith Maud Eton)
(1865–1914)

from *Leaves from the Mental Portfolio of an Eurasian*

When I look back over the years I see myself, a little child of scarcely four years of age, walking in front of my nurse, in a green English lane, and listening to her tell another of her kind that my mother is Chinese. "Oh, Lord!" exclaims the informed. She turns me around and scans me curiously from head to foot. Then the two women whisper together. Tho the word "Chinese" conveys very little meaning to my mind, I feel that they are talking about my father and mother and my heart swells with indignation. When we reach home I rush to my mother and try to tell her what I have heard. I am a young child. I fail to make myself intelligible. My mother does not understand, and when the nurse declares to her, "Little Miss Sui is a story-teller," my mother slaps me.

Many a long year has past over my head since that day—the day on which I first learned that I was something different and apart from other children, but tho my mother has forgotten it, I have not.

I see myself again, a few years older. I am playing with another child in a garden. A girl passes by outside the gate. "Mamie," she cries to my companion. "I wouldn't speak to Sui if I were you. Her mama is Chinese."

"I don't care," answers the little one beside me. And then to me, "Even if your mamma is Chinese, I like you better than I like Annie."

"But I don't like you," I answer, turning my back on her. It is my first conscious lie.

I am at a children's party, given by the wife of an Indian officer whose children were schoolfellows of mine. I am only six years of age, but have attended a private school for over a year, and have already learned that China is a heathen country, being civilized by England. However, for the time being, I am a merry romping child. There are quite a number of grown people present. One, a white haired old man, has his attention called to me by the hostess. He adjusts his eyeglasses and surveys me critically. "Ah, indeed!" he exclaims, "Who would have thought it at first glance. Yet now I see the difference between her and other children. What a peculiar coloring! Her mother's eyes and hair and her father's features, I presume. Very interesting little creature!"

I had been called from my play for the purpose of inspection. I do not return to it. For the rest of the evening I hide myself behind a hall door and refuse to show myself until it is time to go home.

My parents have come to America. We are in Hudson City, N.Y., and we are very poor. I am out with my brother, who is ten months older than myself. We pass a Chinese store, the door of which is open. "Look!" says Charlie, "Those men in there are Chinese!" Eagerly I gaze into the long low room. With the exception of my mother, who is English bred with English ways and manner of dress, I have never seen a Chinese person. The two men within the store are uncouth specimens of their race, drest in working blouses and pantaloons with queues hanging down their backs. I recoil with a sense of shock.

"Oh, Charlie," I cry, "Are we like that?"

"Well, we're Chinese, and they're Chinese, too, so we must be!" returns my seven-year-old brother.

"Of course you are," puts in a boy who has followed us down the street, and who lives near us and has seen my mother: "Chinky, Chinky, Chinaman, yellow-face, pig-tail, rat-eater." A number of other boys and several little girls join in with him.

"Better than you," shouts my brother, facing the crowd. He is younger and smaller than any there, and I am even more insignificant than he; but my spirit revives.

"I'd rather be Chinese than anything else in the world," I scream.

They pull my hair, they tear my clothes, they scratch my face, and all but lame my brother; but the white blood in our veins fights valiantly for the Chinese half of us. When it is all over, exhausted and bedraggled, we crawl home, and report to our mother that we have "won the battle."

"Are you sure?" asks my mother doubtfully.

"Of course. They ran from us. They were frightened," returns my brother.

My mother smiles with satisfaction.

"Do you hear?" she asks my father.

"Umm," he observes, raising his eyes from his paper for an instant. My childish instinct, however, tells me that he is more interested than he appears to be.

It is tea time, but I cannot eat. Unobserved I crawl away. I do not sleep that night. I am too excited and I ache all over. Our opponents had been so very much stronger and bigger than we. Toward morning, however, I fall into a doze from which I awake myself, shouting:

> *"Sound the battle cry;*
> *See the foe is nigh."*

My mother believes in sending us to Sunday school. She has been brought up in a Presbyterian college.

The scene of my life shifts to Eastern Canada. The sleigh which has carried us from the station stops in front of a little French Canadian hotel. Immediately we are surrounded by a number of villagers, who stare curiously at my mother as my father assists her to alight from the sleigh. Their curiosity, however, is tempered with kindness, as they watch, one after another, the little black heads of my brothers and sisters and myself emerge out of the buffalo robe, which is part of the sleigh's outfit. There are six of us, four girls and two boys; the eldest, my brother, being only seven years of age. My father and mother are still in their twenties. "Les pauvres enfants," the inhabitants murmur, as they help to carry us into the hotel. Then in lower tones: "Chinoise, Chinoise."

For some time after our arrival, whenever we children are sent for a walk, our footsteps are dogged by a number of young French and English Canadians, who amuse themselves with speculations as to whether, we being Chinese, are susceptible to pinches and hair pulling, while older persons pause and gaze upon us, very much in the same way that I have seen people gaze upon strange animals in a menagerie. Now and then we are stopt and plied with questions as to what we eat and drink, how we go to sleep, if my mother understands what my father says to her, if we sit on chairs or squat on floors, etc., etc., etc.

There are many pitched battles, of course, and we seldom leave the house without being armed for conflict. My mother takes a great interest in our battles, and usually cheers us on, tho I doubt whether she understands the depth of the troubled waters thru which her little children wade. As to my father, peace is his motto, and he deems it wisest to be blind and deaf to many things.

School days are short, but memorable. I am in the same class with my brother, my sister next to me in the class below. The little girl whose desk my sister shares shrinks close against the wall as my sister takes her place. In a little while she raises her hand.

"Please, teacher!"

"Yes, Annie."

"May I change my seat?"

"No, you may not!"

The little girl sobs. "Why should she have to sit beside a——"

Happily my sister does not seem to hear, and before long the two little girls become great friends. I have many such experiences.

My brother is remarkably bright; my sister next to me has a wonderful head for figures, and when only eight years of age helps my father with his night work accounts. My parents compare her with me. She is of sturdier build than I, and, as my father says, "Always has her wits about her." He thinks her more like my mother, who is very bright and interested in every little detail of practical life. My father tells me that I will never make half the woman that my mother is or that my sister will be. I am not as strong as my sisters, which makes me feel somewhat ashamed, for I am the eldest little girl, and more is expected of me. I have no organic disease, but the strength of my feelings seems to take from me the strength of my body. I am prostrated at times with attacks of nervous sickness. The doctor says that my heart is unusually large; but in the light of the present I know that the cross of the Eurasian bore too heavily upon my childish shoulders. I usually hide my weakness from the family until I cannot stand. I do not understand myself, and I have an idea that the others will despise me for not being as strong as they. Therefore, I like to wander away alone, either by the river or in the bush. The green fields and flowing water have a charm for me. At the age of seven, as it is today, a bird on the wing is my emblem of happiness.

I have come from a race on my mother's side which is said to be the most stolid and insensible to feeling of all races, yet I look back over the years and see myself so keenly alive to every shade of sorrow and suffering that it is almost a pain to live.

If there is any trouble in the house in the way of a difference between my father and mother, or if any child is punished, how I suffer! And when harmony is restored, heaven seems to be around me. I can be sad, but I can also be glad. My mother's screams of agony when a baby is born almost drive me wild, and long after her pangs have subsided I feel them in my own body. Sometimes it is a week before I can get to sleep after such an experience.

A debt owing by my father fills me with shame. I feel like a criminal when I pass the creditor's door. I am only ten years old. And all the while the question of nationality perplexes my little brain. Why are we what we are? I and my brothers and sisters. Why did God make us to be hooted and stared at? Papa is English, mamma is Chinese. Why couldn't we have been either one thing or the other? Why is my mother's race despised? I look into the faces of my father and mother. Is she not every bit as dear and good as he? Why? Why? She sings us the songs she learned at her English school. She tells us tales of China. Tho a child when she left her native land she remembers it well, and I am never tired of listening to the story of how she was stolen from her home. She tells us over and over again of her meeting with my father in Shanghai and the romance of their marriage. Why? Why?

I do not confide in my father and mother. They would not understand. How could they? He is English, she is Chinese. I am different to both of them—a stranger, tho their own child. "What are we?" I ask my brother. "It doesn't matter, sissy," he responds. But it does. I love poetry, particularly heroic pieces. I also love fairy tales. Stories of everyday life do not appeal to me. I dream dreams of being great and noble; my sisters and brothers also. I glory in the idea of dying at the stake and a great genie arising from the flames and declaring to those who have scorned us: "Behold, how great and glorious and noble are the Chinese people!"

My sisters are apprenticed to a dressmaker; my brother is entered in an office. I tramp around and sell my father's pictures, also some lace which I make myself. My nationality, if I had only known it at that time, helps to make sales. The ladies who are my customers call me "The Little Chinese Lace Girl." But it is a dangerous life for a very young girl. I come near to "mysteriously disappearing" many a time. The greatest temptation was in the thought of getting far away from where I was known, to where no mocking cries of "Chinese!" "Chinese!" could reach.

Whenever I have the opportunity I steal away to the library and read every book I can find on China and the Chinese. I learn that China is the oldest civilized nation on the face of the earth and a few other things. At eighteen years of age what troubles me is not that I am what I am, but that others are ignorant of my superiority. I am small, but my feelings are big—and great is my vanity. . . .

I am living in a little town away off on the north shore of a big lake. Next to me at the dinner table is the man for whom I work as a stenographer. There are also a couple of business men, a young girl and her mother.

Some one makes a remark about the cars full of Chinamen that past that morning. A transcontinental railway runs thru the town.

My employer shakes his rugged head. "Somehow or other," says he, "I cannot reconcile myself to the thought that the Chinese are humans like ourselves. They may have immortal souls, but their faces seem to be so utterly devoid of expression that I cannot help but doubt."

"Souls," echoes the town clerk. "Their bodies are enough for me. A Chinaman is, in my eyes, more repulsive than a nigger."

"They always give me such a creepy feeling," puts in the young girl with a laugh.

"I wouldn't have one in my house," declares my landlady.

"Now, the Japanese are different altogether. There is something bright and likeable about those men," continues Mr. K.

A miserable, cowardly feeling keeps me silent. I am in a Middle West town. If I declare what I am, every person in the place will hear about it the next day. The population is in the main made up of working folks with strong prejudices against my mother's countrymen. The prospect before me is not an enviable one—if I speak. I have no longer an ambition to die at the stake for the sake of demonstrating the greatness and nobleness of the Chinese people.

Mr. K. turns to me with a kindly smile.

"What makes Miss Far so quiet?" he asks.

"I don't suppose she finds the 'washee washee men' particularly interesting subjects of conversation," volunteers the young manager of the local bank.

With a great effort I raise my eyes from my plate. "Mr. K.," I say, addressing my employer, "the Chinese people may have no souls, no expression on their faces, be altogether beyond the pale of civilization, but whatever they are, I want you to understand that I am—I am a Chinese."

There is silence in the room for a few minutes. Then Mr. K. pushes back his plate and standing up beside me, says:

"I should not have spoken as I did. I know nothing whatever about the Chinese. It was pure prejudice. Forgive me!"

I admire Mr. K.'s moral courage in apologizing to me; he is a conscientious Christian man, but I do not remain much longer in the little town.

I am under a tropic sky, meeting frequently and conversing with persons who are almost as high up in the world as birth, education and money can set them. The environment is peculiar, for I am also surrounded by a race of people, the reputed descendants of Ham, the son of Noah, whose offspring, it was prophesied, should be the servants of the sons of Shem and Japheth. As I am a descendant, according to the Bible, of both Shem and Japheth, I have a perfect right to set my heel upon the Ham people; but tho I see others around me following out the Bible suggestion, it is not in my nature to be arrogant to any but those who seek to impress me with their superiority, which the poor black maid who has been assigned to me by the hotel certainly does not. My employer's wife takes me to task for this. "It is unnecessary," she says, "to thank a black person for a service."

The novelty of life in the West Indian island is not without its charm. The surroundings, people, manner of living, are so entirely different from what I have been accustomed to up North that I feel as if I were "born again." Mixing with people of fashion, and yet not of them, I am not of sufficient importance to create comment or curiosity. I am busy nearly all day and often well into the night. It is not monotonous work, but it is certainly strenuous. The planters and business men of the island take me as a matter of course and treat me with kindly courtesy. Occasionally an Englishman will warn me against the "brown boys" of the island, little dreaming that I too am of the "brown people" of the earth.

When it begins to be whispered about the place that I am not all white, some of the "sporty" people seek my acquaintance. I am small and look much younger than my years. When, however, they discover that I am a very serious and sober-minded spinster indeed, they retire quite gracefully, leaving me a few amusing reflections.

One evening a card is brought to my room. It bears the name of some naval officer. I go down to my visitor, thinking he is probably some one who, having been told that I am a reporter for the local paper, has brought me an item of news. I find him lounging in an easy chair on the veranda of the hotel—a big, blond, handsome fellow, several years younger than I.

"You are Lieutenant——?" I inquire.

He bows and laughs a little. The laugh doesn't suit him somehow—and it doesn't suit me, either.

"If you have anything to tell me, please tell it quickly, because I'm very busy."

"Oh, you don't really mean that," he answers, with another silly and offensive laugh. "There's always plenty of time for good times. That's what I am here for. I saw you at the races the other day and twice at King's House. My ship will be here for——weeks."

"Do you wish that noted?" I ask.

"Oh, no! Why—I came just because I had an idea that you might like to know me. I would like to know you. You look such a nice little body. Say, wouldn't you like to go out for a sail this lovely night? I will tell you all about the sweet little Chinese girls I met when we were at Hong Kong. They're not so shy!"

I leave Eastern Canada for the Far West, so reduced by another attack of rheumatic fever that I only weigh eighty-four pounds. I travel on an advertising contract. It is presumed by the railway company that in some way or other I will give them full value for their transportation across the continent. I have been ordered beyond the Rockies by the doctor, who declares that I will never regain my strength in the East. Nevertheless, I am but two days in San Francisco when I start out in search of work. It is the first time that I have sought work as a stranger in a strange town. Both of the other positions away from home were secured for me by home influence. I am quite surprised to find that there is no demand for my services in San Francisco and that no one is particularly interested in me. The best I can do is to accept an offer from a railway agency to typewrite their correspondence for $5 a month. I stipulate, however, that I shall have the privilege of taking in outside work and that my hours shall be light. I am hopeful that the sale of a story or newspaper article may add to my income, and I console myself with the reflection that, considering that I still limp and bear traces of sickness, I am fortunate to secure any work at all.

The proprietor of one of the San Francisco papers, to whom I have a letter of introduction, suggests that I obtain some subscriptions from the people of Chinatown, that district of the city having never been canvassed. This suggestion I carry out with enthusiasm, tho I find that the Chinese merchants and people generally are inclined to regard me with suspicion. They have been imposed upon so many times by unscrupulous white people. Another drawback—save for a few phrases, I am unacquainted with my mother tongue. How, then, can I expect these people to accept me as their own countrywoman? The Americanized Chinamen actually laugh in my face when I tell them that I am of their race. However, they are not all "doubting Thomases." Some little women discover that I have Chinese hair, color of eyes and complexion, also that I love rice and tea. This settles the matter for them—and for their husbands.

My Chinese instincts develop. I am no longer the little girl who shrunk against my brother at the first sight of a Chinaman. Many and many a time, when alone in a strange place, has the appearance of even an humble laundryman given me a sense of protection and made me feel quite at home. This fact of itself proves to me that prejudice can be eradicated by association.

I meet a half Chinese, half white girl. Her face is plastered with a thick white coat of paint and her eyelids and eyebrows are blackened so that the shape of her eyes and the whole expression of her face is changed. She was born in the East, and at the age of eighteen came West in answer to an advertisement. Living for many years among the working class, she had heard little but abuse of the Chinese. It is not difficult, in a land like California, for a half Chinese, half white girl to pass as one of Spanish or Mexican origin. This the poor child does, tho she lives in nervous dread of being "discovered." She becomes engaged to a young man, but fears to tell him what she is, and only does so when compelled by a fearless American girl friend. This girl, who knows her origin, realizing that the truth sooner or later must be told, and better soon than late, advises the Eurasian to confide in the young man, assuring her that he loves her well enough not to allow her nationality to stand, a bar sinister, between them. But the Eurasian prefers to keep her secret, and only reveals it to the man who is to be her husband when driven to bay by the American girl, who declares that if the halfbreed will not tell the truth she will. When the young man hears that the girl he is engaged to has Chinese blood in her veins, he exclaims: "Oh, what will my folks say?" But that is all. Love is stronger than prejudice with him, and neither he nor she deems it necessary to inform his "folks."

The Americans, having for many years manifested a much higher regard for the Japanese than for the Chinese, several half Chinese young men and women, thinking to advance themselves, both in a social and business sense, pass as Japanese. They continue to be known as Eurasians; but a Japanese Eurasian does not appear in the same light as a Chinese Eurasian. The unfortunate Chinese Eurasians! Are not those who compel them to thus cringe more to be blamed than they?

People, however, are not all alike. I meet white men, and women, too, who are proud to mate with those who have Chinese blood in their veins, and think it a great honor to be distinguished by the friendship of such. There are also Eurasians and Eurasians. I know of one who allowed herself to become engaged to a white man after refusing him nine times. She had discouraged him in every way possible, had warned him that she was half Chinese; that her people were poor, that every week or month she sent home a certain amount of her earnings, and that the man she married would have to do as much, if not more; also, most uncompromising truth of all, that she did not love him and never would. But the resolute and undaunted lover swore that it was a matter of indifference to him whether she was a Chinese or a Hottentot, that it would be his pleasure and privilege to allow her relations double what it was in her power to bestow, and as to not loving him—that did not matter at all. He loved her. So, because the young woman had a married mother and married sisters, who were always picking at her and gossiping over her independent manner of living, she finally consented to marry him, recording the agreement in her diary thus:

"I have promised to become the wife of —— —— on —— ——, 189——, because the world is so cruel and sneering to a single woman—and for no other reason."

Everything went smoothly until one day. The young man was driving a pair of beautiful horses and she was seated by his side, trying very hard to imagine herself in love with him, when a Chinese vegetable gardener's cart came rumbling along. The Chinaman was a jolly-looking individual in blue cotton blouse and pantaloons, his rakish looking hat being kept in place by a long queue which was pulled upward from his neck and wound around it. The young woman was suddenly possest with the spirit of mischief. "Look!" she cried, indicating the Chinaman, "there's my brother. Why don't you salute him?"

The man's face fell a little. He sank into a pensive mood. The wicked one by his side read him like an open book.

"When we are married," said she. "I intend to give a Chinese party every month."

No answer.

"As there are very few aristocratic Chinese in this city, I shall fill up with the laundrymen and vegetable farmers. I don't believe in being exclusive in democratic America, do you?"

He hadn't a grain of humor in his composition, but a sickly smile contorted his features as he replied:

"You shall do just as you please, my darling. But—but—consider a moment. Wouldn't it be just a little pleasanter for us if, after we are married, we allowed it to be presumed that you were—er—Japanese? So many of my friends have inquired of me if that is not your nationality. They would be so charmed to meet a little Japanese lady."

"Hadn't you better oblige them by finding one?"

"Why—er—what do you mean?"

"Nothing much in particular. Only—I am getting a little tired of this," taking off his ring.

"You don't mean what you say! Oh, put it back, dearest! You know I would not hurt your feelings for the world!"

"You haven't. I'm more than pleased. But I do mean what I say."

That evening the "ungrateful" Chinese Eurasian diaried, among other things, the following:

"Joy, oh, joy! I'm free once more. Never again shall I be untrue to my own heart. Never again will I allow any one to 'hound' or 'sneer' me into matrimony."

I secure transportation to many California points. I meet some literary people, chief among whom is the editor of the magazine who took my first Chinese stories. He and his wife give me a warm welcome to their ranch. They are broadminded people, whose interest in me is sincere and intelligent, not affected and vulgar. I also meet some funny people who advise me to "trade" upon my nationality. They tell me that if I wish to succeed in literature in America I should dress in Chinese costume, carry a fan in my hand, wear a pair of scarlet beaded slippers, live in New York, and come of high birth. Instead of making myself familiar with the Chinese-Americans around me, I should discourse on my spirit acquaintance with Chinese ancestors and quote in between the "Good mornings" and "How d'ye dos" of editors.

> "Confucius, Confucius, how great is Confucius, Before Confucius, there never was Confucius. After Confucius, there never came Confucius," etc., etc., etc.,

or something like that, both illuminating and obscuring, don't you know. They forget, or perhaps they are not aware that the old Chinese sage taught "The way of sincerity is the way of heaven."

My experiences as an Eurasian never cease; but people are not now as prejudiced as they have been. In the West, too, my friends are more advanced in all lines of thought than those whom I know in Eastern Canada—more genuine, more sincere, with less of the form of religion, but more of its spirit.

So I roam backward and forward across the continent. When I am East, my heart is West. When I am West, my heart is East. Before long I hope to be in China. As my life began in my father's country it may end in my mother's.

After all I have no nationality and am not anxious to claim any. Individuality is more than nationality. "You are you and I am I," says Confucius. I give my right hand to the Occidentals and my left to the Orientals, hoping that between them they will not utterly destroy the insignificant "connecting link." And that's all.

1909

❖

Anonymous

(late nineteenth century)

ONE FARMER'S WIFE

I was an apt student at school and before I was eighteen I had earned a teacher's certificate of the second grade and would gladly have remained in school a few more years, but I had, unwittingly, agreed to marry the man who is now my husband, and tho I begged to be released, his will was so much the stronger that I was unable to free myself without wounding a loving heart, and could not find it in my heart to do so. . . .

I always had a passion for reading; during girlhood it was along educational lines; in young womanhood it was for love stories, which remained ungratified because my father thought it sinful to read stories of any kind, and especially love stories.

Later, when I was married, I borrowed everything I could find in the line of novels and stories, and read them by stealth still, for my husband thought it a willful waste of time to read anything and that it showed a lack of love for him if I would rather read than to talk to him when I had a few moments of leisure, and, in order to avoid giving offense and still gratify my desire, I would only read when he was not at the house, thereby greatly curtailing my already too limited reading hours. . . .

It is only during the last three years that I have had the news to read, for my husband is so very penurious that he would never consent to subscribing for papers of any kind and that old habit of avoiding that which would give offense was so fixed that I did not dare to break it.

The addition of two children to our family never altered or interfered with the established order of things to any appreciable extent. My strenuous outdoor life agreed with me, and even when my children were born I was splendidly prepared for the ordeal and made rapid recovery. . . .

Any bright morning in the latter part of May I am out of bed at four o'clock; next, after I have dressed and combed my hair, I start a fire in the kitchen stove, . . . sweep the floors and then cook breakfast.

While the other members of the family are eating breakfast I strain away the morning's milk (for my husband milks the cows while I get breakfast), and fill my husband's dinnerpail, for he will go to work on our other farm for the day.

By this time it is half-past five o'clock, my husband is gone to his work, and the stock loudly pleading to be turned into the pastures. The younger cattle, a half-dozen steers, are left in the pasture at night, and I now drive the two cows a half-quarter mile and turn them in with the others, come back, and then there's a horse in the barn that belongs in a field where there is no water, which I take to a spring quite a distance from the barn; bring it back and turn it into a field with the sheep, a dozen in number, which are housed at night.

The young calves are then turned out into the warm sunshine, and the stock hogs, which are kept in a pen, are clamoring for feed, and I carry a pailful of swill to them, and hasten to the house and turn out the chickens and put out feed and water for them, and it is, perhaps, 6:30 a.m.

I have not eaten breakfast yet, but that can wait; I make the beds next and straighten things up in the living room, for I dislike to have the early morning caller find my house topsy-turvy. When this is done I go to the kitchen, which also serves as a dining room, and uncover the table, and take a mouthful of food occasionally as I pass to and fro at my work until my appetite is appeased.

By the time the work is done in the kitchen it is about 7:15 a.m., and the cool morning hours have flown, and no hoeing done in the garden yet, and the children's toilet has to be attended to and churning has to be done.

Finally the children are washed and churning done, and it is eight o'clock, and the sun getting hot, but no matter, weeds die quickly when cut down in the heat of the day, and I use the hoe to a good advantage until the dinner hour, which is 11:30 a.m. We come in, and I comb my hair, and put fresh flowers in it, and eat a cold dinner, put out feed and water for the chickens; set a hen, perhaps, sweep the floors again; sit down and rest and read a few moments, and it is nearly one o'clock, and I sweep the door yard while I am waiting for the clock to strike the hour.

I make and sow a flower bed, dig around some shrubbery, and go back to the garden to hoe until time to do the chores at night. . . .

I hoe in the garden till four o'clock; then I go into the house and get supper . . . when supper is all ready it is set aside, and I pull a few hundred plants of tomato, sweet potato or cabbage for transplanting . . . I then go after the horse, water him, and put him in the barn; call the sheep and house them, and go after the cows and milk them, feed the hogs, put down hay for three horses, and put oats and corn in their troughs, and set those plants and come in and fasten up the chickens. . . . It is 8 o'clock p.m.; my husband has come home, and we are eating supper; when we are through eating I make the beds ready, and the children and their father go to bed, and I wash the dishes and get things in shape to get breakfast quickly next morning. . . .

All the time that I have been going about this work I have been thinking of things I have read . . . and of other things which I have a desire to read, but cannot hope to while the present condition exists.

As a natural consequence there are daily, numerous instances of absent-mindedness on my part; many things left undone. . . . My husband never fails to remind me that it is caused by my reading so much; that I would get along much better if I should never see a book or paper. . . .

I use an old fashioned churn, and the process of churning occupies from thirty minutes to three hours, according to the condition of the cream, and I always read something while churning. . . .

FOUR

Modern Voices

During the twentieth century, many women felt free of the conventions—and the accompanying restrictions—of Victorian times. The New Woman grew into the modern woman (the flapper, the hoydenish and boyish and outspoken girl who no longer cared what her society thought of her behavior). With new freedoms came new voices, and even in the privacy of the letter or the diary change was evident. When painter Georgia O'Keeffe (1887–1986) wrote to her friend Anita Pollitzer in 1915, her letters spoke about her sense of her developing art, her individual need to express the natural beauty that surrounded her. They were a highly idiosyncratic expression, remote from the clamor of The Great War that was simultaneously sounding through the world.

American writers have frequently written about themselves. Beginning with Ben Franklin's autobiography, the memoir became a popular form for both women and men, and *Memories of a Catholic Girlhood* by Mary McCarthy (1912–1989) is among the most famous. As this excerpt shows, McCarthy turns inward, finding her story in her own reaction to people's treatment of—and naming of—her. The narrative is not external or plot-centered, but rather trained on the reactions of the protagonist-author, one and the same person. Characteristic of writing at mid-century, McCarthy's memoir is also concerned with the impact of formal religious belief—and its accompanying pain—on the psyche. Of the many books that marked her successful writing career, among them a novel, *The Group*, McCarthy's autobiography may be her most lasting.

Leslie Marmon Silko (b. 1948) draws from the long tradition of American autobiography to write the multi-voiced memoir, *Storyteller*. Combining poetry, song, memoir, fiction (the story "Storyteller" is often anthologized), art work, and a gallery of portraits of friends and relatives, the mixed-form text has become a resource for all kinds of readers, and a model for all kinds of writers. Silko, who is part Laguna Indian and part Mexican, insists on fusing cultures and forms native to both cultures with mainstream Western literary forms. While her novels, *Ceremony* and *Almanac of the Dead*, have been well-received, *Storyteller* is a remarkable text that moves beyond the individually autobiographical in its creation of a world.

Pat Mora (b. 1942), known primarily as a poet and essayist, captures several strains of American letters in her moving letter to a young Chicana writer. Speaking of the difficulties of being outside the dominant culture, yet reaffirming the joys of living a creative life as she learns the craft of words, Mora touches the reader deeply through seemingly simple, but always poetic, language. A Chicana from El Paso, Texas, Mora now lives in Cincinnati, Ohio, where she continues to write and mother her family; in 1993 her essays appeared in *Nepantla: Essays from the Land in the Middle.* The simplicity of her well-chosen words does not suggest naïveté, but a hard-won courage to say difficult things directly.

These selections suggest that the relatively straightforward model of the letter or memoir has been enriched by including cultural history in private writing in a number of ways. In the work of both Silko and Mora, representative of the best contemporary women's writing, the reader sees landscape and community, human interaction and personal interrogation, woven into writing that almost defies generic classification. What remains in that writing is excellence.

❖

Georgia O'Keeffe
(1887–1986)

TO ANITA POLLITZER

Charlottesville, Virginia—*October 1915*

ANITA

—Living just seems wonderful tonight—for no apparent reason—and again for no reason except that I happen to want to—I must tell you about it—

Adelaide and I walked through the woods this afternoon—just following paths for three or four hours

When I came in your letter was slipped under my door with the Steiglitz clipping in it—You can laugh all you want to about my wondering what Art is—

Yes—Laugh

I believe some wise old fool says its good for the soul so maybe it will help—

Anita—you can have that flower study you like if it doesnt get in the Water Color Show—and I think it will not—I am just wanting it hung for curiosity—And if it gets in and isn't sold you can have

it—if you want it. I am always through with my things—when they
are—after I've made them—I don't want the darned thing—

It is all very well to laugh—I laugh too—But you get mightily
twisted with your self at the tale end of the earth with no one to talk
to—The thinking gets more serious when you wonder and fight and
think alone—Of course I have thought what you say about it—but
some times hearing some one say it again—just the phrasing—gives
you a starting point for a new idea. I don't know that my heart or
head or anything in me is worth living on paper—We ought to be
as busy making ourselves wonderful—according to your theory—as
we are with expressing that self—

Can you imagine me sitting down and faking a letter to you every
few days. You must fancy me fond of curious amusements—but I
know you dont think Im doing that. Certainly Im glad Im here—
Im really enjoying the loneness of it. I don't know that Im doing
anything—but it doesnt matter.

Would you like to see some of Adelaides work? I think you would
get a large amount of enjoyment out of it so I am going to send you
some and ask for suggestions. Anita—I just cant tell you how much
fun I got out of the Steiglitz clipping—

SAME AS EVER—
GEORGIA.

I am using all the scraps of paper I have tonight because I haven't
any other and forgot to get it.

Anita I am sleepy and can't write any more tonight—

It feels like squeezing blood out of a turnip—and I like only to
write you when its an overflow.

LOVINGLY

Canyon, Texas—September 11, 1916

Tonight I walked into the sunset—to mail some letters—the whole
sky—and there is so much of it out here—was just blazing—and
grey blue clouds were riding all through the holiness of it—and the
ugly little buildings and windmills looked great against it

But some way or other I didn't seem to like the redness much so
after I mailed the letters I walked home—and kept walking—

The Eastern sky was all grey blue—bunches of clouds—different

kinds of clouds—sticking around everywhere and the whole thing—
lit up—first in one place—then in another with flashes of lightning—
sometimes just sheet lightning—and some times sheet lightning with
a sharp bright zigzag flashing across it—. I walked out past the last
house—past the last locust tree—and sat on the fence for a long
time—looking—just looking at—the lightning—you see there was
nothing but sky and flat prairie land—land that seems more like the
ocean than anything else I know—There was a wonderful moon.

Well I just sat there and had a great time all by myself—Not even
many night noises—just the wind—

I wondered what you are doing—

It is absurd the way I love this country—Then when I came
back—it was funny—roads just shoot across blocks anywhere—all
the houses looked alike—and I almost got lost—I had to laugh to
myself—I couldnt tell which house was home—

I am loving the plains more than ever it seems—and the SKY
Anita you have never seen SKY—it is wonderful—

Mary McCarthy
(1912–1989)

NAMES
from *Memories of a Catholic Girlhood*

Anna Lyons, Mary Louise Lyons, Mary von Phul, Emilie von Phul, Eugenia
McLellan, Marjorie McPhail, Marie-Louise L'Abbé, Mary Danz, Julia
Dodge, Mary Fordyce Blake, Janet Preston—these were the names (I can still
tell them over like a rosary) of some of the older girls in the convent: the
Virtues and Graces. The virtuous ones wore wide blue or green moire good-
conduct ribbons, bandoleer-style, across their blue serge uniforms; the beautiful ones wore rouge and powder or at least were reputed to do so. Our class,
the eighth grade, wore pink ribbons (I never got one myself) and had names
like Patricia ("Pat") Sullivan, Eileen Donohoe, and Joan Kane. We were in-
elegant even in this respect; the best name we could show, among us, was
Phyllis ("Phil") Chatham, who boasted that her father's name, Ralph, was
pronounced "Rafe" as in England.

Names had a great importance for us in the convent, and foreign names,

French, German, or plain English (which, to us, were foreign, because of their Protestant sound), bloomed like prize roses among a collection of spuds. Irish names were too common in the school to have any prestige either as surnames (Gallagher, Sheehan, Finn, Sullivan, McCarthy) or as Christian names (Kathleen, Eileen). Anything exotic had value: an "olive" complexion, for example. The pet girl of the convent was a fragile Jewish girl named Susie Lowenstein, who had pale red-gold hair and an exquisite retroussé nose, which, if we had had it, might have been called "pug." We liked her name too and the name of a child in the primary grades: Abbie Stuart Baillargeon. My favorite name, on the whole, though, was Emilie von Phul (pronounced "Pool"); her oldest sister, recently graduated, was called Celeste. Another name that appealed to me was Genevieve Albers, Saint Genevieve being the patron saint of Paris who turned back Attila from the gates of the city.

All these names reflected the still-pioneer character of the Pacific Northwest. I had never heard their like in the parochial school in Minneapolis, where "foreign" extraction, in any case, was something to be ashamed of, the whole drive being toward Americanization of first name and surname alike. The exceptions to this were the Irish, who could vaunt such names as Catherine O'Dea and the name of my second cousin, Mary Catherine Anne Rose Violet McCarthy, while an unfortunate German boy named Manfred was made to suffer for his. But that was Minneapolis. In Seattle, and especially in the convent of the Ladies of the Sacred Heart, foreign names suggested not immigration but emigration—distinguished exile. Minneapolis was a granary; Seattle was a port, which had attracted a veritable Foreign Legion of adventurers—soldiers of fortune, younger sons, gamblers, traders, drawn by the fortunes to be made in virgin timber and shipping and by the Alaska Gold Rush. Wars and revolutions had sent the defeated out to Puget Sound, to start a new life; the latest had been the Russian Revolution, which had shipped us, via Harbin, a Russian colony, complete with restaurant, on Queen Anne Hill. The English names in the convent, when they did not testify to direct English origin, as in the case of "Rafe" Chatham, had come to us from the South and represented a kind of internal exile; such girls as Mary Fordyce Blake and Mary McQueen Street (a class ahead of me; her sister was named Francesca) bore their double-barreled first names like titles of aristocracy from the ante-bellum South. Not all our girls, by any means, were Catholic; some of the very prettiest ones—Julia Dodge and Janet Preston, if I remember rightly—were Protestants. The nuns had taught us to behave with special courtesy to these strangers in our midst, and the whole effect was of some superior hostel for refugees of all the lost causes of the past hundred years. Money could not count for much in such an atmosphere; the fathers and grandfathers of many of our "best" girls were ruined men.

Names, often, were freakish in the Pacific Northwest, particularly girls' names. In the Episcopal boarding school I went to later, in Tacoma, there was a girl called De Vere Utter, and there was a girl called Rocena and another called Hermoine. Was Rocena a mistake for Rowena and Hermoine for Hermione? And was Vere, as we called her, Lady Clara Vere de Vere? Probably. You do not hear names like those often, in any case, east of the Cascade Mountains; they belong to the frontier, where books and libraries were few and memory seems to have been oral, as in the time of Homer.

Names have more significance for Catholics than they do for other people; Christian names are chosen for the spiritual qualities of the saints they are taken from; Protestants used to name their children out of the Old Testament and now they name them out of novels and plays, whose heroes and heroines are perhaps the new patron saints of a secular age. But with Catholics it is different. The saint a child is named for is supposed to serve, literally, as a model or pattern to imitate; your name is your fortune and it tells you what you are or must be. Catholic children ponder their names for a mystic meaning, like birthstones; my own, I learned, besides belonging to the Virgin and Saint Mary of Egypt, originally meant "bitter" or "star of the sea." My second name, Therese, could dedicate me either to Saint Theresa or to the saint called the Little Flower, Soeur Thérèse of Lisieux, on whom God was supposed to have descended in the form of a shower of roses. At Confirmation, I had added a third name (for Catholics then rename themselves, as most nuns do, yet another time, when they take orders); on the advice of a nun, I had taken "Clementina," after Saint Clement, an early pope—a step I soon regretted on account of "My Darling Clementine" and her number nine shoes. By the time I was in the convent, I would no longer tell anyone what my Confirmation name was. The name I had nearly picked was "Agnes," after a little Roman virgin martyr, always shown with a lamb, because of her purity. But Agnes would have been just as bad, I recognized in Forest Ridge Convent—not only because of the possibility of "Aggie," but because it was subtly, indefinably *wrong*, in itself. Agnes would have made me look like an ass.

The fear of appearing ridiculous first entered my life, as a governing motive, during my second year in the convent. Up to then, a desire for prominence had decided many of my actions and, in fact, still persisted. But in the eighth grade, I became aware of mockery and perceived that I could not seek prominence without attracting laughter. Other people could, but I couldn't. This laughter was proceeding, not from my classmates, but from the girls of the class just above me, in particular from two boon companions, Elinor Heffernan and Mary Harty, a clownish pair—oddly assorted in size and shape, as teams of clowns generally are, one short, plump, and baby-faced, the other tall, lean, and owlish—who entertained the high-school department by calling attention to the oddities of the younger girls. Nearly every school has such a pair of satirists, whose marks are generally low and who are tolerated just because of their laziness and non-conformity; one of them (in this case, Mary Harty, the plump one) usually appears to be half asleep. Because of their low standing, their indifference to appearances, the sad state of their uniforms, their clowning is taken to be harmless, which, on the whole, it is, their object being not to wound but to divert; such girls are bored in school. We in the eighth grade sat directly in front of the two wits in study hall, so that they had us under close observation; yet at first I was not afraid of them, wanting, if anything, to identify myself with their laughter, to be initiated into the joke. One of their specialities was giving people nicknames, and it was considered an honor to be the first in the eighth grade to be let in by Elinor and Mary on their latest invention. This often happened to me; they would tell me, on the playground, and I would tell the others. As their intermediary, I felt myself almost their friend and it did not occur to me that I might be next on their list.

I had achieved prominence not long before by publicly losing my faith and regaining it at the end of a retreat. I believe Elinor and Mary questioned me about this on the playground, during recess, and listened with serious, respectful faces while I told them about my conversations with the Jesuits. Those serious faces ought to have been an omen, but if the two girls used what I had revealed to make fun of me, it must have been behind my back. I never heard any more of it, and yet just at this time I began to feel something, like a cold breath on the nape of my neck, that made me wonder whether the new position I had won for myself in the convent was as secure as I imagined. I would turn around in study hall and find the two girls looking at me with speculation in their eyes.

It was just at this time, too, that I found myself in a perfectly absurd situation, a very private one, which made me live, from month to month, in horror of discovery. I had waked up one morning, in my convent room, to find a few small spots of blood on my sheet; I had somehow scratched a trifling cut on one of my legs and opened it during the night. I wondered what to do about this, for the nuns were fussy about bedmaking, as they were about our white collars and cuffs, and if we had an inspection those spots might count against me. It was best, I decided, to ask the nun on dormitory duty, tall, stout Mother Slattery, for a clean bottom sheet, even though she might scold me for having scratched my leg in my sleep and order me to cut my toenails. You never know what you might be blamed for. But Mother Slattery, when she bustled in to look at the sheet, did not scold me at all; indeed, she hardly seemed to be listening as I explained to her about the cut. She told me to sit down: she would be back in a minute. "You can be excused from athletics today," she added, closing the door. As I waited, I considered this remark, which seemed to me strangely munificent, in view of the unimportance of the cut. In a moment, she returned, but without the sheet. Instead, she produced out of her big pocket a sort of cloth girdle and a peculiar flannel object which I first took to be a bandage, and I began to protest that I did not need or want a bandage; all I needed was a bottom sheet. "The sheet can wait," said Mother Slattery, succinctly, handing me two large safety pins. It was the pins that abruptly enlightened me; I saw Mother Slattery's mistake, even as she was instructing me as to how this flannel article, which I now understood to be a sanitary napkin, was to be put on.

"Oh, no, Mother," I said; feeling somewhat embarrassed. "You don't understand. It's just a little cut, on my leg." But Mother, again, was not listening; she appeared to have grown deaf, as the nuns had a habit of doing when what you were saying did not fit in with their ideas. And now that I knew what was in her mind, I was conscious of a funny constraint; I did not feel it proper to name a natural process, in so many words, to a nun. It was like trying not to think of their going to the bathroom or trying not to see the straggling iron-grey hair coming out of their coifs (the common notion that they shaved their heads was false). On the whole, it seemed better just to show her my cut. But when I offered to do so and unfastened my black stocking, she only glanced at my leg, cursorily. "That's only a scratch, dear," she said. "Now hurry up and put this on or you'll be late for chapel. Have you any pain?" "No, no, Mother!" I cried. "You don't understand!" "Yes, yes, I understand," she replied soothingly, "and you will too, a little later. Mother Superior will tell you about it some time during the morning. There's nothing to be afraid of. You have become a woman."

"I know all about that," I persisted. "Mother, please listen. I just cut my leg. On the athletic field. Yesterday afternoon." But the more excited I grew, the more soothing, and yet firm, Mother Slattery became. There seemed to be nothing for it but to give up and do as I was bid. I was in the grip of a higher authority, which almost had the power to persuade me that it was right and I was wrong. But of course I was not wrong; that would have been too good to be true. While Mother Slattery waited, just outside my door, I miserably donned the equipment she had given me, for there was no place to hide it, on account of drawer inspection. She led me down the hall to where there was a chute and explained how I was to dispose of the flannel thing, by dropping it down the chute into the laundry. (The convent arrangements were very old-fashioned, dating back, no doubt, to the days of Louis Philippe.)

The Mother Superior, Madame MacIllvra, was a sensible woman, and all through my early morning classes, I was on pins and needles, chafing for the promised interview with her which I trusted would clear things up. "*Ma Mère*," I would begin, "Mother Slattery thinks . . ." Then I would tell her about the cut and the athletic field. But precisely the same impasse confronted me when I was summoned to her office at recess-time. *I* talked about my cut, and *she* talked about becoming a woman. It was rather like a round, in which she was singing "Scotland's burning, Scotland's burning," and I was singing "Pour on water, pour on water." Neither of us could hear the other, or, rather, I could hear her, but she could not hear me. Owing to our different positions in the convent, she was free to interrupt me, whereas I was expected to remain silent until she had finished speaking. When I kept breaking in, she hushed me, gently, and took me on her lap. Exactly like Mother Slattery, she attributed all my references to the cut to a blind fear of this new, unexpected reality that had supposedly entered my life. Many young girls, she reassured me, were frightened if they had not been prepared. "And you, Mary, have lost your dear mother, who could have made this easier for you." Rocked on Madame MacIllvra's lap, I felt paralysis overtake me and I lay, mutely listening, against her bosom, my face being tickled by her white, starched, fluted wimple, while she explained to me how babies were born, all of which I had heard before.

There was no use fighting the convent. I had to pretend to have become a woman, just as, not long before, I had had to pretend to get my faith back— for the sake of peace. This pretense was decidedly awkward. For fear of being found out by the lay sisters downstairs in the laundry (no doubt an imaginary contingency, but the convent was so very thorough), I reopened the cut on my leg, so as to draw a little blood to stain the napkins, which were issued me regularly, not only on this occasion, but every twenty-eight days thereafter. Eventually, I abandoned this bloodletting, for fear of lockjaw, and trusted to fate. Yet I was in awful dread of detection; my only hope, as I saw it, was either to be released from the convent or to become a woman in reality, which might take a year, at least, since I was only twelve. Getting out of athletics once a month was not sufficient compensation for the farce I was going through. It was not my fault; they had forced me into it; nevertheless, it was I who would look silly—worse than silly; half mad—if the truth ever came to light.

I was burdened with this guilt and shame when the nickname finally found me out. "Found me out," in a general sense, for no one ever did learn the particular secret I bore about with me, pinned to the linen band. "We've got a name for you," Elinor and Mary called out to me, one day on the playground. "What is it?" I asked, half hoping, half fearing, since not all their sobriquets were unfavorable. "Cye," they answered, looking at each other and laughing. " 'Si'?" I repeated, supposing that it was based on Simple Simon. Did they regard me as a hick? "C.Y.E.," they elucidated, spelling it out in chorus. "The letters stand for something. Can you guess?" I could not and I cannot now.

The closest I could come to it in the convent was "Clean Your Ears." Perhaps that was it, though in later life I have wondered whether it did not stand, simply, for "Clever Young Egg" or "Champion Young Eccentric." But in the convent I was certain that it stood for something horrible, something even worse than dirty ears (as far as I knew, my ears were clean), something I could never guess because it represented some aspect of myself that the world could see and I couldn't, like a sign pinned on my back. Everyone in the convent must have known what the letters stood for, but no one would tell me. Elinor and Mary had made them promise. It was like halitosis; not even my best friend, my deskmate, Louise, would tell me, no matter how much I pleaded. Yet everyone assured me that it was "very good," that is, very apt. And it made everyone laugh.

This name reduced all my pretensions and solidified my sense of *wrongness*. Just as I felt I was beginning to belong to the convent, it turned me into an outsider, since I was the only pupil who was not in the know. I liked the convent, but it did not like me, as people say of certain foods that disagree with them. By this, I do not mean that I was actively unpopular, either with the pupils or with the nuns. The Mother Superior cried when I left and predicted that I would be a novelist, which surprised me. And I had finally made friends; even Emilie von Phul smiled upon me softly out of her bright blue eyes from the far end of the study hall. It was just that I did not fit into the convent pattern; the simplest thing I did, like asking for a clean sheet, entrapped me in consequences that I never could have predicted. I was not bad; I did not consciously break the rules; and yet I could never, not even for a week, get a pink ribbon, and this was something I could not understand, because I was trying as hard as I could. It was the same case as with the hated name; the nuns, evidently, saw something about me that was invisible to me.

The oddest part was all that pretending. There I was, a walking mass of lies, pretending to be a Catholic and going to confession while really I had lost my faith, and pretending to have monthly periods by cutting myself with nail scissors; yet all this had come about without my volition and even contrary to it. But the basest pretense I was driven to was the acceptance of the nickname. Yet what else could I do? In the convent, I could not live it down. To all those girls, I had become "Cye McCarthy." That was who I was. That was how I had to identify myself when telephoning my friends during vacations to ask them to the movies: "Hello, this is Cye." I loathed myself when I said it, and yet I succumbed to the name totally, making myself over into a sort of hearty to go with it—the kind of girl I hated. "Cye" was my new patron saint. This false personality stuck to me, like the name, when I entered public high school, the next fall, as a freshman, having finally persuaded my grand-parents to take me out of the convent, although they could never get to the bottom of my reasons, since, as I admitted, the nuns were kind, and I had made many nice new friends. What I wanted was a fresh start, a chance to begin life over again, but the first thing I heard in the corridors of the public high school was that name called out to me, like the warmest of welcomes: "Hi, there, Si!" That was the way they thought it was spelled. But this time I was resolute. After the first weeks, I dropped the hearties who called me "Si!" and I never heard it again. I got my own name back and sloughed off Clementina and even Therese—the names that did not seem to me any more to be mine but to have been imposed on me by others. And I preferred to think that Mary meant "bitter" rather than "star of the sea."

1957

❖

Leslie Marmon Silko

(1948–   )

from *Storyteller*

Grandma A'mooh used to tell me stories she remembered hearing when she was a girl. One time, she said, some Navajos came and ran off a big herd of Laguna sheep. The Laguna men all got together and went after them. The Navajos were headed north but they couldn't travel very fast because they were driving all those sheep ahead of them. So finally, a little way past Paguate toward Moquino, they caught up with the Navajos. But the Lagunas didn't harm them or take them captive. They just asked the Navajos why they had taken the sheep, and the Navajos said it was because they were very hungry and had nothing to eat. So the Lagunas told them that next time they needed food to come ask for it instead of stealing it and the Laguna people would be happy to give them something. Then the Lagunas gave them five or six sheep and let them go. Grandma was always proud of this story because her uncles and grandfather had been there.

At Laguna Feast time, on September 19, Navajo people are welcome at any Laguna home regardless of whether they are acquainted or not. When Navajo people knock, they are invited in to eat as much as they want. And no matter how much they eat, they are never refused another helping of bread or chili stew.

Many of the Navajo people would come back to the same houses year after year for Laguna Feast until finally they were good friends with the Laguna families and they would bring nice gifts when they came. Grandpa Hank had a friend like that, an old man from Alamo. Every year they were so glad to see each other, and the Navajo man would bring Grandpa something in the gunny sack he carried—sometimes little apricots the old man grew or a mutton shoulder. Grandpa would walk around the store and gather up things for his friend—coffee and sugar and a new pair of Levi's—things like that. I remember the last time the old Navajo man came looking for my grandpa. He came into the store and looked for Grandpa where Grandpa always stood, behind his desk in the corner. When he didn't see him, the old man asked for him and then we told him, "Henry passed away last winter." The old Navajo man cried, and then he left. He never came back anymore after that.

1981

❖

Pat Mora
(1942–   )

TO GABRIELA, A YOUNG WRITER

The enthusiasm and curiosity of young writers is source of energy. In one sense, we are all fledgling writers. With each new piece, we embark on the mysterious process again, unsure if we can describe or evoke what is in our minds and hearts. Sometimes it is difficult to convince those under thirty that the struggle never ends, that art is not about formulas. Maybe that continuing risk lures us. Luckily, octogenarians such as movie director Akira Kurosawa or Mexican painter Rufino Tamayo show us that we need never retire, and that what we have to share near the end of our lives may be far more lyrical than our early efforts in any art form. A sad truth about art is that it is unlinked to virtue. Wretches can write well while saints produce pedestrian passages.

I like to share what little I know, to encourage beginning writers. When a friend asked if I'd give her thirteen-year-old daughter some advice, I wrote her.

DEAR GABRIELA,

Your mother tells me that you have begun writing poems and that you wonder exactly how I do it. Do you perhaps wonder why I do it? Why would anyone sit alone and write when she could be talking to friends on the telephone, eating mint chocolate chip ice cream in front of the TV, or buying a new red sweater at the mall?

547

And, as you know, I like people. I like long, slow lunches with my friends. I like to dance. I'm no hermit, and I'm not shy. So why do I sit with my tablet and pen and mutter to myself?

There are many answers. I write because I'm a reader. I want to give to others what writers have given me, a chance to hear the voices of people I will never meet. Alone, in private. And even if I meet these authors, I wouldn't hear what I hear alone with the page, words carefully chosen, woven into a piece unlike any other, enjoyed by me in a way no other person will, in quite the same way, enjoy them. I suppose I'm saying that I love the privateness of writing and reading. It's delicious to curl into a book.

I write because I'm curious. I'm curious about me. Writing is a way of finding out how I feel about anything and everything. Now that I've left the desert where I grew up, for example, I'm discovering how it feels to walk on spongy fall leaves and to watch snow drifting *up* on a strong wind. I notice what's around me in a special way because I'm a writer, and then I talk to myself about it on paper. Writing is my way of saving my feelings.

I write because I believe that Mexican Americans need to take their rightful place in U.S. literature. We need to be published and to be studied in schools and colleges so that the stories and ideas of our people won't quietly disappear. Although I'm happy when I finish the draft of a poem or story, deep inside I always wish I wrote better, that I could bring more honor and attention to those like the *abuelitas,* grandmothers, I write about. That mix of sadness and pleasure occurs in life, doesn't it?

Although we don't discuss it often because it's depressing, our people have been and sometimes still are viewed as inferior. Maybe you have already felt hurt when someone by a remark or odd look said to you: you're not like us, you're not one of us, speaking Spanish is odd, your family looks funny.

Some of us decide we don't want to be different. We don't want to be part of a group that is often described as poor and uneducated. I remember feeling that way at your age. I spoke Spanish at home to my grandmother and aunt, but I didn't always want my friends at school to know that I spoke Spanish. I didn't like myself for feeling that way. I sensed it was wrong, but I didn't know why. Now, I know.

I know that the society we live in and that the movies, television programs, and commercials we see all affect us. It's not easy to learn to judge others fairly, not because of the car they drive, the house they live in, the church they attend, the color of their skin, the language they speak at home. It takes courage to face the fact that we all have ten toes, get sleepy at night, get scared in the dark. Some families, some cities, some states, and even some countries foolishly convince themselves that they are better than others. And then they teach their children this ugly lie. It's like a weed with burrs and stickers that pricks people.

How are young women who are African American, Asian American, American Indian, Latinas, or members of all the other ethnic groups supposed to feel about themselves? Some are proud of their cultural roots. But commercials are also busy trying to convince us that our car, clothes, and maybe even our family are not good enough. It's so hard today to be your self, your many interesting selves, because billboards and magazines tell you that beautiful is being thin, maybe blonde, and rich, rich, rich. No wonder we don't always like ourselves when we look in the mirror.

There are no secrets to good writing. Read. Listen. Write. Read. Listen. Write. You learn to write well by reading wonderful writing and by letting those words and ideas become part of your blood and bones. But life is not all books. You become a better writer by listening—to your self and to all the colors, shapes, and sounds around you. Listen with all of your senses. Listen to wrinkles on your *tía's,* your aunt's, face.

Writers write. They don't just talk about writing just as dancers don't just talk about dancing. They do it because they love it and because they want to get better and better. They practice and practice to loosen up just as you practiced and practiced when you were learning to talk. And because you practiced, you don't talk the way you did when you were three.

Do you know the quotation that says that learning to write is like learning to ice-skate? You must be willing to make a fool of yourself. Writers are willing to try what they can't do well so that one day they can write a strong poem or novel or children's book.

After a writer gains some confidence, she begins to spend more and more time revising, just as professional ice-skaters create and practice certain routines until they have developed their own, unique style. You probably don't like rewriting now. I didn't either until a few years ago.

How or why a book or poem starts varies. Sometimes I hear a story I want to save, sometimes it's a line, or an idea. It would be as if you saw someone dance and you noticed a step or some special moves and for a few days you didn't actually try the steps, but off and on you thought about them. Maybe you even feel the moves inside you. And then one day you just can't stand it anymore and you turn on the music and begin to experiment. You don't succeed right away, but you're having fun even while you're working to get the rhythm right. And slowly you loosen up, and pretty soon you forget about your feet and arms, and you and the music are just moving together. Then the next day you try it again, and maybe alter it slightly.

My pen is like that music. Usually I like to start in a sunny spot with a yellow, lined tablet and a pen. I have a number of false starts like you did dancing. I'm working but having fun. Alone. The first line of a poem is sometimes a hard one because I want it to be an interesting line. It may be the only line a reader will glance at to decide whether to read the whole piece. I'm searching for the right beginning. I play a little game with myself. (This game works with any kind of writing.) I tell myself to write any line no matter how bad or dull, because I can later throw it away. If I sit waiting for the perfect line, I might never write the poem. I'm willing to make a fool of myself. So I start, usually slowly. I write a few lines, read them aloud, and often start again. I keep sections I like and discard the uninteresting parts. The next day I read my work and try to improve it. I'm trying to pull out of myself the poem or story that's deep inside. It's important not to fall in love with the words you write. Pick your words or phrases, and then stand back and look at your work. Read it out loud.

You and I are lucky to be writers. So many women in history and even today who could be much better writers than I am have not had that private pleasure of creating with words. Maybe their families think writing is a waste of time, maybe they don't believe in themselves, maybe they have to work hard all day and then have to cook and clean and take care of their children at night, maybe they've never been taught to read and write.

I hope that you develop pride in being Mexican American and that you discover what you have to say that no one else can say. I hope that you continue writing, Gabriela.

1993

550

PART VI

Bodily Pleasures

Woman as caretaker. Woman as domestic helpmate. Woman as mother, wife, friend, nurturer. So many of the identities women take on are about giving sustenance, about feeding others, literally and metaphorically. Who feeds women?

Throughout this collection, we have seen women writers in various roles—as artists preeminently, but also as intellectuals, activists, political commentators, social critics, visionaries. We end this collection on a light note, with a tribute to women's bodily pleasures, including a celebration of cooking as an act that can be self-sustaining as well as nurturing of others. Women's bodies are so often arrayed for the pleasure of others, but here, in erotica as well as in cookery, women exult in themselves, in their own sensuality and in the sensual worlds they create.

The language in these selections is as spirit-lifting as it is body-rich. "Today is the first day of October," writes the "Captain's Lady" in 1871, before giving away her recipe for "Jamaican Schrimp." "It is a veritable gold and crimson fantasy as far as the eye can see." Or Emily Dickinson writes of "Wild Nights—Wild Nights!" in a sexy, celebratory mood so different from that conveyed by the view of her as the virgin poet in the white dress, lowering cookies from her bedroom window to the neighborhood children in the street below:

> *Rowing in Eden—*
> *Ah, the Sea!*
> *Might I but moor—Tonight—*
> *In Thee!*

In what lover is Dickinson dreaming of mooring? The imagery here is as classically female as the ocean, even though the lover remains (historically) unknown.

We can delight here in Dickinson's delight: "Wild nights should be / Our luxury!" And we invite the reader to enjoy these simple and exquisite pleasures,

beautifully rendered by a baker's dozen of women writers who understand that
it can be as blessed to receive as it is to give. Enjoy!

O N E

Recipes

Family recipes are one legacy of women to their friends and relatives, offering
up treasured cooking secrets as an inestimable inheritance. Gifts of love, recipes have throughout history been enclosed in personal letters or tucked into
boxes of food. From the eighteenth century, they have also been collected into
booklets, printed and either distributed or sold, with profits sometimes ear-
marked for the club or charity that created the cookbook. This use of recipes
as a gesture of friendship has also been one way women communicate with
one another.

Recipes have served as a way to salvage something permanent from the
almost constant labor of preparing food. For the "Captain's Lady," cookbook
and memoir are almost indistinguishable. The recipe comes with a story of
longing for the return of her beloved. Love and food are intertwined, as they
are for Alice B. Toklas, who cooked Sunday dinners for Gertrude Stein, and
for the artists and writers they entertained in their famous apartment in Paris.
Toklas cooked *American* food on Sundays, simple dishes she had "eaten in
the homes of the San Joaquin Valley in California—fricasseed chicken, corn
bread, apple and lemon pie."

The eroticism of food is powerful. But food often has a spiritual significance
as well. Edna Lewis's "Sunday Revival Dinner" commemorates "our most
important social event of the summer season," a revival dinner that remembers
the slave past and celebrates freedom: "The fruits of our hard labor were now
our own, we were free to come and go, and to gather together for this week
of reunion and celebration." And Zarela Martinez, a Mexican chef who lives
and cooks in New York City, provides her recipe for bread served on the Day
of the Dead as a way to remember her past and to explain to Anglo-Americans
this "happiest, most life-affirming holiday." As Martinez notes, "it is the celebration of memory, the time when we really feel we are speaking to and
embracing those whom we have lost."

❖

THE LAST RETURN FROM THE SEA

from *The Captain's Lady's Cookbook*

October 1, 1871

Today is the first day of October. It is a veritable gold and crimson fantasy as far as the eye can see. Such splendor, such magnificence: the golden sun rising from the smoke hazed mountains transforming them into a wonderland of riotous colours then continuing on in its orbit ever upward radiating in the vast heavens of cerulean blue.

I arose early this morning just as the mists were rising above the water and the sun was breaking through. All morning I felt a strange inner unrest, a feeling of unrestrained joy and expectation. Could this be the day? I carefully made my most perfect lemon meringue pie and then left it to cool. I hastily dressed in a soft emerald green velvet riding habit. I donned a tocque of green ostrich plumes and then set off on my favourite chestnut bay, Star. I called to Dutchess, the terrier and Moira and Rori, the Irish setters; we set off at a fairly brisk pace through the perfect wood down to the pond. There, rivulets of dew were evaporating in the warmth of the sun. The pond, so still, faithfully reflected the iridescent images of all that it captured within its depths: the trees, the leaves, the sun, the sky. Shy deer daintily sipped the cool water, joined by rabbits and an occasional mother fox and her pretty cubs. I had a basket with me containing bread for the fish, birds and animals and small treats for the horse, the dogs and myself. As the morning wore on, we walked further into the peaceful wood to the holy place my Captain and I had made. There by the small shrine to St. Francis, I knelt and prayed, "Please send my Captain safely home, today." As I rose and turned, I thought I saw a vision, but no! There he was running to me through the wood, the sunlight catching the glint from his golden hair. I immediately ran to him with the dogs at my side barking for joy. It was as if we were in a dream. Then I was in his strong arms: that magic circle of love and contentment. My Captain lifted me onto the horse, took the reins, and we started home.

My Captain is home, nevermore to venture forth to sea. I will now be able to gaze at him to my heart's content, everyday. My love has returned. My life is complete.

Jamaican Schrimp

4 lbs. large Gulf schrimp. Cook about 3 lbs. fresh tomatoes. Then puree them. Add

1¹/₂ tsp. turmeric	1 tsp. cumin
1 tsp. coriander	red pepper to taste
1 tsp. ginger	salt to taste

Cook for about 20 minutes, in large pan. Serve with 4 cups cooked rice. For a savoury, dip in English Grey's Chutney.

The Captain brought this receipt back from Jamaica.

Alice B. Toklas

(1877–1967)

from *The Alice B. Toklas Cook Book*

Before coming to Paris I was interested in food but not in doing any cooking. When in 1908 I went to live with Gertrude Stein at the rue de Fleurus she said we would have American food for Sunday-evening supper, she had had enough French and Italian cooking; the servant would be out and I should have the kitchen to myself. So I commenced to cook the simple dishes I had eaten in the homes of the San Joaquin Valley in California—fricasseed chicken, corn bread, apple and lemon pie. Then when the pie crust received Gertrude Stein's critical approval I made mincemeat and at Thanksgiving we had a turkey that Hélène the cook roasted but for which I prepared the dressing. Gertrude Stein not being able to decide whether she preferred mushrooms, chestnuts or oysters in the dressing, all three were included. The experiment was successful and frequently repeated; it gradually entered into my repertoire, which expanded as I grew experimental and adventurous.

BASS FOR PICASSO

One day when Picasso was to lunch with us I decorated a fish in a way that I thought would amuse him. I chose a fine striped bass and cooked it according to a theory of my grandmother who had no experience in cooking and who rarely saw her kitchen but who had endless theories about cooking as well as about many other things. She contended that a fish having lived its life in water, once caught, should have no further contact with the element in which it had been born and raised. She recommended that it be roasted or poached in wine or cream or butter. So I made a *court-bouillon* of dry white wine with whole peppers, salt, a laurel leaf,* a sprig of thyme, a blade of mace, an onion with a clove stuck in it, a carrot, a leek and a bouquet of *fines herbes*. This was gently boiled in the fish-kettle for 1/2 hour and then put aside to cool. Then the fish was placed on the rack, the fish-kettle covered and slowly brought to a boil and the fish poached for 20 minutes. Taken from the fire it was left to cool in the *court-bouillon*. It was then carefully drained, dried and placed on the fish platter. A short time before serving it I covered the fish with an ordinary mayonnaise and, using a pastry tube, decorated it with a red mayonnaise, not coloured with catsup—horror of horrors—but with tomato paste. Then I made a design with sieved hard-boiled eggs, the whites and the yolks apart, with truffles and with finely chopped *fines herbes*. I was proud of my chef d'oeuvre when it was served and Picasso exclaimed at its beauty. But, said he, should it not rather have been made in honour of Matisse than of me.

Picasso was for many years on a strict diet; in fact he managed somehow to continue it through the World War and the Occupation and, characteristically, only relaxed after the Liberation. Red meat was proscribed but that presented no difficulties for in those days beef was rarely served by the French except the inevitable roast fillet of beef with *sauce Madère*. Chicken too was not well considered, though a roast leg of mutton was viewed with more favour. Or we would have a tender loin of veal preceded by a spinach *soufflé*, spinach having been highly recommended by Picasso's doctor and a *soufflé*, being the least objectionable way of preparing it. Could it not be made more interesting by adding a sauce. But what sauce would Picasso's diet permit. I would give him a choice. The *soufflé* would be cooked in a well-buttered mould, placed in boiling water and when sufficiently cooked turned into a hollow dish around which in equal divisions would be placed a Hollandaise sauce, a cream sauce and a tomato sauce. It was my hope that the tri-coloured sauces would make the spinach *soufflé* look less nourishing. Cruel enigma said Picasso, when the *soufflé* was served to him.

1954

*Note. The leaf must come from Apollo's Laurel (Laurus Nobills), better known outside France as the bay.

Edna Lewis
(1916–   )

SUNDAY REVIVAL DINNER
from *The Taste of Country Cooking*

Baked Virginia Ham
Southern Fried Chicken
Braised Leg of Mutton
Sweet Potato Casserole
Corn Pudding
Green Beans with Pork
Platter of Sliced Tomatoes with Special Dressing
Spiced Seckel Pears
Cucumber Pickles
Yeast Rolls
Biscuits
Sweet Potato Pie
Summer Apple Pie
Tyler Pie
Caramel Layer Cake
Lemonade
Iced Tea

This menu is typical of what we would serve at our most important social event of the summer season. It was a time when the garden and field vegetables were at their peak, chickens the perfect size for frying, and it was a time for the first cooked hams of the season The linen-covered picnic tables would be filled with an array of meats cooked to a crispy, deep brown, corn puddings, baked tomatoes, pork-flavored green beans, sweet and pungent beets, cakes, pies, and ice cream followed by iced drinks and watermelon slices, all served free to the visiting guests and relatives home on vacation.

Revival Week

Anticipation of Revival Week began with the first spring planting. Revival was like a prize held out during the long, hot summer days when work stretched from the morning's first light until late evening.

556

Our Revival Week always began on the second Sunday in August. Memories of slavery lingered with us still, and Revival was in a way a kind of Thanksgiving. There was real rejoicing: The fruits of our hard labor were now our own, we were free to come and go, and to gather together for this week of reunion and celebration.

At the beginning of August, the first harvest was usually over. The work horses and stock were driven to the large community pasture to graze peaceably for the rest of the summer. Only the milking cows and riding horses remained behind. With the field work finished, my father and the other men in the community were able to spend time getting things in order around the house in preparation for Revival Week. The first chore was to lay in a supply of wood for all the extra cooking that would be taking place. Any needed repairs on the summer kitchen were made, the main room was freshly wallpapered, the fireplace and chimney whitewashed. Whitewash also brightened up the outside trim, the fence posts, and even the trunks of the trees that grew around the house.

Although I didn't think about it at the time, I wonder how my mother made it each year to Revival Sunday, with so much to do and without ever varying from the calm and quiet manner that was her nature. Until the field work, which she loved, was over, she had no time to begin her own important preparations for Revival Week. And so, during the week leading up to second Sunday, as well as doing her regular household chores and caring for her brood of chickens, guinea hens, turkeys, and ducks, and her own vegetable garden, she would cut out and sew new dresses of white muslin for the six of us and our two adopted cousins as well as for herself, usually finishing the last buttonholes and sashes late Saturday night in between the cooking that she would have begun for the next day's noontime dinner at the church.

For my brothers and sisters and me, this was a week full of excitement, with friends and relatives arriving each day from distant cities—Washington, Philadelphia, New York. There were new cousins to play with and we could count on at least one trip into town in the buggy or in the back of the farm wagon to buy staples my mother would be needing, such as vanilla, spices, and sugar. Our own farm and garden yielded all of the flour, butter, lard, meat, vegetables, and fruits that we could use.

My mother never started her cooking until late on the eve of Revival Sunday. By this time she would have everything gathered in and laid out that she would need, and, I guess, a carefully planned schedule laid out in her mind as well. When we were bathed and turned into bed, no pies or cakes had yet been made. But when we came hurrying down on Sunday morning, the long, rectangular dining-room table would be covered with cakes ready to be iced and pie dishes lined with pastry dough to be filled and baked. While we counted them and excitedly discussed our special favorites and how many slices of each we could eat, my mother was out in back feeding her fowl. When she came in she would make us breakfast, standing at the stove with her everyday calm. Then she would help us dress, tie on our ribbons, and send us to sit on the porch until noontime with firm warning to sit quietly so that our new clothes would not get mussed. It would seem a very long morning.

Mother would return to the kitchen to continue her cooking. Because she liked to arrive at the church with the food piping hot, my father would attend the morning service alone and then come back for us as soon as it was over. We would be so excited as we climbed into the surrey. I remember how very special I felt in my new dress which helped me overcome the discomfort of having to wear shoes for the first time since March when school had let out. After we were all squeezed in, my father would load on the carefully packed baskets of food. The savory aroma of fried chicken, so warm and close, always pricked our appetites and long before we reached the church, which was only two miles distant, we would be squirming impatiently, though silently.

The churchyard would be filled with people as we drove up; I felt as though everyone was looking at us. My father would drive straight up to one of the long tables that were stretched out in a line under the huge, shady oak trees alongside the church. My mother would spread out a white linen tablecloth before setting out the baked ham, the half-dozen or more chickens she had fried, a large baking pan of her light, delicate corn pudding, a casserole of sweet potatoes, fresh green beans flavored with crisp bits of pork, and biscuits that had been baked at the last minute and were still warm. The main dishes were surrounded with smaller dishes of pickled watermelon rind, beets and cucumbers and spiced peaches. The dozen or so apple and sweet potato pies she had made were stacked in tiers of three, and the caramel and jelly layer cakes placed next to them. Plates, forks, and white damask napkins and gallon jars of lemonade and iced tea were the last things to be unpacked.

All along the sixty-foot length of tables, neighbors were busy in the same way setting out their own specialties. There were roasts and casseroles, cole slaw and potato salads, lemon meringue, custard, and Tyler pies, chocolate and coconut layer, lemon cream, and pound cakes.

When all the food had been placed on the tables, an unspoken signal would ripple down the line and we would all stand quietly while the minister spoke a grace of thanksgiving. We always liked him, for he knew to keep it short. When the solemn words ended, neighbor would turn to neighbor and warm handshakes, hugs, and affectionate welcomes would be exchanged.

And then at last everyone would come forth and be served, guests and friends first, children last. Second Sunday always seemed to have been a perfect day, with everyone looking their best, eating and chatting. My mother and the other ladies were eager to see that all of the guests were served, and there was always a special plate for a special friend. We usually stood behind our table admiring all the sights. There would be two more days of feasting during the week besides a round of visiting and entertaining in every home in Freetown. The festivities ended for us on Friday, when the visitors stopped by to thank us and say good-bye, promising to return next summer.

Braised Leg of Mutton

When the miller announced he would butcher a sheep on a Saturday, you understood it would be mutton. It was usually available after the sheep had been sheared. Lambs were never butchered; they were sold off or kept for wool. Mutton, the meat of a sheep three years and older, has a stronger, more exotic flavor than "lamb" and is very delicious when properly prepared.

When buying mutton now, you have to be sure it's from a reliable butcher, and there are few that sell it. Lamb is only a trade name today. It is neither lamb nor is it mutton; it is really a sheep of an age between the two.

Serves 8 to 10

1 leg of mutton	6 to 8 peppercorns
1/2 teaspoon thyme	1 bay leaf
2 teaspoons salt	2 small onions
2 tablespoons soft butter	2 to 3 cloves
1 quart cold water	1 small clove garlic

Take the leg of mutton and trim it close. Saw the small end of the leg bone off as close as possible and, starting at the top end of the leg, pull as much of the skin off as possible or cut it away. Crush the thyme and salt together and mix it with the soft butter. Rub this mixture over the leg of mutton. Leave to set for an hour. Have a heavy oval pot available. Add 1 quart of cold water, the peppercorns, bay leaf, the onions stuck with the 2 or 3 cloves, and the garlic. Set the pot over a medium-high burner and bring to a boil. When boiling, put in the leg of mutton. Cover with a tight-fitting cover and set the pot to cook in a 350° preheated oven for 3 hours, basting every 20 minutes. The long slow cooking will bring out the interesting flavor of the mutton while giving it a rich pale-brown color. When cooked, remove the mutton to a platter and strain the cooking liquid into a saucepan. Set over a burner to heat and to cook down a little if necessary. Pass this heated sauce with the mutton when it is served.

Sweet Potato Casserole

Serves 8 to 10

3 pounds sweet potatoes
$^3/_4$ cup granulated sugar
8 tablespoons ($^1/_2$ cup) butter
$^1/_2$ teaspoon grated nutmeg

1 pint rich milk
3 tablespoons crushed cube sugar

1 3-quart casserole

Place the sweet potatoes (yams are not a good substitute because they are too soft) in a pot of boiling water and cook them until they are barely tender, about 40 minutes. Remove the potatoes from the water and leave them to cool. When they are cold, skin and slice them into $^1/_4$-inch pieces and place the slices in layers in a 3-quart casserole. Over each layer sprinkle about 2 tablespoons of granulated sugar and dot it over with 2 tablespoons butter. Continue this process until all the potatoes are used up, stopping only halfway to sprinkle grated nutmeg over the middle layer. Add in just enough milk (approximately a pint) so that it covers everything but the top layer of potatoes. Finally, dot the top layer with butter, add a sprinkling of nutmeg and the crushed cube sugar. Set in an oven preheated to 350° to cook for 45 minutes. The top should be crusty around the edges, a rich brown color, and crunchy when chewed.

Corn Pudding

Corn pudding was one of the great delicacies of summer and the first corn dish of the season. After helping to thin out the corn and weed it, we watched eagerly for the day when Mother served her rich, aromatic, golden-brown corn pudding. It was always served with a sweet potato casserole made from fresh-dug sweet potatoes. The sauce from both dishes mingled together in the plate combining in a flavor that was memorable. The richness of the dishes reflected the season of the year—a time when there was a plentiful supply of milk, butter, and eggs.

Serves 6 to 8

2 cups corn, cut from the cob
$^1/_3$ cup sugar
1 teaspoon salt
2 eggs, beaten

2 cups rich milk
3 tablespoons melted butter
$^1/_2$ teaspoon fresh-grated nutmeg

1 1$^1/_2$-quart casserole

Cut the corn from the cob into a mixing bowl by slicing from the top of the ear downward. Don't go too close to the cob—cut only half of the ker-

560

nel. Scrape the rest off. This gives a better texture to the pudding. Sprinkle in the sugar and salt, stir well, mix the beaten eggs and milk together, and pour the mixture into the corn. Add the melted butter. Mix thoroughly and spoon the mixture into a well-buttered casserole. Sprinkle over with nutmeg. Set the casserole into a pan of hot water and set this into a preheated 350° oven for 35 to 40 minutes or until set. Test by inserting a clean knife into the center of the pudding. If it comes out clean it is done.

Note: An ingenious way we had to retain the freshness of corn was to stand the ears in a tub of water about 2^1/$_2$ inches deep. When the ear is severed from the stalk, its source of moisture is cut off. By standing the corn in a dish of clean water, the cob continues to absorb moisture.

Pork-Flavored Green Beans

Serves 4 to 5

^{1}/$_2$ pound cured smoked pork shoulder or bacon
1 quart cold water

1 quart canned green beans
Salt and pepper

Wash the piece of pork, removing any salt or residue, and make a number of slices in the meat without separating it into pieces. Put the pork into a 2-quart saucepan of cold water. Set on burner and cook slowly for an hour. Then remove the piece of meat, but keep the stock boiling. Open and drain a quart of canned beans, then add to the boiling stock. Cook rather briskly for 25 to 30 minutes. Add salt and black pepper to taste, but be careful because cured meat usually has enough salt to season the pot. The beans are more flavorsome when cooked earlier and reheated for dinner. Serve hot, garnished with thin slices of the boiled pork.

Biscuits

Makes about 1^1/$_2$ dozen

3 cups sifted flour
1 scant teaspoon salt
^{1}/$_2$ teaspoon baking soda
4 teaspoons Royal Baking Powder
^{2}/$_3$ cup lard

1 cup plus 2 tablespoons buttermilk
(If sweet milk is being used, omit the baking soda and the 2 tablespoons of milk; sweet milk is more liquid than sour and therefore these are not needed.)

Take a large bowl, sift into it the measured flour, salt, soda, and baking powder. Add the lard and blend together with a pastry blender or your fingertips

561

until the mixture has the texture of cornmeal. Add the milk all at once by scattering it over the dough. Stir vigorously with a stout wooden spoon. The dough will be very soft in the beginning but will stiffen in 2 or 3 minutes. Continue to stir a few minutes longer. After the dough has stiffened, scrape from sides of bowl into a ball and spoon onto a lightly floured surface for rolling. Dust over lightly with about a tablespoon of flour as the dough will be a bit sticky. Flatten the dough out gently with your hands into a thick, round cake, and knead for a minute by folding the outer edge of the dough into the center of the circle, giving a light knead as you fold the sides in overlapping each other. Turn the folded side face down and dust lightly if needed, being careful not to use too much flour and causing the dough to become too stiff. Dust the rolling pin and the rolling surface well. Roll the dough out evenly to a ½-inch thickness or a bit less. Pierce the surface of the dough with a table fork. (It was said piercing the dough releases the air while baking.) Dust the biscuit cutter in flour first; this will prevent the dough sticking to the cutter and ruining the shape of the biscuit. Dust the cutter as often as needed. An added feature to your light, tender biscuits will be their straight sides. This can be achieved by not wiggling the cutter. Press the cutter into the dough and lift up with a sharp quickness without a wiggle. Cut the biscuits very close together to avoid having big pieces of dough left in between each biscuit. Trying to piece together and rerolling leftover dough will change the texture of the biscuits.

1976

Zarela Martirez

(*contemporary*)

LOS DÍAS DE LOS MUERTOS
from *Food From My Heart*

I think if I could choose one event to dramatize the spirit of Mexican religion, it would be the Day of the Dead, or actually Days—Los Días de los Muertos, November 1 and 2. To begin with, I assure you that this name does not sound in the least ghoulish or morbid to a Mexican. The Day of the Dead is perhaps our happiest, most life-affirming holiday. It is the celebration of memory, the time when we really feel we are speaking to and embracing those whom we have lost.

For me the Day of the Dead has been an important moment of the year since before I can remember. But even so, I don't think I took in the full dimension of meaning until I was a nineteen-year-old college student traveling—in an unchaperoned group of young people for the first time in my life!—to visit the ceremony on an island in Lake Pátzcuaro, in the state of Michoacán. It was a time in the late sixties when educated Mexicans from all over were suddenly "discovering" the richness of Mexican culture and descending in droves on previously untouched spots. So were many European tourists. So I have to say that the Day of the Dead celebration on the island of Janitzio, probably the most famous in all Mexico, already had a strong note of commercialism. But for me it was an astonishing and very moving pageant dedicated to the continuity of life.

We set out at dusk by motorboat, singing "María Isabel" to the strains of two guitars and one set of bongos and full of the famous local *pescado blanco* (white fish) caught in graceful "butterfly nets." The lake was soon a vast, chilly sea of darkness lit only by a few guide lanterns on canoes making the same journey. But even from far off we saw a yellow-white glow coming from the cemetery. We disembarked into a crowd of visitors and vendors that I couldn't match with anything in our sedate, private family celebration of the day. What a maelstrom! People were selling toys in the shape of laughing skulls; candies made like skeletons; chicle gums (cousins to our chewing gum) in all colors; black, yellow, or white candles; candleholders of shiny black pottery; *copal* (incense) burners. Streams of cheerful family parties pushed past us in the dark and confusion as if en route to a midnight picnic—which isn't too far off the mark.

Janitzio is a rocky island, and the hilly cemetery might have been hard to navigate had it not been so full of lights. It was a carnival lit by thousands of candles. Hundreds of brilliant orange-yellow shapes—high arches or criss-crossed squares—glowed in the darkness above every gravesite. They were *cempasúchil,* yellow marigold strung on ropes or strings, sometimes spelling out names. I had never seen or dreamed of such a fantasy of *cempasúchil.* Huddled in shawls and *rebozos* against the chilly evening, the people settled down to sing and drink and chat on the ground by the graves, half-shadowed revelers watched from the darker shadows by crowds of German or Dutch tourists. They were Tarascan Indians, and for them the strings of flowers were arches framing a passage for the souls of their friends or relatives to return to their earthly resting place on a kind of social visit. This is the whole purpose of the celebration.

Yes, these people were having a nice reunion with their loved ones! They had brought food for the visit, including the favorite dishes of the deceased, and placed them—always in new pottery vessels bought for the occasion—before small altars erected at each grave with a picture of the loved one. They had also taken along any comforts the person might be missing in the next life, such as bottles of liquor and packs of cigarettes, toys and games, and new clothes. I was astonished at the practical range of *ofrendas* (offerings) laid on freshly ironed white embroidered tea towels. Of course we had always visited the family graves on the Day of the Dead, but our celebration had been limited to scrubbing the tombstones and decorating them with zinnias or other autumn flowers and sharing a silent moment of communion.

The full-blown Day of the Dead ceremony, which I was seeing that evening for the first time, is most common in Mexico among the Indian peoples and the more rural *mestizos.* Four hundred years ago it probably would not have seemed strange in most places. At that time many peoples in Mexico celebrated a festival in August and September to ask the intervention of departed ones in warding off early frost. The idea that individual personalities continue after death and can intercede for the living with the great powers fitted well enough with the Spanish Catholic faith to survive the Conquest without much change. The holiday conveniently migrated through the calendar to coincide with the Catholic feasts of All Saints and All Souls Day at the beginning of November. But only the date changed. Nothing disturbed the original basis of the celebration, the belief that dead souls spend a brief period each year on earth on a kind of holiday. It's an opportunity to catch up with those who are dear to you.

The Janitzio celebration begins after dark on November 1 and continues as a graveside vigil until dawn. In other villages there are usually two celebrations. November 1, All Saints, is when the souls of the children arrive home in the villages and are met by welcoming committees of the local mayor and dignitaries along with the town band. The procession leads the children through an arch of *cempasúchil* at the gate of the cemetery and helps them find their graves. Each grave is decorated with images or structures of *cempasúchil* and turned into party sites with candies, toys, new clothing, and white candles, always in new pottery candleholders. On the next day, All Souls, the souls of the adults are welcomed in the same way (except that the candles are black or yellow). Those without surviving relatives are not forgotten—their graves are decorated by townspeople. In some communities the altar with the *ofrendas* is set up at home instead of in the cemetery.

Beyond the favorite foods of the deceased, certain things are traditional for the Days of the Dead that date back to pre-Columbian times, including a sweet pumpkin dessert called *calabaza en tacha* and some forms of *tamal.* In Janitzio people had brought a special kind of *tamal* with duck filling, from the Lake Pátzcuaro wild ducks that are supposed to be harpooned (not shot) for this occasion. But the most famous specialty of the day throughout Mexico is of European origin. In one of those typical Indian-Spanish intermarriages that have shaped our culture, the native peoples came to celebrate the Days of the Dead with a rich, sweet yeast bread on the model of the altar breads that are special feast-day offerings everywhere in Europe from Spain to Sweden. The Mexican imagination put a new spin of fantasy on the idea by shaping the loaves into different images. The famous *pan de muerto* ("bread of death") comes in the shape of human figures, alligators, lizards, and other animals—but most often skulls and cross-bones or teardrops and crosses, gaily decorated with colored sugar crystals.

The following recipe is a typical modern version of the *pan de muerto.* Like the European altar breads, it was originally made with flour, yeast, eggs, sugar, and some aromatic flavoring like orange-blossom water. Today Mexican home bakers often enrich and sweeten the bread with condensed milk.

Pan del Día de Muertos
Bread for the Day of the Dead

2 envelopes dry yeast
$^1/_2$ cup lukewarm water
$3^1/_2$ to 4 cups unbleached all-purpose
flour, or as needed
$^1/_2$ teaspoon salt
9 tablespoons (1 stick plus 1 tablespoon; 5
ounces) unsalted butter, at room
temperature and cut into small
pieces, plus extra for greasing
3 large eggs (2 for the dough, 1 for
glazing the loaves)

3 large egg yolks
$^1/_2$ of 1 can (14 ounces) condensed milk
(about $^7/_8$ cup)
1 tablespoon orange flower water
(available in gourmet stores and
Italian and Middle Eastern
markets)
Sugar or colored sugar crystals for
sprinkling

In a small bowl, dissolve the yeast in the water and let sit in a warm place 5 minutes. Make a sponge by stirring in 4 to 5 tablespoons of the flour. Cover with a damp towel and let sit in a warm place until full of bubbles and about doubled in bulk, roughly 45 minutes.

Combine a scant $3^1/_2$ cups flour with the salt in a large bowl or on a pastry board or clean counter. Cut or rub in the butter with a pastry blender or your fingers until the dough resembles the texture of coarse cornmeal.

Beat together 2 of the whole eggs and the 3 egg yolks. Have ready the condensed milk and orange flower water. Gradually add these ingredients to the dough, working them in with your fingertips. Add the yeast sponge and work it in, adding flour as necessary to make a soft but kneadable dough. Knead on a lightly floured work surface until smooth and silky, about 10 minutes. (Alternatively, use the dough hook of an electric mixer.) Lightly grease a large bowl with butter and place the dough in it, turning to coat both sides with butter. Let sit in a warm place, covered with a damp cloth or plastic wrap, until doubled in bulk, $1^1/_2$ to 2 hours.

Punch the dough down. If not making decorated loaves, shape into 3 equal-sized round loaves. Or, to make 2 decorated loaves, proceed as follows: Cut off about one fourth of the dough and set aside. Divide the rest into 2 equal portions, shaping each into a ball. Place side by side on a greased and floured baking sheet, remembering that the loaves will expand in baking. With the remaining dough, shape skulls and crossbones: First divide the dough into 4 parts; roll 2 pieces between your palms into long, narrow strips for crossbones and cut each in half. Crisscross 2 strips over each loaf. Shape the remaining 2 pieces into 2 small balls for skulls. Lightly press them onto the loaves just above the crossbones (if you have difficulty getting them to stick, make gashes in the loaves with a small, sharp knife and press the balls into the gashes). Lightly cover with damp towels and let rise in a warm place until doubled in bulk, about 1 hour.

Meanwhile, preheat the oven to 375°F.

Beat the remaining egg and brush lightly over the loaves and decorations and bake 40 minutes. When done, the loaves will be golden brown and sound hollow when tapped. Sprinkle the loaves with sugar and return to the oven for about 1 minute to melt it.

YIELD: 3 PLAIN ROUND LOAVES (ABOUT 6 INCHES ACROSS) OR 2 DECO-RATED LOAVES (ABOUT 7 INCHES ACROSS)

1992

T W O

Erotica

Eighteenth- and nineteenth-century fiction often recounts the story of the Fallen Woman who is seduced and then punished for her deed (often cast as a "sin" or a "crime"), typically by abandonment, pregnancy, and death in childbirth. In "The Storm," Kate Chopin (1850–1904) plays with and even parodies this convention. She stubbornly refuses to buy into a sexual double standard, and, instead of a woman being punished for her sexuality, in this story, everyone is better off after an episode of adultery, including the spouses and families of the two people who engage in a burst of extramarital passion as a storm rages outside.

The storm, a classic symbol of passion, is seen again in the poem from *Autumn Sequence* by Jan Freeman (b. 1957): "the bedspread offers buds to play with middle fingers, / the language pours a storm against the stripped branches / lifting the sheet from the floor." Here, Freeman explores the letting and letting-go of passion with the woman she loves. This is also the theme of "Lifting Belly" by Gertrude Stein (1874–1946):

> *Lifting belly is so strong and willing.*
> *Lifting belly is so strong and yet waiting.*
> *Lifting belly is so soothing. Yes indeed.*

The other poets and prose writers whose works are presented in this section—Emily Dickinson (1830–1886), H. D. (1886–1961), Anaïs Nin (1903–1977), Georgia Douglas Johnson (1880–1966), Rita Mae Brown (b. 1944), and Olga Broumas and Jane Miller (b. 1949)—all mimic in words the "yes indeed" of physical love and passion. To quote again from Dickinson's poem (putatively about a bee):

> *Reaching late his flower,*
> *Round her chamber hums—*
> *Counts his nectars—*
> *Enters—and is lost in Balms.*

Emily Dickinson
(1830–1886)

WILD NIGHTS—WILD NIGHTS!

Wild Nights—Wild Nights!
Were I with thee
Wild Nights should be
Our luxury!

Futile—the Winds—
To a Heart in port—
Done with the Compass—
Done with the Chart!

Rowing in Eden—
Ah, the Sea!
Might I but moor—Tonight—
In Thee!

c. 1861   *1891*

❖

COME SLOWLY,—EDEN!

Come slowly—Eden!
Lips unused to Thee—
Bashful—sip thy Jessamines—
As the fainting Bee—

Reaching late his flower,
Round her chamber hums—
Counts his nectars—
Enters—and is lost in Balms.

c. 1860   *1890*

❖

VOLCANOES BE IN SICILY

Volcanoes be in Sicily
And South America
I judge from my Geography—
Volcanos nearer here
A Lava step at any time
Am I inclined to climb—
A Crater I may contemplate
Vesuvius at Home.

1914

❖

Kate Chopin
(1850–1904)

THE STORM
A Sequel to "The 'Cadian Ball"

I

The leaves were so still that even Bibi thought it was going to rain. Bobinôt, who was accustomed to converse on terms of perfect equality with his little son, called the child's attention to certain sombre clouds that were rolling with sinister intention from the west, accompanied by a sullen, threatening roar. They were at Friedheimer's store and decided to remain there till the storm had passed. They sat within the door on two empty kegs. Bibi was four years old and looked very wise.

"Mama'll be 'fraid, yes," he suggested with blinking eyes.

"She'll shut the house. Maybe she got Sylvie helpin' her this evenin'," Bobinôt responded reassuringly.

"No; she ent got Sylvie. Sylvie was helpin' her yistiday," piped Bibi.

Bobinôt arose and going across to the counter purchased a can of shrimps, of which Calixta was very fond. Then he returned to his perch on the keg and sat stolidly holding the can of shrimps while the storm burst. It shook the wooden store and seemed to be ripping great furrows in the distant field. Bibi laid his little hand on his father's knee and was not afraid.

II

Calixta, at home, felt no uneasiness for their safety. She sat at a side window sewing furiously on a sewing machine. She was greatly occupied and did not notice the approaching storm. But she felt very warm and often stopped to mop her face on which the perspiration gathered in beads. She unfastened her white sacque at the throat. It began to grow dark, and suddenly realizing the situation she got up hurriedly and went about closing windows and doors.

Out on the small front gallery she had hung Bobinôt's Sunday clothes to air and she hastened out to gather them before the rain fell. As she stepped outside, Alcée Laballière rode in at the gate. She had not seen him very often since her marriage, and never alone. She stood there with Bobinôt's coat in her hands, and the big rain drops began to fall. Alcée rode his horse under the shelter of a side projection where the chickens had huddled and there were plows and a harrow piled up in the corner.

"May I come and wait on your gallery till the storm is over, Calixta?" he asked.

"Come 'long in, M'sieur Alcée."

His voice and her own startled her as if from a trance, and she seized Bobinôt's vest. Alcée, mounting to the porch, grabbed the trousers and snatched Bibi's braided jacket that was about to be carried away by a sudden gust of wind. He expressed an intention to remain outside, but it was soon apparent that he might as well have been out in the open: the water beat in upon the boards in driving sheets, and he went inside, closing the door after him. It was even necessary to put something beneath the door to keep the water out.

"My! what a rain! It's good two years sence it rain' like that," exclaimed Calixta as she rolled up a piece of bagging and Alcée helped her to thrust it beneath the crack.

She was a little fuller of figure than five years before when she married; but she had lost nothing of her vivacity. Her blue eyes still retained their melting quality; and her yellow hair, dishevelled by the wind and rain, kinked more stubbornly than ever about her ears and temples.

The rain beat upon the low, shingled roof with a force and clatter that threatened to break an entrance and deluge them there. They were in the dining room—the sitting room—the general utility room. Adjoining was her bed room, with Bibi's couch along side her own. The door stood open, and the room with its white, monumental bed, its closed shutters, looked dim and mysterious.

Alcée flung himself into a rocker and Calixta nervously began to gather up from the floor the lengths of a cotton sheet which she had been sewing.

"If this keeps up, *Dieu sait* if the levees goin' to stan' it!" she exclaimed.

"What have you got to do with the levees?"

"I got enough to do! An' there's Bobinôt with Bibi out in that storm—if he only didn' left Friedheimer's!"

"Let us hope, Calixta, that Bobinôt's got sense enough to come in out of a cyclone."

She went and stood at the window with a greatly disturbed look on her face. She wiped the frame that was clouded with moisture. It was stiflingly hot. Alcée got up and joined her at the window, looking over her shoulder. The rain was coming down in sheets obscuring the view of far-off cabins and enveloping the distant wood in a gray mist. The playing of the lightning was incessant. A bolt struck a tall chinaberry tree at the edge of the field. It filled all visible space with a blinding glare and the crash seemed to invade the very boards they stood upon.

Calixta put her hands to her eyes, and with a cry, staggered backward. Alcée's arm encircled her, and for an instant he drew her close and spasmodically to him.

"*Bonté!*" she cried, releasing herself from his encircling arm and retreating from the window, "the house'll go next! If I only knew w'ere Bibi was!" She would not compose herself; she would not be seated. Alcée clasped her shoulders and looked into her face. The contact of her warm, palpitating body when he had unthinkingly drawn her into his arms, had aroused all the old-time infatuation and desire for her flesh.

"Calixta," he said, "don't be frightened. Nothing can happen. The house is too low to be struck, with so many tall trees standing about. There! aren't you going to be quiet? say, aren't you?" He pushed her hair back from her face that was warm and steaming. Her lips were as red and moist as pomegranate seed. Her white neck and a glimpse of her full, firm bosom disturbed him powerfully. As she glanced up at him the fear in her liquid blue eyes had given place to a drowsy gleam that unconsciously betrayed a sensuous desire. He looked down into her eyes and there was nothing for him to do but to gather her lips in a kiss. It reminded him of Assumption.

"Do you remember—in Assumption, Calixta?" he asked in a low voice broken by passion. Oh! she remembered; for in Assumption he had kissed her and kissed and kissed her; until his senses would well nigh fail, and to save her he would resort to a desperate flight. If she was not an immaculate dove in those days, she was still inviolate; a passionate creature whose very defenselessness had made her defense, against which his honor forbade him to prevail. Now—well, now—her lips seemed in a manner free to be tasted, as well as her round, white throat and her whiter breasts.

They did not heed the crashing torrents, and the roar of the elements made her laugh as she lay in his arms. She was a revelation in that dim, mysterious chamber; as white as the couch she lay upon. Her firm, elastic flesh that was knowing for the first time its birthright, was like a creamy lily that the sun invites to contribute its breath and perfume to the undying life of the world.

The generous abundance of her passion, without guile or trickery, was like a white flame which penetrated and found response in depths of his own sensuous nature that had never yet been reached.

When he touched her breasts they gave themselves up in quivering ecstasy, inviting his lips. Her mouth was a fountain of delight. And when he possessed her, they seemed to swoon together at the very borderland of life's mystery.

He stayed cushioned upon her, breathless, dazed, enervated, with his heart beating like a hammer upon her. With one hand she clasped his head, her lips lightly touching his forehead. The other hand stroked with a soothing rhythm his muscular shoulders.

The growl of the thunder was distant and passing away. The rain beat softly upon the shingles, inviting them to drowsiness and sleep. But they dared not yield.

The rain was over; and the sun was turning the glistening green world into a palace of gems. Calixta, on the gallery, watched Alcée ride away. He turned and smiled at her with a beaming face; and she lifted her pretty chin in the air and laughed aloud.

III

Bobinôt and Bibi, trudging home, stopped without at the cistern to make themselves presentable.

"My! Bibi, w'at will yo' mama say! You ought to be ashame'. You oughtn' put on those good pants. Look at 'em! An' that mud on yo' collar! How you got that mud on yo' collar, Bibi? I never saw such a boy!" Bibi was the picture of pathetic resignation. Bobinôt was the embodiment of serious solicitude as he strove to remove from his own person and his son's the signs of their tramp over heavy roads and through wet fields. He scraped the mud off Bibi's bare legs and feet with a stick and carefully removed all traces from his heavy brogans. Then, prepared for the worst—the meeting with an over-scrupulous housewife, they entered cautiously at the back door.

Calixta was preparing supper. She had set the table and was dripping coffee at the hearth. She sprang up as they came in.

"Oh, Bobinôt! You back! My! but I was uneasy. W'ere you been during the rain? An' Bibi? he ain't wet? he ain't hurt?" She had clasped Bibi and was kissing him effusively. Bobinôt's explanations and apologies which he had been composing all along the way, died on his lips as Calixta felt him to see

573

if he were dry, and seemed to express nothing but satisfaction at their safe return.

"I brought you some shrimps, Calixta," offered Bobinôt, hauling the can from his ample side pocket and laying it on the table.

"Shrimps! Oh, Bobinôt! you too good fo' anything!" and she gave him a smacking kiss on the cheek that resounded. "*J'vous réponds*, we'll have a feas' to-night! umph-umph!"

Bobinôt and Bibi began to relax and enjoy themselves, and when the three seated themselves at table they laughed much and so loud that anyone might have heard them as far away as Laballière's.

IV

Alcée Laballière wrote to his wife, Clarisse, that night. It was a loving letter, full of tender solicitude. He told her not to hurry back, but if she and the babies liked it at Biloxi, to stay a month longer. He was getting on nicely; and though he missed them, he was willing to bear the separation a while longer—realizing that their health and pleasure were the first things to be considered.

V

As for Clarisse, she was charmed upon receiving her husband's letter. She and the babies were doing well. The society was agreeable; many of her old friends and acquaintances were at the bay. And the first free breath since her marriage seemed to restore the pleasant liberty of her maiden days. Devoted as she was to her husband, their intimate conjugal life was something which she was more than willing to forego for a while.

So the storm passed and every one was happy.

1898

❖

Gertrude Stein
(1874–1946)

from LIFTING BELLY

Part II

Lifting belly. Are you. Lifting.
Oh dear I said I was tender, fierce and tender.
Do it. What a splendid example of carelessness.
It gives me a great deal of pleasure to say yes.
Why do I always smile.
I don't know.
It pleases me.
You are easily pleased.
I am very pleased.
Thank you I am scarcely sunny.
I wish the sun would come out.
Yes.
Do you lift it.
High.
Yes sir I helped to do it.
Did you.
Yes.
Do you lift it.
We cut strangely.
What.
That's it.
Address it say to it that we will never repent.
A great many people come together.
Come together.
I don't think this has anything to do with it.
What I believe in is what I mean.
Lifting belly and roses.
We get a great many roses.
I always smile.
Yes.
And I am happy.
With what.
With what I said.

This evening.
Not pretty.
Beautiful.
Yes beautiful.
Why don't you prettily bow.
Because it shows thought.
It does.
Lifting belly is so strong. . . .

Lifting belly is so kind.
To me there are many exceptional cases.
What did you say. I said I had not been disturbed. Neither had we. Lifting
    belly is so necessary.
Lifting belly is so kind.
I can't say it too often.
Pleasing me.
Lifting belly.
Extraordinary.
Lifting belly is such exercise.
You mean altogether.
Lifting belly is so kind to me.
Lifting belly is so kind to many.
Don't say that please.
If you please.
Lifting belly is right.
And we were right.
Now I say again. I say now again.
What is a whistle.
Miracle you don't know about the miracle.
You mean a meteor.
No I don't I mean everything away.
Away where.
Away here.
Oh yes.
Lifting belly is so strong.
You said that before.
Lifting belly is so strong and willing.
Lifting belly is so strong and yet waiting.
Lifting belly is so soothing. Yes indeed.
It gives me greater pleasure. . . .

1915–1916

Georgia Douglas Johnson
(1880–1966)

I WANT TO DIE WHILE YOU LOVE ME

I want to die while you love me
While yet you hold me fair,
While laughter lies upon my lips
And lights are in my hair.

I want to die while you love me
And bear to that still bed
Your kisses—turbulent, unspent,
To warm me when I'm dead.

I want to die while you love me
Oh, who would care to live,
'Til love has nothing more to ask
And nothing more to give.

1928

❖

H. D.
(1886–1961)

SEA ROSE

Rose, harsh rose,
marred and with stint of petals,
meagre flower, thin,
sparse of leaf,

more precious
than a wet rose
single on a stem—
you are caught in the drift.

577

Stunted, with small leaf,
you are flung on the sand,
you are lifted
in the crisp sand
that drives in the wind.

Can the spice-rose
drip such acrid fragrance
hardened in a leaf?

1916

❖

Anaïs Nin
(1903–1977)

MANDRA, II
from *Little Birds*

I am invited one night to the apartment of a young society couple, the H's.
It is like being on a boat because it is near the East River and the barges pass
while we talk, the river is alive. Miriam is a delight to look at, a Brunhilde,
full-breasted, with sparkling hair, a voice that lures you to her. Her husband,
Paul, is small and of the race of the imps, not a man but a faun—a lyrical
animal, quick and humorous. He thinks I am beautiful. He treats me like
an objet d'art. The black butler opens the door. Paul exclaims over me, my
Goyaesque hood, the red flower in my hair, and hurries me into the salon
to display me. Miriam is sitting cross-legged on a purple satin divan. She
is a natural beauty, whereas I, an artificial one, need a setting and warmth
to bloom successfully.

Their apartment is full of furnishings I find individually ugly—silver can-
delabra, tables with nooks for trailing flowers, enormous mulberry satin poufs,
rococo objects, things full of chic, collected with snobbish playfulness, as if to
say "We can make fun of everything created by fashion, we are above it all."

Everything is touched with aristocratic impudence, through which I can
sense the H's fabulous life in Rome, Florence; Miriam's frequent appearances
in *Vogue* wearing Chanel dresses; the pompousness of their families; their
efforts to be elegantly bohemian; and their obsession with the word that is
the key to society—everything must be "amusing."

Miriam calls me into her bedroom to show me a new bathing suit she has bought in Paris. For this, she undresses herself completely, and then takes the long piece of material and begins rolling it around herself like the primitive draping of the Balinese.

Her beauty goes to my head. She undrapes herself, walks naked around the room, and then says, "I wish I looked like you. You are so exquisite and dainty. I am so big."

"But that's just why I like you, Miriam."

"Oh, your perfume, Mandra."

She pushes her face into my shoulder under my hair and smells my skin.

I place my hand on her shoulder.

"You're the most beautiful woman I've ever seen, Miriam."

Paul is calling out to us, "When are you going to finish talking about clothes in there? I'm bored!"

Miriam replies, "We're coming." And she dresses quickly in slacks. When she comes out Paul says, "And now you're dressed to stay at home, and I want to take you to hear the String Man. He sings the most marvelous songs about a string and finally hangs himself on it."

Miriam says, "Oh, all right. I'll get dressed." And she goes into the bathroom.

I stay behind with Paul, but soon Miriam calls me. "Mandra, come in here and talk to me."

I think, by this time she will be half-dressed, but no, she is standing naked in the bathroom, powdering and fixing her face.

She is as opulent as a burlesque queen. As she stands on her toes to lean towards the mirror and paint her eyelashes more carefully, I am again affected by her body. I come up behind her and watch her.

I feel a little timid. She isn't as inviting as Mary. She is, in fact, sexless, like the women at the beach or at the Turkish bath, who think nothing of their nakedness. I try a light kiss on her shoulder. She smiles at me and says, "I wish Paul were not so irritable. I would have liked to try the bathing suit on you. I would love to see you wearing it." She returns my kiss, on the mouth, taking care not to disturb her lipstick outline. I do not know what to do next. I want to take hold of her. I stay near her.

Then Paul comes into the bathroom without knocking and says, "Miriam, how can you walk around like this? You mustn't mind, Mandra. It is a habit with her. She is possessed with the need to go around without clothes. Get dressed, Miriam."

Miriam goes into her room and slips on a dress, with nothing underneath, then a fox cape, and says, "I'm ready."

In the car she places her hand over mine. Then she draws my hand under

579

the fur, into a pocket of the dress, and I find myself touching her sex. We drive on in the dark.

Miriam says she wants to drive through the park first. She wants air. Paul wants to go directly to the nightclub, but he gives in and we drive through the park, I with my hand on Miriam's sex, fondling it and feeling my own excitement gaining so that I can hardly talk.

Miriam talks, wittily, continuously. I think to myself, "You won't be able to go on talking in a little while." But she does, all the time that I am caressing her in the dark, beneath the satin and the fur. I can feel her moving upwards to my touch, opening her legs a little so I can fit my entire hand between her legs. Then she grows tense under my fingers, stretching herself, and I know she is taking her pleasure. It is contagious. I feel my own orgasm without even being touched.

I am so wet that I am afraid it will show through my dress. And it must show through Miriam's dress, too. We both keep our coats on as we go into the nightclub.

Miriam's eyes are brilliant, deep. Paul leaves us for a while and we go into the ladies' room. This time Miriam kisses my mouth fully, boldly. We arrange ourselves and return to the table.

1979

❖

Rita Mae Brown
(1944–   )

SAPPHO'S REPLY

My voice rings down through thousands of years
To coil around your body and give you strength,
You who have wept in direct sunlight,
Who have hungered in invisible chains,
Tremble to the cadence of my legacy:
An army of lovers shall not fail.

1971

❖

Olga Broumas and Jane Miller
(1949–   )

SHE DIDN'T THINK
WE WERE MARRIED

She didn't think we were married in any traditional sense so didn't hesitate to apply first to one and then the other the awkward silences which her colorful beauty could be felt to fill, as in panavision, setting a slower mood for the spectator perhaps but quickening her pulse. *Don't leave,* she didn't whisper, nor *stay with me,* but rather shifted her hair as one shifts an entire pose left to right close-up, taking a minute, triggering the free association where every promise lost or denied finds its place. Blue skies, tawny beach, sea-green and berry stain. By year's end she would bring us one of her first architecture assignments, in the manner of the Japanese masters, the arrangement of dots in disorder. Impressionable and expressive, she lined the corridors with butcher paper, unable to avoid herself and, hence, design—wool-bodies, lace, the infinite destinies of flakes, ceramic porosity, wormwood. She would hide sea, sand and boat by hanging the sheet upside down. Told to watch water boil, stray rain, to unrehearse them, she did it many times and in her mind, until by ear first fathomed disarray.

1985

❖

Jan Freeman
(1957–   )

FIFTEEN
from *Autumn Sequence*

Next to the white window
half in the white light,
what can I say now, love love, cherish me?
Twin our mouths,
a perfect semblance?
Who touches stained glass holds one blue forearm,
one red elbow, yellow shoulder;

stay away, that vicious capacity shows itself
between the comic gestures; no perfume, no washing:
each morning two foam pillows mimic the texture,
the bedspread offers buds to play with middle fingers,
the language pours a storm against the stripped branches
lifting the sheet from the floor,
setting an imagined picture against the lamp base.
I stretch myself over each blue mountain.
A rainbow, one section, hung from a string that day.
One cotton bag hung from the low promising cloud
sways while I count each equation:
your smile where the scarring snips the wound free,
more open than any moon, any dark ring, crescent, visible, invisible,
oh love:
let me.

1993

ACKNOWLEDGMENTS

The editors and publisher gratefully acknowledge permission to reprint the following material:

Adams, Abigail: A letter from *The Book of Abigail and John: Selected Letters of the Adams Family, 1762–1784*, edited by L. H. Butterfield. Published by The Belknap Press of Harvard University Press. Copyright © 1975 by the Massachusetts Historical Society. Reprinted by permission of the publisher.

Allen, Paula Gunn: "Kopis'taya (A Gathering of Spirits)" from *The Sacred Hoop* by Paula Gunn Allen. Copyright © 1986, 1992 by Paul Gunn Allen. Reprinted by permission of Beacon Press.

Anderson, Laurie: From *United States* by Laurie Anderson. Copyright © 1984 by Laurie Anderson. Reprinted by permission of HarperCollins Publishers, Inc.

Angelou, Maya: "Woman Me" from *Oh Pray My Wings Are Gonna Fit Me Well* by Maya Angelou. Copyright © 1975 by Maya Angelou. Published by Random House, Inc. in 1975 and by Virago Press in 1988. Reprinted by permission of the publishers.

Awiakta, Marilou: "Amazons in Appalachia" from *Selu: Seeking the Corn Mother's Wisdom* by Marilou Awiakta. Published by Fulcrum Publishing, 350 Indiana St., #350, Golden, CO 80401 (1–800–992–9208) in 1993. Reprinted by permission of the publisher.

Barney, Natalie: From a letter by Natalie Barney to Liane de Pougy from *Portrait of a Seductress: The World of Natalie Barney* by Jean Chalon, translated by Carol Barko. Reprinted by permission of Librarie Ernest Flammarion.

Broner, E. M. "The Ceremonies of Community" from *The Telling* by E. M. Broner. Copyright © 1993 by E. M. Broner. Reprinted by permission of HarperCollins Publishers, Inc.

583

Brooks, Gwendolyn: "Religion" from *Children Coming Home* by Gwendolyn Brooks. Copyright © 1991 by Gwendolyn Brooks. Published by The David Company, Chicago. Reprinted by permission of the author.

Broumas, Olga and Jane Miller: Untitled poem from *Black Holes, Black Stockings* by Olga Broumas and Jane Miller. Copyright © 1985 by Olga Broumas and Jane Miller. Published by Wesleyan University Press. Used by permission of the University Press of New England.

Brown, Rita Mae: "Sappho's Reply" from *Poems* by Rita Mae Brown. Copyright © 1971, 1973 by Rita Mae Brown. Published by The Crossing Press, Freedom, CA. Reprinted by permission of the publisher.

Cather, Willa: "Old Mrs. Harris" from *Obscure Destinies* by Willa Cather. Copyright 1930, 1932 by Willa Cather and renewed 1958, 1960 by the Executors of the Estate of Willa Cather. Reprinted by permission of Alfred A. Knopf, Inc.

Chesnut, Mary Boykin: Diary entry dated Aug. 26, 1861 from *Mary Chesnut's Civil War* edited by C. Vann Woodward. Copyright © 1981 by Yale University Press. Published by Yale University Press. Reprinted by permission of the publisher.

Childress, Alice: "Men in Your Life" from *Like One of the Family* by Alice Childress. Copyright © 1956. Renewed 1984 by Alice Childress. Used by permission of Flora Roberts, Inc.

Chopin, Kate: "The Storm" from *The Complete Works of Kate Chopin*, edited by Per Seyersted. Reprinted by permission of Louisiana State University Press.

Cliff, Michelle: "A History of Costume" from *The Land of Look Behind* by Michelle Cliff. Published by Firebrand Books, Ithaca, NY. Copyright © 1980 by Michelle Cliff. Reprinted by permission of the publisher.

Clifton, Lucille: "the thirty eighth year" from *Good Woman: Poems and a Memoir 1969–1980* by Lucille Clifton. Copyright © 1987 by Lucille Clifton. Reprinted with the permission of BOA Editions, Ltd., 92 Park Ave., Brockport, NY 14420.

Cofer, Judith Ortiz: "What the Gypsy Said to Her Children" by Judith Ortiz Cofer from *Woman of Her Word: Hispanic Women Write* edited by Evangelina Vigil Pinon. Reprinted with permission of the publisher Arte Publico Press.

584

Cooper, Anna Julia. From *A Voice from the South* by Anna Julia Cooper, with an Introduction by Mary Helen Washington. The Schomburg Library of Nineteenth-Century Black Women Writers. Copyright © 1988 by Oxford University Press, Inc. Reprinted by permission.

Dickinson, Emily: Poems #341 and #754 from *The Complete Poems of Emily Dickinson* edited by Thomas H. Johnson published by Little Brown & Co. Copyright 1929, 1935 by Martha Dickinson Bianchi. Copyright renewed 1957, 1963 by Mary L. Hampson. From *The Poems of Emily Dickinson,* edited by Thomas H. Johnson published by The Belknap Press of Harvard University Press. Copyright 1951, © 1955, 1979, 1983 by the President and Fellows of Harvard College. Reprinted by permission of the publishers and the Trustees of Amherst College.

Dove, Rita: "Daystar" from *Thomas and Beulah* by Rita Dove. Published by Carnegie-Mellon University Press. Copyright © 1986 by Rita Dove. Reprinted by permission of the author.

Forché, Carolyn: "As Children Together" from *The Country Between Us* by Carolyn Forché. Copyright © 1981 by Carolyn Forché. Reprinted by permission of HarperCollins Publishers, Inc. and Jonathan Cape Ltd.

Freeman, Jan: "Fifteen" from "Autumn Sequence" from *Hyena* by Jan Freeman. Published by Cleveland State University Poetry Center in 1993. Reprinted by permission of the author.

Gellhorn, Martha: "Last Words on Vietnam, 1987" from *The Face of War* by Martha Gellhorn. Copyright © 1988 by Martha Gellhorn. Reprinted by permission of Grove/Atlantic, Inc. and Aitken, Stone & Wylie Limited.

Gerstenberg, Alice: *Overtones* by Alice Gerstenberg is published in a single acting edition by Baker's Plays, 100 Chauncy Street, Boston, MA 02111.

Glaspell, Susan: *Trifles: A Play In One Act* by Susan Glaspell. Copyright 1951 by Walter H. Baker Company. Reprinted by special arrangement with Baker's Plays, 100 Chauncy Street, Boston, MA 02111.

Goldman, Emma: From a letter from Emma Goldman to Ben Reitman dated Sept. 27, 1908 located in the Ben L. Reitman Papers, Special Collections, the University Library, The University of Illinois at Chicago. Reprinted by permission of Ian Ballantine, Executor of the Estate of Emma Goldman.

Gordon, Mary: "More Than Just a Shrine" by Mary Gordon from *The New York Times Magazine* November 3, 1985. Copyright © 1985 by The New York Times Company. Reprinted by permission.

H. D.: "Sea Rose" from *Collected Poems 1912–1944* by H. D. Copyright © 1982 by The Estate of Hilda Doolittle. Reprinted by permission of New Directions Publishing Corp.

Harjo, Joy: "Remember" from *She Had Some Horses* by Joy Harjo. Copyright © 1983 by Joy Harjo. Used by permission of the publisher, Thunder's Mouth Press.

Harper, Frances E. W.: From a letter by Frances E. W. Harper to John Brown from *A Brighter Coming Day* edited by Frances Smith Foster. Published by The Feminist Press in 1990.

Hurston, Zora Neale: "Sweat" by Zora Neale Hurston. First published in *Fire!* in 1926. Reprinted by permission of the Estate of Zora Neale Hurston.

Jacobs, Harriet: From *Incidents in the Life of a Slave Girl* by Harriet Jacobs, with an Introduction by Valerie Smith. The Schomburg Library of Nineteenth-Century Black Women Writers. Copyright © 1988 by Oxford University Press, Inc. Reprinted by permission.

Jen, Gish: "In the American Society" by Gish Jen. First published in *The Southern Review.* Copyright © 1986 by Gish Jen. Reprinted by permission of the author c/o Maxine Groffsky Literary Agency.

Kiowa Prayers: Documents 1–7 from *Women and Religion in America, Volume 3: 1900–1968* by Rosemary R. Ruether and Rosemary S. Keller. Copyright © 1986 by Rosemary R. Ruether and Rosemary S. Keller. Reprinted by permission of HarperCollins Publishers, Inc.

Larsen, Nella: "Freedom" by Nella Larsen is reprinted from *The Sleeper Wakes: Harlem Renaissance Stories by Women*, edited by Marcy Knopf and published by Rutgers, The State University, 1993.

Le Guin, Ursula K.: From "May's Lion" by Ursula K. Le Guin. First published in *The Little Magazine.* Copyright © 1983 by Ursula K. Le Guin. Reprinted by permission of the author and the author's agent, Virginia Kidd.

Le Sueur, Meridel: "Women Are Hungry" first published in *The American Mercury*, March 1934. Reprinted by permission of the author.

Lerner, Gerda: "One Farmer's Wife" as edited by Gerda Lerner from *The Female Experience: An American Documentary* edited by Gerda Lerner, Bobbs-Merrill, 1977. Reprinted by permission of Gerda Lerner.

Lewis, Edna: "Sunday Revival Dinner" from *The Taste of Country Cooking* by Edna Lewis. Copyright © 1976 by Edna Lewis. Reprinted by permission of Alfred A. Knopf, Inc.

Lim, Genny: *Bitter Cane* from *The Politics of Life: Four Plays by Asian Women*, edited by Velina Hasu Houston. Published by Temple University Press in 1993. Copyright © 1993 by Genny Lim. Reprinted by permission of the author.

Lorde, Audre: "Song for a Thin Sister" from *Undersong: Chosen Poems Old and New*, revised edition, by Audre Lorde. Copyright © 1992, 1982, 1976, 1974, 1973, 1970, 1968 by Audre Lorde. Published in the U.S. by W. W. Norton & Co., Inc. in 1992 and in Great Britain by Virago Press in 1993. British edition copyright © 1993 Estate of Audre Lorde. Reprinted by permission of the publishers.

Lyon, George Ella: "The Foot-Washing" by George Ella Lyon. First published in *Appalachian Journal*, Vol. 9. No. 4 (Summer 1982). Copyright Appalachian Journal/Appalachian State University. Used by permission of the publisher.

Martinez, Zarela: "Los Dias de Los Muertos" from *Food From My Heart* by Zarela Martinez. Copyright © 1992 by Zarela Martinez. Reprinted with the permission of Macmillan Publishing Company.

McCarthy, Mary: "Names" from *Memories of a Catholic Girlhood* by Mary McCarthy. Copyright © 1957 and renewed 1985 by Mary McCarthy. Reprinted by permission of Harcourt Brace & Company and A. M. Heath & Company Ltd.

Mirikitani, Janice: "Suicide Note" from *Shedding Silence* by Janice Mirikitani. Copyright © 1987 by Janice Mirikitani. Used by permission of Ten Speed Press, P.O. Box 7123, Berkeley, CA 97407.

Mora, Pat: "To Gabriela, A Young Writer" from *Nepantla* by Pat Mora. Copyright 1993. Published by The University of New Mexico Press. Reprinted by permission of the publisher.

Morrison, Toni: "Recitatif" by Toni Morrison. Copyright © 1983 by Toni Morrison. Published in *Confirmations: Stories By Black Women*, compiled by Amiri Baraka and Amina

Baraka. Published by William Morrow & Co. in 1983. Reprinted by permission of International Creative Management, Inc.

Naylor, Gloria: "Lucielia Louise Turner" from *The Women of Brewster Place* by Gloria Naylor. Copyright © 1980, 1982 by Gloria Naylor. Used by permission of Viking Penguin, a division of Penguin Books USA Inc.

Nin, Anaïs: From *Little Birds: Erotica* by Anaïs Nin. Copyright © 1979 by Rupert Pole as trustee under the last will and testament of Anaïs Nin. Reprinted by permission of Harcourt Brace & Company and Penguin Books Ltd.

O'Connor, Flannery: "A Late Encounter with the Enemy" from *A Good Man Is Hard to Find and Other Stories* by Flannery O'Connor. Copyright 1953 by Flannery O'Connor and renewed 1981 by Regina O'Connor. Reprinted by permission of Harcourt Brace & Company and Harold Matson Company, Inc.

O'Keeffe, Georgia: From *Lovingly Georgia: The Complete Correspondence of Georgia O'Keeffe and Anita Pollitzer*, edited by Clive Giboire. Copyright © 1990 by Tenth Avenue Editions. Letters of Georgia O'Keeffe copyright © 1990 by the Estate of Georgia O'Keeffe. Reprinted by permission of Simon & Schuster, Inc.

Oates, Joyce Carol: "Extenuating Circumstances" by Joyce Carol Oates. Copyright © by The Ontario Review, Inc. Reprinted by permission of John Hawkins & Associates, Inc.

Olsen, Tillie: "Oh, Yes" from *Tell Me A Riddle* by Tillie Olsen. Copyright © 1956, 1957, 1960, 1961 by Tillie Olsen. Reprinted by permission of Delacorte Press/Seymour Lawrence, a division of Bantam Doubleday Dell Publishing Group, Inc. and the Elaine Markson Literary Agency, Inc.

Ozick, Cynthia: "The Shawl" from *The Shawl* by Cynthia Ozick. Copyright © 1980, 1983 by Cynthia Ozick. First published in the *New Yorker*. Reprinted by permission of Alfred A. Knopf, Inc. and Jonathan Cape Ltd.

Plath, Sylvia: "Lady Lazarus" from *Ariel* by Sylvia Plath. Copyright © 1963 by Ted Hughes. Copyright renewed. Reprinted by permission of the publishers HarperCollins Publishers, Inc. and Faber and Faber Ltd.

Quindlen, Anna. "The Good Guys" by Anna Quindlen from *The New York Times* April 11, 1993. Copyright © 1993 by The New York Times Company. Reprinted by permission.

TOPICAL LISTING OF CONTENTS

Childhood and Adolescence (Living in the Family)

Shaping an Identity

Love Relationships

Mothering

Aging

AUTHOR INDEX